THE ECONOMIC WEAPON

THE ECONOMIC WEAPON

The Rise of Sanctions as a
Tool of Modern War

NICHOLAS MULDER

Yale

UNIVERSITY PRESS

New Haven and London

Yale University Press books may be purchased in quantity for educational, business, or promotional use. For information, please e-mail sales.press@yale.edu (U.S. office) or sales@yaleup.co.uk (U.K. office).

Book epigraph: G. W. F. Hegel, *Lectures on the Philosophy of History*, transl. J. Sibree (London: Henry G. Bohn, 1857), 298.

Set in Janson type by Tseng Information Systems, Inc.
Printed in the United States of America.

Library of Congress Control Number: 2021939589
ISBN 978-0-300-25936-0 (hardcover : alk. paper)

A catalogue record for this book is available from the British Library.

This paper meets the requirements of ANSI/NISO Z39.48-1992 (Permanence of Paper).

10 9 8 7 6 5 4 3 2 1

Napoleon, in a conversation which he once had with Goethe on the nature of Tragedy, expressed the opinion that its modern phase differed from the ancient, through our no longer recognizing a destiny to which men are absolutely subject, and that Policy occupies the place of the ancient Fate [*La politique est la fatalité*]. This therefore he thought must be used as the modern form of Destiny in Tragedy—the irresistible power of circumstances to which individuality must bend.

—G. W. F. HEGEL, *Lectures on the Philosophy of History*

Contents

Acknowledgments

AS I GRAPPLED WITH the history of economic sanctions, I incurred many debts to mentors, colleagues, interlocutors, friends, and family, all of whom helped give shape to this book and bring it into existence.

Throughout my time in the doctoral program in history at Columbia, I was immeasurably aided by my supervisor, Mark Mazower. An early enthusiast of the project, he subtly and incisively commented on many drafts and has provided a lasting model for how to think and write, historically and otherwise. The encouragement, energy, and generosity of Adam Tooze powered much of this project and made the last decade an invigorating experience. I would like to thank Susan Pedersen, whose seminar first inspired me to examine the impact of the Great War blockade and whose teaching and advice set an edifyingly high standard of scholarly commitment. I owe a debt to Samuel Moyn, who asked acute questions and helped expand the project toward the history of international law. I would also like to thank Lisa Tiersten for her kind support and always valuable advice. Natasha Wheatley got straight to the point with terrific advice on how to write the history of an actual thing. I also profited greatly from talking, reading, and learning with Charly Coleman, Victoria de Grazia, Martha Howell, Małgorzata Mazurek, Timothy Mitchell, Camille Robcis, and Carl Wennerlind.

My colleagues at Cornell have been extraordinarily welcoming since my arrival in Ithaca. I am particularly grateful to Ray Craib, Cristina Florea, Maria Cristina Garcia, Durba Ghosh, Larry Glickman, Tamara Loos, Aziz Rana, Russell Rickford, Robert Travers, Aaron Sachs, and Claudia Verhoeven. A manuscript workshop allowed me to take in the helpful insights of Jamie Martin and Stefan Link. I also want to thank Robert Boyce,

Patricia Clavin, David Edgerton, and Patrick Weil for reading and criti-
cizing portions of the argument. Stimulating questions, conversation, and
critique came from Fritz Bartel, Deborah Cohen, Mario del Pero, Nicolas
Delalande, Michel Erpelding, Jeremy Friedman, Stefanos Geroulanos,
Michael Geyer, Georgios Giannakopoulos, Daniel Immerwahr, Simon
Jackson, Kostis Karpozilos, Duncan Kelly, Jan Lemnitzer, Jörn Leonhard,
Fredrik Logevall, Charles Maier, Reid Pauly, Morten Rasmussen, Jenni-
fer Siegel, Quinn Slobodian, Leonard Smith, Anders Stephanson, Marc
Trachtenberg, and Karin van Leeuwen. For helpful comments, insights,
and camaraderie, I am grateful to Benjamin Abrams, David Adler, Nader
al-Atassi, Thomas Bottelier, Danielle Carr, Anusar Farooqui, Ted Fertik,
Yakov Feygin, Pierre-Christian Fink, Freddy Foks, Kate Jackson, Anton
Jäger, Jeremy Kessler, Madhav Khosla, Aden Knaap, Max Krahé, Johannes
Lenhard, Dominik Leusder, Chase Madar, Clara Mattei, Flavien Moreau,
Ben Mueser, Timothy Nunan, Orçun Okan, Charles Petersen, Victor
Petrov, Ryan Rafaty, Jerome Roos, Apratim Sahay, Maja Spanu, Daniel
Steinmetz-Jenkins, Jan Stöckmann, Boyd van Dijk, Jens van 't Klooster,
Camila Vergara, Darius Weil, Madeline Woker, and Alexander Zevin.

While conducting archival research in France, the United Kingdom,
Germany, Switzerland, the Netherlands, and the United States, I benefited
from the financial support of the Prins Bernhard Cultuurfonds; the Social
Science Research Council's International Dissertation Research Fellowship (IDRF); the Columbia-Sciences Po Alliance Fellowship, enabling an
affiliation with the Centre de recherches internationales (CERI) and Sciences Po's département d'histoire, where I was supervised and helped by
Jérôme Sgard; the Chateaubriand Humanities and Social Sciences (HSS)
Fellowship of the French Embassy in the United States; and the research
funding of the Hoover Institution Archives.

My thanks are also due to those who hosted, assisted, and enter-
tained me during this research trajectory: Grey Anderson, Nils Mangin,
Birthe Mühlhoff, Alexandra Persegol, the Pisani-Ferry family, and Danilo
Scholz in Paris; Stephen Wertheim in London; Hunter Dukes and Emma
Vehviläinen in Cambridge; Ana Bogdan, Thomas Meaney, Saskia Schäfer,
and Jonas Tinius in Berlin; Yahya Khan and Yusra Mirza in Geneva; Alexander Clapp and Xenia Kounalaki in Athens; Daniel da Costa, Diana van
Everdingen, and Arnoud van Thiel in Amsterdam; Elisabeth Rubinfien
and Daniel Sneider in Palo Alto; and Ugo Mattei in Berkeley.

The project improved significantly as a result of talks and presen-
tations at the Columbia Global Center in Istanbul; St Anthony's Col-

lege, Oxford; the Institute for Historical Research in London; Sciences Po in Paris; the German Historical Institutes in Paris and Washington; the Universities of Tilburg, Amsterdam, and Copenhagen; a workshop with Charles Bright and Michael Geyer organized at Columbia University with Ted Fertik and Adam Tooze; Harvard's International History Conference; and the Yale ISS Grand Strategy Workshop. I am grateful to Jonathan Eyal at the Royal United Services Institute for hosting me in conversation and to Mattias Fibiger for the opportunity to present a chapter to the BGIE unit at Harvard Business School.

At Yale University Press, I would like to thank my editor, Seth Ditchik, as well as Karen Olson, Kristy Leonard, Bojana Ristich, and two anonymous readers, for their interest, patience, assistance, suggestions, and extraordinarily efficient handling of the publishing process.

Finally, I owe much to my closest friends, family, and loved ones in the Netherlands, Belgium, New York, Ithaca, and elsewhere in the world. Thanks to the love, good judgment, wit, and curiosity of Sophie Pinkham, I was able to sustain and finish the project. This book is dedicated to my parents, Denise van de Leur and Taco Mulder, who have always supported me, up close and from afar, and helped me figure out the most important things. Of course, any errors that remain in the work are wholly my own.

Abbreviations

Organizations and Institutions

AA	Auswärtiges Amt (German Foreign Ministry), a.k.a. Wilhelmstraße
ABA	American Boycott Administration
ABC	Allied Blockade Committee
AMTC	Allied Maritime Transport Council
ARA	American Relief Administration
ATB	Advisory Committee on Trading and Blockade in Time of War (UK; CID subcommittee)
BoT	Board of Trade (UK)
CFI	Commission financière inter-ministérielle (France)
CIB	Commission inter-ministérielle de Blocus (France)
CID	Committee of Imperial Defence (UK)
Comité R	Comité de restriction de l'approvisionnement de l'ennemi (France)
CSDN	Conseil supérieur de la défense nationale (France)
CSG	Conseil supérieur de guerre (France)
DLfV	Deutsche Liga für Völkerbund (Germany)
EFO	Economic and Financial Organization (League of Nations)
FO	Foreign Office (UK)
FEA	Foreign Economic Administration (U.S., 1943–1945)
FPA	Foreign Policy Association (U.S. think tank)
IBC	International Blockade Committee (League of Nations)
ICRC	International Committee of the Red Cross (NGO)

LCL	Le Crédit Lyonnais (French bank)
LEP	League to Enforce Peace (U.S. NGO, 1915–1919)
LNU	League of Nations Union (UK NGO)
LON	League of Nations (also Société des Nations [SDN])
MAE	Ministère des affaires étrangeres (French Ministry of Foreign Affairs), a.k.a. Quai d'Orsay
MEW	Ministry of Economic Warfare (UK, 1939–1945)
OHL	Oberste Heeresleitung (German high command, 1914–1918)
OKW	Oberkommando des Wehrmachts (German high command, 1933–1945)
PCIJ	Permanent Court of International Justice (1922–1946)
RWM	Reichswirtschaftsministerium (Germany)
SC	Supreme Council (inter-Allied)
SCE	Section de contrôle économique (French economic intelligence)
SEC	Supreme Economic Council (inter-Allied)
TCH	Trade Clearing House (UK commercial intelligence)
TEA	Trading with the Enemy Act (in effect in UK, 1914–1919 and 1939–1945; in effect in U.S., 1917–today)
UDC	Union of Democratic Control (UK political movement)
WILPF	Women's International League for Peace and Freedom
WTD	War Trade Department (part of UK Ministry of Blockade)
WTID	War Trade Intelligence Department (part of UK Ministry of Blockade)

Introduction

Something More Tremendous Than War

C AN WAR BE BANISHED from the earth? Throughout modern history, world peace has been a powerful ideal. It has also been one of the most elusive. Each major war produced its share of cynics as well as visionaries. Pessimists saw war as an inescapable part of the human condition. Optimists viewed growing wealth, expanding self-government, and advancing technology as drivers of slow but steady moral progress. This veering between hope and desolation took on a new urgency after the unprecedented destruction of World War I. The victors created a new international organization, the League of Nations, which promised to unite the world's states and resolve disputes through negotiation. The collapse of the global political and economic order in the 1930s and the outbreak of a second world war have made it easy to dismiss the League as a utopian enterprise. Many at the time and since concluded that the peace treaties were fatally flawed and that the new international institution was too weak to preserve stability. Their view, still widespread today, is that the League lacked the means to bring disturbers of peace to heel. But this was not the view of its founders, who believed they had equipped the organization with a new and powerful kind of coercive instrument for the modern world.

That instrument was sanctions, described in 1919 by U.S. president Woodrow Wilson as "something more tremendous than war": the threat was "an absolute isolation . . . that brings a nation to its senses just as suffocation removes from the individual all inclinations to fight. . . . Apply this economic, peaceful, silent, deadly remedy and there will be no need for force. It is a terrible remedy. It does not cost a life outside of the nation boycotted, but it brings a pressure upon that nation which, in my judgment, no modern nation could resist."[1] In the first decade of the League's existence, the instrument described by Wilson was often referred to in English as "the economic weapon." In French, the Geneva-based organization's other official language, it was known as "*l'arme économique.*" Its designation as a weapon pointed to the wartime practice of blockade that had inspired it. During World War I, the Allied and Associated Powers, led by Britain and France, had launched an unprecedented economic war against the German, Austro-Hungarian, and Ottoman empires. They erected national blockade ministries and international committees to control and interrupt flows of goods, energy, food, and information to their enemies. It was the severe impact on Central Europe and the Middle East, where hundreds of thousands died of hunger and disease and civilian society was gravely dislocated, that made the blockade seem such a potent weapon. Today, more than a century after the Great War, these measures have a different but more widely known name: economic sanctions.

How economic sanctions arose in the three decades after World War I and developed into their modern form is the subject of this book. Their emergence signaled the rise of a distinctively liberal approach to world conflict, one that is very much alive and well today. Sanctions shifted the boundary between war and peace, produced new ways to map and manipulate the fabric of the world economy, changed how liberalism conceived of coercion, and altered the course of international law. They caught on rapidly as an idea propounded by political elites, civic associations, and technical experts in Europe's largest democracies, Britain and France, but also in Weimar Germany, in early Fascist Italy, and in the United States. But then as now, sanctions aroused opposition. From the outbreak of war in 1914 until the creation of the United Nations Organization in 1945, a diverse assortment of internationalists and their equally varied opponents engaged in a high-stakes struggle about whether the world could be made safe for economic sanctions.

When the victors of World War I incorporated the economic weapon into Article 16 of the Covenant of the League of Nations, they transformed it from a wartime to a peacetime institution. Like other innovative aspects of the League's work in the realms of global economic governance, world health, and international justice, sanctions outlived the organization itself and continued as part of the United Nations after World War II.

Since the end of the Cold War their use has surged; today they are used with great frequency. In retrospect the economic weapon reveals itself as one of liberal internationalism's most enduring innovations of the twentieth century and a key to understanding its paradoxical approach to war and peace. Based on archival and published materials in five languages across six countries, this book provides a history of the origins of this instrument.

The original impulse for a system of economic sanctions came at the 1919 Paris Peace Conference from the British delegate, Lord Robert Cecil, and his French counterpart, Léon Bourgeois. These men were unlikely partners. Cecil, an aristocratic barrister and renegade member of the Conservative Party, was a fervent free trader who became Britain's first minister of blockade during the war; Bourgeois, the son of a republican watchmaker, worked his way up the professions to become a Radical Party prime minister in the 1890s and advocated a political theory of mutual aid known as "solidarism" (*solidarisme*). But despite these different backgrounds, both Cecil and Bourgeois agreed that the League could, and should, be equipped with a powerful enforcement instrument. They envisioned deploying the same techniques of economic pressure used on the Central Powers against future challengers of the Versailles order. Such recalcitrant countries would be labeled "aggressors"—a new, morally loaded legal category—and be subjected to economic isolation by the entire League. The methods of economic warfare were thus repurposed and refined for use outside a formally declared state of war. What made interwar sanctions a truly new institution was not that they could isolate states from global trade and finance. It was that this coercive exclusion could take place *in peacetime*.

The significance of the birth of economic sanctions lies in this momentous shift in the meaning of war and peace. A coercive policy that used to be possible only in time of war—isolating human communities from exchange with the wider world—now became possible in a wider range of situations. Commercial and financial blockade, a policy developed as a form of economic war, was reconceived as a prophylactic against war. By carving out the space in which international economic sanctions have been used for the last century, the League thus had a much more profound impact on modern history than is usually assumed. Indeed, this book argues that the struggle to create and use the weapon of sanctions deeply shaped the interwar world and thereby the structure of the political and economic order that we inhabit today. For one thing, it marked the international emergence of a new form of liberalism, one that worked through a technical and administrative apparatus of lawyers, diplomats, military experts, and economists. These officials' work, first in wartime and then after 1919, had far-reaching effects. In a period when European governments granted suffrage and extended welfare and social insurance, sanctions made them see other populations as suitable targets of coercive pressure. Long-standing traditions, such as the protection of neutrality, civilian noncombatants, private property, and food supplies, were eroded or circumscribed. Meanwhile, new practices, such as police action against aggressor states and logistical assistance to the victims of aggression, arose. All of this amounted to a major and complex transformation of the international system.

Today, economic sanctions are generally regarded as an alternative to war. But for most people in the interwar period, the economic weapon was the very essence of total war. Many sanctionists regretfully noted the devastating effects of pressure on civilians but nonetheless wholly accepted them. Woodrow Wilson held that if "thoughtful men have . . . thought, and thought truly, that war is barbarous, . . . the boycott is an infinitely more terrible instrument of war."[2] William Arnold-Forster, a British blockade administrator and ardent internationalist, admitted that during the Great War "we tried, just as the Germans tried, to make our enemies unwilling that their children should be born; we tried to bring about such a state of destitution that those children, if born at all, should be born dead."[3] Internationalists were exceedingly honest about this awful reality for a good reason. By deliberately spelling out the horror of enforced deprivation, they hoped to dissuade revisionist states from even thinking about challenging the Versailles order. A fear of being blockaded would keep the peace.

The initial intention behind creating the economic weapon was thus *not* to use it. To interwar internationalists, economic sanctions were a form of deterrence, prefiguring nuclear strategy during the Cold War. Of course, sanctions were not nearly as immediately destructive as nuclear weapons. But for anyone living in the pre-nuclear decades of the early twentieth century, they raised a frightening prospect. A nation put under comprehensive blockade was on the road to social collapse. The experience of material isolation left its mark on society for decades afterward, as the effects of poor health, hunger, and malnutrition were transmitted to unborn generations. Weakened mothers gave birth to underdeveloped and stunted children.[4] The economic weapon thereby cast a long-lasting socioeconomic and biological shadow over targeted societies, not unlike radio-active fallout. Feminist politicians and scholars in particular recognized this during the Great War itself, and many pursued an energetic campaign against the economic weapon's targeting of civilians. The women's movement played an active role in the international history of sanctions, largely opposing and moderating their force—although also sometimes supporting them as preferable to war.

The economic weapon was not the only interwar practice to instill fear in civilians. In 1923, future British prime minister Ramsay MacDonald warned that "the next war will be worse than ever. There will be blockade and, what is more, there will be the air raids, with poisonous gases, which will simply devastate whole towns and whole countrysides."[5] Both airplanes and poison gas were feared for the indiscriminate fashion in which they wounded and killed. But their effect was in the first place psychological. Aerial bombing during World War I killed about fourteen hundred civilians in Britain and several hundred on the continent—out of a total death toll in the range of 20 million.[6] Air power had the ability to strike terror and was used as a cheap form of colonial control in the 1920s. Only the advent of the four-engined bomber in the late 1930s, however, made strategic bombing possible.[7] Gas also became a highly feared weapon. But during the Great War it was not used on civilians, and on a generous estimate it killed about ninety thousand (or 7 percent) of the estimated 1.2 million soldiers affected by it.[8] Moreover, chemical weapons were unambiguously banned as weapons of war by international agreement in 1925, a mere decade after their introduction on the battlefield.

If we compare the three major anti-civilian weapons of the interwar period—air power, gas warfare, and economic blockade—it becomes clear that blockade was by far the deadliest. In World War I, 300,000–400,000 people died of blockade-induced starvation and illness in Central Europe, with an additional 500,000 deaths in the Ottoman provinces of the Middle East affected by the Anglo-French blockade.[9] Before World War II these hundreds of thousands of deaths by economic isolation were the chief man-made cause of civilian death in twentieth-century conflict. Yet unlike aerial bombing and gas warfare, the lethal effects of blockade were remarkably difficult to render visible and condemn, even to their direct users. Arnold-Forster worried that "the economic weapon is one which is so infernally convenient to use that it naturally commends itself to those who sit in offices. Pens seem so much cleaner instruments than bayonets, and can be handled by the amateur with so much less exertion, so much less realisation of the consequences."[10] Sanctions were attractive not just because of their potential power, but also because they were easy to use for their handlers. Their coercive power was administered not out of the cockpit of a bomber or through the breech of a cannon but from behind a mahogany desk. Sanctions, an American commentator argued, were special because their "field of operations is not a visible terrain; but a force is exerted just the same."[11]

Precisely because sanctions combined concrete and ineffable qualities, they raised the question of *how* they changed the behavior of those exposed to them. Wilson warned that a boycott could cripple a modern trading nation's standard of living. But he ultimately pinned his hopes "not only on the physical pinch, not only the fact that you cannot get raw materials and must stop your factories, not only the fact that you cannot get credit, that your assets are useless," but on the mental force of being placed under sanctions, "the still greater pinch that comes when a nation knows that it is sent to coventry and despised." Ignoring their physical effects, Wilson claimed their true power was psychological; sanctions worked because "it is the soul that is wounded much more poignantly than the body."[12] Sanctions were a useful antidote to war exactly because in the modern world, being quarantined from global commerce was an unbearable form of imprisonment.

Rather than restoring the liberal certainties of the prewar world, the introduction of sanctions in 1919 meant that the post–World War I international order bore the permanent imprint of economic warfare. This involved a sustained effort to make economic pressure against civilians both technically legal and politically legitimate. International law had long been a paradigm for thinking about the use of force and questions of war and peace. But domestic legal institutions were affected too. States acquired new powers of control over private economic interests. Despite the internal logic of legal principles, during the rise of sanctions the law functioned less as a constraint on politics than as a field of contestation in its own right. In this domain, disputes over the boundaries of regulation, emergency powers, economic coercion, and the use of force were central.

Changes in international and domestic law had serious political, even strategic, consequences. As became clear during World War I, the hermetic encirclement of a modern trading state required controlling what its nationals did everywhere in the world. Effective isolation also depended on the power to stop third countries from trading with the enemy state. This desire to make economic sieges impregnable clashed with two older internationalist principles: freedom of the seas and legal neutrality. Sanctionists therefore began to redefine international law to restrict free navigation as well as neutral trading rights. Every state, company, and individual had to join in isolating the aggressor. This changed the status of private trade, foreign investment, and capital flows in the world economy. International firms, merchants, bankers, and investors grew wary of peacetime sanctions as they struggled to reconstruct and protect their global networks in the wake of the war. They desired a legal and economic order that was free from political interference and protected their businesses and assets from the risk of interruption, devaluation, or seizure. The history of sanctions is a prime example of how legal institutions shaped material outcomes and affected the tissue of globalization and the everyday lives of civilians. Law was no mere abstraction or scrap of paper but a core domain for the elaboration of statecraft and strategy.

Aside from new legal justifications, putting sanctions into effect prompted policymakers to engage in novel technical interventions. This book examines how interwar sanctionists developed mechanisms for energy control, blacklisting, import and export rationing, property seizures and asset freezes, trade prohibitions, and preclusive purchasing, as well as financial blockade, the precursor to modern financial sanctions. The complexity of these techniques makes clear how much economic warfare depended on intelligence gathering and knowledge production. To cut off an entire country from the dense linkages that sustained global exchange, it was necessary to map the worldwide fabric of material flows connecting it to the rest of the world. But in the 1920s, the administrative state in many European countries was still in its infancy. The progress of sanctions came to depend not just on new legal powers, but also on more accurate statistics. In combining the quest for power with the elaboration of knowledge, sanctions were a quintessential form of so-called biopolitics—the state management of human lives and livelihoods—under conditions of advancing globalization.

Sanctions also raised great questions about Europe's relationship to the wider world. For all the lofty talk about ending war among the great powers, in times of diplomatic crisis it became clear that they were often aimed at smaller states. French cabinet minister Étienne Clémentel opined in 1917 that by controlling and withholding raw materials "the united states of Europe, of America, of Asia could find the sanction, vainly sought in the force of arms, which would impose peace on unruly peoples as on predatory peoples."[13] Despite their supposed universality, League sanctions were considered suitable for use mainly against peripheral European states and "semi-civilized" countries. Justifying the infliction of pain from a distance came easily to European elites accustomed to managing colonial empires overseas and defending class rule at home. In 1919, the Soviet republics of Russia and Hungary were the first states to be subjected to Western blockades without an official declaration of war. In subsequent years two border conflicts in the Balkans were defused with threats of economic sanctions. Yugoslavia was made to desist in its invasion of Albania in 1921, while the Greek dictator Theodoros Pangalos was dissuaded from starting war with Bulgaria in 1925. In the years that followed Turkey, China, and Japan each appeared in the crosshairs of the economic weapon. As global imperial powers, Britain and France were prepared to go much further in pressuring Asian peoples than fellow Europeans. Only in the 1930s did European challengers such as Italy and Germany come into view.

Sanctionists originally conceived the economic weapon as a tool for keeping the peace within Europe. Many believed that if the ability to use sanctions had existed in July 1914, it could have held back Austria-Hungary and Serbia from dragging the continent into war. But the fact that post–World War I sanctions were usually considered against the periphery made them appear less a new peacekeeping practice than the latest disciplinary mechanism of Western empire. The limited enthusiasm for sanctions in the rest of the world meant that their operation was extraordinarily sensitive to continued agreement among the core League states. It was this uneasy combination of expansive material potential and constrained political legitimacy—a form of dominance without hegemony—that began to cause problems in the 1930s.[14] "Collective security," as the League's system of mutually supporting sanctions and aid became known, envisioned a world in which the sovereignty of each state was equally inviolable.[15] But this was difficult to reconcile with the imperial and hierarchical order of the thirties.

The rise of sanctions was thus bound up with the wider transformation of war, liberalism, law, and empire in the interwar years. As a result, sanctions played an important role in the crisis of globalization that erupted in the 1930s. The breakdown of the post–World War I order had many causes: waning enthusiasm for democracy, the popularity of revolutionary communism and rising fascism, the shock of the Great Depression, and the failure of disarmament efforts. Given these headwinds, it is hardly surprising that stability was shattered and the world slid toward a new global conflict. But this familiar story takes on a new quality when we integrate the history of sanctions into it. Interwar sanctions differed in their effects as the global situation changed. During the 1920s, war fatigue, reconstruction, and a return to growth allowed the economic weapon to play a stabilizing role. But amid the deteriorating circumstances of the 1930s, its effects became destabilizing. Examining how these structural shifts shaped the effect of sanctions forces us to reconsider what was fragile about the interwar order. Conceived during an era of high globalization, sanctions politicized the post–World War I world economy in new ways, creating fault lines that began to crack when conditions took a turn for the worse after the depression. During the 1930s, many countries reacted to the deteriorating economic environment by launching programs of internal self-strengthening and autarky. Rather than stopping this nationalist tide and the risk of war that it entailed, sanctions reinforced it. Although this counterproductive effect was widely recognized at the time, it has not been systematically examined by historians. In doing so, this book outlines a new perspective on the interwar crisis of globalization.

One of the dominant interpretations of the interwar crisis centers on the role of hegemonic stability.[16] In this view, the early twentieth-century world was caught in a transition between hegemons: on the one hand, the fading imperial power of Britain, and on the other, an ascendant but immature United States, which shirked responsibility for a leadership role commensurate to its economic size. The danger of this interregnum became apparent during the Great Depression, when the international economic order entered a deep crisis marked by nationalism and disintegration. Hegemony theorists emphasize that it was only in the wake of World War II that the United States came to provide a stable international monetary and financial system—the Bretton Woods system—enabling an "embedded liberalism" of national welfare states.[17] But in the 1930s, they argue, there was not yet a great power available to provide the global public goods needed to save liberalism.

That the interwar world was riven by profound tensions has also been the point of departure for historians who emphasize competitive dynamics as a cause of breakdown. This realist-materialist vein of analysis has focused on the escalation propelled by uneven economic growth and industrial development, on the one hand, and military rivalry and ideological struggle, on the other. The depression opened a window for nationalist revival that was seized by states fearful of the dominant liberal capitalist powers. Instead of unity under a benevolent U.S. umbrella, autonomy projects in the 1930s envisioned autarkic regional spheres of influence ruled by heavily armed empires. The historians in this group tend to regard international organizations such as the League as a well-intentioned sideshow to the central tragedy of full-spectrum power politics.[18]

The story of how a hegemonic vacuum and ideological-economic rivalry produced spiraling insecurity is important. But it needs to be integrated with the research of historians of interwar internationalism in the last decade. These scholars have recovered the ambitious scope of early twentieth-century efforts in global governance, from refugee settlement and public health to drug prohibition, colonial supervision, and financial advising.[19] In emphasizing economic sanctions as another signal innovation of interwar internationalism, this book follows in the tracks of this growing literature. However, it shifts our attention back to the realm of international security. Charting the development of sanctions demands that we take seriously a capacity that hegemonists, competitive realists, and historians of interwar internationalism all consider to have been lacking in the League: coercive force.

For this is what the economic weapon ultimately was. In its style and self-presentation the League may have been opposed to power politics. But there was a remarkable continuity between the coalition that had starved Central Europe into defeat during World War I and the elite policymakers who flocked to Geneva after the conflict. Indeed, personnel was policy; the blockaders of the Great War were the internationalists of the 1920s and inspired the sanctionists of the 1930s. Memories of blockade loomed very large in the imagination of interwar Europeans, and its renewed use against peace breakers represented a daunting threat to small nations. As early as 1920, the head of the League's Information Section, the American journalist Arthur Sweetser, declared that "if it is charged that the League is powerless because of lack of actual military or naval forces, it may easily be retorted that it possesses against a Covenant-breaking state a force far more subtle and more powerful, the force of economic strangulation."[20] The internationalists in Geneva, as well as those in London, Paris, Moscow, and Washington, did not shy away from the threat and use of massive economic force.[21]

To be sure, practical and strategic questions dogged the actual implementation of sanctions. But fear of economic isolation was more powerful than the League's ability to deploy it quickly. Wartime experience and internationalist discourse combined to give the economic weapon an ideological force far beyond its material readiness. Economic blockade acquired, in the words of the French jurist René Cassin, "a permanent potentiality" (*une virtualité permanente*).[22] Interwar Europe was haunted by this specter of sanctions.

Whereas the threat of sanctions sufficed to restrain smaller states, it backfired against authoritarian states powerful enough to consider challenging the League. Deterrence broke down when Fascist Italy risked confrontation by invading Ethiopia in 1935. Internationalist enforcement swung into action to implement Article 16 of the League Covenant. For the first time economic sanctions were deployed at scale as three-quarters of the world's states severed most of their commercial links with Italy. The sanctions failed to hurt Benito Mussolini's regime quickly enough to save Ethiopia from conquest and occupation. Italy had prepared to withstand shortages. Nevertheless, Mussolini had to launch a campaign for comprehensive anti-sanctions autarky (*autarchia*) to survive financial attrition. Sanctions so depleted Italian economic strength that Il Duce could not consider another offensive war for several years.

The Italo-Ethiopian War is often interpreted as a defeat for internationalism at the hands of fascism and imperialism. But from a strategic-material perspective it is better seen as the moment when the first major use of economic pressure dramatically raised the stakes of using sanctions as a tool to maintain world order. The League sanctions were seriously worrying to other revisionist states. Officials in Nazi Germany became convinced they would be the next target. In early 1936 a regime-wide drive began to achieve "blockade resilience" under the Four-Year Plan. Japan, too, started to worry about its prospects for regional autonomy. To both Berlin and Tokyo, territorial expansion became a way to enhance self-reliance, mobilize popular support, and retain strategic independence. Conquest appeared as an avenue of escape from the anxiety of living under the Damoclean sword of international blockade. Over time, the seeming inevitability of economic war prompted both Adolf Hitler and the Japanese leadership to secure resources by any means available. The internationalist search for more effective sanctions and the ultra-nationalist search for autarky thereby became locked in an escalatory spiral. Of course, the economic weapon was only one among several causes of the outbreak of World War II; its threat interacted with existing aggressive impulses and other influences. But while historians have given plenty of attention to conventional military factors, as well as the ideological, political, economic, and social origins of war, the role of sanctions in shaping the aggression of fascist and militarist powers in the late 1930s has not been sufficiently examined.[23]

That sanctions played an unintentional destabilizing role in the interwar collapse is all the more tragic since the League's Article 16 entailed more than prohibitive measures alone. During the Great War, the phrase "economic weapon" also denoted a positive agenda to *provide* other societies with material resources rather than depriving them. Between 1916 and 1920 this logistical function was fulfilled by inter-Allied organizations such as the Allied Maritime Transport Council (AMTC) and the Supreme Economic Council (SEC), which simultaneously mobilized resources for the Entente through the same world markets from which they were severing the Central Powers.[24] The provision of supplies to allies was indissolubly linked with the interdiction of supplies to the enemy. These policies, diametrically opposed in their effects, were two sides of the same economic weapon.

John Maynard Keynes, one of the architects of inter-Allied war finance and a famous critic of economic punishment, saw great promise in these positive tools as early as 1924. But despite interest from certain British internationalists and financiers, in the interwar years France was the only major state to consistently support a permanent mechanism to provide emergency financing to the victims of aggressive war. If small nations could rely on the material backing of a broad alliance in case they were attacked, such a guarantee would itself function as a deterrent to potential aggressors. This economic plan to prevent aggression produced the Convention on Financial Assistance in 1930, an internationalist initiative that has been all but forgotten. But due to political disagreements and fiscal conservatism, the convention never went into force. The result was that the League talked up the threat of blockade against aggressors without putting in place an aid mechanism for their victims—a highly unstable combination that was easily breached. The fragility of international institutions stemmed from this imbalance of focus, which prioritized discipline and punishment—in the form of austerity at home and sanctions abroad— while neglecting expansion and solidarity, both in domestic welfare and in foreign aid.

As World War II erupted, the wisdom of the positive economic weapon was appreciated anew. The Roosevelt administration began to direct financial assistance to Latin America and China in 1938–1939 to counter German and Japanese influence.[25] But the idea that solidarity with the beleaguered was just as important as the punishment of aggressors found its most consummate expression in the global provision program of Lend-Lease, begun in early 1941. Centered on the United States, both sanctions and supply thus survived the interwar years to be reincorporated into the United Nations Organization when it was founded in 1945. The history of this positive economic weapon grew out of early twentieth-century war economics. Yet as the negative instrument of sanctions has come to dominate modern geopolitics, the shared origins and complementary function of these two approaches has been overlooked.

The interwar history of sanctions is instructive for our twenty-first-century world in another way as well. Sanctions exploited the economic networks of interwar globalization but ultimately undermined its political foundations. Today, as the world economy reels from financial crises, nationalism, trade wars, and a global pandemic, sanctions are aggravating existing tensions within globalization. That sanctions are intended to promote international stability is, unfortunately, no defense against this risk: unintended negative consequences can be just as destructive as premeditated harms. Interwar history should sharpen our sense of what the stabilizing power of provision could have done if it had not been overshadowed by the destabilizing effects of deprivation, real and imagined.

For as long as humans have organized themselves politically, they have used material channels to persuade, cajole, and coerce each other. Sanctions are often traced back to Thucydides's account of rival city-states in ancient Greece. In his *Peloponnesian War*, he records Athens's commercial ban against merchants from the Greek port city of Megara in 432 BC—an event that international relations scholars have proclaimed the first case of economic sanctions in history.[26] But besides scholarly disagreement over the exact nature of the Megaran decree, such claims about ancient origins construct misleading continuities across space and time.[27] A purely state-centered definition excessively widens the definition of "sanctions" to any economic policy with a political aim without considering how these practices function, both materially and morally, in the international system in which they are deployed.

Two distinguishing characteristics of modern economic sanctions are their link with the enforcement of norms and the international legal and economic imagination behind them. For much of medieval and early modern history, the word "sanction"—derived from the Latin verb *sancire*, meaning to ratify or to underwrite—connoted approval. In the medieval church and at the courts of Catholic monarchs, for example, it was common to issue "pragmatic sanctions" to endorse special cases of royal inheritance by female heirs. But the term started to acquire another, slightly different, meaning in the late nineteenth century. As the world grew economically integrated to an unprecedented degree, the question of what principles underpinned this international order became more pressing. This is when the term "sanction" acquired its second meaning of guarantee or enforcement. Because the nineteenth-century international system was ruled hierarchically by a group of great powers and governed by European principles of law, their sanctions were conceived of as punitive measures to uphold "civilization" against "barbarism." In its scale and nature, this order was totally different from the Aegean world inhabited by ancient Athenians. The modern meaning of economic sanctions—that is, to use material exclusion from the world economy to protect international norms—was unimaginable before the economic and cultural conditions created by globalization beginning in the mid-nineteenth century.

While economic pressure is an age-old weapon, economic sanctions to enforce visions of international order are a distinctly modern innovation. This narrower definition of "sanctions" helps to distinguish them from related but distinct tools of policy regarding trade, industry, development, technology, and aid. Tariffs, for example, are often referred to as "trade sanctions." But they differ in crucial ways from the economic sanctions whose history is traced in this study. Customs tariffs are forms of legislation that shield a given economy or domestic industry from competition. Economic sanctions, by contrast, are offensive in nature. Although some of their aspects can be enforced through domestic legislation, their object is located beyond the borders of the states using them; it is one or more *other* national economies that are placed under sanctions. Tariffs function like taxes: they make exchange more expensive and difficult but do not prevent it categorically. Sanctions, on the other hand, prevent all entry or exit of a given commodity, and in this they reflect the blockade techniques that inspired them. The key difference is that sanctions are restrictions on exchange imposed on their target from the outside; they seek to exert *force* over other actors at a distance.

What tariffs have in common with sanctions is that they are both located on a spectrum of prohibition. As practices of prohibition expanded during the early modern period, so did the vocabulary to describe them. The *embargo*—from the Spanish verb *embargar*, meaning to arrest—emerged during the sixteenth century as a royal order to seize enemy ships at anchor in Habsburg ports.[28] But the degree to which European states enforced these restrictions differed significantly. It was not uncommon for merchants to maintain trade with countries at war with their own government. As Spain fought its rebellious Dutch provinces in the Eighty Years' War (1568–1648), Dutch traders continued to sell to Spanish territories, even when Spanish embargoes prevented them from buying anything in return. In their eyes, making money by trading with the enemy was no betrayal of the fight for independence but a way to accumulate the wealth that sustained it. The logic of commerce therefore competed with the logic of war and often won.

In the mid-seventeenth century the term "blockade" entered most European languages as a term for besieging cities, islands, and territories. Two factors circumscribed the use of blockades. The first was that blockade was a belligerent act; it depended on the existence of a state of war. To exercise the rights of blockade, states had to formally declare war. Blockades were thus a form of combat, not a mere administrative matter. Jonathan Swift reported a British army officer in the 1720s insisting that "the Army is the only School for Gentlemen. . . . Damn me, I would be glad by God to see any of your scholars with his Nouns, and his Verbs, and his Philosophy, and Trigonometry, what a Figure he would make at a Siege or Blockade."[29] So long as a state of war obtained, it was permissible to apply ruthless pressure against civilians. However, when a peace treaty was signed, the blockade had to be lifted and all trade freedoms restored.

A second limitation to blockade was material. Economic war in the early modern period aimed primarily to degrade the income and resources of rival states; to starve citizens who in many places were self-reliant in food production was possible only in highly localized sieges of individual towns or small city-states. The relatively self-sufficient character of most larger agrarian states meant that their exposure to external pressure was limited. Cutting off trade in manufactures and colonial raw materials could inflict considerable damage. But most countries' trade dependence was not widespread or profound enough to enable wars to be won through material pressure alone.

The limited reach of interdependence before the nineteenth century made early modern economic pressure qualitatively and quantitatively different from modern economic sanctions. But from the Napoleonic era onward, Britain began to exploit commercial channels in a more systematic way. At the Congress of Vienna in 1814–1815, Foreign Secretary Lord Castlereagh proposed to give weight to the conference's international declaration against the slave trade by organizing a non-purchase campaign against goods made with slave labor. Spain, Portugal, and France could thereby be forced to phase out the trans-Atlantic slave trade. Although the proposal did not come to fruition, it demonstrated a growing awareness that trade restriction could be used for humanitarian objectives.[30]

On the whole, however, severing nations from worldwide exchange went against the grain of the greater freedom of flows that accompanied nineteenth-century capitalist expansion. Historians now widely characterize the years between the 1840s and 1914 as the "first great era of globalization."[31] What has been less recognized is that an important legal pillar of this process was the growing body of law that protected private property from inter-state conflict. This separationist theory of war and commerce drew on strong currents of Enlightenment thinking. Jean-Jacques Rousseau's *On the Social Contract* (1762) argued that "War then is not a relationship between one man and another, but a relationship between one State and another. . . . Any State can only have other States, and not men, as enemies."[32] In the Napoleonic era this view became the basis for the so-called Rousseau-Portalis Doctrine, which held that individual civilians were not responsible for the actions of their governments. Private property in war was therefore inviolable by the state as a public entity. The doctrine quickly became dominant in national law, statecraft, and diplomacy across continental Europe.

To modern eyes, nineteenth-century wars protected commerce and finance to a degree that is almost unbelievably generous. During the Crimean War between Britain and Russia (1854–1856), Her Majesty's Treasury continued to fulfill its payment obligations to the tsarist government on old loans. Meanwhile, Russia dutifully paid interest to owners of its sovereign debt living in Britain.[33] A British government minister saw it as beyond dispute for "civilised nations that public debts should be paid to an enemy during war."[34] In the treaty ending that war, the Paris Declaration of 1856—the first multilateral treaty open to signature by any country—the maritime foundations of globalization acquired a further layer of protection through the creation of a category of "free goods" that were immune to seizure on the high seas.[35] But war on land enjoyed similar protections. As they led a revolt against rule from Vienna, Italian noblemen continued to draw regular income from their estates in Austrian-held Lombardy.[36] After unification, Italy signed treaties with Austria-Hungary and the United States that rendered civilian property immune from seizure in conflict. Arch-militarist Prussia honored these principles even as it fought a series of short, brutal wars to unify Germany in 1864–

1871.[37] Rare cases of politically motivated financial restrictions, such as Bismarck's 1887 loan ban (*Lombard-Verbot*) against Russia, proved the general rule that geopolitics and market regulation usually remained separate. The Russian government promoted the inviolability of private property on land by belligerents, a principle that was generalized in the Second Hague Treaty of 1907.[38] Both old and new European elites could support the separation of war from commerce: to aristocrats purely military wars satisfied the demands of honor while preserving their landed wealth, whereas the bourgeoisie could learn to live with periodic armed conflict if property and contract retained their integrity. The economic thinker Karl Polanyi described this nineteenth-century arrangement as one that "guarded with extreme rigor against a general war while providing for peaceful business amid an endless sequence of minor ones."[39] By erecting a barrier between public war and private economic life, laissez-faire liberalism made economic sanctions as a state policy affecting all of economy and society nearly impossible.[40]

Over the course of the nineteenth century two developments began to put this segregated system of war and commerce under pressure. The first was Europe's growing imperialism, which routinely broke down its central barrier by waging war on the livelihood of entire peoples outside the "civilized" world. One manifestation of this was the rise of pacific blockade, the nineteenth-century practice that most resembled twentieth-century sanctions. As their commercial influence on other continents grew, Britain and France began to exploit the considerable gray area between formal peace and open war. The first time that they imposed a blockade without declaring war was to help Greek insurgents revolting against the Ottoman Empire in the 1820s. In the following decades, these brief episodes of maritime pressure were increasingly accompanied by more aggressive actions, such as raids and naval bombardments. Common reasons for doing so were debt repayment and the protection of European citizens and property abroad. Between 1827 and 1913, imperial powers used pacific blockade to bend weaker states to their will at least twenty-three times.[41] This form of economic pressure short of war took advantage of the discrepancy in power between European empires and smaller states in Latin America, Mediterranean Europe, the Balkans, and Southeast Asia. While the measure was, in the words of one British diplomat contemplating how to make Venezuela repay its debts, "totally inapplicable in the case of a Great Power," it was nonetheless "suitable to the case of a recalcitrant petty State in controversy with Great Powers of overwhelming strength, who, while desiring to obtain proper redress, are unwilling to dismember or destroy a puny antagonist."[42]

European imperialists never had a monopoly on the use of economic pressure, however. In fact, the state-centered tradition of embargoes and blockades from which sanctions would emerge had a civil society counterpart. This was the organization of economic non-interaction by political and social movements against foreign oppressors or moral injustices. American colonists and British Quakers had used such tactics in the eighteenth century. Organized non-intercourse as a global phenomenon therefore existed before it had a proper name: the boycott.[43] The term originated in a famous case in 1880 in which the Irish Land League, which fought for the rights of landless peasants, used a policy of non-interaction to pressure Charles Boycott, the despotic agent of an absentee landlord, into making concessions to rural tenants. Soon his name was widely used as a noun and verb; it entered the French language one year later and by the end of the decade was used in Spanish, Italian, Portuguese, Swedish, German, Dutch, and even several Asian languages.[44] The rapid proliferation of the term itself in the 1880s shows that boycotts were directly linked to the globalization of trade and information in the late nineteenth century. As steamships and telegraph networks allowed faster travel and communication and the circulation of print media exploded, groups from the Chinese Boxer rebels to the Indian Swadeshi movement and Polish nationalists used these technologies to organize campaigns of private economic pressure.

The second trend that undermined the separation of commerce and war was growing internal opposition among European elites. British common law justices had never liked the Enlightenment separationist theory. As one judge, John Nicholl, argued in 1800, "There cannot exist, at the same time, a war of arms and a peace of commerce."[45] On this view, a state of war suspended the foundations of private economic life and allowed the seizure and suspension of all enemy property and contracts. British Conservatives and navalists wanted to give the Royal Navy free rein to interdict global commerce; they chafed at restrictions imposed by international law, whose separationist rules they secretly planned to repudiate in case of war.[46] In France, a new generation of naval thinkers, the *jeune école*, saw the revolutionary upheaval of the Paris Commune as evidence that wars could be won by triggering social unrest on the enemy's home front.[47] They argued for an all-out offensive against commercial supply lines, as well as artillery bombardment of civilian population centers. This orientation was consonant with strategic thinking in the United States, which had won the Civil War against the Confederacy by waging total war on land and mounting a naval blockade of Southern cotton exports. American elites thus agreed with British and French navalists that in an age of industrialism and globalization, civil society was a legitimate target of war. Alfred Thayer Mahan, the American naval theorist who was the most widely read military thinker of the late nineteenth-century world, argued that property engaged in commerce was "the life-blood of national prosperity . . . and as such it is national in its employment, and only in ownership private. To stop such circulation is to sap national prosperity; and to sap prosperity, upon which war depends for its energy, is a measure as truly military as is killing the men whose arms maintain war in the field."[48]

These fin-de-siècle visions of open war against civilian economies were bleak. But in some ways these anti-separationists were merely thinking the material realities of a globalized world through to their logical conclusions. It was precisely the laissez-faire ideal of an apolitical international economy totally insulated from war that was historically novel. This project displayed a distinctively nineteenth-century faith in the progress of trade and law as hallmarks of Western civilization. Separationism was embraced by liberal politicians in Great Britain but also by German bureaucrats, Belgian and French international lawyers, Italian aristocrats, and Russian generals, as well as bourgeois merchants from Bremen to Bombay to Buenos Aires.

As a result, by the beginning of the twentieth century it seemed to many that the arteries of global trade and finance were a vital force holding back the possibility of a large-scale conflict. Economic sanctions were only an elusive hope, one of many utopian schemes populating the newspapers, cafés, and lecture halls of the period. The sanctionist idea became popular in the international arbitration movement, a loose group of jurists in Europe and the United States who wanted to end the occurrence of war by submitting all inter-state disputes to a neutral arbiter, ideally a world court. But to be effective, this arbiter had to possess some "sanction" or guarantee its judgments were respected by non-compliant states.[49] Under domestic law, states had a variety of punishments for lawbreakers. But in international politics, it was much less clear how one could punish an entire state. In 1906, a group of French arbitrationists proposed sanctions with an economic content.[50] Boycotts and the temporary freezing (sequestration) of foreign property were put forward as options. The lawyer Jacques Dumas argued that "the sanction of bills would be more efficacious than the sanction of bullets."[51] More aggressive options, such as intervention by international naval and land forces, were controversial.[52] These were clearly a form of war, not a way to stop it. "If arbitration leads to war," another jurist objected, "the question of pacification will not have advanced at all."[53]

The possibility of exploiting economic interdependence to uphold law and preserve peace was thus being considered in arbitrationist circles. The first attempt to generalize this insight came from the eccentric merchant-turned-internationalist Léon Bollack. A Frenchman who had created his own universal language, launched a gold coin as international currency, and proposed to unite Britain and France in a confederation called Westia, or Ouestie, Bollack put forward another idea in 1911: a "global law of customs boycott." Under this law, if a country refused to respect an arbitration verdict, all other arbitrationist states could punish it by refusing entry to its goods, expropriating its foreign property, and blocking its financial transfers.[54] In September 1912, Bollack presented this idea to the Universal Peace Congress in Geneva.[55] Its goal was straightforward: *"tuer la guerre,"* to kill war.

Bollack's idea attracted immediate criticism from other arbitrationists who saw the world economy with its division of labor as a complex organism to be protected. One of them, the Hungarian sociologist André de Maday, warned that it was dangerous to envision "the complete isolation of a people, and especially . . . the interruption of international communication." Was it wise, he asked, to inflict a "crying injustice," such as preventing food imports, on a civilian population, saving it from war only to subject it to famine instead?[56] Dumas agreed, proclaiming that the boycott was "an institution of the past" and that modern morality regarded it as "an injustice, to penalize individuals for the faults and missteps of governments."[57]

The arbitrationist debate about economic sanctions was a theoretical discussion of a tool that at the time existed only on paper. Maday and Dumas had delivered prudential critiques of economic sanctions, the first but certainly not the last such warnings in history. By contrast, Bollack's utopianism appeared wildly out of touch with growing geopolitical tensions around the world. Arbitrationism proved too weak politically to prevent European governments from embarking on war in July 1914. Yet in an unexpected twist, the war ended up making one of the movement's ideas a reality. The total war advocates in most European states gained the upper hand over the proponents of continuing business as usual. Property was seized, shipping lanes were blockaded, bank accounts were frozen, and private firms were placed under close surveillance. The world economy was subjected to the ruthless logic of strategic victory using all means available. But after four years of grinding global conflict the victors did, in fact, create an international mechanism to protect peace with economic sanctions. The answer to the arbitrationist puzzle—how to make international law binding—emerged from the way that the Entente waged a new kind of industrial, commercial, and financial warfare. Economic sanctions arose where the conditions of advanced globalization encountered the techniques of total war. How this sudden shift changed the world is the story told in this book.

The Economic Weapon is composed of three parts, each of which examines a consecutive phase in the history of sanctions and adopts a distinct focus to do so. Part I, "The Origins of the Economic Weapon," covers the blockade project pursued by Britain and France from 1914, spanning the Great War and the immediate postwar years up to the restoration of trade with Bolshevik Russia in 1921. Chapter 1 charts how the evolving wartime politics of blockade presented new challenges and opportunities for intervention in a deeply interdependent world economy, from the management of neutral trade to the interdiction of finance. Chapter 2 examines how the economic weapon took shape between 1917 and the drafting of the League's Article 16 sanctions procedure at the Paris Peace Conference in early 1919. It was in this period that blockade administration changed from an instrument of state policy to a technocratic internationalism, rendered more effective after U.S. entry into the conflict on the Allied side. This chapter shows how this globe-spanning control over raw materials inspired the idea of using international resource boycotts after the war. It also documents how the Versailles negotiations among Woodrow Wilson, Robert Cecil, and Léon Bourgeois unintentionally produced a league of nations that could apply blockade-style sanctions without declaring war on aggressor states. Chapter 3 studies the first peacetime use of economic pressure by the Allies in 1919 as they blockaded revolutionary Communist regimes in Russia and Hungary. This episode launched a public debate across Europe about the ethics of economic war on civilians. Vocal campaigns by feminist, humanitarian, leftist, and liberal groups eventually helped persuade the Allies to moderate economic pressure on Central and Eastern Europe for fear of driving populations into the hands of political radicals instead of toward bourgeois stability.

Part II, "The Legitimacy of the Economic Weapon," is an institutional history of how national elites and the technocrats in the League managed the powerful but incomplete system that took shape during the 1920s. Beginning with the League's convening of an International Blockade Committee in 1921 and ending with the international crisis over Manchuria in 1931, Chapters 4 and 5 trace how the option of economic sanctions appeared in virtually every international crisis of this period. There was a profoundly imperial dimension to the way the economic weapon operated in this period. Threats of economic sanctions successfully restrained border wars in the Balkans, convinced Turkey to give up territorial claims in Iraq, and were continuously considered against striking workers and anticolonial nationalist resistance in China. Chapter 6 shows how the struggle to secure wider legitimacy for sanctions against civil society and private economic interests led to a deep but underappreciated political rift within Western liberal elites. This split between sanctionists and neutralists weakened the imperial-internationalist consensus on which the League rested and complicated its relations with external powers, especially the United States.

Part III, "Economic Sanctions in the Interwar Crisis," assesses the role of the economic weapon in the global crisis of the 1930s and 1940s, from the Great Depression until the end of World War II. Chapter 7 investigates the difficulties of implementing sanctions from Manchuria to South America and the fraught efforts to deter a set of powerful challenges to the post–World War I order from Japan, Nazi Germany, and Fascist Italy. Chapter 8 reconsiders the most famous interwar use of the economic weapon, the League sanctions against Mussolini's regime during the Italo-Ethiopian War, arguing that this crisis produced a new understanding of sanctions focused on attrition. But why did sanctions not prevent the return of conflict and the eventual outbreak of another world war? Answering this question requires us to look beyond narratives of the 1930s as an ideological struggle between liberalism and totalitarianism or democracies and dictatorships. Instead, the analysis presented here advances a more hard-nosed view of how economic pressure spurred competition for raw materials, financial reserves, and territory. Chapter 9 suggests that the intensification of autarky in the mid-1930s can be understood as driven in part by a general "blockade-phobia," brought on by memories of economic war and kept alive by sanctions. Chapter 10 provides a materialist interpretation of World War II as a conflict revolving around the construction of coalitions for resource control. When, after 1941, Anglo-French economic warfare was supplemented by the U.S. Lend-Lease program, unifying coercion and aid into a single constellation, the sanctionists belatedly attained the collective security that had eluded them in the 1930s. The book concludes by examining how the legacy of the interwar economic weapon shaped the post-1945 international order and what this history means for our twenty-first-century present as the widespread use of sanctions today raises new questions about the politics of globalization.

PART I

The Origins of the Economic Weapon

CHAPTER ONE

The Machinery of Blockade,

1914–1917

A T THE END OF August 1914, three weeks into the war, the German diplomat Kurt Riezler wrote a letter to his fiancée, Käthe Liebermann. Trained as a classicist in Munich, Riezler had already spent several years as personal political adviser to the the head of government, Chancellor Theobald von Bethmann-Hollweg. At age thirty-two, he embodied the peremptory confidence of Wilhelmine Germany's ruling elite. From his post at the imperial army headquarters, he reassured Käthe that "everything is going well, the question of provision is also being taken care of and we will not starve. The English will certainly hold on *to the bitter end* like they did against Napoleon I, but we will set up a Continental System in a more refined way than Napoleon."[1]

Riezler's invocation of Napoleonic history was understandable. In August 1914, it seemed that European history was repeating an older pattern. Once more, Britain faced a powerful land empire aiming for continental dominance. And again, it used its maritime power to restrict its terrestrial opponent's access to world trade, forcing the opponent — then France, now Germany — to create a self-sufficient European economic bloc. But beyond these similarities, the comparison obscured more than it illuminated. In material terms the world in which Riezler lived was not at all like that of the 1800s. The intervening century had seen an unprecedented expansion of trade, integration of markets, rise in industrial production, urbanization of society, and democratization of institutions. As a result, when the Triple Entente of Britain, France, and Russia embarked on economic war against the Central Powers, Germany and Austria-Hungary (joined a few months later by the Ottoman Empire and Bulgaria), it did so under conditions vastly different from those of the Napoleonic era. Severing its continental enemies from external markets led the Entente to develop a system of economic surveillance and control without historical precedent.

What resulted was a transnational enterprise to master something far larger than a single rival empire: the global trading system. The experience of managing this apparatus from 1914 to 1918 convinced Allied policymakers that economic pressure was a force so powerful that it could prevent future wars. But how did this policy develop to the point that it acquired such war-stopping allure? The administrative history of the blockade is well known.[2] Yet how the wartime blockade shaped the economic weapon that emerged at the Paris Peace Conference has been much less examined.[3] In the process of learning how to wage economic war, British and French officials and their allies began to exploit interdependence. To do this they intervened in the infrastructure of the world economy. This involved gathering intelligence, producing qualitative and quantitative knowledge, and devising policy instruments with which to enforce the isolation of their enemies. Although building the economic weapon required vast reservoirs of knowledge, how to use this information remained an inescapably political choice.[4] Rival institutions, individuals, and interests therefore clashed in the management of economic warfare. But it was precisely this flexibility in using its levers for political ends that over time strengthened the appeal of blockade as a model for future sanctions.

The blockade became one of the most consequential experiments in global economic governance of the twentieth century. Building their economic weapon in a thoroughly interconnected world launched the Allied blockaders on a voyage of discovery. There is no better way to illustrate this process than to delve deeply into the blockade enterprise itself. This chapter provides an overview of the development of the Allied blockade but focuses on two particularly illuminating learning experiences: the control of raw materials and the emergence of financial blockade. These policies became the wartime predecessors to later commodity embargoes and financial sanctions. A focus on minerals and money brings out how closely the material and financial dimensions of economic pressure were intertwined. Our journey therefore begins with a small but essential commodity in world trade in 1914: the mineral ore known as manganese.

Manganese and Globalization

Manganese is a chunky, silver-gray metal found in lumps and arteries in the earth's crust. It has long been known to have the capacity to harden iron objects. In nineteenth-century Central Europe, blacksmiths used small amounts of manganese when smelting pig iron in their furnaces to produce a tougher, shiny product called *Spiegeleisen* (mirror iron). What allowed it to become a key mineral was the revolution in modern steel manufacturing launched by the discovery of the Bessemer Process in the 1850s. Tinkering in the hills of Gloucestershire, Henry Bessemer and Robert Mushet developed a method to produce steel that involved de-oxidizing molten pig iron by adding manganese to it, radically improving its quality and preventing rust and corrosion. Manganese thus became a preferred input for alloys used to manufacture strong yet relatively cheap stainless steel. By the 1890s, electric furnaces using high-grade manganese ore could turn out prime industrial metal.

In the early twentieth century, Germany was the second-largest steel-maker in the world, after the United States. Accounting for half of all West European and almost a quarter of global production, its steel industry was dominated by conglomerates such as Krupp, which manufactured every-thing from hulls, girders, and beams to plating, pipes, track, and helmets.[5] But the raw materials that went into this prodigious output came largely from outside Germany. Iron ore arrived in trains from France and Lux-embourg and coal from the Ruhr region itself. Steadily improving supply lines meant that Krupp plants were fed by a continuous flow of inputs de-livered throughout the year from all over the world. This allowed the firm to achieve an enormous yearly steel production while operating on very small inventories; in 1913, Krupp held stocks of raw materials that covered just two months of production.[6]

Despite its leading position in European steel making, German in-dustry thus depended on overseas supply. Manganese, which had very few European mines, was a case in point. Most of the world's manganese came from the Chiatura mines in Georgia, then part of the Russian Em-pire. British India, which had deposits on the Malabar coast, provided the second-largest supply. In 1913, combined output of Russian and Indian mines came to two million tons, some 90 percent of global production.[7] The third- and fourth-largest producers were Brazil, which exported about 183,000 tons of manganese in 1913 and 1914, and Spain, which pro-duced just 21,000 tons, less than 1 percent of global output.[8] Commensu-rate with its share of global steel output, Germany consumed a quarter of the annual world production of manganese. All in all this meant that over half a million tons of manganese ore arrived in Germany in 1912—nearly two-thirds from Russia, a quarter from India, 6 percent from Spain, and 4 percent from Brazil.[9]

The needs of German steel producers drove considerable manganese imports. *Where* the ore came from, however, was determined by a variety of factors. Transport infrastructure was one of these. The mid-nineteenth-century transportation revolution had dramatically lowered freight rates for oceanic transport. Despite major railway investment in recent decades, maritime transport often remained cheaper than overland supply. For a solid bulk good like manganese, even small distances by rail added significantly to the wholesale price. By the time Russian ore reached the Black Sea port of Poti, just 180 kilometers from the mining pit at Chiatura, its unit price had tripled from 10 to 30 francs per kilo due to the dire state of tsarist railways in Georgia.[10] German firms imported from Brazil because it was often cheaper to have mineral ores sent overseas from Latin America than to transport them overland from Russia. Krupp's main plants were located in the Ruhr Valley in western Germany, connecting them to world markets via the Rhine River through the Netherlands. In the 1880s and 1890s a wave of European investment in Brazilian railroads further increased the ease of access and hence competitiveness of Latin American ores compared to those from Russia, which, as noted, relied on much poorer railways.

Physical and political conditions of production also shaped supply. Indian manganese benefited from the low cost of colonial labor on the subcontinent.[11] Although plentiful, the Russian manganese mines at Chiatura were a hotbed of revolutionary agitation. The young Georgian Iosif Jugashvili—later known as Stalin—started his political career as a Bolshevik by organizing mining workers in the region.[12] Finally, the quality of the material mattered. Manganese-holding ores with higher concentrations of the pure chemical element were prized since smaller amounts were then needed to produce a unit of steel. Brazilian mines held high-quality ores of 50 percent purity, whereas Russian deposits were cheaper but low-grade. All these reasons—good infrastructure, political stability, and high-grade ores—ensured that the Brazilian export of manganese to Germany remained viable and reasonably competitive.

Krupp's procurement of Brazilian manganese involved a complex chain of transactions. The steel firm sent orders with desired amounts to its London agent, who matched requirements with the offers of suppliers in the global mining industry concentrated in the British capital. After dispatching this order to a given mine, the agent arranged trade financing by forwarding the order to Krupp's bank, Deutsche Bank. As the second-largest bank in the world, Deutsche Bank was able to dispense the trade credit through a special Latin American subsidiary, the Deutsche Ueber-seeische Bank, which operated locally under the name Banco Alemán Transatlántico.[13] Meanwhile, manganese ore was being dug up in large pit mines in the state of Minas Gerais in the Brazilian interior.[14] One such ex-cavation site was located at Itabira, where the British-owned Itabira Iron Ore Company had operated a mine since 1911.[15] This pit was connected to the main inland railway of Brazil, the state-owned Estrada de Ferro Cen-tral do Brasil, which ran through the state capital of Belo Horizonte.[16] From Belo Horizonte, bulk cargo trains carried the manganese three hun-dred miles (five hundred kilometers) southeast to the national capital, Rio de Janeiro. Itabira Iron Ore's sales desk in Rio received a bill of exchange from the Banco Alemán Transatlántico on behalf of Krupp. This bill was effectively a promise that the company would be paid for the manganese ore shipment once it had been received by its user. Because it was issued and underwritten by Deutsche Bank, a large bank that could disburse the amount paid to the mining company if demanded, the bill was itself a means of exchange that could be sold for cash. (Highly rated bills of ex-change could even be used to pay for other goods as if they were money.)

In Rio, the ores were transferred from railcars onto steamships, ready for their trip through the heart of the global trading system—the world's oceans. Britain, Germany, the United States, and Norway all operated large merchant marines to ferry goods between Latin America and Europe. Merchant vessels involved in such long-distance transport required insur-ance. This risk protection was provided by the British firm Lloyd's, the world's major marine insurer, at its exchange in London. The trade also relied on an adequate supply of fuel. Both the Brazilian locomotives that brought manganese to the coast and the Norwegian steamers that ferried ores across the Atlantic used coal as their main source of energy. Almost 90 percent of the coal imported by Brazil came from Britain. British coal traders sold coal directly to shipping companies and privately owned coal depots (so-called bunkers) around the world. Insurance, fuel trading, and storage were all dominated by firms based in the British Isles.[17] Any steamer departing from Rio with ores destined for Europe was therefore quite likely to be powered by carboniferous rock dug out of the soil of Wales and shipped southward across the Atlantic before being burned on the northward journey. From Brazil it took three weeks for the average steamer to arrive in Rotterdam, the Dutch transit port for the West European riverine trade. There the manganese ore would be transferred to another railcar or river boat for the final 130 miles (210 kilometers) to the Krupp plant in Essen, where steelworkers used high-tech blast furnaces to smelt it and iron ore into hardened stainless steel.

The material supply chain in minerals trading had a financial counterpart in an international chain of payments. Krupp's high-speed order system meant it would usually find buyers for its finished steel product by the time inputs arrived at the plant. This allowed the company to invoice its clients for the cost of manganese imports. With this prospective payment it cleared its trade debt to Deutsche Bank. In the four to six weeks between the mining of the manganese in Brazil and its physical delivery in Essen, Deutsche Bank would bear the risk of price shifts and ultimate payment on its balance sheet. To offset the money tied down in this way, the bank borrowed from other banks in the London money market, such as the French Crédit Lyonnais. While the commodity shipment it had financed was being transported across the Atlantic, this left Deutsche Bank free to conduct other lending business.

As a result, a single import of raw materials from Minas Gerais to the Ruhr could easily involve seven parties in six different countries other than Krupp and the Itabira Iron Ore Company: the Brazilian government and its state railroad, a Norwegian shipping firm for transport, Lloyd's to underwrite the ore shipment and another British company to supply bunker coal, a Dutch railroad operator carrying the shipment to Germany, Deutsche Bank to finance Krupp's initial purchase, and a French multinational bank to extend the short-term liquidity allowing Deutsche Bank to cover its trade credit. The complexity of this single supply and payments chain shows how intricate the architecture and infrastructure of fin-de-siècle globalization had become by the time that the war broke out. Moreover, depending on the vantage point of the observer, the transaction assumed a variety of guises. From the most straightforward point of view, the supply and final use of the manganese made it a Brazilian-German exchange. But in legal-corporate terms the example considered here appeared as Anglo-German trade since a British-owned mine supplied a German steel company. Trade statistics helped clarify what was going on but only up to a point. Import and re-export through entrepot economies such as the Netherlands was a confounding factor. Since the manganese shipment would be registered by customs officials when it crossed national borders, in international trade statistics the Itabira-Krupp delivery would show up twice, as Brazilian-Dutch trade *and* Dutch-German trade.

The Itabira-Krupp manganese contract was a very normal transaction in the highly globalized environment of 1914. Most of the inputs for high-value-added industries such as chemicals, shipbuilding, and electrical manufacturing involved much more complex supply chains. This ecosystem of private interactions was minimally regulated by governments even as their economies heavily relied on these trading networks. The British Board of Trade (BoT) and the German Imperial Customs Office kept statistics about the shipments involved (such as the coal being shipped from Wales to Brazil and the manganese crossing by rail into the Ruhr), but these conveyed only part of the process. The most knowledgeable people involved were the mining company officials and bankers in London who made crucial transactions in support of the trade. But even they had limited control over certain aspects, such as a shipment's Norwegian maritime part and Dutch rail-bound part. The case of a simple steamer full of manganese thus gives a sense of the bewilderingly complex networks, exchanges, ties, and movements that underpinned global trade in 1914. If a war broke out, then how could this system be controlled to prevent the ore reaching Germany? This was the practical question that led Britain and France to begin building the blockade machinery that inspired modern sanctions.

Building the Blockade

Britain clearly occupied a pivotal position in this global economic system. Although Krupp did not think of itself as being engaged in trade with Britain when it sourced manganese ore from Brazil, the expertise, resources, and influence of British firms and banks sustained every aspect of its business. The centrality of London to the prewar world economy is difficult to overstate. In 1912 the City of London financed roughly 60 percent of the world's trade through its discount market, where short-term trade credit was extended and settled in the form of bills of exchange.[18] At least £4 million in such bills came due every day.[19] London brokers and acceptance houses were carrying over £350 million in bills of exchange on their books when the war broke out, one-fifth of which was owed to them by German and Austro-Hungarian borrowers.[20] Britain possessed the world's largest merchant marine, and its shipping companies carried 55 percent of the world's seaborne trade.[21] Two-thirds of global maritime insurance contracts were handled in Britain.[22] Due to its enormous coal exports, Britain was also the world's premier energy exporter; in the words of one historian, it was "the Saudi Arabia of 1900." Over three-quarters of the eighty million tons of coking coal, the fuel used by 96 percent of the world's cargo vessels, came from the British Isles.[23] At any one time, about twenty million tons were kept in British ports, with a further twenty-five million tons kept across a network of British-controlled bunker depots from the Falkland Islands to Gibraltar, and much of the rest was maintained and supplied by private British firms to local bunker depot owners.[24] Moreover, 70 percent of the global telegraph cable network was composed of lines operated by British companies.[25] Britain's infrastructural power over the lifeblood of globalization—goods, money, energy, and information— was therefore immense.

Before the war British naval planners had intended to use this power to launch a coordinated strike at the financial and commercial nervous system of the German economy.[26] But in the first weeks of war the Admiralty's plans for such an "economic Schlieffen Plan" were defeated.[27] The blockade that did emerge therefore came to be managed primarily by the Foreign Office rather than by the Admiralty. Even though it was enforced by the Royal Navy's surface fleet, the blockade ended up in civilian as much as military hands.[28] Economic pressure remained influenced by naval staffs, while implementation would henceforth be handled by civilian bureaucrats. This had two implications. The first result was that blockades and sanctions became matters of statecraft as much as military strategy. The second was that a less onerous legal form of pressure was chosen than a full blockade. The economic "blockade" of the Central Powers was in fact a system of *contraband control*, a policy looser than a full legal blockade.[29] A full blockade would have allowed the Entente to prohibit *all* maritime traffic in and out of enemy ports. By contrast, contraband control was a regime of inspection that seized only prohibited cargoes and goods destined or intended for enemy use. It depended on the ability of a belligerent to stop ships anywhere on the high seas. This was a capacity that only the Royal Navy possessed.[30] What allowed Britain to use this power was its declaration in November 1914 that the North Sea was now a war zone. The British and French governments defended this de facto policy of "distant blockade"—impossible under the rules of the 1856 Paris Declaration—by arguing that the changed conditions of modern maritime warfare necessitated a distant blockade plus contraband control. They justified breaking the letter of the law by invoking its spirit.[31] Although Britain was slow to unfold the machinery of blockade, by early 1915 it found willing partners in the French. In February, Germany declared a campaign of unlimited submarine warfare against Allied merchant shipping. This impelled the British government to step up its efforts to isolate Germany and coordinate more closely with the French in the process.[32]

The blockade administrators soon realized that more than just Anglo-French collaboration was required. Contraband control focused primarily on goods traveling to Europe's main neutral economies: the Netherlands, Switzerland, the three Scandinavian countries, and Spain. Continuous diplomacy was required to manage the conflicts that arose with these states. The Dutch government, for example, could not cease trade with either Britain or Germany lest it violate its status as a neutral power.[33] Yet to the Foreign Office and Admiralty, the Dutch transit trade to western Germany was a costly loophole that had to be closed.[34] In November 1914, a group of Dutch businessmen and bankers created the Nederlandsche Overzee Trustmaatschappij (Dutch Overseas Trust Society, NOT). Private traders in the NOT pledged that all goods they imported were destined for domestic consumption and would not be re-exported to Germany. This assuaged British worries about German foreign trade being diverted through the Netherlands while allowing the Dutch government to retain its official neutrality. A year later, the Société suisse de surveillance économique (SSS) was established to manage Swiss external trade in a similar fashion. In coordination with British diplomatic representatives, the SSS used the power of Swiss law to force private firms and businesspeople to abstain from economic relations with the Central Powers. Although the NOT and SSS were not under the direct control of Entente governments, they functioned to satisfy an Anglo-French strategy. These bodies were products of the Dutch and Swiss willingness to curtail their countries' economic sovereignty as a price for staying out of the largest war in European history.[35]

To understand the blockade as a governance system, it is instructive to examine how it obtained, processed, and disseminated information. In Britain, the kernel of the entire strategy was the so-called Trade Clearing House (TCH), a section of the Treasury's newly created War Trade Department (WTD). In February 1915, the TCH set to work with thirty staff members scouring all the sources at its disposal: German newspapers, customs records, reports from diplomatic missions, intercepted cables, shipping manifests, and hearsay from traders in the City of London. Unsurprisingly, the volume of information passing through the TCH be-

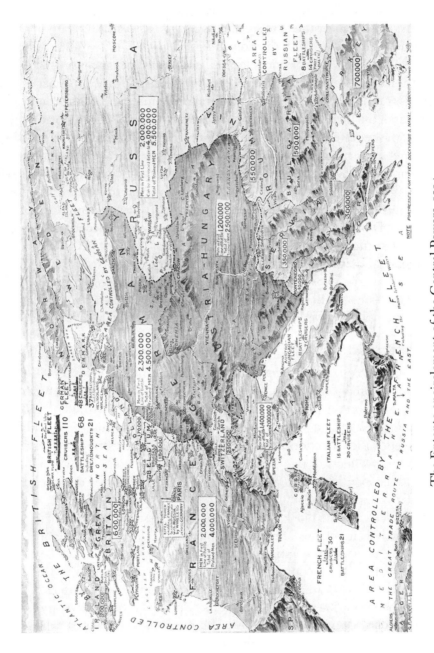

The Entente encirclement of the Central Powers, 1914.

Map by G. F. Morrell in the *Birmingham Gazette*. National Library of Wales.

came torrential within a matter of months; by September, total staff nearly quintupled to 145 people.[36]

Meanwhile, the WTD handled all the applications for import and export licenses from merchants who wanted to obtain permission to circumvent the blockade. Merchant firms and banks that wanted to keep trading had to disclose all their extant business dealings and were recruited into the intelligence-gathering network operated by the TCH.[37] Under the British Trading with the Enemy Act of August 1914, the WTD also acquired the power to confiscate enemy property and investments across the British Empire.[38] By January 1917, it could seize any foreign security—enemy or neutral—held in the City of London.[39] The Treasury thereby gained substantial control over a sector of the British economy that before the war had been largely self-regulating and unsupervised except by the Bank of England. The activities of the WTD and the TCH produced a stream of information and recommendations that ended up in front of the Restricting of Enemy Supplies Committee. This inter-ministerial committee brought together delegates from the Foreign Office, Admiralty, and the BoT and would make final decisions on policy. Its deliberations then passed to the Contraband Committee, which provided expert opinion on whether the proposed measures were in accordance with the international maritime law of blockade.[40]

The Foreign Office naturally looked abroad for ways to block the Central Powers' trade. It controlled a worldwide network of embassy officials, legation staff and local consuls, and agents. At the start of the war, Britain's foreign diplomatic personnel numbered just 414 individuals worldwide, only one-third of whom were career diplomats.[41] The remainder were local consuls, legation staff, and semi-official representatives involved in private business. Traditional upper-class diplomats balked at the idea of granting these men on the ground, whom they regarded as unreliable social climbers, any discretion to wage economic war.[42] But the Foreign Office was ill-prepared to engage in full-time blockade administration. British officials abroad thus had to improvise, and they began to report extensively on the activities of foreign companies trading with Germany and Austria-Hungary, as well as foreign ships transporting goods from Asia and Latin America to Central Europe.[43]

The center of the French blockade apparatus in the first three years of the war was the Committee for the Restriction of Enemy Commerce and Provisions (Comité de restriction des approvisionnements et du commerce de l'ennemi). Known as the "Comité R," it was created in March

1915 within the Foreign Ministry (Quai d'Orsay) and counted nine members, both military officers and civilian bureaucrats.[44] During the war it published 195 weekly reports on the Central Powers' economic situation based on information gathered by the Section de contrôle économique (SCE), a small office in the cabinet of the minister of war that collated information from mail and telegraph censors.[45] The head of the SCE, Jean Tannery, saw his organization as an "intelligence service on commerce in contraband of war."[46] The Quai d'Orsay also built up a considerable foreign information-gathering network by early 1916, consisting of forty-nine consular stations worldwide, thirty-two of them in crucial neutral and transit zones around Europe.[47] Despite these broadly parallel institution-building efforts, the French blockaders' approach to the blockade differed from that of their colleagues across the Channel in one respect. In British circles a business-as-usual attitude was prevalent. Foreign Office and Treasury officials were wary about risking Britain's great commercial and financial standing by pressing and antagonizing neutral and third countries too much. By contrast, the French blockaders thought vigorous economic pressure against the enemy was impossible without some pecuniary loss to the Entente. To them the British spirit of risk avoidance was irreconcilable with victory in the economic war.

Economic Total War

By late 1915 the Entente's blockaders had not achieved the comprehensive economic isolation of their enemies. On the European battlefields, the Central Powers were holding out in France, Belgium, the Alps, and Gallipoli and advancing deep into Russia and the Baltics. In their parliaments and press, the Entente governments were being accused of lacking the determination to prosecute the war effectively. French prime minister Aristide Briand visited London in January 1916 to make the case for increased cooperation. His British counterpart, Herbert Asquith, and his cabinet agreed on the need for a more vigorous economic war. On 23 February 1916, all the British bodies hitherto involved in contraband control were merged into a single organization with ministerial status: the Ministry of Blockade. Nominally part of the Foreign Office, the ministry was in fact a fully autonomous branch whose roots spread across the British state, also gobbling up the Treasury's TCH, now renamed the War Trade Intelligence Department (WTID).[48]

As the head of the Ministry of Blockade, Asquith appointed Lord

Lord Robert Cecil, ca. 1915. Library of Congress.

Robert Cecil (1864–1958), Viscount Cecil of Chelwood. Cecil was a an inspired choice for the job. He came from the aristocratic inner sanctum of the British political elite, having been born the third son of the Marquess of Salisbury, one of the most powerful Conservative prime ministers of the nineteenth century. Educated at Eton and Oxford, Cecil practiced law for two decades before entering politics as a Conservative MP in the 1906 general election, when the Liberals swept back into power after almost two decades in opposition. Within his party, Cecil stood out as an ardent supporter of free trade. In the fight over tariff reform, he sided with Asquith's Liberals against the protectionist Conservatives led by Joseph Chamberlain and Lord Lansdowne.[49] Cecil's political career was a kind of measured family rebellion; he took particular pride in opposing the more reactionary imperialist tendencies of the Tory party, led by his own cousin, Arthur Balfour. Despite his patrician origins Cecil was not without a populist streak himself. He relished long speeches, enjoyed personal interviews with journalists, and maintained an extensive correspondence with fellow internationalists in dozens of countries. But even at the height of his later extra-parliamentary campaigning for the League, which would earn him a Nobel Peace Prize in 1937, he never lost his standing as a consummate insider in the British ruling class.

At first sight, it may seem odd that a committed free trader like Cecil spent the war unfolding a sprawling system of restrictions on global commerce. But in wartime Britain this was not at all unusual. In fact, the most fervent free traders in the Liberal and Conservative Parties (including Lloyd George, Edward Grey, and Lord Curzon) were also the chief supporters of all-out war on German foreign trade. The reason for this was their belief in the primacy of economic interdependence. Edwardian elites were highly aware of their country's reliance on export earnings and imported food. The British population was especially foreign-fed: more than 65 percent of its caloric consumption came from overseas.[50] Because Cecil and his peers saw commerce as the glue that bound the civilized world together, manipulating those ties seemed an obvious way to change the behavior of its aberrant members. The war reformulated the role of the British state in managing trade in a more activist and interventionist manner, but it did not change the underlying primacy of commerce that had united prewar free traders.[51]

Cecil's ministerial appointment made him the supremo of British economic warfare. He described his job as "really much more than a blockade . . . the organization of all sorts of economic and commercial pressure on our enemies."[52] The Ministry of Blockade systematized and centralized the economic war against the Central Powers. At the core of this shift in economic warfare was an epistemic as much as an organizational transformation.[53] British blockaders understood their own maturation as the outcome of a process of learning how to produce actionable knowledge. In interwar studies of the blockade, this was described as a progression from a primitive "evidential" system to a more advanced and "scientific" so-called statistical system. This innovation came from within the blockade apparatus, and it was largely driven by one man, Cecil's subordinate and close associate, William Arnold-Forster.

William Arnold-Forster (1886–1951) came from a background distinct from but not dissimilar to Cecil's. Born into a prominent family of Liberal Unionist politicians, his great-uncle was the famous Victorian poet and critic Matthew Arnold. His father, Hugh, had been adopted by the Quaker

wool industrialist William Forster and become a Liberal Unionist MP before being appointed state secretary for war in Arthur Balfour's Conservative cabinet in 1903.[54] His son Will thus grew up in a liberal-imperialist
household at the core of the British elite. He joined the Royal Naval Vol-
unteer Division in December 1914 and subsequently served in the Trade
Division of the Admiralty, becoming its representative on the Contraband Committee, where he served as Admiralty representative alongside
Cecil, who represented the Foreign Office. The Contraband Committee
kept files about cargoes en route to enemy ports and would dispatch Royal
Navy vessels to intercept these shipments. Its basic operating method was
to undertake discrete interventions in the global trading system based on
leads about contraband.

In this position, William Arnold-Forster became the architect of an
epistemic revolution in economic warfare. The principal drawback of the
Contraband Committee's evidentiary approach was the enormous effort it
required. Both intelligence analysts and inspectors were chronically over-
worked. Since searches at sea were difficult, many ships had to be allowed
to pass unless they were clearly engaged in illicit trade. During 1915, Rear
Admiral Dudley de Chair's Tenth Cruiser Squadron operated eighteen
armed merchant cruisers that stopped no fewer than 3,098 vessels in the
North Sea—an average of eight interceptions per day. Of this total number, 743 ships (a quarter of all ships stopped) were sent into port for closer
inspection.[55] At the main British Channel ports equipped for such inspection, Kirkwall and the Downs, Royal Navy personnel would check the
cargo manifests, telegraph their contents to the Contraband Committee,
and physically inspect the vessel. But ships came in all sizes, and time constraints required tough decisions. To inspect a large passenger liner carrying five hundred passengers required a Royal Navy crew of ten officers and
twenty sailors to work nonstop for at least eighteen hours.[56] In the same
amount of time, many smaller vessels could have been searched. Besides
the inevitable errors in intelligence processing and execution, there simply
was no way to control all the maritime traffic entering neutral ports with
such a small force.

Arnold-Forster realized that vast amounts of trade to neutral countries was ending up in enemy hands. To save men and resources on inefficient pinprick inspections, he proposed to cast the net much wider. In 1915
he began to plead with the Admiralty to replace the evidential approach
with a statistical method that became known as the rationing system.[57]
The WTD used prewar consumption levels to produce quarterly and

annual estimates of "normal" levels of imports by neutral states. Instead of looking for proof that individual ships were transporting contraband, Arnold-Forster argued, Britain should restrict neutrals from importing more than their prewar average for any given good. Any imports exceeding the established rations would result in an embargo on further trade in those commodities.

From the British point of view, the rationing system improved control over world trade. But for the neutrals it created major problems. The WTD's estimates often underestimated actual neutral needs, which had increased due to the wartime dislocation of domestic industry and world trade.[58] But the statistical blockade system also had an inherent tendency to produce lower rations over time. In the case of the Netherlands, the WTD concluded in early 1916 that Dutch imports of linseed, lubricating oil, and gasoline during the final quarter of 1915 had exceeded the normal quantities. The Royal Navy immediately blocked further imports of these goods.[59] However, the WTD also reduced rations of goods of which Dutch imports had turned out *lower* than their allotment in the preceding quarter. Rations of maize, rye, oilcake, cotton, and refined petroleum were accordingly adjusted downward. The British officials reasoned that if the Dutch had shown that they could satisfy their needs with fewer imports than estimated, this meant that the existing ration was too high and should be reduced.[60]

As a result, under the rationing system there was almost no way for neutrals to maintain existing levels of imports without either incurring penalties for exceeding the ration quantities or seeing those quantities ratcheted down for not having been used fully. The new system completely reversed the burden of proof that international law required belligerents to meet. Ordinarily, the blockader had to prove that goods were in fact destined for the blockaded. By 1916, Britain often declared neutral imports that exceeded a self-picked norm to be contraband until proven otherwise. This broke with the traditional interpretation of belligerent rights under international law. But as a way of preventing potential contraband from reaching Germany it was much more efficient than the older system. Based on aggregate statistics rather than specific evidence, the British state had shifted the operating logic of the blockade from a legal to an economic basis.

Arnold-Forster's epistemological revolution ended what he later called "the early, unscientific stages of the blockade."[61] It laid the groundwork for later additions of new policy tools. In early 1916, the blockade apparatus consisted of a physical maritime barrier, an import-export licensing scheme, and a mechanism for rationing the imports of neutral countries. With the unification of various organs under Cecil's Ministry of Blockade, three new tools were added. The first was the introduction of blacklists. A publicly available Statutory List registered firms that were known to trade with enemy entities.[62] Any firm on this list was ipso facto in violation of British law and could have its cargoes impounded and assets seized under the Trading with the Enemy Act. Besides the Statutory List, the ministry also maintained three secret blacklists: one for bankers, one for ships, and one for firms that were suspected of trade with the enemy. The French also maintained *listes noires*, which were regularly updated by an inter-ministerial commission. American firms that traded with Germany were usually kept on the secret blacklist while the British and French blockade bureaucrats gathered further information about their activities. Political concern about antagonizing Washington prompted a second measure intended to deal with American trade in particular: the introduction of navigation certificates or "navicerts." These were permits with which foreign exporters could obtain passage through the maritime blockade if they registered their cargo with a local British embassy.[63]

Finally, by the spring of 1916 the Ministry of Blockade had set up a powerful energy control mechanism based on British-owned and British-supplied bunker coal all over the world.[64] Bunker control, which came into effect in March 1916, was run by a small section of the BoT known as the Unofficial Coal Committee. It demanded that neutral vessels stop in British ports for cargo inspection as a condition for being supplied with coal. Shipments far from Europe were inspected by local consuls or Royal Navy attachés. Ships cleared to receive coal were added to a White List. The prospect of being denied coal was a powerful incentive for neutral firms to register their cargoes and avoid trade with the Central Powers. Bunker control soon became the most effective way to bring difficult-to-track vessels into a growing database of world shipping.

Simultaneously, the French developed a fourth tool of blockade. If controlling trade between neutrals was not always possible, then buying these countries' supplies of specific commodities outright could be the best way to prevent them from being obtained by the enemy. This practice of "preclusive purchasing" first emerged at Briand and Asquith's January 1916 meeting in London. A committee for foreign purchases (*comité des achats à l'étranger*) was created in the French Ministry of War.[65] The only thing that constrained preclusive purchasing was monetary resources.

With French government spending already stretched to its limit to support the war effort, Britain borrowed on international markets, chiefly in New York, to obtain the funds with which crucial commodities could be bought.[66]

By August 1916, the Comité R had become a full department (*sous-direction*) in the French Foreign Ministry. It included statistical, technical, and translation sections; a cryptography desk and a printing office; and at least 35–40 permanent staff members by the end of the year.[67] The French Ministry of Blockade (Ministère du Blocus) and the economic administrators in Paris tried to conceptualize a guiding strategy for the blockade and cast this into a permanent structure. The French were also much more efficient than the British in their use of manpower, administering all blockade-related activities with just 53 persons (of whom 26 were female clerks and typists), compared to the 1,880 functionaries working under Cecil at the Ministry of Blockade and the Foreign Office.

This parsimony was largely due to Jacques Seydoux, an archetypal Quai d'Orsay civil servant and "the linchpin of the blockade effort" within the French state. Seydoux (1870–1929) was born into a Protestant family belonging to the liberal Parisian bourgeoisie. Educated at the École libre de sciences politiques, he worked as a diplomat in London, Berlin, and Athens before the war propelled him into the position of assistant director of blockade.[68] Seydoux was determined to defeat Germany, but he also wanted to use the blockade bodies to mobilize resources for postwar reconstruction, a task that he thought would necessarily involve all European countries. This forward-looking and pragmatic attitude locked Seydoux in an institutional struggle with Étienne Clémentel (1864–1936), the technocrat who served as minister of industry, commerce, post, and telegraphs. An imperious, confident, and self-aggrandizing figure, at the Paris Economic Conference in June 1916 Clémentel pushed through an inter-Allied resolution to permanently restrict German commerce after the war, against the will of Quai d'Orsay diplomats.[69] But his scattered responsibilities meant he never saw this plan through to the end. This allowed Seydoux to reposition France as a more constructive partner in economic warfare. From March 1916 onward the so-called Comité permanent international d'action économique convened in Paris with representatives from Britain, France, Italy, Russia, Serbia, Japan, Portugal, and (later) Romania to unite national blockade measures.[70] After American entry into the war an Allied Blockade Committee (ABC) was created for the same task. Even if most of the resources and intelligence in the blockade system flowed to

London, Paris remained an important locus of decision making among the wider coalition partners in the Entente.

The uses and limits of the blockade system become clear if we return to the example at the beginning of this chapter: what happened to shipments of Brazilian manganese to Germany? As blockade administrators tracked minerals, they made substantial advances but also encountered serious problems. As early as October 1914, manganese had been added to the British and French lists of goods considered "absolute contraband"—that is, goods that always served a military purpose and were thus readily seizable.[71] Prewar commercial statistics clearly conveyed Germany's dependence on manganese imports from Russia, India, Spain, and Brazil.[72] French economic intelligence composed a more detailed, though still imperfect, understanding of German production since the start of the war.[73] Tannery's analysts estimated that the total needs of the Central Powers amounted to roughly one million tons per year by late 1916; deducting their small estimated reserves, they expected the Germans to face a mounting shortfall.[74]

The war rearranged available routes of access to manganese suppliers. Since India was part of the British Empire and the Central Powers were fighting Russia on the Eastern front, Germany lost access to the two largest suppliers of the mineral ore. It was now wholly dependent on small amounts from neutral Spain and from the Jakobeny mine in Austrian-controlled Bukovina.[75] By the end of 1916, 90 percent of global production was controlled by the Reich's opponents. As rising shipping rates raised the cost of ocean transport from India and rail transport from Russia was severed, Brazilian manganese mines were uniquely well positioned to profit from this global disruption. Buoyed by high prices, Brazilian production rose from 183,000 tons in 1914 to 310,000 tons in 1915, reaching 350,000 tons in 1916 on the back of surging American demand. Enormous Entente munitions and materiel orders were reconfiguring the U.S. economy for war production.[76] Producing one ton of steel required fourteen pounds of manganese, and total U.S. imports from Brazil rose from 63,000 tons in 1913 to 468,000 tons in 1917.[77]

Two years into the war, German industry had been effectively shut off from its prewar supplies. French intelligence reported that German agents had tried to stockpile and smuggle manganese but that their hidden shipments had been intercepted by British naval patrols.[78] A combination of intelligence gathering, estimation, diplomatic coordination with allies and neutrals, and old-fashioned maritime power helped tighten the blockade of this key metal. But the blockaders' success did not immediately throttle their enemies' war effort. The reversion to lower-grade steel by German and Austrian war factories took time to make itself felt on the battlefield. Moreover, the Central Powers reacted to the shortage by shifting their aims. As we shall see, with their overseas supply cut off, German generals, bureaucrats, and industrialists focused on overland access to one region above all: Russia.

Blockade and Future Enforcement

Minister of Blockade Robert Cecil described his job as the management of "a blockade of an entirely novel character that nobody had ever tried to carry out in the history of the world before."[79] He unabashedly defended Britain's right to invasively manage global flows of goods, money, and information. To American newspaper readers, Cecil explained that Britain must be able to intercept transatlantic mail and telegraph messages.[80] In the second half of 1916, he also began to think more concretely about what the blockade project could mean for the future of international cooperation.[81] That September, he penned a memorandum to Lloyd George's cabinet on the challenge of preserving postwar peace. Cecil presented a counterfactual question: could the escalation of the July Crisis of 1914 have been avoided? When Austria-Hungary declared war on Serbia, not all options for a peaceful resolution had been exhausted. Cecil felt a negotiated settlement, either through a great power conference or some sort of arbitration procedure, could have resolved the crisis. Still, it remained difficult to compel the quarreling parties to respect the outcome of such a procedure. Cecil wrote:

> If, however, an instrument could be found which would exert considerable pressure on a recalcitrant Power without causing excessive risk to the Powers using it, a solution of the difficulty might perhaps be found. *I believe that in blockade as developed in this war such an instrument exists.* No doubt for its full effect an overwhelming naval power is requisite. But much could be done even by overwhelming financial power, and with the two combined no modern State could ultimately resist its pressure. Suppose in July 1914 it had been possible for the Entente Powers to say to Germany and Austria, unless the ultimatum to Serbia is modified or a conference is called, we will cut off all commercial and finan-

cial intercourse from you, it is very doubtful whether the Central Powers would have proceeded. If the United States could have been induced to join in such a declaration, the effect would have been enormously increased.[82]

This memorandum was the first proposal by a British cabinet official to transpose the blockade into a peacetime mechanism to prevent war. Cecil's idea would shape long-term plans for an international organization.[83] Yet his apparatus was only one branch of economic governance developed during the war. Vast efforts to mobilize global resources in support of the Entente war effort had also taken shape. Since early 1915, a small coterie of officials at the Treasury that included the young John Maynard Keynes had worked to link the balance sheets of the Entente economies together. By 1916, credits from Wall Street were fueling massive Anglo-French arms procurement in the United States. A novel intergovernmental body to manage shipping tonnage, the AMTC, was created under the British civil servant Arthur Salter and the French businessman Jean Monnet. By 1918 the AMTC had enlisted much of the global merchant marine to supply the Entente war economy.[84] International economic cooperation worked to deprive the enemy and provide resources to alliance partners at the same time. This strategic duality bore some resemblance to Napoleon's Continental System of 1806-1813, which the French historian Albert Sorel once described as a "two-trigger machine" (*machine à double détente*) to ruin Britain's foreign trade while constructing a new continent-oriented economic system.[85] Allied economic internationalism during World War I functioned in a similar way: Cecil, Arnold-Forster, and Seydoux focused on interdiction of resources to the enemy, while Salter, Keynes, and Monnet managed their mobilization for the alliance.

   That the two faces of this Janus-like global project complemented one another did not mean that there was agreement on how it should develop or to what end. Many believed that if the contraband control system against the neutrals was pressed too hard, access to these countries' resources would be lost. Moderates such as Seydoux believed that a fine balance should be maintained between closing off world-economic possibilities to the Central Powers and realizing them for the Entente. Yet hardliners such as Clémentel and the French interventionists around him pushed for both more inter-Allied integration *and* increased pressure on the Central Powers. It was in this context that the concept of "the economic weapon" (*l'arme économique*) first gained traction in 1917.[86] Clémentel's chief adviser, the economic historian Henri Hauser, spelled out the term's meaning in a memorandum for French cabinet communication with the Wilson administration. In Hauser's view, the Entente's economic union fulfilled five distinct roles: first, that of a "combat weapon" to undermine the Central Powers' morale; second, "a first-rate guarantee for peace negotiations"; third, "a measure of persuasion and attraction with regard to neutrals"; fourth, "an instrument of mutual aid in view of Allied economic recovery and development"; and fifth, perhaps most important of all, "one of the foundations and most effective guarantees of the new international order that will have to be founded after this war."[87]

This vision contained an important tension. Either the economic weapon could become an impartial instrument of peace or it could retain its offensive character and aim at the "industrial ruin" of specific threats, especially Germany. What was difficult was to combine these two aims into a single mechanism, especially if it was to acquire broad legitimacy after the war in the eyes of the defeated countries.[88] What set French internal disputes apart from divisions in the British government was that the disagreement concerned not the viability of the economic weapon but the ultimate intentions behind it. Should it be used to continue power politics or to transcend them? This question would hang over the entire interwar history of sanctions and would be a major bone of contention in Anglo-French relations. In a meeting with British officials in August 1917, Clémentel suggested a scheme for inter-Allied control of global raw materials to force Germany to accept peace. In his view commodity control was a powerful instrument for the preservation of peace in the name of a postwar international organization or arbitration. "In the future, would it not be in this control of raw materials," Clémentel asked, "that the united states of Europe, of America, of Asia could find the sanction, vainly sought in the force of arms, which would impose peace on unruly peoples [*peuples turbulents*] as on predatory peoples [*peuples de proie*] and would this not be the best constraint to guide toward arbitrage?"[89] His hierarchical language spoke volumes about the world order Clémentel was committed to preserving.

The wartime experience of Greece shows how the blockade remained embroiled in old-fashioned power politics and could function as a more refined instrument of it. Officially neutral, Greece was riven between a pro-Allied faction under republican prime minister Eleftherios Venizelos and a pro-German clique of officers around King Constantine, brother-in-law of the German Kaiser. In late 1916 this split escalated into a de facto civil war. To press Constantine into joining the war on the Allied side, the French government extended the general European blockade system to the royalist areas of Greece, especially the Peloponnese, but without declaring war. Britain soon joined this policy, seizing Greek ships in Allied ports. Since the population of Old Greece depended on food imports, this pacific blockade caused severe hunger. Civilian mortality in Athens doubled in early 1917. In June the king abdicated, and the Allies ended their blockade; Venizelos quickly formed a new government that led the country into war on their side. On the brink of world war, economic pressure had been politically efficacious but highlighted Greece's subordinate status in the international order.[90] Europe's great powers had used pacific blockades against the country in 1827, 1850, and 1886. While in 1917 Cecil and Clémentel staked out lofty visions for the future use of such techniques, to the Greek population the economic deprivation of that year was reminiscent of the plight of their nineteenth-century ancestors.

Financial Blockade

In its early years, Allied blockade policy focused on the interception of physical goods and seizure of foreign property. Over time, bunker control also brought energy under the control of the blockaders. What remained largely untouched, however, was the most dynamic element of the world economy: the global financial system. Although world trade between Central Europe and the rest of the world had slowed considerably, Germany and Austria-Hungary still found sources of funds abroad. Large money flows continued to pass through financial centers in neutral countries. Between February and March 1916, for example, the British Treasury recorded over $11 million in wire transfers from Wall Street to various neutral European banks.[91] One circular noted that "Dutch and Scandinavian banks are putting through business of incredible magnitude. Small banks in places like Amsterdam, Rotterdam, Copenhagen, Christiania, Bergen, Malmö, Trondjhem and Stockholm put through as much business in a day as they would in a month of normal times. There is no other basis possible for all this finance than trading with Germany."[92] Cecil's Ministry of Blockade wanted to stop these flows. But it lacked both the necessary personnel and the methods to obtain systematic financial intelligence from the City of London.

The City banker E. F. Davies suspected that many trades through London involving neutral banks in fact hid profits from German firms overseas being repatriated to the Reich.[93] Davies recommended that the ministry develop a policy for the financial blockade of Germany by recruiting experienced traders from the City to spot such suspicious transactions.[94] Imposing more bureaucracy and blocking a certain amount of trades would cause the City to lose some of its foreign exchange business. But the gains in the efficacy of the blockade were, in Davies's eyes, far larger. "Some people," he thought, "look at the pecuniary side of the matter, without considering that it is better to lose money for six months and wage war successfully than to make money and endanger the Empire."[95]

Cecil appointed Davies to lead a newly created Finance Section. He brought with him a small coterie of like-minded bankers from Barclays and the Hong Kong and Shanghai Banking Corporation (HSBC). The Finance Section developed a stamp-authorization scheme for neutral-to-neutral financial transfers through London.[96] Because orders to transfer money and securities were sent by post or by telegram, a financial blockade was in effect a communications blockade: whoever controlled postal routes and undersea telegraph cables also controlled payment flows. Mail censorship and signals interception thus became instrumental to severing enemy banks from the global financial system. The Finance Section compensated for its limited personnel by placing the burden of enforcement on financial institutions themselves. From May 1916 banks in Allied countries were made to sign guarantees that their accounts would not be used "for any business which will in any way, either directly or indirectly, assist or be for the benefit of an enemy of Great Britain or her Allies."[97] Blockade administrators thereby held the prospect of blacklisting, prosecution, and forced closure over the heads of private bankers. The Finance Section created its own intelligence-gathering network by developing a rudimentary system of mandatory reporting: select banks incorporated under British law had to report their weekly flows to and from neutral countries.[98] The role of banks in greasing the wheels of trade meant that the Finance Section also learned much about commercial goings-on. In a memorandum to Lord Cecil, Davies reported that "Every consignment of goods crossing the seas which is financed in the United Kingdom under credits established with British Banks can be followed by the Finance Section . . . including the names of the consignors and consignees, ports of shipment and destination, names of steamers, and dates of sailing, etc."[99]

In the late summer of 1916, Sir Adam Block succeeded Davies as the head of the Finance Section.[100] Block was an experienced banker who had spent a long time in the Ottoman Empire, where he had served as chief dragoman (interpreter) of the British Embassy and as an administrator in the Ottoman Public Debt Administration.[101] He immediately proposed a crackdown on Swiss banks, which he saw as duplicitous financiers of the Kaiser. In conversations with French blockade officials, he also proposed cutting off all American money orders to neutrals that passed through London. The French government was taken aback by the impetuousness of Block's approach.[102] Their Commission financière inter-ministérielle (Inter-Ministerial Finance Commission) was run largely by French central bank officials but also included private bankers such as Octave Homberg, another veteran of colonial finance who had chaired the Banque de l'Indochine and Banque de l'Union Parisienne, and negotiated the first inter-Allied loan of the war on Wall Street in 1915.[103] The commission, supplied with intelligence by the analysts of Tannery's SCE and in frequent contact with Jacques Seydoux's blockade desk at the Quai d'Orsay, drove forward the partial financial blockade targeting neutral countries that was constructed in 1917.

Latin America was a large supplier of raw materials to European industry, but it was equally important to Britain and Germany as a destination for foreign investment.[104] Financing new ventures in this high-growth market was a very profitable activity for the banks involved; in 1913 Deutsche Bank's regional subsidiary, the Banco Alemán Transatlántico, brought in one-sixth of the revenue and net profits of its parent conglomerate.[105] Five German banking consortiums had created their own subsidiary banks in the region between 1886 and 1912.[106] As long as this considerable German banking and business in Latin America continued, a blockade focused narrowly on physical goods trade failed to dent the Reich's global economic position. The financial blockaders thus began to seek ways to prevent the German repatriation of overseas profits to the besieged metropole. But enforcing such a policy confronted administrators in Paris and London with the difficulties of intervening in the early twentieth-century financial system without damaging their own economies. A striking case study is the Franco-British effort in late 1917 to stop German financial transfers from Argentina and punish the French and Dutch banks that facilitated them.

At the center of this affair stood Crédit Lyonnais, the great success story of French fin-de-siècle finance. Founded in 1863 with a capital of 20 million francs, fifty years later it had grown into the world's largest bank, with total assets of 2.85 billion francs (£113 million).[107] As a multi-continental banking conglomerate, it provided short-term trade credit and

long-term capital to firms in eastern and southern Europe, Russia, the
Middle East, Latin America, and Asia. The French megabank conducted
Latin American business through its Madrid branch, which transacted
with German, Dutch, and Swiss banks active in the region. National allegiance mattered little in this domain, and Crédit Lyonnais held in trust a
portfolio of securities that belonged to Banco Alemán Transatlántico.[108]

Most Latin American finance was conducted by the subsidiaries of
major European banks. One of the Crédit Lyonnais's counterparties was
a subsidiary of the Rotterdamsche Bank, which had been established in
March 1914. It opened its first branch in Buenos Aires in October as the
Banco Holandés de la América del Sud. A Brazilian branch in Rio followed in 1916.[109] Banco Holandés first appeared in the intelligence funnel
of the French blockaders in February 1916, when its Buenos Aires branch
bought 4.3 million marks' worth of gold on behalf of the Disconto Gesellschaft, the second-largest bank in Germany. Disconto had for some time
been trying to sell gold to the Argentine government to raise money for
German war expenditures.[110] Because there was not yet a coherent Entente financial blockade policy in place, both Dutch banks and Argentina
were free to transact as they wished. No action was taken. But the Latin
American branches of European banks were an obvious future target for
blockade administrators.

By the late summer of 1917, the entry of the United States into the
war changed the situation. The Allied powers now controlled the world's
three main financial centers—New York, London, and Paris—and could
mount a more forceful campaign of financial pressure. In early September, Adam Block of the Ministry of Blockade's Finance Section argued for
more stringent controls on neutral banks at the French inter-ministerial
financial committee in Paris. "Experience has shown," he claimed, "what
a powerful weapon is constituted by the inscription on black lists and the
exclusion of all relations with the Allies; before such a threat, a great majority of neutral banks will accept our conditions."[111] Block wanted a blan-
ket ban on transactions between Allied citizens and neutral citizens who
had any kind of relation with the Central Powers. His French colleague
Octave Homberg was more cautious. A general embargo against large
neutral banks, he thought, ran the risk of backfiring. Forced to choose between the two rival alliances, banks that were heavily involved in business
with the Central Powers would probably cut their ties with the Entente
rather than cease lending to Germany. In that case, Homberg warned,
"The weapon that we will have forged will turn itself against us."[112] He

thought that a more subtle approach was needed: a blacklist-style system of discretionary prohibitions not against banks as a whole but only against specific suspicious transfers, justified as a measure to target arbitrageurs speculating against Allied currencies.[113]

These more capillary sanctions were soon applied to transatlantic transfers between Latin America and European neutrals. As Allied financial pressure on Brazil increased, the Banco Holandés's Rio branch became the conduit for profit transfers to Spain; German merchants likely hoped that its Dutch affiliation would shield them from the blockaders. From intelligence gathered on the spot by consular personnel, the French blockaders learned that the Banco Holandés had links with the German trading house Bromberg & Company and demanded its inscription on the blacklist.[114] On 14 August, the Dutch bank's Rio branch sent 180,000 Spanish pesetas (£8,500) from an account held by the Deutsche Sudamerikanische Bank to the Madrid branch of Crédit Lyonnais. A similar-sized payment through the Banco Holandés followed nine days later, followed by a half-million-peseta (£23,900) wire transfer in September. Upon noticing these payments, the French embassy in Madrid requested that the bank, which was clearly sending enemy funds to Europe, be added to the blacklist.

By October 1917 a file had been drawn up on the Dutch bank. Banco Holandés used five different names to undertake transactions for various Latin American subsidiaries of several major German banks such as Deutsche Bank, Dresdner Bank, A. Schaaffhausen'scher Bankverein, and Darmstädter und Nationalbank. The Dutch bank's three branches in Amsterdam, Rio, and Buenos Aires were soon added to the French blacklist.[115] The plot thickened when it was discovered that there were two French nationals on the Banco Holandés's board of directors. To the members of the French financial blockade committee the most troubling aspect was not even the presence of fellow Frenchmen on the board of a blockade-violating bank but the fact that Crédit Lyonnais, an institution they considered their national pride, had allowed Germans to use foreign front accounts.

Bringing Crédit Lyonnais's Madrid branch to heel posed another challenge. After the French blockaders had frozen its correspondent accounts with neutrals, Spanish courts had become involved. They were now ordering Crédit Lyonnais to fulfill its contractual obligations to its counterparties, as Spanish clients were suing the French bank for nonpayment. Its Madrid branch directors pleaded with the financial blockade committee for permission to make the payments that had fallen into arrears. But the committee was steadfast: "Crédit Lyonnais, a French corporation, must conform to the French law and could not defend any better before the Spanish courts a refusal to pay than by invoking this obligation."[116] What was at stake in the Crédit Lyonnais–Banco Holandés affair was how much power nation-states could exercise over the globalized private financial sector. Could the French government force the world's largest bank to reconfigure its international business in the national interest?[117] Before 1914 Western governments often assisted bankers in international affairs as financial houses acquired significant political influence in Europe, Asia, Africa, and the Americas. Inter-Allied war finance was highly dependent on a small group of New York–, London–, and Paris-based bankers. The extension of the blockade into the financial world brought about a local inversion of this relation, rendering banks vulnerable to political decisions about the intensity with which economic warfare should be pursued. In legal terms the French state had little difficulty forbidding *direct* transfers from French banks to enemy nationals. But this was trickier in the case of payments *between neutral banks*, on which the plumbing of Allied war finance also relied.

Nonetheless, by intervening forcefully in specific cases without erecting permanent controls, the financial blockaders set an example while leaving the banking sector in charge of its own compliance. Financial blockade was primarily a surveillance mechanism, although this did not, in the view of the committee, "diminish in any manner that the financial establishments take their own precautions and police themselves. It is they who are the best equipped to survey their correspondents and their agencies and the Government does not have the task to substitute itself for them."[118] Compliance would be the banks' own responsibility. Even as global economic war decisively ended the laissez-faire world of the nineteenth century, private interests remained to a large degree masters of their own house. But where the limits of state intervention lay would emerge as a recurring problem in the design of sanctions in the decades to come.

CHAPTER TWO

The Birth of Sanctions from the Spirit of Blockade, 1917–1919

E
CONOMIC ISOLATION LEFT A powerful impression on those who experienced World War I. "Blockade delivers blow upon blow, now here, now there, till every bone in the national body is broken," wrote Russian shipping entrepreneur Boris Kadomtsev as he looked back on the events of 1917. In his view, "Many histories of war would have to be entirely rewritten if the influence of the Blockade in the affairs as well as in the 'history of the world' were to be given its true place."[1]

World history indeed took a decisive turn in the first four months of that year. In fact, it was as much economic pressure by the Central Powers as by the Allies that was responsible. When Germany blocked the Danish Sound and the Ottoman Empire closed the Turkish Straits, Russia lost the main arteries connecting its vast economy to the outside world. Before the war a quarter of the world's grain trade had passed through the Dardanelles.[2] With its merchant marine bottled up in the Black Sea and the Baltic by this dual blockade and its Arctic ports accessible only six months a year, the Russian economy came under tremendous strain.[3] Without sufficient export earnings or imports of coal and food, by early 1917 the railways could no longer adequately supply the world's largest army and the sizeable civilian population.[4] In March a revolution overthrew the tsarist state in Petrograd. In the same weeks, the German decision to try to bring

England to its knees by restarting unrestricted submarine warfare brought on a second turning point: the United States entered the war on the Allied side as an associated power.[5]

Russia's revolution and Germany's unleashing of U-boats against Atlantic shipping were crucial events in the blockade of the Central Powers. As the tsarist armies collapsed, the eastern rampart in the economic siege of Central Europe crumbled. Vast Eurasian resources now beckoned. Securing these raw materials seemed to offer Berlin and Vienna an escape from material attrition. At the same time, U.S. entry into the conflict enormously strengthened the alliance of the Allied and Associated Powers. Washington did not just control vast quantities of raw materials, food, and capital. Congress also passed its own version of the British Trading with the Enemy Act, beginning a campaign of expropriation against "alien property."[6] As Latin American governments followed suit in declaring war, Germany lost much of its foreign investment in the Western Hemisphere. Finally, the arrival of U.S. troops set the clock ticking on the timespan in which Germany could achieve battlefield victory on the Western front.

As the war entered its final year, economic war thus assumed a paramount importance. In these months, between late 1917 and the summer of 1918, talk about the power and promise of "the economic weapon" reached a peak in Britain, France, and the United States. Raw materials control seemed a war-winning weapon as well as a way to keep a defeated Reich docile. "The economic weapon, the most decisive, which can, without a drop of blood, bring the aggressor to his knees, will be used," wrote the French newspaper editor Léon Bailby in 1918. "The threat will be understood in Germany . . . and that the League of Nations is no longer a utopia, because it brings out into the open an irresistible weapon."[7] Nor were the Allies alone in perceiving resource control as pivotal. As they negotiated and then exploited peace in the East, the German leadership too became fixated on the resources of the Black Sea and Caucasus region, launching several quixotic expeditions to acquire the raw materials necessary to withstand any future blockade. Yet in the fall of 1918 it was not immediate shortage but battlefield exhaustion and the collapse of morale among German soldiers in the West that broke the Reich's resistance.

These dramatic reversals of fortune transformed expectations of what victory would look like in the final two years of the war. They also deeply shaped blockade policy and by extension the sanctions of the future League of Nations. Germany's rush for resources in the East convinced the Allies to maintain the blockade after the Armistice in November 1918; the last restrictions would not be fully lifted until July 1919, after a new republican government signed the Versailles Treaty. Simultaneously, the widespread perception that the world order now hinged on the global balance of raw materials spurred a flurry of Allied proposals for sanctions mechanisms. Regardless of what shape these would take, it was clear that the new international organization being crafted at the Paris Peace Conference would "rule by economic pressure."[8] The eventual provisions of Article 16 of the League's Covenant were a compromise solution, with all the imperfections of backroom diplomacy. For one thing, it was very much an open question whether blockade had in fact won the war for the Allies. Another issue was that neither Cecil nor his French counterpart Léon Bourgeois had envisioned a league that was dependent on economic sanctions alone. Both believed that some military intervention capacity, even if only a minimal one, had to be created. Nor had the British intended sanctions to be a peacetime instrument; in line with their common law tradition, they preferred to wage economic war openly. But at the Paris Peace Conference the role of U.S. president Woodrow Wilson and his legal adviser, David Hunter Miller, blocked European intentions on both counts. Economic sanctions thereby took on an institutional form that was unexpected, while their ideological appeal as a history-shaping weapon grew massively and probably beyond proportion.

The Involuntary Autarky of the Central Powers

The governments of Germany and Austria-Hungary had long maintained they were invincible in the face of the enemy's blockade. Chancellor Bethmann-Hollweg declared early in the war that "the economic unit from Arras to Mesopotamia cannot be crushed."[9] His inclusion of the Middle East in the Central Powers' besieged land fortress was apposite. When the Ottoman Empire entered the war in November 1914, it too became a target of Entente economic warfare. Unlike in the North Sea, where enemy mines and submarines necessitated the use of a contraband control system, in the Mediterranean the British and French navies could actually institute an effective blockade and declared one against the Ottoman Empire.[10] The Anglo-French blockade of Anatolia and the Levant devastated the food economy of Greater Syria. It has not received the historical attention that it deserves, especially in light of the fact that it likely contributed to as many civilian deaths as the blockade of Central Europe.[11] Estimates of the total deaths among the inhabitants of Greater Syria between 1915 and 1918 range from 350,000 to 500,000.[12] One historian has estimated that as much as 18 percent of the population of Ottoman Syria, or one in six inhabitants, died during the war.[13] The Ottoman Empire was a net importer of grain, bringing in eighty-eight thousand tons of cereals in 1913–1914, all of which were cut off by the Anglo-French blockade. Requisitioning of grain and animals by the Ottoman army weakened the distribution of food and effectively severed towns from the surrounding countryside. On top of this, a locust attack hit the region in 1915, with swarms the size of Manhattan consuming the food intake of forty-two million humans in a single day.[14] After the harvest of 1916 was severely reduced, famine conditions took hold. Ottoman exploitation and locusts caused serious hardship. But it was the blockade that massively compounded the dislocation of regional agriculture, causing a food crisis to tip into starvation and eventually mass civilian deaths. This is clear from the fact that after early 1917, Ottoman regions such as Transjordan, which were connected by Arab trading networks to maritime supplies of food, were less affected by famine than Syria and Lebanon, which remained under both Ottoman control and formal blockade.[15] From December 1915 until October 1918 no ships, not even neutral ones, were permitted to cross the Mediterranean blockading line upheld by the British and French navies.[16] In December 1916 the USS *Caesar*, an American vessel bound for Beirut with two thousand tons of aid, including grain, was intercepted and its cargo diverted to Salonika and Alexandria.[17] The "effective" and thereby lawful character of the blockade was one of the major causes of its deadliness. In comparison to the contraband control used against Germany, in the Mediterranean the formal legality of blockade increased its lethality.

Yet exposure to blockade produced only limited change within the Ottoman state. In part this was because the Ottoman elite actively welcomed the starvation of groups such as Armenians and Arabs that it considered internal enemies or seditious subjects.[18] Within the German elite, however, there was great concern about the problems that prolonged material isolation posed for the national economy and popular welfare. The wartime economic organization that emerged in 1915–1916 was shaped by the effects of this external pressure. As the Entente devised new methods to turn control of the raw materials and food resources into weapons, the Central Powers drew lessons from the blockade about wartime economic organization and the utility of conquest.[19] Almost without exception, German commentators criticized the British blockade as illegal and in violation of international law.[20] For the nationalist right, the blockade confirmed its suspicions that Britain was a perfidious empire that would defend its hegemony at all costs.[21]

When it came to ideas about the postwar order, the German experience of economic encirclement by blockade produced two broad responses. One was the call for a return to a liberal legalism. The exclusionary resolutions of the Paris Economic Conference of June 1916 provided a perfect target for such arguments. Clémentel's harsh measures made the Entente appear as a mercantilist alliance unwilling to grant Germany equal standing in the world economy. These proposals openly renounced many of the principles of economic liberalism and equality—such as most-favored nation status, protection of property and patents, and equitable market access—for which the Allies claimed to be fighting. German economists were quick to note the discrepancies.[22] The Reichstag's famous Peace Resolution of 19 July 1917 demanded an end to Germany's economic isolation in any settlement. It was the only hope that the political center—the coalition of social democrats, liberals, and centrist Catholics—had of rebuilding a prosperous German economy with a global presence. To them economic peace (*Wirtschaftsfrieden*) was the key prerequisite of any political peace.

The other line of response was more radical. It was the onset of blockade in full force in 1916 that drove a growing interest in the idea of *Mitteleuropa*, a German-led central European economic zone. As talk of an "economic weapon" in Paris and London increased in 1917, the scope of German ambition in the East rose proportionately.[23] Erich Ludendorff and his staff at the Supreme Army Command (Oberste Heeresleitung; OHL) began to see expansionary autarky as the most viable strategy for long-term security. Ludendorff concluded that "a three-years' war was only possible because we had in Germany abundant coal, and so much iron and food that together with what we could obtain from occupied territory and neutral countries, we could, by practising the most rigid economy, manage to exist in spite of the hostile blockade. Only by offensive action . . . had we been able to exist; we should certainly have been lost had we remained within our own frontiers."[24] In his assessment, comprehensive economic warfare had changed the minimal requirements for hegemony. A state that did not possess vital raw materials, or reliable access to them, could survive prolonged war only by seizing territory containing those resources through conquest. At a September 1917 meeting about German demands for possible peace negotiations, Ludendorff stated:

> I am of [the] opinion that it is desirable that we should try to get a peace before the winter sets in, so long as it brings us those essentials we need to secure our economic position hereafter and gives us an economic and military position which allows us to face another war of defence without anxiety. . . . Without Rumania and the other occupied areas, we should have been in a critical position with regard to food. Even with Rumania it has been serious enough. . . . We must, therefore, have an increase of territory. That territory can only be found in Courland and Lithuania, which offer good agricultural opportunities.[25]

The more an all-consuming war seemed inevitable, the more German and Allied war aims became locked in a mutual process of radicalization.[26] Allied economic warfare did not only respond to a fixed set of German goals. The shifting pressure of the blockade actively shaped those goals as they changed the strategic and political objectives of the German elite.

The Economic Consequences of Brest-Litovsk

The February Revolution in Russia raised the prospect that the largest land army of the Entente would cease to fight in the war. If the eastern pillar of the war effort collapsed, the entire Allied grand strategy for conducting the war had to be revised. Sir William Robertson, the British chief of the Imperial General Staff, wrote a memorandum on the possibility of a Russian collapse in May 1917. "One of the most important results of Russia making peace," Robertson warned, "would be to relieve the blockade of Germany by allowing her to procure supplies from Russia." Although he noted that the value of Russian resources depended on the state of the railway system, the speed of Russian demobilization, and the domestic need for food supplies, he estimated that "in course of time substantial relief must undoubtedly be expected."[27]

In the absence of a battlefield decision, the main road to victory—the economic blockade of the Central Powers—would be fatally undermined if the encirclement broke in the East. Christabel Pankhurst, the most prominent suffragette supporter of Lloyd George's war effort and the editor of the nationalistic journal *Brittania*, even traveled to Petrograd to personally appeal to Alexander Kerensky's Provisional Government to honor the Entente and continue a war of attrition against the Central Powers.[28] But in August, the British war cabinet agreed that "possibly the stalemate in the military operations might become so complete that it might be necessary to fall back on a passive defensive; to hold the line with the smallest number of men compatible with safety, and thus to release as much manpower as possible for industry, and simply to rely upon blockade to bring about the collapse of the enemy, just as often occurred in the case of a siege."[29]

From this perspective, the Allied military intervention in Russia that began in December 1917 was a means to preserve the economic encirclement of Germany. In London, Foreign Secretary Arthur Balfour was maneuvering to get an expeditionary force off the ground. He wanted to keep the siege intact by finding local military proxies, "various Cossack organizations to the North of the Caucasus and Armenians to the South [who] control [the] richest grain-growing districts of the country and almost all coal and iron. . . . While war continues a Germanized Russia would provide a source of supply which would go far to neutralize effects of Allied blockade."[30]

When negotiations for a peace between Russia and the Central Powers started at Brest-Litovsk, the Allies followed them closely. In Austria-Hungary, public attention focused on the need for a "bread peace" (*Brotfrieden*) to provide food for the empire's cities.[31] Once the size of the territories that Russia would cede to the Central Powers became clear in early 1918, Allied elites were shocked. For some the Brest-Litovsk Treaty changed the entire outcome that could reasonably be expected from the war.[32] Winston Churchill wrote that "no one at this time saw any prospect of a speedy end to the war, and there seemed no reason to doubt that the Germans and Austrians would have the time—as they certainly had the power—to draw new life almost indefinitely from the giant Empire prostrated before them."[33] Robertson likewise thought the best outcome that Britain could now secure would be to "gain terms of peace which would render the future position of the British Empire reasonably secure."[34] When the treaty was signed in March, the WTID's chief German expert, William G. Max-Muller, noted that the enemy was emboldened by "the knowledge that he has burst the barrier that we had built round him, and is no longer dependent on his own resources. . . . It would be a grave mistake to underestimate the effect on Germany's economic position of her achievements in the East." But, Max-Muller continued, "Though Germany may get food from Russia, and also coal, iron, oil, flax, leather, etc., there are many essential raw materials, such as cotton, wool, jute, silk, rubber, and countless other commodities of which we shall still be in a position to deprive her."[35]

The chief French strategy-making body, the French Supreme War Council (Conseil supérieur de guerre; CSG), took a very pessimistic view of the peace in the East. It declared that "the events in Russia modify profoundly the physiognomy of the war and will modify the physiognomy of the peace. The axis of German policy has been moved." It was not German navalism that threatened the world; the real menace was Berlin's imminent control over the Eurasian landmass. "One should not have any illusions," the French staffers warned; "a Germany obtaining economic domination over the Balkans, Russia, and all of Western Asia has won the war and become master of the Old World."[36]

Indeed, German industrial interests were pushing the Reich government to secure manganese deposits in Ukraine and the Caucasus.[37] Eighty percent of Russian production came from the Georgian Chiatura mines; the remaining 20 percent was mined at Nikopol in Ukraine, another territory put under German influence by the Treaty of Brest-Litovsk.[38] A German engineer noted that proven deposits amounted to 30 million tons in the Caucasus and 11 million tons in Ukraine, but estimated reserves in the former were eight times larger than proven ones—some 240 million tons. Such an estimate amounted to at least forty-two years' worth of manganese at 1917 consumption levels, enough to supply Ruhr steel manufacturers until 1959.[39] Unsurprisingly, the Kaiser and his generals saw a trans-Caucasian expedition to obtain Georgian manganese and Caspian oil as a top priority.[40]

As the Allies grasped the size of the prize obtained by Germany at Brest-Litovsk, they veered between despondent and self-assured views of the future of blockade. In late November 1917, the prominent Tory politician Lord Lansdowne voiced his opposition to the government's economic war policy in an open letter to the editor of the *Daily Telegraph*. "While a commercial 'boycott' would be justifiable as a war measure, and while the threat of a 'boycott' in case Germany should show herself utterly unreasonable, would be a legitimate threat," Lansdowne opined, "no reasonable man would, surely, desire to destroy the trade of the Central Powers, if they will, so to speak, enter into recognizances to keep the peace, and do not force us into a conflict by a hostile combination."[41] He proposed making a genuine offer of economic peace to Berlin. The next month, the Conservative speaker of Parliament, James Lowther, went further and criticized the idea of a postwar boycott of Germany: to "cut her off altogether and treat her as though she were a leper . . . that would be a way of carrying on the war, and although it would not be with the weapons we were now using, there would be the same hatred and struggle between one combination of nations and another, and it would leave the world divided."[42]

Against such hopes of returning to prewar commercial normalcy, Cecil continued to project his total economic war beyond the war's end, with the full backing of Prime Minister David Lloyd George. The liberal *Economist* magazine, under the patriotic management of Hartley Withers, who had replaced the previous editor, the pro-peace Francis Hirst, wholly endorsed the intransigent cabinet position.[43] "The threat to enforce an economic boycott is a very strong card in the hand of the Allied Powers," the paper wrote, "and one which may legitimately be used to the full to shorten the war or to bring about a real peace. . . . A ruinous boycott of an unrepentant Germany is no idle threat."[44] Cecil defended the economic weapon as the best instrument of a future league of nations, citing Henry VII's disciplining of restive noblemen after the Wars of the Roses as an example: "How did a strong English King finally gain ascendancy and control over the warring Barons?" Cecil asked. "He instituted a central body which enforced decrees on the Barons largely by economic means."[45]

A similar determination to achieve total victory was palpable in Paris, where the elections of November 1917 brought to power the radical republican Georges Clemenceau on a platform committed to "integral war" (*guerre intégrale*). Clemenceau's stance attracted broad support, even from his political opponents. The monarchist Léon Daudet affirmed that "without total war, the blockade, which rightly claimed—at least until the Russian defection—to encircle and starve Germany, was and could only be a word."[46] The French right thought that the weapon of resource control should be used in a merciless fashion to bring German imperialism to heel. Edmond Laskine, columnist for the legitimist newspaper *La Liberté*, suggested a staggered boycott: if Germany made peace within six months, its products would be banned from Allied markets for five years afterward; if it fought for another year, they would be boycotted for a decade. Laskine was confident that "after Brest-Litovsk Germany is and remains excluded from the *Weltwirtschaft* [world economy]. Lenin and Trotsky can give imperial Germany the keys to Riga or even to Petrograd: but the keys to international trade are not within their reach."[47]

Despite this nationalist zeal, Clemenceau's cabinet viewed German economic domination of Eastern Europe as a very serious threat. This prompted two fateful French decisions in March and April 1918. The first was to continue the blockade after any eventual armistice. The cabinet's bureau of economic studies advised that because Eastern resources could sustain a virtually limitless German war effort, economic pressure should continue even after a cease-fire with Berlin.[48] On this basis, French block-aders received permission to continue their efforts until German hege-mony in Eurasia was overturned.[49] This was a crucial contingent event with great significance for the subsequent history of sanctions. In fact, by convincing the Allies to maintain the blockade beyond the end of hostili-ties, it was the peace of Brest-Litovsk in the East, not the Treaty of Ver-sailles in the West, that began the creation of modern economic sanctions as measures outside of war.

Clemenceau's second decision was to tighten the financial blockade of Russia in response to its exit from the Entente. Petrograd's peace deal with Germany was particularly concerning to the French because of their vast financial interests in Russia; a quarter of the entire French stock of for-eign investment was in tsarist government bonds and private enterprises.[50] Following the February Revolution the Provisional Government not only continued to pay interest on old tsarist debts held by foreigners, but also borrowed substantial new funds on the Paris money market.[51] After the Bolshevik seizure of power, the French state stepped in to guarantee inter-est payments to investors.[52] But this policy became untenable when, in February 1918, the Bolsheviks repudiated Russia's entire 14.8-billion-ruble foreign debt.[53]

The largest debt default in history disproportionately affected a block of 1.5 million middle-class savers who held 43 percent of all French capital in Russia.[54] Yet what worried the French public even more than the default itself was the possibility that imperial Germany might materially benefit from it. Although few observers in early 1918 expected Lenin and Trot-sky's Bolsheviks to last very long in power, many did fear that in despera-tion the Communists might surrender Allied economic assets to Germany. What the Treaty of Brest-Litovsk put at stake was not just physical control of territory, but also legal title to hundreds of firms owned and financed by Western investors. The French Ministry of Blockade received word that German buyers were already prowling neutral markets for oppor-tunities to purchase these enterprises. Its economic intelligence section warned that "it is an established fact that the Germans have been looking for some time to acquire the shares of the firms that find themselves in re-gions occupied by them, as a way to assure themselves of the majority of their capital and to take over control of these firms."[55]

In response to this threat—a hostile takeover if ever there was one—the French National Assembly passed the most far-reaching capital controls of the war. The law of 3 April 1918, written jointly by the finance and war ministries and rushed through parliament, effectively forbade French investors from selling specific financial assets to foreign parties. An initial list of firms to which the law applied had already been drawn up in late March, containing dozens of majority French–owned firms in the Balkans and the Ottoman Empire.[56] Octave Homberg, the banker in charge of the French financial blockade, wrote to Clemenceau that the 3 April law would "prevent the export from France of the assets of enterprises situated in Russia, in Turkey, in Romania and in Serbia, where French capital has an interest, and in which the enemy is looking to acquire a preponderant influence."[57] Since the Ministry of Finance was already paying rentiers interest on defaulted Russian state debt, its financial controls affected stakes in Russian industrial, mining, railway, timber, oil, and agricultural enterprises that were easy to sell and hence likely to end up in enemy hands.[58] But by preventing French savers from selling the defaulted debt elsewhere, even at a steep discount, the financial blockade reinforced the loss of wealth inflicted by the Bolshevik default. This spurred fierce popular anti-communist sentiment that would leave a deep mark on French politics in the interwar period.

Allied anxieties about Eastern resources increased further on 7 May, when delegations from the four Central Powers signed the Treaty of Bucharest with Romania. Among its economic clauses was the Romanian government's extension of a ninety-year lease of its oil reserves to German firms. The treaty also installed German civil servants in Bucharest to oversee Romanian ministries.[59] The country's resources could be rapidly tapped. Seventeen months of military occupation had allowed repairs and infrastructural improvements to progress; by the spring of 1918 some 370 oil wells were in operation, with another 136 wells under construction. In February, Romania sent 277 trainwagons of oil a day to Germany and Austria-Hungary; by May the rate had risen to 400 trainloads a day.[60] The country was rapidly becoming a cornerstone of the Central Powers' ability to resist resource blockade.[61] But in the long run, more was needed. As the Kaiser reminded his generals in characteristically clipped language, "We went into Ukraine to get food."[62] In June, a German force arrived in Tbilisi to secure the long-awaited ore and oil reserves of the Caucasus.[63]

The German spring offensives on the Western front showed that the Reich still possessed serious fighting power.[64] A conflict that had moved little for years now changed into mobile warfare, combining assault tactics with unprecedented artillery barrages and poison gas to achieve an overwhelming material and psychological effect. In the face of early German military successes, Allied elites reassured themselves of eventual victory by emphasizing that the global balance of forces still overwhelmingly favored them. The British classicist Alfred Zimmern, then working in the political department of the Foreign Office, rhapsodized about the economic weapon, "the most powerful in the varied armory of the Allies. . . . No human power can prevent it from ultimately . . . bringing victory, final and decisive, to the Allied cause."[65] Zimmern approvingly quoted Ludendorff's deputy, General Hugo von Freytag-Loringhoven, who had admitted that "the power of radical decision of a world-war has slipped away from the armies. The strategical situation is conditioned by the world-economic situation."[66] This same admission was also seized upon by a pseudonymous British author, Atticus, who noted that "the experience of the blockade, reinforced now by the collaboration of nearly all the great producing countries of the world, has taught us to look to economic armaments as a practicable substitute for armed force in dealing with future offenders against the world's peace."[67] That British commentators cited German generals shows the close enmeshing of wartime strategy and postwar order. As the prospect of an international system in which blockade would play a recurring role dawned, the stakes of victory rose.

Contemporary French estimates give a sense of the picture of the balance of global economic resources, shown in table 2.1. Allied countries had a combined population of 1.18 billion, whereas the Central Powers had 160 million in their own territories and another 212 million in occupied and aligned territories in Belgium and Eastern Europe—372 million all together.[68] Even with the latter group included in the resource base of the Central Powers, the balance still strongly favored the Allies, who controlled majority shares of twenty-six out of thirty-one key commodities. This included monopolies in cotton and jute and semi-monopolies in cane sugar, rice, silk, hemp, nickel, aluminum, rubber, and tea. The Central Powers controlled majorities in only five commodities: barley, rye, beet sugar, flax, and manganese.[69]

The French Comité R summarized these facts about the global distribution of essential commodities in a series of widely circulated reports titled "L'arme économique des Alliés."[70] After this careful stock-taking of global commodities, its conclusion was clear:

> The cover of the Eastern and Southeastern countries (the Russian Empire, Romania, and Persia) in an economic struggle will be useful to Germany; it will not manage to give her victory. . . .

Table 2.1. The Economic Weapon of Raw Materials, 1918

Commodities	Allied and Associated Powers (annual production in thousands of tons)	Central Powers and Occupied Territories (annual production in thousands of tons)	Allied Share of World Total (%)	Central Powers' Share of World Total (%)
Foodstuffs				
Wheat	64,382	36,215	61	34
Barley	12,775	19,488	37	60
Rye	3,910	38,227	9	86
Maize	85,904	12,242	86	13
Oats	34,833	26,505	54	41
Cane sugar	6,923	0	94	0
Beet sugar	1,868	4,370	27	64
Rice	94,330	106	94	0.1
Fibers				
Wool	138	97	59	41
Cotton	4,659	0	100	0
Silk	229	16	93	6
Flax	192	1,134	14	85
Hemp	912	88	91	9
Jute	1,482	0	100	0
Rubber	130	0	91	0
Minerals				
Iron	96,000	45,000	61	29
Copper	747	62	73	6
Lead	1,000	172	73	13
Zinc	1,513	678	62	27
Nickel	389	14	95	3
Aluminum	529	10	98	2
Manganese	918	1,424	39	60
Chrome	114	20	85	15
Combustibles				
Oil	39,231	11,744	69	20
Coal	847,000	338,000	70	29
Stimulants				
Tea	354	0	72	0
Cocoa	187	7	74	3
Tobacco	660	211	70	22
Coffee	805	0	79	0

[For] Germany, an economic war after the cessation of the hostilities will be very hard . . . [against] a group of states that controls more than half of the grain and lead; nearly two-thirds of the wool; more than two-thirds of iron, zinc, and oil; more than four-fifths of maize, copper, and tin; and the quasi-totality of rice, cotton, silk, jute, rubber, and nickel that the world produces each year.[71]

French military officers waxed lyrically about the possibilities for an "economic League of the Allies" to contain German commercial influence.[72] The economic weapon also became an increasingly popular idea in the United States, both among legislators and in the private sector. In February, Representative Patrick Kelley introduced a bill in Congress to boycott German goods as well as those American firms that continued trade with Germany after the end of the war.[73] Walter Berry, the head of the American Chamber of Commerce in Paris, declared to a group of French and Allied cabinet ministers, ambassadors, and generals that "it is urgent that the economic bottling-up of Germany become a categorical imperative of Allied policy. . . . It is not solely primary materials, indispensable commodities to Germany that the Allies dispose of; we possess the world market." Using this preponderant power to organize a boycott, Berry thought, was "the effective weapon to wipe out Junkerism without trace."[74] When the U.S. Chamber of Commerce proposed this peace-preservation tool to its members, it received support from American chemical and pharmaceutical companies eager to trounce their German competitors. But there were also dissenters. The National Association of Manufacturers called the boycott idea "not only futile but vicious," and the International Seamen's Union of America also rejected it.[75] Industries and workers hoping for a recovery of world trade steadfastly opposed a postwar economic weapon as a form of counterproductive belligerence.

Democracy and the Economic Weapon

By 1918, the Allied and Associated Powers were committed to a total war aimed not just at their opponents' military defeat, but also at the transformation of their political institutions. The radicalization of war aims to include political-ideological change was clear in the trajectory of U.S. president Woodrow Wilson. Although sympathetic to Anglo-American naval power, he was initially hesitant about economic pressure because he identified it with a long history of European imperialism and gunboat diplomacy.[76] Wilson saw the 1902–1903 Anglo-German pacific blockade of Venezuela as a violent European intrusion into a Western Hemisphere kept peaceful by the Monroe Doctrine.[77] Any future peace, he proposed in February 1917, should be founded on four principles: political independence, territorial integrity, economic peace, and arms limitations. Economic peace entailed a "mutual guarantee against such economic warfare as would in effect constitute an effort to throttle the industrial life of a nation or shut it off from equal opportunities of trade with the rest of the world."[78] This starting position was similar to the *Wirtschaftsfrieden* proposals of the Reichstag majority coalition and British Conservatives like Lansdowne and Lowther.

But U.S. secretary of state Robert Lansing raised an obvious problem with such a ban. Economic warfare often lay in the eye of the beholder. Was the imposition of tariffs a form of war? The United States had had heavily protected markets for the entirety of the nineteenth century and justified tariffs based on the existence of similar measures in other countries. Moreover, who would be the impartial judge of whether economic hostility had occurred? In response, Wilson changed the third point on his wish list for a peace settlement. He gave it a much more commercial character, saying that there should be a ban only on countries conspiring to deprive others of the "fair and equal opportunities of trade."[79] Two months before entering the war, Wilson therefore began to warm to measures of economic coercion such as blockades, embargoes, and boycotts. He spoke the language of formal equality but took an increasingly sympathetic view of economic warfare against Germany. This first became clear in August 1917, when Pope Benedict XV issued his "Note to the Heads of the Belligerent Peoples," a seven-point peace proposal that included disarmament but also "the institution of arbitration, with its lofty peacemaking function, according to the standards to be agreed upon and with sanctions to be decided against the State which might refuse to submit international questions to arbitration or to accept its decisions."[80] On the fundamental question of peace and its enforcement, Pope Benedict agreed with the arbitrationists.[81] The international order should have a legalist-sanctionist character.[82] The pope also called for "every obstacle to the ways of communication between the peoples [to] be removed" by ensuring "the true freedom and common use of the seas."[83]

Yet the belligerents' responses to Benedict's note were overwhelmingly negative. The German government said it would only support a peace that respected German interests; Britain announced its adhesion would be conditional on German policy toward Belgium; and France ignored Benedict's note outright. Wilson's adviser, Colonel Edward House, insisted that Wilson should seize the initiative and "take the peace negotiations out of the hands of the pope and hold them in [his] own."[84] On 27 August, Wilson wrote a devastating reply to the pope in which he outlined a political theory of economic pressure. The president rejected Benedict's proposal as an impossible return to the status quo ante. All "free peoples of the world" were fighting against Germany's "vast military establishment controlled by an irresponsible government which . . . secretly planned to dominate the world." The German people too had been victims of this aggressive clique, which was now their "ruthless master." America opposed "all exclusive and egoistic economic leagues" like the 1916 Paris Economic Conference. Yet having broken the trust of the world, the German population would need to provide guarantees to other peoples. The "participation upon fair terms in the economic opportunities of the world [of] the German people" would be conditional on "if they will accept equality and not seek domination." Wilson suggested that proof of such intent depended on a credible democracy emerging in Germany. Until that time, he said, "We cannot take the word of the present rulers of Germany as a guaranty of anything that is to endure, unless explicitly supported by such conclusive evidence of the will and purpose of the German people themselves."[85]

Wilson effectively refused to negotiate with any German government before the Kaiser abdicated. Until that time, Germany would continue being subjected to an expanding economic blockade. The democratic morality of this position seems odd: if the German people were themselves the victims of a militarist government, why should they suffer exclusion for the behavior of the regime? Yet this would be to misunderstand Wilson's distinction. Separating the populace from its rulers was not an expression of moral principle but a performative political act. By setting up the German people against the imperial government, he hoped to provoke them to assert their popular sovereignty in the most radical way: by overthrowing the emperor.[86] The only "conclusive evidence of the will and purpose of the German people" that would meet Wilson's test was a democratic revolution against the imperial German state. This meant that the future of the economic blockade was now tied to regime change in Berlin.[87] On 27 October 1917, Colonel House wrote to Wilson that the economic isolation of Germany should be maintained after the peace unless the Reich democratized. Wilson soon accepted House's position and even added another condition: without German democratization, there would be no extension of the Open Door (equal trade access to non-Western markets) for Central European countries.[88] In his Fifth State of the Union Address on 4 December, the president laid out the logic of conditionality in American economic pressure in its clearest form. "German power," he said, "a Thing without conscience or honor or capacity for covenanted peace, must be crushed and, if it be not utterly brought to an end, at least shut out from the friendly intercourse of the nations."[89] Wilson continued:

> The worst that can happen to the detriment of the German people is . . . that if they should still, after the war is over, continue to be obliged to live under ambitious and intriguing masters interested to disturb the peace of the world, men or classes of men whom the other peoples of the world could not trust, it might be impossible to admit them to the partnership of nations which must henceforth guarantee the world's peace. . . . It might be impossible, also, in such untoward circumstances, to admit Germany to the free economic intercourse which must inevitably spring out of the other partnerships of a real peace. But there would be no aggression in that; and such a situation, inevitable because of distrust, would in the very nature of things sooner or later cure itself, by processes which would assuredly set in.[90]

Strikingly evident here was Wilson's belief in the ability of economic incentives to shape the behavior of human populations. His democratic theory of the economic weapon presupposed an ideal citizen who was, if not exactly an Anglo-American capitalist, then at least in most respects a *homo economicus*. This implied that ordinary Germans were peaceful traders waiting to be liberated from a war-mongering autocratic Kaiser. Yet Wilson did not think that the German population was without blame: it had deceived itself and acquiesced in its own subjugation. For that reason, Wilson acted both as an advocate of popular sovereignty *and* as a tough prosecutor of total war. The German people, he believed, would be induced to change their government; his trust in "processes which would assuredly set in" professed his faith in the inevitable forward march of democracy as a political practice linked with private enterprise and free trade. It was inconceivable to Wilson that any reasonable self-governing people would in the long run refuse to accept whatever conditions barred them from access to the global marketplace.

The link between economic pressure and the behavior of populations would become a crucial element of interwar economic sanctions: by acting on the will of the people, governments would be forced to constrain destabilizing behavior in the international sphere. By connecting commercial exclusion to the promotion of democratic government, American internationalists formulated a new set of arguments about how economic war in fact served the cause of peace. In this regard Wilson's thinking was distinct from that of his European allies. Franco-British interest in the economic weapon stemmed less from a desire to change Germany's political constitution than from fears of strategic and economic rivalry. The British liberal newspaper editor A. J. Spender was convinced that "the commercial and industrial magnates of Germany thoroughly understand the immense power in the hands of the Allies through their . . . control of a large part of the raw materials of the world" but felt that "they are powerless to influence their Government."[91] Elites in Paris and London worried about the power of conglomerates like Krupp, AEG, and BASF rather than constitutional details.[92] By contrast, Wilson made German reincorporation into the global market conditional on the downfall of its militaristic monarchy. Wilson was the first statesman to cast the economic weapon as an instrument of democratization. He thereby added an *internal* political rationale for economic sanctions—spreading democracy—to the *external* political goal that Cecil, Clémentel, and European advocates of sanctions had aimed at: inter-state peace. This aspect of the "Wilsonian moment" was less a set of political ideals to be realized than a set of constitutional conditions to be followed by smaller nations, on pain of coercive exclusion from the global market.[93]

Sanctions were already part of Wilson's famous Fourteen Points speech to Congress on 8 January 1918. The second point, a call for "absolute freedom of the navigation upon the seas," contained the important caveat "except as the seas may be closed in whole or in part by international action for the enforcement of international covenants."[94] This raised expectations that Wilson would fulfill the hopes of an important U.S. arbitrationist group, the League to Enforce Peace (LEP). Its treasurer, Herbert Houston, argued that "economic pressure is a powerful and peaceful way to insure peace, while an international police force is likely to be a warlike way to provoke war," a view that he claimed enjoyed "the support of the business men of America."[95] Another LEP member, the wealthy Boston merchant Edward A. Filene, noted that "the deterrent effect of organized non-intercourse . . . would make war less likely."[96] For American commercial elites this legalism was not only compatible with peace, but also with their interest in maintaining a Western Hemisphere in which U.S. influence remained dominant.[97] No one in the LEP ever considered the possibility of economic sanctions being imposed against the United States itself. When they spoke about international law enforced by economic pressure, legalists on both sides of the Atlantic took for granted that it would operate in the world order they had themselves built—one that was entirely congruent with empire.

Against the legalist template, Wilson formulated an international order that was quite different in form.[98] The league that Wilson would present in draft version to the British and French delegations in Paris in January 1919 was organized like a parliament and looked nothing like a world court envisioned by the legalists in the LEP. The discussions of the legislative body of Wilson's ideal league would stabilize international politics by bringing to bear something the president thought even more powerful than economic pressure: "the moral force of the public opinion of the world."[99] There would be no set procedure through which to administer economic sanctions. Committed to using blockade to produce democratic revolution in Germany and Russia, Wilson wanted the league to be a political union to project this ideological program around the world.

Wartime Sanctions Schemes

Statesmen and policymakers were not alone in conceptualizing sanctions during the war. In Allied countries a range of intellectuals, journalists, lawyers, economists, and other experts also discussed the possibilities that blockade offered for global governance. This enthusiasm took hold long before the impact of economic pressure itself could be gauged. The British barrister F. N. Keen, for example, saw Allied war finance as the possible foundation for an international bank to fund the forces of peace. In his view "the power which such an institution would wield, either for purposes of fiscal or financial boycott, would be enormous."[100] Another focal point of debates about international order after the war was the Bryce Group, a coterie around the Liberal Party stalwart Viscount Bryce.[101] Two figures in this circle's orbit made perceptive early proposals for internationalizing the blockade. John Atkinson Hobson was well known for his attack on imperialism as a system in which the interests of finance capital and export industry drove international conflict, a critique of global capitalism eventually taken up by Lenin.[102] Norman Angell was equally renowned for *Europe's Optical Illusion*, his paean to fin-de-siècle economic interdependence and its peace-promoting possibilities.[103] As both men recognized, the world war accentuated rather than ended the dynamics of Edwardian globalization.[104]

In Hobson's view, an organized economic weapon was worth developing precisely because "the conditions for its rapid and concerted application have never hitherto existed." Under threat of being severed from world markets, he thought that "every section of the industrial and commercial community would bring organized pressure on its Government to withdraw from so intolerable a position and to return to its international allegiance."[105] The ultimate foundations of imperialism—the inordinate political influence of organized export-industrial and financial interests— could thus be turned into a solution for international strife. Like Hobson, Angell accepted the primacy of material forces in world politics, but he had a stronger appreciation for ideological and psychological factors. He began from the fact that the outbreak of war had thrown Britain into the worst financial crisis in a century:

> All this gives a mere hint of what the organised isolation by the entire world would mean to any one nation. Imagine the position of a civilized country whose ports no ship from another country would enter, whose bills no banker would discount, a country unable to receive a telegram or a letter from the outside world or send one thereto, whose citizens could neither travel in other countries or maintain communication therewith. . . . We have little conception of the terror which such a policy might constitute to a nation. . . . But if this machinery of non-intercourse were organized as it might be, there would be virtually no neutrals, and its effect in our world to-day would be positively terrifying.[106]

Angell's ideal for the world economy was an "economic World-State," a set of overlapping and interacting networks that tied together most global economic, social, cultural, and technical life. In his 1915 book, *The World's Highway*, he argued that the ideal countermeasure to aggressive war was the "worldwide exclusion of both the culture and the commerce of the aggressor, not merely during a war, but until such time as the aggressive policy were modified." As a first step, Angell proposed turning British seapower into a global enforcer in return for the United States' surrendering its neutral rights to unencumbered trade, a scheme he called the "internationalisation of trade control."[107] Only the United States, he thought, was large and wealthy enough to survive independently in the modern world. But this latent self-sufficiency meant that America necessarily had to be included in a global system of sanctions. Its size made it potentially able to withstand a boycott but also made it the decisive player in directing such pressure against any state in the world.

Neither Hobson nor Angell thought that international economic sanctions were without risk, however. Hobson warned that "the extreme pressure of the boycott might lead to forcible reprisals by the boycotted State which would, in fact, precipitate war."[108] Angell recognized that organized economic coercion would destabilize "the strong international currents which division of trade and labor, irrespective of frontiers, have in the last few generations set up. . . . There might result between nations a sort of competition for self-sufficingness which, ill directed, might conceivably end in buttressing that immoral nationalism that was one of the causes of the war."[109] As we shall see, these warnings about the risks of sanctions stimulating autarky and fomenting war were underappreciated at the time by other internationalists.

The war also created many advocates of sanctions on the European continent. The Italian polymath Eugenio Rignano envisioned a "federal council of Europe" whose "international sanction" stipulated that the participating countries should "strike the rebel state by breaking diplomatic relations and interrupting all economic and commercial links with it."[110] Rignano's book circulated in France during the war, where it was picked up and cited by intellectuals active in the French government. Edgard Milhaud, a professor of political economy who was close to the socialist leaders Léon Blum and Albert Thomas, explicitly endorsed economic sanctions in an April 1916 speech to the French National Study Committee (Comité national d'études; CNE), a group of experts convened by the government as an informal think tank to prepare plans for the postwar order.[111] "Peoples already dispose of a powerful weapon to impose respect for conventions to those among them tempted to violate them. That weapon is the boycott," Milhaud proposed.[112] He thought that the forty-four signatory states to the two Hague conventions formed such a powerful bloc that a collective embargo could not be resisted.[113]

Milhaud's report, which incorporated Rignano's ideas and elaborated them in the context of the blockade, was first discussed by the CNE on 10

April 1916.[114] Its ideas were taken up and realized by the committee's president, former prime minister Léon Bourgeois. An important figure in early twentieth-century French politics, Bourgeois was the chief exponent of a form of liberal socialism called solidarism. Based on fin-de-siècle sociological theories about mutual interdependence, solidarism emphasized the need for collective action to enhance individual liberty and promoted the building of a modern social and fiscal state to do so.[115] Bourgeois subscribed to the arbitrationist view that the entire world should be united under a single judicial authority. One consequence of this universalist attitude was the disappearance of neutrality. If all links with an aggressor had to be severed, then that meant, as Bourgeois said, that "there [would] no longer be neutral states."[116] His committee debated various modalities of isolation. Diplomatic exclusion was not enough; economic restrictions were also needed. All commerce between the international community and the violating state should be prohibited; contracts should be suspended or terminated; the property of enemy subjects should be confiscated. Finally, economic exclusion of the aggressor went hand in hand with economic mutual aid among the states imposing the sanctions. The application of Bourgeois's solidarism to international politics meant that weaker members would be financed, fed, supplied, and supported by the entire community.[117] International solidarity against the isolated aggressor could be constructed through material aid. This focus on provision shows that the economic weapon was not only a destructive tool. From the outset the French conception of *l'arme économique* included a solidaristic component of economic assistance, modeled on the wartime inter-Allied organizations.

Yet there was also a serious coercive element in the French plan. It decreed an automatic and across-the-board cessation of economic interaction with aggressors. But from mid-1916 onward, French officials were clear that they did not think that economic sanctions exhausted the tools of a future league of nations. The organization needed its own military force. To Bourgeois, military sanctions were a logical consequence of the creation of real supranational authority. Just like individuals who agreed to join civil society gave up their private right to use force against one another, nations creating a new international body would transfer their resort to violence to a sovereign that policed all of them equally.

As chair of the CNE, Bourgeois skillfully disseminated these ideas in a way that established him as the chief French theorist of sanctions. In July 1917 he was appointed to lead a full inter-ministerial commission to design the French blueprint for a postwar international organization. The Bourgeois Commission was composed of fifteen officials, mainly military and diplomatic experts, but it also included two major arbitrationist lawyers, the law professors and Nobel Peace Prize laureates Paul d'Estournelles de Constant and Louis Renault.[118] There were strong disagreements within the commission between supporters of an alliance-based system and advocates of a more impartial international legal order. Bourgeois defended himself against military accusations that his juristic plans were weak and useless in the harsh world of power politics. "Are we idealists?" he noted in the first meeting. "Dreamers? No, unfortunately we are *realists!* Shaped all too much by the bloody ordeal that saddens humanity. There is a real, primordial, vital interest, superior to all interests: peace. Only law can establish it. We must assure the organization of law."[119]

The anti-German hardliners were not easily convinced. In September 1917, most commission members felt that "it is a matter of economically isolating the rebel Power and in that regard we find ourselves in agreement with what the Allies agreed at the [Paris] Economic Conference of 1916."[120] But during the following months the persistent Bourgeois managed to push a strongly legalist and arbitrationist agenda through his commission. Its first draft charter for the league was presented to Clemenceau in June 1918. In addition to provisions for an international military force and a permanent general staff, it included a wide array of legal, economic, and military sanctions.[121] These were drafted by two jurists in the Ministry of Blockade, André Weiss and Fernand Pila. They envisioned at least four different kinds of economic sanctions. The first was *blockade:* the cessation of all commercial relations with the transgressor state. The second was the more specifically legal measure of *embargo,* which entailed the confiscation of enemy goods, cargoes, investments, and property on the territory of league member states. Third, the offending state could be deprived of access to *raw materials* vital to its economic functioning. Finally, a similar ban would be issued to affect its ability to obtain *external finance* abroad, especially public loans. Foreign creditors could call in outstanding credits to the state in question, thereby putting its government budget under pressure. Weiss and Pila mentioned that these measures were inspired by the "Allied economic blockade" and noted the congruence of their ideas with those of Cecil.[122]

The Bourgeois Commission underlined that "this simple sketch shows that the 'League of Nations' will not be a disarmed organization."[123] Crucially, Weiss and Pila always intended economic sanctions as *complementary* to military sanctions. As a last resort, the league would intervene militarily by sending a multinational force to subdue the aggressor state. Such intervention would be legitimate because it was undertaken "in the service, not of dynastic interest or the spirit of conquest, but of the safeguarding of law."[124] The proposed league army took its inspiration from the wartime command of French marshal Ferdinand Foch, who from 1917 onward led the Inter-Allied Command of British, French, Italian, and American troops on the Western front.[125] But this idea of multinational peacekeeping expeditions immediately ran into strong Anglo-American opposition. Norman Angell conjured up the image of "Cossacks camping in Central Park to secure the enforcement of an international decision hostile to the will of the whole American people and secured in the International Congress as the result of a snap vote in which a combination of Japanese, Haytian, Siamese and Turkish delegates had managed to secure the voting balance!"[126] This reluctance to binding international security commitments had to be overcome. Bourgeois tried to anticipate as many Anglo-American objections as possible: that the league usurped war-declaring powers from Congress; that it led to entangling alliances; that it violated the Monroe Doctrine; that European monarchies and non-democracies lacked good faith because of their political systems. The French even prepared to encounter the humanitarian view that "the system of economic boycotting of a recalcitrant nation is inhumane because it makes noncombatants suffer: women, children, old people."[127] In Bourgeois's view, an organization that was universal, reliable, and automatic in its interventions would be so reliably effective that these costs could be avoided.

Another French *solidariste* and friend of Bourgeois was anthropologist Marcel Mauss.[128] A draft document from 1918 found in his personal files contains an ingenious plan for automatic international sanctions. It introduced the concept of "contraband of peace," defined as all foreign property and commercial goods based in or traversing another nation's territory. In case of a treaty violation, this wealth could be seized and auctioned off by the nation proven in the right by an international organization. Mauss's hope was that this threat would strengthen peace since "in this way public opinion would be strongly stimulated by the risk of financial loss entailed on the class engaged in international commerce, and the government inclined to disregard its international obligations would become very unpopular even with its own citizens."[129] "Contraband of peace" did not become part of the French negotiating package for the Peace Conference. But it shows how French internationalist schemes in 1917–1918 all agreed that whatever the nature of economic sanctions, they should be based on reliable and hence credible deterrence.

In Britain, a deterrence-based economic weapon also attracted support from the left. The labor-supporting journalist Henry Noel Brailsford did not hide his excitement that "raw materials, including foodstuffs, have become the pivot of world-politics. . . . With an international control over the flow of raw materials across frontiers, the League would recruit every civilized State in its ranks. With the power to stop this flow, it would have a sanction at its command which every State must dread."[130] South African defense minister Jan Smuts expressed a similar position in his pamphlet *The League of Nations: A Practical Suggestion*, published in December 1918.[131] At the center of his plan was an official moratorium on war: a mandatory waiting period in international disputes during which recourse to war was forbidden. As nerves calmed, diplomacy and arbitration could take their effect. To Smuts, "The breaker of the moratorium . . . [would] become ipso facto at war with all the other members of the League, great and small alike, which will sever all relations of trade and finance with the law-breaker." Smuts agreed with the French that the economic weapon would work as a deterrent since "the effect of such a complete automatic trade and financial boycott will necessarily be enormous."[132]

The Paris Peace Conference offered a unique opportunity to institutionalize wartime policies of economic pressure in a more constructive guise. The Allies' victory in the fall of 1918 solidified their case for blockade as a tool of peacekeeping. Smuts was representative of Allied policymakers when he contended that "the experience of this war has shown how such a boycott . . . has in the end availed to break completely the most powerful military Power that the world has ever seen; and the lesson is not likely to be lost on future intending evildoers."[133] Since events had demonstrated that economic pressure could defeat a feared industrial nation like Germany, it was reasonable to think it had the potential to subdue any challenger to the new postwar order.

In making this assumption, the pioneers of economic sanctions foreclosed a question that was not fully resolved at the time: was the blockade decisive in bringing about the Allied victory? In 1918-1919 there was never any attempt to pursue a systematic study of the effects of blockade along the lines of the Strategic Bombing Survey examining Allied air war in the 1940s.[134] Lacking the methodological sweep and data used by mid-century social scientists, historians of the Great War have been divided on the question.[135] First of all, it is important to acknowledge that measuring the effects of blockade on socioeconomic life is not the same as appraising their efficacy in winning the war. The final months of Wilhelmine Germany suggest a complex relationship between effects and efficacy. To begin with, it was military supremo Ludendorff himself who in late September 1918 lost his nerve after the capitulation of Bulgaria, begging the civilian government in Berlin for an armistice.[136] As he sought to save the army by ending the war, politicians at home were in fact calling for an all-out war of popular resistance against the Allies.[137] In short, frontline troops demoralized by military defeat, not ravenous citizens driven to revolt by the blockade, were the crucial agents who pressured the country toward an armistice.[138] Germany's food situation actually improved from July to September 1918 due to the good harvest that year and the influx of supplies from Eastern Europe.[139] But these improvements were nullified by setbacks on the Western front, where all the gains of the Spring Offensive evaporated and the Allies cut deep into German-held territory. Ludendorff had hoped to repeat the shock-and-awe tactics that had knocked Russia out of the war in 1917 but instead saw his own soldiers lose the will to fight and grow increasingly restive.[140]

The efficacy of blockade was partially limited by how the German economy worked. Germany was not as dependent on overseas food supplies as Britain.[141] Precisely for this reason, the war affected Germany more negatively by conscripting millions of agricultural workers—responsible for providing three-quarters of ordinary caloric consumption—than by severing access to foreign imports, which provided just a quarter of the prewar total.[142] More broadly, the blockaders underestimated the fungibility of resources in a complex industrialized economy. Blockade prevented Germany's large export industries from selling to world markets. It thereby released labor and inputs for use elsewhere.[143] The mobilization of economy and society for total war was ridden with problems, but there is little doubt about its productive achievements: in 1918 war production was higher than in any preceding year. The paradox of the German collapse that summer was that a fighting force plentifully equipped with shells and guns suffered a comprehensive breakdown in morale.[144] A clear causal chain between economic pressure and military defeat is difficult to construct.

Blockade therefore played at most a supporting role in the outcome of World War I.[145] Ultimately, battlefield setbacks and the internal tensions of Central European societies mobilized for total war were more crippling than economic encirclement. Why, then, has the opposite conclusion—that blockade *was* decisive—persisted in interwar politics and in much subsequent historical writing? Part of the answer is that the defeated themselves helped to exaggerate its impact. The first in-depth study of the war produced in the 1920s and 1930s, the Carnegie Endowment's mammoth 150-volume *Economic and Social History of the World War,* drew heavily on the assessments of former German and Austro-Hungarian state officials. These administrators were keen to blame external forces for internal collapse instead of drawing attention to their own failures in war-economic planning.[146] More important, German nationalists spent the postwar years spreading the infamous stab-in-the-back legend, blaming the empire's defeat on civilian betrayal, to emphasize that the army remained undefeated. This myth dovetailed with the Allied argument that blockade had vitally demoralized the German home front.[147] Loudly proclaiming the damage caused by blockade was also a favorite tactic in Weimar politicians' charm offensive to lower Germany's reparations burden, revise the Versailles Treaty, and attract foreign capital.[148] In private, German officials admitted that the blockade had not caused as much damage as their own propaganda claimed.[149] Humanitarian campaigns rightly drew attention to civilian suffering but at the cost of further reinforcing the notion that hunger had caused Central Europe's social order to collapse.[150]

What mattered most for interwar history was that all sides came to believe that blockade had been decisive to the outcome of the war.[151] For the internationalists such as Cecil, Smuts, Bourgeois, and Wilson, questioning the efficacy of economic war was politically self-undermining. It directly impeded the plausibility of the economic sanctions that they wanted to craft at the Paris Peace Conference. As Arnold-Forster, who served there as the British Admiralty representative, later put it, "We succeeded in bringing death through privation to some 760,000 people in Germany alone up to the Armistice. . . . We brought our enemy to his knees. . . . This blockade weapon is more indivisible and far more deadly than had formerly been supposed."[152] Even though historians now see a death toll between 300,000 and 400,000 as a more realistic estimate, what was politically consequential in the interwar period was the fearsome specter of blockade that persisted in European historical memory.[153]

This blockade myth profoundly shaped political and strategic thinking for the rest of the twentieth century. Belief that economic pressure produced victory in 1918 became an article of faith for the supporters of economic sanctions. Ten years after the armistice, Cecil and Arnold-

Forster remained convinced that targeting "the commerce of our enemies" provided "that pressure which gave us the victory in the late War and will do so again."[154] Belief in the power of the economic weapon had become an internationalist political commitment. And the Allies' war-winning weapon had one very clear institutional heir: the League of Nations. But the precise nature of the League's economic sanctions owed much to the political compromises struck during the months-long negotiations at the Peace Conference.

The Drafting of Article 16

As we have seen, the British, French, and American statesmen who shaped the Covenant of the League of Nations—Cecil, Bourgeois, and Wilson—had all formulated specific ideas about economic sanctions in the run-up to the peace negotiations. Of the three, Cecil was probably in the best position to see his plans through. Not only had he been the British Empire's minister of blockade, but he had also been given plenty of freedom by Lloyd George to craft the league in broad agreement with British policy.[155] A special league study committee chaired by Lord Phillimore had presented its findings to the British cabinet in March 1918. After Cecil merged his own ideas with Phillimore's recommendations, the "Cecil draft" placed a blockade-like security mechanism at the heart of the British negotiating position.[156] It also supported military sanctions—i.e., the ability for the league to organize armed intervention. Yet in this respect the British draft did not go as far as the French design for a permanent international military staff "to foresee and prepare" an expeditionary force.[157] League member states, Cecil and Phillimore thought, should organize armed intervention on a case-by-case basis.

The first meeting that Cecil had with the Americans, on 9 January 1919, suggested that London and Washington did not see eye to eye on this question of military sanctions. When Wilson's adviser, Colonel House, read out the scheme that he had drawn up with the U.S. president, Cecil was struck by the fact that it depicted blockade alone as sufficient to enforce arbitration. The Americans did not envision a military backstop. When he raised the point that "the compulsion was to be only by economic means," House admitted that he personally thought that armed intervention should be available to the league if necessary.[158] It was not clear, however, if Wilson would agree to this. The first draft that the American president had shared, based on advice from his secretary of state, Lansing, and legal adviser, David Hunter Miller, prescribed "a complete economic and financial boycott, including the severance of all trade or financial relations," as well as "the prohibition of all intercourse" with an aggressor.[159] That the economic weapon would give the league its punch was something on which all the great powers agreed. What divided them was whether it would be the only instrument to do so.[160]

Wilson opposed military sanctions because he believed that the United States should not get entangled in alliances with European powers, a conviction further buttressed by his advisers. Lansing and Miller based their thinking on the U.S. Constitution, which reserved the right to declare war for Congress alone. Since these powers could not be delegated in advance to any supranational organization, they suggested that any proposed "union of the nations to prevent aggressions and international wars" should be a "negative covenant" rather than a "positive guaranty." In other words, the league should bind countries *not* to act aggressively rather than commit them to common action against aggression.[161]

Military sanctions were not the only divisive issue. A second question was whether the use of the league's sanctions mechanism would entail *war* against the Covenant-breaker. Unintentionally, the negotiations here produced an innovation in international law: the possibility of using economic coercion against a state without being at war with it. Jan Smuts had already suggested in his pamphlet that sanctions could be cast as policing actions, refusing law-breaking states their belligerent rights to fight back.[162] But the British delegation had changed its stance on this for legal reasons: under common law, His Majesty's Government could not claim the authority to institute coercive economic measures without officially declaring war. In Paris, Cecil therefore proposed that any violation would "by itself" (ipso facto, in the technical phrase) create a state of war between the transgressing state and the league.[163] Regardless of whether league economic sanctions would work like a formal effective blockade or like the more ambiguous system of contraband control developed during the world war, the British state thus saw them as *belligerent* measures. As a form of use of force by states, sanctions formed part of the legal temporality of war by their very nature. Cecil believed in a foundational dichotomy between war and peace as distinct states; "the conditions of a League of Nations in peace time and an Allied Council in war time are entirely different," he wrote in his diary during the conference.[164]

As he had made clear in his 1916 memorandum, Cecil believed troublesome governments would avoid going to war if they had certain knowledge that doing so would bring terrible consequences. His conception of the economic weapon, like that of Smuts, was based on deterrence. The credible threat of a merciless economic siege had to be made abundantly clear for this to work. So Cecil's first proposal explicitly rejected all legal constraints on action against aggression: "The naval, military and economic operations undertaken . . . shall be carried out without regard to any limitations hitherto imposed on belligerent States by any convention or rule of international law."[165] The deterrent effect of the economic weapon would be stronger if all legal restrictions on economic warfare were done away with.

Wilson's adviser David Miller thought that this legal *carte blanche* was a "drastic provision," and in his first meeting with Cecil at the Hotel Majestic on 21 January he opposed the British proposal.[166] A firm American legalist, Miller was concerned not just about the economic weapon's proposed break with existing international law. He took special issue with the ipso facto war doctrine in the British draft. Guarding their legislative independence, Miller argued that the decision to go to war belonged to a sovereign people and could be made only in concrete cases. It could never, in his eyes, be made to start automatically if certain conditions were met; in the United States only a declaration of war by a majority in Congress could do this. On both these points, Miller succeeded in pushing Cecil and Wilson to adopt a milder formulation instead. This formed the basis for Wilson's second draft. Instead of creating an automatic state of war, this document prescribed that states violating the Covenant were "deemed to have committed an act of war against all the members of the League."[167] By 27 January, the merger of the Wilsonian and British drafts produced a new Cecil-Miller draft.

The modification made on Miller's behest was small in content but large in meaning. Indeed, it is difficult to overstate its significance for the modern history of economic sanctions. By making possible coercive sanctions without creating a state of war, the Cecil-Miller draft for the first time broke the long-standing link between the power to blockade and the condition of belligerence. Although subsequent drafts always defined aggression as an *act of war*, they no longer specified that the league response against it would take place in a *state of war*. A new modality for the use of force—non-belligerent economic coercion—thus entered world politics at the highest level in January 1919.[168]

Further negotiations in early February determined two more aspects of league sanctions. One was the concept of the enemy. In the January drafts, the targets of economic pressure had been specified as "*subjects* of the Covenant-breaking State." The newer versions instead talked about *nationals*. This mattered because many states had used the emergency of the world war to designate inhabitants of their territories as "enemy aliens" based on their ethnic or racial characteristics instead of their civic status.[169] Economic sanctions based on the nationality principle would not spare the assets of citizens of the aggressor state residing abroad, even if they had only tenuous links to their government. The second change was to specify in more detail what Wilson's "complete economic and financial boycott" entailed. Here the technical experience of the blockade ministries found its way directly into the league's founding text: severance of trade, financial relations, personal travel, and other forms of economic interaction between the aggressor and all other countries would all be prohibited.[170]

By the first week of February 1919, the basic outline of the league's economic weapon had taken shape. It had been largely, although not solely, an Anglo-American process. The elaborate French scheme had been significantly watered down. In plenary sessions the idea of military sanctions applied by an international expeditionary force was blocked by the British and American delegations. Bourgeois once more emphasized the realism underpinning his solidarism; without its own armed forces, he submitted, the league "will be nothing but a dangerous façade." But Wilson countered that "if we organize from now on an international force, it will seem like we are substituting international militarism for national militarism."[171] Bourgeois could not win against such determined Anglo-American opposition. The French statesman was in ill health at the Peace Conference; during his meetings with Cecil at the Hotel Majestic he sat wrapped in fur rugs against the winter cold.[172] One French desideratum that did make it into the Covenant was the league's economic support mechanism for attacked countries, encapsulated in the third paragraph of the sanctions article.[173] But no concrete action to determine the distribution of benefits and burdens was decided in Paris. It would take until the second half of the 1920s before this positive economic weapon was further developed.

Although there was now an Anglo-American-French deal on the table, the league's economic sanctions mechanism still needed international legitimation. In late March, Cecil and Bourgeois met with a group of thirteen neutral countries (Argentina, Chile, Colombia, Denmark, Netherlands, Norway, Paraguay, Persia, Salvador, Spain, Sweden, Switzerland, and Venezuela) to discuss the proposed sanctions articles. Most neutrals thought that the sanctions before them were too far-reaching, forcing them to join economic pressure campaigns against their will. The Dutch wanted more "precise regulations for the military and economic action of the League." Cecil, keen to avoid any excessively stringent British commitment, rebuffed this outright. Denmark was happy to join in economic measures but would not allow foreign troops on its territory. Cecil and Bourgeois retorted that this was incoherent since economic sanctions required taking a side and would end Danish neutrality anyway; Copenhagen simply had to choose between neutrality and joining the economic weapon. The Swedish delegation thought that the economic sanctions proposed were "too severe," suggesting instead "an increasing scale of economic pressure."[174] But these small European neutrals had little leverage with which to force the great powers to accept their demands. They ultimately approved the Covenant, hoping to modify it in their interest once the League of Nations had been established. The final version of the article, now labeled number 16 of the Covenant, read as follows:

> Should any Member of the League resort to war in disregard of its covenants under Articles 12, 13 or 15, it shall ipso facto be deemed to have committed an act of war against all other Members of the League, which hereby undertake immediately to subject it to the severance of all trade or financial relations, the prohibition of all intercourse between their nationals and the nationals of the covenant-breaking State, and the prevention of all financial, commercial or personal intercourse between the nationals of the covenant-breaking State and the nationals of any other State, whether a Member of the League or not.

Both the Americans and the British could recognize their own designs in this text. Wilson got his wish by having a council composed of great powers decide whether an act of war had been committed. This preserved U.S. discretionary power over the league's rule by economic pressure. For his part, Cecil saw the hermetic nature of the sanctions—applied to all commerce, finance, and communications—as proof that they constituted "the severest blockade by all other members of the League."[175]

The Versailles Treaty was signed in July 1919, and the Covenant of the League of Nations entered into force in January 1920. By leaving economic sanctions as the main disciplinary tool, the drafters of the Covenant staked much on a single instrument. The League's security system came to rest on a much narrower basis than many internationalists had hoped. This contingent outcome contains some of the roots of the troubled interwar history of sanctions as an instrument against aggression. As a policy possible in peace but without organized armed force to back it up, the economic weapon had to assume a role in the postwar order that was larger than most of its supporters had intended. As a result, much was expected of it—perhaps too much.

CHAPTER THREE

The Peacewar, 1919–1921

I N EARLY 1919, Central Europe was so exhausted that it seemed to
be consuming itself. A U.S. doctor who had traveled to Austria-
Hungary reported on 16 January that the "blockade had done its
work. Absolutely nothing left. Every clock in Prague gone, melted
for the metals."[1] In freezing Vienna, Henry Brailsford witnessed "children
dressed in suits neatly made from sacks. In many hospitals children had
to be wrapped in paper, for want of sheets and blankets." Whereas before
the war, Vienna had "lived on the coal of Bohemia, the wheat of Croatia
and the meat of Hungary, . . . now stands it alone." Brailsford expected
that "Austria is doomed to death if the blockade continues for many weeks
more."[2]

These reports captured the peculiar situation of the months between
the Armistice and the signing of the Versailles Treaty. Although the war
of arms had officially ended, the economic war continued. The blockade machinery kept large parts of Europe in a chokehold of deprivation.
While Allied statesmen and their advisers in Paris were talking, walk-
ing, dining, and debating, they kept in place many of the policies of economic pressure developed during the war. Simultaneously, they began to
organize relief efforts. Food, clothing, and medicine eventually began to
enter the politically stable parts of Europe. Significant as these programs
were, they addressed problems caused in no small part by Allied blockade
policy. Moreover, in the spring and summer of 1919, Germany's republican government in Berlin, the Bolshevik regime in Petrograd, and the

Hungarian Soviet Republic in Budapest all remained under blockades that were carried over from war into peacetime. Drafting the League's economic sanctions was thus no innocent parlor-room affair. Article 16 and the men who drafted it were deeply implicated in the ongoing use of economic coercion and provision.

Blockade and its counterpart, humanitarian relief, both belonged to the wartime economic weapon. In the post-Armistice months they functioned as complementary instruments in the shaping of the postwar order. This chapter shows that continued economic war after the end of hostilities aroused considerable controversy in many countries, triggering debates about the ethics of targeting civilians and the role of economic factors in stabilizing politics and society. Both the power to feed and to starve lay in the hands of the SEC, an executive organ just below the Allied heads of government. However, the use of economic pressure in peacetime was beset with problems. Who would suffer most from being deprived of access to trade? Would blockade-caused hunger and socioeconomic collapse stifle Bolshevism or spur it? And who determined when the isolation of the defeated and revolutionary states of East and Central Europe would end?

The continuation of the blockade against Germany and Austria-Hungary has not escaped the attention of historians.[3] Humanitarian efforts to feed Europeans in this period have also been well documented.[4] Less appreciated are the distinct class politics of blockade. The economic campaign against Bolshevism was a form of counterrevolution on the cheap and at a distance. Classic studies by historians Arno Mayer and Charles Maier show how European elites regained their grip on power after the upheaval of the wartime years and the radical groundswell of the Russian Revolution.[5] Material pressure against civilian populations deserves to be seen as an essential tool in this stabilization of the bourgeois social order in Europe. Wilson's wartime hope—to use material pressure to transform rival states' internal political character—found its most consummate expression in this period. As such, the postwar blockades and embargoes of the 1919–1921 period also need to be seen as core dimensions of domestic conflict in the aftermath of the Armistice.[6] Robert Gerwarth has emphasized how civic strife in this era brought forth a "new logic of violence," a desire to exterminate enemies both internal and external.[7] The years following the world war were indeed filled with highly visible forms of violence: street fighting on the barricades of Berlin and Munich, Fascist *squadristi* breaking up Italian farm and factory occupations, Freikorps soldiers roving through Baltic swamps on anti-communist crusades, ethnic clashes in the Caucasus, and desperate refugees huddled on the quays of a burning Smyrna. The drama of these events has tended to hide the effects of the slow grind of deprivation and deflation enforced from afar—first by inter-Allied bodies during the Peace Conference, then, as the spread of revolution was blocked, against the Soviet state in Russia.[8]

Postwar economic pressure had another effect that persisted in the interwar period: it began to dissolve the timeworn distinction between the state of war and that of peace. Observing European geopolitics in 1920, the Franco-British humanitarian Edmund Morel worried about the deep uncertainty caused by the policies that had created a condition he called "peacewar." "The essential purpose of 'War,'" he wrote, "is the destruction of human life and economic resources, and that purpose is being carried out to-day with diligent activity by certain Governments which, nevertheless, protest that they are not 'at war.'" Morel criticized what he saw as "the scientific destruction, by the weapon of blockade, of Russian men and women and children. It is destroying them in various ways, depriving them as far as it can of food, clothing, fuel, light, soap, medical necessities, and means of transport—in short, of the things without an adequate possession of which mankind contracts disease, and perishes. No more cruel, bestial, calculated, cowardly and altogether diabolical method of destruction of human life has ever been devised."[9] Morel was wrong to attribute the misery to Allied policies alone; both the Reds and the Whites fighting each other in the Russian Civil War bore responsibility for the country's suffering. But his broader point was accurate: in a world where economic coercion became more normalized, the meaning of the terms "war" and "peace" was thoroughly destabilized.

The Blockade of Hungary

In the early morning hours of 4 April 1919, a train pulled into Budapest's Keleti Station. Having traveled via Switzerland and Austria, it was guided onto a side track and surrounded by armed guards. On board was South African general Jan Smuts, the former Boer rebel turned factotum of the British Empire. Smuts had left Paris three days earlier with a small retinue of advisers including the young diplomat Harold Nicolson, a high-society fixture of the Bloomsbury Group, and the radical Liberal MP Josiah Wedgwood. Their mission was to negotiate with the new Communist regime that had come to power in Budapest two weeks earlier. Not wanting to recognize the Hungarian Soviet government, Smuts refused to leave the wagon-lit. So its leader, the Communist Béla Kun, came on board the train to talk. Their initial meeting produced no result, however. Smuts proposed an armistice, but his condition for lifting the Allied blockade was a serious one: Hungary had to cede all of Transylvania to Romania. Kun, who had been born in Transylvania as Béla Kohn and just two weeks earlier had been dwelling in a Hungarian prison cell, made a counter-proposal. To prevent Hungary's dismemberment, he suggested the Allies occupy Transylvania as a neutral zone and force the Romanians to withdraw east. Yet Smuts was uncompromising: without the unconditional cession of Transylvania, there would be no end to Hungary's economic isolation. These terms the Hungarian Communists found hard to accept.[10]

The negotiations went nowhere. Nicolson, thirty-three years old like Kun, described his interlocutor as "the Jew Bolshevik" with "the face of a sulky uncertain criminal," and he was repelled by the Hungarian foreign minister, József Pogány, a "little oily Jew—fur coat rather moth-eaten—stringy green tie—dirty collar."[11] Smuts decided that he could not take the Hungarian Communists seriously, and the Allied mission departed after a twenty four-hour stay. The "stalemate of mutual non-recognition" between the Allies and the Hungarian Soviet state continued, but events in Central Europe changed rapidly.[12] Three days later, Nicolson had returned to Paris and was enjoying the comfort of his rooms in the Hotel Majestic, where he took a "much-needed bath," just as the Romanian Army invaded Transylvania and began its advance on Budapest to crush Hungary's revolutionaries.[13]

Smuts's abortive negotiations to lift the blockade of Hungary were the result of political events that had caught the Allies by surprise. At the start of the year, the British cabinet had been planning to reduce economic pressure on Hungary's Social Democratic government, which had come to power in November and was desperate to restore the import of foreign goods. When asked in mid-March about the future of the blockade by his cousin, Foreign Secretary Balfour, Cecil replied that though some restrictions still existed, "the blockade of German-Austria & Hungary [should] be raised from the earliest possible date."[14] This changed when the Hungarian Social Democrats reacted radically to a French proposal for negotiations that entailed grave territorial losses for Hungary.[15] The minority Communists were allowed into government, with Béla Kun becoming prime minister. Kun proclaimed a Hungarian Soviet Republic, hoping to realize a political revolution and strengthen Hungary's hand in peace talks with the Allies by attracting Russian Bolshevik support. His revolutionaries were not the only ones to exploit the political chaos of the post-Armistice period to maximum effect. In armistice talks with the Austro-

Hungarian Empire in November 1918, Allied negotiators had specified that they would not recognize any successor states until a general peace treaty determining new inter-state borders came into effect. This created a legal vacuum in which Béla Kun's unrecognized government could be isolated by economic blockade without the need to declare war against it. The Allied blockade began on 28 March, enforced in Vienna by a commission that controlled all shipments down the Danube and at the downstream end of the river by Serbian and Romanian forces.[16]

Although Smuts had been unyielding about the blockade in the negotiations with Kun, he was also the first to suggest a change in policy. "I have no doubt," he wrote two weeks after returning, "that the only proper course is to remove the blockade as soon as possible from all Central European countries and to issue a public declaration to that effect. The blockade and famine are now the principal allies of Bolshevism and the proper way to fight anarchy in those countries is to remove the blockade, assist with food, and pave the way to the resumption of normal conditions."[17] Smuts was making an emerging prudential argument: if hunger caused Bolshevism and the blockade perpetuated hunger, then it should be lifted as soon as possible. Nicolson, however, persuaded the British cabinet to wait and see. In early May, he wrote that if "Kun succeeds in forming a stable and moderate Government, the blockade will presumably be raised immediately," but if "the Terrorists come into power, I presume that we will wish to maintain existing restrictions."[18]

The problem with this reasoning was that "stable and moderate" government was hard to imagine without first restoring Hungarian access to world markets. Nicolson's support for blockade was undermining the very stability he claimed to seek. The SEC left the door open to both continuing the blockade and lifting it, declaring that there would be no objection to a raising of the barriers "as soon as the political situation permitted."[19] But in practice the Allies wanted Béla Kun to submit to their demands or else end his government. By mid-May, Hungary was fighting Yugoslav forces in the south, Romanian armies in the east, and Czechoslovak troops in the north. Kun rallied a disparate array of forces for national defense and beat back first the Czechs and subsequently Romania's advance as well.[20] In light of these developments, Nicolson declared his support for continuing the blockade to Cecil and Smuts:

> While feeling that it is extremely inhumane to exert pressure on enemy civil populations by such indirect means as blockade, I

think it should be realised that whatever food is allowed to reach Hungary will be used by Bela Kun in a preferential manner so as to benefit his supporters as against the bourgeoisie. . . . I admit that it is most unpleasant to feel that women and children are starving in Hungary simply because we persist in the blockade, but I feel that it would be illogical to reverse our policy at the very moment when we most need to maintain all possible pacific means of pressure on our enemy.[21]

Eyre Crowe, the Foreign Office's specialist on Germany, had an even tougher line than Nicolson, arguing that it was "out of the question that we should recognize Bela Kun. The proper policy for us is to bring about his fall."[22] Thus the blockade of the Hungarian Soviet Republic was maintained not only by Romanian, Czech, and Yugoslav armies in the field, but also by the Allies on Hungary's western border. In July, Jacques Seydoux strengthened the blockading ring by sending French troops from Bavaria to eastern Austria to man border controls, joining a small Italian contingent already active there.[23]

The forces arrayed against Kun's government soon became overwhelming. After a retreat in July, the end came on 3 August, when Communist-controlled Budapest fell to the Romanian Army. This presented a new set of problems for the Allied Supreme Council. As their capital was being ransacked by Romanian troops, the Hungarian people had to be kept well-disposed toward the Allies. Here Herbert Hoover, the head of the American Relief Administration (ARA), weighed in. Hoover hoped that Hungarian trade unions could fortify a new non-Soviet democratic administration. But he did not offer the carrot of aid without a corresponding stick. He advised that the blockade should be lifted for two weeks, allowing for better social and economic conditions in which Hungarian moderates could sort out a stable government. If the Hungarians did not use this period to conform "by demobilizing and doing what the Council wished, the Blockade could be re-imposed."[24] As for the counterproductive looting by Romanian soldiers, Hoover's fellow American delegate on the Council, Under Secretary of State Frank Polk, made it clear that the Romanians too would have to be issued with an "economic threat," an idea supported by Balfour on behalf of the British.[25] This predilection for liberally imposing material restrictions on others led to some striking contradictions. While the Allies threatened economic sanctions against Hungarians unless they chose the correct democratic government, and against Romanians for despoiling their opponent's capital, they reminded the Serbs they had "a humanitarian duty" to lift an embargo on shipping food supplies from their territory to a famished Hungary.[26]

Peacetime blockade in the dynamic circumstances of 1919 required direct enforcement on the ground. Controlling these blockade lines took more effort now than during the war itself. Beyond Central Europe, the Allied economic war against the Ottoman Empire continued in the form of restrictions on trade in the eastern Mediterranean, Black Sea, and Red Sea regions.[27] On top of this, the question of what to do with economic pressure on Bolshevik Russia loomed. These policies had first been adopted in 1917–1918 to preserve the encirclement of Germany and gradually morphed into a strategy for containing Bolshevism and perhaps even overthrowing it by assisting its opponents in the Russian Civil War.[28] As the Royal Navy pressed forward into the Baltic and Black Seas after the Armistice, the possibility of blockading Russia directly presented itself. The decision fell to the new British minister of blockade, the Liberal politician Cecil Harmsworth, an old member of Prime Minister Lloyd George's secretariat.[29] Throughout the spring Harmsworth corresponded with Robert Cecil in Paris about the continuation of the blockade of Germany and Soviet Russia while he fended off questions from the House of Commons about the extension of economic war into peacetime. In February a special Anglo-French-Italian-American Eastern Blockade Committee (Comité du blocus de l'Orient), chaired by Jacques Seydoux, was brought into being to unify the blockades of Central Europe, the Ottoman Empire, and southern Russia. Under Seydoux's oversight, a low-profile but iron cordon was upheld from the Baltic Sea along the Polish and Austrian borders through the eastern Balkans to the Aegean islands—where special customs posts were installed to stop contraband—and thence to the Red Sea coast of southern Arabia, where the British wanted to continue blockade to make restive Arab tribes submit to the Allies.[30]

French and British military officials were the main advocates of increased pressure on Lenin's government. The head of the French military mission in Russia saw "an even more rigorous blockade of the European and Siberian borders" as "the most fearsome weapon up to the present."[31] In late March, the Royal Navy attaché in Paris proposed an official blockade of the Black Sea coast held by the Bolsheviks. Harmsworth realized that this was politically impossible without an official British declaration of war on the Soviet government. A pacific blockade "could be treated by [the Soviets] as an act of war" and would cause an undesirable escalation of the situation. Harmsworth decided on a subtler form of interdiction, using the existing Admiralty mechanism of bunker control—the scheme controlling which ships received coal from British depots—to stop merchant vessels supplying Bolshevik-controlled ports.[32]

Yet the main obstacle to using blockade as a weapon against revolutionary communism was not legal but humanitarian. Visitors to Russia recounted scenes of deep misery among the civilian population. In April, the Russian Red Cross in Petrograd appealed to its American counterpart for grain and supplies to feed children in the capital. This led to fierce discussion on the SEC about how to reconcile humanitarian considerations and anti-communist goals. Cecil's private secretary, Walford Selby, harshly rebuffed the Soviet call for assistance, which he thought a "pathetic appeal to which a deaf ear may be turned."[33] Selby saw the Bolsheviks themselves as entirely to blame for the situation in Russia and suggested that nothing should be sent to Russia until they had relinquished power. Edward Wise, the British Food Controller's delegate on the SEC, agreed that some pressure had to be kept on Russia. But he added, "I regret it, for I don't believe really that we shall kill Bolshevism by allowing children to starve or die for lack of drugs or medicine." Wise felt that an immiserating blockade was no way to undermine a revolutionary government that owed its power to popular anger about poverty and squalor. But as an experienced administrator of deprivation and convinced anti-Bolshevik, Cecil did not budge. His comment on Wise's confession was terse: "I see no other alternative."[34]

Considering his record in sternly enforcing blockade in peace as well as in war, Cecil's reputation as a Nobel Peace Prize–winning statesman who experienced a "wartime conversion" that made him a "pacifist and internationalist" is not accurate.[35] He was as hard-nosed about power as any member of the British war cabinet. When the SEC recommended to Allied leaders in April that the blockade of Germany should be lifted as a gesture of goodwill to the German delegation arriving in Paris, Cecil explained his tough position to Harmsworth: "It is perfectly clear that the blockade has enfeebled Germany, which is what it was designed to do," he wrote with some irritation. "Our object was and is, not to do what is best for Germany but what is best for ourselves, by bending the German will to our own so that they will sign our Peace terms."[36]

Cecil soon began to support relief efforts to feed Germany. But this shift shows that in 1919, blockade and humanitarianism were often supported not by opposed factions but by the same people. Another promi-

Food Controller E. F. Wise's note to Robert Cecil,
17 May 1919. Wise writes, "I don't believe really
that we shall kill Bolshevism by allowing children to
starve or die for lack of drugs & medicine."
The National Archives of the UK.

nent internationalist of this period, future U.S. president Herbert Hoover,
had a similarly complex relation to economic pressure. Hoover was an
enterprising and pragmatic figure. In many respects he was the polar
opposite to the high-handed and moralistic Wilson. Although he owed his
charitable reputation to his wartime role in organizing the Committee for
the Relief of Belgium and the food supply of northern France, Hoover did
not think that starving civilians was wrong in principle.[37] Tactical assessments rather than morality guided his views. As the Armistice was being
signed in late 1918, Hoover wrote to Wilson that for the time being, "It
is a positively necessary fact that we have continuance of the embargo."[38]
When the German Revolution produced left-wing radicalism, he quickly
came to oppose the blockade of the Reich as counterproductive. Hoover
also pivoted to supplying rather than depriving Germany because of indi-
cations that U.S. farmers were suffering from a glut of pork and dairy supplies and needed a large outlet for their products.[39] Yet when Bolsheviks
seized power, as in Béla Kun's Hungarian Soviet Republic, he supported
a full blockade of these radicals. Hoover's humanitarian credentials were

further boosted by the assistance he organized during the Russian famine in 1921–1922.[40] Around this time, he lost faith in the efficacy of economic pressure as a political instrument—a skepticism that marked his entire subsequent political career. But, as we shall see, Hoover and many European humanitarians came to oppose the blockade because of their anti-Bolshevism, not in spite of it. An illustrative example of this attitude was the head of the Danish Red Cross Society in Paris, a humanitarian official who encouraged the Allied armies in their fight against the Bolsheviks, a party who "employ absolute terrorism, and are completely devoid of any humanitarian sentiment. . . . We absolutely have to act before it is too late, and before all of Europe is affected by this disease, which is as contagious, and ten times more terrible than the Spanish flu, because it is the absolute overthrow of society as a whole."[41]

The Domestic Politics of Blockade

It was easy to make a case for ending economic pressure on prudential grounds. Winston Churchill, then Britain's state secretary for war, had opposed the German and Russian blockades from the start. "It is repugnant to the British nation," he told Parliament, "to use this weapon of starvation which falls mainly upon the women and children, upon the old, the weak, and the poor, after all the fighting has stopped—one moment longer than is necessary to secure the just terms for which we have fought." Ideally the Allies should use their land forces as a pressure tool, for "without this power we have no means whatever of influencing or guiding the course of events in Europe except by starving everybody into Bolshevism."[42] Continuing it would "throw Germany into the arms of the Bolsheviks and so give the Soviet Government of Russia a fresh lease on life."[43] The aim behind unofficially blockading Russia while reestablishing trade with Germany was precisely to avert such a German-Russian behemoth.[44]

How long Germany and Russia would remain economically isolated was not a question only of foreign policy and strategy, but also of domestic politics. West European publics were increasingly critical of using force against Russia. Democratization and demobilization both limited what the Allied governments could do. On the one hand, further deprivation was likely to fan revolutionary fervor. "This Bolshevist germ," one British MP noted, "becomes very infectious in countries which are suffering from food shortage."[45] Relief was clearly the soundest way to forestall further leftist revolts. Yet the enormous demobilization process in which Britain was engaged prevented an immediate lifting of the blockade. Of the 3.5 million men in uniform that the British Army deployed in ten countries in November 1918, it demobilized over 2.7 million in the twelve months thereafter.[46] The same applied to France, which was eager to demobilize its armed forces so domestic reconstruction could begin.[47] As the size of armed forces was being rapidly reduced, London and Paris both faced the problem of how to maintain pressure on Germany until the peace treaty had been signed.

The blockade apparatus, enforced by the Royal Navy and directed by the SEC in Paris, seemed the obvious answer to this conundrum. Cecil wrote to Harmsworth that it was "the easiest and cheapest method of applying pressure to Germany" and eased the difficulties of keeping men under arms. What Hoover, American public opinion, and British merchants calling for the immediate lifting of all restrictions misunderstood was that the blockade was not meant to obstruct trade but that it was "an implement of war and a lever for securing the results of war."[48] If the entire machinery of control and guidance was dismantled, it could not easily be rebuilt quickly. Cecil therefore insisted that it be maintained. But the policy of economic war in peace disturbed quite a few British Conservatives. Churchill was not the only one to voice misgivings. Lord Lansdowne, who had opposed Lloyd George and Cecil in 1917 with his call to moderate the economic war and reach a peace of understanding with Germany, thought that continuing blockade until a peace treaty was signed was foolish. "How long is this process of turning the screw, of using the weapon of starvation, likely to last?" Lansdowne asked. "If we are to go on with the starving policy until [the] welter of difficult international questions has been cleared up, I am afraid that we shall find . . . that there will be nobody left with whom to come to terms at all."[49] Such prudence among the Conservatives was not due to any special sympathy for Germany. It was driven by their fear of revolution and desire to quickly reestablish a stable social order. The Conservatives also sought to contain some of the radical effects of a Liberal Party–led total war on hierarchies of property, work, and gender. Blockade targeted women and children, not men in uniform. It widened the remit of war beyond a professional class of men trained in the use of violence. The Conservative critique of total war sought to restabilize these old distinctions.

Blockade and economic sanctions were topics of intense debate among women in this period too. In Britain, Christabel Pankhurst and the nationalist suffragettes of the Women's Party were unrelenting advocates of blockade. At one point they had even called for Cecil's resignation for failing to pursue the economic war of attrition with sufficient vigor.[50] Margaret Jourdain defended starvation blockade based on its "respectability" as a long-standing and legitimate method akin to siege warfare.[51] After the Armistice the U.S. publication *The Woman Patriot* warned about "a vast seething mass of anarchy, extending from the Rhine to the Siberian wastes" and declared that "the Allies can scarcely afford to feed, police and govern Germany and Russia while 'soviets' are contending for their various views and talking instead of working."[52]

Most women's groups, however, were active in opposition to economic war. In Germany, working-class women had borne the brunt of the deprivation caused by the blockade.[53] This experience had encouraged their civic claims on the state, contributing to the German Revolution and to the social hopes vested in the new republican government.[54] Some of the most scathing criticisms of the blockade in Britain came from the Women's International League for Peace and Freedom (WILPF), especially its political thinkers, Helena Swanwick and Agnes Maude Royden.[55] Royden condemned economic pressure as "a graceful phrase for torture; and thinking of the women I know in England whose babies are born dead, from 'economic pressure' on their mothers, I ask myself if these are indeed the means by which we shall convert the German people from a false idea."[56] At the WILPF's founding congress in The Hague in April 1915, the organization had adopted a charter that called for an equitable peace settlement founded on freedom of the seas. Although women's groups demanded an end to the war and were horrified by the treatment of food as contraband, they did not reject all kinds of pressure. The boycott, long popular among social movements seeking change, was still considered an essential tool of women's politics. Thus the American Jane Addams called at the Hague congress for women to "unite in bringing social, moral and economic pressure to bear upon any country which resorts to arms instead of referring its case to arbitration and conciliation."[57]

After the Armistice, women's organizations across Europe launched a major campaign against the continuation of the blockade. British feminist Ethel Williams visited Vienna and reported about the effects on children to audiences in Britain.[58] The WILPF's British branch organized a rally on Trafalgar Square that attracted thousands of attendants, condemning the blockade as "extermination which begins with the children."[59] They also organized humanitarian shipments of food and milk to the continent together with the Red Cross. By the time a second WILPF congress took place in Zurich in May 1919, the realities of hunger and starvation had changed the members' priorities. For the WILPF it was an absolute priority that the remaining policies of blockade, "a disgrace to civilization," were ended.[60]

Feminist groups and thinkers were particularly concerned about economic blockade and sanctions because of the effects of the war on public health and social and demographic structure.[61] Their concern with issues of reproduction made the grievous effect of hunger on maternal and child health particularly worrying. Nutritionists had made new advances in documenting the effects of deficient feeding on infant development.[62] The WILPF and its sister organizations in Central Europe were therefore intervening in multiple debates at once: not only about the meaning of war and peace, but also about the future political and social order of the continent and the responsibilities of modern government.[63] When Addams and fellow pacifist feminists returned from the Zurich congress to Paris in May 1919, ending blockade policies remained one of their main goals. Addams recalled that "Mr. Hoover's office [in Paris] seemed to be the one reasonable spot in the midst of the widespread confusion; the great maps upon the wall recorded the available food resources and indicated fleets of ships carrying wheat from Australia to Finland or corn from the port of New York to Fiume. And yet even at that moment the hunger blockade, hitherto regarded as a war measure, was being applied both to Hungary and Russia as pressure against their political arrangements, foreboding sinister possibilities."[64]

For Addams, Royden, Swanwick, and other members of the WILPF, the postwar feminist campaign against the blockade was the starting point of a broader critique of international institutions. By failing to provide a materially secure economic peace, the League perpetuated many of the rivalries that had emerged during the war. "Economic hostility, having been legitimatized by the food blockades of the war," Addams argued, "was of necessity being sanctioned by the very commissions which were the outgrowth of the Peace Conference itself."[65] War in general damaged the society that female labor and care maintained and reproduced, and economic war particularly so since it "destroyed everything that mothers have begun."[66]

The feminists' opposition to sanctions put them at odds with the mainstream of British politics, which saw economic pressure as good insofar as it allowed the demilitarization of domestic society. Compared to armed war, economic pressure avoided the need to draft large numbers of young men as conscripts. It could be directed by bureaucrats and operated through laws, courts, and administrators. Nonetheless, blockade attracted the opposition of organized sections of the British workforce because it was being used against a proletarian state. In January 1919, British social-ists had started the "Hands Off Russia" campaign. Public and parliamen-tary anger grew when the Lord Privy Seal refused point blank to answer questions from the House of Commons about the blockade's legality.[67] Cecil Harmsworth denied that a blockade in the strict sense of the term existed.[68] But a growing unease was palpable about the reconfiguration of war and peace that had occurred at the Peace Conference. In the eyes of many in the radical free-trade wing of the Liberal Party, such as Josiah Wedgwood, maintaining a blockade without a parliamentary vote for war was an affront to constitutional principle.[69] By doing so in the absence of an official state of war, they worried, Lloyd George's government was also acting in breach of international law.[70] The Union for Democratic Con-trol (UDC), an important pressure group for a more accountable foreign policy, published appeals by Russian notables calling for an end to the blockade and aid for the reconstruction of their country.[71] Its position was that a de facto economic war in the absence of de jure war was both im-moral and illegal. Edmund Morel, one of the group's leading figures, gave speeches around the country attacking the "new system of peace-making . . . [which] condemned entire populations to economic ruin and sought, by the cumulative enactments of the Peace of Paris, to complete the pro-cess of strangulation by blockade imposed as a war-weapon."[72] In France, prominent writers and publishers, including Anatole France, Georges Du-hamel, Henri Barbusse, and Gaston Gallimard, protested against the iso-lation of Russia as the Allies' "great crime."[73]

Despite this growing domestic opposition, the Allied governments made a final concerted push to isolate Soviet Russia from the international economy in the fall of 1919. On 9 October, they issued a diplomatic note to Germany demanding that Berlin join their economic embargo against Russia. If their hope was to boost the League's untried "economic pressure weapon," then the gambit was a failure.[74] The war had created deep Ger-man revulsion about blockade against civilian populations. The social-democratic newspaper *Vorwärts* wrote of a proposal that was "criminal and unethical to a special degree."[75] Foreign minister Hermann Müller spoke out against imposing on the Russians the same deprivation that Germany had endured for four years. "We know on the basis of our experiences that Bolshevism is fed precisely by such coercive methods as the Allies want to use today. We truly got to know the hunger blockade first-hand."[76] Despite its many grave internal disagreements, the Weimar Republic's political elite was almost uniformly opposed to joining the blockade of Russia.[77] On 29 October, its centrist coalition government officially rejected the Allied note. The blockade of Soviet Russia had reached its peak, but it would take a while longer to crumble.

Ending the Blockade of Soviet Russia

Time was not on the Allies' side during the postwar blockades of 1919–1921. As governments tried to restore the prewar gold standard, they launched a short but intense recession that caused global deflation and lower incomes across much of the world economy. In this context, the continued dislocation of trade led to growing calls by exporters to reconnect with the Russian economy. Rumors that merchant mariners from Scandinavia were asking their governments to ignore the Allied blockade of Russia showed the policy of exclusion was disintegrating.[78] On 16 January 1920, the SEC decided to lift a part of the blockade by permitting trade with Russian farmers' cooperatives. What this meant was open to some dispute. *Pravda* wrote that "the question of the lifting of the blockade still entails many obscurities."[79] The Quai d'Orsay thought that "the reprise of commerce with Russia appears to be the best means to eliminate the most extreme forms of Bolshevism in Russia itself" but that trade with "the Russian cooperatives does not imply any negotiation with the Soviet government, and also not the recognition thereof."[80] Allied leaders were at pains to explain that interaction was not the same as acceptance. The farmers' cooperatives, they argued, were chosen as preferred trading partners precisely because they were associations that were purely economic in character.[81] But the Soviet Politburo of course saw things differently. Two veteran Bolsheviks, Leonid Krasin and Maxim Litvinov, were appointed to lead the central cooperatives' organization, Centrosoyuz. Their hope was to visit European countries to engage in commercial negotiations that would benefit the entire Russian economy.[82]

British leaders hoped that limited exchange would soften and dull Bolshevism more effectively than maximum economic pressure. Lloyd George explained to the House of Commons: "We have failed to restore Russia to sanity by force. I believe we can save her by trade. Commerce has a sobering influence in its operations. The simple sums in addition and subtraction which it inculcates soon dispose of wild theories. The Russian with his head in the clouds finds he is cold, and discovers that he is not clad and that he is hungry. . . . There is but one way—we must fight anarchy with abundance."[83] Lloyd George subscribed to a version of the older liberal idea of *doux commerce*, the notion that trade is inherently civilizing. Yet there was also a strong link in this reasoning between calculative rationality and the abandoning of "wild theories." Practical accounting to meet immediate needs would tame revolutionary passions. In his speech to the Commons, he invoked the need to feed Europe with Russian grain as a major practical reason to start trade with the farmers' cooperatives. "When people are hungry," he argued, "you cannot refuse to buy corn in Egypt because there is a Pharaoh on the throne."[84] The language of civilization and commerce that he used was political; Lenin, he implied, was a brutal despotic ruler from antiquity. But the language was deployed in favor of depoliticized economic exchange since resuming trade with Russia was not tantamount to recognizing the Soviets as equal partners.

The Soviet leaders, on the other hand, realized that rebuilding their ravaged economy gave them a certain amount of leverage. Their search for advanced technology and investment capital from foreign suppliers would prove too tempting for many cash-strapped Western bankers and businesses to resist. Managing this import power wisely was the way out of economic isolation.[85] Litvinov had emphasized the importance of Soviet resources to European reconstruction in preliminary talks with the Allies in Copenhagen in the spring of 1920.[86] The emergence of the Soviet Union opened a new dimension in the politics of economic pressure.[87] A state committed to world revolution proved able not just to withstand isolation, but also to break through the blockade and direct economic pressure itself. The Soviet use of a government monopoly on foreign trade to withhold commodities from Europe was a state-driven application of the economic weapon against other countries.

But socialist ideas about economic pressure always coexisted with older, bottom-up strategies in which populations used boycotts and coordinated strikes against governments and businesses.[88] Two factors made the aftermath of World War I a particularly propitious time to think about how the statist and civic versions could be used in concert. The first was wartime labor mobilization in European economies. Economic sectors that saw the largest surges in labor activism during the war—steel production, coal mining, arms manufacturing, railroads, dockyards, and shipbuilding—were also the most strategically vital to the British, French, and Italian governments. The second was the founding of the Communist

International (Comintern) in Moscow in March 1919.[89] A revolutionary state in Russia and working-class civil society across Europe could now find a new unity of purpose by using economic pressure against capitalist elites. The Comintern first attempted to mobilize this transnational power in response to Allied intervention against the Russian and Hungarian revolutions. Trade unions of Britain, France, and Italy had made far-reaching plans for an international general strike, set to begin on 20 July 1919. Factional disputes among the national workers' movements had derailed the initiative.[90] Yet economic pressure by organized labor continued to be a worrisome prospect to those in power. Having administered an unprecedented naval blockade, the British elite was understandably troubled by the increasing militancy of shipbuilders and dockworkers. The political arm of the British workers' movement, the Labour Party, made no secret of its preparedness to cripple the British economy with strikes if its political demands were not met.

Arnold-Forster, having helped Cecil during the war and served as Admiralty representative at Paris, left the government in 1919 and joined the UDC and the Labour Party. He remained an ardent internationalist and felt that the League of Nations was the only institution that could legitimately wield the terrible instrument of blockade. Precisely for this reason, the British government's ambiguity on the isolation of Russia was dangerous. Arnold-Forster underscored that because the economic weapon was "less conspicuous and less obviously expensive, and, unless steps are taken, less subject to democratic control," there was a serious need to make its use more accountable.[91] If sanctions would be primarily aimed at civilian populations, then citizens should also be the ultimate directors of economic pressure. Unlike in previous conflicts, naval blockade would be secondary to administrative measures like energy, communications, and export controls. Full mastery of the economic weapon required public oversight of the bureaucracy of the modern warfare state.

If the British government and the League did not open their decision making to popular input, the working classes would take matters into their own hands, Arnold-Forster warned:

> Instead of a refusal of service, or national strike, organised by national Governments, we shall come to international strikes organised by international Labour movements. Unless the League makes haste to democratise itself, the Transport Workers of the world, or the Seamen's Union, or the Coal Workers, will be filch-

William Arnold-Forster, contributor
to the UDC journal *Foreign Affairs*,
July 1920. University of Iowa.

ing away the League's economic weapon, and settling such questions as whether [Russian White general] Denikin is to have
supplies for a war against revolutionary Russia. . . . Unless the
League's Constitution is revised, there is a real danger that it may
abuse its economic powers in the same sort of way as the Paris
Conference did in dealing with Hungary and Russia.[92]

If economic war could not be extinguished, Arnold-Forster thought that
it should be made subject to maximum popular control.

That organized labor could exercise powerful economic pressure to
restrict militarism was also made clear by events in Central and Eastern
Europe. In March 1920, the militarist Kapp-Lüttwitz coup against the
Weimar German government was stopped by a massive general strike.[93]
The Social-Democratic Party (SPD) organized a nationwide walkout of
German public- and private-sector workers, crippling the ability of the
right-wing putschists to establish a military dictatorship. This general
strike was the largest ever seen in Germany—and probably anywhere in

the world by this point.[94] The Polish-Soviet War that erupted that spring provided more proof of the power of grassroots economic pressure. After Polish forces invaded Soviet Ukraine and took Kiev, Lenin and Trotsky called on Western workers to stop the invasion. In May, dockworkers and stevedores at the East India docks in London refused to supply coal to ships bringing munitions to Poland.[95] This spontaneous action soon attracted wider support. Trade union leader Ernest Bevin called for a boycott by workers producing and transporting weapons for wars that "outrage our sense of justice."[96] When, in early August, the Red Army's counter-offensive into Poland had brought it to the gates of Warsaw, class tensions grew in Britain and France. Anglo-French staff talks discussed offering military aid to Poland, and Whitehall considered a declaration of war against the Soviets. But on 9 August 1920, the Labour Party and the British Trades Union Congress (TUC) warned that "the whole industrial power of the organised workers will be used to defeat this war."[97] Lloyd George took the power of the unions to shut down Britain's trading economy extremely seriously. In the event, the Red Army was stopped by Polish defenses in front of Warsaw and a ceasefire was soon agreed. The British labor movement had not ended the conflict by itself. But its words and actions had created a climate of opinion in Britain that enabled the de-escalation of the war against Bolshevism.[98]

Moreover, in the aftermath of the Polish-Soviet War the intense public political pressure on Lloyd George to end the blockade of Russia was beginning to pay off. In March 1921, a trade agreement restored prewar economic relations between the United Kingdom and Russia. Article 1 of the Anglo-Soviet agreement stipulated that "Both parties agree not to impose or maintain any form of blockade against each other and to remove forthwith all obstacles hitherto placed in the way of the real trade between the United Kingdom and Russia."[99] The Allied attempt to starve Russians into turning against Bolshevism had failed. British, French, and American political elites now chose a new means with which to pursue this end. Instead of depriving the Bolsheviks of resources, the Allies began to supply them, making a show of the abundance that capitalism had to offer.[100] When serious famine erupted in southern Russia later that year, Western humanitarians came to the help of the Soviet government.[101]

Lloyd George's transformation from blockader to trader was an acknowledgment that forging commercial connections could have a stronger impact on the behavior of underdeveloped and isolated countries than severing them from external trade.[102] Despite his commitment to ruthless blockade during the war, from 1920 onward Lloyd George prioritized economic suasion over economic force. His defense of trade with the Soviets derived from the constructive, activist nature of his liberalism. In his view, liberal subjects were not naturally created to be rational, law-abiding capitalist entrepreneurs and workers. They required exposure to the mores of the market. The penury of the postwar period was an opportunity to cultivate the Russians and other semi-civilized peoples as nascent capitalist subjects.[103] Lloyd George saw reasonable peoples as non-ideological and practically minded, which meant that they had abandoned childish beliefs in revolution and transcendence. As he put it to the press in defense of the Anglo-Soviet treaty, "Lenin begins to realise that he has to trade. He thought he could run his country on some theories of Karl Marx. What does he find? Starvation, famine, and his railways completely out of repair. You cannot patch up locomotives with Karl Marx's doctrines."[104]

Whatever outposts of political radicalism remained in Europe were now besieged enclaves that no longer posed a threat to the overall social order; in the words of Charles Maier, they were "proletarian La Rochelles confronting a bourgeois hinterland."[105] Yet although radical socialist revolution failed in Western Europe, the Soviet Union persisted and even managed to expand ties with the rest of the world that had been damaged by three years of undeclared economic war. As one French diplomat wrote, Leonid Krasin had "renounced the violent method and [thinks] that Russia can be well constituted as a 'communist oasis' in a bourgeois Europe, with which it will find itself in peaceful relations and commercial ties and that its example will suffice to convert."[106]

By 1921 elites in Allied countries, Central Europe, and the Soviet Union were worried about being fatally weakened by organized economic pressure, whether this was external (sanctions, blockade, or capitalist encirclement) or internal (strikes and boycotts by workers) in nature. Blockades had usually been tools of state power. But as the domestic debates about blockade show, undeclared economic wars in peacetime become subject to interest group competition, class disputes, and democratic contestation. Once politicized by the war, the economic weapon was now an instrument without a single operator. The postwar period raised profound debates about which states, classes, and social groups should be deprived of material sustenance and who should decide on the terms of isolation and integration. The Allied campaigns to isolate Kun's Hungary and Bolshevik Russia were also the first uses of peacetime economic sanctions to achieve regime change in other states. In this regard they prefigured the period after World War II, when internal objectives began to overtake inter-state objectives as the main reason for the use of sanctions. Yet if ideological change toward liberalism was the aim of these policies, then economic pressure singularly failed to achieve such Wilsonian hopes. Aid proved far more effective a tool of stabilization than blockade. As one British diplomat concluded after visiting the deprived cities of Germany in 1919, "It is better to feed an idealist than to fight him. It is only those who fast who see visions."[107]

PART II

The Legitimacy of the Economic Weapon

CHAPTER FOUR

Calibrating the Economic
Weapon, 1921–1924

I N JULY 1920, the League's most powerful organ, the Council, met
in the northern Spanish coastal city of San Sebastian. British foreign
secretary Arthur Balfour emphasized what he thought the organization needed most. "We must have an economic blockade," he announced to the assembled journalists. "No nation would destroy itself in
these civilized times by inviting such a penalty," Balfour predicted. "It is
not likely it will often be used, since it is not probable the League will often
be defied."[1] Balfour's view of how League sanctions would work—first and
foremost as a deterrent—was the dominant one among internationalists in
the decade after World War I. As more countries joined the League, this
deterrent effect was bound to grow. The French had always envisioned
an organization "tending to the universal" (*tendant à l'universel*).[2] But this
remained an aspiration rather than a reality. As ex-belligerent and revolutionary states, neither Germany nor Soviet Russia were members. Even
more problematic was that in March 1920 the Versailles Treaty, and with it
the legal basis of the new organization in Geneva, had been rejected by the
U.S. Senate. This meant that the Council, the League's executive organ,
would have not five but only four permanent members—Britain, France,
Italy, and Japan—with its four non-permanent members elected by the
Assembly, the League's legislature, for three-year periods.

The Council's Article 16 procedure against aggressors was not the only multilateral coercive instrument at the disposal of the three large European states, Britain, France, and Italy. Under the Versailles Treaty these countries, as well as Belgium, a non-permanent Council member, were earmarked to receive German reparations payments. If Germany was found guilty of non-compliance, tough enforcement measures of an economic or military nature could be used. Sanctions as they emerged in the post–World War I order were therefore marked by a constitutive tension. Within the League, sanctions were supposed to help preserve universal peace. But in practice, their implementation would be in the hands of the same European great powers that used separate Versailles Treaty sanctions to pursue their own particular interests in the reparations question. By using similar methods in both domains, Britain, France, and Italy were professing universalism while practicing power politics at the same time.

Discussions of the economic weapon in the early 1920s were shot through with this fundamental ambiguity: would sanctions be another instrument of great power competition or a means of transcending it? In August 1921 the League convened a special expert body, the IBC, to adjudicate the meaning of Article 16 and calibrate its functions more precisely. The ink on these IBC resolutions was barely dry when the first crisis erupted in which the article's deterrent function was put to the test. A well-timed League sanctions threat in November compelled Yugoslavia to break off its creeping invasion of northern Albania. Sanctions prevented what could have spiraled into the fourth Balkan war in a decade. This successful display of unity stood in marked contrast with the use of sanctions to enforce Versailles Treaty reparations claims against Germany. Beginning in early 1921 the Allies forcefully seized German ports and customs posts, a process that escalated into the occupation of the Ruhr industrial region. The inter-Allied discord sown by the Ruhr crisis caused further problems for the deterrence of League sanctions when Italy, now ruled by the Fascist Benito Mussolini, embarked on a punitive expedition against the Greek island of Corfu in 1923. It seemed that imperial hierarchy, not the norm that sovereign states were equal, was the stronger influence on peacetime economic pressure.

The International Blockade Committee

During the Peace Conference, Cecil and Bourgeois had assuaged the worries of smaller countries about great power dominance by promising that member states' precise obligations under the Covenant would be worked out at the first League meetings in Geneva in the fall of 1920.[3] Many states therefore welcomed the decision by its secretary-general, the British Foreign Office diplomat Eric Drummond, to push the economic weapon to the front of the League's agenda.[4] In December, Drummond wrote that a special group of experts would sketch precise "plans which enable the League to use the weapon of international economic and financial blockade."[5] This blockade commission would be balanced between great powers and smaller countries, mimicking the structure of the Council. Drummond's Secretariat asked Cuba, Norway, Spain, and Switzerland to join the expert body. Since the non-permanent Council members for the 1920–1923 period were Belgium, Brazil, China, and Greece, this meant that the smaller countries in the League now had three European and one Latin American representative to defend their interests.

While preparing for the internationalization of the economic weapon, Paris and London were rearranging their state capacity and changed their strategic outlook. In the face of a large budget deficit and no relief on debts incurred during the war, British expenditure cuts and demobilization had forced the Ministry of Blockade to be disbanded in July 1919. When pressed on the efficacy of the blockade in the House of Commons, Cecil confessed, "I believe we succeeded, but the machinery which had to be established was elaborate, and I am sure it cannot be established usefully now."[6] Even if Britain had wanted to institute a comprehensive blockade on the wartime model, it now lacked the civilian administration and intelligence infrastructure needed to do so.

British liberalism had long harbored a strong antipathy to land armies, conscription, generals, and anything else that reeked of militarism. An excessively strong army would not only be a costly burden on a thriving private economy. It would also spur nationalism and aggressive behavior, all of which clashed with the values of open-mindedness, rationality, and peace. Liberals were much fonder of the Royal Navy, which they saw as a purely defensive instrument to protect the empire and its lines of transport and communication. David Edgerton has argued that liberal internationalism in interwar Britain was always accompanied by a distinct "liberal militarism."[7] The economic weapon played a role in both, appearing as "sanctions" in the former and "blockade" in the latter. Blockade was attractive because its cost to Britain was very low, as was its visibility to the British public. As Arnold-Forster put it, "Blockade in its present form offers a new problem to the pacifist philosopher. . . . When the aggressor

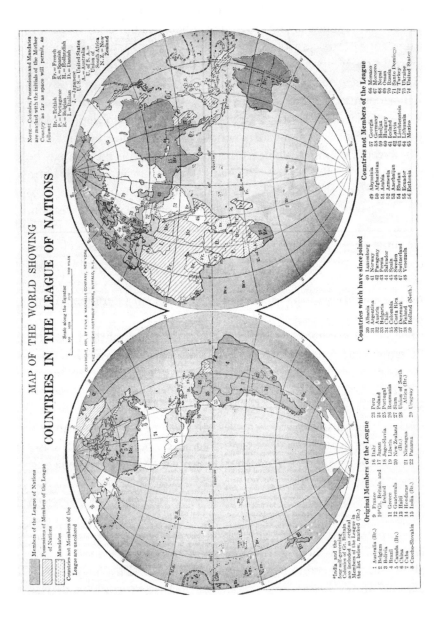

Member states of the League of Nations in April 1921.
Originally published in *Literary Digest*. Cornell University Library.

has to go on sticking his bayonet into the passive resisters, . . . even he will come to see in time that the process is unpleasant. But in the case of blockade there is no such direct contact with the results to act as a check. . . . Lord Curzon's pen will replace the invader's bayonet and there will be no distressing scream audible in Downing Street. Blockade is so convenient."[8] The possibility of inflicting terrible suffering on civilians from a distance by bureaucrats was morally abhorrent to Arnold-Forster. Yet to most British internationalists like him, the lack of a League army made the economic weapon the organization's main instrument by default. Arnold-Forster's case for blockade was an internationalist-democratic one. As the architect of the "scientific" statistical blockade system, he admitted that it was a terrible measure capable of killing hundreds of thousands of people. But if it was internationalized under League control, its potential power might be great enough to assure peace.

The French began thinking about how to perform such internationalization in early 1921, in preparation for the IBC meeting that fall. The Foreign Ministry's review was conducted by the commercial relations desk under Seydoux, a department that had developed out of the wartime blockade apparatus.[9] A functionary more self-effacing than Cecil, who had a penchant for bold vision and oration, Seydoux preferred to work out deals away from the public eye.[10] While the British administrative capacity to institute blockade was shrinking, he convinced his superiors that French national security depended on permanent preparedness for economic warfare. In February 1921 an inter-ministerial subcommittee for the study of blockade was formed. Chaired by the French ambassador to the League, Jean Goût—another former blockade administrator—it brought together representatives from the ministries of foreign affairs, commerce, finance, agriculture, and war; the navy; and the army. The committee worked from the premise that the "dogma of a short war" had left France unprepared in 1914 and delayed its ability to bring economic pressure to bear on Germany and Austria-Hungary. In its eyes, what was needed was "an economic organization that will have, without delay, a staff and is likely to function from the mobilization onward."[11]

The subcommittee drafted lists of industrial raw materials and foodstuffs to be stockpiled and discussed how peacetime blockade might be used. It was possible that an aggressor would respond to a sanctions regime by invading smaller nations around it.[12] Of course, this was precisely the fear that countries like Denmark, the Netherlands, and Switzerland had about deploying the League's economic weapon against Germany. French military planners pushed the civilian administrators to consider a preventive blockade merely when it seemed a country would embark on aggression.[13] The idea of economic pressure as a first-strike strategy, an economic Schlieffen Plan, remained appealing. Yet the feasibility of this approach seemed increasingly in question. As a growing number of civilian and military technocrats came to realize in the interwar years, when actually applied, the power of economic pressure lay in exhaustion through attrition, not paralysis through rapid action. The economic war of 1914–1918 had not fulfilled hopes that material interdiction would cause rapid social collapse; certainly neither the Allied blockade nor the German submarine war had had this effect within any short timeframe that was politically exploitable. However, internationalists seeking to strengthen sanctions deterrence kept emphasizing their quick-acting effects, leading to a relative overestimation of material pressure among strategists and historians.[14]

At any rate, the civilian officials on Goût's inter-ministerial subcommittee knew that a preemptive blockade would be diplomatically and legally impossible. They opposed the military's quick-acting version of the policy as a threat to the hard-won peace and political stability in Europe. Preventive blockade was never proposed in Geneva. Yet Seydoux and Goût did think that an economic sanctions mechanism should be automatic, comprehensive, and supported by as many member states as possible. What they were seeking to defend was a middle ground between the military hardliners in their own country and the growing tendency toward continental disengagement of the British Foreign Office.[15]

The IBC convened in Geneva in late August 1921. The committee was composed of eight members, four from the great powers (Britain, France, Italy, and Japan) and four from the wartime neutral countries: Cuba, Norway, Spain, and Switzerland. Most were experts on foreign economic and legal affairs. Cuba sent its ambassador to Germany, Aristides de Aguero y Bethancourt, an old revolutionary comrade of José Martí and Máximo Gómez and one of Cuba's main spokesmen in international affairs.[16] The Spanish delegate, Pablo Garnica Echevarría, a former banker and Liberal Party deputy, had resolutely laissez-faire economic views; like Aguero, he defended neutral rights against a strong blockade mandate for the League.[17] The remaining two neutrals, Norway and Switzerland, had sent experts on maritime affairs and international law: Christian Sparre, a former Royal Norwegian Navy admiral and parliamentarian for the liberal Venstre party who strongly defended freedom of the seas; and Max Huber, a professor of international law at the University of Zurich and the Swiss

The International Blockade Committee in Geneva, August 1921. Seated,
from left to right, are Jean Goût (France), Aristides Aguero y Bethancourt
(Cuba), William Finlay (Britain), Pablo Garnica Echevarría (Spain), Max
Huber (Switzerland), Christian Sparre (Norway), and Minoru Oka (Japan).
Courtesy of the United Nations Archives at Geneva.

Foreign Ministry's chief legal adviser.[18] Given the importance attached
to the IBC in Paris, the French government sent Goût himself. An experienced Quai d'Orsay insider, he had been head of the Foreign Ministry's Asian department and deputy head of the blockade department during the war and had contributed to designing French League proposals.[19]
The British seat was taken by Sir William Finlay, a distinguished lawyer
who had served as a legal adviser on various blockade committees during
the war and was Lloyd George's lord chancellor from 1916 to 1919.[20] The
other two permanent Council members on the IBC were the former Italian finance minister Carlo Schanzer and Dr. Minuro Oka, a civil servant
and journalist who had run the commerce and industry department at the
Japanese Ministry of Agriculture and Commerce and who led the Japanese
League of Nations Association.[21]

Over the course of nine sessions across six days, the IBC focused on three key questions. First, *when* would economic sanctions be deployed? Second, *who* would decide that sanctions should be imposed? Finally, *how* would League member states implement them? These questions were deeply political, and the committee treated them as such.[22] It became clear that the most sensible interpretation of Article 16 was at once narrow and open-ended. The narrowness was applied to the actions that would trigger them. Sanctions, the IBC agreed, should only be a response to aggression as defined in Article 10 of the Covenant: "armed action" against the "territorial integrity" or "political independence" of a member state. This definition excluded internal rebellions, coups, civil wars, and minority questions as conflicts that justified using sanctions. Only violating inter-state peace between sovereigns would be a cause of sanctions use. At the same time, the sanctions measures themselves were defined as pliable by the IBC. League members, the committee held, were free to engage in *acts of war* in retaliation, but they could decide for themselves if this brought them into a *state of war* with the aggressor.[23] This distinction satisfied both Britain and France. It allowed Paris to institute economic sanctions as a peacetime policing measure. Simultaneously, London could use its considerable naval power as a deterrent without having to resurrect the wartime blockade apparatus. Individual government discretion over whether sanctions created a state of war also benefited the neutrals, which could impose light measures without forsaking their neutrality. The committee removed some anxiety by claiming that notwithstanding the whole debate over the meaning of pressure in war and peace, Article 16 was "essentially economic in nature."[24] On the question of who decided on sanctions, it vested absolute power in the League Council.

Besides these formal and procedural concerns, the deeper question that the IBC was broaching was how the economic weapon should be calibrated. If it was possible to resolve an international crisis without taking coercive measures, so much the better. But exactly how strong and quick should League sanctions be to have an optimal deterrent effect? As Finlay and his superiors at the Foreign Office were aware, optimal deterrence was not necessarily maximal deterrence.[25] If the sanctions were immediately devastating, they might be so strong that they could not be used lightly; doubts might then arise about whether the economic weapon would actually be used at all. Conversely, if the sanctions were too measured, they might not work quickly enough or draw into question the Council's willingness to escalate further.

The problems and dislocations caused by the wartime blockade had deeply marked the outlook of many neutral countries. On the insistence of the neutral delegates, the IBC stipulated that food embargoes should be used only as a last resort just short of war. This was not the only way in which public opinion shaped the economic weapon, however. The committee viewed "publicity" as key to the deterrent function of sanctions. That is, they would work only if the Council's sanctions decision was openly announced for all the world to hear. The IBC expected that on receiving news of impending sanctions, "public opinion in the country which has been declared a Covenant-breaker will also be aroused, and that, in consequence, a new political orientation may be adopted, thus making a return to a normal situation possible. The result will be that the conflict will be brought to an end without it becoming necessary to put the sanctions in force."[26]

This argument about the effect of sanctions on public opinion was a powerful rationale, aligning the operation of democracy with the cause of peace. Yet its core premise was that "public opinion," if it could find coherent and timely expression within an aggressor state, was influenced primarily by economic factors. The prospect of material damage rather than moral stigma would induce publics to restrain their governments' aggressive behavior. Identifying public opinion with the primacy of commercial motives was no doubt appealing to the bourgeois officials on the IBC. Still, their conviction that a population's fear of falling living standards could preserve peace was striking. Would the *doux commerce* of economic exchange always trump the *amour-propre* that encouraged nationalism and aggression? In light of the deep distrust and division left behind by the war, many commentators were skeptical. Even Norman Angell, the most famous early twentieth-century proponent of the softening commerce argument, concluded that same year, "What we have seen in recent history is not a deliberate choice of ends with a consciousness of moral and material cost. We see . . . a whole continent given over to an orgy of hate, retaliation, the indulgence of self-destructive passions. . . . No indictment of human reason could be more severe."[27]

Sanctions under the Versailles Treaty

While these discussions about Genevan sanctions were taking place, a different sort of sanction was being put into effect under the Versailles Treaty to pressure Germany into reparations payments. The Allied Reparations Commission was due to announce in May 1921 the total size of the indemnity to be paid. Up to that point, Berlin had a bad record of making payments both in money and in goods. On 3 March, British prime minister Lloyd George held an address at St. James's Palace that circulated widely around Europe. Unless Germany accepted Allied payment proposals or matched them with a similarly good proposal of its own, he warned, the Allies would impose economic sanctions on Germany.

The French government considered several sanctions. First, its occupation of the Rhineland could be extended beyond its currently envisioned end in 1934.[28] Second, more German territory could be seized. Third, it could impose "customs sanctions" by levying duties on goods traffic on the Rhine and on assets like railways, mines, and forests.[29] A combination of the second and third options seemed the most appealing. French occupation authorities had identified the ports of Duisburg, Ruhrort, and Düsseldorf as the key economic hubs through which most coal produced in the Ruhr region was exported abroad—some twenty million tons per year, a figure over two-thirds of annual French production.[30] If customs stations could be erected there to tax coal exports via riverboat at their source of loading, the burden would hit the wealthy German industrialists seen as responsible for the non-fulfillment of reparations. Moreover, the revenues from this export tax could be used to relieve French finances.

In the early morning hours of 8 March, French troops occupied Düsseldorf, Duisburg, and Ruhrort. In the Reichstag the German chancellor, Constantin Fehrenbach, of the Catholic Center Party, announced that "the Allied governments have decided upon and have already put into action . . . the so-called sanctions. I will start by translating this word into the proper German. They are nothing but acts of violence. The praiseworthy concepts of law have nothing to do with these actions." Fehrenbach then delivered an appeal to the German people to face the sanctions with bravery, just as they had faced the wartime blockade. "The German people need to prove the height of their resilience, the expansion of their patience, and their faithful endurance. . . . It is uplifting for us . . . to observe which spirit reigns in these threatened territories: the spirit of determination."[31] Sanctions were criticized across the entire German political spectrum for different reasons, depending on the outlook of the parties concerned: for being a tool of League imperialism to crush class struggle (the socialist USPD); as an attack on German workers and a blow for the understanding of peoples (the social-democratic SPD); as an economic impediment to the need to reestablish commerce and economic growth (the centrist-liberal DDP); as breaches of law, civility, and good standards of conduct among nations (the Center Party); or as a cloaked attack on the national health of the German people, unjustly placed under economic quarantine in peacetime (the right-nationalist DVNP).[32]

Yet the uniform condemnation of sanctions by German politicians did not mean that all critics supported the government. The left was scathing about the class politics of Fehrenbach's appeal to the German people to tighten their belts. Such injunctions to steadfastness were deceptive so long as the upper and middle classes were unwilling to make their own sacrifices in facing down the sanctions. Former doctor and USPD deputy Julius Moses called the German elite a "racketeerocracy" (*Schieberokratie*) that used the sanctions to cover up its own failures. On reparations, the government was engaging in "theater diplomacy" as an excuse not to deliver the public services and living standards that the German people deserved. Right-wing politicians liked to decry how sanctions affected the health of the German people, but they refused to make the public expenditures needed to aid the weakest.[33]

Germany appealed to Geneva to block the Rhine port occupations. The Allied sanctions, Berlin claimed, were violations of the international peace protected by the Covenant. Germany was not a member state, so it did not enjoy full representation in the organization. But under the Covenant's Article 17, even non-member states could benefit from inter-state arbitration if they were prepared to temporarily assume the duties of membership. German foreign minister Walter Simons sent a note to Secretary-General Drummond asking for an Article 17 conciliation procedure to "obtain the immediate lifting of the measures of violence taken by the Allies." French officials were incensed that Germany, as a non-member, dared to ask for the Council to convene.[34] Seydoux wrote a note defending the French sanctions in which he argued that "to occupy peacefully a territory, to assign to the payment of the debt of a debtor State the receipts of the customs rights of that State or certain sums due to the recalcitrant nation, are measures that have for long been practiced and consecrated by the custom of states . . . to force recalcitrant States to execute their obligations or their commitments."[35] While Seydoux was right that such measures had been used in preceding decades, this logic blithely extended gunboat diplomacy from the semi-colonial periphery to Europe itself.

Such desires to "Ottomanize" Germany were by no means restricted to France, a long-standing rival of German power in Europe. Even small nations, which otherwise had a strong stake in the protection of formal equality among states, were tempted to accept imperial hierarchies in the use of economic pressure when they could secure benefits by doing so. Danish conservatives wanted to occupy the north German province of Schleswig, including the Kiel Canal, which connected the North Sea to the Baltic. Such a move, they argued, would find broad support in Scandinavian countries and allow Germany's creditors to control a major waterway, just as Britain and France operated the Suez Canal in Egypt.[36] Belgian foreign minister Henri Jaspar proposed the blockade of Hamburg, Germany's main seaport, and the seizure of its maritime customs income as a form of collateral.[37] Talk about the impending seizure of Hamburg was so common in the spring of 1921 that the Czechoslovaks asked French prime minister Aristide Briand if he could at least administer the port with the commercial interests of their landlocked country in mind.[38] This enthusiasm for unequal punishment implied a remarkable reversal. In 1902–1903 Germany had joined the pacific blockade of Venezuela. Less than two decades later, it was in danger of becoming the target of the same unequal procedure.[39]

In an effort to render the German government more cooperative, the Allies decided in August 1921 to end the Ruhr port occupations and customs posts. However, this relief was conditional on Berlin's official acceptance of the legality of previous measures. Nothing that had been done in terms of territorial occupation could be held against them, whether inside or outside the League, now or in the future. This set a precedent for future measures of isolation, taxation, the seizure of assets, and military occupation as legal peacetime economic sanctions. But the tension caused by these moves dissipated somewhat as the League engaged in a successful use of sanctions that seemed to warrant the internationalists' belief in deterrence.

Saving Albania

As the second League Assembly opened in September 1921, a political crisis was brewing over the independence of Albania. The small country had been created by the European great powers in the wake of the Balkan Wars of 1912–1913. To rule its mixed population of Sunni Muslims, Roman Catholics, and Orthodox Christians, the great powers picked a German prince, Wilhelm of Wied. Crowned in March 1914 as Prince Vidi I of Albania, he left the country just seven months later to fight on the Eastern front.[40] Albania disintegrated along sectarian lines and narrowly escaped partition at the hands of Italy, Greece, and Yugoslavia during the Peace Conference through a last-minute intervention by Woodrow Wilson.[41]

Northern Albania near the border with Yugoslavia, 1921. From Rose Wilder
Lane, *Peaks of Shala* (New York and London: Harper and Brothers, 1923).
University of Virginia.

Albanian independence was threatened not only by internal instability,
but also by the expansionist ambitions of the Serb-dominated Kingdom
of Yugoslavia to its north. Part of the reason for this was that fixing the
northern border between the countries, a process begun in 1913, was not
complete when the world war erupted, and the task remained unfinished.[42]
Serb forces used this uncertainty to exploit local divisions among northern
Albanian clans, bringing a large chunk of the country under their control.
Reports of Serbian brutality in northern Albania grew in 1920, even as the
country was admitted to the League in December. An arbitrationist friend
of Bourgeois wrote to him that "the extermination of the Albanian race
. . . will not be anything but a great crime committed after many others
since the war, but this crime will have been committed with the complicity
of the Great Powers. . . . History will not pardon it."[43] The conflict escalated in July 1921, when a Catholic chieftain called Marka Gjoni declared
an autonomous "Republic of Mirdita" in the country's north. Entering
Albania with a band of twelve hundred fighters and Russian and Serbian
mercenaries, funded and equipped by the Yugoslav government, Gjoni
claimed to defend the freedom of Christians against the "Turkish agents,"

"Bolsheviks," and "Kemalists" he alleged controlled the central government in Tirana.[44] By September a simultaneous Yugoslav ground offensive conducted "with great vehemence using perfected means of warfare" had destroyed 157 villages and endangered Albania's survival as a state.[45]

With the international press terrified about the prospect of another Balkan war, the Assembly heard representatives from both sides.[46] Britain backed the government of Albanian prime minister Pandeli Evangjeli and confirmed its commitment to his country's independence. On 8 November, Lloyd George sent a telegram to Drummond in which he declared that the Yugoslav invasion threatened peace; if the government of Prime Minister Nikola Pašić refused Geneva's mediation, he would propose economic sanctions.[47] Whitehall thus raised the prospect of an Article 16 sanctions regime against Yugoslavia.[48] Lloyd George also brought forward the next Council meeting by two days to increase the pressure on Belgrade. Before the House of Commons, he said that "if the raids and slaughter did not stop at once," the Yugoslavs would face a Royal Navy blockade of the Adriatic and the severance of diplomatic relations.[49] As Yugoslav troops advanced, the British threat was reported across Europe and the United States.[50] At the Council meeting of 17 November, open to the public and attended by reporters, British ambassador Herbert Fisher consciously formally delivered Lloyd George's threat of economic sanctions.[51] These overt announcements bought the time necessary to let diplomacy do its work. A League commission of inquiry with experts from Finland, Luxembourg, and Norway fixed the northern border by mid-November, which allowed the hostilities to die down.[52] As long as the border remained unclear, it was technically difficult to claim that Yugoslav conduct was an act of aggression against Albanian territorial integrity. To avoid this legal awkwardness, Léon Bourgeois, who followed the crisis closely from Paris, privately concluded that it would be better if Article 16 would not actually have to be applied.[53] But his worries were unnecessary. Before the end of the month, the Yugoslav government had backed down and withdrawn its troops behind the new border.

The Yugoslav-Albanian crisis of 1921 showcased how League intervention in an escalating conflict could preserve peace. The episode buttressed Albania's contested statehood; a country whose invasion could not go unpunished was indeed a genuine sovereign state.[54] More important, it vindicated internationalist hopes that the economic weapon had a genuine and powerful effect. The threat of an economic cutoff had worked to de-escalate the situation. As the League's deputy secretary-general Frank

Paul Walters later wrote, "There can be little doubt that Albania owed her survival as an independent State to the action of the League . . . and to the threat of sanctions so unexpectedly sounded forth from London. This last was, indeed, of doubtful legality: but it was completely effective."[55] *The Economist*, whose editor, Walter Layton, was closely tied to the Genevan internationalist milieu in the interwar years, claimed that the episode was "the first illustration of the use of the League's special weapon—the economic blockade."[56] Despite its large army, Pašić's government had been "amenable in a more than proportionate degree to economic sanctions. The mere threat of reference to the League set the dinar falling on the London market, and this is what induced the Jugoslav Government to give way so promptly."[57]

This economic analysis was true in that Yugoslavia realized it could not afford another war. But the threat of blockade left a bitter aftertaste in Belgrade. The Yugoslav delegate to the Council, Bošković, said that "the threat of using against the Serbs, Croats, and Slovenes Article 16 of the pact was particularly painful for the *amour-propre* of his country."[58] The economic weapon acted on the national political imagination as much as on a rational assessment of economic interest. It would work against a small Balkan state unable to fight the great powers. But could the same be said about a medium-sized, second-tier power? Would an aggressive dictator bow to a sanctions threat? This problem would arise sooner than the deterrence theorists anticipated.

The Ruhr and Corfu

If the Allies' wartime blockade had been an economic operation with a military purpose, the Ruhr occupation of 1923 was the inverse: a military operation with an economic purpose.[59] As an ultimate means of securing reparations, it had been considered for years beforehand. Lloyd George, in a moment of frustration, had suggested it in 1920.[60] Seydoux, far from a rigid anti-German hardliner, told his colleagues that "the real sanction, the one that we have been thinking about since the month of January 1920, is the occupation of the Ruhr."[61] At a Paris meeting in August 1921, Prime Minister Briand had made it clear to Lloyd George and Italian prime minister Ivanoe Bonomi that the last-minute German acceptance of the ultimatum had been the only thing that had prevented him from ordering the seizure.[62] By April 1922 the British consulate in Cologne was picking up fears among the Rhenish population of an impending French invasion.[63]

Such drastic action would certainly cause major tensions with Britain and the United States. But on the Allied Reparations Commission, France could count on the support of Belgium and Italy, two allies equally eager to obtain more resources for postwar reconstruction.

The French Foreign Ministry had first considered economic sanctions as enforcement measures in the spring of 1921. Its inter-ministerial sub-committee had considered and rejected territorial seizure as a form of economic sanction. "Pacific occupations," it noted, "have never been effective except regarding countries unable to defend themselves. . . . Such measures could not as a result be adopted in the majority of cases."[64] Moreover, occupying other countries' cities and lands was not legally defensible because Article 10 of the Covenant protected the territorial integrity of all League member states. However, there were two reasons for seeing Germany as an exception. The first was the fact that the Reich was not a member state and had been demilitarized; it was not officially protected by the Covenant and did not have a large enough army to defend itself. The second was the fact that, as Seydoux had already pointed out, the Versailles Treaty explicitly allowed for reprisals in case of German non-payment. The relevant section of the treaty, Paragraph 18 of Annex II of Part VIII, concerning reparations, allowed the Allies to take "economic and financial prohibitions and reprisals, and in general such other measures as the respective Governments may determine to be necessary in the circumstances." It was on Paragraph 18 that the legal case for the occupation as an economic sanction was built.[65]

Briand's cabinet had ordered the preparation of plans for a Ruhr invasion to gain control of lucrative economic assets, chiefly coal mines and steel factories, but also dyestuff plants, state forests, and customs posts on the Rhine.[66] The French Army under Marshal Foch had finalized these plans as early as May 1921.[67] Eighteen months later, Briand's successor, Raymond Poincaré, made one last attempt to obtain British support for implementing economic sanctions.[68] Whitehall rejected this proposal. Still, the Ruhr occupation was no unilateral undertaking. When Germany failed to make scheduled deliveries of coal and timber, France obtained a three-to-one vote in its favor on the Allied Reparations Commission before it initiated the occupation as a sanction. A sixty-thousand-strong force of Belgian and French troops began crossing into the Ruhr on 11 January 1923.[69] Soon the French military authorities were engaged in a tug-of-war with the government in Berlin over coal deliveries from German industrialists. The working class did not turn out to support the French against Ruhr capitalists. Instead, the occupation boosted German nationalism, uniting a broader swathe of the population than before behind calls to protect the fatherland.[70]

Most British commentators understood the Ruhr occupation as a demonstration of force intended to signal French resolve. Only a few perceptive analysts in the Foreign Office and Treasury recognized that it in fact had an ulterior economic aim. Occupying the Ruhr was first and foremost a way to obtain payment *in kind* from a recalcitrant Germany by extracting large amounts of coal, steel, goods, and customs revenue from the region. In the summer of 1922, Poincaré told French lawmakers that since military sanctions did not bring in any money, the challenge was "finding the best sanctions"—that is, the most monetarily rewarding ones.[71] Payment, not punishment, was the main objective. A second aim of the occupation was to raise the costs of non-compliance for Germany. Berlin should stop sabotaging the reparations payments through inflation and evasion. As the British councilor at the embassy in Berlin explained to Foreign Secretary George Curzon, "The real question before us is not a moral one, but merely whether the occupation . . . will hit them so hard as to make them willing to agree to anything rather than suffer it to continue."[72]

The French saw their operation as the multilateral enforcement of a right to payment in peacetime.[73] The occupation was the result of taking a certain kind of economic rationality to its logical extreme. Once the coercive extraction of resources, revenues, and profits entered the realm of the possible, there was always a temptation to double down: if Germany did not comply, this simply meant the pressure of occupation was not yet strong enough to change its behavior. As resistance to occupation grew, this mindset began to appear dangerous. Even the liberal *Economist* suggested that "the hedonistic calculus is not the whole of human nature. If Germany were entirely cool-blooded and cool-headed, she might lie down under this treatment for fear of worse. But all the news that comes from Germany points to a closing of the ranks, and a rapidly rising temper, and history shows that whenever a community is driven beyond a certain extremity it fights without counting the cost."[74] This admission that there were limits to what economic coercion could achieve was formulated in opposition to French policy. Yet the British government's expectations about how the economic weapon had restrained Yugoslavia and would deter other would-be aggressors were based on much the same idea.

The European tensions caused by the Ruhr occupation were further increased by another act of occupation with imperial characteristics in the Mediterranean. In August 1923, the Italian general Enrico Tellini, head of the commission for the demarcation of Albania's southern border, was killed by bandits in the Epirus region of northwestern Greece. Mussolini demanded an apology from Athens, as well as the payment of damages, burial with full military honors, and a thorough investigation of the murder by the Greek government. When the Greeks agreed to some but not all these conditions, Il Duce took matters into his own hands. In a brazen display of aggression, Mussolini sent an Italian naval squadron to Greek waters. On 31 August these ships bombarded Corfu, killing twenty civilians and wounding dozens, and landed a five-thousand-strong army regiment on the Ionian island.[75]

Mussolini's punitive expedition coincided with the fourth League Assembly in Geneva. But Italy's ambassador on the Council, Antonio Salandra, refused to discuss the issue. As a result, the Italo-Greek conflict was referred to the Conference of Ambassadors—a smaller diplomatic forum consisting of Britain, France, Italy, and Japan, with the United States in an observer role—that had emerged from the inter-Allied Supreme War Council. France, seeking to avoid international scrutiny of its own Ruhr occupation, supported this move to take the dispute out of the public limelight of the League.

The British government was particularly dismayed at the Italian escalation. Whitehall immediately started to investigate the application of sanctions under Article 16, as it had done during the Yugoslav-Albanian war two years earlier. There was a strong desire on the part of the cabinet and the public to proceed with at least some sanctions. *The Times* wrote that "nations which have valuable commercial interests abroad, and which depend for many necessaries upon foreign commerce and upon foreign finance will assuredly think twice and think coolly, before they expose themselves to the risk of incurring penalties so severe."[76] Cecil advocated a full blockade of Italy, prompting the *Daily Mail* to call him a warmonger.[77] Yet the institutions in charge of administering sanctions were more hesitant. The Treasury argued that the only way of blocking Italian access to international financial markets and commerce would be to reintroduce the system of control and surveillance instituted during the wartime blockade. It was expected that this would be possible only if popular opinion firmly supported harsh action against Italy.[78] The Admiralty reminded the cabinet that an actual blockade would be impossible without first neutralizing the Italian fleet, an offensive operation that would entail open war.[79] Yet the real problem lay in comprehensiveness. Without American participation in an embargo, the Italians would be able to continue to access world markets.[80] Some of the U.S. press was fiercely condemnatory, but on the whole there was little appetite for intervention against Mussolini.[81]

Mussolini was gambling on the fact that by not declaring war on Greece, he could get away with the occupation of Corfu. Franco-Belgian policy in the Ruhr lent some support to military occupation as a coercive measure. Mussolini had no treaty rights to invoke but only the past practice under international law that nations could resort to so-called reprisals in case of injury. Italy, he emphasized, did not want to initiate a war. Nonetheless, to the Italians the British press discussions about an Article 16 sanctions procedure were worrying. Salandra picked up rumors in Geneva that an anti-Italian bloc was forming in the Assembly, led by the Norwegian internationalist Fridtjof Nansen.[82] The Italian Navy began to consider what a war against Greece and Yugoslavia supported by Great Britain would require.[83]

Fortunately, the Conference of Ambassadors managed to bring the Corfu crisis to a negotiated end without economic sanctions or naval action. Greece apologized and acceded to most Italian demands, including the payment of 50 million lire in damages, and Mussolini could claim a victory for Italian honor. But the incident showed that even a dominant maritime power like Britain could not muster the policy coordination to effectively implement economic sanctions wholly by itself. Without the United States in the League, British sanctions risked forcing the empire to block the foreign trade of the world's largest economy. What had been possible against Yugoslavia in 1921—defusing a crisis through a sanctions threat—proved too difficult and risky against Italy in 1923.

Franco-British discord over the Ruhr occupation had ensured that no sanctions warning was ever issued, which was probably for the better. Helena Swanwick of the UDC felt that "the threat of sanctions in relation to the Corfu incident would have made worse an already bad situation."[84] As Peter Yearwood has argued, the episode demonstrated that "the sanctions articles of the Covenant [were] ineffective, at least when agreement between France and Great Britain was lacking."[85] British strategic analysts concluded in the wake of the Corfu incident that effective peacetime blockades would be much more difficult to achieve because neither American nor Soviet participation was likely, and the blockaders would face far larger civilian merchant marines.[86] The efficacy of the wartime economic weapon had hinged on a favorable geopolitical alignment that could no longer be taken for granted in the 1920s.

Italy was the key swing vote in the Allied Reparations Commission, which had authorized the sanction of the Ruhr occupation under the Versailles Treaty. In return, Mussolini expected France to defend his right to occupy Corfu as a reprisal against Greece. There was more to this than

Fascist rodomontade. Italian officials saw their country as belonging to an inner circle of imperial great powers. This was not without reason. Italy was one of four permanent Council members; contributed expert personnel to the League's various organs; and possessed an African colonial empire in Libya, Eritrea, and Somaliland.[87] It had also acquired control over the Greek-inhabited Dodecanese Islands through the Treaty of Lausanne in 1923 and ruled this archipelago through a governor in a colonial fashion.[88]

Given this deeply imperial relation to lands inhabited by Greeks, it is not difficult to see why Italians felt entitled to shell and seize Corfu in a display of gunboat diplomacy. Italian elite and public opinion saw the bombardment and occupation of a Greek island as a perfectly proportional response to the injury the country had suffered. The Italians were exploiting the narrow definition of war in the Covenant to avoid triggering Article 16.[89] Mussolini also listed past reprisals by Britain and France against Qing Formosa (1885) and Siam (1893), as well as the international blockades of Crete (1897), Venezuela (1902–1903), and Montenegro (1913) as examples of international enforcement that justified his actions.[90] Indeed, as the British jurist Frederick Pollock observed during the Corfu crisis, "If Signor Mussolini cared for technical precedents," then Britain's own past practice "would be more than enough for him."[91] An American lawyer similarly pointed out the inconsistency in the British position on the Ruhr, where Whitehall opposed sanctions for treaty enforcement even though "England has invoked them many times."[92] Corfu and the Ruhr were both episodes that brought the unpleasant imperial past of economic coercion back into an organization that claimed to have put the savage world of power politics behind it.

Building the economic weapon of sanctions involved preparation by bureaucrats, economists, military officers, and jurists: identifying targets for economic pressure and then outlining the policy levers to be deployed. Yet an additional effort was needed to make sure that the *object* to be pressured by sanctions—a country, a population, a social class, a region, or a movement—possessed the right characteristics to obtain the desired effect. The use of sanctions under the Versailles Treaty in 1921–1923 confronted the same problem in practice that the IBC faced in theory: how could people be made responsive to sanctions? Not all peoples and societies were inherently materialistic in ways that made them amenable to economic sanctions. The construction of sanctions was therefore not just an effort to devise an effective instrument, but also a project to fashion a responsive object. Would populations change their collective behavior due to shocks to their material conditions? When they refused to bend to external pressure, this led sanctionists to expressions of frustration and pleas to continue experimenting. During the reparations saga, for example, the *Daily Telegraph* concluded that "The psychology of the Germans is so curious that 'sanctions' which might be decisive with a more self-respecting people seem to have small effect upon them. The humiliation of seeing their towns and provinces occupied by foreign soldiers leaves them unmoved. It remains for the Allied Government to devise an appeal to the material interests of this remarkable people which cannot be disregarded, and then to leave Marshal Foch and his gendarmerie to carry it into effect."[93] Making the economic weapon a measure that could shape state behavior, enforce norms, and guarantee security depended on this labor of construction—devising an appeal to the material interests of remarkable peoples, whether they were Soviets or Hungarians or Yugoslavs or Germans or Italians. But after five years of use, sanctions seemed as likely to spur nationalism as they were to increase international solidarity. In the grand Pavlovian experiment of building sanctions, calibrating pressure correctly to obtain the desired effect proved very difficult.

Uncertainty lay not only in the response of a country targeted by sanctions. The economic weapon also allowed its users to maximally exploit the gray zone around the boundary of war and peace. Indeed, different interpretations about where sanctions fell on the spectrum of force actively weakened this boundary in the 1920s. The adjudication of this question at the Paris Peace Conference and by the IBC in favor of optional belligerence had enormous political consequences. For the remainder of the interwar period, Britain and France, the two military powers most responsible for implementation, were free to decide whether they saw sanctions as wartime or peacetime measures. The French concluded from the Corfu crisis that coercive measures were permitted if they were not intended as acts of war.[94] The British came away from the same crisis with the exact opposite impression: a full blockade would require institutions and laws that were available only by assuming wartime powers. That such different views about how to use sanctions persisted in the two most powerful democracies in Europe made it more difficult for the League as a whole to achieve its goal of preserving peace.

CHAPTER FIVE

Genevan World Police, 1924–1927

I N AN INTERDEPENDENT WORLD economy, sanctions could provide security only if almost all states participated in them as part of
a global system. In the League's early years, two congenital defects
had prevented it from developing such quasi-universal reach. The
first was the U.S. abandonment of the organization, placing the world's
largest economy outside the circle of Article 16 upholders. The second
issue was the European tension caused by the struggle over reparations
from Germany. By 1924, however, international affairs entered calmer
waters. A new blueprint for the stabilization of the German economy, the
Dawes Plan, used American finance to lower the temperature of European
politics. Eventually, Britain, France, and Italy even agreed to let Germany
into the League by 1926. The middle years of the 1920s thus raised hopes
that Geneva would become the headquarters of a global sanctionist security order.

But diplomats and internationalists from European and American
countries disagreed about how tightly knit the resulting system had to be
and about which countries would be on the hook to enforce it.[1] The first
major initiative of this period, the so-called Geneva Protocol, tried to
strengthen the Covenant by linking economic sanctions to judicial arbitration and the regulation of armaments.[2] Its most enthusiastic proponents envisioned a transatlantic security order in which the manpower of
the French Army, the cruisers of the Royal Navy, and the dollar loans of
Wall Street would provide interlocking security instruments. Such visions

went too far for the British Conservative cabinet and the U.S. Republican administration, and the protocol failed.

Britain and France were left free to develop their own approaches to the economic weapon. French governments continued to advocate automatic sanctions procedures; failing that, they wanted a stronger mechanism to provide assistance to the victims of aggression. Planners at the Advisory Committee on Trading and Blockade in Time of War (ATB), an important British planning organ, went in the other direction. Toning down the severity of blockade techniques, they moved them out of the realm of wartime measures and into a new policy category that they called "economic pressure."

That the mere threat of sanctions could work to secure peace was shown once again in October 1925, when the League used such a warning to defuse a short border war between Greece and Bulgaria. British and French officials also considered using economic blockades against Turkey, China, and the Soviet Union to speed up treaty negotiations, quash nationalist uprisings, and retaliate in diplomatic quarrels. These plans showed that it was easier to use material pressure unilaterally to enforce hierarchical order against smaller Eurasian states than to bring it to bear multilaterally in disputes involving other great powers. In this regard, the sanctionists faced a problem in the form of Germany, a neutralist state with revisionist objectives. When it was admitted to the League as a new permanent Council member in 1926, Germany was exempted from joining in sanctions procedures against other states. Even as it grew larger, the League thus suffered from a growing gap between official commitment and effective policy, as the gulf separating the virtual threat of sanctions from the real application of economic pressure widened.

The Geneva Protocol

The origins of the Geneva Protocol lay in growing dissatisfaction with the IBC compromises on sanctions struck in 1921. The committee's resolutions had made sanctions optional, their pacific or belligerent nature discretionary, and their application gradual. This made them less onerous to impose for member states. Yet the flexible nature of the IBC resolutions was difficult to reconcile with the actual language of the Covenant, which was much more forceful and uncompromising about the use of the economic weapon. An opportunity to expand the League's security function emerged in early 1924, when Britain and France both embraced a more progressive domestic political course. In January, the Scottish trade unionist Ramsay MacDonald became the first Labour Party prime minister in British history. Shortly afterward socialist Édouard Herriot became prime minister in France; he supported the League wholeheartedly and promoted the "internationalisation of security."[3] More encouraging still for the prospects of renewed internationalism was the arrival in Europe that summer of a group of American League enthusiasts, including James Shotwell from the Carnegie Endowment, General Tasker Bliss, and Wilson's former legal adviser, David Hunter Miller, who together worked out an "American plan."[4] At its heart lay a novel approach to combating aggression. Rather than circumscribe the term's meaning with a specific definition, Shotwell and his colleagues proposed that "aggression" should simply be any act that a majority of the Council agreed to designate as such.

The task of synthesizing MacDonald's and Herriot's ideas about arbitration with Shotwell's plan into what became known as the Geneva Protocol fell to two Europeans: the Czech foreign minister Edvard Beneš and the Greek jurist-diplomat Nikolaos Politis. Beneš hammered out a twenty-one-article protocol, with an automatic sanctions procedure in Article 11. The protocol incorporated all the Article 16 sanctions of the Covenant—economic, financial, transport, communications, and travel bans—but for the first time specified what the assistance promised in paragraph 3 meant. Signatories would aid the attacked state by "the provision of raw materials and supplies of every kind, openings of credit, transport and transit." In addition, Article 12 of the Geneva Protocol envisioned that the League's Economic and Financial Organization (EFO) should help to study and prepare Genevan sanctions. Although hitherto the EFO had been a technical organ that produced economic analysis, advised national governments, and supervised postwar reconstruction finance, Beneš and Politis proposed that it should make "plans of action for the application of the economic and financial sanctions against an aggressor State."[5]

Within the EFO, there was interest in playing a more active role in the implementation of sanctions. Upon taking charge of the organization in 1919, its head, the former inter-Allied shipping administrator Arthur Salter, had already pointed out that the economic weapon depended on accurate information; at the time he had proposed that a special "Blockade Intelligence Council" was needed to identify the weaknesses of individual states and monitor the effects of sanctions.[6] One of Salter's staffers, the Scottish statistician Alexander Loveday, continued this search for "information concerning the commercial interdependence of different countries." Loveday saw sanctions intelligence as crucial not only to estimate the effects on the targeted county, but also "to ascertain the probable weak spots in the blockade barrier." He took an early interest in financial blockade. In the interlinked world economy of the 1920s, he was convinced that the duration of sanctions would be decided by "the dependence of the blockaded state on foreign banking credits" and that a blockade intelligence council therefore "must rely upon information collected at the moment from the great money centres of the world."[7]

As one historian has put it, the Geneva Protocol united "a battery of collective sanctions behind a tripwire that was provided by the American definition of aggression."[8] This change was significant because it entailed a strong security commitment from Britain, the empire most concerned with preserving its discretionary power over the economic weapon. British naval power was making headlines at that very moment. In the highly publicized "Empire Cruise" of 1923–1924, eight Royal Navy battlecruisers and light cruisers circumnavigated the globe over the course of ten months.[9] If the protocol could put this force at the League's disposal to enforce sanctions, it would be a tremendous victory for internationalism.

Whatever doubts the British Admiralty harbored about the Geneva Protocol were due primarily to strategic goals. In the 1920s the Royal Navy was confident it could win a war against any naval power except the United States. Assuming the role of League police force would weigh it down with more obligations than its competitors. The Admiralty thought that the protocol meant "the assumption of such great responsibilities . . . [that] would involve the gravest risks to the fleet on which the safety of the Empire depends."[10] Trade protection and securing the British Empire's maritime lines of communication had to remain chief priorities.[11] The Admiralty faced a serious dilemma: it could preserve parity with the growing U.S. Navy at the cost of abandoning internationalism, or it could become Geneva's blockader-in-chief but lose its strategic autonomy. This military tension between the navy's long-term strategy and Britain's internationalist commitments remained present throughout the interwar years.

In October 1924, Ramsay MacDonald lost power to the Conservatives under Stanley Baldwin, who would remain in power for the next five years. The Tories were much less predisposed than Labourites to make concessions that ran counter to Britain's imperial interests. Less than a month after the Geneva Protocol had been drafted, serious political resistance to it emerged in London. One ranking Foreign Office diplomat complained that the original Article 16 had tricked Britain into overcommitting; the Covenant had been rushed through without enough discussion, "like Minerva sprung completely equipped from the head of Jupiter," and now the protocol would do the same.[12] As the main internationalist in the British cabinet, Cecil vehemently disagreed. He noted that the economic sanctions of Article 16 were regarded "by all the Continental nations as their sheet anchor" and that for "the Foreign Office to play fast and loose with our obligations under the Covenant . . . would be really disastrous."[13] Cecil tried to convince the skeptics that the Geneva Protocol was a logical response to fill the security vacuum created by the Anglo-American veto against a League army in 1919.[14]

Aristide Briand, now France's foreign minister, also lobbied the British establishment. Both countries had an strong interest, he argued, "in seeing two elements linked: the French army and the British navy," a duumvirate that together could respond to "conflicts that might arise in all regions of the globe."[15] However, the French government felt that economic power behind the League would have even more heft "in the form of mutual assistance than in the form of sanctions."[16] Emphasizing the positive economic weapon of supply had several advantages. It avoided the disputes with Washington that negative sanctions would inevitably cause. At the same time, it roused the commercial instincts of U.S. export firms and banks, and channeled them toward beleaguered states. Finally, mutual aid appeared more attractive than risking national armed forces in an intervention. This was the conclusion that Elliott Felkin, Salter's secretary in the EFO, reached after consulting John Maynard Keynes. Felkin came away from talking to Keynes convinced that a financial assistance mechanism could hold strong appeal to the British elite. "An obligation of this kind might involve Great Britain in the liability of guaranteeing twenty or thirty million pounds," he thought. "[It] would be much more inclined to run the risk of losing a sum like this in the interests of general security and welfare than to assume an obligation to send the Navy, under whatever method of pacific or quasi-pacific blockade, to places where there would be a definite risk of being embroiled in war."[17]

But the Committee of Imperial Defence (CID), Britain's highest strategic decision-making body, was far more skeptical of the protocol than both the French and the EFO. It recommended to Baldwin's cabinet that the entire initiative should be abandoned: Britain should not, under any circumstances, be forced to intercept the foreign trade of the United States. The CID took the view that "[any] position of being bound on behalf of the League to interrupt financial, commercial and personal relations between citizens of the United States and those of some other country ought not to be prolonged."[18] Such a confrontation risked grave diplomatic damage.[19] Moreover, the British strategists feared that the protocol would turn the EFO into the "economic and financial section of a General Staff," a possibility that would tie Britain's hands in strategic terms and was thus unacceptable.[20] France and the other continental European states supporting the protocol saw the British approach as unbalanced, inconsistent, and unreliable. To the French military, the "English tendencies . . . can be summarized in the following formula: 'a bit of blockade, the least possible economic assistance, no military assistance at all, and a lot of disarmament.'"[21] Beneš and Politis went further, arguing that the only thing that would deter an aggressor was the prospect of facing war with the entire League. Five years after Wilson and Miller had removed the concept of ipso facto war from the Covenant, the question of automatic war against aggression was back on the table.

On the point of automaticity, Shotwell's "American plan" was less helpful than his European backers realized. By using economic sanctions to discriminate against aggressors, it departed from traditional U.S. neutrality.[22] But to make them palatable to the political elite in Washington, Shotwell made sanctions optional (or "permissive," as he labeled them). Turning the French argument for automatic sanctions on its head, he argued it was precisely "the threat of uncertainty as to what the other states might do [that functioned] as an effective agency for keeping an aggressive state from proceeding to the overt act of war."[23] David Hunter Miller also defended "permissive" sanctions as more efficacious because of their uncertain gravity.[24] Shotwell's and Miller's sanctions were thus based on a deterrence theory quite different from that envisioned by internationalists in Britain, France, and Geneva. They saw ambiguous sanctions rather than crystal-clear sanctions as the more powerful deterrent since a would-be aggressor could not prepare against an unpredictable counter-measure in advance.[25]

The question of deterrence also provoked disagreement between the League and feminist organizations. When it became clear that the sanctions of the protocol's Article 11 would include food shipments, the WILPF's Emily Balch wrote to the EFO. Balch said that she dreaded seeing "hunger blockades admitted as one of the possible new weapons of international control." She trusted that experts could devise a form of financial pressure that would work through the wallet, not the stomach. Such a policy would in her view have "a stronger moral basis." But Balch went beyond common ethical arguments against food blockades. She also argued that sanctions against civilians were ineffective; they simply failed to change the behavior of bellicose governments. "It is not the hunger of women, children and the poorest and weakest that troubles the war-making elements," Balch wrote. "The well-to-do, the powerful and the army will always have food enough even under a blockade famine."[26]

Balch's objections bothered League officials, especially Elliott Felkin. He was opposed to any qualification of the League's right to stop food shipments as an economic sanction. The IBC resolution declaring food blockades a "last resort" had been a mistake, Felkin thought. It was "superficially more humane," yet "in the end it is more humane to stop all imports." The logic of blockade as a war-prevention measure was total. Felkin believed that "it is the starvation of the general population and in particular of the poorest people which is likely to cause such trouble in the aggressor country that it must give way." Promoting a popular uprising, whether through public opinion or in the form of bread riots, was the very point of sanctions. Balch's argument that the powerful would manage to insulate themselves from starvation could be turned around; if food going into a blockaded country would benefit the rich and powerful anyway, then a full food blockade made more sense than a special exemption for civilians. Felkin ended by insisting on the necessity of mercilessness if sanctions were to preserve peace through deterrence:

> I think personally that we should make sanctions as automatic and as terrible to the entire government, fighting forces and civil population of the aggressor state as we can without resorting to arms or landing ourselves in such trouble with neutrals as to entail the breaking up of our system of sanctions owing to their opposition, and I think that the more successful we are in making life in the aggressor state intolerable to the ordinary man & woman the more likely are we in a modern democratic state to break down the resistance of the recalcitrant state or indeed prevent a potential aggressor from becoming recalcitrant.[27]

Balch's critique did not change League policy. But it did produce a crystalline statement of the logic behind the internationalist belief that only total sanctions were a viable deterrent.

While British and French sanctionists encountered humanitarian objections from their own civil societies, American opponents of the Geneva Protocol advanced racial and geopolitical reasons. The protocol contained a clause that allowed the Permanent Court of International Justice (PCIJ), created by the League in 1920, to adjudicate "domestic questions" — an amendment that had been introduced by Japan. Since Congress had just passed the infamous Immigration Act of 1924 (also known as the Asian Exclusion Act), this led many to fear that the United States would be dragged before an international tribunal for its racist immigration laws.[28] The domestic questions clause seized the U.S. public imagination. As Arthur Sweetser, the highest-ranking American in Geneva, observed, "American judgment of the Protocol is almost exactly the reverse of the truth. . . . 75% of American attention has been directed to the domestic question as regards Japan, migration, etc., 20% to the question of sanctions which are decidedly contrary to America's traditional policy; and about 5% to the question of compulsory arbitration and peaceful settlement of disputes."[29] By extending police power to member states on every continent, the protocol also threatened the Monroe Doctrine, Washington's historic claim to preponderance in the Western Hemisphere. The possibility of European cruisers enforcing League sanctions in Latin America was abhorrent to Secretary of State Charles Evans Hughes.[30] His suspicion only grew upon hearing Beneš's explanation of what the protocol's arbitration and sanctions obligations would mean for U.S. interventions in the region. Asked if actions such as the pacific blockades, occupations, and raids against Mexico in 1914–1916 would be allowed, Beneš plainly replied that Mexico, as a member state, had the right to appeal to Geneva. If aggression had occurred, then the Council could impose economic sanctions against the United States.[31] Unsurprisingly, the Coolidge administration steadfastly refused to endorse the protocol.

Between October 1924 and September 1925, the protocol was signed by nineteen states.[32] The remaining thirty-five League member states did not sign. In March 1925, a Council meeting exposed the deep fissures among the great powers. Briand made an impassioned plea for accepting the protocol, but Foreign Secretary Austen Chamberlain elaborated Britain's "insuperable" objections. Italy joined this skepticism, while Japan postponed a verdict. The Geneva Protocol was never ratified. Despite the best efforts of the League's staff, France, and a coalition of European countries, by mid-1925 economic sanctions were still as qualified and optional as they had been in 1921.

Germany and League Sanctions

As we have seen, sanctions were an integral part of the reparations system under the Versailles Treaty. One formal step to Germany's reintegration into the European order as a formal equal was thus the removal of this unequal structure of enforcement. When it agreed to the Dawes Plan in August 1924, Germany accepted Allied oversight, in return for American capital and protection against grave sanctions like the Ruhr occupation.[33] Sanctions would be possible only in response to a "flagrant breach" (*manquement flagrant*) of the Versailles Treaty, an event defined so strictly that Berlin was unlikely to suffer them.[34] The Dawes Plan also opened the way for Germany to eventually become a member of the League.[35] From September 1924, getting a seat at the table in Geneva became a consistent aim of German foreign policy.[36]

German desires to join the victors of the world war in their internationalist organization were not unconditional, however.[37] The nationalist liberal Gustav Stresemann, briefly chancellor in 1923 and thereafter foreign minister until his death in 1929, was committed to restoring Germany's old political and economic power on the European continent. Yet Stresemann's softer brand of revisionism did not risk open confrontation; he preferred to work through international organizations rather than against them.[38] With regard to economic sanctions, Germany tried to carve out a distinct space for itself in the League. As a prospective permanent Council member, it had the ability to decide when Article 16 sanctions would be used. But the crucial condition of entry set by Berlin was that it would not be required to participate in those sanctions. As long as the Versailles Treaty limited German armed forces, joining in an embargo without possessing an army was too dangerous for a country located in the heart of Europe.

To understand the reasons for this ambivalence—entering the League but not its collective security mechanism—it is also important to grasp how Germans understood the functioning of sanctions within the organization.[39] Many in the Weimar German elite saw the League of Nations essentially as a political federation (*Bund*). The immediate precursors to the modern German state had taken this form, both the German Federation (1815–1866), created by the Vienna Congress, and the short-lived North German Federation (1866–1870). As a loosely aligned group of states that had outlawed war among each other, the League also bore a strong functional similarity to the Holy Roman Empire, the Christian-constitutional super-federation that had existed in Central Europe for a millennium from Charlemagne to Napoleon.[40] In fact, there was no country in the world whose domestic constitutional history so closely resembled that of the League, especially its sanctions procedures, as Germany itself. Just as the Covenant condemned aggression and prescribed conflict resolution by the Council, so under the imperial constitution the Holy Roman emperor had been charged with preserving the so-called perpetual peace of the land (*Ewiger Landfrieden*). Any state or ruler in the empire that broke this peace by going to war with another state could be subjected to a disciplinary procedure known as imperial execution (*Reichsexekution*), in which an intervention force was assembled from contributions by other states within the empire.[41]

This tradition of imperial intervention had a profound influence on German thinking about Article 16; in the interwar period, the League's sanctions procedures were invariably referred to in German as a "League execution" (*Bundesexekution*).[42] Stresemann had personal experience with the Weimar Republic's federal intervention procedure; his crackdown against Saxony's leftist state government in October 1923 cost him the chancellorship.[43] Ironically, joining the League would submit Germany to a superior power that could threaten his country with similar coercive powers. Even though the Dawes Plan enabled an escape from the clutches of Versailles Treaty sanctions, Germany still faced a larger challenge: how could it peacefully regain its former power without becoming the target of an international Article 16 *Bundesexekution* directed from Geneva?

During the negotiations leading up to the Locarno Treaties in early 1925, German diplomats pointed out to their British and French counterparts that they could not preserve neutrality *and* contribute to sanctions at the same time. Since participation in economic sanctions meant taking sides in a conflict, joining an embargo could invite an attack. But Stresemann also sought to preserve Weimar Germany's relationship with the Soviet Union, which had provided an export market for manufactures, credit, and military advisers. Commenting on the future of the alliance, Stresemann said that "as a *Realpolitiker* it depends for me not in the first place on whether the League of Nations formally waives vis-à-vis Germany the use of Article 16."[44] Protecting ties with Moscow was a matter of honoring older treaty commitments that predated Germany's arrival in Geneva. Moreover, as one German diplomat wrote, "Germany will . . . be constantly in the position, not just to refuse participation in a League execution against Russia, but in general to make such a *Bundesexekution* impossible."[45] After all, as a permanent Council member, Berlin could block the unanimity required to initiate an Article 16 procedure.

Even so, it was more constructive for Germany to use its influence to shape the League's current and future sanctions practice. Two of Stresemann's key advisers, the diplomats Bernhard von Bülow and Friedrich Gaus, emphasized that League sanctions were not yet fully developed and thus presented opportunities as well as constraints for Germany to exploit.[46] During talks in the Swiss lakeside town of Locarno in October 1925, Stresemann obtained his desired exemption from participation in sanctions in Annex F of the eponymous Locarno Treaty.[47] While not formally endorsing the possibility of German neutrality, Britain, France, and Italy gave Berlin a provision that it could invoke to justify non-participation in sanctions. This helped Stresemann convince the SPD and the moderate wing of the nationalist DNVP to support the Locarno Treaty.[48] It also formed the basis of his defense of the treaty against attacks by hard-right nationalists in the Reichstag.[49]

Germany's special carve-out was accepted by other League members. To the French politician Joseph Paul-Boncour, a believer in Bourgeois's solidarism and a strong advocate of collective security and economic assistance under Article 16, German adherence to the Covenant was another step on the road to making the League a universal organization. "From now on, in a conflict, there will no longer be neutrals among the member states," Paul-Boncour wrote. "Only Russia remains an open breach. . . . [Locarno] unifies mandatorily, with the exception of Russia—and pending her arrival, even her—all the productive nations that encircle the possible aggressor."[50] Neutrals were also content with Annex F, since it created a precedent for exemptions from participation in League economic sanctions. The Danes, for example, thanked the Germans for helping them because "the obligations of the members to participate in League executions and League sanctions have definitely been made milder."[51]

Yet neutral membership of an organization which, in its attitude to aggression, was fundamentally anti-neutral, remained an incongruent position. "If [Germany] is fortunate enough to escape the Scylla of the Executors, then it will all the more surely fall victim to the Charybdis of the Executed state," wrote one German commentator.[52] The Weimar Republic's ambivalent attitude to League sanctions was further complicated by Stresemann's diplomacy in Eastern Europe. The first step in his *Ostpolitik* was to reaffirm the alliance with the Soviets through a new treaty in April 1926. This Treaty of Berlin explicitly banned Germany and the Soviet Union from using economic boycotts or blockades against one another, further eroding Berlin's sanctionist duties as a League member.[53] British and French internationalists noticed that Germany had made contradictory commitments to Geneva and Moscow. Arnold-Forster made an unsuccessful appeal to German citizens to join the sanctionist majority on the Council.[54] But since there was no crisis in which to test Berlin's commitments, the issue was covered up. As it began its seven-year membership in the League (1926–1933), Germany was relieved from participation in economic sanctions while anchoring its neutrality in an anti-sanctions constellation with the USSR.

Grand Strategy and the ATB

In the aftermath of the world war, policymakers in Britain and France struggled to design measures to isolate recalcitrant countries effectively without provoking war.[55] Legally a full blockade would mean initiating war, but the whole point of sanctions was to prevent war. Making sanctions non-belligerent was possible only if economic pressure was fine-tuned very precisely. This strategic issue confronted governments of all political stripes. Between 1924 and 1929, Baldwin's Conservative government relied on the experience of the wartime pioneers of international blockade, such as Robert Cecil and William Arnold-Forster. These men, known to the outside world as passionate internationalists, thus worked at the same time as consummate insiders of the British "warfare state."[56]

In terms of their attitudes to the use of force, the difference between British liberal internationalism and imperialist unilateralism was much smaller than is often supposed. The economic weapon allowed the CID to rethink how the British Empire could use its material power against potential opponents.[57] CID chairman Maurice Hankey gave this specific task to the ATB, created in 1923.[58] The purpose of such "grand strategy" was to manage decline, not avert it, and Cecil and Hankey were in close touch as they confronted the reality of this fact.[59] Their main disagreement was about how British liberal civilization was best defended. Cecil proposed a combination of international organization, naval power, and a good dose of general disarmament, whereas Hankey stressed preserving a certain "military spirit" to stem decadence among the population. "Just as we are prone to wonder at the spectacle of the camps of the Roman armies filled by barbarians at a time when the Italian cities were crowded with men on the dole," he wrote in a letter to Cecil, "so the historians of the future may be puzzled at the phenomenon of an army . . . which cannot complete its ranks at a time when one million males are receiving unemployment benefit."[60] It was not surprising that elite concerns about the martial resilience of British society surfaced at the same time as its establishment was developing new forms of force aimed at breaking the moral cohesion of other populations.

Questions of political economy deeply shaped the priorities of the British Empire in the interwar period. Financial and commercial strength was the backbone on which army, navy, and air force all depended for funding and force maintenance.[61] To this end the government reduced inflation, brought sterling back onto the gold standard in 1925, made deep budget cuts, and tried to create propitious market conditions for private interests to flourish.[62] The ATB operated at the intersection of this process involving both armaments and economic adjustment. In early 1926, Hankey asked Cecil on behalf of Prime Minister Baldwin to chair the ATB. A unique planning role unifying civil servants and military officers across different ministries and all branches of the armed forces was thus in the hands of the nation's most prominent League supporter.[63] As the Treasury's top economist, Ralph G. Hawtrey, put it in May 1926, "The blockade organisation was really a fourth Fighting Service," and hence "a separate political head in charge of it might be advisable."[64]

Hawtrey's presence on the ATB shows how economists also played a growing role in the development of interwar sanctions policy. A leading theorist of credit money and trade, Hawtrey was close to the bankers and merchants in the City of London throughout his forty-three years at the Treasury.[65] On the ATB he often made common cause with the comptroller-general of the Department of Overseas Trade, Sir Edward Crowe.[66] Hawtrey and Crowe analyzed the economic weapon and the international economy in which it operated from the point of view of practitioners. It was thus no surprise that they often thought of money as the prime instrument of British influence; as they averred in 1924, "Finance might be our best weapon."[67] But as civil servants, they were aware of the tensions involved in building a weapon that leveraged the private networks of the British economy in times of austerity. Crowe saw himself in "an unenviable position, being on the one hand a representative of a department that desired to increase the trade of the country, whilst on the other he was a member of a Committee interested in the preparation of the most perfect machine possible for the enforcement of blockade measures in war."[68]

The ATB was in fact so prolific that its work had to be divided into subcommittees. Its Legal Subcommittee included Cecil Hurst, the Foreign Office legal adviser who was probably the first to use the term "the economic weapon" in 1912, as well as A. Pearce Higgins, the Whewell Professor of International Law at Cambridge University.[69] Senior military officers were also involved. At least one Royal Navy representative, usually the head of the Admiralty's Plans Division, would sit on the committee as the chief intelligence conduit for its deliberations. Together with the BoT, the Admiralty formed a Standing Committee on Bunker Control to examine the future of coal supply measures. After surveying bunker depots in some 220 ports worldwide, this group concluded that the growing use of oil-fired ships in the global merchant marine was making coal-based bunker control "of very little value in future wars."[70]

Over the course of the 1920s the ATB planners began to dissociate economic coercion from open conflict. To counter the Admiralty's objections that blockade would lead to war, the committee sketched two distinct modalities of the economic weapon. One was the classic weapon of blockade with all its naval and legal accoutrements. The other was what became known as "economic pressure" and was sometimes referred to as "commercial blockade." To defend this instrument, Cecil underscored the difference between using force in a direct physical sense and applying pressure in indirect ways. Indirect pressure operated at a distance and was virtual rather than physical. It affected not human bodies but aspects of the social and economic world around them: market liquidity, business and consumer confidence, price levels, public morale, and communal cohesion. Cecil claimed that no more than 20 percent of the wartime blockade he had directed "was enforced by physical measures taken by the Admiralty. It was mainly carried out by economic pressure."[71]

Yet the difference between "hard" physical and "soft" economic measures was to some degree artificial. For a blockaded state, British legislative trade restrictions had the same effect as a Royal Navy cruiser intercepting inbound cargo: both prevented resources from reaching the population and created artificial scarcity. The distinction between "physical" and "economic" measures was therefore one that meant more for the users of sanctions policy than for their object. Talking about "economic pressure" allowed civilian bureaucrats to lay claim to blockade as *their* policy domain. Sanctions were considered economic, nonviolent, pacific, and civilian in nature, distinguishing them from physical, violent, belligerent military measures. They came to be conceived of as a political rather than a military instrument, were integrated into diplomatic practice, and could be administered by technocrats rather than professional soldiers.[72] As ATB chairman, Cecil admitted that "a great part of our measures for exerting economic pressure in the last war were illegal, or rather, extralegal."[73] He made it clear he was shaping a policy instrument that transcended the existing division of labor within the British state as well as international law.

Arnold-Forster, too, was finding a receptive audience for his sanction-ist ideas in Geneva and London. At the EFO, Felkin regularly consulted him during the discussions about the Geneva Protocol. Arnold-Forster's status as an expert on the economic weapon rested not only on his prac-tical familiarity with British wartime measures, but also on his grasp of the legal ramifications of sanctions, both domestic and international. In his view the British Trading with the Enemy Act of 1914 provided a suit-able template for domestic legislation. This law allowed for the immedi-ate sequestration of enemy property, the cancellation of all contracts with subjects of enemy nationality, and their loss of legal personality before domestic courts. Its advantage was that it suspended rather than eviscer-ated rights of property and contract, allowing for a quick reversion to nor-mality once a crisis had passed.[74] Effective domestic laws had to be quick, act uniformly across all spheres of society, be applicable without a state of war, capable of gradual increase in severity, and "suspensory rather than destructive of commerce."[75] International law also provided large oppor-tunities for innovation in sanctions. By having broken during the war with long-standing principles of the law of blockade without putting firm new ones in their place, Britain and France had created a normative vacuum around the question of who could economically isolate whom, for what purposes, and under which conditions. Arnold-Forster drove this point home in lectures to the Royal United Services Institution and the think tank Chatham House.[76] Sanctionism had to seize new possibilities wher-ever it encountered them.

Blockade and Sanctions in the East

While preparatory work for British and League economic sanctions took up a large part of the ATB's interwar activity, the committee was also called upon by the cabinet in urgent crises. During the 1920s these oc-curred predominantly along the Eurasian seam where the British and So-viet empires intersected.[77] These episodes produced studies of economic pressure against Turkey, China, and Soviet Russia that give valuable in-sight into British thinking about sanctions.

Turkey had remained a target for the economic weapon after the Allied blockade of the Ottoman Empire was lifted in 1918. During the Greco-Turkish War in the early 1920s, British and French policymakers considered if they should respond to "the Asian problem" by inflicting economic pain on Turkish nationalists, and they aired these considerations fairly openly in the press. "One does not think of the use of force," wrote one French republican newspaper, "but of the possibility of a blockade of the coasts of Asia Minor."[78] British officials continued to keep the option of sanctions in reserve during the tense negotiations in Lausanne, Switzerland, about the borders of the new Turkish republic, especially when talks briefly broke down in early 1923.[79] The Turkish delegation carefully maneuvered among three forces: Britain's overwhelming territorial interest in the oil-rich Iraqi province of Mosul; the French desire to retrieve some of their investment in the prewar Ottoman debt, of which they held 60 percent; and nationalist hardliners in Ankara who opposed any kind of "colony peace" with the West.[80]

Although the Lausanne Treaty restored Turkish independence and a French-brokered deal was eventually reached on the Ottoman debt, the dispute over Mosul Province had to be referred to the Council for arbitration.[81] To the British government, economic sanctions were an obvious way to bring pressure to bear on Ankara if it did not drop its claims to the territory. *The Economist* compared the Turkish case with that of Yugoslavia two years earlier: "It may be doubted whether the economic weapon, even if wielded with its full force, will have the like effect upon the Turks. Of course, the Turks want, like any other nation, to reconstruct their economic life on something like a Western standard, but they may value their territorial aims more, and may elect, rather than abandon them, to see Anatolia sink to the economic level of Afghanistan or Abyssinia. And if they do not fear the economic sanctions of the League, still less do they feel its moral authority."[82] The efficacy of sanctions could, in other words, be seen as a function of the degree to which countries were prepared to embrace liberalism.

In December 1925, Balfour asked the ATB to analyze the prospects for economic sanctions against Turkey.[83] The Baldwin cabinet's concern was that the Mosul dispute would trigger an Anglo-Turkish war—possibly after the PCIJ ruled in favor of British Iraq and Turkey refused to accept the verdict. After studying the Turkish economy, the committee's conclusions were pessimistic. Since the country had long land borders, it was relatively immune to maritime blockade. Moreover, it depended only to a small degree on seaborne trade for its hard currency earnings. Consequently, League sanctions would "do no more than cause annoyance, inconvenience, and possibly a moral effect in that it would demonstrate that the world was against her."[84] Nonetheless, Foreign Secretary Austen Chamberlain carefully conveyed the impression that the three European powers on the Council would impose material sanctions if pushed. This certainly contributed to Turkey's decision not to defy the League, and the Mosul dispute was resolved in April 1926, when Britain offered Turkey a share of oil royalties in the region for the next twenty-five years.[85]

A more acute crisis for the British imperial presence in Asia began in the summer of 1925 as Chinese discontent about foreign rule in Western concessions and treaty ports broke into open revolt after a police massacre in the International Settlement of Shanghai.[86] The centerpiece of this popular uprising, coordinated by the Chinese Nationalist and Communist Parties, combined in the "First United Front" and receiving Soviet funding and advisers, was the Canton–Hong Kong general strike that began in June.[87] Owing to a high degree of local labor organization, the Canton–Hong Kong strike committee, led by the seamen's and tram workers' unions, quickly brought together a large coalition. Landing-stage workers, steamship repairers, construction workers, carpenters, smiths, cobblers, butchers, grocers, restaurant and tea house servers, cooks, tailors, seamstresses, maids, laundry workers, barbers, and housemaids working in the diplomatic quarter all went on strike. By July some 250,000 laborers out of Hong Kong's population of 600,000 had ceased work.[88] Public utilities, transport, and industrial production ground to a halt. Marketplace trading and shipping activities were severely reduced. After Hong Kong governor Reginald Stubbs tried to punish the Cantonese supporters of the strike by banning food and gold exports to the countryside, the strike committee instituted a full boycott of the colony.[89] The damage inflicted on European business was severe. In October, the British government extended a £3 million emergency credit to Hong Kong to prevent an acute liquidity crisis. It was, in the words of the French writer André Malraux, "a war of a totally new kind . . . undertaken by the anarchic power of southern China, against the very symbol of British domination in Asia, the military rock from where the fortified empire surveys its herds."[90]

The Canton–Hong Kong general strike greatly worried British and French authorities.[91] At the CID, Maurice Hankey saw the unrest as a dangerous red barbarism fostered by Russian communism to conquer the Eurasian landmass. China, he thought, was "almost in chaos. Any day you may get some movement which compels intervention and brooks no delay—a massacre in Canton or Pekin, another siege of the legations. Xenophobia has broken out in China every 20 or 25 years for the last century. Force has always been needed to restore the situation."[92] Hankey's first instinct was to break up the strike with a blockade. The Foreign Office contacted the French government to discuss economic sanctions against the Chinese Nationalists. Since the beleaguered Anglo-French concession in Guang-zhou was located on an island, the Foreign Office and Admiralty envisaged subjecting the city itself to a naval blockade—in effect, encircling the en-circlers. Having just stabilized the European situation and finished their troop withdrawal from the Ruhr, Seydoux and Goût at the French Min-istry of Foreign Affairs had little desire to start a war in East Asia. How-ever, the French argued that the League's handling of the Corfu crisis had produced a useful legal precedent to exploit. As long as economic counter-measures did not target another state directly, they could be cast as a legal form of reprisal. They commented that "a blockade of the port of Can-ton by British vessels does not appear to have to constitute an act of war; this will be a coercive measure destined to modify or remove regulations [i.e., the Chinese boycott] that hamper British commerce."[93] Counter-revolutionary policing could thus be dressed up as a measure to enforce non-discrimination.[94]

The question of blockade became more urgent as the strike wore on. In March 1926, Cecil chaired a special meeting of the ATB on the possibility of instituting a blockade of the approaches to Canton.[95] The Cantonese countryside imported only a few external necessities, such as fuel supplies, illuminants, and fats and oils, whose cutting off would have an effect. But the local population would probably revert to subsisting on locally grown rice and firewood, whose availability depended on the quality of the harvest, not the Royal Navy. Ex-governor Stubbs argued that everything depended on whether the Chinese merchant class would be able to influence the Nationalist leadership. Since they were the social stratum that the Nationalists taxed to support their armed struggle and the strike, "the present position of the merchants—both political and finan-cial—might prove an essential factor in the problem of what would be the effect of the blockade." By contrast, Stubbs thought that "the labouring classes would be able to get on somehow in spite of the blockade, and . . . the hardships inflicted might only enrage them."[96]

At the heart of the problem that the ATB confronted was the social target of the economic weapon. Stubbs and other committee members agreed that the ideal object of economic sanctions was a mercantile agent whose behavior was guided by profit and loss. However, working-class power posed an obstacle to this behaviorist logic. If Cantonese merchants were indeed in charge, economic pressure could motivate this commercial class into pushing the Nationalists to compromise. But if the working classes controlled the strike, then economic sanctions might well bolster their resolve, risking escalation into a fully fledged popular war against foreign imperialism.

As the strike gradually fell apart in the spring of 1926, so did the urgency to intervene. Leadership struggles among the Nationalists led Chiang Kai-shek to arrest the strike committee. Moreover, local merchants, peasants, and workers were increasingly dissatisfied with the harsh enforcement of the boycott against Hong Kong and the Shameen.[97] Despite this, the general strike had demonstrated its formidable power, "a most effective economic weapon, as both the Japanese and the British in China have reason to know," in the words of *The Economist*.[98] Over the course of fourteen months, Hong Kong's trade fell by 80 percent, and the colony lost an estimated £100 million in income.[99] By contrast, Canton's trade boomed and the Nationalists emerged stronger and richer than before.[100]

Many in the British establishment saw the hand of the Soviet Union behind the disturbances in China and regarded Moscow as waging a shadow war against the British Empire.[101] In May 1927, a British police raid on the London office of the Soviet trade delegation and All-Russian Cooperative Society—also known as Arcos, the chief agency for British-Soviet trade—led to the severing of diplomatic relations between the two countries.[102] Austen Chamberlain admitted that "the actual moment chosen for the breach was an accident" but that its effects in aggravating Soviet distress were nonetheless "opportune."[103] At any rate, the affair convinced Stalin that the imperialist powers were united in a "capitalist encirclement" of the USSR, which they were strangling in a "financial blockade."[104] Despite there being no such actual policy on the part of the British government, the option was certainly being considered by the ATB, which studied in November how to respond to a possible Soviet invasion of Afghanistan.[105] Since recovering from civil war and famine, the Soviet Union had become self-sufficient in foodstuffs and was rapidly regaining its old export position in raw materials such as grain, ores, flax, timber, and oil. This made it virtually impervious to commodity cutoffs; vital inputs could easily be obtained in neighboring countries. The Soviet reliance on external finance for industrialization was a pressure point that could be targeted. But it would be difficult for British action by itself to have an appreciable effect, especially if Germany and the United States remained potential sources of funds. For these reasons, Cecil and Hawtrey concluded that "blockade is most unlikely to deal a deciding blow."[106]

This judgment was echoed by the German banker Carl Melchior, a friend of Keynes who visited Moscow in November 1927. Melchior reported to the EFO: "If it would be possible . . . to unite the capitalist powers in a kind of economic and financial blockade against Russia, . . . then such a move would bring Russia in an extraordinarily difficult economic and financial position, but it would in my view not lead to the downfall of the current government. The Russian people would then, as long as this situation remains, tighten their belts one or two notches."[107] Despite many plans and attempts to coerce them materially, peoples on the Eurasian landmass remained an intractable object for the economic weapon.

The Virtual and the Real Economic Weapon

Since no League economic sanctions were implemented in the 1920s, it is easy to conclude that the instrument remained marginal. Indeed, diplomatic historian Zara Steiner has argued that since none of the international disputes in the 1920s "involved the use of sanctions . . . the League's security system was never tested."[108] But to look only at instances of actual implementation is to miss an important dimension of the history of the economic weapon. As we have seen, the dominant conception of sanctions among interwar internationalists depended initially on deterrence through the threat of use, either explicit (as against Yugoslavia in 1921) or implicit (as against Turkey in 1925). A narrow definition of "use" that excludes this prospective aspect of economic sanctions does not grasp their power in international politics in the period.

The importance of the virtual dimension of the economic weapon was proven once more in October 1925, when a Greco-Bulgarian border skirmish was defused before it could escalate into a war between two League member states.[109] This incident, also known as the War of the Stray Dog, was so successfully contained that it became a *cause célèbre* in the League's peace literature. In Steiner's account, the great powers' "combined pressure on the Greeks proved sufficient without invoking Article 16. . . . Great-power solidarity rather than the sanctions weapon determined the outcome."[110] While the peaceful outcome of the episode is beyond dispute, the actual deliberations in Geneva belie this upbeat account of events. A sanctions package against Greece was not only prepared and discussed during the crisis, but its display to the government in Athens was also crucial in de-escalating the tensions.

Exactly what happened at the border crossing at the Bulgarian town of Petrich in Thrace on 19 October is disputed; in the most credible account,

Greek dictator General Theodoros
Pangalos after his coup d'état, 1925.
Sueddeutsche Zeitung Photo/Alamy
Stock Photo.

a Greek soldier chasing his dog across the border was shot and killed by
Bulgarian sentries, leading to an exchange of gunfire. Greece was ruled by
Theodoros Pangalos, a stern, truculent general who had come to power
in a coup in June 1925 and fashioned his regime after that of Mussolini.[111]
Pangalos was an ardent Greek nationalist, and the Petrich incident created
an opportunity to shore up his precarious popularity that was too good to
miss, especially since the Paris Peace Treaties had reduced Bulgaria's army
to just twenty thousand men, and the government in Sofia had few great
power allies. By 22 October, several battalions of Greek forces had advanced ten kilometers into Bulgarian territory on a thirty-kilometer-wide
front and had begun bombarding Petrich.[112]

   As both sides mobilized for war, Bulgaria appealed to the League for
mediation. In Geneva, Drummond agreed with Aristide Briand that a

Council meeting would take place in Paris on 26 October to discuss measures to contain the crisis. But many officials in the League Secretariat worried that the situation would escalate before then. To prevent this, they sent telegrams to the Bulgarian and Greek governments urging them to avoid military action until a Council decision had been reached.[113] These dispatches had their effect, and a serious Greek attack on Petrich scheduled for the morning of 24 October was avoided "in the nick of time," as Arthur Salter put it in his later report on the crisis.[114]

In the days before the Council meeting in Paris, Drummond and Salter were busy designing the sanctions to be used if Pangalos did not withdraw his troops. Salter drafted a note to the British, French, and Italian governments asking them to send warships to make a demonstration off the coast of Athens. This was meant to prepare for "the application of economic sanctions which the Council may recommend in accordance with Article 16." Rather than tone down this display of force, Drummond asked if "it [is] certain that the presence of ships . . . will have sufficient effect?"[115] Salter made it clear that a naval demonstration "would be preparation for economic pressure, and a clear warning that serious and practical steps for its application were in progress. If the warning by itself were not sufficient the pressure would be applied progressively . . . until finally the whole coastline was blockaded."[116]

Although fleet action was thus the first step, the EFO also studied economic sanctions. Salter had organized the League's £12.3 million refugee resettlement loan to Greece in 1924 and was thus deeply familiar with its economy.[117] Since suffering a financial crisis in the 1890s, Greek finances had been closely supervised by Western creditors, so instituting a financial blockade would require temporarily ignoring their interests. On the other hand, Greece's dependence on imported food made it highly vulnerable to commercial blockade.[118] In this case, Salter, Drummond, and their colleagues did not consider U.S. neutral shipping a major problem of sanctions implementation; the trade flows concerned were small, and they assumed that they could count on the goodwill of the American public.[119]

Greece was the more likely target of sanctions but not the only possible one. In the event that the government of Prime Minister Aleksandar Tsankov in Sofia should refuse a League directive to resolve the crisis or escalate matters into open war, Salter also commissioned an EFO study of Bulgarian economic vulnerabilities. Bulgaria was heavily dependent on foreign creditors, to whom it had mortgaged most of its domestic revenue streams.[120] Sanctions against its trade would dry up customs income and thereby force Sofia to default on its debt. But beyond this modest effect on the "psychological basis of the exchange position," the country seemed fairly impervious to external pressure. The EFO observed that Bulgaria was "a very poor, very primitive, and a self-supporting country," with total exports and imports of only $76 million (compared to total Greek trade of $204 million); annual imports were just $8 per capita. No other European countries except Lithuania and Estonia had so little total trade with the outside world. This very low trade dependence clearly came as something of a surprise to the analysts in Geneva, who speculated that the incident at the Greek border must have been caused because the plentiful cereal harvest had made Bulgarians "habituated to working during the summer and fighting during the autumn months."[121]

Meanwhile, the Council meetings on 26 and 27 October progressed. Chamberlain agreed with Briand and the Italian representative Vittorio Scialoja on a gradated sanctions package and communicated it to the Greek government: if Greek troops had not left Bulgarian territory within sixty hours, diplomatic relations would be severed, followed up shortly afterward by a fleet demonstration and, finally, if Pangalos did not yield, a full blockade. By the morning of 28 October, Athens had surrendered.[122] This stabilization allowed the Council to send a commission of inquiry that settled the frontier dispute by early December. The successful sanctions threat not only convinced Pangalos to back down, but also boosted the Council's credibility in openly preparing for sanctions against Turkey several months later, enabling the peaceful settlement of the Mosul dispute.

These deterrence crises forced the League officials to assess how sanctions functioned within international law. The Greco-Bulgarian incident prompted the head of the League's Legal Section, the Dutchman Joost Adriaan Van Hamel, to write a long report on how the organization's police action worked as a form of coercion short of war. A progressive liberal, Amsterdam law professor, and advocate of close Dutch alignment with Britain, Van Hamel thought that the League's internationalist praxis was creating its own legal paradigm.[123] Before the world war, international law had regarded a state of war as impossible without a formal declaration of war. But in his view, "It would, however, be a great mistake to admit that League action should be restricted by such technical conceptions. . . . Under the League of Nations regime, various terms of a legal nature acquire a different meaning from that formerly associated with them. They will be governed by new rules still to be drawn up . . . [including] the application of the so-called 'rules of war' when applied in a collective action organised by the League. It would also apply to the application of the economic weapon of the League, which is not necessarily governed by the older rules in existence on the subject of blockade."[124]

Van Hamel saw the removal of legal constraints as a way to strengthen the deterrent effect of the League's economic sanctions. "The economic weapon is one which works better by being kept in store," he wrote. "Prudent League action should in most cases refrain from applying it or from leading up to its application, and thereby showing its weaknesses. On the other hand, it should always be there theoretically organised, and the possibility of its application never be doubted."[125] League officials thus advanced a conception of sanctions that relied on their force as a powerful abstraction. Indeed, they felt that sanctions might work better as an abstraction than when they were actually applied. But the danger of relying on their potential damage was that an aggressor would call the League's bluff.

The elaboration of economic sanctions in the mid-1920s was marked by a tension. On the one hand, certain interpretative questions remained unresolved, and domestic legislation to implement sanctions was lacking in most countries. On the other hand, the very public efforts to make economic sanctions central to global security raised their profile in politics, public debate, and the business world beyond their actual proportions. The deterrence theory of economic sanctions had been shown to work, but perhaps it worked *too* well. If threatened too much, states might choose to defend themselves against sanctions. By the late 1920s, as international tensions over tariffs, migration, and naval armament were rising, League officials were beginning to become aware of the enormous shadow that the economic weapon cast over the prosperity of the Roaring Twenties. EFO secretary Felkin thought that "the immediate need now is not to increase sanctions, but to devise every possible means of making it unnecessary to bring the enormous sanctions of Article 16 into operation."[126] The rhetoric of sanctions did more than express the new reality of interwar politics; over time it also came to influence that reality.

CHAPTER SIX

Sanctionism versus Neutrality,

1927–1931

T HE POINT OF ARTICLE 16 was to enable, as a German diplomat put it, "the war of all against war."[1] The economic weapon
had the political task of stabilizing the postwar order. But in the
eyes of many internationalists it also had a moral and legal purpose: to punish the crime of aggression. While the Covenant had mentioned aggression, it was not until the Eighth Assembly in 1927 that the
League officially condemned aggressive war.[2] By this time, negotiations
were under way for an international treaty outlawing war as an instrument
of national policy. This agreement, the Paris Peace Pact or Kellogg-Briand
Pact, was signed in August 1928.[3] Succeeding where the Geneva Protocol
had failed, the pact was a promising advance for the cause of international
peace. Its only flaw was that it lacked a clear method of enforcement. In
the late 1920s, internationalists therefore sought to harmonize the League
and the Paris Pact, using the sanctions of the former to uphold the latter's
ban on war. Cecil and Arnold-Forster envisioned such a union of Geneva
and Washington as "an international *posse comitatus.*"[4]

To make this project of institutional synthesis work, however, several
outstanding questions had to be resolved. First, it was necessary to reach a
grand bargain between the world's two premier naval powers, Great Britain and the United States. Unless there was some kind of agreement on
the meaning of freedom of the seas, it was possible that Washington would

refuse to join economic sanctions against an aggressor and continue trading with outcast states. In that case, Britain faced a dilemma: accept U.S. neutrality and undermine the economic weapon or enforce it to the hilt and thus restrict American foreign trade—by force if needed. The clash between British blockade and U.S. neutral rights had been a major bone of contention during the world war, and a renewed confrontation over this issue—what Norman Angell called "the Satanic contingency"—remained possible throughout the interwar years.[5] Second, the question remained to what extent economic sanctions would interdict food supplies to civilians. Humanitarians wanted to protect noncombatants from a starvation blockade. But economic sanctions fed a fundamental uncertainty about "what the acts of coercion would be against a nation at war against the world," as U.S. internationalist James Shotwell described it.[6] Third, the growth of international business and finance in the boom of the Roaring Twenties had made the private sector equally concerned with protecting its property, contracts, and investment decisions from sanctions.[7] Two German authors even proposed to extend the Paris Pact to international business to create "a Kellogg Pact for private property."[8] Sanctionism began to affect not only geopolitics and the ethics of war, but also the stability of global capitalism.

This chapter traces how the project to reconcile the Covenant and the Paris Pact solved some of these issues while failing to address others. On the whole, the achievement of the sanctionists was less to build a fully functioning edifice of their own than to contain and defeat alternative visions of international order that avoided sanctions or restricted their effects, especially the doctrine of neutrality, which depoliticized trade and investment. These alternative orders show the stakes of the sanctionist endeavor. Sanctionists used liberal language to reconceptualize war making and peacekeeping. One of their key innovations was to create a new distinction between "public" and "private" wars. "Public wars" were coalition wars against aggression with the backing of international law. By contrast, a "private war," any unauthorized use of force by a single state, was now rendered illegal and labeled a form of aggression.

The sanctionists' recourse to a classical dichotomy of liberalism, the public-private distinction, fosters the impression that they were liberals whereas their enemies were anti-liberal. In fact, the struggle between sanctionism and neutrality is better understood as a competition not between liberalism and illiberalism but between politicization and depoliticization. Many sanctionists were left-leaning and wanted to bring politics into new domains. British Liberals and Labourites, French radicals and republicans, and American Progressives and New Dealers all rejected the idea that politics and the economy were separate realms.[9] Private economic relations among individuals and among firms were a legitimate object of intervention, both at home (through taxes and regulation) and abroad (in the form of tariffs and sanctions). Conversely, some of the most fervent neutralist opponents of sanctions were early neoliberal thinkers who wanted to insulate capitalism by instituting a fundamental separation between the realm of private property and the domain of state sovereignty.[10]

Sanctionists politicized the international economy to a new degree. Armed with the concept of aggression, they destroyed many old nostrums: distinctions between civilians and noncombatants, state property and private property, and neutrals and belligerents were recast as obstacles to fighting evil. Indeed, sanctionists argued, under early twentieth-century globalization *all* forms of trade, transport, and finance could strengthen national economic power, thereby contributing to an aggressor's ability to wage war and resist international norms. Hence the only meaningful economic war against such an opponent was an unlimited one. It was a testament to this major shift in the liberal outlook that by 1929, figures from the heart of the British ruling class such as Cecil and Arnold-Forster could rhetorically ask, "What is 'private' property?" as an argument for abolishing that very concept in wartime.[11] At the same time, the ambitious interventionist agenda of this sanctionist liberalism was undermined by its reliance on the conservative economics of the gold standard and budgetary austerity. The development of the economic weapon accentuated this basic tension within interwar liberalism, a disjuncture that became most clear in the fate of the League's financial plan to prevent war.

The Convention on Financial Assistance

The positive economic weapon was contained in Article 16's third paragraph, which promised that member states would "mutually support one another in the financial and economic measures." French policymakers had always emphasized that the collective provisioning aspect of the economic weapon was equally important to its sanctions component.[12] In the 1920s, the question was how many of the world war's logistical mobilization structures could be re-created within the parameters of the League as part of a sanctions procedure against an aggressor.

John Maynard Keynes was one of the early advocates of this policy.

After working to arrange inter-Allied finance for the Treasury during World War I, Keynes had advised Cecil at the Paris Peace Conference. On the SEC in the spring of 1919, he had become a strong critic of the continuation of the blockade, which British policymakers had, he felt, "grown to love for its own sake."[13] In 1924, when the Secretariat and EFO were trying to pass the Geneva Protocol, Elliott Felkin had asked him for his views on sanctions.[14] Keynes was skeptical of negative measures of interdiction. "The more things are thought about the more shall we be inclined to depend upon positive assistance to the injured party as compared with reprisals against the aggressor," he wrote, because "positive measures would be much more impressive when the time came than negative acts which would always run the risk (1) of not being efficacious and (2) of not being easily distinguished from acts of war."[15] Keynes strongly believed that the economic weapon should focus on provision instead of deprivation. Felkin had championed his idea, but the protocol's failure put it out of reach for the time being.

Within the League, the positive economic weapon was advocated by three states that wanted the organization to have a stronger security-providing function: France, Finland, and Poland. After Léon Bourgeois's death in 1925, the spirit of his *solidarisme* persisted in the French League delegation, which pushed for economic aid to countries threatened by aggressors. France's Superior National Defense Council (Conseil supérieur de la défense nationale; CSDN) had noted in 1926 that the Locarno Treaty, though a step toward improved international security, was not yet sufficient. What was most needed were "practical tools to assure the rapid designation of the aggressor and the efficacy of assistance measures provided in Article 16 of the Covenant."[16] French enthusiasm for an expanded financial aid weapon dovetailed with its national war-fighting strategy, the so-called economic action abroad scheme.[17] The Third Republic planned to obtain supplies and raw materials from its own colonies, financed by borrowing in London. It would also draw on the resources of its British sister empire to sustain land and naval campaigns.[18] French strategists envisioned the creation of "consultative organs of the Council for all measures concerning sanctions or international cooperation. . . . One could thus have the germ of a financial council, a food council, a navigation council, etc."[19] From Paris's viewpoint, the long-term threat against which the League should guard was the revival of German military power in Western Europe. For Finland, which had become independent from Russia after a brief but bloody civil war in 1918, the Soviet Union posed the main threat. Poland, facing both these states, regarded Soviet armament and restored German power as equal causes for concern.

The problem for the Poles and Finns was how to obtain meaningful assistance quickly if they were attacked by larger neighbors.[20] Poland had entered military alliances with France and Czechoslovakia in the 1920s and built up a small domestic arms industry but remained dependent on Western support for its survival.[21] Finland was far away from industrial democracies that might protect it from attack, and it would have to import military equipment, ammunition, and raw materials from abroad. It was this disadvantageous position that motivated the plan presented to the League by Finnish delegates Rafael Erich and Rudolf Holsti in September 1926.[22] Erich and Holsti proposed that a state under attack should receive short-term subsidies for arms purchases and be granted a long-term emergency loan to sustain its economy and self-defense while international action against the aggressor got under way. As another Finnish official put it, their mechanism offered a policy of "insurance against war."[23]

The Finnish proposal coincided with a more general attempt by small European states to upgrade the League's security framework. In December, Belgian statesman Henri de Brouckère delivered a report in which he critically reassessed all that had been done to develop economic sanctions.[24] Brouckère thought that the blueprint provided by the 1921 resolutions of the IBC had taken far too lenient a view of states' duties to impose sanctions under Article 16. Why should the League wait for the crime of aggression to occur? The entire spirit of the Covenant clearly allowed Geneva to take any measures necessary to avert conflict, Brouckère argued.[25] The Council's powers to take *preventive* coercive measures had to be construed very widely to include pacific blockade, naval demonstrations, and gradual economic pressure. Brouckère outlined three reforms to strengthen economic sanctions. First, the financial assistance provisions in the third paragraph of Article 16 should be institutionalized, as the Finns proposed. Second, because "the effective application of an economic blockade presupposes the possession of a vast amount of accurate information on the economic and financial relations between States," the EFO should gather sanctions intelligence.[26] Third, the League had to dispel all doubts about its legal power to comprehensively sever an aggressor state from the world economy. It should claim the largest possible remit for use of force in peacetime—effectively a revival of the nineteenth-century doctrine of pacific blockade. These three measures would increase the helpfulness of economic sanctions to victims through assistance; render them immediately effective against the aggressor through superior information;

and make them unassailable by non-League members through comprehensive legal isolation.

The Brouckère proposals delighted French diplomats in Geneva, who
were glad to see their solidarist sanctions agenda receive support from Belgium, the Netherlands, Czechoslovakia, Poland, Romania, and Greece.[27]
German diplomats, however, had just guided their country into the League
on the assumption that its sanctions mechanism would be kept weak. In
their eyes the Brouckère reform proposals were exactly what should be
avoided. In the German Foreign Ministry, Stresemann's adviser, Bernhard von Bülow, suspected that the organization of assistance was merely
"a cover for the military and economic aims of the French."[28] It could become, he feared, a coalition for the "economic mobilization of the League
of Nations."[29]

Besides German opposition, a positive assistance mechanism faced a
number of practical challenges. Direct subsidies to distressed states were
unworkable since the League lacked its own monetary reserves.[30] Under
the interwar gold standard, countries could build up their foreign exchange
reserves to cover initial emergency purchases. But such self-insurance was
expensive. Moreover, weak developing economies would be far less able
to accumulate funds in this way than rich exporters. Even if a state under
direct attack possessed enough reserves, it was doubtful if these could be
converted quickly into liquid funds. In fact, the already feeble creditworthiness of small states in financial markets was likely to plummet further
in such crisis circumstances. Finally, the gold standard itself would likely
interfere with emergency war finance, as the world had experienced in August 1914; in times of stress central banks would be forced to raise interest rates to stem gold outflows, making money dear just when economic
mobilization and national defense required it to be cheap and plentiful.

The EFO's Financial Committee studied the Finnish memorandum
but proposed a different solution. This body was composed of leading
European financiers—investment bankers like Carel ter Meulen, Henry
Strakosch, and Carl Melchior, as well as treasury advisers such as Otto
Niemeyer and André de Chalendar—many of whom had advised the
League's financial reconstruction program for Austria in 1922-1926.[31]
Based on the Austrian experience, they outlined a scheme to backstop national public debt in emergency situations. A state that fell victim to aggression would borrow by itself but could strengthen its credit by "as-
sociating" it with that of stronger states. The total amount of such an
international guarantee for a national loan would be divided into specific
tranches based on the economic weight of the guarantors. This jointly

held liability would function as a shared financial commitment against aggression, in which "universal participation would be a powerful moral deterrent." The financiers proposed £50 million as a maximum initial guarantee.[32] Another line of defense could be constituted by a second-tier "super-guarantee" borne by the financially strongest member states. The Financial Committee's mechanism was meant to bolster distressed states by making the League act as a conduit for private capital while acting as its ultimate guarantor.[33] This plan became known as the Convention on Financial Assistance.

There were more ambitious financial schemes under discussion in 1927. The initial Finnish proposal had mentioned subsidies that could be immediately disbursed. Yet as Finnish central bank chairman Risto Ryti admitted, the League's accumulation of such funds would withdraw a large amount of gold from global markets—putting the viability of the international gold standard at risk.[34] This is why Ryti supported the idea put forward by Otto Niemeyer of the British Treasury: League states should contribute their own sovereign bonds to a special "sanctions fund" established at a reliable central bank, such as the Swiss National Bank, so that in case of an invasion these high-quality assets could be sold for cash or used as collateral for borrowing. Carl Melchior went further than Niemeyer, proposing a "League of Nations Financial Institute"—a legally distinct special-purpose vehicle—that could issue its own debt instrument, to avoid financial market speculation against weaker individual states.[35] Poland's delegate even suggested opening the convention to non-member states in a bid to bring Wall Street into the business of anti-aggression finance.[36]

Support for a financial assistance weapon grew steadily. But Brouckère's second reform—enlisting the EFO in data production for sanctions—encountered more resistance. Its only supporter was French treasury official André de Chalendar.[37] Most officials on the economic and financial committees were orthodox laissez-faire liberals who rejected the idea that the EFO should chart the global economy "with an eye to having such intelligence at hand in case of future Article 16 procedures." The Financial Committee insisted to Drummond that gathering sanctions intelligence would place the EFO's ordinary collection of financial and commercial statistics in a sinister light.[38] If data were being harvested to design more effective sanctions, then the League was engaging in geopolitical planning under the cover of scientific inquiry. Would member states consent to sharing economic data if they might be used in the future to hurt them more successfully? The financial experts worried about the consequences for the League's integrity as a neutral technocracy. The chair of the economic committee, the French philologist and commerce specialist Daniel Serruys—another veteran of the wartime blockade bureaucracy—told Drummond that "it would not be expedient to contemplate collecting any information other than that which it already possesses."[39] In contrast to the faith in interventionism prevalent in the Secretariat, in the League's economic arm a more permissive economic attitude in favor of free exchange remained dominant.[40] Serruys saw no use in adding to the EFO's responsibilities by shouldering the group with the task of resolving crises that politicians, not economists, had caused.[41] This strong opposition to letting economic advisers deal with security questions dashed the body's prospects as a possible headquarters of sanctions planning. British worries that continental bureaucrats would turn the EFO into an "economic General Staff" were thus unfounded: the commerce experts in Geneva opposed such a political role for their organization just as much.

Even though the idea of sanctions intelligence gathering was rejected, the Convention on Financial Assistance continued to gain supporters. The scheme's most avid proponent on the Financial Committee was Henry Strakosch. An Austrian-Jewish immigrant to Britain, Strakosch had become a successful banker and executive in the South African mining industry, as well as an omnibus financial adviser across the British Empire and League member states.[42] Like Keynes, with whom he was friendly despite their disagreement about the gold standard, Strakosch believed the positive and negative sides of the economic weapon against aggression should be balanced. The League's aim should be "the closing of foreign markets to the aggressor and the opening of them to its victim." Since a state fighting for its survival might see its creditworthiness fall in its hour of greatest need, bringing it to the brink of collapse, the priority was to ensure that an international emergency loan was "acceptable to the investing public of the chief financial centres of the world."[43]

As designed by Strakosch, the convention therefore had a threefold guarantee. First, the distressed state would issue whatever debt it needed on the security of its own revenues. The private banks that underwrote this loan would transfer half the money raised to a trustee, which in the case of the League was the Swiss National Bank. This would constitute a reserve out of which the loan's principal and interest would be paid to investors. If sufficient, then the scheme would work as a simple sovereign debt operation by a single state. However, if the distressed state could no longer meet the interest payments or was in danger of defaulting, a second line of defense was constituted by the states involved in the convention. These so-called guarantors would divide the loan into tranches and place

special guarantee bonds with the trustee central bank, assuming responsibility for servicing the loan if a desperately fighting borrower was unable to pay. As Strakosch pointed out, by spreading out the costs of annual
interest payments among dozens of League guarantors, the costs to each
individual state would be kept very low, if they even had to pay anything at
all. The convention fixed the *total* annual loan service guarantee at £4 million; at then prevailing interest rates of 6–7 percent, this meant the convention could backstop roughly £57–67 million in international loans in
a given year. This was a very substantial amount for smaller states. But if
even such a contingent and modest burden proved too much, the convention provided a third safeguard in the form of a small group of financially
very powerful states such as Britain, France, Germany, and Japan. These
"super-guarantors" promised to service and repay the loan shares if any of
the original guarantors failed.

Keynes found that the entire scheme was "excellent and precisely
meets the case." His only concern was speed; he thought it vital that once
the guarantors had deposited their bonds, "everything should be able to
go ahead very promptly without further reference to them."[44] Strakosch
argued that the convention was "an immensely better way of bringing
the force of the League to bear than by any such schemes as an international army or air force, or by any kind of blockade against the aggressor. It is more spectacular and more practically useful."[45] Strakosch
used his position as chairman of *The Economist* to publicize the convention
widely among financiers in the City of London and to the British public.[46]
The League Assembly accepted it in September 1930, led by Britain and
France. By the end of the following year, a total of thirty states had signed
the convention.[47] But the initiative was fatally undermined by linking its
entry into force to the successful passing of an international disarmament
treaty. When the long-awaited World Disarmament Conference failed in
1933 amid a broad collapse in international cooperation, the Convention
on Financial Assistance died as well. The League thus never managed to
transform its inherited experience in war finance and its acquired knowledge of lending programs into a positive financial weapon in the interwar
years.

Kellogg-Briand and Freedom of the Seas

The Kellogg-Briand Pact, signed in August 1928, entailed the renunciation
of war as an instrument of national policy.[48] However, Britain, France, and
the United States affixed their signature to the pact only with important

specifications and reservations. For one, as U.S. secretary of state Frank Kellogg made clear, self-defense was still a justification for recourse to arms. The exercise of this right could be determined by countries themselves, and it applied not just to attacks on U.S. territory, but also against U.S. interests worldwide.[49] The British government made an explicit reservation for resorting to wars to defend regions "of special and vital interest" to its empire, where it retained "freedom of action."[50] Signing away one's right to embark on war was considerably easier when the bar for invoking self-defense was also lowered.[51] The incompleteness of the ban was not the only issue, however. There was also an internal problem. Under Kellogg-Briand, it was possible for the League to engage in a war of collective enforcement against a treaty-violating aggressor. Such a "public war" would have a coalitional character. But as a non-member state, the United States did not regard League decisions as binding, making it unclear if it would respect Geneva's sanctions. Indeed, American merchants and ships might well invoke neutrality to violate an embargo. This would force the League blockaders to choose between permitting such circumvention or declaring war on the United States.[52]

Kellogg distinguished between "being in war" and blockade as an act of war; the latter did not imply the former. But Whitehall was increasingly concerned about whether the United States would tolerate an expansive British blockade in the case of a League or international economic war against an aggressor.[53] Baldwin's Conservative cabinet was so worried about the blockade issue that it ceased to support any attempt to expand League sanctions. "Unless the United States were a party to that arrangement," Foreign Secretary Austen Chamberlain declared in Geneva in the fall of 1927, "its logical result would be war with the United States—a fantastic method of attempting to preserve the peace of the world."[54]

The European and American advocates of sanctions now stood at a crossroads. The prospect of a U.S.-League clash over sanctions threatened to derail the efforts of internationalists on both sides. As *The Economist* commented in early 1928, "It seems to be felt that to allow an international crisis to reach the pass at which sanctions have to be applied would be a confession of failure—not to speak of the separate and still unsolved problem of applying economic sanctions to a member of the League without a clash with the United States over the inevitable interference with American trade."[55] The Paris Pact agreed on that year prompted internationalists to attempt a grand transatlantic bargain on enforcement measures.

The proposed sanctions platform behind Kellogg-Briand revolved around one of the oldest concepts of world ordering and international law: freedom of the seas. In essence a new free seas doctrine had already been formulated a decade earlier. The second of Wilson's Fourteen Points called for "Absolute freedom of navigation upon the seas, outside territorial waters, alike in peace and in war, except as the seas may be closed in whole or in part by international action for the enforcement of international covenants." In 1918 his adviser, Colonel House, had pushed the British to accept this formula, but to little effect. Even as House threatened to conclude a separate peace with Germany unless London accepted Wilson's freedom of the seas, Lloyd George was unmovable. "We would be sorry," the British prime minister had said, "but we could not give up the blockade, the power which enabled us to live."[56] After Wilson's death in 1921, the idea of a revamped freedom of the seas had continued to circulate among internationalists. The possibility of a clash between the Kellogg-Briand Pact and the Covenant made British promoters of economic sanctions—Cecil and Arnold-Forster in the United Kingdom and Salter and Felkin in Geneva—focus on a basic quid pro quo deal: Britain would promise to use its naval power only in "public" wars and blockades with League authorization if in return the United States would support these international sanctions. In the spring of 1928, Salter sought out American support for this plan by contacting the foreign affairs expert Raymond Buell. Having fought in the U.S. Army in World War I, Buell had completed a doctorate at Princeton and taught government at Harvard before, at the age of thirty-two, becoming director of research at the Foreign Policy Association (FPA), an interest group pushing the U.S. government in a more active internationalist direction. Buell had identified the issue of American compliance with League sanctions in a series of perceptive bulletins in the spring of 1928 that had attracted the attention of European sanctionists.

Salter proposed to hold a conference to codify maritime law in the interest of world peace. He wanted to distinguish between "private" war and "public" war (he also referred to the latter as "police" or "international" war). In a private war, the old rules of blockade and contraband would apply: only weapons and munitions transports would be restricted. But, Salter wrote, "the blockade rights in a 'public' war should be of the widest possible extent—as wide as ever claimed by any belligerent in past wars, or wider—and that, in case of such action of an international police character and such only, a pacific blockade should have just as full consequences as regards neutrals as a blockade in a formal war."[57] Salter wanted a public blockade to be as unrestrained as possible. It should be deployable in peacetime, total in scope, and apply to all countries, including neutrals.

In an analogy with U.S. domestic law enforcement, Salter told Buell that even if it did not join League action, Washington should not "help the aggressor State by insistence on it being supplied with resources. . . . Gun-running should in such cases be regarded as at least as disreputable as rum-running."[58] At a time when Prohibition was still in effect, this was a salient comparison: banning alcohol was a moral as well as a legal project, involving new forms of control, surveillance, and enforcement measures that reached deep into U.S. households.[59] Making economic sanctions against aggression an international norm would require a similar moralization of a domain hitherto left to private law: global commerce and finance.

Salter's suggestions were soon given a more public platform by Arnold-Forster. His hope was "to secure the widest discretion for the League, but to make private economic pressure more and more difficult; powers tolerable in a policeman would be insupportable in a mere high-wayman fighting for his own hand."[60] In a paper co-authored with Cecil and read at Chatham House, Arnold-Forster put forward this idea in a more developed form. Britain should surrender its belligerent rights in private wars in exchange for unlimited rights to use economic coercion in public wars. Arnold-Forster simultaneously wrote the Labour Party's official policy on sanctions in the run-up to the May 1929 general election.[61] The British left, he contended, should stand "for the complete renunciation of the right of private war and . . . for the full acceptance of the new doctrine of Freedom of the Seas, i.e., that the high seas should be closed by international agreement for the enforcement of international covenants."[62] On the American side, Buell and David Miller advocated that the U.S. government adopt the same doctrine to guide its international obligations. Washington did not have to join the League. If lawmakers felt that a country designated an aggressor by the Council also violated the Kellogg-Briand Pact, it was sufficient to stop protecting private commerce with the guilty party and not hinder League sanctions.[63] Miller thought that Kellogg-Briand "links the United States to the League of Nations as a guardian of peace."[64] If this congruence between the Paris Peace Pact and the Covenant was achieved, then the option of neutrality for the world's major powers was effectively removed.

Yet there was a domestic hindrance. The U.S. government had no legal mechanism for using external economic pressure in a *discriminatory* way—that is, against one warring side in a conflict but not the other. The

Shotwell-Miller group busied itself addressing this legislative lacuna. To do so they enlisted the help of two congressmen, Representative Stephen Porter (R-Pennsylvania) and Senator Arthur Capper (D-Kansas). On 11 February 1929, Porter and Capper simultaneously proposed resolutions in the House and the Senate for "an embargo on arms shipments to nations violating the peace compact." The Capper Resolution was based largely on a draft written by Shotwell.[65] Both of the proposed bills activated an arms embargo, the Porter Resolution if the president found a country to be *involved* in war, the Capper Resolution when a country was *declared* to have violated the Kellogg-Briand Pact. The Capper Resolution was therefore the more discriminatory economic sanctions bill; it explicitly punished warring states for violating the ban on war. In doing so, it offered the possibility of unifying League and American action against aggression.[66]

American internationalists feverishly promoted the Capper Resolution; Nicholas Murray Butler, president of Columbia University, was an early and vocal proponent. But U.S. arms manufacturers put up stiff resistance to the proposed legislation, and the House of Representatives tabled the bill.[67] Paul Claudel, the French ambassador in Washington, compared American business opposition to the embargo resolutions to "masons and entrepreneurs protest[ing] against firemen, because they stole the bread from their plate."[68] Indeed, manufacturing interests had good reason to oppose export controls.[69] Following events from a distance, the Soviet newspaper *Izvestia* wrote that "in the idea of Senator Capper, and in particular in the idea of Porter, the question of sanctions must be decided by the President of the United States," whereas League sanctions were "in the hands of the Anglo-French bloc. That is the fundamental difference between the system of the League of Nations and the system that is proposed on the basis of the Kellogg Pact by a group of American politicians."[70] Another stumbling block was the fact that European navalists still opposed all international guarantees of free navigation. The French Navy, for example, thought that it would be very dangerous to allow troublesome states to resupply themselves freely. "It goes without saying that a nation animated by aggressive intentions will take all precautions before unleashing war," French naval analysts wrote. "In these conditions, it would be capable of using at full capacity the raw materials that it could attain from abroad." French strategists therefore concluded that unimpeded navigation almost always constituted "a considerable advantage in favor of the aggressor state and to the detriment of the attacked state."[71]

British admirals were also steadfastly opposed to any freedom of the seas doctrine, even the one with internationalist qualifications that Wilson had introduced in 1918. The most important British naval strategist of the early twentieth century, Julian Corbett, had worked on the Phillimore Committee, which had drafted the first British blueprint for the League. His main critique of freedom of the seas was that it would deprive liberal maritime states of the power to use sanctions to bring recalcitrant countries to heel. "When the whole world has become to so large an extent possessed of a common vitality, when the life of every nation has become more or less linked by its trade arteries with that of every other," he wrote, "the force of an oecumenical sea interdict has become perhaps the most potent of all sanctions." Returning to a pre-1914 world of free seas was tempting "when men had not yet driven home to them what sea-power actually meant for the cause of peace and freedom and for the punishment of international criminality," but it was also politically and strategically naïve.[72] Smaller nations, Corbett thought, should support making the League of Nations a true system of collective security instead of clinging to their old habits of neutrality and free navigation. A decade after the Paris Peace Conference, Admiralty figures were full of contempt for freedom of the seas, which they saw as a dangerous doctrine, "a rallying cry in the past of weaker sea Powers . . . [that] Britain could never accept; were she to do so, she would at once renounce her power in the world."[73]

By the late 1920s, the issue of freedom of the seas had split liberal states on the Atlantic seaboard: Britain and France in opposition, the United States and small European trading states such as the Netherlands, Norway, and Sweden in favor. The latter group's resistance showed that despite growing enthusiasm, the sanctionist agenda encountered opposition from neutralist liberal countries. What did their alternative order consist of? As we shall see, neutrality formed a moral and legal universe of its own, one in which war was a state of hostility to be contained in space and time. One of the characteristics of a world of neutrals was that society, economy, and infrastructure were insulated from state coercion as much as possible.

The Erosion of Neutrality

To understand why economic sanctions clashed with neutrality, it is key to grasp that the European neutrals' shared diplomatic orientation stemmed from a common economic model. Switzerland, the Netherlands, Sweden, Norway, and Denmark were all highly open export economies; the former two also had sizable financial sectors engaged in overseas lending. These economies were all strongly committed to freedom of the seas, neutrality, relatively free trade, and the gold standard. Their desire to avoid military entanglements also produced strategic alignments, most notably the Convention of Oslo, a seven-country free-trade agreement with political overtones that united the Fennoscandian states and the Low Countries in the 1930s.[74]

Neutrality, the sanctionists argued, was an archaic institution. In a world where economic globalization had interwoven production chains and money flows, the moral implications of trade were undeniable. It was nonsensical to afford private commerce any cover if it facilitated resources flowing to an enemy.[75] The first British theorist of "grand strategy," Major-General John Frederick Charles Fuller, fulminated against the wartime conduct of neutral states, "vampires [that] were feasting on the blood of the battlefields. . . . As long as international law is so worded as to permit of neutrals trading like ghouls on the blood of the belligerents, international law is immoral and, consequently, it is a virtuous act to destroy it. To foster it is not only to place a premium on greed and cowardice but also on moral prostitution."[76]

Fuller's pugnacious outlook put him on the radical right of British politics. In the 1930s he drifted into the orbit of Mosley's British Union of Fascists. But the aversion to neutrality was also found among British internationalists of a liberal and progressive stripe. To further confound matters, in continental Europe defenders of neutrality ranged across the political spectrum. The Norwegian journalist Victor Mogens declared that no world peace would be possible before freedom of the seas and private property protection had become a general doctrine and "until it is rendered impossible for a State to wage war against non-combatants, the peaceful population of another country, its old men, women, and children, by means of the frightful weapon of starvation."[77] Though this might appear as a plea for humanity from a small Scandinavian state, Mogens was a robust conservative who would later lead the right-wing nationalist Fatherland League. The strongest criticism of his argument came from William Arnold-Forster, a Labour Party member who denied the possibility of distinguishing between state and civilian supplies. "Every attempt thus to cut in half the weapon of blockade is doomed to failure, for the distinctions on which it rests do not really exist," he argued, invoking Ludendorff's view that the lesson of the world war was that "army and nation were one."[78] The fact that neutrality could make nationalists look like pacifists and liberals sound like Ludendorff shows that the different stances on this issue were dictated by geopolitical and economic preferences, not just legal and moral principle.

Arnold-Forster saw clearly, and early on, what would result from pushing discriminatory sanctions against aggression to their logical conclusion. Either belligerence would disappear, since all enforcement would become policing action against bandit states, or else neutrality would have to be abolished, to make public war a universal affair without impartial bystanders. "It is better," he concluded in a lecture to the Royal United Services Institute in 1925, "to press on towards a League of all Nations when there will be either no belligerence, or else, in effect no neutrality, than to spend our labour in renewed attempts to reconcile the old irreconcilable conflict between belligerent and neutral interests."[79] Yet since League action might have to go beyond sanctions and escalate into actual war, it was neutrality rather than belligerence that was the most likely to be sacrificed. Eventually each country would have to side either with the League or with the aggressor; there was no third option.

From the point that economic interdependence forged inescapable connections, the opponents of neutrality also derived strong moral arguments. Neutrality was simply "irreconcilable with the idea of the solidarity of peoples," one contemporary jurist averred.[80] In the wake of World War I, the violent conquest of small countries by their larger neighbors was no longer a regional affair. Due to the international nature of news media and the formation of public opinion, atrocities and the treatment of ethnic minorities were becoming a prime concern of national publics in League states. In such an omniconscious world, it was felt by many that standing by idly as war ravaged the earth was a moral failure, not just a political one.[81]

The dynamic global frontier of partiality and neutrality in the late 1920s lay in Central and (South)east Europe. The region's politics revolved around the alignment of the small states between the Soviet Union and Germany (*Randstaatenpolitik*) and the question of who could organize the League's sanctions apparatus against whom.[82] Designating a state as an aggressor would bring an international coalition into being. Finland's campaign for financial assistance under Article 16 sought to secure funding in case of a war with the Soviet Union. German diplomats keen to preserve the German-Soviet relationship observed the Finns' stance with dismay. Stresemann's adviser, Bülow, felt that "Finland's physiognomy in Geneva is no longer that of a neutral Nordic small state, but that of an extreme and goal-oriented advocate of security and sanctions efforts."[83]

For Weimar Germany, the armaments restrictions of the Versailles Treaty meant that invoking neutrality was the only way to stay out of a war. The Allies' right under Article 213 of the Versailles Treaty to inspect

German factories and military installations for violations of the disarmament provisions meant that the possibility of sanctions against Berlin remained. During talks in The Hague in January 1930, French prime minister André Tardieu and British chancellor of the exchequer Philip Snowden made it clear to German foreign minister Julius Curtius that economic and financial pressure were not off the table.[84] Even though he insisted on German neutrality on nearly every international issue, Curtius feared what he suspected were French efforts to "organize the sanctions war of the League of Nations" against Germany.[85] For a long time, the United States had displayed financial benevolence toward Germany, often against French and British wishes. But by 1930, the U.S. government was regarded by German policymakers as neutral in name only. Bülow thought that Geneva was ultimately beholden to an increasingly influential group of American internationalists eager to use sanctions for every problem. The Capper and Porter Resolutions showed that the United States was on its way to abandoning neutrality and would soon begin to discriminate in the use of economic pressure. Once the "Washington group" (*Washingtoner Kreis*) had given its approval, he expected that the sanctions apparatus of the League would impose blockades on European states. "The Genevan dependence on Washington would be starkly exposed," Bülow thought, but "against this, Geneva will then have, when it proceeds to blockade and sanctions, a strong backing."[86] Even if he overestimated Anglo-French-American cooperation, Bülow's diagnosis of an emerging global liberal sanctionist bloc was clearly daunting to countries like Germany that had been exposed to economic pressure in the past.

In fact, sanctions were a source of tension rather than concord in Anglo-American relations. When the Labour Party won the British general election in May 1929, returning Ramsay MacDonald to power, liberal internationalists in Britain rejoiced. MacDonald reestablished diplomatic relations with the Soviet Union, and in October 1929 he visited the United States, the first British prime minister to do so.[87] His American counterpart was Herbert Hoover, probably the most renowned humanitarian internationalist in the world, who had been elected Republican president in November 1928.

Hoover supported MacDonald's push for disarmament and fiscal rectitude, but he was wary of global policing plans based on economic blockade.[88] On the eleventh anniversary of the end of the Great War, Armistice Day 1929, Hoover launched a counterproposal: food ships should enjoy immunity and be allowed to pass through blockades. "Born of a poignant personal experience," Hoover said, "I have held that food ships should be made free of any interference in times of war. I would place all vessels laden solely with food supplies on the same footing as hospital ships. The time has come when we should remove starvation of women and children from the weapons of warfare." To the statesmen of Britain, France, Japan, Italy, and the other smaller naval powers, Hoover argued that such protection would promote disarmament since it was "the fear of an interruption in seaborne food supplies [that] has powerfully tended toward naval development in both importing and exporting nations."[89]

Hoover's proposal to insulate food supplies from global power politics was well received in neutral countries. A Swiss newspaper wrote that "when one wants to appreciate the significance of this idea, one should recall in what strong opposition to the foundations of the League of Nations it stands." The League used "an economic war, which contains a hunger blockade," but Hoover's idea would mean that "the odious starvation of the civilian population of the enemy will henceforth no longer be a weapon of war," the German mission in Bern enthusiastically reported.[90] But the U.S. proposal never gained traction in the League Council, where the major European powers quickly publicly opposed it.[91] Britain rebuffed the idea outright.[92] The French government regarded the food ship exemption as a disguised strategic ploy with a "humanitarian appearance" that has in reality "without a doubt been nothing but an episode in Anglo-American naval rivalry."[93] While armament restrictions were successfully agreed on at the London Naval Conference, Hoover's initiative went nowhere.

Throughout the 1920s, sanctionists were consciously anti-humanitarian as they wagered their project on making Anglo-American navalism a cornerstone of world order. Although not all their efforts to reconcile the Covenant and the Paris Pact met with success, rival attempts to impose humanitarian checks on the use of starvation as a threat and weapon were clearly blocked. The demise of Hoover's food ship proposal meant that by the end of the decade the sanctionists remained more powerful than the neutralists. As the French ambassador in Washington wrote to Paris, the prospect that sanctions would be used to enforce the Paris Peace Pact had "a problematic and spectral existence. . . . If the phantom has been exorcised from the domains of the real, it continues to haunt the region of the possible."[94]

The fall of 1929 was an enjoyable time for Elliott Felkin. The EFO's number two visited Barcelona's International Exposition on behalf of the American Chambers of Commerce. After talking shop during the day, in the evening he joined the other attendees in feasting on stuffed chicken, foie gras, and langoustines aboard the steamship *Victoria Eugenia*. As believers in *doux commerce*, they saw the restoration of the gold standard and of growth in industry, trade, and finance as signs of a prosperous future. While Felkin and his fellow internationalists rejoiced, a German professor arrived in Barcelona to deliver a lecture at the congress of the European Federation of Culture. He sharply attacked his contemporaries' faith in untrammeled economic integration, calling their optimistic vision that consumption and wealth accumulation would promote political stability both illusory and dangerous.[95] The professor argued that under the League the victors of the war had stripped their defeated opponents of their sovereignty.[96] Sanctions were the dark side of liberalism, a superficially neutral tool that in fact hid old-fashioned power politics.

The speaker in question, Carl Schmitt, was an infamous illiberal jurist who opposed the Weimar Republic and welcomed the rise of the Nazis. His stark analysis of the interwar system has had a strong appeal for critics of liberalism then and since.[97] However, in his fervor to attack liberalism, Schmitt misrepresented the process under way. The late 1920s were marked not by a sinister liberal plot orchestrated through the League, but by a hybrid condition of transition from one political-legal order to another. The new "public" system of collective security and League sanctions was chafing against an older "private" system of limited war, neutrality, and humanitarian law. It was precisely the uneasy coexistence of these two paradigms between 1927 and 1931 that made the period's politics so disorienting. But this was not, as Schmitt suggested, a struggle between liberalism and some anti- or non-liberal alternative; in his preference for the older separationist system, Schmitt was in fact aligned with many classical liberals and future neoliberals.[98] The divide between sanctionism and neutrality expressed not a conflict between liberalism and its enemies but a clash between opposing paradigms *within* liberalism itself.

Schmitt was also wrong in his portrayal of ideological conflict. Interwar sanctions were decidedly not a brutal Anglo-American imposition on a previously harmonious European order. They had strong intellectual and ideological roots on the continent itself. Because of the U.S. rejection of the Versailles Treaty, in the interwar decades the economic weapon remained primarily a European and specifically an Anglo-French project, administered through Geneva when possible and bilaterally when necessary.[99] Unlike modern sanctions, the economic weapon did not function to protect democracy or liberal values. Its first and foremost function was the defense of the territorial order created in 1919. Article 16 sanctions were triggered by attacks against sovereign member states of the League, not by domestic human rights abuses or the dismantling of liberal institutions. In this regard, the sanctionist system between the wars differed profoundly from the principles of liberal internationalism as we recognize them today.[100]

Although the sanctionists did not establish a hermetic order by the start of the 1930s, they were in a position to stop alternative projects from succeeding—arrangements in which sanctions had no place, in which their effects were contained, or in which economic coercion was banned outright. The only durable victory for the opponents of sanctions was an unexpected one within the bureaucracy of the League itself: the EFO's refusal to gather economic intelligence to design sanctions.

Ultimately, the ambivalence between sanctionism and neutrality was unsustainable not just because their underlying philosophies were incompatible. The capitalist restoration of the Roaring Twenties was built on weak foundations, and the world economy was tottering. A downturn in global commodity prices had already begun in 1927–1928. As Felkin and Schmitt savored Barcelona's autumn sun, a massive financial crash took place on Wall Street, marking the onset of the Great Depression. The global slump politicized much more than just international economic relations; the League system and the Paris Peace Treaties also came under tremendous strain as nations launched radical bids for autonomy. One of the most promising extensions of Article 16, the Convention on Financial Assistance championed by Keynes and Strakosch, arrived too late to be implemented. This left the sanctionists with negative instruments to punish aggression but little support to dispense to its victims. As a result, economic sanctions would face their most serious challenges yet in the 1930s.

PART III

Economic Sanctions in the Interwar Crisis

CHAPTER SEVEN

Collective Security against
Aggression, 1931–1935

"THE MOST IMPORTANT PROBLEM in the science and art of government today," wrote the Geneva-based American professor Pitman Potter in April 1932, "[is] the problem of organizing and operating a system of sanctions in international government."[1] Although sanctions had existed for over a decade, around the time Potter was writing, a new name emerged for the edifice to which they belonged: "collective security." The phrase became the marching banner for the armed defense of international treaties and stability, and sanctions were its most important weapon.[2] This orientation emerged for a good reason: the following decade saw attempts to prevent or stop war with sanctions from Latin America to Africa and from Europe to East Asia as a militarist Japan, Nazi Germany, and Fascist Italy all embarked on programs of rearmament, territorial expansion, and empire building.

Were interwar internationalists wrong to believe that economic pressure could fulfill this role? Many contemporary commentators and historians have depicted League sanctions as weak and ineffective, arguing that they were merely a way to signal commitment to peace and condemn aggression.[3] E. H. Carr's foundational text of international relations realism, *The Twenty Years' Crisis* (1939), held that the League's sanctions were misguided since the countries imposing them were not prepared to use military force as an ultimate backstop.[4] In his account of the Great Depression as a failure of hegemonic stability, Charles Kindleberger claimed that the sanctions lacked "any lead from the United States or Britain" and therefore "failed."[5] Zara Steiner's authoritative work on interwar international history argues that the British government publicly affirmed its support for sanctions but lacked the resolve to carry them out.[6] The implication of these verdicts is clear: preventing the slide into world war in the 1930s stood or fell with the success of sanctions, and in this regard the League proved too feeble. This general impression of impotence pervades historical literature and memory of the 1930s. The picture of a well-intentioned but naïve League provides a neat backdrop for an upbeat and progressive *Bildungsroman*-style narrative about the modern international order that took shape after 1945.[7] In this view, the League lacked sanctions with hard power, whereas the United Nations learned from its weaknesses and was backed by real force.[8]

As the next chapters will show, a closer look at the key crises of the 1930s reveals that the problem with sanctions was less their inherent weakness than their considerable but unpredictable strength. The Japanese invasion of Manchuria and northern China in 1931–1932 began a decade of argument among American, British, French, and Dutch policymakers about whether to deploy economic sanctions against Tokyo.[9] That these were not applied was largely from fear of encouraging further Japanese military action. Nevertheless, pro-League internationalists emerged from the Manchurian crisis determined to take the political fight for enforcing peace and a sanctions-wielding U.S. state to the next level. In Britain, Robert Cecil personified the assertive politics of collective security as figurehead of the League of Nations Union (LNU), a civil society group that by 1933 had acquired over a million members.[10] Broadly backed by left and liberal opinion, it took a much more forceful internationalist position than the Conservatives, who regarded Cecil and his colleagues as "bloodthirsty Pacifists."[11]

Although it suffered setbacks, there were important moments when the League seemed to gain in power. In 1934 the Soviet Union joined the organization as a Council member, emboldening anti-fascists across Europe, who hoped it would enable economic pressure on Nazi Germany. When the following spring Soviet diplomats moved to form a sanctionist front against Nazi rearmament, Western governments demurred because they feared the trade backlash against their own economies. Yet in October 1935, the League showed it was capable of imposing sanctions on

Mussolini's Italy for its invasion of Ethiopia. In a groundbreaking episode, examined in chapter 8 below, most of the world's sovereign states united in the first multilateral economic sanctions regime in history. Once more, however, concern about pushing the aggressor into general European war led sanctions designers to moderate their approach, producing a gradualist package that deliberately avoided harsher measures.

There were many diplomatic, economic, and technical challenges to forming successful sanctionist coalitions, but their problems also had a deeper structural root. This was the shakiness of the meaning of war and peace, an unstable legacy bequeathed by the world war that was aggravated by the use of force in peacetime. Sanctions were so strongly tied to the total war from which they emerged that they could appear as indistinguishable from war. This was true for nationalist governments but also for the sanctionist states seeking to restrain them. In the former, the prospect of economic isolation enabled and accelerated popular and economic mobilization against the outside world. In the latter, imposing sanctions required bringing the state onto a quasi-wartime footing in the name of preserving peace. As a British commentator pointed out in 1931, "Unless the various Governments are armed with the necessary powers, economic sanctions cannot be generally applied. . . . At present all this has not been done. . . . This means that the economic weapon is not ready for action."[12] The succession of international crises from Manchuria to Ethiopia would raise the stakes of such sanctions preparedness to new heights.

Manchuria and the Prospect of Sanctions

On 21 February 1930, five notables met at the Harvard Club in midtown New York to consider the meaning of economic sanctions for U.S. foreign policy. As one of them put it, the Kellogg-Briand Pact had elevated "the problem of economic sanctions to the level of a real issue in American political and economic life." The United States had signed a treaty to outlaw aggressive war. But it had not embraced any formal responsibility to counter it in the world, unlike the members of the League committed to Article 16. The United States was not the only state outside the League that had a role to play in making sanctions more hermetic. The Soviet Union, Brazil, and Mexico also mattered. Among them, these four countries had a prime financial market, an enormous export trade in foodstuffs and manufactured goods, most of the world oil supply, and large quantities of every crucial war material: Brazilian rubber, Mexican oil, American copper and cotton, and Soviet manganese and platinum.[13]

The Harvard Club gathering produced an initiative that was financed by the Twentieth Century Fund, a think tank established by Edward Filene in 1919. A successful Boston-based department store owner, Filene had been a prominent backer of the LEP in 1915–1918. His Twentieth Century Fund united Wilsonian internationalists, arbitrationists, and prominent U.S. lawyers, businessmen, and government officials. In August 1931, Filene invited Columbia University president Nicholas Murray Butler to chair the so-called Committee on Economic Sanctions.[14] Groundwork for its studies had already been prepared by the jurist John Whitton and the economist Frederick Tryon; the fund planned to publish its full report in spring 1932, to coincide with the World Disarmament Conference in Geneva. Although an escalating economic and financial crisis was spreading across Central Europe, the League Assembly that convened in September 1931 still took place in an atmosphere of peace. Cecil even told those assembled in Geneva that "scarcely ever has there been a period in the world's history when war seemed less likely than it does at the present."[15]

Eight days later, on Friday, 18 September, this notion was shattered. In an infamous false-flag attack, the Mukden Incident, Japanese army officers bombed the South Manchurian Railroad as a pretext to take over large parts of the region. On the same weekend, a mutiny among Royal Navy sailors in Scotland led to panic on the London Stock Exchange and in currency markets, forcing the British government to take sterling off the gold standard on Monday, 21 September. In a single weekend both the international political and economic orders suffered serious shocks. Japan's invasion of Manchuria after the Mukden Incident triggered a "Far Eastern crisis."[16] Before the League had time to act, Chinese students began to organize a popular boycott against Japanese goods.[17] This grassroots non-purchase campaign had noticeable effects. By November, just two months after the invasion, Japanese exports to Manchuria had fallen 68 percent from their 1930 levels; exports to northern, central, and southern China were down by 24, 17, and 10 percent, respectively.[18] An American journalist in China described the mass boycott as a "mighty economic weapon . . . a peculiarly fierce kind of war in which the entire spiritual strength of the nation is mobilized."[19]

The immediate problem that confronted Western policymakers was that neither the Japanese nor the Chinese governments were unified actors. Chiang Kai-Shek's government in Nanjing was facing a significant challenge from a rival clique of Kuomintang (KMT) generals in Canton, and the two sides disagreed on how to deal with the Japanese.[20] Japan's civilian cabinet in Tokyo was more moderate than military hardliners in Manchuria, who were acting independently and mobilizing popular support in Japan itself. Foreign Minister Kijuro Shidehara was highly regarded by his Western colleagues, especially U.S. secretary of state Henry Stimson, for his cooperative attitude at the 1930 London Naval Conference. But his position was increasingly tenuous as even many Japanese liberals balked at the restrictions being imposed by Western tariffs, immigration quotas, and peace treaties.[21] Ultra-nationalist army officers attempted two coups d'état in 1931 alone, reducing the room for maneuver for Japanese moderates like Shidehara. Given these rifts within both Japanese and Chinese elites, it was unclear who was making decisions and whose response to material pressure mattered more.

Due to this opacity, a League inquiry into the incident attracted broad support from President Hoover in Washington, French prime minister Pierre Laval, and Ramsay MacDonald and his foreign secretary, John Simon, in Britain. Cecil and Salter wanted more forceful League action: a declaration that Japan had acted as the aggressor and deliberation about sanctions to be imposed under Article 16.[22] Initially Geneva did little as leaders on all sides expected that a negotiated solution to the dispute was within reach; it helped that neither China nor Japan recognized the conflict as an official war.[23] A further obstacle was that American representatives sent to Geneva and Paris appeared uninterested in international cooperation. Briand, who chaired the Council, repeatedly asked U.S. ambassador Charles Dawes to attend, but the former general and financier could not be bothered to cross the Seine. Arthur Sweetser described these failed meetings of November and December 1931 as "[among] the damndest opera-bouffe incidents in diplomatic history."[24]

American opposition to sanctions was complex. As a long-standing opponent of blockade, Herbert Hoover thought that sanctions were an act of war.[25] A business-oriented internationalist of a conservative cast, he did not want the world of commerce to be disturbed by political interference. Stimson was more inclined to restrain Japan, but his State Department was split on the issue of sanctions. Under Secretary William Castle, who had served as ambassador to Japan, supported Hoover in viewing sanctions as an aggressive act of war.[26] Another group of diplomats around the chief of the Division of Far Eastern Affairs, Stanley Hornbeck, formed a pro-sanctions camp. Hornbeck was the first U.S. policymaker to study the potential of a U.S. sanctions campaign against Japan in December 1931. To him, the attraction of sanctions lay in the grossly uneven trade relationship. As the destination of 40 percent of Japan's foreign trade, the U.S. market was much more important to Tokyo than vice versa; Japan attracted just over 4 percent of U.S. exports. Hornbeck thought the economic damage from sanctions would become serious within three months. Within half a year, the imperial government would have to negotiate a settlement with China and the West. Japan's export industries and shipping "would be wrecked immediately by an economic boycott."[27]

Trade was at the center of Manchurian sanctions discussions — and for understandable reasons. By early 1932, the deepening Great Depression was causing a very rapid contraction of world trade. The U.S. economy maintained the largest export trade by value, at $2.37 billion, just ahead of Germany ($2.19 billion), Britain ($2.07 billion), and France ($1.19 billion).[28] But American industrial interests were strongly opposed to reducing their exports further by engaging in embargoes or boycotts. The labor economist George Soule held that the material and demographic constraints already affecting Japan had been underestimated; an American boycott would provoke a violent counter-reaction. It was possible that Tokyo would succumb to sanctions "like a broken-down panhandler faced with a policeman's club," Soule thought, "but it is more likely that a proud people like the Japanese, opposed by the hostility of the world, would believe that they must now make themselves impregnable by consolidating a great Eastern empire or sink to an ignominious existence as a disgraced and second-rate power."[29] By forcing a choice between humiliation and a fight for survival, he warned, sanctions would empower Japan's hardliners. In Britain, the ATB's first report on Japan's economic vulnerabilities reached a similar conclusion: with American and Soviet participation, a combination of import, export, and financial restrictions might have a strong effect, but it could not be ruled out that "sanctions might drive Japan into open war."[30]

Notwithstanding political and economic doubts, the Manchurian crisis produced a noticeable shift in feminist views of economic pressure. Cecil campaigned together with the WILPF to hold Japan accountable for its aggressive forays into Chinese territory after January 1932. In the United States, Emily Balch proposed a peaceful private boycott of Japanese goods that would force business to reconsider support for aggression but avoid a hunger blockade of the population. In a meeting with Stimson's assistant, she proposed that a "voluntary boycott" would find broad support among politically active women who cared for world peace.[31] In the immediate aftermath of the world war, feminist political organizations had overwhelmingly rejected economic sanctions. But by 1931–1932 they had grown closer to the bolder positions taken by pro-League internationalist groups such as the League of Nations Association in America and the LNU in Britain.[32] Still, Balch and others supported a boycott only if it did not "stir up a movement of mass hatred and war spirit." Dorothy Detzer, the head of the U.S. branch of the WILPF, reassured Balch that there was "no danger of precipitating a war with Japan."[33] Detzer, an important pacifist lobbyist for arms embargo legislation on Capitol Hill in the 1930s, was joined in this view by Vera Micheles Dean, a Russian émigré political scientist who edited the sanctionist news bulletins of Raymond Buell's Foreign Policy Association.[34]

Together these civil society groups created the American Boycott Association (ABA) in the spring of 1932. Through an intensive nationwide campaign involving activists, community organizers, church groups, news circulation, and public events, the ABA drummed up support for a pressure campaign against Japan. This achievement reversed the political dynamic of the post–World War I confrontation between democracy and economic pressure. During the long "peacewar" of 1918–1921, popular movements had mobilized against the anti-Soviet blockade while Allied elites wanted to maintain it. A decade later, grassroots campaigning by the U.S. outlawry of war movement and its League sister organizations in Britain had shifted into a strong movement in favor of boycotts and sanctions while conservative ruling elites opposed this policy. Part of this shift was due to the changed context of international politics: by the early 1930s the question was no longer how to end a world war but how to prevent small wars from escalating. The growing distance in space and time from total war led many liberals, leftists, and feminists to a new assessment of the uses of force: commercial pressure was distinct from war and preferable to a repetition of it. By contrast, social agitation had left conservatives more convinced that, as one of them suggested, "The national boycott, in and of itself, *is* war. . . . Perhaps the idea should be tracked down that boycotting is nothing but an improvement, a late development indeed, of the art of war."[35]

Amid this discussion, the Committee on Economic Sanctions, chaired by Nicholas Butler, released its report, *Boycotts and Peace*, in April 1932.[36] It presented the fullest case yet for U.S. participation in international sanctions. The committee's thinking about the economic weapon was also influenced by the European discussions of the previous decade. Deterrence theory had underpinned sanctions in the 1921 IBC resolutions, the Shotwell-Miller 1924 plan, and the ideas of Arnold-Forster, Cecil, and Felkin throughout the 1920s. This logic was also the basis of the Butler committee's report. As *Boycotts and Peace* argued, "General knowledge, in any country considering aggressive action, that world-wide economic sanctions might be invoked against it, would certainly call into action the fears of all business and industrial interests in that country; and their influence, exercised entirely directly and within the country, would in many cases suffice to turn the scale against the contemplated aggression."[37] The report unleashed a frenzy of debate about economic sanctions in the U.S. public sphere.[38] Butler explicitly pitched it as a case for boycotting Japan, attempting to sway the Hoover administration from its opposition to sanctions.[39]

Boycotts and Peace also provoked a debate about sanctions between Raymond Buell and the famous progressive philosopher John Dewey, then at Columbia. At issue was the question "Are Sanctions Necessary to International Organization?"[40] Buell argued that sanctions were a necessary corollary to any system of international order and that establishing deterrence was key. The Japanese, he argued, had observed the weak Western response to the anti-imperial revolts of 1925–1927 and concluded that events in China would not warrant international sanctions. If sanctions had been forcefully implemented at the time, then Japanese industrialists would have immediately stopped the army from further escalation in Manchuria. Buell extended this lesson to the start of the world war: like Cecil, Angell, and Sweetser, he was convinced Germany would have restrained Austria-Hungary from attacking Serbia in July 1914 if it had known a ruthless blockade would be the consequence.

At its core, however, Buell's argument was not based on historical experience but on a new philosophy of the international order. The failure to establish sanctions decisively as the basis of world peace would mean the continuation of might making right—the "war system." To inaugurate a new, better order, something as powerful but not as horrendous as war was needed. Moral pressure alone was not strong enough. Buell accepted the risk of collateral damage but also denied that it was possible in moral terms "to separate a government from the individuals under its jurisdiction." In his view, once under sanctions, "the people of a country can escape from the hardships of an international boycott by causing its government to live up to its international obligations."[41] Whether any mechanism for popular input existed was an open question; in any case, it was up to populations to change their governments' behavior by whatever means available.

Dewey questioned Buell's analogy between the state system and domestic society. Punishment under civil law could not be readily transposed to the international sphere. For Dewey, a moral community could institute punitive measures only on the basis of a preexisting agreement about core values. But to expect that this process could be applied in reverse in international politics was to put the cart before the horse. A more cohesive global morality had to coalesce first as a result of historical and cultural development; only after this would states accept collective measures of coercion. Imposing sanctions before such a consensus existed sowed further division. Dewey argued that no moral community could be created by force; it had to emerge organically through increasing interaction and exchange.[42]

Ultimately, the United States did not impose sanctions on Japan in the Manchurian crisis. It did, however, adopt an official doctrine of non-recognition toward the Japanese-supported state of Manchukuo. Washington's refusal to recognize territory taken by conquest was a measure improvised by Henry Stimson in response to the Japanese Army's violent attack on Shanghai in January 1932.[43] Hoover supported this "Stimson Doctrine" after the fact as a form of condemnation that did not risk war. In November, the League-sponsored Lytton Inquiry, which investigated the Mukden Incident, designated Japan as the perpetrator. Lytton's report identified Manchukuo as "territory occupied by Japan," not an independent state, and recommended the entire League adopt non-recognition. This prompted Japan to leave the League in March 1933—the first Council member to do so.[44]

In many ways this was an unexpected turn of events. At the beginning of the 1930s Japan had seemed firmly committed to Genevan internationalism. With a liberal foreign policy and a restrictive financial policy keeping militarism in check, the country was experiencing a "golden age of constitutionalism" and was in the process of "becoming a second England."[45] But even before the invasion of Manchuria, many Japanese officials had been hesitant about the League, seeing it as an organization with ingrained prejudices against them. At the Paris Peace Conference many members of the Japanese delegation felt Article 16 was much more likely to be used against their country than against Britain or the United States.[46] On the IBC in 1921, Minoru Oka had somewhat watered down the stringency of sanctions. In the following years, Tokyo had tried to create more consideration abroad for Japan's special geographical position as a resource-poor Asian island power, but without success. At the same time, while its departure from Geneva over the Lytton Report was a setback, it was not an irreversible step toward war with the West.[47] The Japanese Privy Council emphasized its desire to maintain friendly relations with other great powers and to continue participation in disarmament schemes. Leaving the League was not a choice for untrammeled belligerence or renewed isolation but a turning away from an organization that many Japanese saw as insensitive to their interests in East Asia.[48]

The Far Eastern crisis provoked debates in Western democracies that primed politicians, policymakers, and publics for the future use of economic sanctions. By 1933, both sides had begun to hone their arguments: advocates, that sanctions were preferable to war and that they could exploit key weaknesses; critics, that they were difficult to coordinate, likely to backfire, or ineffective in the face of responses such as nationalism, trade diversion, and stockpiling.

A Spiral of Insecurity

As Japan left the League, European states confronted the Nazi takeover in Germany. Hitler's *Machtergreifung* on 30 January 1933 was the result of a dangerous combination of economic crisis, political opportunism by authoritarian German conservatives, and the armed forces' desire to escape Versailles Treaty restrictions on armaments.[49] In an alarming display of their anti-Semitic worldview, Nazi storm troopers began to target Jewish-owned businesses within weeks of coming to power. The regime officially declared a boycott on 1 April.[50]

Just as in the Manchurian case, civil society preceded governments in calling for economic pressure on Germany. Jewish organizations in the United States were quick to organize protests against this discrimination. After convincing figures such as Senator Robert Wagner and American Federation of Labor president William Green to condemn Nazi policies, the American Jewish Congress took the lead in organizing an anti-Nazi boycott.[51] But this campaign failed to attract official government support, and among Jewish organizations in various countries there were fears that a general boycott of Nazism would aggravate the regime's violence.[52]

Hitler's coming to power ended the relative moderation in the Franco-British attitude toward sanctions on Germany that had prevailed from 1926 to 1932. In Britain, the work of Butler's American Committee on

Economic Sanctions and the Buell-Dewey debate had sparked a renewed interest in sanctions among journalists, foreign policy experts, and officials.[53] In the spring of 1933, Chatham House convened a special working group on economic sanctions that included jurist John Fischer Williams, disarmament advocate Philip Noel-Baker, liberal sinecurist Philip Kerr (Lord Lothian), long-standing prime ministerial secretary Thomas Jones, and professor-internationalist Alfred Zimmern. Government bureaucracies and military planning staffs like the ATB and CSDN no longer had a monopoly on the topic of sanctions, which was being taken up by broader groups of experts and commentators, especially at official and private think tanks and foundations.[54] In the British internationalist milieu, there were hopes that the incoming administration of Franklin Roosevelt would be more receptive to the use of economic pressure than its predecessor had been.

The sense that a new wind was blowing in Washington was strengthened by Norman Davis, Roosevelt's envoy to the World Disarmament Conference in Geneva. On 22 May, Davis declared to the world that the United States would not block or undermine any common action against an aggressor. If it agreed that aggression had taken place, then America would no longer insist on its neutral rights to defeat a League blockade or sanctions regime. Advocates of U.S.-League cooperation were overjoyed by Davis's speech. The French ambassador in Washington thought that it constituted "immense progress." U.S. cooperation was valuable in itself, but it also allowed Paris to overcome the long-standing British excuse for rejecting an automatic sanctions mechanism: that an absolute economic weapon would risk war with the United States.[55] To the French government, the rapidly growing political challenge of Nazi Germany made closer transatlantic alignment on this question a necessity.

That same month, British planners first studied German economic weaknesses. MacDonald instructed the ATB to investigate how economic pressure might prevent German rearmament. Since rebuilding its armed forces would violate the military clauses of the Versailles Treaty but not constitute inter-state aggression, an Article 16 procedure to trigger a general League embargo was impossible. Accordingly, the ATB planners had to assume that any campaign of economic pressure would take place outside the League and without a state of war. Only domestic measures by directly interested countries would be possible; participation would thus be restricted to, at best, Britain, France, Belgium, Poland, and the Little Entente of Czechoslovakia, Yugoslavia, and Romania. This group could not mount hermetic pressure, and German trade would probably evade the restrictions by being rerouted through third countries. Prohibitions on exports might merely divert German sales elsewhere; nor was the Reich very dependent on these seven European democracies for crucial imports. Under such constrained conditions it was "highly problematical whether . . . it would be possible to exert economic pressure on Germany which would be effective."[56]

The paradox of economic pressure on Germany in 1933 is that the Nazi regime anticipated it long before Western democracies were capable of concerted action. To the Nationalist Socialists, the foreign boycotts and protests were attributed to a nebulous Jewish world conspiracy that co-ordinated external pressure against them. This paranoia assumed greater proportions because of the many channels through which Germany was still materially dependent on the rest of the world: its external creditors, its imports of raw materials, and the capital of foreign investors.[57] In June the regime declared a partial moratorium on foreign debt repayment while embarking on a racial purge of its leading economic sectors.[58] To preserve its limited foreign exchange reserves, the Reich government began to re-strict drastically the amount of money that could be taken out of Germany and placed its industrial chambers of commerce under state control.[59] In August, bureaus for foreign exchange control (*Stellen für Devisenbewirt-schaftung*) began to restrict German citizens' purchases of tickets on for-eign ocean liners, effectively instituting a state ban on using U.S. and Brit-ish shipping companies.[60]

Germany's first major step toward a break with the Versailles order came on 14 October 1933, when the failure of disarmament talks sent Hitler into a rage. Lashing out against the outside world, the Führer an-nounced that Germany would withdraw from both the disarmament talks and the League of Nations. This brazen move was confirmed by the Ger-man foreign minister, Konstantin von Neurath, in a letter to the League's new secretary-general, the Frenchman Joseph Avenol. Within the Ger-man government the decision, though not unexpected, caught many un-prepared. Many German state officials and military officers in the 1920s and early 1930s detested the Versailles armaments restrictions and dis-trusted the League. But they did agree on one thing: the organization's sanctions power had to be taken very seriously.

Stresemann's old adviser, Bernhard von Bülow, had long worried about the threat of League sanctions. Having begun his career in the Kaiser's diplomatic service and rising to the rank of state secretary in the Weimar years, the chaos caused by the Nazi seizure of power thrust Bülow into effectively leading the Foreign Ministry.[61] In March 1933, he sketched the geopolitical landscape that Germany confronted. Since Britain possessed a "strong political, moral and financial position" and France remained "by far the strongest military power in the world," Germany should avoid provoking these countries.[62] Still, it was possible to slowly reduce vulnerabilities without infuriating the world's major powers. The key lay in focusing economic relations toward (south)eastern Europe, which formed an ideal expansionary zone. The small economies along the Danube were too dependent on sales to Germany to participate in sanctions against Berlin; furthermore, the overland and riverine links that sustained this trade could not be severed by blockade in case of war.[63] Bülow thought that "the existing dependence on the outside world . . . could not be gotten rid of"; nor, however, would this be desirable since it removed Germany's best "opportunities for political influence" vis-à-vis smaller countries.[64]

Throughout the year Bülow and Reich defense minister Werner von Blomberg tried to avoid international affronts. However, Hitler's unplanned departure from the League in October forced his military officials to prepare for the contingency of international retaliation.[65] On 25 October, Blomberg issued a directive to the army and navy commands and the air minister to prepare for defensive action "in the event of hostile sanctions."[66] Defense ministry planners expected that this would be a "sanctions war" under Article 16, involving everything from economic restrictions to blockade to the invasion and occupation of German territory. In fearing sanctions would inaugurate a war to crush Germany, the army was overestimating the severity of the League's reaction. Avenol and his secretariat in Geneva were taken aback by the decision and did not contemplate any immediate disciplinary action; at any rate, Hitler quickly moved to mollify Paris by suggesting Franco-German reconciliation.[67] But the sudden break prompted a military preparation that had lasting consequences. By interpreting sanctions as an existential threat to the Reich requiring a military response, the German military initiated what one of its historians has called "a spiral of insecurity whose end could not be foreseen."[68]

The departures of Japan and Germany meant that the League had lost two of its five permanent Council members in just seven months. Only Britain, France, and Italy remained as major powers upholding the Versailles order. It is tempting to conclude that the absence of any sanctions against Germany displayed these measures' weakness. Yet the months after

the Nazi departure suggest that their force was still something to be reck-
oned with. Instead of following Hitler in defying the League, in January 1934 Mussolini called specifically for "the elimination of sanctions
from the Covenant." While the Fascist leader obviously preferred a weaker
international organization, the fact that he tried to defuse its enforcement
mechanism suggests that these powers were significant to him. Mussolini
claimed he wanted the League to be a more practical organization, one
less devoted to preserving the status quo, and that "the present sanctions
should therefore be abolished or replaced by another system."[69] Secretary-
General Avenol's openness to working with dictatorships indicated that
Genevan internationalism was shifting from a liberal to a more apolitical
footing friendly to authoritarian governments.[70] But Fascist attempts to
disarm rather than ignore League sanctions hint at a continued trepida-
tion behind their brash show of self-confidence.

Embargo Ambiguities

One reason that revisionist states worried about the League's power to restrict trade was that in 1933–1934 a growing segment of the U.S. elite was
visibly exploring ways to cooperate with London, Paris, and Geneva in
this domain.[71] These American internationalists set their sights on passing legislation for embargoes on exports of armaments, munitions, and
war materiel.

Presidential power to impose arms embargoes had emerged in the
realm of the Monroe Doctrine as early twentieth-century administrations tried to police revolutionary and civil wars in Central America.[72]
The idea of a *discriminatory* embargo against one side or country in a conflict came from the Wilsonian tradition of righteous internationalism,
however. David Miller and Columbia law professor Joseph Chamberlain
had first proposed the idea in 1925–1926.[73] As Chamberlain put it, "There
would seem to be no reason why a nation could not make use of this economic weapon as a means of redress. . . . There is no customary international law under which a state is compelled to permit trade with other
states, so that the embargo could not be considered as a legal wrong committed against the state using it."[74] Early embargo proposals were forms
of domestic economic regulation with foreign policy goals; they were imposed on U.S. firms, not on foreign traders. A discriminatory embargo
against aggressors was first proposed in Congress in 1927, but neither this
proposal nor the 1929 Capper and Porter Resolutions to enforce the Paris

Pact with weapons bans were written into law. During the Manchurian crisis, internationalist attempts to institute a discriminatory embargo on Japan were successfully resisted by the arms industry. In March 1933, the return of a Democratic administration raised European expectations that a shift in policy might be possible.[75] The French Foreign Ministry hoped embargo legislation could change from an "instrument of national policy" to "a means of international cooperation."[76]

American advocates of collective security through arms control faced real difficulties. The tenth attempt to pass an embargo law, sponsored by Congressman Sam McReynolds, passed the House in April 1933. But one month later its Senate version was amended by California senator Hiram Johnson to apply the embargo impartially to *all* belligerents in a conflict.[77] This small modification entirely changed the meaning of state restrictions on foreign trade. Banning arms exports to *both* sides of a war turned what had been intended as a discriminatory embargo into an impartial war containment measure. It was a victory for the neutralists rather than the sanctionists. Johnson's amendment in turn became the bedrock of the Neutrality Acts of 1935, 1936, and 1937, which applied equally to all belligerents. In doing so, U.S. neutrality legislation undermined the discriminatory nature of the League's economic weapon against aggression.

Despite encouraging speeches, the United States therefore turned out to be at best a half-hearted sanctions partner, and at worst a totally obstructionist power. As the worldwide political situation worsened, European qualms about this aloofness became more acute. In November 1934, British prime minister Stanley Baldwin promised at a speech in Glasgow that "never so long as I have any responsibility in governing the country will I sanction the British Navy being used for an armed blockade of any country in the world until I know what the United States of America is going to do."[78] Indecision was diplomatically frustrating. But it also undermined the entire logic of deterrence that sanctionists saw as the real basis for a potent economic weapon.

Nonetheless, international arms embargoes developed significantly in this period. In September 1932, a war had erupted between Bolivia and Paraguay over the arid border region of the Gran Chaco. Fueled by Western arms exporters keen to find an outlet for their wares, the Chaco War escalated into a prolonged campaign of grueling marches, siege warfare, and envelopment battles in scrublands and dusty riverbeds—the bloodiest inter-state war in Latin America's twentieth-century history.[79] An early Franco-British proposal for a League arms embargo against Bolivia and

Paraguay was put before the Council in February 1933. But the executive body in Geneva could not decide so long as U.S. arms manufacturers remained outside any interdiction scheme.[80] By the summer Bolivia and Paraguay had mobilized 250,000 men. Capitalizing on desires to keep the League from interfering with Latin American affairs, U.S. internationalists made common cause with neutralists in Congress to restrict arms to both belligerents.[81] This led to the successful U.S. adoption of a Chaco embargo law in May 1934.

This initiative triggered a wider response. Instead of acting through the League, France and Britain now coordinated an international arms embargo outside of the Geneva circuit. By December 1934, twenty-seven countries had passed legislation banning weapons exports to the two Latin American nations. Accusations of cheating and evasion were widespread, but eventually most governments managed to force their arms-exporting firms to respect the controls.[82] In January 1935, the Chaco embargo took an unforeseen twist. League-sponsored armistice talks between the warring parties resulted in a ceasefire agreement, but only the Bolivian government in La Paz accepted this deal. Now that the country had complied with international norms, the international arms embargo on Bolivia was lifted.[83] Yet this left in place the restrictions against Paraguay, which was gripped by fears that it might soon become the target of an Article 16 sanctions procedure.[84] For a small landlocked country, the effect of international restrictions on arms imports by the world's major industrial countries was very disconcerting.[85] Indeed, faced with the external pressure of an arms embargo, Paraguay acted as Japan and Germany had done before and left the League in February. Although it had vanquished Bolivian troops in the field, the country's economy was too weakened to sustain the war much longer. In June 1935, the government in Asunción ended the conflict on favorable terms.

The general sweep of the Chaco embargo inspired the U.S. neutrality legislation adopted in August 1935.[86] Internationalists have castigated the neutralists for their parochial thinking and "isolationism."[87] But the 1930s arms embargoes were not so much a constraint on economic statecraft as an instance of it.[88] By imposing exports controls on the world's largest manufacturing economy, neutralists were, whether they saw it or not, making significant material interventions in world trade as well as geopolitics. This entanglement weakened the neutralists. Sanctionists in the Roosevelt administration suffered short-term defeat but in the long run had the wind in their sails. After 1935, when the legislative reform of the

Second New Deal coincided with the first Neutrality Act, all the neutralists could dispute was the aim of state control of commerce, not the intervention itself. Once it was accepted that the U.S. government should regulate trade with warring states *to avoid war*, it was only a short distance to regulating trade *to stop war*. Neutrality legislation, intended as a roadblock against U.S. global interventionism, eventually became a stepping-stone in its rise to primacy instead.

The Soviet Union and Sanctions

The international Chaco arms embargo had one unusual participant: the Union of Soviet Socialist Republics. In 1934 Stalin and his commissar for foreign affairs, Maxim Litvinov, initiated a new turn in Soviet foreign policy and came out in support of collective security.[89] On 18 September, three months after joining the Chaco embargo, the Soviet Union officially entered the League as a permanent Council member next to Britain, France, and Italy. Soviet participation was a sign that Geneva was not fatally crippled after the departures of Japan and Germany the previous year. More importantly, Moscow's adherence to the Covenant seriously increased the leverage of the organization's economic pressure. The Soviet government's trade monopoly meant that it would have no problems overcoming private resistance to commercial restrictions. Moreover, as ATB analysts concluded in the aftermath of the German break with Geneva, the Nazi regime continued to have fragilities that could be targeted.[90] Sanctions against German exports could reduce its foreign exchange earnings enough to throttle Hitler's planned rearmament. The ATB surmised that if Germany's already falling foreign trade shrank further, the regime would have to choose between allocating scarce reserves to importing food and civilian necessities or to the army's raw materials needs.[91] Indeed, by the summer of 1934, the Reichsbank held barely a week's worth of hard currency with which to finance purchases abroad, suggesting that banning German goods from major export markets would have had an immediate effect on the capacity to pay for imports.

Whether this damage would have sufficed to topple the Nazis is open to debate. But it certainly seems it would have thrown a serious wrench into Germany's economic recovery and rearmament at a crucial point in the consolidation of the regime. Bülow was concerned that "Without mobilizing a single man or firing a single shot, [our opponents] can place us in the most difficult situation by setting up a financial and economic blockade against us, either covert or overt."[92] What held Britain back from taking such action was not just political caution among the Conservative elite. ATB sanctions planners identified two material risks. One was the damage that sanctions on an economy of Germany's size would inflict on Britain's own foreign trade. The other issue was financial entanglement. British banks held an average of £40–60 million in German short-term debt, on which the Reich dutifully paid interest. Any financial blockade would cause default and require these assets to be written off, damaging the balance sheets of British financial institutions. Financial pressure could thereby unintentionally trigger a solvency crisis for the City of London.

The cunning German finance minister and Reichsbank chairman Hjalmar Schacht was aware of this threat of contagion and exploited British banks' proximity to the Reich to deflect London's political opposition to Nazi policies. Germany's debtor leverage against Britain was further strengthened by Schacht's New Plan, introduced in September 1934. This moved German trade relations onto a bilateral footing. Using a clearing system in which reciprocal deliveries of goods were tallied up and only the difference was settled in currency, the New Plan restricted foreign exchange expenditure to an absolute minimum.[93] The New Plan was not designed to counter economic sanctions, but by conserving precious monetary reserves, it reduced the risk that blows to foreign trade would force the abandonment of political goals. In this Germany was not alone: all medium-sized states that engaged in rapid rearmament in the 1930s confronted balance-of-payments issues, as they found that the quantity of currency reserves acted as a material constraint on their foreign policy. Sanctions planners increasingly took note of this widespread foreign exchange weakness and designed measures to aggravate it.

The Soviet arrival in Geneva thus opened possibilities for anti-German sanctions. But the united anti-German front was threatened by the shifting and unstable position of Italy. The Great Depression had radicalized Fascist foreign policy.[94] In the fall of 1932, Mussolini and his minister of colonies, Emilio De Bono, began planning the conquest of Ethiopia. Haile Selassie's East African monarchy became the fixture of Fascist plans for imperialist expansion and colonial settlement.[95] In February 1934, the Italian leadership set the date for invasion at the end of the monsoon rains in the early fall of 1935. Military buildup had to begin immediately. What hampered this process was not the League but Hitler. Mussolini was becoming worried about growing Nazi influence in Austria, whose independence he considered foundational to Italian security. The Italian Army had prepared a blueprint, Plan 34, for a military invasion of the Alpine republic if a Nazi insurgency broke out in Austria. That summer, German subterfuge indeed threatened to bring Austria under Nazi influence. After the assassination of Chancellor Engelbert Dollfuß in a botched German-supported coup in July, Mussolini massed several divisions in Tyrol and threatened to invade unless the existing regime remained in place. Hitler backed down. But these tensions in the Alps significantly delayed Rome's plans for colonial war in Africa, as the reinforcement of Italian forces in Eritrea was put on hold pending the stabilization of the European situation.[96] Only in December 1934, after a skirmish between Italian and Ethiopian border troops occurred at Wal Wal in the Ogaden Desert, did Mussolini order preparations for the planned invasion to continue.

While Italian reinforcements arrived in East Africa, and the League appointed a commission to investigate the Wal Wal incident, Hitler pushed his defiance of the Versailles Treaty further. In March 1935 he re-instituted general conscription in the Reich, expanding the Reichswehr from 100,000 to 300,000 men. The French government was in the final stages of concluding a mutual assistance treaty with the Soviet Union and proposed to capitalize on this impending alliance by stopping Germany's rearmament with targeted sanctions. Paris wanted to steer clear of a food blockade that would enable Nazi propagandists to claim the League was trying to "starve out the German people." But when it came to the raw materials essential for armaments production, Britain, France, and the Soviet Union were in a powerful position. The three states possessed a substantial part of the world's manganese, chromium, nickel, and magnesium carbonate and controlled flows of bauxite, wolfram, and molybdenum into the Reich.[97]

In April 1935 the French government put this plan before Britain and Italy at a meeting at the Piedmontese lakeside town of Stresa. The proposal's anti-German sanctions focused on mineral restrictions in collaboration with the Soviets, whose heft in trade negotiations was growing due to the German need for their raw materials during rearmament.[98] Shortly afterward, German diplomats indicated to the British that they would consider mutual non-aggression pacts. The Stresa coalition seemed capable of scaring Hitler. "It means that Germany is willing to play, that she is worried about the idea of a general economic boycott," wrote the *New York Times'* Moscow correspondent Walter Duranty, "that the big and hitherto successful bluff that Germany has put up against the rest of Europe is not proof against the German fear that Stresa may hit Germany on her tender spot, namely, foreign trade and raw materials and finance."[99]

As defenders of the European status quo, Britain and France held the key to deciding where collective sanctions against aggression should be focused.[100] They faced a choice between halting Germany's erosion of the Versailles Treaty in Europe or stopping Mussolini's preparations for aggression in Africa. To contain Nazi rearmament, the liberal democracies needed to preserve a working relationship with Italy. Implementing Article 16 required unanimity on the Council, meaning that Italy's permanent seat gave Mussolini a crucial role in approving sanctions against Hitler.[101] But if the League had to check Fascist encroachment against its African member Ethiopia, reining in Rome took precedence over the containment of Germany. The latter prospect was disliked by the French elite, for whom Germany remained the ultimate threat to European peace. During the 1920s France had guarded against this danger by orchestrating the Little Entente in East-Central Europe.[102] But Hitler's rapidly growing power meant that no plausible containment plan could work without a strong eastern pole. The League's most viable anti-aggression coalition was therefore a replica of the Triple Entente of 1907–1917, except that Britain and France were now in alliance with the Soviet Union rather than tsarist Russia.[103]

France's mineral sanctions scheme at Stresa was the first Western proposal to build on the Soviet turn to collective security. Litvinov was prepared to join the Western democracies in the defense of Article 16 but had to struggle to overcome deep-seated anti-communist attitudes in Western capitals.[104] Stalin also took the German threat seriously, supporting talks with Paris and Prague that supported French-Soviet and Czechoslovak-Soviet mutual assistance treaties.[105] The question that remained was whether Britain would accept Moscow as a real partner. In May 1935, Anthony Eden became the first British foreign minister to visit the Soviet Union. Conversing with Stalin in the Kremlin, Eden pointed out Britain's small size on the map, compared to the enormous expanse of the USSR. "Yes, a small island," Stalin responded, "but a lot depends on it. If this small island tells Germany, 'We will not give you money, raw materials, metal,' peace in Europe would be guaranteed."[106]

In London, Soviet ambassador Ivan Maisky also pursued a joint Anglo-French-Soviet sanctions effort to nip Nazi expansion in the bud. The problem, once again, was Italy. Mussolini's pro-League policy against Germany in Europe clashed with his anti-League policy in East Africa. As a Council member, Italy could not be allowed to attack another sovereign member state. But how could the Fascists in Rome be forced back into a European coalition against the Nazis? Maisky suggested that if Baldwin was a clever imperialist, he should explicitly threaten sanctions on Italy, including the closure of the Suez Canal. This would cut off the shortest sea route to supply the Fascist expeditionary force in East Africa and force Mussolini to the negotiating table; perhaps Il Duce could be bought off with an ex-German mandate territory under French or British control? "Not only would the prestige of the League of Nations be considerably raised," Maisky thought, "but the united front of Great Britain, France, Italy and the USSR against the German threat would be consolidated, and the paths to relative calm in Europe would be opened."[107]

Difficulties of Deterrence

Could the situation have turned so favorably? Throughout his preparations for war against Ethiopia, Mussolini remained deeply distrustful of Germany. When he heard about Nazi agitation against him in May 1935, Mussolini wrote to the Italian consul in Munich that "all bridges with Germany are broken. If she wishes to co-operate for the peace of Europe, so much the better; otherwise we will crush her, for in the future we stand completely on the side of the Western powers."[108] This was not mere braggadocio. In June, the French and Italian military staffs drew up plans for a combined trans-Alpine invasion of Bavaria if Hitler annexed Austria.[109] At Stresa, MacDonald had reaffirmed that London would stand with Paris and Rome against Germany as guarantors of the Versailles and Locarno treaties.[110] Most contemporary analysts expected Hitler's next provocation to come in Austria or against Danzig in Poland or Memel in Lithuania. All these actions would suffice to trigger Article 16 sanctions led by the four permanent members of the Council: London, Paris, Rome, and Moscow.[111]

But behind closed doors the British elite was much less enthusiastic about internationalism. Whitehall preferred to strike a deal with Germany to keep threats to its global imperial position—such as Italy's menace to East Africa—under control. The chiefs of staff were worried about the readiness of the empire's armed forces and insisted that "this country should not become involved in war within the next few years. We cannot urge too strongly . . . that no opportunity should be lost to avert the risk of war."[112] London also rebuffed the Franco-Soviet plans for mineral sanctions against Nazi Germany. When the ATB finally reviewed the Stresa sanctions plans in early June, it dismissed them as "ineffective."[113] But the three reasons cited for this decision—a backlash against British foreign trade, leakage to opportunist countries, and the risk of financial crisis to London—showed that a lack of force was not the problem for British planners. Only evasion through third countries really constituted a weakness, and even this was a soluble problem if diplomatic effort was put into enforcement. In fact, both the fear of commercial blowback and concerns about a City of London meltdown testified to the very substantial side effects of sanctions rather than to their weakness. Politicians might prevaricate about their commitments. But to those who grappled with the concrete options for exploiting interdependence in the 1930s, it was clear that despite the Great Depression the economic weapon still possessed considerable power. The bluster of fascist leaders and the fecklessness of some of their democratic rivals were self-interested denials of this reality.

Internationalist civil society groups committed to the League and opposed to fascism most resolutely proclaimed the power of economic sanctions. In the spring and summer of 1935, growing center-left political support for these measures was apparent in Britain. During the preceding months, the LNU had mobilized some eleven million voters to take part in the Peace Ballot, a privately organized referendum about support for Geneva and its peace agenda. On 27 June, Cecil personally announced the results at Royal Albert Hall, and these surprised even him: an overwhelming majority expressed support for economic sanctions (10 million yes votes against 600,000 "no" votes) and, if necessary, even military sanctions (6.7 million "yes" votes against 2.3 million "no" votes). On the whole, 86.8 percent of the eleven million respondents supported the economic weapon, and three-quarters backed military action.

The announcement of the Peace Ballot's results did exactly what Cecil and the LNU leaders had hoped. Overnight, the electoral calculus among the British elite changed. With an enormous constituency that was unabashedly internationalist and in favor of economic pressure and even military force, the Conservatives changed tack and began to speak more positively about sanctions. By this time, a very broad left-liberal bloc already supported immediate sanctions on Fascist Italy as it prepared for war. Some MPs even called for Britain to close the Suez Canal.[114] British and French labor unions also came out in favor of sanctions, as did the Communist parties in the Third International, which backed Moscow's collective security line to the hilt.[115] Only a few leftists opposed both Mussolini's impending aggression and the League sanctions that would be deployed against it. The Trinidadian Trotskyist C. L. R. James attacked Stalin's arguments for the economic weapon as "criminal nonsense." James declared that the working-class movement to which he belonged would "support Abyssinia as Lenin supported Afghanistan against Britain, [but it] will not allow itself to be caught in the Imperialist trap" by supporting the defense of the British Empire and Geneva's sanctions.[116] Against state-directed sanctions, James supported the emancipatory potential of the boycott, which he called "workers' sanctions."[117]

Considering the quickly shifting debate surrounding the possibility of sanctions against Italy, was the deterrence of the economic weapon in 1935 weak or strong? The retrospective perception that League sanctions were a paper tiger is not reflected in the accounts of contemporaries. In the months leading up to the Italo-Ethiopian War, the growing resolve to use sanctions against Mussolini was palpable. Spurred by the Peace Ballot, the Tories took more direct action to stem the escalation of conflict. On 25 July, pending the results of a League inquiry into the Wal Wal incident, Britain imposed an embargo on the export of arms to both Italy and Ethiopia, joining France, Switzerland, Belgium, and Czechoslovakia.[118] Stanley Baldwin was a cautious Conservative imperialist much warier of collective security than the internationalists around Cecil. But in the heady atmosphere of the times he too started to deliver ebullient defenses of the economic weapon. After returning to office in May, Baldwin affirmed that countries that threatened international peace would face the combined strength of Britain and the United States; "the immediate power of the uniform blockade, and a refusal to trade or lend money, would be a sanction that no country on earth would dare face."[119] In Vienna, the economic journalist Karl Polanyi aptly described the rising mood of international vigilance against aggression: "In the Anglo-Saxon parts of the world a pacifist-sanctionist religion is doing the rounds. . . . It fights for peace, but not for the status quo. It stands for conservative dynamism."[120]

CHAPTER EIGHT

The Greatest Experiment in
Modern History, 1935–1936

THE FASCIST INVASION OF Ethiopia was the first occasion on which the League's economic weapon was put into full operation. Sanctions against Mussolini had been anticipated for months due to border skirmishes and the Italian troop buildup in East Africa. By September 1935, governments around the world expected Geneva to take action if war broke out. They were right to presuppose that if an Article 16 sanctions procedure was implemented, its target would be the Fascist regime in Rome. At the annual Assembly on 11 September, both French prime minister Laval and British secretary for league affairs Anthony Eden publicly announced their intention to use economic sanctions if Il Duce attacked.[1] After Mussolini invaded Ethiopia on 3 October, the League wasted little time in designating Italy the aggressor and hashed out a package of sanctions that was brought into effect six weeks later. Its under secretary-general, the Irishman Sean Lester, described it as the start of "the greatest experiment in modern history."[2]

League sanctions did not compel Italy to break off its war, nor did they save the government of Emperor Haile Selassie or the independence of the Ethiopians. Italy's conquest was completed by the end of spring 1936. Amid acrimony and dejection, the last measures were lifted by July. The conventional interpretation is that sanctions in the Italo-Ethiopian War were a fiasco that sounded the death knell of the League—and with it, the disintegration of collective security as a whole.[3] Historian A. J. P. Taylor expressed this view most forcefully: "The real death of the League," he argued, "was in December 1935, not in 1939 or 1945."[4] While the failure of the League to contain aggression is undeniable, its wider implications are more complex. In the interwar history of sanctions, three particular aspects of the episode stand out. The first is that the actual use of peacetime economic sanctions inaugurated a new phase in their development, forcing a change in how the force of the economic weapon was conceived. For a decade after the world war, it was the virtual threat of material isolation that had sufficed as a peace-ensuring device. This deterrence had worked against Yugoslavia in 1921 and Greece in 1925. What differed in 1935 was that sanctions confronted a relatively large industrialized state that was both ideologically and materially invested in militarism and colonial conquest. This forced sanctions out of the virtual domain and into the realm of actual application.

Second, the need to move from abstraction to action involved a redesign of economic pressure. One measure that the League's sanctions planners proposed but never implemented was an oil embargo against Italy.[5] Mussolini was rightly fearful of this option. Even if it is dubious whether this policy would have been immediately effective, Il Duce certainly seems to have believed it would spell the end of his African adventure.[6] But to judge the sanctions by the yardstick of the potential energy blockade overlooks the actual model on which British and French policymakers had pinned their hopes: a finance-focused approach to sanctions rather than a resource-based one. Economists rather than naval experts were the driving force behind this design. Their "Treasury theory" of sanctions aimed to hit aggressor states where they were weakest: in their foreign exchange reserves. The trade collapse of the Great Depression had rendered hard currency in short supply, and the way to drive this stock down further was to block Fascist *exports* from world markets. Pressure on the balance of payments was at the heart of the Treasury theory, whose novelty has been missed by the evocativeness of the more classical "Admiralty theory" of throttling imports of key commodities. But as economic historians have shown, in the harsh world-economic environment of the 1930s foreign exchange reserves *were* a key commodity.[7] The advantage of currency-draining sanctions was that they were less onerous to the states using them and less immediately provocative to their targets. But this gradualism was also their main weakness: by tightening the budgetary constraints on warfare without immediately barring its possibility, export bans enabled Mussolini, and other aggressors after him, to take high-risk decisions for ruthless conquest rather than to moderate their aims.

The third key aspect of the Italo-Ethiopian sanctions is the influence that they exerted on the strategic situation faced by revisionist states like Italy, Nazi Germany, and Japan. Far from being derided as ineffective, League sanctions were observed in these countries with apprehension and anxiety. Their turn to autarky had begun under the impact of the Great Depression but was strengthened by sanctions. Even if imperfectly exe-cuted, the League sanctions showed that internationalist coalitions could quickly coalesce to organize economic pressure that might well be ex-panded, reviving fears of a repetition of the 1914–1918 blockade.

These three points suggest that the Italo-Ethiopian War did not end collective security so much as open a new chapter in its development. Brit-ain and France did not just craft a new approach to the economic weapon in 1935–1936. They came close to extending it laterally when the Roosevelt administration tried to modify its neutrality legislation. The other oppor-tunity that was narrowly missed was expanding anti-aggression measures in depth by organizing financial and logistic help to the Ethiopians. Both options foreshadowed the reinvention of internationalist alliance warfare that would mark the next decade.[8] Attritional sanctions did not prevent the conquest of Ethiopia, but they seriously deformed the Italian econ-omy, forcing difficult choices on the Fascist regime and shaping the au-tarkic orientation of German and Japanese elites as well. After 1935, these states mobilized themselves on a wartime footing and fought and funded conflicts in Spain and China in an increasingly desperate effort to escape their material vulnerabilities.[9]

Interdependence and the Great Depression

To understand the politics of economic sanctions in the 1930s, we must first grasp how the world economy in which they intervened was affected by the Great Depression. The global slump was a shocking, transforma-tive event and a watershed in modern economic history. As commodity prices fell, farmers and firms went bust; stock markets crashed while in-vestors panicked, banks failed, and cabinets tottered. Governments re-sponded by raising tariff barriers, defaulting on their debts, leaving the gold standard, adopting capital and exchange controls, and engaging in competitive currency devaluations. These dramatic shocks ended the lib-eral economic order that had been built up since the mid-nineteenth century. What the depression did not end, however, was the basic fact that major industrial economies were materially dependent on the rest of the world. The 1930s saw massive shifts in the world-economic landscape, but the potential of sanctions was less affected by them than one would expect.

Trade, often taken as a proxy for the slump as a whole, is an illustrative example. As the EFO's annual surveys showed, world trade fell precipitously from $68.6 billion in 1929 to $23.4 billion in 1934.[10] This collapse was severe in monetary and commercial terms, but it was less marked in material terms. Whereas world trade fell by two-thirds measured *by value* at market prices, the decline *in volume* of actual goods exchanged was about one-third.[11] Between 1924 and 1929 the volume of global commerce had grown at the very high rate of 6 percent per year.[12] Even the sizable subsequent collapse meant that the physical volume of world trade fell not to any pre-globalization low but to the very high levels of integration of the immediate pre–World War I era. For most of the 1930s, the total volume of world trade remained *above* its 1913 level.[13] Moreover, most of the trade volume decline caused by the depression occurred in high value-added manufactured goods. Trade volumes in raw materials and food were less affected and rebounded quickly.[14] In other words, the 1930s witnessed a virtually undiminished physical quantity of commodities circulating around the world—not to mention other important benchmarks of globalization, such as migration.[15] The notion of a drastic and unqualified interwar "deglobalization" is thus misleading; insofar as it applies, it is to price levels, capital, and monetary indicators rather than to the circulation of people, production, and commodities.[16]

By the late 1930s world trade had also become much more regionally distributed than in the fin-de-siècle years. In 1913 Europe accounted for nearly 60 percent of global exports. By 1937 its share had shrunk by almost a quarter, whereas the Americas, Africa, Asia, and Oceania all gained in global market shares.[17] The faith that European elites had placed in the economic weapon during the war reflected the confidence bestowed by the continent's dominant trade position in the 1910s. A quarter century later, non-European economies had claimed a more active role in the global market. Supposed interwar deglobalization is thus more accurately described as the "de-Europeanization" of a world economy that remained deeply global.[18]

In general, how the downturn affected overall trade values and volumes was less important to sanctions than how it shaped specific sectors. The depression had mixed effects on interdependence in transport,

Table 8.1 Countries Ranked by Size of Merchant Marines, 1914 and 1937

Rank	1914	GRT (millions of tons)	Share of Global Total (%)	1937	GRT (millions of tons)	Share of Global Total (%)
1.	Britain	21	50.4	Britain	20.6	37.9
2.	Germany	5.5	13.2	United States	12.4	22.8
3.	United States	5.4	13	Japan	4.5	8.3
4.	Norway	2.5	6	Norway	4.3	7.9
5.	France	2.3	5.5	Germany	3.9	7.2
6.	Japan	1.7	4	Italy	3.2	5.9
7.	Italy	1.7	4	France	2.8	5.2
8.	Netherlands	1.5	3.6	Netherlands	2.6	4.8
	Total	41.6		Total	54.3	

energy, and minerals. Shipping was both an economic sector and a form of global infrastructure not fully captured in export statistics, yet one that was crucial to enforcing sanctions. In the 1930s the largest merchant marine was the British transport fleet, followed by the American and Japanese fleets, which had boomed during World War I. Smaller competitors such as the German, Norwegian, Italian, French, and Dutch fleets each constituted 3–4 percent of global tonnage. Germany and Italy retained a fairly strong position despite the downturn in international maritime transport. As table 8.1 shows, the interwar period had been a growth phase for the shipping industry.[19] But the global merchant marine shrank for four consecutive years from 1932 to 1935, meaning that overall tonnage in 1937 had fallen back to its 1921 level, when Allied fleets had been swelled by wartime construction.[20] Since the early postwar years, the rise of the Japanese, Norwegian, and German fleets by the late 1930s was noticeable. The problem for sanctionists was not the deglobalization of oceanic traffic, but the increasing dispersal of control: by the late 1930s the three revisionist powers (Italy, Germany, and Japan) controlled about 20 percent of global tonnage, and the tonnage of ships under a "neutral" (Dutch, Norwegian, or U.S.) flag doubled from fifteen million tons in 1914 to at least thirty million tons.[21]

Technological change further complicated global commodity control on the seas. Most new merchant vessels built after the war were powered by fuel oil—also known as heavy oil—which they used to heat steam boilers or power internal combustion engines. Between 1914 and 1934, the number of coal-powered merchant vessels fell from 88 to 51 percent of global tonnage, and the number of oil-powered ships grew from 3 to 46 percent of the world's cargo fleet.[22] As the ATB had recognized in the mid-1920s, this meant that a system of coal bunker control was no longer feasible in a future conflict.[23] Oil production was too diffuse and located largely outside the British Empire, in countries such as the United States, the Soviet Union, Venezuela, and Mexico.[24] The only way to turn fuel control into a global disciplinary tool was for the British and Americans to cooperate with the Dutch, who through Royal Dutch Shell controlled important shares of Middle Eastern and Southeast Asian oil production, especially the major source of oil in East Asia—the Dutch East Indies.[25]

The Anglo-American-Dutch preponderance in the global oil market was emblematic of a wider concentration in global minerals production. In 1938, ten countries controlled 71 percent of the world's minerals; four countries held 52 percent of known reserves; and the United States by itself had 29 percent of global minerals at its disposal. Britain and France did not possess many minerals in their metropolitan territories other than coal and iron, but they controlled large amounts in their colonial empires and informally through British and French private companies operating abroad. If these shadow corporate holdings were included in their national totals, the effective concentration of minerals was even more extreme, implying Anglo-American control of over 51 percent and a U.S.-British-French-German-Soviet oligopoly comprising 74 percent of global supply.[26] As table 8.2 shows, the "minerals premium" conferred by formal and corporate empire was especially large for the United Kingdom, which held only 4.5 percent of global mineral reserves in the British Isles but possessed 21.6 percent through overseas territories and companies in Latin America, Africa, the Middle East, and Asia. All together, the League of Nations saw its members' control of the most important commercial minerals remain stable over the course of the 1930s, at slightly over half of global supply.[27] While the share of the revisionist anti-Comintern powers grew, by 1936 it was still less than a quarter of what the League controlled; the Soviet arrival in Geneva compensated for Japan's and Germany's departures.

The League was thus a potentially powerful apparatus of resource control. But the core states behind the Genevan order, Britain and France,

Table 8.2. Possession of Key Minerals, 1929 and 1936

	Share of Global Total in 1929 (%)	Share of Global Total in 1936 (%)
League of Nations	53.5	52.4
Revisionist powers (Germany, Italy, Japan)	9.6	11.6
United States	34.2	29.0
British Empire	21.2	21.6
Soviet Union	3.8	9.2
Germany	7.1	8.2
French Empire	7.8	6.0
Canada	5.2	5.4
Metropolitan France	5.9	4.7
United Kingdom	4.6	4.5
Japanese Empire	1.2	2.9
South Africa	3.3	2.6
Mexico	3.0	2.5
Australia	1.6	1.9
Italy	1.3	1.5

Note: Minerals counted here are the twenty-eight "major minerals of commerce": aluminum, antimony, chromite, copper, iron, lead, manganese, mercury, nickel, tin, tungsten, zinc, asbestos, barite, china clay, coal, fluorspar, graphite, gypsum, magnesite, mica, nitrates, petroleum, phosphates, potash, pyrites, sulphur, and talc.

could not make this dominance effective on their own. They needed the cooperation of the United States as well as the Soviet Union, the state that had most significantly improved its raw materials situation in the 1930s as it recorded breakneck growth in the first two Five-Year Plans.

That very phenomenon, extensive economic growth, provided another reason for the continued power of sanctions. Economists began to realize that what mattered in a war economy was not just the supply of raw materials but the rate at which they were consumed. In this regard the forces of population growth, urbanization, and rising living standards rendered the structure of interwar societies more fragile. On an annual basis, industrial economies in 1930 consumed twice as much coal and nine times as much oil as they had done in 1900.[28] This heightened material through-put meant that shortages of raw materials would bite more quickly than before. Finally, importing at elevated rates also required sufficient currency reserves. Given how unevenly such reserves were distributed, some countries were much more vulnerable to sanctions than others. As *The Economist* wryly noted, "Access to the world's natural resources is generally free, except in time of war, to all comers who can pay for them—like the Ritz Hotel."[29]

The Admiralty and Treasury Theories of Sanctions

Fascist Italy had been in the crosshairs of British and French strategic planners for some time. Their first studies (produced in 1931 and 1933, respectively) were encouraging. Admiralty analysts contended that "the most favorable target for the Economic Weapon is a country which is highly industrialised, largely dependent on foreign foodstuffs and raw materials, and whose military strength exceeds its power of economic resistance . . . [meaning] that it is easier to wear down its civil population by economic methods than to compel its military forces to submission by strength of arms."[30] Italy's economy fit these criteria well, as it drew raw materials largely from overseas using the seventh-largest merchant marine in the world. In fuel, external supply was crucial to the Italian economy: 47 percent of its coal and 99 percent of its oil were supplied through maritime transport.[31] Naval planning, informed by wartime inter-Allied blockade, naturally leaned toward a sanctions strategy focused on interdicting commodities.

Given the need for political flexibility in confronting revisionist states like Italy and Germany, there were drawbacks to this "Admiralty theory" of sanctions. To begin with, acquiring control over entire categories of commodities produced in various locales around the world required large diplomatic coalitions. Moreover, the depression had caused tensions over unfair competition, tariff wars, and resource monopolies to run high. Whatever goodwill remained for the use of economic sanctions might well evaporate if the entire project ended up producing mechanisms for the permanent control of certain goods on world markets. For these reasons, civilian sanctions planners gravitated toward a different sanctions design, one that was lighter in touch but, it was hoped, more effective at a lower political cost.

This "Treasury theory" of sanctions deemphasized restricting vital

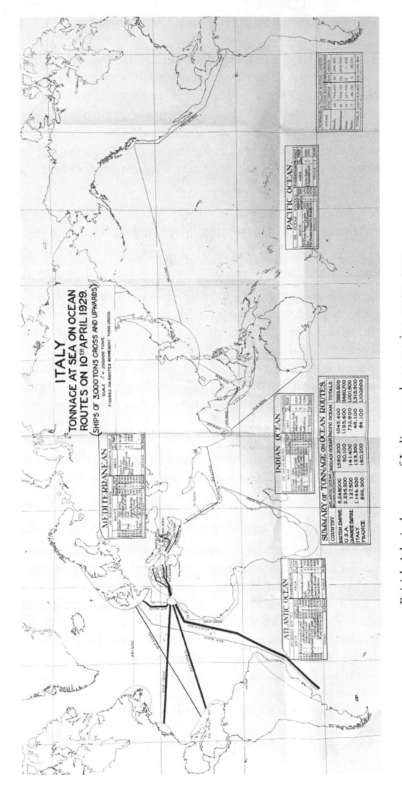

British Admiralty map of Italian merchant marine routes, 1929.
The National Archives of the UK.

commodities. Instead it sought to exploit Italy's weak balance-of-payments position. It was common knowledge in London that Rome had been unable to access international financial markets for sovereign borrowing for some time. The only links between Wall Street and the City of London, on the one hand, and the Italian economy, on the other, ran through private banks. As signs of impending war grew during 1935, many American and British bankers cut down the amount of credit that they were offering Italian borrowers. Even major industrial firms such as tire manufacturer Pirelli, carmaker Fiat, and the chemicals conglomerate Montecatini were being denied twelve-month financing for their import needs by the Bank of England and London merchant banks.[32] ATB analysts pointed out that "the distrust of Italy's position which is universal abroad is, in fact, already imposing something in the nature of a financial blockade upon Italy."[33] In this distressed situation, the real lever that British sanctionists could exploit was Italy's limited capacity to pay simultaneously for military expenditures *and* vital imports, both of which were financed from a limited pool of earnings.

Ex-League chief Eric Drummond, who had been appointed British ambassador in Rome, reported that Italy had spent £11.5 million on its military reinforcements in the first six months of 1935. Once another fifty-thousand-man contingent of the expeditionary force had arrived in Africa, expenditures would rise to £40 million per year. Given that in July the Bank of Italy held only £92 million sterling (5.5 billion lira) in reserves, military and civilian outlays were now directly competing for the same reduced supply of funds. Just as in the case of Nazi Germany, the ATB therefore concluded that foreign exchange reserves were the weakest link in the entire Fascist economy. It recommended that sanctions should target the source of Italy's reserve accumulation—its exports—as much as its imports. If all League members closed their markets to its exports, Italy's annual hard currency earnings could be reduced by as much as 73 percent.[34]

From this point of view, allowing Mussolini to continue reinforcing his army corps in the Horn of Africa merely gave him more rope with which to hang himself. Once sanctions kicked in, maintaining a larger mechanized European army abroad would require vast quantities of money for food, fuel, clothing, transport, and maintenance, all of which would increase the drain on Italy's fragile government budget and monetary reserves. Another ATB report on how to apply economic pressure directly on the Italian armies put it as follows:

Italian ships delivering supplies to the Eritrean port of Massawa during
the military buildup three months before Mussolini's invasion of Ethiopia,
July 1935. Smith Archive/Alamy Stock Photo.

Apart from the possibility of acute difficulties arising in the actual
zone of operations in East Africa owing to the lack of such necessaries as water, cereals and petroleum products, Italy's difficulties
would probably first manifest themselves in a general shortage of
the foreign exchange resources necessary to purchase her essential requirements rather than in particular shortages of particular articles. . . . Therefore, it would appear to be unnecessary to
take exceptionally drastic measures designed to prevent Italy from
obtaining particular essential requirements . . . provided that a
reasonable assurance could be obtained that she pays through the
nose for any supplies which she does secure.[35]

This aim to make the aggressor "pay through the nose" emerged as a distinct model of how sanctions could cut short ambitions for war. It was a
theory of attrition rather than a deterrent. The British and French governments expected that in the face of an economic threat, Mussolini would
not budge as quickly as Pašić and Pangalos had done in the 1920s. But they

were confident that they could wear down Italian endurance while staying clear of actual war.[36] On the basis of this estimation, British foreign secretary Samuel Hoare and French prime minister Pierre Laval agreed at the League Assembly in mid-September to rule out more invasive sanctions, such as an oil embargo, closure of the Suez Canal, or a naval blockade, as unnecessarily provocative.[37]

In France, policymakers also began to favor an attritional strategy targeting exports. When the CSDN studied the possibilities for sanctions against Germany in 1935, its priority was avoiding the appearance of starving the German people. French planners thought that "the most barbaric sanctions [are] those that aim at food, and to a lesser degree at textiles," an industry that employed a large number of Germans. Wrecking this manufacturing sector might produce unemployment and strikes, but this social effect would not guarantee the weakening of German military production that French strategists were seeking to achieve. Cutting off vital commodities would not work quickly enough because of the German "genius for replacement [génie de l'Ersatz]." Thus the CSDN concluded that a "boycott of German exports appears preferable to blockade or embargo measures."[38]

The extensive preparation for sanctions in Paris and London in 1935 shows that neither government was caught unawares by Italy's decision to embark on war or by the need to impose sanctions in response. By August, English-language newspapers were already explaining to their readers how economic sanctions against Italy would work.[39] British and French strategists were entirely prepared.[40] For his part, Mussolini had gone too far to back down. With over four hundred thousand men already on the African continent, Fascist Italy had invested so much in the venture that its military buildup had acquired a momentum of its own. Mussolini had relayed the invasion order to his forces in East Africa on 27 September; the attack was planned for dawn seven days later.[41]

War in East Africa

On 3 October 1935, Italian troops invaded Haile Selassie's empire in a double pincer movement, southward from Eritrea and westward from Somalia. Watched by an international community ready to take action against them, they needed to obtain territorial results quickly. Nearly half a million strong, Italian commander Emilio De Bono's army was the largest military force ever sent to the African continent by a European state, numbering three hundred thousand Italian troops, eighty-seven thousand askaris, and one hundred thousand laborers employed in road building and other work-creation schemes.[42] On the way to the Ethiopian capital, Addis Ababa, De Bono intended to pause periodically to reinforce his army before pushing on, in a leap-frogging movement, to conserve strength and avoid overstretched supply lines.

The caution of De Bono's land-based campaign plan stood in stark contrast to the risk entailed in its maritime foundations. Italy's invasion was supplied in an intercontinental operation ferrying a constant stream of troops, materiel, and provisions from Italian ports through the Suez Canal to its two bridgeheads in Eritrea and Somalia—a total distance of between 2,200 and 3,600 kilometers (1,370–2,240 miles). It was risky for any state at an intermediate level of economic development to undertake a sustained military effort across such distance, let alone to do so across sea lanes controlled by other countries and on the basis of limited financial strength.[43]

Despite the fact it had invaded Ethiopia without a declaration of war, Italy was declared the aggressor by the League within four days. On 7 October, the Council ordered the creation of a committee comprising eighteen member states that would study, compose, and report on a package of sanctions under Article 16. The Portuguese diplomat Augusto de Vasconcellos was appointed chair of this "Committee of Eighteen" or Coordination Committee. In the space of two weeks, his group outlined a package of five economic sanctions: an arms embargo, a financial freeze, an import embargo, a range of export prohibitions on specific commodities and goods, and a mutual support fund. The sanctions went into effect on 18 November and were applied fairly consistently by fifty-two out of fifty-eight League member states. It was a remarkable feat of transnational coordination. Article 16 had finally been put to the test against aggression. In an air of nervous excitement, the Geneva correspondent for the *New York Herald Tribune* wrote that "the remarkable and unprecedented achievement of getting nearly fifty sovereign states to agree on collective measures for taking sanctions . . . has enormously enhanced the prestige of the League. All the observers on the Geneva scene within the last fortnight have had the impression that they have been witnessing world history in the making and that a new power in international affairs has taken shape invisibly."[44]

Influenced by the economic reasoning of French and British officials, the most cutting element of Vasconcellos's package was not so much Proposal IV, "embargo on exports to Italy," which could be extended to coal and oil, but Proposal III, "refusal of Italian goods," the embargo directed against Italian foreign exchange earnings.[45] Indeed, the aim of draining means of payment is evident from an important detail of the import embargo that was circulated to all sanctionist governments: the only good of Italian origin allowed into League states was gold or silver bullion and coin, which formed the bedrock of the Bank of Italy's capacity to pay and borrow.[46] Once Mussolini accepted sanctions as the cost of imperial expansion, the geopolitical confrontation between Italy and the sanctionist front in the League turned into a race between military success and material resistance. In other words, the success of the sanctions campaign in 1935–1936 hinged on whether Italy's armored columns could reach Addis Ababa before League sanctions against its exports drained the country's financial reserves.[47] By preventing Italy from selling into nearly fifty national markets, the Coordination Committee, furnished with data by the British Admiralty, was hopeful that Italian export revenues could be substantially driven down.[48] Optimists took heart in British estimates that ordinary earnings could be reduced by as much as 70 percent.[49] Mussolini seemed to have stumbled into the trap laid for him by the sanctionists and was now exhausting Italy's strength in an endurance test he was bound to lose.[50]

The attritional logic of the import embargo made several assumptions. One was that the invaders would not conquer Addis Ababa before the onset of the summer rains, which in Ethiopia lasted from May to September. Most European military experts believed that taking a country with the mountainous terrain and size of Ethiopia required more than one dry season.[51] By that time, the BoT and the Admiralty expected that Italian foreign exchange reserves would have been exhausted and Mussolini would be financially unable to prosecute his war. At the Treasury, economists Ralph Hawtrey and S. D. Waley forecast that if sanctions reduced Italian export revenues by 75 percent, the Bank of Italy's reserves would fall by between £68 million and £108 million, allowing for just 9–15 months' worth of imports before they were exhausted.[52] French military intelligence likewise estimated that with a monthly import financing requirement of at least 500 million lira (£8.4 million), Italy could not hold out for more than ten months.[53] With no external loans forthcoming from either Wall Street or London, this would cause insuperable problems for the regime. There was thus a common expectation in London and Paris that squeezing Italian exports would force Mussolini to the negotiating table within a year, before he would be able to claim Ethiopia.

Indeed, toward the end of 1935 and into the early months of 1936 there were clear signs that the import embargo was working. As destinations for Italian exports were closed off, the Fascist regime was forced to cut imports drastically to preserve foreign exchange. But given Italy's structural current account deficit, the fall in the currency and gold reserves was nonetheless heavy. Even before the invasion had been launched the Bank of Italy's reserves had fallen by £78 million ($379 million) as it had spent heavily to cover the enormous military buildup in East Africa.[54] In June 1935 the central bank had suspended the mandatory reserve coverage ratio, which prescribed that 40 percent of the money supply had to be backed by gold.[55] But while this allowed for increased domestic spending, it could not increase the hard currency needed to pay for imports. Between October 1935 and August 1936, reserves plummeted further, from £67 million to only £37.5 million.[56] Mussolini devalued the lira by 25 percent a week after the sanctions took effect, but since it had been overvalued before, this did little to improve export competitiveness. From November 1935 to July 1936, Italy exported a mere £37.7 million worth of goods, compared to £59 million in the same period one year earlier—a 35 percent reduction. Yet even strict rationing could only shrink imports by 22 percent in the same period.[57] Absent foreign financing, eventually a balance-of-payments breakdown would result.

At the League, Vasconcellos's sanctions committee did not yet extend "Proposal IVa," the export embargo, to oil and coal exports to Italy. Expecting a long military campaign and accepting the EFO's estimate that the import embargo would financially exhaust Italy by the late summer of 1936, the committee postponed a decision on oil sanctions on 6 November.[58] The reason for this was that the success of an oil embargo depended entirely on the American government. At the time, U.S. oil companies controlled 60 percent of global oil production. Although they were not a major prewar supplier of Italy, they could easily divert their exports there to meet increased demand.[59] The Coordination Committee was in contact with Washington about possible oil restrictions; Secretary of State Cordell Hull had notified Vasconcellos on 26 October that a U.S. arms embargo had gone into effect under the Neutrality Act passed in August.

Yet there were tensions between the cautious U.S. neutrality policy and the League's economic sanctions regime.[60] Roosevelt asked businessmen to join in a "moral embargo" against Mussolini but took no legislative action to restrict American trade with Fascist Italy.[61] The ambassador to Italy, William Phillips, wrote on 14 November that even if the major U.S. oil companies would agree to restrict their sales to Italy, their 150 smaller competitors would still not adhere to such a soft constraint. Their power to supply the Fascist war economy was considerable: Italy needed about eight thousand tons of fuel a day for both civilian use and military operations, and small U.S. firms could supply eighty thousand tons a day.[62] For this reason, Phillips suggested waiting for an initiative from Geneva before joining any oil embargo.

This reticence became a self-fulfilling prophecy, however, since the League would agree to oil sanctions only if Washington would join them. Stanley Hornbeck, leader of the State Department sanctionists since the Manchurian crisis, insisted that so long as the United States remained noncommittal, the League itself would be obstructed; "the question whether the League powers decide to apply sanctions may turn upon the matter of our giving at this time the intimation of our position. . . . If we give that intimation, we assist the League. If we withhold that intimation, we probably assist and encourage Mussolini."[63] American internationalists mounted a press campaign for intervention to aid Ethiopia. At the Foreign Policy Association, Raymond Buell had been calling for emergency action by the executive to stop raw material shipments since September.[64] During the sanctions regime, his colleague Vera Dean also consistently argued for closing the loopholes in the sanctions constituted by the nonparticipation of the United States and Germany.[65]

Cracks in the internationalist front against Fascist Italy were beginning to appear. On 8 November, Maisky reported that his friend in the Foreign Office, Robert Vansittart, had expressed the hope that the war in Africa would be over by Christmas. It was an odd thing to say for the permanent under secretary for foreign affairs; given the attritional logic of the import embargo and the impossibility of a military victory in the field before the end of that year, this could only mean that British diplomats were hoping for some kind of deal. On 14 November, Baldwin's Conservatives were reelected after campaigning on a pro-League platform. Now that deterring Mussolini had failed and sanctions were in place, London and Paris were hesitant to push the economic measures further and risk open war. This reflected the view of the sanctions gradualists in Samuel Hoare's Foreign Office as well as that of French prime minister Laval and the Quai d'Orsay. Neither wanted to provoke an attack by Mussolini on their own empires by cornering the Italian leader with more economic pressure.[66]

After the British general election, secret negotiations began in Paris between Laval and Hoare about a deal to divide Ethiopia that would surrender most of Haile Selassie's territory to the Italian empire.[67] The public mood at the end of November was still strident; one newspaper declared that "Anglo-French unity, in the spirit of the World War entente cordiale, thanks to Fascist imperialism, is again an accomplished fact"; yet as Maisky noted, "The potion was brewing in the imperialists' infernal kitchen."[68] On 9 December news of the territorial deal was leaked to the press, and an international outcry ensued. The Hoare-Laval Pact was received in many quarters with consternation and came to epitomize the duplicity of imperialist motives that undercut the noble solidarity of the League.

Yet the sanctions effort did not end on the announcement of the Hoare-Laval Pact. In fact, the British and French governments were forced to disavow their own secret plan, testifying to the strength of public opinion against Mussolini. Moreover, the attritional logic of the sanctions package remained relentlessly at work. The window of opportunity for a Fascist victory in East Africa continued to shrink. In November, Haile Selassie's troops had fought the Italians to a standstill at Enderta; by mid-December, the Ethiopians launched a counter-offensive at Dembeguina Pass, capturing dozens of tanks and field guns and thousands of Italian prisoners.[69] De Bono's military campaign was flagging. But whether this could be turned into a victory for the League depended on whether and how the sanctions against the Fascist regime could be expanded.

Energy and Infrastructure

While a vicious war raged in East Africa, intense sanctions diplomacy was taking place around the prospect of a League oil embargo. Vasconcellos's Coordination Committee discussed energy sanctions again on 1 January 1936 and appointed an experts' committee to study the efficacy of such a measure. But a decision on the embargo itself was once more postponed because of the unclear American position. U.S. oil shipments to Italy had risen 446 percent in December 1935 compared to one year earlier. The Fascist armies were clearly benefiting from American petroleum.[70] If this supply was cut off, the Ethiopians might be able to follow through on their recent successes. Collective security advocates fixed their hopes on the expiration of the U.S. Neutrality Act that had been passed in August; unless renewed or replaced, the law would lapse by 29 February 1936—leaving the United States free to intervene.

The main hope of internationalists on both sides of the Atlantic was that a revised Neutrality Act would include discriminatory embargo powers, enabling Roosevelt to join international sanctions against Italy. But even a second-best solution—a new law that allowed U.S. *non-interference* in the League's punitive measures—would be helpful. A third option was to use the Neutrality Act's export prohibitions in a discretionary way. If U.S. lawmakers placed the right items on the embargo lists, these would hit Italy severely and not affect Ethiopia much, even if the former were not openly designated as the aggressor. The French ambassador in Washington thought that there were "serious chances" that the embargo lists would be expanded to include petroleum and cotton in particular.[71]

This stealth discrimination proved hard to implement, however. To placate neutralist opinion in Congress, the State Department dropped the requirement that the new legislation distinguish between aggressors and victims.[72] In Paris, Laval, who had hoped for Roosevelt's collaboration, felt "regret that these propositions, placed under the sign of neutrality, aban-don . . . the idea of a discrimination between the aggressor state and the state victimized by aggression."[73] But even the fallback option of tweak-ing the embargo lists faced unprecedented scrutiny from U.S. senators. "When you give an absolute discretion to the President, he may select such articles as he desires," argued California senator Hiram Johnson, "and it gives him an opportunity, by the selection, to pick the aggressor, and to do as he sees fit in regard to the conflict."[74] Led by Johnson, the Senate struck from the bill the sections granting the president discretion over raw ma-terials exports. Dejected, the French ambassador informed Paris that the neutralists had realized these powers were "a sort of encouragement to the President to associate himself with the sanctions of the League of Nations and notably with the embargo on petroleum."[75] Ethiopia's fate seemed to hinge on arcane details of U.S. legislation. In early February, four months into the war, Italian forces still had not advanced beyond Mekelle in north-ern Ethiopia, barely one-sixth of the nine-hundred-kilometer distance to Addis Ababa.[76] War correspondents reported a frustrated impatience among the troops about their lack of progress.[77]

On 12 February, the Senate broke the deadlock by rejecting the option of a new bill and extending the old Neutrality Act until 1 May 1937. Com-pounding this setback, Vasconcellos's expert committee delivered its re-port on the oil embargo the same day. The League experts estimated that if fully implemented and assuming U.S. exports remained at their prewar level, oil sanctions would exhaust Italy's fuel supply in three and a half months. But as U.S. oil exports to Italy were rising, the actual effect of sanctions would take longer to set in. As a result, the oil sanctions option was shelved. The same week, Italian forces went back on the offensive, supported by chemical weapons, and the prospects for Ethiopian survival grew very dim.

British and French internationalists found that Soviet diplomats were ardent proponents of collective security, more so than the aloof Americans. As the fourth Council member, the USSR had dutifully cut off supplies of chromium, manganese, and iron ore to Italy. Litvinov also supported bans on coal and steel.[78] Yet under the influence of Stalin's domestic agenda, Soviet economic diplomacy was not consistent, and exports of other non-sanctioned items continued.[79] In February 1936, the USSR also stopped oil shipments, not to Italy but rather to Germany, which it considered the biggest threat to world peace.[80] As Soviet diplomats pointed out in their correspondence with the League, the government monopoly on foreign trade was extremely useful in directing sanctions policy for a state with great power ambitions.[81]

What other options for pressure against Italy were on the table? Without a doubt, the largest spanner that could have been thrown into the works of the Fascist economy was an infrastructural one: closing the Suez Canal to Italian ships. By the summer of 1935 Italy was the single biggest user of the canal after Britain itself.[82] The canal was governed by the 1888 Treaty of Constantinople, a holdover from British rule over Ottoman Egypt; it specified that the canal would be open to civilian and military vessels of all nations, neutral and belligerent, in times of peace and war. The waterway was thus effectively demilitarized by international agreement.[83] But by the 1930s, many sanctionists felt that stopping aggression should allow the League to override older treaty law. Since sanctions effectively removed neutrality, they reasoned that the Covenant's Article 16 should trump the Treaty of Constantinople.

The problem was that this view had a fragile basis in contemporary jurisprudence.[84] In fact, the most important interwar judicial decision on neutrality, the so-called Wimbledon Case, adjudicated by the PCIJ in 1923, had affirmed that states had to honor the territorial neutrality of treaty-governed waterways.[85] Most legal experts tended to agree.[86] In 1935, the Italians gambled that Britain, France, and the other signatories to the Treaty of Constantinople would respect its provisions in their response to the Ethiopian crisis. To make sure, Mussolini repeatedly announced that Rome would consider any move to close the canal tantamount to a declaration of war. For both legal-political and strategic reasons, British and French planners therefore ruled out the closure of the canal during their last-ditch peace negotiations in August and September 1935.[87] That such an obvious lever to halt Italy's aggression in East Africa was not used understandably frustrated sanctionists in Britain and the United States. Raymond Buell argued that the uncertainty about sanctions that plagued world politics should be resolved by internationalizing the Suez Canal, as well as the Panama Canal, which was then in American hands, and perhaps the Turkish Straits as well.[88]

Other forms of interdiction and nuisance were also examined. The ATB, for example, studied the payment of canal dues to the Suez Canal Company.[89] To conserve foreign exchange, Italian ships often paid these transit fees on credit; by October 1935 the sum owed by Italy to the Franco-British firm was considerable, and a company demand that duties be paid on the spot "could be considered as a form of sanction."[90] But by far the most dramatic form of sanction that the British government contemplated was restricting water supplies to Italian East Africa. De Bono's expeditionary force had amassed large freshwater stores in the British-controlled ports of Aden, Port Sudan, and Mombasa.[91] A ban on the export of these stores would have required enormous logistical improvisation at prohibitive expense. Ultimately, however, the ATB decided against a "water blockade" of the Italian Army because it saw this as a military action rather than a commercial prohibition. Here an imperial prejudice clearly shaped British thinking about the economic weapon. When it had considered economic pressure against Chinese Nationalists in the 1920s, the ATB had few qualms about proposing cutting off food and fuel as part of a pacific blockade against the Chinese population.[92] Yet in a confrontation with another European colonial power, merely closing a canal in breach of international treaties or stopping the private sale of water constituted a military act rather than an "economic" one. This double standard goes some way toward explaining why sanctions, which had worked against small Balkan states in the 1920s, ran into problems when their target was a fellow European empire engaged in colonial war. Their coercive nature was carefully acknowledged when applied to great powers but blithely accepted when they affected semi-sovereign states and colonial populations.

Discussions about where sanctions crossed from the economic into the military domain point to a broader League anxiety about not going to war with Italy. But from a strategic point of view, the challenge facing internationalism went beyond Mussolini. Germany and Japan constituted far larger threats to the existing European and imperial order in Europe and East Asia. In March 1936, Hitler marched his troops into the Rhineland in brazen violation of the Versailles Treaty. German armed forces now stood once more on the French border. Having implemented a moderate economic sanctions package against Italy, Britain and France struggled to find the will, strategy, and popular support to retaliate against Hitler's legally less significant, but strategically more threatening, provocation in the Rhineland.[93] Anthony Eden was the only cabinet member still pushing for an extension of the oil embargo, which he proposed once more in March. But international attention to the plight of the Ethiopians had dissipated. Selassie's armies suffered a string of serious defeats in the spring. On 5 May, Fascist troops entered Addis Ababa, which the emperor had left days earlier. A dispirited League Council voted in July to lift sanctions on Italy, which had been in effect for 241 days.

When the ATB reviewed the sanctions after the end of the Italo-Ethiopian War, it concluded that "the deterrent effects upon Italy of the sanctions policy adopted were negligible, chiefly because the Ethiopian resistance collapsed before the sanctions had attained their full effect and also because Italy was able, by anticipatory accumulation and evasion of the economic pressure placed upon her, to find sufficient stocks to meet her military requirements."[94] Through a combination of export diversion, stockpiling, national saving, and military luck, the Italians completed their war of conquest before confronting bankruptcy. Nevertheless the close-run nature of the war in its first few months, the damage that sanctions wrought on Italy, and the effect of the U.S. recommitment to neutrality at the crucial turning point in February 1936 should not be underestimated. Mussolini later told Hitler that "if the League of Nations had followed the advice of Eden to extend sanctions against Italy to oil, then in the space of eight days we would have had to retreat in Ethiopia. It would have been an unmistakable catastrophe for me."[95]

The Italo-Ethiopian War made visible the stakes of deploying economic sanctions against aggression. The address that the exiled emperor Haile Selassie delivered to the League Assembly in Geneva on 30 June 1936 asked a tough question: in the wake of the brutal Fascist conquest, could small states still expect their sovereignty to be respected, or would they be forced "to accept the bonds of vassalship"?[96] His *cri de coeur* has rightly gone down in history as a brave defense of international morality to a morally bankrupt organization. What is rarely mentioned, however, is that Selassie ended his speech by explicitly indicting the League for its failure to provide positive material assistance to Ethiopia. What the emperor castigated was Geneva's frugality in the face of danger. As he pointed out, the two Central European nations that had benefited from financial reconstruction programs in the 1920s, Austria and Hungary, were also among the six member states that had refused to implement the Coordination Committee's sanctions. Yet Italy's invasion had not led to more than a meager recommendation to implement the support measures of the third paragraph of Article 16.[97]

John Maynard Keynes had also emphasized before the invasion that what Ethiopia needed was international funding for its defense, not just sanctions. While he supported the embargoes on Italy, Keynes argued that a guaranteed loan to Addis Ababa would "revolutionize the effectiveness of Ethiopian defense" and put "an entirely different complexion on the Italian prospects."[98] During the following months, Ethiopia had fruitlessly attempted to secure such material assistance. Its delegation praised Finland's pioneering role in the Convention on Financial Assistance when it first asked the League for financial support for arms purchases in November 1935.[99] After Selassie went into English exile in Bath, Ethiopian diplomats demanded the maintenance of sanctions against Italy, but also requested a guarantee for a £10 million loan to continue the resistance from abroad—yet no other countries supported the proposal.[100] The international abandonment of Ethiopia showed not only the difficulties of moving from threatening sanctions to using them. It also starkly exposed the limits of material solidarity among states in the politically distrustful, economically austere 1930s.[101]

This material failure did not necessarily diminish the political prominence of sanctions, however. The Italo-Ethiopian War showed that the economic weapon was capable of mobilizing a broad segment of left, liberal, and centrist opinion in Western democracies. The American journalist Constantine Brown wrote that "the net moral result" of the Ethiopian sanctions was that "pacifists are becoming militarists and vice versa, hardboiled soldiers and admirals are becoming pacifists."[102] The sanctionist camp, which included communist, socialist, and liberal internationalists, saw the first use of Article 16 as proof of its cardinal importance to world order. As Vera Dean put it, "The Ethiopian affair reveals not the breakdown of League machinery . . . but the bankruptcy of leadership in League states."[103] Sanctionists thought the League's action to stop Mussolini had failed because it had not been prepared to use decisive force in defense of the existing order. German émigré economist Moritz Bonn felt that much more significant coercion could have been used, and thus "It cannot be said that sanctions failed. For pressure which has not been exercised cannot have failed."[104]

To the most hard-nosed internationalists the value of sanctions did not depend on whether they could save Ethiopia. In their view the question was if they could break Italy. In April 1936, Jan Smuts, one of those present at the creation of the League's economic weapon in 1919, wrote that sanctions were "bleeding Italy white" and "must prove effective if persisted in to the bitter end." Displaying a stubborn belief in their deterrent function, Smuts argued that depriving Italy of the spoils of conquest would be a more effective way of prohibiting future conquest than stopping actual war itself. "If they could not prevent the war," he thought, "they could yet save the peace."[105] Rather than abandon their instrument, sanctionists were adjusting their sense of the political resolve required to make it work. If de-escalating crises was not always possible, sanctions might have to be used for strategic containment, grinding down aggressor states in the long run.

Reflection on the Ethiopian case thus tended to make internationalists *more* outspoken proponents of coercive sanctions. Norman Angell, a reliable weathervane of the dominant mood in early twentieth-century Anglo-American liberalism, thought that "the truth in this matter has been turned upside down by false slogans [such as] 'Sanctions mean war.' . . . It is uncertainty about sanctions which invites war. Sanctions, if certain and effective, mean peace."[106] Angell proposed that the League should simply make explicit what had been implicit in its organization all along: that it was a hegemonic coalition to pool economic power for the defense of peace by whatever means necessary. To the Next Five Years Group, a discussion circle of British Liberals and Conservatives who had come together in the ebullient internationalist summer of 1935, Angell explained what he felt the lessons of the Ethiopian War were:

> The world has so shrunk that no nation can any longer defend itself by its own power. In the last war we had Twenty Allies, and needed them. . . . Even with the help of France, of Russia, of Italy, of Japan, aided by the economic resources and finally the naval and military power of America, it was a near thing. . . . So any form of armed defence in the modern world involves us in military and naval co-operation with foreign states; alliances. If the putative

enemy makes alliances, we too must make them in order to wield equivalent power. We must make them or drop out of the race.[107]

As a cooperative architecture, then, the League was hardly defeated in 1936. Many of its supporters saw collective security and alliance politics not as opposed but as complementary aspects of the same project. This resolve guaranteed that economic pressure would continue to have an important role in the armory of internationalism even as it appeared to have failed. In fact, the influence of sanctions on international history was beginning to make itself felt in inadvertent ways.

CHAPTER NINE

Blockade-phobia, 1936–1939

I N 1936, THE CZECH writer Karel Čapek published his satirical
novel *War with the Newts*. The book begins with the discovery, off
the coast of Sumatra, of a knot of highly intelligent newts. Capable
of performing labor, using tools, and acquiring language, the newts
are quickly consigned to perform slave labor for humans. But their integration into civilization creates tensions, from working-class discontent
about low-wage newt competition to feminist calls for newt emancipation.
Eventually, the newts' desire to create swamps for dwellings by inundating
coastal regions leads them into war with the humans:

> It was a strange war, if in any way it can be called a war. . . . The
> British Admiralty violated the peaceful business relations with the
> Newts by preventing the boat *Amenhotep* from discharging a cargo
> of explosives which had been ordered; the British Government
> by forbidding supplies of any kind first began the blockade of the
> Salamanders. The Newts could not complain of these hostile acts
> at The Hague, because the London Convention had not given the
> Newts the right to bring forward complaints, nor at Geneva be-
> cause they were not members of the League of Nations.[1]

The British blockade backfires as the newts launch a counter-blockade,
sinking their opponents' shipping and bringing Britain to the brink of
starvation. *War with the Newts* clearly recalled World War I, when Čapek's

Central European homeland was hit by blockade and Germany retaliated with submarine warfare, as well as the more recent struggles of the League against aggression. These themes show that many people in the 1930s expected future wars to be started, fought, and won by economic pressure. The League sanctions against Italy in 1935–1936 had brought this possibility to the forefront of global politics. Čapek's fable about the insurgency of "Global Salamandrism" points to the central role of blockade in the interwar imagination.

The economic sanctions imposed in 1935–1936 revived a latent blockade-phobia that had first taken root in World War I. In Fascist Italy, but also in Nazi Germany and in militarized Japan, the episode accelerated the search for a very specific form of economic autarky: resilience against sanctions or a blockade that cut off imports of raw materials. This defensive reaction unleashed a highly unstable dynamic. Since none of these three countries—united after 1936–1937 through the Anti-Comintern Pact—was self-sufficient in crucial raw materials, their search for immunity against blockade strengthened their inclination toward territorial conquest. As their strategic ambitions grew, the threat and application of new sanctions only increased the urgency of securing resources at all costs. Economic pressure, meant to restrain aggressive expansion, now began to accelerate it. A vicious cycle therefore materialized in the second half of the 1930s as sanctions and self-defeating bids for autarky reinforced each other.

This escalatory dynamic was unintended. But it was hardly unforeseen. The destabilizing effects of nationalist fears of blockade had been anticipated in the 1910s by liberal internationalists such as Hobson and Angell. In 1924, EFO staffer Alexander Loveday suggested it was worth studying how "the position of a blockaded country may be greatly strengthened if it is able at once to invade a neighboring country which is an important source of supply for some necessary raw material."[2] Interwar scholars recognized the "nightmare of raw materials" (*cauchemar des matières premières*) as a distinct phenomenon of their times.[3] Historians have shown how the belligerence of Germany, Italy, and Japan was driven by economic, commercial, and strategic insecurities.[4] But there has not been much systematic investigation of how remembered and anticipated blockades, sanctions, and autarkic strategies interacted in the run-up to World War II.[5]

Studying how sanctions and autarkic expansion affected each other is complicated by two factors: economic crisis and ideology. The disintegrating effects of the Great Depression, on the one hand, and the internal radicalization of Fascist regimes, on the other, were undeniably very important drivers of escalation in the 1930s.[6] Any account of how Fascists and militarists revolted against the interwar order must take both into account. Yet it is precisely at the intermediate level of perception and policymaking, where foundational material shocks connected with sweeping ideological impulses, that sanctions produced unintended effects by connecting memories of the 1914–1918 blockade with the economic demands of future war.

The failure of League sanctions to save Ethiopia from Italian imperialism has somewhat obscured the fact that the measures had severe repercussions for Italy. As we saw in chapter 8, the sanctions-induced drain on monetary reserves came close to triggering a serious crisis. The Fascist regime survived exposure to the economic weapon only by using its controlled trade system to impose savage rationing and deflation. But these emergency measures were eclipsed by Mussolini's policy of *autarchia*, a deliberate anti-sanctions strategy announced in November 1935 and further elaborated in the spring of 1936. A series of ambitious autarkic plans (*piani autarchici*) tried to achieve self-sufficiency in food and lower import needs in textile, coal, and oil production. By forcing an unstable mixture of military armament, export promotion, and civilian austerity on the weak Italian economy, the sanctions had lasting effects on the strategic possibilities open to Mussolini's regime. Economic stabilization could be attempted only at the risk of social unrest. But actual autarky remained out of reach, and Italy fell ever deeper into dependence on Germany. Mussolini attempted to resolve these tensions with further adventures to secure resources such as iron ore from Spain and oil from Albania. Ultimately, the effect of the sanctions created a choice between painful stability and risky expansion that was consistently resolved in favor of the latter—with fatal consequences.

German autarkic thinking had deep national roots but was strengthened by the memory of blockade during the world war and the effects of the Great Depression.[7] The significance of the League sanctions of 1935–1936 was that they further reinforced the Nazi belief that German power was existentially threatened by the possibility of a cutoff of raw materials imports.[8] Sanctions occurred at a crucial moment in the internal politics of the regime and hastened preexisting plans toward self-sufficiency as the drive for "defensive autarky" radicalized into a more demanding, war-oriented objective: blockade resilience (*Blockadefestigkeit*).[9] Nazi blockade-phobia provided an impetus to three initiatives in the realms of economic, foreign, and strategic policy. First, the Four-Year-Plan, outlined in the spring and unveiled in the late summer of 1936, aimed at "raw materials freedom" (*Rohstoff-Freiheit*) by the construction of massive capacity for the synthetic production of oil, rubber, and fibers, and the exploitation of domestic iron ore. Second, German diplomats and bureaucrats further pursued a politically motivated foreign trade policy aimed at creating unseverable overland links with Central and East European countries. Third, Hitler focused on territorial expansions that offered not just security, but also resource benefits for Germany—first by extending support to Franco's Spanish Nationalists in the summer of 1936 and thereafter in the annexation of Austria in 1938 and Czechoslovakia in 1939 as he prepared for a wider European war of conquest.

Japan was in some ways the most unlikely candidate for radicalization. Although the country had left the League in 1933, it had emphasized its friendly intentions toward the West and was kindly disposed toward Ethiopia. Japan had continued to trade freely throughout the global downturn, but as an import-reliant island state and the most trade-dependent of the three revisionist powers, it had a strong interest in resource security. What derailed Japanese plans for economic development and autarky was the unplanned outbreak of prolonged war with Chiang Kai-Shek's Chinese Nationalists in 1937. Just as Italy's African war rendered its economy more fragile, so Japan's entanglement in China increased its exposure to Western economic pressure. This situation provoked, as the chief historian of Japan's autarkic turn puts it, "a perverted search for self-sufficiency which would ultimately lead to war with the West and ruin for Japan."[10]

From Autarchy to Autarky

The effects of sanctions on world politics in the 1930s have been difficult to ascertain amid the general disorder caused by the Great Depression. The global crisis of the liberal economic system drastically undermined the international political order.[11] The world economy of the 1930s was riddled with intrusive and coercive measures; tariffs, export subsidies, import quotas, exchange controls, clearing agreements, and boycotts were commonly used in many countries. This makes it difficult to isolate the effect of economic sanctions as a specific vector of instability. Even contemporaries sometimes struggled to distinguish them. During Council discussions about imposing sanctions on Germany in April 1935, Portuguese ambassador Da Mata asked, "Do not we all live in a period when import and export restrictions, quotas, licences and many other similar measures are applied indiscriminately to friendly States? . . . Are we not all suffering from permanent economic sanctions?"[12] Amid the breakdown of international cooperation caused by the depression, this confusion was understandable. Trade wars with economic motives had become hard to tell apart from sanctions used for political ends.

This analytical problem extends to registering the impact of sanctions on national policy. Policies of economic nationalism were pursued by many states, even those without revisionist ambitions that thus had little reason to fear League sanctions.[13] On closer inspection, however, it is possible to distinguish specific reactions to sanctions that go beyond general protectionist policies. In 1937, the Italian liberal economist Luigi Einaudi made a helpful distinction between the meaning of "autarchy" as opposed to "autarky." The ancient Greek term *autarchy*, he pointed out, derived from the words αὐτός (self) and ἀρχή (rule). It had been used by Stoic philosophers to denote independence, a political state of self-rule, or a psychological condition of self-command. This concept was distinct from *autarky*, which combined αὐτός with the verb ἀρκέω (to suffice) and entailed material self-sufficiency. As Einaudi pointed out, "autarchy" was not just a different goal from "autarky." The two aims could very well clash with each other in practice. Political independence could often be sustained only through connections with other states and support from other communities. An attempt at full autarky, then, might lead to the collapse of autarchy. For this reason, Einaudi criticized the Fascist response to sanctions, the self-reliance policy labeled *autarchia*, not just as an etymological error, but also as a step that would endanger the very political autonomy that Italy sought to achieve by it.[14]

Einaudi's distinction between independence-enhancing *autarchy* and the more radical self-sufficiency of *autarky* is a useful way to think about economic policies in the 1930s. As Stefan Link has argued, no state in this period aimed at full material independence from the outside world—a goal that was inherently unachievable for industrial countries.[15] Common to the economic nationalism of the period was that it sought to restructure societies' engagement with international markets and finance; national coalitions pursued autarchy to achieve "trade and investment relationships over which they [were] able to exert greater political control than previously."[16] Autarchy therefore manifested itself in protectionist practices such as tariffs, licensing, quotas, and subsidies. It might also entail import-substituting industrialization, default on external debts, and barter and clearing agreements to save external currency. Many Latin American, Asian, and East-Central European states initiated such policies in the 1930s and pursued them far into the twentieth century.[17]

By 1935–1936, the effects of the global slump were still noticeable but beginning to recede. As the EFO's *World Economic Survey* showed, world trade was still 18 percent below its 1929 peak but showed a "rather marked increase in the last quarter of 1935."[18] The beginning of economic sanctions against Italy in that period stimulated a number of policies that, for all their subsequent inadequacies, were aimed at autarky in the second, more radical, sense. The aim of this policy, which was first described by German commentators in 1934 as raw materials freedom, was to avoid economic dependence on imports of primary materials along international routes that could be severed by sanctions or blockade.[19] Raw materials freedom was perfectly compatible with continued exports to the rest of the world. What it aimed to avoid was the risk of a Great War–style commodity blockade—an external cutoff of vital inputs.

To grasp the reasoning behind raw materials freedom, it is important to note that autarchic protectionism offered little defense against sanctions. Tariffs could protect a domestic market from foreign goods, thereby shielding native producers from external competition. But protection against foreign merchandise did nothing to protect against the severance of inflows. As consumers of raw materials, even strongly protectionist countries could be highly dependent on the outside world. In fact, the collapse of global commodity prices in the depression had made raw materials more affordable, further enabling the import of primary inputs from wherever they could be sourced most cheaply. As economist Felice Guarneri, the foreign exchange minister of Italy from 1935 to 1939, observed, most countries were happy to be "protectionist as producers, but free-trading as consumers."[20] Escaping sanctions required the creation of a protected source of supply. Autarchic economies based on protectionism were not sanctions-proof, but autarkic economies focused on "raw materials freedom" might be.

Yet achieving "raw materials freedom" was a formidable challenge. In 1931 the American geologist and minerals expert Charles Leith held that "no nation is really self-contained as to war supplies, and . . . with the vastly increasing demands of modern warfare, essential supplies in huge quantities must be obtained from all quarters of the globe. . . . The problem of adequate preparation . . . is probably beyond the power of the strongest nation."[21] Stockpiling went some way toward reducing the danger. But they were helpful mainly for those states that were already self-sufficient in major materials, such as the United States.[22] For vulnerable countries, a more appealing approach was to move supply lines to overland routes that were easier to protect. Germany's increasing orientation in the second half of the 1930s toward a Southeast European space for economic expansion (*Ergänzungsraum*) was one example of this, allowing Yugoslav copper and iron ore, Romanian grain and oil, and Hungarian livestock and bauxite to be shipped along the Danube or moved by rail.[23] Japan's "yen bloc" connected its home islands with China, Taiwan, Korea, and Manchuria via sea lanes, requiring increased naval protection.[24] Italy focused on imports of coal across the Alps from Germany, iron ore shipped from Spain, and oil transported from Albania.[25]

The most ingenious path to raw materials freedom was through synthetic production. From the 1920s onward, chemical techniques such as the Bergius and Fischer-Tropsch processes made it possible to turn coal into liquid fuels by using pressure, heat, hydrogen, and a catalyst.[26] The German military took a strong interest in this technology and advocated for its adoption for economic and strategic reasons in the Weimar Republic and later in Nazi Germany.[27] Fuel hydrogenation was extremely inefficient, producing fuels vastly more expensive than natural oil supplied from overseas by tanker ship. But oil tankers could easily be stopped by sanctions and blockade, something that the League had actively and openly discussed in the limelight of world media in early 1936.[28] The extent to which countries pursued synthetic fuel is therefore a useful indication of the influences on their autarkic policies. Britain, for example, also built two large coal-to-liquid plants. But by 1938 it opted for maritime oil imports because of cost considerations; in light of its large navy, oil from coal was, as David Edgerton has shown, "a 'double insurance policy' which made no sense."[29] By contrast, Italy launched its own hydrogenation program in 1936, while the Japanese military began even larger efforts in synthetic oil production, building the third synthetic fuel plant in the world after Germany and Great Britain. That these regimes, which were significantly less wealthy than Britain, nonetheless pursued costly synthetic fuel investments indicates that they desired genuine raw materials freedom. Autarky was not just a nationalist catchphrase but a real material goal.

While synthetic fuel projects were one of the most prominent instruments of autarky, they were far from the only one. Synthetic fibers also reveal the impact of sanctions on economic policy; arguably they had even greater significance in the event that imports were severed. In the 1930s the textile industry was a pillar of industrial employment, creating jobs for one-fifth of the German, one-third of the Japanese, and fully half of the Italian industrial workforce.[30] Unemployment in this sector was a threat to social stability, something these regimes, as well as British and French sanctions planners, all understood.[31] Imports of raw cotton, wool, and silk took up a substantial share of the national import bill. Replacing them with synthetic substitutes such as rayon, nylon, and staple fibers was politically and financially beneficial.[32] There was also a strategic reason. Raw wool was the world's fifth-most-traded material by value after cotton, coal, petroleum, and wheat, and it came disproportionately from British imperial dominions: Australia, New Zealand, and South Africa together furnished three-fourths of the annual clip in 1936.[33] Despite their mundane appearance, synthetic fiber production was thus an important defensive bulwark in the face of possible British or League sanctions.

Italian *Autarchia* as Anti-Sanctions Strategy

Italy's first autarchic policies were rooted in the experience of World War I, when delayed deliveries of American grain and British coal had fanned widespread social unrest. Mussolini resolved that such an interruption of supplies should never be repeated. Accordingly, Il Duce had launched his "Battle for Grain" (Battaglia del grano) in 1925. In a large-scale process involving farmers, agronomists, industrial corporations, and families, agricultural policy was turned into a central plank of the regime's agenda for the transformation of Italy.[34] The Battle for Grain was the first move toward "alimentary sovereignty" that marked Fascist Italy into the 1940s.[35] Italy's dependence on imported food had already fallen substantially when League sanctions were imposed. In 1930 the country still imported 3.64 million tons in cereals; by 1933 this had fallen to 1.49 million tons.[36] Italy benefited from record harvests in 1933 and 1937, making it self-sufficient in wheat, although this was a temporary rather than a structural achievement.[37] By 1938, Italy produced 94 percent of its foodstuffs domestically, and daily per capita consumption peaked at 2,734 calories—a figure not reached again until the 1950s.[38]

A second stage of autarchy began in 1934 as Italy confronted the fallout of a domestic financial crisis and the unemployment shock of the Great Depression.[39] The conquest of Ethiopia was partly a response to the legitimation crisis that the slump caused for the regime. As the country rearmed, however, the overvalued lira came under pressure. Devaluation was not an option for Mussolini. Having arduously returned to the gold standard in 1927 at the exchange rate of 92.46 lira per pound sterling—the famous *quota novanta*—he was committed to protecting his own prestige as well as the savings of patriotic rentiers.[40] But as Italy began to experience growing capital flight, rearmament and preparations for the invasion could not be continued without creating administrative controls over trade. By February 1935 this system had been expanded to nearly all strategic materials and included barter agreements to save foreign exchange as well as controls on civilian imports.[41] But in May Guarneri was brought in from the industrial lobby Confindustria to run the trade control apparatus, now designated the Office for Exchange and Currencies (Sovraintendenza agli scambi e valute). Guarneri became one of the most powerful technocrats in the regime, wielding the power to allocate export subsidies, restrict any imports, and spend the country's precious foreign exchange and gold reserves.[42] Additional room for maneuver was created by the Bank of Italy's suspension of gold coverage in July and the cessation of foreign debt payments in August.

League sanctions were thus imposed after Italy had already departed from a liberal commercial policy to deal with the financial consequences of preparing its economy for war.[43] Italy survived the sanctions due to the existence of this system, which allowed Guarneri to practice strict reserve management and Mussolini's finance minister, the aristocratic fencing champion Paolo Thaon di Revel, to implement severe austerity.[44] Italy's dependence on its monetary reserves was dramatically illustrated by the social participation of women and children in national autarkic rituals. One month after the sanctions entered into force, Queen Elena joined with Mussolini's wife, Rachele, to inaugurate a new special holiday, the Giornata della Fede, in which women offered their wedding rings and jewelry to the state.[45] Il Duce called upon women to turn "every Italian family into a fortress of resistance," and although the results were meager—some 2,262 kilos of gold, worth about $2.8 million, were collected—the social fervor displayed in the battle against international sanctions was pronounced.[46] Meanwhile, young children roamed the nation's streets, junkyards, and homes to gather cutlery, utensils, broken bicycles, and other forms of scrap metal that could be recycled for smelting.[47] The gold and metal collection drive was an example of how the regime used the sanctions to launch broad social mobilization while simultaneously undertaking financial retrenchment. The national campaign for *autarchia*

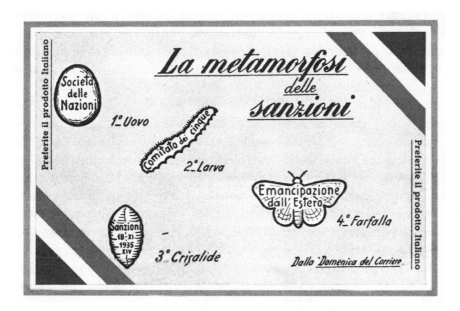

Italian postcard showing "the metamorphosis of sanctions" as Italian
autarky develops from the ovular stage of the League of Nations to the
larval stage of the Genevan Committee of Five, to the chrysalid stage of
economic sanctions, to finish as a butterfly that has reached "emancipation"
from the outside world. Originally published in *Domenica del Corriere*, 1936.
Copyright © Fototeca Gilardi/Age Fotostock.

"Anti-sanctionist triptych" calling on Italians to
deliver gold, scrap metal, and savings to the state as
it resists external pressure. Artwork by Mario Sironi,
published in the Fascist newspaper *Il Popolo d'Italia*,
28 November 1935. Biblioteca di storia moderna e
contemporanea (Rome).

was declared the day after the sanctions went into effect. The slogan was chiseled into marble in public monuments, adorned propaganda posters, and guided the rewriting of history books.[48] Many policies large and small were declared to be part of an anti-sanctions (*anti-sanzionista*) policy or a form of "counter-sanctions" (*controsanzioni*).[49]

Italy's turn to autarky after November 1935 was a continuous effort with limited success rather than an actual achievement. Full self-sufficiency was always impossible for a country as poor in raw materials as Italy. But the core issue was a lack of agreement about economic priorities within the regime. Stabilizing the economy in the wake of the shock of sanctions demanded a different set of policies than protecting it from future sanctions. As Alessio Gagliardi has shown, Italian autarky was torn between two deeply contradictory impulses: a financial "currency autarky," emphasizing trade balance and reserves, and an "integral economic autarky" that focused on the availability of raw materials.[50] This ambivalence was, in fact, a mirror image of the changing approaches of League sanctions planners: integral economic autarky functioned as a defense against Admiralty-style resource sanctions while currency autarky attempted to ward off Treasury-style commercial sanctions. On the whole, the practical direction of Italian autarky was highly unstable and inconsistent.

Initially it seemed that the conservative wing of the regime might prevail. The aim of Guarneri's policies of import limitation and export promotion and of Thaon di Revel's budgetary austerity was to regain economic balance. After the Bank of Italy was effectively nationalized in June 1936, lira devaluation in September was meant as a further step in this direction.[51] Guarneri saw the sanctions as an occasion for a conservative stabilization that would also resolve Italy's pre-embargo financial crisis. He told the French financial attaché in Rome that sanctions had "allowed the government to create a 'pathos' that has greatly contributed to making the people and the ruling class accept the restrictions imposed on Italy by the economic and financial situation."[52] By 1937, his monetary bureaucracy had been scaled up to a full Ministry of Exchange and Currencies.[53] Sanctions, Guarneri hoped, would serve as a regime-strengthening device, enabling the state to push through the unpopular measures needed to return to normalcy.

But conservative stabilization quickly reached an aporia. In part this was because of long-standing weaknesses. Italy had long had a structural balance-of-payments deficit—"probably since the conquest of Carthage," one observer joked.[54] In ordinary times this was offset by the invisible earnings of emigrants and from tourists and shipping, while on the capital account Italy was dependent on U.S. and British finance. The drying up of external funds could be compensated by recycling corporate earnings through the state's two industrial-financial conglomerates, IMI and IRI.[55] But this did not resolve the problem of external balance. Even when some basic economic links with Britain and France were restored in the fall of 1936, these bilateral agreements were based on trading levels that were far too low to sustain adequate imports. A policy of trade balance therefore inevitably resulted in the savage repression of civilian living standards.

Moreover, by producing a lopsided recovery, Guarneri and Thaon di Revel's retrenchment failed to stem the radicalization of Fascist foreign policy and actually further encouraged it. Austerity put the development or "realization" of imperial territories in Africa out of reach.[56] From 1936 to 1939 government spending was trimmed down from 23.5 percent to 19.4 percent of GDP. But since the burden of adjustment fell almost entirely on civilian imports and private consumption, falling effective demand had to be offset by higher military expenditures. Armaments spending actually went up *after* the Italo-Ethiopian War and kept growing.[57] Even rearmament could not proceed, however, without greater raw material imports, especially of coal, iron ore, and oil. Instead of providing satiety, conquering Ethiopia had left Italy with a military Moloch that, as a result of the belt-tightening of sanctions, demanded to be fed in other ways.

The expansionists in the regime began to push for new interventions and conquests. In November 1936, Eric Drummond and his deputy, Gladwyn Jebb—the future secretary-general of the United Nations—reported to London from their post in Rome that because of the dire economic situation created by the import reductions needed to withstand sanctions, "the probability that [Italy] unites with Germany and Japan in some dirty adventure [is] far from negligible."[58] Italy's ostensible escape from sanctions was in fact paving the way toward future conquest, radicalization, and war.

The trajectory of this radicalization is better appreciated by contrasting Italy's eye-catching "autarkic plans" with their practical results, which continued to necessitate opening up new sources of raw materials. There were some modest successes. The production of synthetic fibers and textiles was stimulated as a way to reduce imports of raw wool and cotton.[59] In this Italy was helped by its early interest in rayon, an artifact of collaboration with the British fibers and chemicals firm Courtaulds in the 1920s. Courtaulds and the German Vereinigte Glanzstoff-Fabriken (VGF) together owned most of the shares of Italy's largest synthetic fibers producer, the Milan-based SNIA Viscosa. SNIA managed to become the leading rayon producer in the world, supplying over half of global output by the second half of the 1930s.[60] SNIA also developed a wool substitute from casein, the fiber found in skimmed milk, known as Lanital ("Italian wool"). Lanital was paraded around global fashion circuits, used in military uniforms, and marketed as one of the new "textiles of the empire," although its quality was noticeably inferior to real wool.[61] Still, its use allowed raw wool imports to be cut by 20–25 percent.[62]

Energy proved a tougher nut to crack. The Fascist regime experimented with the use of methane as a fuel for streetcars and trains.[63] Extracted from deposits in northern and central Italy, by 1938 methane could provide the energy equivalent of about forty thousand tons of oil — 10 percent of annual gasoline consumption.[64] The growing use of hydroelectric power in the north of the country also allowed for lower coal and oil consumption.[65] But despite impressive propaganda efforts, Italy's mineral situation remained a fundamental obstacle to its imperial ambitions.[66]

Coal was a case in point. Coal production remained insufficient to fulfill national demand; the difference was made up by imports from Germany, continental Europe's largest coal producer. Fascist coal policy focused on the Sulcis region of southwestern Sardinia. In this swampy and malaria-infested backwater, the Carbosarda company, led by Guido Segre, had first begun developing coal mines in the summer of 1935. Earlier geo-engineering projects, especially the 1932 settlement of the Pontine Marshes, set the tone.[67] After the imposition of League sanctions, Mussolini accelerated attempts to transform the Sulcis region into an "Italian Ruhr."[68] Segre's new coal company, the Azienda Carboni Italiani (A.Ca.I), began building a new town around the Sulcis coal field, which was officially founded on 5 November 1937 as Carbonia, the city of coal.[69] Architects designed a town that soon began to receive migrants from Veneto, the Marche, Sicily, and Abbruzzo. From 1935 to 1939, the company's workforce grew from 1,060 to 14,965 miners, while annual coal production rose from 77,000 tons to 1.16 million tons.[70] Istrian mines on the Adriatic added another 1 million tons. But three years into *autarchia*, Italy still imported six times as much coal as it produced itself.

Oil was an even larger conundrum. In the wake of the sanctions the Fascist regime pursued two parallel strategies: the development of oil fields in Albania and synthetic production. The core of Italy's Albanian oil industry was centered on the town of Kuçovë (Cucciova), where a concession had been secured from King Zog in 1928. The Italian Company for Albanian Oil (AIPA) was created to exploit and transport the oil to

The AIPA oil field at Petrolia in Albania, 1939.
MARKA/Alamy Stock Photo.

Italy and started to develop the town in 1935.[71] Just like its Sardinian hard-carbon equivalent, fuel extraction at Kuçovë became a propaganda project for Mussolini, who renamed the town Petrolia, the city of oil. An eighty-kilometer-long pipeline was built to transport oil to the port city of Vlöre, whence it was shipped across the Adriatic for intensive refining—an important process given the poor, tarry quality of raw Albanian petroleum. Foreign Minister Galeazzo Ciano cajoled Albania into becoming an Italian protectorate in the spring of 1939, hoping that the territory would be a stepping-stone for wider resource extraction in the Balkans, where German firms had already expanded their presence.[72] By this time, the Petrolia field was producing two hundred thousand tons of fuel a year. Albania had effectively become a petrocolony of the Fascist empire, with oil constituting two-thirds of its export volume.[73]

Carbonia and Petrolia were high-profile components of Mussolini's *autarchia* program, combining colonization with a gambit for industrial high modernity. But the League sanctions also prompted Italy to start a synthetic fuel program. A specialized consortium, the Azienda nazionale idrogenazione combustibili (ANIC), was launched by Italy's state oil firm, AGIP, AIPA, and Montecatini, the country's chief engineering and chemicals conglomerate.[74] Using German fuel hydrogenation technology, ANIC set up two coal liquefaction plants and two refineries in Livorno and Bari.[75] ANIC's first production target was to liquify 2.34 million tons of low-grade lignite coal into 50,000 tons of fuels. The problem, as the company notified the government's autarky committee, was that there was too little surplus coal available in Italy to meet this goal. The most that could be allocated to hydrogenation was a mere 578,000 tons from the Arno Valley mines in Tuscany. Between June 1938 and December 1940, just 4 percent of Italy's refined fuel was derived from coal hydrogenation, whereas more than a third came from Albanian wells. Given these delays, overseas dependence remained ineluctable: 43 percent of Italian oil supply in this period came from Mexico.[76] ANIC's production peaked in 1939, when it delivered 374,000 tons of refined products—half of the annual target. By the time Mussolini joined the war in the summer of 1940, Italian oil stockpiles amounted to just one month's worth of consumption.[77]

Since Italy thus never achieved self-sufficiency or even a basic freedom from raw materials imports, it could only secure growing resources by expanding its sphere of influence. Ciano's takeover of Albania was one example of this trend, but the country had too little to offer to significantly buttress Italy's long-term resources and was too poor to absorb Italian exports. A more substantial expression of how post-sanctions autarky impelled Mussolini toward war was his intervention in the Spanish Civil War, which started in late 1936. By supporting Francisco Franco's Nationalists against the Republican government, Italy found a way to maintain ideological fervor, offload its armaments production on a willing purchaser, and obtain raw materials in return. Fascist-Nationalist trade was conducted covertly through SAFNI, a Chilean nitrates firm incorporated in Rome. To Mussolini, Spain's main economic value lay in the large deposits of iron ore contained in the Moroccan mines controlled by the Nationalists. In return for a very large military aid channel, Franco's regime increased its exports of ores to Italy from just 6,000 tons in 1936 to 397,000 tons in 1938—a fifth of Italian industry's annual requirements for steelmaking.[78] From early 1938 onward, Franco paid Mussolini for weapons deliveries in pounds sterling earned by selling ore to the British, thereby providing Italy with a valuable source of foreign exchange.[79] What limited the size of Italian gains in Spain was not so much Iberian supply but the fact that—as in the Balkans—the Germans had gotten there first. In its rage for resources, the Third Reich was squeezing out its smaller ally.

This was not the first time that friction emerged between Rome and Berlin. League sanctions had created closer commercial ties between Italy and Germany, the major European economy that did not join the Genevan embargo. But on closer inspection this alignment was far from beneficial for either side.[80] Sanctions had caused conflict in 1936 because the clearing-based trade systems that governed Italian-German trade required balanced flows in both directions. As Italy cut its imports dramatically to withstand the economic siege, it thus bought fewer German goods.[81] Since the Reich had a long-standing trade surplus with Italy, German firms demanded payment in hard currency for any further deliveries. Guarneri saw this as "the manifestation of a fundamentally unfriendly attitude."[82] Eventually, a compromise was found, but tensions remained considerable, not least because Mussolini knew that the Germans, who scrupulously observed neutrality during the Italo-Ethiopian War, had opted to make money by supplying weapons and ammunition to Haile Selassie on the eve of the war.[83]

By 1938–1939, the two countries were once again at loggerheads as they pushed into the same economic zones. Simultaneous expansion put the attainment of autarky further out of reach, especially for Italy. In April 1939, a new clearing agreement was signed that included resources from imperial territories: Albanian oil controlled by Italy could now be traded for Czech industrial exports directed by Germany. But behind the scenes, the Germans realized that Mussolini should be kept *out* of war; Italy's massive dependence on oil imports would destroy the already precarious balance of fuel supply and demand within a German-dominated continental European economy.[84] Insofar as Italy gained a respite from sanctions by trading with Germany, it did so only at the cost of worsening its structural problems. Mussolini's strategic options were being narrowed by decisions taken in Berlin—altogether a recipe for war rather than peace.[85]

The radical and unbalanced measures taken to escape sanctions permanently militarized Italy. Guarneri tried to hide these tensions by giving the outside world an impression of happy improvisation. To *Time* magazine, he invoked Marie Antoinette, whose "notion was that if the people could not have bread they might have to eat cake. . . . Italians may have to wear natural silk, of which Italy produces plenty, instead of cotton, of which we produce little or none."[86] On the second anniversary of the League embargo, "the Italian Schacht" still boasted to the *New York Times* that "sanctions, while they gave [me] sleepless nights, are the best thing that ever happened to Italy."[87] But by the time he was dismissed by Mussolini in October 1939, it was clear that Guarneri's anti-sanctions policy had no more rescued Italy from crisis and war than Marie Antoinette's dietary suggestion had staved off the French Revolution.

Nazi *Blockadefestigkeit*

Hitler's drive to restore German power within Europe was both aided and threatened by the League sanctions against Italy. In the short run, Nazi Germany benefited as British and French attention focused on the war in East Africa. Punishing Italy not only broke the Stresa front that had threatened sanctions against Germany in early 1935. It also allowed Hitler to find an opportune moment to move ahead with his revisionist campaign to overturn the Versailles Treaty restrictions on German armament and territorial sovereignty. But over the long run the situation facing the Nazi regime was clearly not improved by Geneva's show of economic force against an aggressor state. In this broader context, the sanctions reaffirmed Hitler's desire to achieve independence from global sources of supply. Due to scientific advances in the 1920s, Germany possessed the technologies to at least attempt moving toward the goal of raw materials freedom, especially in synthetic fuel and rubber.[88] German autarky policy had begun to develop more rapidly in the early 1930s in realms ranging from agricultural research to synthetic production.[89] What limited this were the financial and political costs of repressing civilian consumption and investment in pursuit of faster rearmament, a balance managed since 1933 by finance minister and Reichsbank chairman Hjalmar Schacht.[90]

Mere days after the Italian invasion of Ethiopia, German diplomats began to anticipate the possibility that the "sanctions powers" might cut off raw materials to Germany to avoid their transshipment to Italy.[91] Military analyst Hans Steinberger warned about the "notorious partiality of Geneva. . . . The risk of an interdiction of commerce and credit is thus possible."[92] Foreign Ministry officials were convinced that the sanctions process was "doubtlessly being initiated by particular governments with the tendency to turn it into a sort of trial mobilization [*Probemobilmachung*] for the case of any future conflict with Germany."[93] The perception that the sanctions against Mussolini showed what would be in store for the Reich quickly spread to Hitler and leading officials in the armed forces, Foreign Ministry, economic bureaucracy, and Nazi Party. On 21 November, three days after League measures went into effect, Hitler received the French ambassador, André François-Poncet, and proceeded to lecture him on what the sanctions meant. "If economic compulsion were employed to achieve political ends, the result would be that every State would try even harder than before to make itself economically independent of other States," Hitler said, warning François-Poncet that "after her present experiences Italy would continue to strive for autarky by every means." More ominously, he warned that the German government "would draw the logical consequences from the repressive measures decided by the League of Nations."[94]

Germany immediately experienced the indirect effects of League sanctions. Goods such as butter, margarine, and other foodstuffs became more expensive as the sanctions powers limited the amount sold on world markets.[95] This put immediate pressure on the German balance of payments, prompting the Foreign Ministry's economic department to consider "protection against unfortunate consequences of this kind resulting from economic warfare."[96] Bernhard von Bülow, the *éminence grise* of the Wilhelmstrasse, wrote that "our sole concern is whether, and how, we can autonomously protect ourselves against the direct or indirect repercussions of the sanctions procedure on our own raw materials situation," adding that Germany could not "allow its own requirements of foodstuffs and raw materials to be endangered as the result of the proceedings of the Sanctions Powers."[97]

On 6 December, the Reich Defense Council, an inter-ministerial strategic planning body created by Hitler two years earlier, convened at the War Ministry in Berlin.[98] The army's chief planner for national defense, Alfred Jodl, declared that in light of recent developments, "war no longer exists. Yet all states arm themselves more strongly than before. Economic or military sanctions are used. . . . Whoever pronounces the ominous word 'mobilization' has lost the war at a political level. Thus all states avoid the word mobilization." To Jodl, sanctions indicated that dangerous territory was ahead in which force might be used at any moment. Chairman Wilhelm Keitel ended the meeting by demanding that all government departments study Italy's experience of sanctions to produce "suggestions" for German policy.[99] The next day, Schacht delivered a speech in which he described sanctions as a "problematic invention of the League of Nations . . . which reinforce[s] the desire for autarky." Schacht concluded that "whereas a lot of economic nationalism was really prestige autarky," only an actual "defensive autarky" (*Verteidigungsautarkie*) could protect against future sanctions.[100] By December 1935, German policymakers were already moving from observation of the effects of sanctions to planning pathways toward immunity against them.

The discussions about extending sanctions to oil in January and February 1936 were observed from Germany with concern.[101] That month the Soviet Union ceased oil shipments to the Reich, citing insufficient payments.[102] Experts warned that the raw materials situation was still far away from the attainment of the necessary reserves and domestic synthetic fuel capacity needed to withstand prolonged economic isolation or war.[103] If Geneva created an international apparatus for the control of global petroleum shipments, this could easily be deployed against the Reich. The German ambassador in Rome, Ulrich von Hassell, reported on Valentine's Day that even if League oil sanctions were not "going to be resolved upon, [they] would remain in suspension like the sword of Damocles."[104]

Only the peace appeal to Italy and Ethiopia made on 2 March by Vasconcellos's Coordination Committee, coupled with another postponement of a decision on oil sanctions, made it clear that this threat would, for the time being, remain in abeyance.[105] Keen to exploit the opening, Hitler announced the remilitarization of the Rhineland on 7 March. He gambled correctly that amid the fragile global recovery from the Great Depression, putting pressure on two outlaw states at once would be too much for the sanctionist coalition. Indeed, the ATB counseled the British cabinet against imposing sanctions on Hitler. As the third-largest goods importer in the world after Britain and the United States, Germany was an important export market for smaller European economies, so "the effect on world trade of economic sanctions against Germany would be much more serious than the effect of economic sanctions on Italy."[106]

After getting away with militarizing the Rhineland, Hitler began to put German self-sufficiency on a long-term footing. Under Schacht, rearmament had taken place within the bounds of balance-of-payments constraints. Hitler ended this policy of relative moderation in April 1936 by appointing Hermann Göring as special commissar for raw materials and foreign exchange — the two prime targets of current and future sanctionists. As Göring began to sketch a plan to make Germany self-sufficient and war ready, Schacht objected, invoking financial obstacles.[107] But having already endorsed the goal of autarky as a legitimate response to sanctions and other threats, he was in a weak position to resist. At the next Reich Defense Council meeting on 14 May, Keitel, Jodl, Bülow, and other officials acknowledged Göring's new mandate and immediately mentioned "Italy's measures against the sanctions" as policies that could "solve also our difficult problems concerning the armament economy," including through "blockade organization."[108]

The Four-Year Plan that emerged over the summer and was revealed in September was therefore shaped by the regime's ongoing analysis of what sanctions meant for Italy.[109] One of the Plan's cardinal aims was the achievement of "blockade resilience" (*Blockadefestigkeit*).[110] Its official publication claimed that "the recognition that a 67-million-strong people cannot be dependent on the mercy of its neighbors, either in peace or in war, and that nutritional or raw material factors can get it into distress just because of a 'peaceful' blockade or economic war, must bring a responsible state leadership to the decision to provide a remedy to this."[111] Under Göring's supervision, attaining autarky acquired an explicit time horizon: fuel independence in eighteen months (i.e., by March 1938) and readiness to wage war by September 1940.[112] In a speech to leading industrialists in December, Göring reminded his audience that in 1914-1918 Germany had possessed "insufficient counter-measures." What was needed most was that "*the daily bread* must be absolutely guaranteed. It is more important than guns and grenades." The Reich also needed to accumulate raw materials for industry on home ground. "Imagine only that we would no longer obtain any Swedish iron ore, if it should fall into Jewish hands!"[113] This was a telling form of paranoia; even in the world war, these supplies had never been interrupted, as Sweden remained neutral and the German Navy retained control of the Baltic. It was a political decision from Stockholm to sever trade that worried Göring. Tied together in an anti-Semitic worldview, peacetime economic sanctions and wartime blockade had morphed into a single threat.[114] As one German geopolitical analyst wrote, "It requires an especially cool juristic mind to keep the difference between sanctions and openly hostile acts effective for longer than a few weeks."[115]

Germany's trade with Eastern and Southeastern Europe could not be easily severed by Western powers and therefore fit snugly into the strategy to attain blockade resilience.[116] Yugoslavia produced valuable iron ore, copper, and tin; Hungary supplied bauxite, livestock, and wheat; and Romania had long been an important source of grain and oil.[117] The main problem in obtaining food, crucial minerals, and fuel from this region was that it required a countervailing export drive. As one economist explained, "For the further progress of the recovery it is necessary to procure the foreign exchange surpluses needed to cover the increased raw materials requirements by expanding German exports."[118] The military's economic staff put it even more simply: "Without exports, no foreign exchange," and "Without foreign exchange, no rearmament."[119] Exports therefore continued to be crucial.[120] Creating a Europe-wide "greater economic space" that enjoyed raw materials freedom would still involve selling German goods to Latin America, Asia, and Africa.[121] To Nazi economic officials, *Blockadefestigkeit* was thus perfectly compatible with continued trade prowess. Getting to this goal in fact depended on accumulating foreign exchange by continuing the export of high-value-added manufactures at scale.[122]

By 1937, however, it was clear that Southeast European economies were not buying enough from Germany to finance the enormous quantities of raw materials demanded by heavy industry to meet the production targets of the Four-Year Plan.[123] Commodities could be obtained on world markets. But Hitler rejected expanding intercontinental imports as long as the Royal Navy could interdict supply lines, arguing that "it was more a question of security of transport than one of foreign exchange."[124] The Ethiopian precedent was never far from his mind. In September, the Führer insisted that "a people of great military power can become the victim of an economic blockade. We got to experience this danger in its full immediacy when 52 states in Geneva decided on criminal economic sanctions against Italy. . . . We will never forget this."[125] Germany obtained some material benefits from its support for Franco in the Spanish Civil War, but this too required fragile naval and air supply.[126] It was the annexation of Austria in March 1938 that temporarily improved Germany's strategic situation by expanding its trading links in Southeastern Europe and doubling the Reichsbank's reserves, pushing back the foreign reserve constraint on German armament by another year.[127]

In the meantime, Britain and France had started preparing for open economic war. The first British study of economic warfare against Germany was compiled in July 1938.[128] It concluded that Germany had built up considerable stocks and that a proper blockade would have to encompass perhaps as many as nineteen neutral states—a significant increase from the five neutrals managed by Cecil's Ministry of Blockade. By early September, as he traveled to Munich to determine the fate of Czechoslovakia, French prime minister Édouard Daladier had CSDN-produced plans ready to "assure from the start a close blockade of the adversary" if war broke out.[129] But rather than risk war, Daladier and Chamberlain chose to surrender Edvard Beneš's state to Hitler. Nazi Germany thereby not only avoided a campaign against the 1.25-million-strong Czechoslovak Army that it may well have lost. It also captured 3.5 billion Reichsmarks' worth of gold, foreign currency, and stockpiled raw materials.[130] Analysts at the Quai d'Orsay's commercial desk warned that "the Hitlerian state sees in the new resources of which it will dispose the means to impose its political hegemony on Europe. . . . Escaping from the danger of an economic blockade, Nazism could be tempted to launch other adventures and to place new Western powers before the blackmail of war."[131]

The self-sufficiency gained by conquest was tenuous. By early 1939, the German war economy was in better shape than it had been in 1914. Economic diplomacy had created a trading bloc in precisely those countries that lay in the blockade-free zone of Southeastern Europe.[132] Synthetic fuel production could supply a third of peacetime German oil consumption, with imports from Romania just sufficing to cover the rest.[133] On paper, Germany had thus reached a measure of resilience against peacetime sanctions. This was conditional, however, on two factors. The first was the absence of military mobilization, as active operations massively increased resource consumption; oil demand, for example, would rise by 60 percent. The second was that the resource-providing alliances that Berlin had built up would remain stable. In case of either a military mobilization or a negative diplomatic realignment, Germany would run immediately into problems. Further sources of raw materials could be secured only by force.

Ultimately, German blockade-phobia drove the regime to such ex-

tremes that blockade resilience was undermined. Nazi aggression provoked foreign responses that imperiled autarkic goals as soon as they were
attained. In his famous Reichstag address on 30 January 1939, Hitler ominously forecast that war in Europe would spell the destruction of the Jews,
but he also warned that "when foreign statesmen threaten us with economic countermeasures, . . . then all I can do is to assure them that this
would lead to a desperate struggle for economic survival."[134] Around this
time, the United States was shifting to a posture of "armed unneutrality"
and extending support to London and Paris in their stance against
Hitler.[135] The Nazi occupation of Czechoslovakia led Roosevelt and Treasury Secretary Henry Morgenthau to impose a retaliatory tariff on German goods, costing 85 million Reichsmarks in export revenues.[136] By April,
one of Göring's Four-Year Plan officials warned that "the economic war
against the anti-Comintern powers under the leadership of Great Britain,
France, and the USA, which has already been conducted secretly for a long
time, has now been finally revealed; as time passes it will become more
and more severe."[137] In this pattern of "temporal claustrophobia," desperate decisions for conquest brought into being the economic pressure that
the Nazis were trying to escape, causing greater problems of supply that
propelled the regime forward to its inevitable defeat and destruction.[138]

The debate in Western capitals between sanctionists and appeasers
was therefore happening on the basis of a mistaken assumption. Both
camps believed in a similar materialist calculus: if costs and benefits were
balanced correctly, then Hitler would behave as a more rational member
of the international system.[139] What this underestimated was the autonomous force that the specter of blockade had acquired in Hitler's mind
and, as a result of the Four-Year Plan, throughout the Nazi regime. When
Reich economics minister Walter Funk emphasized in May that the Four-
Year Plan and foreign trade were not contradictory but complementary
policies, the *Financial Times* interpreted this as a sign that "Germany did
not think of relinquishing her position in the world economy" and that
"the blockade as an economic weapon had lost its terror."[140] But the fears it
inspired were very much alive in the minds of the Nazi leadership. In their
imagination the boundary between war and peace, and thus between sanctions and blockade, had broken down.[141] Even before the start of general
European war, German publicists and officials were retroactively describ-
ing the League embargo against Italy as a "sanctions war" (*Sanktionskrieg*)
directed by Britain and France.[142]

To liberal states, Article 16 was still a tool to prevent or constrain war. But Nazi ideology saw the origins of sanctions in wartime blockade as a foretaste of where these policies would eventually return. When the Swiss diplomat and League high commissioner Carl Burckhardt visited Hitler at his Bavarian summer residence on 11 August, the Führer told him, "I need Ukraine, so that they cannot again starve us out like in the last war."[143] Within two weeks, German diplomats had signed the Molotov-Ribbentrop Pact with the Soviets, securing large deliveries of Caucasian oil and Ukrainian grain. On 22 August, Hitler declared to his generals that these supplies from the East meant that "we do not need to fear blockade."[144] But this was not a sign that de-escalation was imminent. It was the calm before the storm. At this late stage, Hitler was merely reassuring his subordinates that no external intervention could derail the next campaign of conquest he had lined up in his flexible step-by-step plan to make Germany the dominant power on the European continent.[145] The invasion of Poland began one week later.

Japan's Struggle with Economic Pressure

Japan's interest in autarky, like that of Germany and Italy, had roots in World War I. From studying that conflict, its military elite had become convinced that the fate suffered by imperial Germany—a national model since the Meiji restoration—at the hands of the Allied blockade had grave implications for their own country.[146] Influenced by the experience of total war, a generation of young officers, chief among them Kanji Ishiwara, wanted to develop the material and territorial base from which Japan could survive a future "continuous war," an attritional conflict of long duration.[147] In the protectorate of Manchukuo, established in 1932, Ishiwara and his fellow "total-war officers" sought to create a resource-intensive industrial base.[148] The East Asian continent was thus expected to provide the base for a "strategic autarky" that the Japanese home islands lacked.[149]

Despite the ultra-nationalists' obsession with Manchukuo, Japan continued to practice relatively free trade and retained a deeply interdependent position in the world economy. This was largely due to the influence of its finance minister, Korekiyo Takahashi, whose commitment to reflation and state-driven investment spurred an economic boom in the mid-1930s.[150] Japanese economic openness was, to some degree, baked into its growth model: its industrial power depended on the steel, textile, and silk industries, which required copious amounts of iron ore, cotton, wool, and raw silk from abroad. The civilian fleet was the world's third-largest

merchant marine and provided additional income by operating much of
the intra-Asian tramp trade. Moreover, Japan was not an automatic ally of
Germany or Italy. In fact, much of the Japanese population sympathized
with the Ethiopians' plight at the hands of Italian imperialism.[151] At the
same time, the Italo-Ethiopian War was widely regarded as a sign that
global great power struggle was accelerating and that Japan might have to
create a Tokyo-centered economic sphere in East Asia.[152]

As Europeans awaited Geneva's decision on oil sanctions in February
1936, ultra-nationalist army officers assassinated Takahashi. The young reform bureaucrats who gained power after his death pursued a more intensive pace of rearmament. A tense situation arose, as Japan's increasingly
statist and militarized economy was highly connected to international
trading partners.[153] Military expansion sucked in so many raw materials
that the price structure of the balance of trade was altered; imported coal
and iron ore prices went up much more than export prices, creating resource shortages where they did not exist before.[154] More dangerous was
that to supply these growing quantities of raw materials, Japan depended
disproportionately on the United States and the British Dominions, the
states most likely to oppose its bid for East Asian power. In 1936, the U.S.
and British empires supplied 72 percent of Japan's iron ore, 92 percent of
its scrap iron, 90 percent of its manganese ore, 97 percent of its copper, 85
percent of its zinc, 86 percent of its raw cotton, 70 percent of its oil, and
74 percent of its rubber.[155]

The disjuncture between Japan's economic entanglement and its growing political divergence from the West posed a sanctions risk. But different
factions in its elite were divided on the primary threat. Ishiwara and the
total-war officers were focused on the Soviet Union, which remained im-
placably opposed to Japanese expansion on the Asian landmass.[156] By contrast, the Imperial Japanese Navy was more concerned about the United
States, whose imperial presence in the Philippines and on Pacific islands
blocked southward expansion. Both the Soviets and the Americans might
use economic pressure against Japan, the former through its Council seat
in Geneva, the latter together with its European and Chinese allies. To
prepare against this eventuality, Japan studied Mussolini's *antisanzionista*
campaign. The Ministry of Commerce and Industry sent a secret mission
to Italy to study its anti-sanctions measures; the Japanese technocrats took
a particular interest in Guarneri's foreign-exchange-saving methods.[157]

Italian anti-sanctions defenses had not only a prospective but also an
immediate use. Just as the Japanese economy started to run up against
capacity limits, Takahashi's death broke the Finance Ministry's ability

to resist military demands for spending increases.[158] Massive purchasing abroad ensued in 1936, causing an import surge that further overheated the economy and rapidly drove up inflation. Domestic industrial management could no longer be separated from control over foreign trade. To curb this spending, the government imposed a licensing system for the control of foreign exchange in January 1937.[159] Japan's empire also became a testing ground for autarky technologies developed with the aid of military funding. Industrialists and Manchukuo's planners courted bids by IG Farben to supply German fuel hydrogenation technology that could unlock the enormous coal basins of northeastern China and the Korean peninsula.[160] By the summer of 1937, the total-war officers and reform bureaucrats were on their way to achieving a single united plan for national autarky, to be approved by the Diet.

It was the situation in China that derailed these plans for long-term self-sufficiency. On 7 July 1937, a Japanese garrison became embroiled in skirmishes with Chinese forces allied to Chiang Kai-Shek's Nationalists at the Marco Polo Bridge west of Beijing. Had Japan still belonged to the League, the incident would have been a perfect quarrel for Geneva to negotiate. There were plenty on both sides who opposed escalation. But in mid-1937 it was the Chinese Nationalist leaders rather than the Japanese who felt that time was not on their side. Chiang worried about holding together a disparate patchwork of forces in northern China, where Japanese commercial interests were expanding. At a luncheon in Washington on 10 July, his finance minister, H. H. Kung, told the State Department that "China was preparing for what he felt was an inevitable war with Japan, . . . [since] with the passage of each year Japan would become as compared with China comparatively stronger."[161]

Chiang ordered six divisions north on 9 July. Five days later the Japanese prime minister, Prince Fumimaro Konoe, announced he was mobilizing troops in response. Within the Japanese leadership, opinion on China was sharply divided. The total-war officers in Manchukuo wanted to become self-sufficient in the long run and needed peace to do so. Ishiwara had been the architect of the 1931 Mukden Incident. But in 1937 he opposed further expansion into China, warning it would become "what Spain was for Napoleon . . . an endless bog."[162] Eventually, a compromise was reached between hardliners and moderates: three divisions would be dispatched to northern China for a short, limited operation, to take no longer than three months and with the goal of forcing Chiang to sue for peace.

By August, the Sino-Japanese War was in full swing even though no declaration of war had been issued by either side.[163] The Chinese mobilized half a million men to defend Shanghai, which became the scene of vicious fighting. After Western dithering over further sanctions during the Italo-Ethiopian War, Chiang was convinced that he should not expect any assistance from Geneva or Washington. This further strengthened his resolve not to compromise with Japan. As Chiang put it to his ministers on 7 August, "In spirit, the United States and Britain would help us . . . but as the Italian case shows, they're not reliable."[164] The lack of positive economic assistance from abroad helped the Nationalist leader decide, based on the local situation, to engage in an all-out war to preserve China's national existence.[165] Nonetheless, he still hoped to receive foreign support.[166] That month the Japanese Navy began a pacific blockade of the southern Chinese coast, a policy it justified as a retaliation against "abuse of the flag" by Chinese vessels ferrying weapons to the Nationalists.[167] Under the guise of an anti-piracy policing measure, Japan became the first non-Western power to use organized economic pressure in an undeclared war; its blockade of China lasted until 1945, making it one of the longest of the twentieth century.[168]

In Washington, Roosevelt was hesitant to declare that a state of war existed between China and Japan since this would trigger an arms embargo under the Neutrality Act, whose third version had been passed that April.[169] The U.S. president was partial to the Chinese and wanted to avoid declaring an impartial arms embargo that would hit the Chinese Nationalists, who imported German and Czech weapons and equipment, much harder than the self-armed Japanese. France argued that as long as there was a chance the conflict could be ended through negotiation, "the specter of sanctions that the application of Article 16 will imply" should be avoided.[170]

Roosevelt's sympathies for the Chinese were increasingly evident. On 5 October, he declared in Chicago that an "epidemic of world lawlessness is spreading," remarking cryptically that "when an epidemic of physical disease starts to spread, the community approves and joins in a quarantine of the patients in order to protect the health of the community against the spread of the disease."[171] This "Quarantine Speech" startled observers around the world.[172] Anti-interventionists in Congress sensed a departure from the neutrality they had fought so hard to preserve. A progressive New Dealer wrote that "the Japanese general staff are no fools and they have undoubtedly accumulated reserve stocks sufficient to keep going for a couple of years. . . . If Mr. Roosevelt tries to lead this Nation into another international Ku Klux flogging of an aggressor, he may find himself, like Wilson, stripped of liberal support, at the mercy of the Tories, and with his domestic reforms discredited and postponed for another generation."[173] Even the *New York Times* was of the opinion that "from the longer view, experience has shown that boycotts and sanctions, or the threat of them, have driven many nations farther along the road to autarchy and tended to reduce international trade still more."[174]

In Europe, however, the quarantine idea was interpreted as a sign that the United States was preparing international economic pressure against Japan. The ATB was quick to analyze Japan's war economy. Although its dependence on international trade was evident, the Ethiopian episode had chastened British confidence in a priori evaluations of the efficacy of sanctions. The Colonial Office civil servant Gerald Clauson warned against the "temptation to . . . establish some form of an equation . . . that the Japanese Exchequer would not be empty until after a certain number of months"—a clear criticism of the Treasury theory of sanctions.[175] But Hawtrey still supported sanctions as a means of financial attrition. In mid-1937, Japan had a foreign exchange reserve of 1.22 billion yen ($351 million). An embargo against Japanese exports, Hawtrey explained, would slow down the rate of reserve accumulation, while increased war production for the Chinese expedition would drive up imports and further drain the pool of foreign exchange.[176] Since intelligence indicated Japan had built up stocks worth six to nine months' consumption, the efficacy of severing raw material imports in the short run was limited.

British policymakers differed on the value of a food blockade, resorting to much wild speculation about whether the Japanese rice-based diet implied a lower vulnerability to nutritional deprivation.[177] Japan had ceased to borrow abroad in 1933, rendering financial sanctions relatively weak; restrictions on its large merchant fleet would affect the British Dominions very negatively.[178] Neither bunker control nor commercial pressure would have an immediate effect, nor would either work without U.S. help and preferably participation from the Netherlands, France, Belgium, Egypt, the Soviet Union, and Argentina as well. Even if such a coalition were assembled, the consequences of using sanctions to drive up unemployment, for example, were ultimately a "psychological question."[179] ATB planners doubted whether Japan would respond in a way they considered economically rational since they were "dealing with an oriental nation, whose habits and character are alien to our own," leaving aside "the impossibility of estimating the probable effects, both material and psychological, upon the subject races of Manchukuo, Formosa and Korea."

Pressure to do something against Japanese aggression kept rising, especially after December 1937, when Japanese aircraft sank the gunboat USS *Panay* on the Yangtze River, killing five and wounding forty-eight passengers. Public opinion in the West turned strongly against Tokyo. The Roosevelt administration demanded the punishment of the perpetrators, and although the president was not prepared to send the U.S. Navy into East China, he was beginning to change his attitude toward economic sanctions.[180] In private, FDR discussed with his advisers how the democracies could fight an undeclared economic war against the Fascist states. If Italy and Japan could wage undeclared war, why not the United States? Roosevelt told Morgenthau that he wanted to use "a technique of fighting without declaring war." This meant avoiding "call[ing] them economic sanctions, but call[ing] them quarantines." He insisted that "we want to be as smart as Japan and as Italy. We want to do it in a modern way."[181] The Treasury legal adviser, Herman Oliphant, described this new form of force projection as "waging peace."[182]

When Morgenthau spoke to his British colleague John Simon about economic action against Japan, British Treasury officials studied the use of exchange controls to drive down Japanese export revenue just as the League import embargo against Italy had done.[183] What rendered this difficult was that both the United States and the British Empire had significant trade surpluses with Japan, earning more foreign exchange by selling to Tokyo than Japan derived by exporting to them. The Treasury's conclusion was therefore the same as that of the ATB: sanctions would have no serious effect for one to two years. This was useless if the point was to make a move that was quick-acting and not mere "economic nagging."[184]

Even though the *Panay* crisis blew over after the Japanese paid an indemnity and apologized, the Sino-Japanese War continued unabated. The problem of how to contain Japan short of going to war persisted. Throughout the spring of 1938, Chinese ex-premier Wellington Koo, a well-connected diplomat and eloquent spokesman for the Nationalist cause, implored Western countries to mobilize financial assistance, whether through Article 16's third paragraph or in the form of direct aid. Litvinov indicated that Moscow supported joint Anglo-French-Soviet assistance. But amid ongoing European rearmament, the British and French governments claimed that they lacked the industrial capacity to produce weapons for an army as large as China's.[185] Thus the emphasis remained on negative rather than positive sanctions. From London, Robert Cecil wrote with grave concern about Japan's continued ability to purchase aircraft in the United States; did Roosevelt not understand "the enormity of this outrage"?[186]

Given the lack of substantial aid, Chinese resistance accomplished much. Strategically, it delayed the implementation of plans for an autarkic East Asian economic zone based on a yen bloc covering Japan, Manchukuo, Korea, north China, and Taiwan.[187] Chiang's abandonment of Shanghai and retreat into the Chinese interior initiated a long-term guerilla war and created a quagmire for the Japanese Army. Konoe's original authorization for a three-month punitive expedition by three divisions at the cost of 100 million yen had, by the spring of 1938, expanded into a twenty-division operation funded by an emergency budget of 2.5 billion yen, 90 percent of ordinary government spending. To equip and fund this force, Japan's civilian industries were subjected to a draconian regime of capital and import controls that all but stifled the country's ability to generate export revenue in international markets.[188]

Time was working against Tokyo. As the army sought an elusive showdown with Chiang's forces, the Japanese economy was hobbled by military outlays and becoming more, not less, dependent on imports from the British Empire and the United States. A faction in the army leadership urged a negotiated solution, but in January 1938 Konoe doubled down on the destruction of Chinese resistance, declaring there would be "absolutely no dealing" with the Nationalist government.[189] Nor was Chiang, who secured $250 million in aid from Moscow, inclined to compromise.[190]

In Washington, Morgenthau had emerged from the December 1937 discussions as a proponent of the use of economic power against aggression. In 1938 he began to dispense financial aid through his gold purchase policy, in which the Treasury bought silver from the Chinese Nationalists and gold from the Spanish Republicans. Officially this was justified as a way to stabilize the yuan-dollar and peso-dollar exchange rates, but in reality it was intended to finance weapons purchases. Morgenthau also cleared a $25 million Reconstruction Finance Corporation loan to China.[191] During the Sudeten crisis in September 1938, Morgenthau convinced Roosevelt that if war came to Europe, France should receive financial support while supplies to the Reich should be cut off to put pressure on the Germans.[192]

As it sought in vain to defeat the Chinese resistance in a decisive battle, Japan began to fight a more brutal war. Fitting its economic planning to suit the new strategic aim of victory in China before a showdown with the Western powers would unfold, the Japanese cabinet passed its own Four-Year Plan in January 1939. This mobilization plan covered all the raw materials of the yen bloc constituted by Japan, Korea, Taiwan, Manchukuo, and north China. The deprivation of civilian industries initiated in the previous year was reversed; through the "link system" exporters who earned more foreign exchange than they spent continued to receive raw materials.[193] Japan hereby avoided the deflation that Guarneri had imposed on Italy.

In the summer of 1939, Britain and Japan edged closer to war after an incident at the British concession in Tientsin. Prime Minister Neville Chamberlain ordered the Royal Navy to prepare for action against Japan rather than Germany.[194] Yet British policymakers remained uncertain about the possibilities of using peaceful economic pressure to bring Japan around. The problem was not an inability to apply the policy but their estimation of its effects. Imperial dominions like Australia, New Zealand, and Canada would protest against stopping trade that was crucial to their national prosperity. Britain's empire, it turned out, could be an obstacle to sanctions as well as an asset. Despite their slow effect, the ATB felt that sanctions targeting Japanese exports were the best way to apply pressure "without laying [ourselves] open to a charge that we are abusing our power over the world's supply of raw materials."[195]

The outbreak of war in Europe in September changed the international economic situation, as London used its war powers in the empire to prioritize supply to the British Isles. British mobilization had unintended consequences. Indian and Australian sales to Japan fell noticeably, and Canada cut nickel exports to Japan.[196] The loss of supplies from the Dominions threw the new Japanese economic strategy into disarray. Maintaining production pushed the country into a deeper dependence on the United States to provide nickel, copper, and machine tools. But U.S. supply too was increasingly unreliable. Roosevelt had first used personal appeals to American manufacturers—so-called moral embargoes—to stop the delivery of aircraft to Japan in July 1938. Imports came under further pressure in mid-December 1939, as U.S. firms ceased supplying aluminum, magnesium, and molybdenum to Japan and halted the transfer of techniques to make high-octane aviation fuel.[197] Hornbeck agitated for the repeal of the 1911 U.S.-Japan commercial treaty, which was allowed to lapse in January.

What was the effect of all these measures on Japan's position? The Imperial Army and Navy had spent years building up stockpiles, providing some cushion against immediate pressure. Officer-administrators in Manchukuo rhapsodized about an imminent "Eastern Autarky," based on the yen bloc's self-sufficiency in coal, iron ore, sulphur, aluminum, salt, and wood.[198] But in the bigger scheme of things, Japan had worked itself into a precarious situation. Invasive controls had gone hand in hand with the destruction of democracy at home, while the Japanese economy was burdened by the army's unlimited and unendable war in China. That conflict uprooted eastern China's economy and society so violently that the goal of long-term self-sufficiency in East Asia was further undermined.[199] Meanwhile, for industrial raw materials such as oil, copper, nickel, and rubber, Japan was by 1940 more reliant on the United States and the Dutch East Indies than it had been in 1935. Conquest was not a sustainable means to autarky. But by provoking economic pressure, it could cause war to escalate.

One of the most acute observers of this unstable situation was Elizabeth Boody Schumpeter, an economic historian who had spent the preceding years studying Japan's Asian empire.[200] In her view, "The relationship between economic pressure, the threat of sanctions, a policy of autarky, and territorial aggression [was] a very involved one, because they act upon one another with cumulative force." In this desperate situation, additional pressure would not induce a change of course. "We cannot assume as so many people do," Schumpeter wrote, "that an embargo or some other form of economic pressure will so discourage the Japanese army that it will pack up and leave China, or that it will cause the Japanese nation quite suddenly to stop supporting its army. Human nature does not react in that way unless on the point of exhaustion."[201] From the State Department, Stanley Hornbeck attacked Schumpeter's claims, which he thought amounted to a "political conclusion."[202] Schumpeter's economic analysis indeed rested on a political understanding of the problem of international peace preservation. She was not opposed to sanctions on principle. But Schumpeter did criticize American sanctionists for failing to think about alternative forms of global order that addressed the root causes of the conflicts that sanctions were meant to stop:

> If sanctions are to become an effective method for insuring collective security, they must be imposed promptly by an international organization which is prepared to implement economic sanctions with force. The international organization must be something more than a means of maintaining the status quo by using collective force against individual force. It must recognize that social and economic security are as important as territorial integrity. If its members are pledged to prevent territorial expansion, they must insure the possibility of industrial and commercial expansion. Only in this way can real collective security be established.[203]

Schumpeter's analysis contained many of the core trends of the 1940s. Providing social and economic security indeed became a cornerstone of renewed internationalism in the following decade. But such positive provision would only emerge as the result of a devastating world war. Japan's aggression, moreover, would soon spread through the Pacific as a result of the U.S. economic sanctions against which Schumpeter had warned so strongly.

CHAPTER TEN

The Positive Economic Weapon,

1939–1945

IN JULY 1941, the Czech economist Antonín Basch delivered a series of lectures at Columbia University. Basch had worked for the Czechoslovak commerce ministry and central bank and attended the world economic conferences of the 1920s and 1930s before moving to the United States. Despite being exiled from his country, now ruled as a protectorate in the Nazi empire, Basch did not think that the aggression of the Axis powers meant that the League had been bound to fail. "The principal lesson of the war," Basch argued in New York, "has been the interrelation today of the whole world economy and the validity of the theses of collective security and an indivisible peace." Rather than expose the bankruptcy of idealism, the war showed that a more ambitious form of global government was needed. He thought that, "The necessity has become apparent of providing in the future for a world organization to prevent any preparation of economic aggression which may pave the way for military aggression."[1]

Basch grasped an important truth about the mid-century moment: the internationalist project of collective security was not discredited by the iniquities of the 1930s but had reconstituted itself and returned more powerfully than before. Collective security did not die; it went to war. The United Nations began in both name and substance as a wartime alliance. It was the full-blown military that the interwar League never fully developed. As the League's chief security instrument in the interwar period, economic sanctions would likewise reappear in the organization of the United Nations Organization that grew out of this structure in 1945.

If sanctions remained more potent than usually assumed, the question must be asked: why did a sanctionist coalition not come together successfully to stop war in the 1930s? As we have seen, a large part of the answer lies in the immense complexity of assembling such an alliance. Ideological competition between democracies and dictatorships regularly clashed with geopolitical aims. The crisis of the thirties is often portrayed as a Manichean confrontation of liberal internationalism and illiberal nationalisms.[2] While the frame is politically evocative, it is not the right way to understand the challenges that collective security faced. The economic weapon created at the Paris Peace Conference in 1918–1919 was designed first and foremost to prevent wars of conquest. It was not concerned with political developments within nation-states or empires. Coups, civil wars, revolutions, ethnic cleansing, and the overthrow of democratic institutions plagued the landscape of interwar politics, but none of these problems triggered the use of economic sanctions.[3]

The focus of sanctionists on stability in inter-state politics, however, got mixed up with the ideological and institutional projects of the interwar world. This created a vexing coordination problem involving at least four sides: first, the main liberal imperial internationalist powers—France, Britain, and their allies; second, the Soviet Union, a half-accepted, half-distrusted authoritarian partner in collective security; third, the largely neutralist but economically all-important United States; and fourth, the revisionist powers of Nazi Germany, Italy, and Japan, each of which had destabilizing intentions but which remained uncoordinated as a group and could thus potentially be played off against each other. By late 1941 the course of the war had resolved this coordination problem by bringing together the first three groups in a direct military and economic partnership against the fourth.

Once a new internationalist front had been assembled, this alliance created institutions of economic coercion and provision that far outstripped those of the 1914–1918 period in scope.[4] From the outset, Britain and France created ministries devoted to economic warfare. This complex of measures included administrative and naval blockade, blacklisting, resource control on every continent, submarine interdiction, and a new and uniquely destructive form of long-range power projection: strategic bombing.[5] The United States and Soviet Union both joined this alliance in 1941, adding global heft to the fight against the aggression of the Axis powers. By the end of that year, the outcome of the conflict was a foregone conclusion. The interwar security system was strengthened not by the insertion of military force into a framework that lacked it, but rather by the full integration of the two great extra-European "flanking powers," the United States and the Soviet Union, into the edifice of collective security.[6] As a creation of the era of total war, economic sanctions therefore persisted in the new disciplinary measures of the UN Charter. But their use would be decided by a small group of major powers in the Security Council: the United States, Great Britain, France, the Soviet Union, and China.[7]

In the history of sanctions, the broad-based revival of economic pressure was not the most significant innovation that took place in the 1940s. After all, the Covenant's Article 16 had kept alive the experience of the expanded blockade measures used in World War I. What was truly new, however, was the belated development of Article 16's positive assistance measures on a massive scale. After first extending financial aid to beleaguered states in 1938, Roosevelt and Morgenthau broke new ground in 1940–1941 with the policy of Lend-Lease, a vast global logistical scheme open to any state willing to join the United Nations' war against Axis aggression.[8] The positive economic weapon, stillborn as a result of the instability and austerity of the interwar years, finally found a material center due to the enormous growth of the U.S. war economy during the early 1940s.[9] War production flooded the world with money and goods, breaking the deadlock of the Great Depression and the sanctions-autarky spiral that it had enabled.[10] Moreover, coordinated provision proved a far stronger alliance-builder than administered deprivation. As the sanctions and competition of the 1930s were displaced by aid and productivity in the 1940s, postwar internationalism acquired solid foundations.[11]

The Winter War and Article 16

Embattled states clung to the League's economic weapon as their main hope for survival amid the existential dangers of the 1930s. Haile Selassie, Wellington Koo, and the Spanish Republican government had all tried to activate Article 16 sanctions against invaders and foreign-backed opponents. Italy had left the League in December 1937, which in principle left Moscow, London, and Paris as the three Council members capable of deciding on sanctions. But the conservative cabinets of Neville Chamberlain

and Édouard Daladier distrusted the Soviet role in the League, despite
Litvinov's repeated assurances that Moscow was committed to collective
security and non-aggression—hence the Soviets' non-invitation to the
Munich Conference in September 1938, where Czechoslovakia was sacrificed to Hitler.[12] At the League Assembly in October, Spain, China, the
Soviet Union, and Mexico were the only states that voted to maintain the
mandatory nature of economic sanctions under Article 16.[13] If no punitive
measures against aggressors were forthcoming, then only aid remained.
But since the 1930 Convention on Financial Assistance had not gone into
force, there was no international mechanism for this. Soviet aid to the
Spanish Republicans and Chinese Nationalists was therefore a purely bilateral policy. But Stalin kept hoping that the old Anglo-French-Russian
alliance would be restored.[14]

As German power grew, London and Paris wanted to prevent another
Brest-Litovsk moment. In March 1939, Britain extended a security guarantee to both Poland and Romania to strengthen the eastern rampart in
an anti-Nazi blockade ring.[15] Chamberlain's and Daladier's preferences
for an alliance with Warsaw also account for why simultaneous efforts
to create an Anglo-French-Soviet alliance failed.[16] When this prospect
diminished in the summer of 1939, Stalin put Soviet interests first and
signed the infamous Molotov-Ribbentrop Pact, a second-best solution to
containing Nazi militarism at the expense of small-state sovereignty.[17] To
the Nazi leadership, the treaty preserved German blockade resilience by
opening up the resources of western Eurasia—animal feed, phosphates,
grain, chrome ore, manganese, nickel, and oil.[18] The German Navy called
Soviet help "so generous that the success of an economic blockade appears
impossible."[19]

But the treaty left Stalin unhappy about Soviet security and keen to
move Soviet defenses further west. Finland, having seen the Convention
of Financial Assistance fizzle out, had meanwhile hedged its bets.[20] In
October, Stalin invited Finnish diplomats to Moscow to propose a land
swap: Helsinki would obtain sizable territories in White Karelia in return
for moving the border closest to Leningrad further northwest so as to expand the Soviet coastline. Misjudging Stalin's desire for strategic access to
the Baltic, the Finns rejected this offer. To bend Finland to his will, Stalin
launched an invasion on 30 November.[21]

The Russo-Finnish War became a litmus test for Western mobilization against the new Nazi-Soviet alliance. Herbert Hoover was at his
home in Palo Alto, California, when a personal appeal for food aid from

Risto Ryti, now Finland's prime minister, reached him three days after the Soviet invasion. Invigorated by the prospect of another humanitarian campaign, Hoover soon embarked on a nationwide tour to rally support for the Finns. "Finland is a little country, carved from the bleak forests of the Far North, scarcely the size of Montana, with but four millions of people," he declared. "For twelve hundred years the Finns have lived in their beloved northland. . . . Now they have been barbarously attacked. . . . They are making heroic defense against appalling hordes of savages."[22] Within six months, Hoover's Finnish Relief Fund raised over $3.5 million in humanitarian aid through private channels.[23] At the Treasury, Morgenthau provided a stronger form of assistance to Finland, extending $30 million in loans through the U.S. Export-Import Bank between December 1939 and March 1940.[24]

On 11 December, Rudolf Holsti addressed the League Assembly in Geneva. This time the Finns received diplomatic support from Britain, France, the Low Countries, and Scandinavia. In the wake of the Nazi invasion of Poland, West Europeans quickly united against an attack they perceived as a similar evil. Even to the left-wing British press, "expelling Russia forthwith from the League . . . would be no injustice . . . since no act of aggression since the last war has been more unprovoked or cynical in character."[25] The assembly also condemned Soviet actions.

When the Council met on 14 December, it voted to expel the USSR from the League under Paragraph 4 of Article 16.[26] Although the lack of a simple majority on the Council meant that the conditions for expulsion had not been technically met, Anglo-French dominance in Geneva ensured that the Soviets were expelled nonetheless.[27] The first months of war in Europe had a galvanizing effect that broke the interwar conception of sanctions as a predominantly negative instrument. The ideas behind the Convention on Financial Assistance seemed freshly relevant. As the U.S. ambassador to Paris reported, "The whole record of the proceedings does not contain one reference to the negative concept of 'sanctions,' [since] the French Delegation had gone to Geneva with the determination to emphasize the positive concept of 'aid.'"[28] Although punitive isolation did not disappear, it was now complemented by the provision of material assistance.

The Winter War was a key moment in the history of Genevan internationalism; the meeting of 14 December 1939 was the last time that the Council convened. It was also the final invocation of the Covenant's Article 16. Henceforth, the economic weapon would reemerge in the comprehensive form it had first assumed in 1914–1918, in which a positive logistical apparatus and a negative interdiction machine operated side by side. But at that stage, the alliance that would harness this material power remained very much up in the air. The place of sanctions in the postwar order would be decided by the political history of the war itself.

This prioritization of assistance to allies instead of deprivation of the enemy was driven by strategic considerations. In September 1939, Britain and France had created a Supreme Allied Council for joint war planning. As in 1914, their strategic thinking considered Germany and the Soviet Union to be single self-sufficient economic bloc. Both the CID and the CSDN saw the two key commodities of this combine as Scandinavian iron ore and Caucasian oil. French intelligence indicated that "the provisioning of Germany in raw materials, especially in iron ore, is so deficient and its financial situation so precarious that one can foresee with some precision the date on which it will have to surrender."[29] The Winter War was causing interruptions in ore shipments across the Baltic. Support for Finland thus became part of a wider strategy against the German-Soviet bloc. In the first months of 1940, London and Paris prepared to send a joint expeditionary force of one hundred thousand British and thirty-five thousand French troops either to Narvik in Norway or to the Finnish port of Petsamo to establish control over the flow of iron ore to the Reich.[30]

An alternative approach to flanking the Nazi-Soviet colossus was to approach it from the south, in the Black Sea region. In the spring of 1940, the alternative to a Scandinavian prong was to bring Turkey into the Allied camp and attack the Soviet Union from the south, either through an aerial attack on the Baku oil fields, a ground invasion with French colonial troops from Mandate Syria, or a landing at Batumi in Soviet Georgia.[31] But in the months before the fall of France the French ruling class was suffering from a profound schism.[32] In the realm of economic pressure, Anglo-French attitudes remained anti-Soviet, not just in ejecting Moscow from the Council, but also in planning for economic war against Moscow during the first nine months of the war. When the Winter War reached a negotiated end in March 1940, the planned expedition to northern Scandinavia was temporarily put on hold. But Hitler had perceived the threat to Swedish ores. In their rapid invasion of Denmark and Norway in April, the Nazis carefully preserved Swedish neutrality while extending the length of European coastline that had to be blockaded by the Royal Navy.[33]

In the United States, Danish and Norwegian communities in the previously neutralist states of the Midwest regarded the Nazi invasion with dismay, allowing Washington to take more serious action than in the Winter War. On 10 April, Roosevelt issued Executive Order 8389, "Protecting Funds of Victims of Aggression," which confiscated all Danish and Norwegian assets held in the United States—some $267 million—under the 1917 Trading with the Enemy Act.[34] This was intended to prevent the German occupiers from accessing these funds, which Washington kept in trust for the Danish and Norwegian cabinets-in-exile in London. A new office, Foreign Funds Control, was created in the Treasury to manage the Scandinavian assets. In the following months its asset freezes systematically followed the Wehrmacht's advance across Europe. By the end of 1940 Foreign Funds Control had sequestered the overseas funds of the Low Countries and France, as well as Romania, Bulgaria, and Hungary. Nazi aggression thus prompted the creation of an economic warfare apparatus within the American state some twenty months before formal war broke out between the United States and Germany.

Economic Warfare Redivivus

Just as in August 1914, the outbreak of war in September 1939 found the British government without a unified economic war strategy. But in institutional terms, the state was better prepared. The ATB felt the organization in charge of blockade "would be one of the most important Departments in the next war" but that it "was really engaged in economic warfare" and should be labeled as such.[35] The Ministry of Economic Warfare came into existence on 3 September under Sir Ronald Cross, a Conservative and parliamentary secretary to the BoT.[36] As the ministry's official historian put it, "economic warfare" was a very recent addition to the vocabulary of international coercion.[37] The ministry got up and running quickly. Several months into its operation, an American journalist described it as "[a] score of Britain's shrewdest bankers and economists, and their 400 assistants" working toward the economic destruction of Nazi resistance.[38] Although Cross was a career politician and civil servant, and most of the ministry's officials were civilian administrators, its intelligence-gathering heart was the Industrial Intelligence Centre under Major Desmond Morton, a military officer.

The ministry's activities fell into three categories. First, "legislative action" included the use of the Trading with the Enemy Act to prohibit as much as possible the interaction with Germany of British firms and foreign firms operating under British law. Private merchants, shipping companies, coal and oil traders, banks, and insurance firms were pressured with the old statutory list system and by legal prosecution from engaging in suspect trade. Second, "diplomatic action" included purchasing agreements and voluntary export restrictions for neutrals. It was only in the third strand of policy, "military action," that the traditional naval practice of intercepting merchant vessels and checking their cargoes persisted.

The slow and indirect approach taken during the first months of the war led to accusations that the ministry was staffed with appeasers. Financial journalist Paul Einzig criticized the blockade for "leaking like a sieve."[39] Arnold-Forster shared his concern that there were too many holes in the blockade. In the spring of 1940 the Netherlands, Belgium, Italy, Sweden, Portugal, and Spain all remained neutral. Only by immediately applying the same statistical system of rationing that he had developed in the last war, Arnold-Forster argued, could the Ministry of Economic Warfare hope to weaken Germany quickly because "the time factor is all-important."[40] Cecil was less convinced of the need for pressure on neutrals and privately advised Cross to be lenient in allowing imports into Germany. He believed that the Reich operated on a very limited base of financial reserves, and "the more the Germans buy from outside, of non-essentials, the less money they will have to spend on munitions of war."[41] For that reason Cecil thought Germany's cash-generating exports, rather than its cash-draining imports, should be the main target of the ministry. The Treasury's foreign-exchange theory that had underpinned sanctions policy in 1935–1939 therefore continued to exert influence in the early stages of the war.[42]

Another improvement on the last war was that the blockade in 1939 was an international project from the start. In June, a twenty-six-man economic mission had arrived in London from Paris to ensure cooperation between the French Ministère du Blocus and the Ministry of Economic Warfare. This Anglo-French executive committee began negotiating the preclusive purchasing of supplies to be kept out of German hands, such as Turkish chrome, Romanian petroleum, Norwegian whale oil, and Mexican lead vanadate.[43] Britain and France also tried to convince the Roosevelt administration to extend its moral embargo policy to include critical war supplies for Germany. Although FDR did not take such action, he did allow the British and French economic warriors to cut their own deals with American firms. U.S. domestic economic policy also helped. The June 1939 Strategic Materials Act had earmarked $100 million for the Departments of the Army and Navy to begin building up stockpiles to safeguard national supply. It was this domestic state-building and war-preparation effort rather than any active interest in blockade or sanctions that allowed the U.S. government to begin withholding important goods and materials from Germany.[44]

Hitler's conquest of Western Europe in the summer of 1940 dramatically changed the circumstances in which economic war was conducted. The fall of France rattled U.S. policymakers into formulating concrete plans for international intervention.[45] The large increase in occupied territory increased the resilience of the Nazi empire.[46] Yet Nazi conquest also made the task of economic warfare easier by reducing the problem of neutral states. By focusing on fewer neutrals, the blockaders could exert more calibrated pressure on them. In Europe, the main focus fell on the mineral-rich and Axis-supplying economies of Portugal, Spain, and Turkey.[47]

An important success was achieved in August, when the United States used sanctions to stop Spain from further widening the war by joining the Axis powers. After the demise of the Third Republic, General Francisco Franco was contemplating allowing Hitler to seize Britain's base in Gibraltar, a move that he hoped would secure economic aid and German support for Spain's imperial expansion in North Africa. The British cabinet wanted to avoid such an alignment at all costs. Accordingly, in July the Ministry of Economic Warfare asked the U.S. government to restrict oil shipments to Spain.[48] Officially this was to prevent their trans-shipment to Germany and Italy, but in practice it was meant to demonstrate Allied resource control to Franco. The interdiction effort was effective because of its manageable size: Spain's monthly fuel demand of fifty thousand tons could be supplied in just ten tanker ships. When two tankers bound for Santander and Bilbao were detained in the port of Houston, the effect on the Spanish fuel stock was immediate and substantial. The American "embargo"—which was more a slowdown than a total blockade—terrified Francoist officials. U.S. companies supplied Spain's entire oil supply, and domestic stocks covered no more than one month, after which the transport system, the fishing fleet, and agricultural production would grind to a halt. As Franco's interior minister Ramón Serrano Súñer warned, even with the rationing of domestic consumption the oil cutoff would soon "caus[e] severe damage to the production of Spain's vital necessities."[49]

The use of tanker control as a form of oil sanctions against Spain coincided with increased U.S. interest in the use of economic coercion to stabilize East Asia. Britain was unwilling to confront Japan without support from the United States. At a dinner in Washington on 18 July, the

British ambassador had sounded out Morgenthau, War Secretary Henry Stimson, and Navy Secretary Frank Knox about Anglo-American sanctions. He feared that without action strong enough to risk war, Japan could not be swayed from its ongoing depredations in China. Morgenthau, Stimson, and Knox were receptive to his argument and proposed an international embargo on oil shipments to Japan from the major British- and U.S.-controlled oil fields servicing the Pacific, mainly in California and the Persian Gulf; it was also hoped that the Dutch would assist by restricting supplies from the Dutch East Indies.

On 25 July, Roosevelt imposed an embargo on exports to Japan but limited its object to aviation fuel and high-grade iron and steel scrap.[50] He did so under the new Export Control Act, which allowed restrictions on exports to other countries in the interest of national security. This constituted a strong foreign economic intervention in East Asia; one journalist described the export controls as "partial use of one of the most powerful economic weapons the United States could aim at Japan."[51] The simultaneous withholding of fuel and iron exports to Japan and Spain in July 1940 was the first time the U.S. government used openly discriminatory economic sanctions in peacetime.[52] Previous restrictions had either been impartial embargoes or voluntary private embargoes more akin to boycotts.[53] Although Roosevelt had allowed the commercial treaty with Japan to lapse in January 1940, it was only in July, after France had fallen and democracy appeared in danger worldwide, that he began to use the New Deal regulatory state to conduct foreign policy through economic pressure in both Europe and Asia. The United States had entered the history of economic sanctions as a primary participant.

The initial effects of Washington's recourse to the economic weapon in Spain were positive. As the Spanish oil supply dwindled, Franco approached Hitler for help. Yet with a continental economy to run, Germany could spare neither oil nor wheat. Franco understood that if he joined the war on Hitler's side, no additional support would be forthcoming. Moreover, the U.S. oil embargo implied a threat of further sanctions on food and other vital goods. After three years of civil war that had devastated Spanish society, these prospects were daunting. Franco let the opportunity to join the Axis pass. On 7 September, restrictions were lifted as quickly as they had been imposed, and U.S. oil shipments to Spain resumed at their normal rate. Oil sanctions thus prevented Francoist Spain from giving in to what its historians have called "the temptation" (*la tentación*) of joining the war and expanding its empire.[54]

The Spanish success contrasts notably with the effects of the onset of U.S. sanctions against Japan. In direct retaliation for Japanese intrusion into French Indochina, where Tokyo was squeezing the Vichy authorities to allow the stationing of troops and procurement of raw materials, Export Control Act restrictions were extended to *all* exports of iron and steel scrap in September.[55] The core of Japan's construction sector and military production, its steel industry, was now starved of inputs. It was increasingly difficult for the advocates of a negotiated settlement in Tokyo to deflect hardliners' warnings that the Americans were stifling their bid for imperial power through an economic war of steadily growing intensity.[56]

The key constraint on Japan's geo-economic position was oil. In 1940, the world's five main oil producers were the United States (with an annual production of 182 million tons), the Soviet Union (29 million tons), Venezuela (27 million tons), Iran (10.4 million tons), and the Dutch East Indies (7.9 million tons); together these countries accounted for some 87 percent of global production.[57] Iranian oil was almost entirely in the hands of British companies, and Venezuela's heavy oil was refined offshore in the Dutch colony of Curaçao before it was ready for export. Both Iran and Venezuela thus fell under effective Anglo-Dutch control. This meant that the only major non-Western oil producer open to Tokyo was the Soviet Union. The Japanese Navy operated a small concession on the island of Sakhalin, but this did not produce more than 160,000 tons per year.[58] After the two countries had fought a short war in Mongolia in the summer of 1939, Soviet-Japanese relations were not good enough to provide Tokyo with sufficient oil.[59] During 1940 Japan twice sent trade delegations to the Dutch East Indies to negotiate the purchase of half of the colony's 3.8-million-ton production. But in their desperation to obtain wider economic relief the Japanese loaded their proposals with so many additional demands that they made their offer too onerous for the Dutch to accept.[60] Other global producers such as Mexico more than tripled their exports of metals and oil to Japan in 1939 and 1940, but by too little to make a difference.[61] Thus Japanese reliance on trans-Pacific supplies of U.S. oil remained its Achilles heel.

Roosevelt's measures to restrict oil to Spain and the flow of raw materials to Japan were an instance of what the British had begun to call "control at source": the preemptive purchasing of supplies at home and in third countries to drive the Axis powers out of world markets. British economic war policy too increasingly aimed at an "oil famine in Europe."[62]

But exhaustion through attrition was not the only strand of economic warfare. The Ministry of Economic Warfare played an important role in preparing for strategic bombing and in planning the air campaign, since its Industrial Intelligence Centre provided targets and economic data to planners in the Air Ministry. As *The Economist* explained, "The Ministry of Economic Warfare was never a mere Ministry of Blockade, and it was always intended that the bombing operations of the R.A.F. should be guided by this ministry's economic experts. . . . Bombing is the accelerator of blockade."[63] After the blockade's slow reduction of inputs made the enemy economy more brittle, the ministry's planners expected it to crack quickly when hit with the force of strategic air power.[64] In the wake of the Blitz, the British War Cabinet approved the bombing of German cities, and the RAF's first "area bombardment" on an enemy urban center, Operation Abigail Rachel, targeted oil refineries around Mannheim on 16–17 December 1940.[65] Henceforth the Allies would use strategic air power to aggravate their economic blockade of the continent.

Lend-Lease as Anti-Aggression Scheme

The Tripartite Pact signed by Germany, Italy, and Japan on 27 September 1940 marked the beginning of a crucial stage in the strategic history of the war.[66] British unwillingness to sue for peace prevented Germany from striking an inter-imperial bargain, as Hitler had wanted. But his incapacity to offer Spain aid in the face of the American oil embargo dissuaded Franco from joining the Axis, blocking German plans for southward expansion into northwest Africa. This moved the Führer's attention back to his obsession with the resources of Russia and Ukraine, which now seemed the only possible foundation for long-term inter-continental competition with Britain and the United States. On 18 December, Hitler made the fateful decision to attack the Soviet Union by mid-1941.[67]

The Nazi decision to strike east was all the more significant in light of the increasing American involvement in the war. Roosevelt's reelection in November 1940 cleared the way for the intensification of U.S. aid to the Allies. Mere days after the vote, Roosevelt approved orders to manufacture twelve thousand aircraft for Britain and began shipping war materiel to Churchill. Simultaneously, Morgenthau initiated the most significant aid yet to China by granting a $100 million loan to the Nationalists—another message to Tokyo that it should give up all expectations of victory in its war in China.[68] If in 1937–1938 Japan had still tried to destroy the Nationalist economy through its "anti-piracy" blockade of the Chinese coast, two years later this local economic war appeared futile. Any intra-Asian trade that Chiang lost to the stranglehold of the Japanese Navy could be compensated by American dollars.

Washington's role in more ambitious schemes to help the embattled states of the world did not go unnoticed. In December, the League deputy secretary-general Frank Paul Walters wrote from Oxford to his colleague Arthur Sweetser: "I have not at all lost hope that the creative urge of 1917–18, which flowed most strongly in America, may re-appear, and if America takes sides in the war more completely than she has yet done—even without becoming a belligerent—it seems to me not only possible but probable that that will happen." Walters, who had been Cecil's secretary during the Paris Peace Conference, thought that in that case "we might see a New Covenant based on effective economic sanctions, instead of the watering-down which inevitably followed in 1921 from America's withdrawal in 1920."[69]

It might seem startling that in the fall of 1940, with Europe under Nazi control and the Blitz in full swing, an official in a defunct, exiled body could have such high hopes for a new international organization based on "effective economic sanctions." But from a long-term perspective, the reasons for Walters's optimism become clearer. Roosevelt had already broken with decades of post-Wilsonian neutrality by using peacetime economic sanctions and was initiating further anti-aggression policies.

On 17 December, the president returned from his post-campaign holiday determined to aid Britain in a more constructive way. Churchill's government, it was becoming clear, would not be able to pay for the enormous weapons and munitions orders it had placed with American firms. With nearly $5 billion in weapons orders already on the books and just $2 billion in unpledged foreign exchange reserves left, the British Exchequer was on track to run out of money by the summer of 1941.[70] The Americans proposed an agreement in which they would lend the guns, ships, and equipment with which Britain and its allies would fight the war on condition they were counted as aid in kind and that the recipients returned them after victory. This allowed U.S. war production and Allied needs to be integrated into a single organization. On 30 December, Roosevelt announced the so-called Lend-Lease program in one of his fireside chats. Over the next weeks, Morgenthau's Treasury prepared a bill that would disburse $7 billion in material assistance.

The Lend-Lease program is often seen as a liberal internationalist

policy that turned the United States into the "arsenal of democracy"—
a phrase coined by Jean Monnet and used by Roosevelt in a radio address
on 29 December—and avoided a repetition of the fraught transatlantic
war debts problem created by World War I.[71] Roosevelt's generosity contrasts with Wilson's aloofness and the stinginess of Republican administrations in the 1920s. But this comparison misses another context that
is equally relevant to understanding Lend-Lease: the League's interwar
efforts to craft a financial mechanism to aid victims of aggression, which
appeared in the 1930 Convention on Financial Assistance. Lend-Lease
provided the logistical edifice that the League had never fully developed.
Its politics are more ambiguous than the "arsenal of democracy" rhetoric
suggests. Instead of a commitment to the defense of democratic institutions worldwide, Lend-Lease was in fact much closer to what Article 16
had envisioned: the financial defense of state sovereignty against invasion,
irrespective of domestic political arrangements.

To receive assistance under the policy, what mattered was not whether
a state was democratic but whether it was currently, or in danger of becoming, a victim of international aggression. By the winter of 1940–1941,
there were plenty of candidates. Mussolini's invasion of Greece in October had led to calls for assistance from Athens, which Roosevelt promised to deliver in December. On 10 February, as the Lend-Lease Act was
being prepared by Morgenthau's financial experts, Roosevelt's economic
adviser, Lauchlin Currie, visited the Chinese government in Chongqing
to promise Chiang $45 million in military equipment.[72] Four days later,
Secretary of State Cordell Hull offered Lend-Lease aid to Turkey and
Yugoslavia as a reward for joining the coalition against the Axis.[73] That the
proposed financial scheme was intended to assist sovereign nations under
external attack became evident at the time of the congressional hearings
about it. Even Hoover, otherwise an implacable critic of Roosevelt's interventionism, affirmed that "we wish our industries to function for Britain,
China, and Greece."[74] A crucial discretionary provision in the bill allowed
Roosevelt to extend future aid to "any country whose defense the president deems vital to the defense of the United States."[75]

At the start of 1941, Britain, China, and Greece were all fighting aggressors. But this is where the similarities ended. Britain remained a major
naval and military power in Europe, and the true value of American aid
was to enable Whitehall to do what it had done in World War I: act as the
disburser of inter-Allied funds.[76] Most prospective Lend-Lease recipients
were not democracies. Both the Nationalist government in Chongqing

"There's Going to Be No Delay on This Production Job." Cartoon by
C. K. Berryman showing President Roosevelt, Treasury Secretary
Morgenthau, and Democratic House and Senate Majority Leaders
Sam Rayburn and Alben Barkley preparing the Lend-Lease Bill to aid
Britain, Greece, and China. Published in the *Washington Evening Star,*
8 January 1941. Library of Congress.

and the Greek state of Ioannis Metaxas were authoritarian regimes; Turkey remained a single-party state under Ataturk's successor, Ismet Inönü;
only Yugoslavia was a functioning democracy at the time of Hull's promise. The rhetoric of democracy espoused by many American boosters of
Lend-Lease was mainly intended for domestic consumption; the initiative
remained largely indifferent toward the internal politics of the aid recipients. As a Council of Foreign Relations study of the program emphasized,
"No quid pro quo concessions regarding . . . political policy should, if they
can possibly be avoided, be demanded. . . . The United States should ask as
offsets only for such things as are likely to make us more efficient agents in
the promotion of world stability."[77]
    A commitment to liberal democracy was therefore not the reason why

Washington began funding the war efforts of other countries in 1941. What was at stake was not domestic freedoms but the national independence of European, Asian, and Latin American states that had not fallen under Axis control. In the history of collective security and economic sanctions, Lend-Lease implemented the positive economic weapon of Article 16 on a vast scale. Indeed, to commentators at the time the policy seemed "the most important single type of economic sanction employed by the United States."[78] The American Federation of Labor described the bill as "the most important legal and economic weapon of defense," a view that was widely held throughout U.S. civil society.[79] One out of every six dollars Washington spent on the war went to the program; put simply, Lend-Lease was the most significant economic scheme against aggression ever created.[80]

The Lend-Lease administration was run on a day-to-day basis by Edward Stettinius, a business executive from U.S. Steel. Weapons deliveries to Europe were ordered within hours of the president's signing of the bill into law on 11 March 1941.[81] The politics of economic pressure and aid that it activated are poignantly illustrated by the situation of Yugoslavia. A constitutional monarchy under Prince Regent Paul, the country's elite had grown disillusioned with the League after the sanctions during the Italo-Ethiopian War had forced Belgrade to cease trade with Italy, which had been its largest trading partner.[82] This had started Paul's drift into the orbit of the Germans, who by 1940 bought the vast majority of Yugoslav exports. Paul had accepted Cordell Hull's offer of Lend-Lease aid. But Hitler had subsequently put tremendous pressure on the regent to sign the Tripartite Pact with the Axis. When Under-Secretary of State Sumner Welles found out about Paul's change of heart, he notified Belgrade that if it joined Germany, the U.S. government would not only refuse Lend-Lease aid, but would also immediately freeze Yugoslav funds abroad.[83] The choice between receiving aid and suffering financial sanctions could hardly have been clearer. Two days after Paul signed the pact, he was overthrown in a British-backed coup by General Dušan Simović. Yugoslav participation in Lend-Lease appeared to have been saved. But before the artillery, ammunition, and supplies shipped from the United States arrived, Simović's military government faced a German invasion.[84] Belgrade fell on 18 April; Athens, on 27 April. Yugoslavia and Greece, the very countries against which Geneva's negative sanctions had been deployed as a deterrent in the 1920s, narrowly missed out on help from the American positive economic weapon in 1941.

This ill-fated Balkan opening to Lend-Lease meant that Britain became the program's first actual beneficiary. John Maynard Keynes was sent to Washington to negotiate the release of Lend-Lease funds. Appropriately, it was Keynes who had told the EFO already in 1924 that he thought "positive assistance to the injured party" was a better use of the economic weapon than "reprisals against the aggressor."[85] In February 1940, he had calculated that Britain had around £1 billion in usable foreign assets at its disposal.[86] Just a year later, London's national defense expenditures had far outstripped this external wealth. The United States had to be convinced to accept deferred earnings. In the first few months of its existence, Lend-Lease aid substantially supported British foreign procurement. Morgenthau was thus more accurate than Monnet and Roosevelt when he called the program an "arsenal for the Empire."[87]

Understandably, internationalists in Britain and the United States rejoiced at this opening of American industrial and financial power to the world's sovereign nations.[88] Historians have recognized that the international institutions created in 1944–1945 owed much to the interwar League and involved more than just American planners.[89] What the correspondence of leading internationalists shows is that the idea of reviving the League in an improved form was already popular in the spring of 1941, at the time when Lend-Lease aid began to flow. Arthur Sweetser, now based in Princeton with exiled members of the EFO, very much grasped the global material foundations of this institution-building project. Sweetser insisted to Buell that American planners should pursue a true "universal approach." He strongly opposed other proposals making the rounds, such as Clarence Streit's call for a U.S.-British politico-military union, which would raise "a definite danger if we set out for what might appear to be a too exclusivist Anglo-Saxon direction of world affairs."[90] Sweetser urged Cecil not "to lose sight of the other democracies, not only such old friends as Scandinavia, Holland, etc., but also . . . of China." A "Pax Anglo-Americana for the next hundred years" was not a legitimate basis for world order and was bound to "build up a counter-alliance."[91]

In 1920 Sweetser had still been enraptured by the League's "weapon of economic strangulation." But he now placed more trust in forging new connections than severing them and believed that the foundations of peace were being laid by "the inventors and the business men who are driving the world together into one indissoluble unit." The spirit of Geneva had taken up temporary residence on the U.S. eastern seaboard, as Sweetser assured Cecil: "We are keeping the spark alive, both in theory and in fact.

I have the profoundest conviction myself that if we can ever bring this war out the way it ought to be brought out, the League will come back into its own infinitely strengthened over the last time, and the world [will] be made eventually to come out into a period of prosperity and hopefulness such as it never has known."[92]

Deprivation and Provision

Hitler's invasion of the Soviet Union on 22 June 1941 closed the grand strategic options of the preceding year.[93] It provided an occasion for Roosevelt to do what Britain and France had not done earlier: bring the Soviet Union into the armed internationalist coalition against fascism. U.S. aid to the Soviets reversed the prevailing orientation toward Moscow that the old Genevan powers had adopted in 1939. In just two years, the Soviet Union went from being an aggressor against Finland—and thus the target against whom an international resupply campaign might be undertaken—to the victim of aggression benefiting from precisely such a scheme. Finland reinitiated war on the Soviets on 25 June in the so-called Continuation War as co-belligerent of the Axis, causing it to undergo the opposite treatment with astonishing rapidity. In April 1941 Helsinki still received loans from the U.S. Export-Import Bank; by June it had to request licenses from Foreign Funds Control to pass through the American financial blockade, which had by now frozen the foreign assets of *every* continental European country.[94]

In the summer of 1941 the negative sanctions weapon and the positive aid weapon went into action simultaneously. Lend-Lease for the Soviets coincided with the escalation of U.S. economic pressure against Japan and the creation of an economic warfare apparatus in the American state. Nazi aggression also reached its genocidal apex in the war of annihilation waged on the Eastern front. The maelstrom of 1941 thus brought together three central strands in the interwar history of economic sanctions: the parallel use of aid and isolation to prevent and contain aggression, the balancing act involved in applying effective coercion short of war, and the effects of blockade-phobia in a world dominated by sanctions.

The Nazi New Order on the European continent was supposed to be much stronger than imperial Germany's brittle hegemony. One German economist proclaimed that "the 'blockade of Europe' is impossible."[95] But bureaucrats in the regime knew this to be false. Although in 1939 the Reich was barely self-sufficient within its prewar borders, by the winter of

1940 the German conquest of Europe had created raw materials and food shortages that rendered a sustained global power struggle with the British Empire and the United States unfeasible.[96] Adding the western territories of the Soviet Union to this bloc would not improve German Europe's blockade resilience unless these lands were subjected to a campaign of racialized mass starvation on an unimaginable scale. The infamous Nazi *Hungerplan*, prepared in the spring of 1941, spelled out the link between blockade security and mass murder with chilling lucidity: "Many tens of millions of people in this territory will become superfluous and will die or must emigrate to Siberia. Attempts to rescue the population there from death through starvation by obtaining surpluses from the black earth region can only be at the expense of the provisioning of Europe. They prevent the possibility of Germany's holding out until the end of the war, they prevent the blockade resilience of Germany and of Europe [*sie unterbinden die Blockadefestigkeit Deutschlands und Europas*]. With regard to this, absolute clarity must reign."[97] The architects of German resettlement in these ethnically cleansed lands—known as Generalplan Ost—were also oriented toward the goal of *Blockadefestigkeit*.[98] Across the German state, the specter of blockade was invoked in the planning for genocide.[99]

Once the largest invasion force in history crossed into the Soviet Union on 22 June, Western governments began to consider aid to Moscow. Two days after Operation Barbarossa began, Foreign Funds Control released $10 million in frozen Soviet orders for aircraft engines and machine tools and began to unfreeze other Soviet assets. Before the month was out, the Soviet ambassador had asked the State Department for a $500 million credit to finance a wide-ranging supply program.[100] A Soviet military mission arrived in Washington to discuss details in early July. As the Luftwaffe was rapidly gaining control of the skies, the Soviet Air Force was in particularly dire need of high-octane aviation fuel.[101] But the size of the assistance needed grew astronomically as the situation on the Eastern front deteriorated. On 18 July, Roosevelt's cabinet saw the first full Soviet aid request, totaling an eye-watering $1.85 billion in supplies: three thousand fighter and three thousand bomber aircraft, twenty thousand antiaircraft guns, fifty thousand tons of aviation fuel, large amounts of gasoline and lubricants, and $50 million in industrial plant.[102]

Even for an industrial powerhouse such as the United States, this was a tall order to fulfill on short notice. What complicated matters more was that the "war of the factories" on the Eastern front coincided with the intensification of the economic pressure campaign against Japan.[103]

U.S. restrictions on exports of iron ore, hydraulic pumps, and lubrication oil to Japan went into effect in December 1940; in January and February 1941, further sanctions followed on exports of copper, zinc, nickel, and potash. These restrictions were undertaken in a stepwise fashion so that they could be justified as measures to safeguard the supplies needed for rearmament.[104] Indeed, the Lend-Lease economy began to suck raw materials, energy supplies, semi-finished goods, and machine tools from all over the world toward the North American continent.[105]

There was still serious disagreement in the Roosevelt administration about how to confront Japan.[106] Hornbeck at the State Department's Far Eastern Division represented the hardliners in favor of "a comprehensive and thoroughgoing program of measures of material pressure."[107] Joseph Grew, the ambassador in Tokyo, was a steadfast supporter of moderation. Grew did not believe "that the deterioration of Japan's economic and financial resources would within a short time cause Japan as a militaristic power to collapse. . . . Up to the present the facts have failed to support the view that Far Eastern conflict can best be avoided by the continued imposition of embargoes on trade and by the blockading of Japan."[108] Most U.S. policymakers came down somewhere between Hornbeck and Grew, recognizing that while sanctions could cause grave economic damage to Japan, they "would not necessarily stop her war machine."[109] The central policy dilemma was whether to impose an oil embargo. Japan had been stockpiling large amounts of fuel. But by the summer of 1941, the global oil supply situation was being seriously complicated by Lend-Lease. The prioritization of shipments to Britain caused an acute crunch in the U.S. tanker fleet.[110] On 20 June, Interior Secretary and Petroleum Administrator for War Harold Ickes announced that henceforth any petroleum-derived product leaving the United States required an export license.[111] Tanker ships were forbidden from departing Atlantic ports except for Britain or Latin American allies. In a repetition of the August 1940 embargo, neutral Spain and Portugal were starting to experience slower deliveries.[112] The demands of Allied rearmament and Japan's need to bankroll and equip a one-million-strong expeditionary army fighting in China now competed for the same North American resources.

Washington's inclination to use trade controls was encouraged by Japanese moves in the Far East. On 24 July, Vichy French authorities transferred two harbors and eight airbases in Indochina to Japanese control. After speaking to Japanese ambassador Kichisaburō Nomura in Washington, the U.S. chief of naval operations, Admiral Harold Stark, believed that the Japanese military would "consolidate their positions, and await world reaction to their latest move." He doubted that they would attack "*unless* we embargo oil shipments to them. . . . They will do nothing . . . until the outcome of the German-Russian war on the continent is more certain."[113] But in Washington, the move into Indochina decided the argument in favor of the sanctionists. On 25 July Roosevelt froze all Japanese assets in the United States and made all exports to Japan subject to control by license.[114] The export license requirement was intended as a "noose around Japan's neck," which [Roosevelt] would "jerk now and then."[115] Five days later, Roosevelt created the Economic Defense Board, the first dedicated body for the conduct of economic warfare.

Roosevelt may not have intended to impose total economic isolation on Japan. But the British and Dutch cabinets soon joined the U.S. asset freeze, and the Netherlands East Indies government also sharply reduced deliveries of bauxite and rubber. While the American president met Winston Churchill off the coast of Newfoundland to draft the Atlantic Charter, the export control apparatus was transformed by Morgenthau and Assistant Secretary of State Dean Acheson. They turned it into a stringent two-tier licensing system that quickly blocked almost all normal exchange with Japan.[116] Tokyo's position was also weakened by its increasing financial isolation: confined to the yen bloc, by the first week of August 1941 Japan was almost totally cut off from the rest of the world economy, having lost 90 percent of its foreign oil supply and 70 percent of its trade revenues in less than two weeks.[117] The seizure of most of its foreign assets meant Japan would eventually run out of foreign currency with which to pay for vital imports and could no longer replenish its fuel reserves on international markets. As a result, the Anglo-Dutch American economic blockade started the clock on the timeframe within which Japan could seize crucial raw materials in Southeast Asia by force. The chief of the naval general staff, Admiral Osami Nagano, told the emperor on 30 July that "because our supplies are gradually diminishing, if we are going to fight, I think the sooner we do, the better."[118] With the oil sanctions in place, he reminded the leadership that the navy alone was burning four hundred tons of fuel oil every hour.[119]

The simultaneous emergence in summer 1941 of relatively tight Allied sanctions against Japan and construction of the enormous Lend-Lease resource conduits to Britain, China, and the Soviet Union dramatically demonstrated the dual nature of the economic weapon. As in World War I, mobilizing resources for allies went hand in hand with withholding them from enemies. What is especially striking is the crucial role of oil as a swing commodity. Of all U.S. aid to the Soviet Union in the first three months after the start of Operation Barbarossa, petroleum products constituted 79 percent by weight (145,000 tons).[120] Since most of this was delivered by tankers from West Coast refineries, the difference between crippling economic sanctions and crucial material aid thus amounted to the subtle rerouting of energy transport across the Pacific—instead of steaming to Yokohama, U.S. tanker vessels now set course for Vladivostok, a few hundred kilometers north. The difference between exclusion and provision was narrow, but its consequences were enormous.

On the evening of 17 September, as the German advance into the Soviet Union was running out of steam, Hitler had dinner at his headquarters with a small circle of intimates. He proclaimed that "the fight for world hegemony will be decided for Europe by the possession of the Russian region; it will make Europe into the place most resilient to blockade in the world [*blockadefestesten Ort der Welt*]."[121] Several days later, he declared that "the myth, that we can be subjugated by a long war, has to be disposed of. We must no longer believe that the passage of time will force us to our knees."[122] Paradoxically, the temporal claustrophobia that had gripped Hitler so profoundly in 1938–1939 seems to have dissipated as the war he had unleashed became larger in scope and duration. Looking back across the recent past, the Führer explained that "insofar as I recognize a material as crucial for war, it will be my full goal that we render ourselves independent in it: iron, coal, oil, grain, cattle, wood, these one must dispose of." The effort to make Europe immune to blockade had been successful: "Today I can say: Europe is autarkic as long as we just prevent that a giant state [*Riesenstaat*] exists farther away that will use European civilization to mobilize Asia against us."[123]

Giant states far away were indeed mobilizing against Hitler by sharing their resources. On 1 October, Roosevelt's envoy W. Averell Harriman arrived in Moscow. In the presence of Stalin's diplomats Vyacheslav Molotov and Litvinov, as well as the British minister of supply, the newspaper magnate and industrialist Lord Beaverbrook, Harriman signed the so-called Moscow Protocol, starting official Lend-Lease deliveries to the Soviet Union. Especially in the provision of trucks, fuel, and aircraft, as well as in machinery and industrial equipment, the program aided both the Soviet military effort and its war economy.[124] In 1941 the international politics of the economic weapon pivoted with amazing speed. As Lend-Lease shipments for the Soviets began to arrive in the Arctic port of Murmansk,

Iranian women beside a Lend-Lease convoy passing through
the "Persian Corridor" into the Soviet Union, 1944.
Everett Collection Historical/Alamy Stock Photo.

Finnish forces launched a ground offensive to cut off the supply lines
ferrying them to besieged Leningrad. It was an ironic twist: Finland, one
of the interwar originators of the League's financial aid weapon, ended up
fighting the wartime instantiation of that very mechanism. In early 1943
the Finnish government cautiously approached U.S. diplomats, expressing
interest in the Atlantic Charter and inquiring about the possibility of obtaining Lend-Lease aid without belonging to the United Nations.[125] The
temptation was obvious and understandable. By war's end, Lend-Lease
deliveries to the Soviet Union totaled over 400,000 motor vehicles, 1.75
million tons of food, 2.6 million tons of oil, and 53 percent of Soviet heavy
ordnance ammunition production.[126] This allowed the Allies to pursue a
global war in which the manpower of the Red Army and the Chinese Nationalists bore the brunt of the fighting.[127]

Allied economic mobilization would win the war but not before
purposive economic pressure backfired by broadening the conflict. The

Anglo-Dutch-American oil sanctions directly prompted a Japanese offensive against Western interests in Southeast Asia. American policymakers felt emboldened by the success of oil sanctions in keeping Franco out of the war; since they had worked against Spain, why not use them against Japan? In October 1941, Hornbeck was satisfied with the sanctions in place; he dismissed concerns that the Japanese leadership would "go on some terrible rampage. . . . [It] has not, in the presence of severe economic pressures, exploded or gone berserk or moved toward a national *juramentado*."[128] Churchill wrote to Roosevelt on 5 November that the Anglo-Dutch-American front had been "brilliantly successful. But our joint embargo is steadily forcing the Japanese to decisions for peace or war."[129]

One month later, Japan struck at Pearl Harbor and attacked across Southeast Asia. It is still a remarkable historical fact that the Japanese imperial elite consciously launched a war that it knew it stood no chance of winning.[130] Like Hitler in the summer of 1939, Japanese leaders were gripped by temporal claustrophobia. But their sense that time was working against them was not imaginary; it was based on the real material depletion caused by economic sanctions and Japan's international isolation within the yen bloc. Unsurprisingly, the main Japanese objective in the 1941–1942 offensive was control over Indonesian oil resources.[131] When Ambassador Hiroshi Oshima met Hitler in January 1942, he told the Nazi leader that Japan would be able to sustain a war of long duration once it had conquered the raw materials of Southeast Asia. As Japanese armies fanned out across the region, Oshima thought Roosevelt's decision to impose sanctions without preparing an armed defense a big mistake, calling it a "downright insane policy." Hitler, all too familiar with the fear of blockade, agreed and added that "if one doesn't want to wait to have one's throat cut, one must strike just beforehand, and Japan rightly recognized and did this."[132]

But short-term success did not change the Axis powers' long-term disadvantage as they faced forces against which they could not win. The wartime alliance of the United Nations officially came into being on 29 December 1941. Its aims had been announced in the Atlantic Charter.[133] Point four of that declaration promised all nations "access, on equal terms, to the trade and to the raw materials of the world which are needed for their economic prosperity." At this time the United States had already committed Lend-Lease funds to over thirty nations. These supplies were the bread, guns, and butter of the UN alliance. By the summer of 1945, when the program ended, Washington had provided over $48 billion in such supplies and received $8 billion through so-called Reverse Lend-Lease.[134] But Roosevelt also launched new government agencies to direct economic pressure on the enemy, such as the Board of Economic Warfare created in December 1941.[135] Consisting of three branches—imports, exports, and analysis—its institutional simplicity was a testament to Washington's commanding material position. Determining which country received what raw materials was to a large extent a matter of managing the internal production and external supply of the U.S. economy. The board's Office of Exports focused on which goods and resources could be spared for shipment to no fewer than thirty-eight different countries, while its Office of Imports managed "foreign sources of critical material supplies."[136] The board's work was based on the premise that "the power of supply can be used as a positive economic weapon in the successful prosecution of the war."[137]

The chairman of the Board of Economic Warfare was Roosevelt's vice president, Henry Wallace. A left-wing New Dealer with agrarian roots, Wallace had ambitious visions for a postwar world in which economic security and a decent standard of living would be made available to every human being. In his famous "Price of Free World Victory" speech on 8 May 1942, Wallace prophesied about a "people's century" and "a century of the common man" for all nations around the world. He reiterated that Roosevelt's "Four Freedoms are the very core of the revolution for which the United Nations have taken their stand."[138] Wallace felt, however, that "we cannot perpetuate economic warfare without planting the seeds of military warfare."[139] Unlike in 1914–1918, the United Nations at war had to be ready to use the power of provision for transformative social ends. Many interwar critics of sanctions saw political conflict as caused in large part by socioeconomic disparities. As Wallace told Ivy Low Litvinov, the British-born wife of the Soviet foreign minister, "The object of this war is to make sure that everybody in the world has the privilege of drinking a quart of milk a day" (a remark to which she responded, "Yes, even half a pint").[140] This was a political-economic agenda quite different from the frugal internationalism of the League founders. Robert Cecil observed such progressive policies with suspicion, explaining that although he supported "a revival of the League in some form or another," he was "most frightened of the Left Wing enthusiasts, who see a great opportunity for trying to use the revived League of Nations for the enforcement of their economic views."[141]

By the spring of 1943 the economic pressure on Europe was being referred to as "the United Nations blockade."[142] The UN war effort involved both economic and air war planners directly targeting enemy civilians and administrators preparing material assistance to those same civilians. The year 1943, for example, saw both the firebombing of German cities and the creation of the United Nations Relief and Rehabilitation Administration (UNRRA).[143] Material provision would flow to every country in the world after the war's end but on terms decided by the Allies. There was no question that the war would end with the enemy's unconditional surrender.[144] Allied schemes for future world organization were built on interlocking monopolies: a global intervention force, strategic resource control, and, following from these, the capacity to use hermetic sanctions against aggressors without neutrality for third countries. Charles Leith, now a mineral consultant for the War Production Board, thought that "the United States must formulate a mineral policy which will encompass sanctions against future aggressors. . . . Some solution to the sanctions problem . . . must be found if Axis rearmament is to be prevented."[145] The "sanctions problem" therefore seemed to be tied to questions of institutional design—how to create something like the League's Article 16 but better—and material stabilization: how to fix the damage done by the war to the world economy.

This was a formidable challenge. When the Bank for International Settlements surveyed the world economy in 1944, it estimated that of a total prewar world trade volume of $46 billion, almost $20 billion had been destroyed, suppressed, or blocked by state restrictions.[146] Massive shifts in production, trade, and distribution had taken place. The Soviet Union suffered twenty-seven million citizens dead and lost 80 percent of its prewar trade and a quarter of its capital stock. But even here the new connections forged by wartime logistics offered a basis for reconstruction: the Soviets also supplied the United States with thirty-two thousand tons of manganese and three hundred thousand tons of chromium under the Reverse Lend-Lease arrangement, sustaining U.S. production of high-quality steel for the entire United Nations.[147] As Allied victory came into view, the question of the economic weapon's role in postwar international organization therefore loomed larger.

Sanctions in a New Multilateralism

On 30 October 1943, the foreign ministers of the United States, Britain, the Soviet Union, and China issued the Moscow Declaration, in which they agreed to establish a postwar security organization.[148] Under the aegis of the LNU, Robert Cecil produced a "Draft Pact for a Future International Authority" that mirrored this four-power structure.[149] Sweetser passed on this draft to State Department planners and in February 1944 conveyed to the British that the Americans found military cooperation the most important element of the postwar order.[150] This was precisely the domain in which Anglo-American agreement had been lacking at the Paris Peace Conference in 1919. Cecil, by now seventy-nine years old, felt that an international organization with military power was absolutely necessary. As he wrote in a letter to his older brother during the war, there were cases in which "nothing short of actual force will stop aggressors."[151]

Cecil's family had become a dynasty of economic warriors. His nephew Roundell Palmer, the third Earl of Selborne—son of his sister Maud—was Britain's minister of economic warfare from February 1942 until the end of the war. Selborne subscribed to the same long-term logic of exhaustion as his uncle. Before the House of Lords, he defended British economic warfare as a giant symphony of attritional instruments, in which "the Navies stop the import of rubber from Malaya, [while] the Air Forces destroy the synthetic rubber factories in Germany." The result was "a vast combined operation against the enemy's fighting power by various methods outside and inside his frontiers."[152] Selborne's views followed Cecil's own musings in 1916 about the blockade as a model for world order, but they went beyond them because of the advent of new technologies and policies. Strategic air power and global resource control enabled modern economic warfare to grind down even the most resilient enemies. If the point was to avoid war, then, as useful as sanctions might be, direct military measures remained the best deterrent. To Cecil the Manchurian and Ethiopian crises had proven that the most important element in war prevention was less the economic weapon itself than "a strong and instructed body of opinion in favour of international organisation, in the first place to prevent aggression if necessary by force."[153] The interwar internationalist hope that economic coercion could transcend military force in world affairs had been chastened; armies, navies, and air forces remained a necessary backstop of global order.

The British government also thought along these lines when it suggested in July 1944 that "the proposed organisation will have to rely, in the main, on the combined military forces of the United Nations and, in particular, of the Four Powers, working together to a common end." What the League had called "public war" was for the UN nothing other than a coalition war by the United States, Britain, the Soviet Union, and China. Economic sanctions, the Foreign Office felt, "might deter potential aggressors, but unless backed by force or the effective threat of it are unlikely to prove an adequate check on a State which is, itself, ready to resort to force."[154] These observations were an admission that economic sanctions were an intermediate tool in the hierarchy of force. The American government also considered sanctions to be "economic, commercial, financial, and other measures of enforcement not involving use of armed force."[155] At the same time, the ladder of coercive measures outlined by the United Nations in 1944–1945 consolidated something the League had not succeeded in establishing: a distinction between uses of force that constituted war proper and forms of coercion, such as economic sanctions, that fell short of war and thus still preserved peace in notional terms.

During this planning phase, the United Nations imagined using future sanctions against the countries it was currently fighting. In 1944 as in 1918, the universal problem of sanctions contained a specific political question: how to deal with Germany. U.S. occupation planning aimed at shock economic liberalization through the dismantling of industrial cartels, exchange controls, and bilateral trade arrangements. A post-Nazi Germany should be so profoundly integrated into world trade that it could never again consider an aggressive bid for autonomy. Germany's ability to export and import should be unrestricted, precisely so that it would remain highly open and hence vulnerable to being disciplined by sanctions.[156]

During inter-Allied talks held at Dumbarton Oaks from August to October 1944, the League sanctions model was reworked. Sanctions were recognized as both war-preventing and war-containing measures. They could be enforced by the UN Security Council, which could punish nonparticipation and enforce general implementation.[157] Military action could be taken to ensure the efficacy of blockades, which could proceed fluidly into war if the Security Council so decided. Sanctions were thereby firmly established midway on the spectrum between moral pressure and military action. The United Nations' major innovation over the League in the realm of sanctions was its introduction of a two-tiered sanctions model. This was based on a Soviet memorandum that ranked different measures of pressure on an increasing spectrum of coercion.[158] First came the "economic pressure" of specific sanctions, then the severing of diplomatic relations, followed by the severance of *all* commercial and financial interaction with an aggressor, including postal, rail, telegraph, and other traffic. These three sets of sanctions were united in the UN Charter's Article 41 as measures "not involving the use of armed force." The more powerful enforcement methods on the Soviet list included the establishment of UN military bases in the territories of victim states, the imposition of sea and land blockade, naval and air force demonstrations, air raids "on particular military objectives of the aggressor state," and, finally, military operations by UN forces. These uses of armed force were prescribed by Article 42, which could be applied when the comparatively milder sanctions of Article 41 "would be inadequate or have proved to be inadequate." Furthermore, Article 42 permitted immediate escalation to military force if the Security Council expected that economic sanctions were unlikely to work. In this realm, too, a major weakness of the League—its adherence to a highly predictable step-by-step procedure for escalation that delayed effective pressure—was corrected. Taken together, these innovations made Articles 41 and 42 of the UN Charter a more forceful, precise, and streamlined sanctions mechanism than the League's Article 16 procedure.[159]

The British, American, and Soviet proposals were put up for discussion before a wider group of countries at the San Francisco Conference, which opened on 25 April 1945, two weeks before the end of the war in Europe. Fifty-one countries were present to determine the details of the functioning of the United Nations Organization; three-fourths of the delegations in attendance, some thirty-eight countries, had been Lend-Lease recipients.[160] As a result, the legitimacy of economic sanctions as an international practice was significantly greater than it had been in 1919, when Cecil and Bourgeois presented their sanctions articles to European neutrals. Moreover, the United Nations seemed a surer protector of state sovereignty now that non-capitalist and non-Western states such as the Soviet Union and China were represented on the Security Council.

It was never in doubt *whether* economic sanctions would return in the post–World War II international order. Even officials of the defunct League, such as Frank Paul Walters, could see as early as December 1940 that what mattered was *how* and *when* effective economic sanctions would emerge as part of any new institutional architecture. Although the League's interwar sanctions are often dismissed as a misconceived experiment, this only reinforces the question of why they reappeared so soon after in the UN Charter. As we have seen, the assumption of failure is itself partially misconceived. Internationalists like Cecil and Sweetser believed that during the 1930s the League had never dared to push collective security to the logical extreme of public war against an aggressor. Many at the San Francisco Conference agreed; the French government, for example, argued that economic sanctions could have prevented a European security crisis in 1935, at the time of the Stresa front, but that "a weakening of wills" had been the problem, not "a defect in [Europe's] institutions."[161] The French elite had felt that Britain in particular had abandoned them in this respect.[162] In 1944–1945, however, France benefited from the unusual generosity of the Allies. Churchill secured Stalin's agreement to grant Charles de Gaulle's government a permanent Security Council seat.[163] Thus the results of the San Francisco Conference ultimately came to reflect something quite close to Léon Bourgeois's original agenda at Versailles: negative economic sanctions *and* positive economic assistance, plus the power to deploy UN military force against aggressors.

The consolidation of economic sanctions in the UN Charter was a victory for a new brand of internationalism. It also constituted a revolution in international law as it had existed for centuries, as those who had lived through the fin-de-siècle period realized. One such observer was the British politician Joseph Kenworthy. An officer in the Admiralty during World War I, Kenworthy had become a vocal critic of the undeclared Allied blockade of Russia in 1919. Like many British Liberals, he felt that undeclared economic war was a despicable instrument for the defense of civilization. By 1944, Kenworthy had left the Liberal Party and was a Labour peer in the House of Lords. During World War II he observed that "in these days, first of all of totalitarian war, and then of war against robber States such as Germany and Japan, the conception of neutrality has largely disappeared. You cannot have neutrals any longer in the old sense in the future, and we shall not have won this war in the political sense if we do not succeed in establishing a system after the war by which in the case of a new aggression or new outburst of lawlessness no neutrals remain."[164]

The classical era of neutrality had indeed ended, and with it, the way that war and peace had functioned in the international order.[165] In the coming era of superpower conflict, the end of neutrality put the independence of small countries back into question. Economic warfare created, in the words of the blockade's main historian, "a world fit, or fit only, for belligerents to live in."[166] Neutralists saw this as a tragic defeat. The American jurist Edwin Borchard attacked the new disposition in 1946, arguing that "the chameleonic epithet 'aggressor' . . . is applied selectively to those particular disturbers of the status quo whom the dominant states happen to dislike. . . . It is responsible for the doctrine of sanctions, designed to bend nations to the will of the ruling group." Borchard was no cynic: the child of German-Jewish immigrants, he despised Nazism and supported Latin American sovereignty, restrictions on the use of force, and development aid. Still, Borchard advocated for "curtailing if not abandoning sanctions, an instrumentality of economic warfare, which widens the gap between the possessing nations and others and constitutes a constant incentive to conflict."[167] At the time of the Paris Peace Conference in 1919 there had been many who had criticized sanctions as the illicit continuation of war in peacetime. But by 1945 the sanctionists were in the majority in Western capitals, and the neutralists were strongly outnumbered. This was not because sanctions were no longer seen as coercive. Rather, after the preceding decade's landscape of savagery, culminating in the horrors of Auschwitz and the devastation of Hiroshima, the spectrum of imaginable violence had expanded so dramatically that sanctions appeared comparatively mild.

By 1945, the material conditions existed in which the idea of ending aggression could acquire real teeth. For the first time, a sizable group of states was able and willing not just to chastise transgressors, but also to organize resources for solidarity. At its head stood the United States, the workshop of the world, its main aid provider, and the rising sanctions-wielding state. In light of its interwar opposition to sanctionism, the U.S. emergence in this role was a remarkable historical reversal.[168] At the same time, the United Nations, an organization whose roots lay in the geopolitical defense against aggression and was held together by the political agnosticism of Lend-Lease, was a diverse collection of regimes. For this reason it was, unlike the League, "never a plausible instrument of ideological warfare."[169] Neither authoritarianism nor empire was an obstacle to UN membership; only wartime support for the Axis was. Spain, for example, was officially put under the diplomatic sanction of non-recognition by the Security Council in 1946. A year later, two American economic war administrators suggested that Franco's dictatorship, "a disreputable Fascist remnant, unfit to be received into respectable international society," could be brought down by economic controls modeled on Washington's oil sanctions against Madrid in 1940; this peaceful coercion could pave the way for a UN "caretaker regime."[170] Spanish isolation lasted until 1950, when Dean Acheson, one of the architects of the fateful U.S. oil embargo on Japan, engineered the country's admission to the United Nations.

The mid-century birth of the international order that we still inhabit today made economic sanctions appear in a new light. The contentious interwar history of the practice was either forgotten, dismissed as a false start, or remembered as a failed idealistic experiment. By contrast, UN embargoes and Cold War–era sanctions were portrayed as a benign alternative to atomic war, an enlightened overcoming of the past. Yet the economic weapon was an interwar creation that was carried over into the postwar world by power politics. What had changed after 1945 was that a novel group of nations had come to agree on a new institutional framework for its use. The history of sanctions also changed in character. Between the wars it had been a predominantly Euro-American affair in which the non-Western world was peripherally involved. For the rest of the century, it would be a global practice in which American power was dominant, while the socialist Eastern bloc and newly independent states in the Third World both resisted and appropriated the tools of economic pressure.

Conclusion

From Antidote to Alternative

E CONOMIC SANCTIONS AS WE know them today emerged a century ago. Toward the end of World War I, organized material pressure emerged as a new answer to an old question: how could war be prevented without resorting to military force? What the victors called their "economic weapon" would be used by the League of Nations to bring wayward states to their senses. After the horrific destruction of the Great War, international institutions adopted techniques of economic war and reframed them as an antidote to war itself. By the end of the war, it was clear that sanctions were likely to become "a permanent part of the machinery of organised mankind."[1]

Seen from the twenty-first century, they have indeed become permanent, but not without important shifts in scope and function.[2] The interwar history of sanctions illuminates our present in three areas. First, it highlights how profoundly liberal internationalism has been shaped by the era of total war between 1914 and 1945. Second, it puts into perspective how the rise of U.S. hegemony has normalized the use of sanctions while widening their goals. Third, it forces us to think about how economic pressure does and does not shape political outcomes, suggesting a key distinction between the *effects* and the *efficacy* of sanctions in global history.

Interwar internationalists sincerely wanted to preserve peace. But since they were unable to erase the memory of civilian suffering caused by the wartime blockade, they decided to embrace this legacy instead. This was the origin of the idea of sanctions deterrence. Knowledge of the horrors of the past would keep future lawbreakers in check. Sanctions deterrence worked to keep peace in the Balkans during the 1920s. But after the Great Depression, as ideological and military rivalry mounted, it came under strain. The Norwegian internationalist Christian Lange worried in 1933 that "where it was possible to use the threat of Article 16 as a preventive of war against small States . . . there was no possibility of using this threat against powerfully-armed States."[3]

Amid rising economic nationalism, peacetime sanctions became more difficult to distinguish from the wartime blockade that had inspired them. In these conditions, sanctions did not stop political and economic disintegration but accelerated it. The English international affairs analyst Helena Swanwick pointed out in 1937 that this meant preparing for war: "If we insist on pursuing a policy of sanctions in Europe as it now is, we must re-arm. . . . What sanctionists will not realize is that the theory of sanctions ties the whole League up to the Balance of Power."[4] Internationalists did not abandon economic coercion as a means of enforcing collective security in the 1940s. But they had to fight another, still more devastating world war before they could establish the policy on a more solid foundation.

Far from being bleeding-heart pacifists, early twentieth-century liberal internationalists were deeply concerned with the use of force. In their eyes, World War I had shattered the old belief that people were inherently peaceful and only their rulers belligerent. The innovation of sanctions was to rely on economic total war to intimidate peoples into restraining their princes. Interwar sanctionists transformed the liberal state, defended the League, attacked neutrality, stigmatized aggression, and justified the threat and application of coercion against civilians. This was a formidable political challenge, and it is not surprising that this project was initially met with resistance.

But the acceptance of sanctions was never a question of narrow legality alone. Since World War II it has become clear that sanctions depend on a substratum of general consent. Economic coercion can find a place in politics if its goals and methods enjoy legitimacy. Multilateral organizations like the United Nations and the European Union have given sanctions a legitimacy that the interwar League of Nations, an organization dominated by empires openly espousing a hierarchy of civilization, never could.[5] But as sanctions have become an accepted tool of liberal international institutions, the threshold for using them has declined. How to respond to the violation of norms remains, ultimately, a political question. In the spring of 1919, Robert Cecil waved away protests against using blockade to overthrow Bolshevism by responding that he saw "no other alternative." Many of today's internationalists, too, see few alternatives. This perception has driven some of the most grievously counterproductive uses of sanctions, most prominently against Iraq in the 1990s, when its strangulation at the hands of the UN Security Council cost hundreds of thousands of lives and permanently damaged the country's social and economic fabric.[6]

These humanitarian nightmares are an important reminder of the lethal early twentieth-century origins of sanctions. But most economic sanctions used today are far more mundane in character. In 2015 a UN official estimated that one-third of the world's population lives in countries that are under some form of economic sanctions.[7] These range from the specific, such as individual travel bans and asset freezes, to more general measures, such as technological and trade restrictions.[8] Today's omnipresent sanctions have traveled a long way from their interwar purpose of preventing war.

This normalization of sanctions as part of the everyday reality of international politics underscores a second point: the consequences of the U.S. rise to global power in the twentieth century. It is a historical irony that the state that between the world wars most fervently opposed economic sanctions has been their most avid user over the last seven decades. In 1929 President Herbert Hoover, a neutralist and humanitarian internationalist, was still able to cast sanctions as a fundamentally un-American practice, an anachronistic form of European-style imperialism. Just over a decade later, Roosevelt's turn to global supremacy went hand in hand with the use of both negative sanctions (oil embargoes) and positive sanctions (Lend-Lease). At the time, the émigré economist Albert Hirschman hoped that the "internationalization of power over external economic relations would go far toward the goal of a peaceful world."[9] America could complete the job begun by Geneva. In practice, the world's de facto sanctionist headquarters quickly moved from the United Nations in New York to U.S. national security institutions in Washington.

America's sanctionism has been shaped by three factors: its unique military dominance, the ideological inflection of Cold War politics, and the role of U.S. financial markets in the world economy. Nuclear weapons and strategic air power made it possible to conceive of deterrence, something that the interwar economic weapon had struggled to project, on a global and existential scale. But nukes also gave economic "peacewar" a new lease on life. The risk of nuclear escalation meant that forms of force that did not trigger conventional war became newly attractive as ways of weakening opposing states.[10] The capitalist Western bloc deployed its economic strength to grind down the long-term growth of the socialist Eastern bloc. This containment took place through multilateral measures such as the Coordinating Committee for Multilateral Export Controls (CoCom).[11] At the level of national policy, the U.S. government transformed the Treasury's Foreign Funds Control. During the Korean War it was renamed and expanded into the Office of Foreign Assets Control (OFAC), the agency that still superintends U.S. sanctions policy today; at the time of this writing, it administers sanctions on over sixteen thousand individuals and organizations.[12]

The aims of economic pressure have expanded too. Interwar sanctions were focused narrowly on the *external* goal of stopping inter-state war. Multilateral and unilateral sanctions since 1945 have usually had *internal* goals: to address human rights violations, convince dictatorships to give way to democracy, smother nuclear programs, punish criminals, press for the release of political prisoners, or obtain other concessions. Since the norms of liberal internationalism have been largely determined by the transatlantic alliance, sanctions objectives are also an index of changing foreign policy concerns. Cold War sanctions and blockades targeted socialist states such as the Soviet Union, Communist China, North Korea, Cuba, and Vietnam.[13] Decolonization challenged the Western monopoly on sanctions, as Asian and African states campaigned for their use against white settler regimes. This culminated in UN sanctions against Rhodesia from 1965 to 1979 and increasing pressure on South Africa thereafter.[14] The Iranian Revolution prompted a U.S. campaign of economic pressure against the Islamic republic that has lasted four decades and continues to this day, with a mixed effect on Tehran's aims and policies.[15] Other Islamist states that incurred major international and U.S. sanctions were Sudan after 1989 and Libya from 1992. These efforts formed part of a wider 1990s shift toward the containment and overthrow of "backlash" or "rogue" states.[16] Often framed around nuclear non-proliferation and human rights concerns, this enduring landscape of sanctions shows little sign of disappearing soon, despite its general inability to produce regime change and serious cost to the populations and economies of the Middle East and East Asia.

The rising incidence and widening aims of sanctions under U.S. hegemony also reflect important shifts in global economic history. Roosevelt's sanctions on Spain and Japan in 1940–1941 were made possible because he governed the largest oil producer in the world. This power slipped from America's grasp due to the rise of the Organization of the Petroleum Exporting Countries (OPEC) in the 1960s and 1970s.[17] The most notable U.S. attempt to manipulate export power was the underwhelming 1980 embargo on grain exports to the Soviet Union.[18] In the long run, however, commodity control was not where Washington's advantage was greatest. Its hegemony derived less from goods trade than from international leadership in corporate, regulatory, technological, and financial structures—an ensemble of capacities that policymakers have come to see as tools of "economic statecraft."[19]

Finance is a particularly potent conduit for pressure. Just as Hawtrey, Strakosch, and Keynes saw the City of London as an essential sanctionist hub in the 1920s, so the pivotal role of Wall Street in the global financial system since the 1970s has provided significant levers for policymakers to exploit.[20] Because the dollar is the premier reserve currency and most popular medium for global trade and debt issuance, a vast segment of international markets and firms falls under U.S. jurisdiction in some way or other. This "weaponized interdependence" has been deepened by the unprecedented interventions of the Federal Reserve since the 2008 global financial crisis.[21] Today, global banks and corporate finance are the frontline of sanctions implementation and compliance. The limits on Washington's use of this financial power are political rather than infrastructural in nature. U.S. policymakers have shown remarkable ingenuity at mastering the plumbing of economic globalization. But the challenge that they face is translating this technical skill into beneficial outcomes in the real world.

This brings us to a final point about sanctions: the difference between economic effects and political outcomes. The policy debate about sanctions has been repeated almost every decade since the League was created in the wake of World War I. At its core has been the perennial question: do economic sanctions work?[22] While the success rate differs depending on the objective, the historical record is relatively clear: most economic sanctions have not worked. In the twentieth century, only one in three uses of sanctions was "at least partially successful."[23] More modest goals have better chances of success. But from the available data it is clear that the history of sanctions is largely a history of disappointment.

What is striking is that this limited utility has not affected frequency of use. To the contrary: sanctions use *doubled* in the 1990s and 2000s compared to the period from 1950 to 1985; by the 2010s it had doubled again. Yet while in the 1985–1995 period, at a moment of great relative Western power, the chances of sanctions success were still around 35–40 percent, by 2016 this had fallen below 20 percent.[24] In other words, while the use of sanctions has surged, their odds of success have plummeted.

But to focus on whether sanctions have *efficacy* in achieving their goals would be to miss their tremendous *effects* on the world's political and economic history. It is vital to distinguish between these aspects.[25] The history of interwar sanctions provides excellent examples of the contrasts and connection between efficacy and effects. Interwar observers often took blockade's visible and horrifying impact on Central Europe as proof that this policy had been essential to Allied victory in World War I. Effects were equated with efficacy without an investigation of the complex links between them. The conflation was politically useful since it boosted trust in the League's ability to keep peace with its fearsome economic weapon. Effects were not a prerequisite of efficacy, however. The most successful interwar sanctions, against Yugoslavia in 1921 and Greece in 1925, involved threats rather than actual application. A depreciated dinar and a humbled general were small prices to pay for the preservation of peace in the Balkans. High efficacy was thus possible in the absence of dramatic effects. In the 1930s, the relationship between effects and efficacy changed yet again. League sanctions against Italy were not effective in stopping Mussolini or saving Ethiopia, but they had marked effects on the Italian regime and the autarkic aims and trajectories of Nazi Germany and Japan. Blockade-phobia meant that the unintended and counterproductive effects of the policy overtook its political goals. It is in this dynamic interaction between effects and efficacy that the true historical significance of sanctions lies, in the era of the world wars as much as in the present.

Perhaps the most confounding aspect of sanctions is that regardless of their technical sophistication, their outcome is never a matter of economic factors alone. Interwar sanctionists assumed state behavior was driven by popular opinion and the material self-interest of populations and elites. But in light of the experience of World War I, this view was dangerously single-minded. Nationalism, fear-mongering, and violent racism surged. Ideals of cultural unity, historic rights to territory, and promises of self-determination and social transformation mobilized millions of Europeans. Given the power of such ideas to move entire societies, how would economic pressure alone dissuade them from repeating such collective struggle? While history shows the power of material calculations, it illustrates equally important countervailing motives. Herodotus ends his *Histories* by recounting how the sixth-century BCE Persians consciously chose *not* to settle in rich and fertile agricultural regions that easily fell under foreign influence, preferring to remain in the rugged mountains of their ancestors; in his words, they "opted to live in a harsh land and rule, rather than to sow a level plain, and be the slaves of others."[26]

The same aspect of economic sanctions that makes them philosophically appealing to liberal internationalism—their reliance on a *homo economicus* rationale—also limits their salience. Economic sanctions do not project only material force; they also project political, social, and cultural values. Sanctions would no doubt work better in a world of perfectly rational, consistently self-interested subjects, but this is not the world that we actually inhabit. Most people in most places at most times make collective choices on the basis of a wider set of considerations. The economic weapon may be a form of politics by other means. But ultimately, stitching animosity into the fabric of international affairs and human exchange is of limited use in changing the world.

Notes

Archives

BA-BL	Bundesarchiv Berlin-Lichterfelde	
BA-MA	Bundesarchiv Militar-Archiv (Freiburg)	
BL	British Library (London)	
	RCP	Robert Cecil Papers
HIA	Hoover Institution Archives (Stanford)	
	SHP	Stanley Hornbeck Papers
KCAC	King's College Archive Centre, Cambridge (UK)	
	AEF	Arthur Elliott Felkin Papers
	JMK	John Maynard Keynes Papers
LOC	Library of Congress (Washington, DC)	
	AS	Arthur Salter Papers
	ND	Norman Davis Papers
LoN	League of Nations Archives (Geneva)	
	ASP	Arthur Salter Papers
	EFO	Economic and Financial Organization
MAE	Ministère des affaires étrangères (La Courneuve)	
	PA-AP	Private archives and papers
PAAA	Politisches Archiv des Auswärtiges Amt (Berlin)	
SHD	Service historique de la défense (Vincennes)	
TNA	The National Archives (Kew, UK)	
	ADM	Admiralty
	AIR	Air Ministry
	CAB	Cabinet
	CID	Committee of Imperial Defence
	FO	Foreign Office
	T	Treasury

Printed Document Collections

ADAP   Akten zur deutschen auswärtigen Politik, 1918–1925; 1925–1933; 1933–1939

DBFP   Documents on British Foreign Policy, 1919–1939

DDI   I Documenti diplomatici italiani, 1918–1935

DGFP   Documents on German Foreign Policy

FRUS   Foreign Relations of the United States

HCPP   House of Commons Parliamentary Papers

IMT   Trial of the Major War Criminals before the International Military Tribunal, 1945–1946

LON   League of Nations Official documents

NCA   Nazi Conspiracy and Aggression, 1945–1946

NMT   Nuremberg Military Tribunals, 1945–1949

Introduction: Something More Tremendous Than War

1. Woodrow Wilson, *Woodrow Wilson's Case for the League of Nations* (Princeton, NJ: Princeton University Press, 1923), pp. 67, 69, 71.

2. Ibid., pp. 71–72.

3. W. Arnold-Forster, "The Future of Blockades—Part II," *Foreign Affairs* 2, no. 3 (September 1920): 38.

4. Mary Elisabeth Cox, "Hunger Games: Or How the Allied Blockade in the First World War Deprived German Children of Nutrition, and Allied Food Aid Subsequently Saved Them," *Economic History Review* 68, no. 2 (2015): 600–631.

5. In House of Commons debate, July 23, 1923, in *Hansard*, vol. 167, p. 82.

6. John Buckley, *Air Power in the Age of Total War* (London: UCL Press, 1999), p. 61.

7. David Edgerton, *England and the Aeroplane: Militarism, Modernity and Machines* (London: Penguin, 2013); Thomas Hippler, *Governing from the Skies: A Global History of Aerial Bombing* (London: Verso, 2017); David Omissi, *Air Power and Colonial Control: The Royal Air Force, 1919–1939* (Manchester: Manchester University Press, 1990).

8. L. F. Haber, *The Poisonous Cloud: Chemical Warfare in the First World War* (Oxford: Clarendon Press, 1986), p. 243.

9. For the Central European figure, see Avner Offer, *The First World War: An Agrarian Interpretation* (Oxford: Clarendon Press, 1989), pp. 33–34; for the Middle East, see Linda Schatkowski-Schilcher, "The Famine of 1915–1918 in Greater Syria," in *Problems of the Modern Middle East in Historical Perspective: Essays in Honour of Albert Hourani*, ed. John Spagnolo, pp. 229–258 (Reading, England: Ithaca Press, 1996).

10. W. Arnold-Forster, "Democratic Control and the Economic War," *Foreign Affairs* 9, no. 1 (March 1920): 11.

11. Garrard Glenn, "War without Guns," *Virginia Quarterly Review* 8, no. 1 (July 1932): 393.

12. Wilson, *Woodrow Wilson's Case for the League of Nations*, p. 72.

13. MAE, Série Guerre 1914–1918, Box A-1276, Rapport sur la conference de Londres, 16–27 August 1917. Unless otherwise noted, all translations are mine.

14. Ranajit Guha, *Dominance without Hegemony: History and Power in Colonial India* (Cambridge, MA: Harvard University Press, 1998).

15. Hans Kelsen, *Collective Security under International Law* (Washington, DC: GPO, 1957).

16. The classic account of the interwar failure of smooth hegemonic transition is Charles P. Kindleberger, *The World in Depression, 1929–1939* (Berkeley: University of California Press, 1973); for a modern update, see Robert Boyce, *The Great Interwar Crisis and the Collapse of Globalization* (Basingstoke: Palgrave Macmillan, 2009).

17. John G. Ruggie, "International Regimes, Transactions, and Change: Embedded Liberalism in the Postwar Economic Order," *International Organization* 36, no. 2 (April 1982): 379–415.

18. The role of uneven and combined development in producing an "insurgency" against liberalism unites the historical work of Adam Tooze: *The Wages of Destruction: The Breaking and Making of the Nazi Economy* (London: Viking, 2006), and *The Deluge: The Great War and the Remaking of Global Order, 1916–1931* (London: Allen Lane, 2014); the role of competitive rearmament is stressed by Joseph A. Maiolo, *Cry Havoc: How the Arms Race Drove the World to War, 1931–1941* (New York: Basic Books, 2010); for a comprehensive diplomatic history of the interwar breakdown, see Zara Steiner, *The Triumph of the Dark: Interwar International History, 1933–1939* (New York: Oxford University Press, 2011); on conjoined but ideologically opposed projects of mass industrialization, see Stefan J. Link, *Forging Global Fordism: Nazi Germany, Soviet Russia, and the Contest over the Industrial Order* (Princeton, NJ: Princeton University Press, 2020).

19. Key contributions to this literature are Iris Borowy, *Coming to Terms with World Health: The League of Nations Health Organisation, 1921–1946* (Frankfurt: Peter Lang, 2009); Paul Knepper, *International Crime in the 20th Century: The League of Nations Era, 1919–1939* (New York: Palgrave Macmillan, 2011); Daniel Laqua, *Transnational Ideas and Movements between the World Wars* (London: Bloomsbury, 2011); Daniel Gorman, *The Emergence of International Society in the 1920s* (Cambridge: Cambridge University Press, 2012); Patricia Clavin, *Securing the World Economy: The Reinvention of the League of Nations, 1920–1946* (Oxford: Oxford University Press, 2013); Glenda Sluga, *Internationalism in the Age of Nationalism* (Philadelphia: University of Pennsylvania Press, 2013); Bruno Cabanes, *The Great War and the Origins of Humanitarianism, 1918–1924* (Cambridge: Cambridge University Press,

2014); Susan Pedersen, *The Guardians: The League of Nations and the Crisis of Empire* (New York: Oxford University Press, 2015); Amalia Ribi Forclaz, *Humanitarian Imperialism: The Politics of Anti-Slavery Activism, 1880–1940* (Oxford: Oxford University Press, 2015); Heidi J. S. Tworek, *News from Germany: The Competition to Control World Communications, 1900–1945* (Cambridge, MA: Harvard University Press, 2019); Diana S. Kim, *Empires of Vice: The Rise of Opium Prohibition across Southeast Asia* (Princeton, NJ: Princeton University Press, 2020); Mira Siegelberg, *Statelessness: A Modern History* (Cambridge, MA: Harvard University Press, 2020).

20. Arthur Sweetser, *The League of Nations at Work* (New York: Macmillan, 1920), pp. 175–176.

21. David Edgerton, *Warfare State: Britain, 1920–1970* (Cambridge: Cambridge University Press, 2006), pp. 66–75; on the emergence of U.S.-led multilateral institutions backed by armed force as a "distinctly American internationalism," see Stephen Wertheim, *Tomorrow, the World: The Birth of U.S. Global Supremacy* (Cambridge, MA: Harvard University Press, 2020).

22. René Cassin, "L'évolution des conditions juridiques de la guerre économique," *Politique étrangère* 4, no. 5 (October 1939): 488–512, 506. In the 1940s, Cassin would become famous as the French co-author of the Universal Declaration of Human Rights.

23. A good overview of the origins of World War II is Robert Boyce and Joseph A. Maiolo, eds., *The Origins of World War Two: The Debate Continues* (Basingstoke: Palgrave Macmillan, 2003); see also Dale C. Copeland: "Economic Interdependence and the Grand Strategies of Germany and Japan, 1925–1941," in *The Challenge of Grand Strategy: The Great Powers and the Broken Balance between the World Wars*, ed. Jeffrey W. Taliaferro, Norrin M. Ripsman, and Steven E. Lobell, pp. 120–146 (Cambridge: Cambridge University Press, 2012), and *Economic Interdependence and War* (Princeton, NJ: Princeton University Press, 2014); an examination of the effect of blockade and economic pressure on German strategic thinking is Erik Sand, "Desperate Measures: The Effects of Economic Isolation on Warring Powers," *Texas National Security Review* 3, no. 2 (Spring 2020): 12–37.

24. Jamie Martin, *Governing Capitalism in the Age of Total War* (Cambridge, MA: Harvard University Press, forthcoming).

25. Eric Helleiner, *Forgotten Foundations of Bretton Woods: International Development and the Making of the Postwar Order* (Ithaca, NY: Cornell University Press, 2014); Ted Fertik, "Steel and Sovereignty: The United States, Nationalism, and the Transformation of World Order, 1898–1941" (PhD diss., Yale University, 2018), pp. 423–506.

26. David A. Baldwin, *Economic Statecraft* (Princeton, NJ: Princeton University Press, 1985), pp. 150–152; Gary C. Hufbauer, Jeffrey J. Schott, and Kimberley Ann Elliott, *Economic Sanctions Reconsidered: History and Current Policy* (Washington DC: Peterson Institute for International Economics, 1990), p. 4.

27. Donald Kagan, *The Outbreak of the Peloponnesian War* (Ithaca, NY: Cornell University Press, 1969), pp. 266–267; G. E. M. de Ste. Croix, *The Origins of the Peloponnesian War* (Ithaca, NY: Cornell University Press, 1972), pp. 225–289.

28. Marjolein 't Hart, *The Dutch Wars of Independence: Warfare and Commerce in the Netherlands, 1570–1680* (London and New York: Routledge, 2014), pp. 134–135.

29. Jonathan Swift, *The Intelligencer,* no. 9 (Dublin: A. Moor, 1729), p. 87.

30. Brian E. Vick, *The Congress of Vienna: Power and Politics after Napoleon* (Cambridge, MA: Harvard University Press, 2014), pp. 204–205.

31. Kevin H. O'Rourke and Jeffrey G. Williamson, *Globalization and History* (Cambridge, MA: MIT Press, 1999); Ronald Findlay and Kevin O'Rourke, *Power and Plenty: Trade, War and the World Economy in the Second Millennium* (Princeton, NJ: Princeton University Press, 2007), pp. 365–428; Harold James, *The End of Globalization: Lessons from the Great Depression* (Cambridge, MA: Harvard University Press, 2009), pp. 10–12; Donald Sassoon, *The Anxious Triumph: Global Capitalism, 1860–1914* (London: Allen Lane, 2019).

32. Jean-Jacques Rousseau, *The Social Contract and Other Later Political Writings,* ed. Victor Gourevitch (Cambridge: Cambridge University Press, 1997 [1762]), pp. 46–47.

33. Olive Anderson, "The Russian Loan of 1855: A Postscript," *Economica* 28, no. 112 (November 1961): 425–426. See also Arnold D. McNair, *The Law of Treaties: British Practice and Opinions* (New York: Columbia University Press, 1938), p. 550.

34. About the Russo-Dutch loan, see House of Commons debate, 1 August 1854, in *Hansard,* vol. 135, p. 1118.

35. Jan Lemnitzer, *Power, Law and the End of Privateering* (Basingstoke: Palgrave, 2014).

36. As A. J. P. Taylor commented, "In that civilized age, it was thought a reasonable demand that political refugees should be allowed to draw enormous revenues from their estates while conducting revolutionary propaganda against the ruler of the country in which the estates lay" (*The Struggle for Mastery in Europe, 1848–1918* [Oxford: Oxford University Press, 1971], p. 71n3).

37. Norman Bentwich, *The Law of Private Property in War, with a Chapter on Conquest* (London: Sweet and Maxwell, 1907), pp. 85–86.

38. "Project of an International Declaration Concerning the Laws and Customs of War," [1874], in Dietrich Schindler and Jiří Toman, eds., *The Laws of Armed Conflicts: A Collection of Conventions, Resolutions and Other Documents* (Dordrecht: Martinus Nijhoff, 1988), pp. 28, 32.

39. Karl Polanyi, *The Great Transformation: The Political and Economic Origins of Our Time* (Boston: Beacon Press, 2001 [1944]), p. 16.

40. The history of twentieth-century neoliberalism was to a significant degree

a sustained attempt to recreate what Quinn Slobodian, following a distinction originally made by Carl Schmitt, has described as the "doubled world" constituted by the separation of the realm of property (*dominium*) from that of sovereignty (*imperium*) (Slobodian, *Globalists: The End of Empire and the Birth of Neoliberalism* [Cambridge, MA: Harvard University Press, 2018], p. 10).

41. Horst P. Falcke: *Die Hauptperiode der sogenannten Friedensblockaden (1827–1850)* (Leipzig: Rossberg'sche Verlagsbuchhandlung, 1891), and *Le blocus pacifique* (Leipzig: Rossberg'sche Verlagsbuchhandlung, 1919); Albert E. Hogan, *Pacific Blockade* (Oxford: Clarendon Press, 1908); J. Teyssaire, *Le blocus pacifique* (Paris: Imprimerie centrale administrative, 1910); Albert Washburn, "The Legality of Pacific Blockade," *Columbia Law Review* 21, no. 5 (May 1921): 442–459.

42. TNA, FO 881/7827, Discussion with Count Metternich on the nature and attributes of pacific blockades, November 21, 1902, pp. 9–10.

43. Lawrence B. Glickman, *Buying Power: A History of Consumer Activism in America* (Chicago: University of Chicago Press, 2009), pp. 116–120.

44. Sidney Tarrow, *The Language of Contention: Revolutions in Worlds, 1688–2012* (New York: Cambridge University Press, 2013), pp. 54–57.

45. Cited in Henry Wager Halleck, *Halleck's International Law: Or Rules Regulating the Intercourse of States in Peace and War* (London: K. Paul, Trench, Trübner, 1908), p. 160.

46. Offer, *The First World War*, pp. 275–281.

47. Thomas Hippler, *Bombing the People: Giulio Douhet and the Foundations of Air-Power Strategy, 1884–1939* (Cambridge: Cambridge University Press, 2013), pp. 14–19; Theodore Ropp, *The Development of a Modern Navy: French Naval Policy, 1871–1904* (Annapolis, MD: Naval Institute Press, 1987), pp. 155–180, 254–280; Arne Roksund, *The Jeune École: The Strategy of the Weak* (Leiden: Brill, 2007); Martin Motte, *Une éducation géostratégique: La pensée navale française de la jeune école à 1914* (Paris: Economica, 2004).

48. Alfred Thayer Mahan, *Sea Power in Its Relations to the War of 1812* (Boston: Little, Brown, 1905), 2:144.

49. Kristina Lovric-Pernak, "Aim: Peace—Sanction: War. International Arbitration and the Problem of Enforcement," in *Paradoxes of Peace in Nineteenth-Century Europe*, ed. Thomas Hippler and Milos Vec (Oxford: Oxford University Press, 2015).

50. Sandi E. Cooper, *Patriotic Pacifism: Waging War on War in Europe, 1815–1914* (New York: Oxford University Press, 1991), p. 108.

51. Jacques Dumas, "Sanctions of International Arbitration," *American Journal of International Law* 5, no. 4 (October 1911): 934–957. See also Dumas, *Les sanctions de l'arbitrage international* (Paris: Publications de la Ligue Inter-Fédérale, 1905).

52. E. Duplessix, *La loi des nations: Projet d'institution d'une autorité internationale* (Paris: Delagrave, 1906), pp. 42–47.

53. L. de Montluc, "La loi des nations," *La paix par le droit* 17 (1907): 18.

54. Léon Bollack, "Le boycottage, instrument de justice internationale," *La Paix par le Droit* 21 (June 1911): 254–263.

55. Léon Bollack, *Comment tuer la guerre: La loi mondiale du boycottage douanier. Rapport présenté à la commission juridique du XIXe Congrès Universel de la Paix (Genève, Septembre 1912) sur les sanctions économiques* (Paris: Published by the author, 1912).

56. M. A. De Maday, "Economic Sanctions in Cases of Violation of International Law," *Advocate of Peace* 75, no. 11 (December 1913): 258–259.

57. Cited in "Bericht über die Verhandlungen des XIX. Weltfriedenskongresses," *Die Friedensbewegung* 1, nos. 19–20 (15 October 1912): 305.

Chapter One. The Machinery of Blockade, 1914–1917

1. Brief Nr. 11 [Koblenz, 27 August 1914], in Guenther Roth and John C. G. Röhl, eds., *Aus dem Großen Hauptquartier. Kurt Riezlers Briefe an Käthe Liebermann, 1914–1915* (Wiesbaden: Harassowitz Verlag, 2016), p. 131.

2. Louis Guichard, *The Naval Blockade* (New York: D. Appleton, 1930); Archibald C. Bell, *A History of the Blockade of Germany and the Countries Associated with Her in the Great War, Austria-Hungary, Bulgaria, and Turkey, 1914–1918* (London: HMSO, 1937); Marion C. Siney, *The Allied Blockade of Germany, 1914–1916* (Ann Arbor: University of Michigan Press, 1957); Marjorie M. Farrar, *Conflict and Compromise: The Strategy, Politics and Diplomacy of the French Blockade, 1914–1918* (The Hague: Martinus Nijhoff, 1974); Eric W. Osborne, *Britain's Economic Blockade of Germany, 1914–1919* (London: Frank Cass, 2004); Lance E. Davis and Stanley L. Engerman, *Naval Blockades in Peace and War: An Economic History since 1750* (New York: Cambridge University Press, 2006), pp. 159–238; Paul G. Halpern, "World War I: The Blockade," in *Naval Blockades and Seapower: Strategies and Counter-Strategies, 1805–2005*, ed. Bruce A. Elleman and S. C. M. Paine, pp. 91–104 (London: Routledge, 2006); Nicholas Lambert, *Planning Armageddon: British Economic Warfare and the First World War* (Cambridge, MA: Harvard University Press, 2012); Isabel Hull, *A Scrap of Paper: Breaking and Making International Law in the Great War* (Ithaca, NY: Cornell University Press, 2014), pp. 141–210.

3. A recent study is Phillip A. Dehne, *After the Great War: Economic Warfare and the Promise of Peace in Paris 1919* (London: Bloomsbury, 2019).

4. Christian Götter, "Von der militärischen Maßnahme zum politischen Machtmittel. Die Evolution der Wirtschaftsblockade im Ersten Weltkrieg," *Militärgeschichtliche Zeitschrift* 75 (November 2016): pp. 359–387.

5. B. Scheffer, *Die Bedeutung der Mangan und Manganeisenerze für die Deutsche Industrie* (Essen: W. Gebhardt, 1913).

6. Lothar Burchardt, *Friedenswirtschaft und Kriegsvorsorge: Deutschlands wirtschaftliche Rüstungsbestrebungen vor 1914* (Boppard am Rhein: Harald Boldt Verlag, 1968), p. 93.

7. SHD 4 N 14, Comité de Restriction de l'approvisionnement et du commerce de l'ennemi (Comité R), "La question des matières premières dans les rapports des Alliés et des Empires Centraux: Le manganèse," No. 1407, 9 November 1918.

8. Winston Fritsch, *External Constraints on Economic Policy in Brazil, 1889–1930* (Basingstoke: Macmillan, 1988), p. 42, table 3.3.

9. *Norddeutsche Allgemeine Zeitung*, 26 April 1918; cited in SHD, 5 N 277, 2ème bureau, Etat-major de l'armée, Section économique, "Note sur les besoins de l'Allemagne en denrées alimentaires et en matières premières d'industrie après la guerre," 24 May 1918, f. 11.

10. SHD, 4 N 14, "La question des matières premières," p. 7.

11. Ibid., p. 4.

12. Stephen Kotkin, *Stalin*, vol. 1: *The Paradoxes of Power, 1878–1928* (New York: Penguin, 2014), pp. 76–78.

13. Werner Plumpe, Alexander Nützenadel, and Catherine Schenk, *Deutsche Bank: The Global Hausbank, 1870–2020* (London: Bloomsbury, 2020), pp. 110–113.

14. Tyler Priest, *Global Gambits: Big Steel and the U.S. Quest for Manganese* (Westport, CT: Praeger, 2005), pp. 23–56.

15. Alzira Alves de Abreu, "Itabira Iron Ore Company," Centro de Pesquisa e Documentação de História do Brasil: http://cpdoc.fgv.br/sites/default/files/verbetes/primeira-republica/ITABIRA%20IRON%20ORE%20COMPANY.pdf. Accessed 15 December 2019.

16. Belo Horizonte had been founded in 1897 amid the frantic economic development of the Brazilian interior, driven by European capital supplied from London, where the Itabira Iron Ore Company was listed on the stock exchange. British and European investors supplied the funding for the operation of the railway, first as a private company and later by lending to the Brazilian government after the railroad was nationalized in 1889. Richard Graham, *Britain and the Onset of Modernization in Brazil, 1850–1914* (Cambridge: Cambridge University Press, 1972), p. 54.

17. John Darwin, *The Empire Project: The Rise and Fall of the British World System, 1830–1970* (Cambridge: Cambridge University Press, 2009), p. 140; Guy E. Snider, *Brazil: A Study of Economic Conditions since 1913* (Washington, DC: GPO, 1920), p. 38.

18. David Kynaston, *The City of London*, vol. 2: *Golden Years, 1890–1914* (London: Vintage, 1995), p. 8.

19. Robert Brand, "Lombard Street and War," *Round Table 2*, no. 6 (March 1912): 249.

20. Richard Roberts, *Saving the City: The Great Financial Crisis of 1914* (Oxford: Oxford University Press, 2013), p. 31.

21. Lambert, *Planning Armageddon*, p. 239.

22. Michael Ball and David Sunderland, *An Economic History of London, 1800–1914* (London: Routledge, 2001), p. 356.

23. David Edgerton, *The Rise and Fall of the British Nation* (London: Penguin, 2018), p. 79.

24. Frederick E. Saward, *The Coal Trade: A Compendium of Valuable Information Relative to Coal Production, Prices, Transportation, at Home and Abroad with Many Facts Worthy of Preservation for Future Reference* (New York, 1914), p. 52; Max E. Fletcher, "From Coal to Oil in British Shipping," *Journal of Transport History* 3, no. 1 (1975): 1–19.

25. Jonathan R. Winkler, *Nexus: Strategic Communication and American Security in World War I* (Cambridge, MA: Harvard University Press, 2009), p. 207.

26. The first in-depth study of this topic was provided by Avner Offer, *The First World War: An Agrarian Interpretation* (Oxford: Clarendon Press, 1989). The most elaborate statement of the fast-acting "economic warfare" thesis is Lambert, *Planning Armageddon*. A good overview is Stephen Cobb, *Preparing for Blockade, 1885–1914: Naval Contingency for Economic Warfare* (Farnham, Surrey: Ashgate, 2013).

27. Lambert's thesis has been disputed by historians who claim that economic warfare in the form of *slow-acting* blockade was the primary war-fighting strategy. Others have argued that "slow" blockade was itself intended to force naval battle with the German fleet and thus merely a means to decisive military confrontation. See John W. Coogan, "The Short-War Illusion Resurrected: The Myth of Economic Warfare as the British Schlieffen Plan," *Journal of Strategic Studies* 38, no. 7 (2015): 1045–1064; Matthew Seligmann: "Naval History by Conspiracy Theory: The British Admiralty before the First World War and the Methodology of Revisionism," *Journal of Strategic Studies* 38, no. 7 (2015): 966–984, and "Failing to Prepare for the Great War? The Absence of Grand Strategy in British Planning before 1914," *War in History* 24, no. 4 (2017): 414–437. The strongest and oldest claim for the importance of blockade as a war-winning strategy was B. H. Liddell Hart, *The Real War, 1914–1918* (Boston: Little, Brown, 1964 [1930]), pp. 471–472. Recent work on the wartime blockade finds "a clear indication that plans for an economic blockade were nowhere near complete" (Osborne, *Britain's Economic Blockade,* pp. 59, 79).

28. Greg Kennedy, "Intelligence and the Blockade, 1914–1917: A Study in Administration, Friction and Command," *Intelligence and National Security* 22, no. 5 (2007): 699–721, esp. 717.

29. Seligmann notes that "While the term 'effective' was not without ambiguity, it was generally understood to mean that a blockading force had to be sufficiently *numerous, strong,* and *proximate* to a stretch of coastline under blockade to be able, in nearly all cases, to physically block entry or exit from the ports and harbors in question. This understanding had various implications, the most important of which was that in the legal sense, there was not and could not be such a thing as a 'distant blockade,' as such a strategy would immediately fail to constitute an 'effective' blockade on the grounds of proximity" ("Failing to Prepare for the Great War?" p. 5; emphasis in original).

30. Farrar, *Conflict and Compromise*, p. 6.

31. The French government admitted the misnomer by placing the term *blocus* in quotation marks in official reports. See, for example, SHD, 4 N 14, Comité R, "Etude sur l'effet des mesures restrictives prises par les Alliés sur les approvisionnements et le commerce de l'ennemi du 1er octobre 1915 au 31 décembre 1916," April 1917, pp. xxxii, 384. (Cited hereafter as SHD, 4 N 14, "Etude sur l'effet des mesures restrictives, 1915–1916.")

32. Georges-Henri Soutou, the preeminent French economic historian of the Great War, has argued that Paris was quick to "pass from a simple maritime blockade to an economic total war" (*L'or et le sang: Les buts de guerre économiques de la Première Guerre Mondiale* [Paris: Fayard, 1989]), p. 146. On Franco-British collaboration, see Elizabeth Greenhalgh, *Victory through Coalition: Britain and France during the First World War* (Cambridge: Cambridge University Press, 2005).

33. Marc Frey, *Der Erste Weltkrieg und die Niederlande: Ein neutrales Land im politischen und wirtschaftlichen Kalkül des Kriegsgegner* (Berlin: De Gruyter, 1998), pp. 110–120.

34. The significance to the Reich of the Dutch ports was not lost on the German general staff, which in its war planning saw the Netherlands as the "windpipe" (*Luftröhre*) of the German economy. See Memorandum by Helmuth von Moltke, 1911, cited in Annika Mombauer, *Helmuth von Moltke and the Origins of the First World War* (Cambridge: Cambridge University Press, 2001), p. 94.

35. Especially useful are Samuël Kruizinga, "Economische Politiek: De Nederlandsche Overzee Trustmaatschappij (1914–1919) en de Eerste Wereldoorlog" (PhD diss., University of Amsterdam, 2011) on the NOT, and Heinz Ochsenbein, *Die verlorene Wirtschaftsfreiheit, 1914–1918: Methoden ausländischer Wirtschaftskontrollen über die Schweiz* (Bern: Stämpfi, 1971) on the SSS.

36. TNA, FO 382/470/136095A, confidential memo, 11 September 1915.

37. G. Kennedy, "Intelligence and the Blockade," p. 706.

38. Nicholas Mulder, "The Trading with the Enemy Acts in the Age of Expropriation, 1914–49," *Journal of Global History* 15, no. 1 (March 2020): 81–99.

39. Hew Strachan, *The First World War*, vol. 1: *To Arms* (Oxford: Oxford University Press, 2001), p. 965.

40. For an overview of the state of the international law of blockade in 1914, see I. Hull, *A Scrap of Paper*, pp. 141–155.

41. Jürgen Osterhammel, *The Transformation of the World: A Global History of the Nineteenth Century* (Princeton, NJ: Princeton University Press, 2014), p. 499.

42. Zara S. Steiner, *The Foreign Office and Foreign Policy, 1898–1914* (Cambridge: Cambridge University Press, 1969); T. G. Otte, *The Foreign Office Mind: The Making of British Foreign Policy, 1865–1914* (Cambridge: Cambridge University Press, 2011).

43. On the occurrence of the policy shifts propelled by growing anxiety among lower-level administrators, see Diana S. Kim, *Empires of Vice: The Rise of Opium Prohibition across Southeast Asia* (Princeton, NJ: Princeton University Press, 2020).

44. MAE, Blocus 1914–1920, Box 267, Comité R, "Constitution du Comité R," 22 March 1915.

45. Ibid., p. 147. "Comité de restriction des approvisionnements et du commerce de l'ennemi. Bulletin hebdomadaire," 30 April 1915–24 October 1917 (Nos. 1–130), thereafter "Bulletin hebdomadaire du Comité de restriction des approvisionnements et du commerce de l'ennemi," 27 October 1917–18 January 1919 (Nos. 131–195).

46. SHD, 7 N 883, Section de contrôle économique, "Note pour le chef du cabinet," 9 January 1915. Mickaël Bourlet: "Jean Tannery (1878–1939) à l'origine de la guerre économique," in *Guerres mondiales et conflits contemporains*, no. 214 (2004): 81–95, and "La section économique du 2ᵉ bureau de l'état-major de l'armée pendant la Première Guerre Mondiale," in *Naissance et évolution du renseignement dans l'espace européen (1870–1940)*, ed. Abdil Bicer and Frédéric Guelton, pp. 117–135 (Vincennes: Société historique de la défense, 2006); Emmanuelle Braud, "Imperatifs stratégiques et économie de guerre: Le renseignement économique militaire en France pendant la Première Guerre Mondiale" (PhD diss., Université de Paris IV-Sorbonne, 2005); Frédéric Guelton, "La naissance du renseignement économique en France pendant la Première Guerre Mondiale," *Revue historique des armées*, no. 4 (2002): 73–88; Ali Laïdi, *L'histoire mondiale de la guerre économique* (Paris: Edition Perrin, 2016), pp. 351–361; Fabien Senger, "La prise en compte de l'intelligence économique par l'institution militaire française au cours du premier conflit mondial (1914–1918)" (PhD diss., Université de Belfort-Montbéliard, 2005).

47. MAE, Blocus 1914–1920, A374–1A, Surveillance de contrabande.

48. G. Kennedy, "Intelligence and the Blockade," pp. 710–711.

49. Gaynor Johnson, *Lord Robert Cecil: Politician and Internationalist* (Farnham, Surrey: Ashgate, 2013).

50. Mancur Olson, *The Economics of the Wartime Shortage: A History of British Food Supplies in the Napoleonic Wars and in World Wars I and II* (Durham, NC: Duke University Press, 1963), p. 74; Cornelius Torp, *The Challenges of Globalization: Economy and Politics in Germany, 1860–1914* (New York: Berghahn Books, 2005), pp. 39–47.

51. The argument that the Ministry of Blockade signified a break with prewar free trade and that Cecil radically changed his *laissez-faire* position is made by Philip Dehne, "The Ministry of Blockade in the First World War and the Demise of Free Trade," *Twentieth Century British History* 27, no. 3 (2016): 333–356; although interwar sanctions and British imperial defense planning until the early 1930s always presupposed strong private free trade as the precondition of successful economic warfare.

52. Robert Cecil, *A Great Experiment: An Autobiography by Viscount Cecil* (London: Jonathan Cape, 1941), p. 40.

53. Michel Foucault, *Security, Territory, Population: Lectures at the Collège de France, 1977–1978* (London: Palgrave Macmillan, 2004), pp. 19–20.

54. William Forster was commonly known as "Buckshot Forster" for his advocacy of harsh repression of the Irish Land League in the 1880s; as state secretary for war, his adoptive son, Hugh Arnold-Forster, would play an important role in the reform of the British Army and the War Office through the Esher Report. "H. E. Arnold-Forster," *Dictionary of National Biography* (London: Smith, Elder, 1912).

55. "Blockade," *Encyclopedia Britannica*, 12th ed. (London: Encyclopedia Britannica, 1922), 30:464–466.

56. Ibid., 30:465.

57. Osborne, *Britain's Economic Blockade*, pp. 93–94.

58. Kruizinga, "Economische Politiek," pp. 255–258, 266–268.

59. TNA, FO 551/4, 25491, War Trade Department, "Statement of the Imports into the Netherlands during the Month of January 1916, Compared with the Quantities to Be Imported under the Rationing Agreement with the N.O.T.," 8 February 1916.

60. Kruizinga, "Economische Politiek," pp. 279–280.

61. BL, RCP MS 51143, Arnold-Forster, "Rationing Neutrals in the Blockade," 3 December 1939, f. 120.

62. Osborne, *Britain's Economic Blockade*, pp. 124–126. The first blacklist was published on February 29, 1916, and included persons and firms in Greece, Morocco, the Netherlands, Norway, Portugal, Portuguese East Africa, Spain, and Sweden.

63. Siney, *The Allied Blockade of Germany, 1914–1916*, pp. 135–142.

64. Osborne, *Britain's Economic Blockade*, pp. 104–105.

65. MAE, Blocus 1914–1920, Box 267, Comité R, Procès-verbal du 18 mars 1916.

66. Marjorie M. Farrar, "Preclusive Purchases: Politics and Economic Warfare in France during the First World War," *Economic History Review* 26, no. 1 (1973): 117–133.

67. MAE, Blocus 1914–1920, Box 266, A 378–1, Borderau d'Envoi, Comité R, 1 January 1917.

68. Stanislas Jeannesson, *Jacques Seydoux diplomate, 1870–1929* (Paris: Presses Universitaires de Paris, 2013), pp. 15–99, 113, 116.

69. For his later publicizing of these schemes, see Étienne Clémentel, *La France et la politique économique interalliée* (New Haven: Yale University Press, 1931); Soutou, *L'or et le sang*, pp. 261–265.

70. MAE, Blocus 1914–1920, Box 98, A 374–2A, Comité permanent international d'action économique, procès-verbaux.

71. The legal classification of manganese happened in stages because of its multiple forms: manganese ore (*ferro-manganèse*) was added on 3 October 1914, manganese metal and its minerals were inscribed on 3 January 1915,

and manganese bioxyde (one of the metal's minerals) was added as a separate category of material on 14 October 1915. In addition, both manganese minerals and ores were added to the list of items under export prohibition in December 1915; SHD 4 N 14, "Etude sur l'effet des mesures restrictives, 1915–1916," pp. 285–286.

72. MAE, Blocus 1914–1920, Box 276, War Trade Advisory Committee, Memorandum D/1902, The present position of the metal industries in Germany and Austria-Hungary in respect of raw materials [fall 1916].

73. SHD, 4 N 14, "Etude sur l'effet des mesures restrictives, 1915–1916," pp. 287–291, 299. Based on how much manganese was used in prewar production, French analysts estimated current German inputs by working backward from known war production numbers. But some uncertainty came from the fact that the amount of manganese needed to produce stainless steel depended on the purity of the ores, which varied by source. Brazilian ore contained 47–50 percent of the physical element and Indian rock between 40–55 percent, whereas the plentiful Russian deposits ranged from 46 percent purity in Ukraine to 49 percent in Georgia, although most of Russia's over one million tons of annual prewar exports consisted of low-grade ores of 40 percent purity. SHD, 4 N 14, Comité R, "La question des matières premières," pp. 3–4, 6–7.

74. French blockade administrators initially disagreed fiercely on whether "artificial manganese" could be produced in sufficient quantities for use in steel mills. SHD 7 N 875, "Note de M. Sayous, chargé de mission en Suisse (resumé et critique)," 15 March 1916, pp. 2, 10. A year later they noted that "without denying the value of German engineers, it is possible to doubt that the use of substitutes will be industrially realizable so as to remedy the current lack of manganese" (SHD, 4 N 14, "Etude sur l'effet des mesures restrictives, 1915–1916," p. 299).

75. Close to the Austrian-Russian border, Jakobeny changed hands four times during the war. J. Robert Wegs, *Die österreichische Kriegswirtschaft, 1914–1918* (Vienna: Schendl, 1979), pp. 56–65; Alexander Watson, *Ring of Steel* (London: Penguin, 2014), p. 327.

76. Adam Tooze, *The Deluge: The Great War and the Remaking of World Order, 1916–1931* (London: Allen Lane, 2014), pp. 215–216.

77. *The Mineral Industry of the British Empire and Foreign Countries: War Period: Manganese (1913–1919)* (London: His Majesty's Stationery Office, 1921), p. 122.

78. SHD, 4 N 14, "Etude sur l'effet des mesures restrictives, 1915–1916," pp. 287–288.

79. Robert Cecil, "Blockade of Enemies," House of Commons debate, 21 March 1918, in *Hansard*, vol. 104, p. 1254.

80. Maurice de Bunsen, *Why Mail Censorship Is Vital to Britain: An Interview with the Rt. Hon. Lord Robert Cecil* (London: J. A. S. Truscott and Son, 1916).

81. Dehne, *After the Great War*, pp. 32–37.

82. TNA, CAB 24/10/GT484, Robert Cecil, "Memorandum on Proposals

for Diminishing the Occasion of Future Wars," n.d. (probably September 1916); reproduced in Cecil, *A Great Experiment*, pp. 353–357; my emphasis.

83. Peter Yearwood, *Guarantee of Peace: The League of Nations in British Policy, 1914–1925* (Oxford: Oxford University Press, 2009), pp. 24–28.

84. Arthur Salter, *Allied Shipping Control: An Experiment in International Administration* (Oxford: Clarendon Press, 1921).

85. Albert Sorel, *L'Europe et la Révolution Française, septième partie: Le blocus continental—Le grand empire, 1806–1812* (Paris: Plon, 1904), p. 114.

86. Séverine-Antigone Marin and Georges-Henri Soutou, eds., *Henri Hauser (1866–1946), Humaniste, Historien, Républicain* (Paris: Presses de l'Université de Paris-Sorbonne, 2006), pp. 39–44.

87. Ibid., p. 159. Hauser wrote that "Inter-Allied control of primary materials can serve the Allies . . . as one of the bases/most effective guarantees of the new international order that we will have to found after this war. Thanks to this control, the country that perturbs the peace could be deprived on the spot and nearly automatically of the primary materials that it needs or that it is in the habit of buying abroad" (cited in SHD, 4 N 14, "Contrôle inter-allié des matières premières. Texte retenu par le Bureau dans les séances des 30 Novembre et 28 Décembre 1917").

88. Soutou, *L'or et le sang*, p. 559. Seydoux wanted Germany to accept Allied peace terms, but in the long run he supported cooperative economic diplomacy. Clémentel was much more worried about Germany's long-term competitiveness and wanted to permanently constrain the Reich's economic resurgence (ibid., pp. 493–494, 507–517).

89. MAE, Série Guerre 1914–1918, A-1276, Rapport sur la conference de Londres, 16–27 August 1917. Cited in Soutou, *L'or et le sang*, p. 485.

90. Mark Mazower, *Greece and the Inter-War Economic Crisis* (Oxford: Oxford University Press, 1991), pp. 44–45.

91. SHD, 7 N 968, Blocus financier, War Trade Department note, "Contrôle des opérations de banque," 15 May 1916.

92. TNA, FO 902/38, Weekly circular of the War Trade Department, 24 January 1916, f. 116.

93. TNA, FO 902/38, "Origin of the Finance Section," letter from E. F. Davies to Mr. Worthington Evans, 19 February 1916, ff. 1–12.

94. Davies gave a concrete example of a suspicious transfer: "A London banker receives an order to send 250,000 Kronor to Scandinavia and credit a Scandinavian banker in sterling for account of a bank in New York. Upon receipt of this order, the operator would possibly think that Scandinavia was withdrawing balances from the United States to avoid losses in the [foreign] exchange [market], but the skilled exchange man would probably institute searching enquiries, because he would know that a German concern established in Buenos Aires or Valparaiso and having made profits might possibly be transferring such profits to New York for transmission from New York through London to Scandinavia and thence to Berlin" (ibid., ff. 5–6).

95. Ibid., f. 12.

96. TNA, FO 902/38, R.C. to Reginald McKenna, 21 June 1916, f. 157.

97. TNA, FO 902/38, "General Guarantee 'A,'" Ministry of Blockade, f. 138. It was expressly stipulated that "By enemy we mean not merely the government of a country at war with Great Britain or her Allies, but we include also any person or firm of enemy nationality and in addition any person or firm on the Statutory Lists published by His Majesty's Government"—an expansive remit that meant that the sanctions applied in the domain of private law between persons and companies as well as public law between nations.

98. TNA, CO 323/714/86, Form M.B.I and M.B.II, Comptroller, Finance Section of the Ministry of Blockade, 29 August 1916, ff. 525–528.

99. TNA, FO 902/38, Memorandum with regard to Finance Section of the Ministry of Blockade, 15 May 1916, f. 144.

100. MAE, Blocus 1914–1920, Box 280, A378-4, Commission financière interministérielle, September 1916.

101. Block rose from being British delegate to the Public Debt Administration to the presidency of its council of administration; he was described by one contemporary as the "Sir Robert Hart of the public debt administration," a reference to the British head of the Chinese Maritime Customs Service (S. A. M. Adshead, *Salt and Civilization* ([Basingstoke: Palgrave Macmillan, 1992], p. 268).

102. Swiss banks did many kinds of operations, but their speculation on the mark was as likely to hurt as it was to benefit the Central Powers, whose exchange rate continued to slide downward on international markets. Financial speculation by banks to eliminate price differentials would affect the German currency more negatively than the dollar and the pound, which preserved their prewar convertibility into gold. MAE, Blocus 1914–1920, A378-4, Blocus financier. Note de M. Sayous (Commission financière inter-ministérielle), Zurich, 2 November 1916.

103. Fabien Cardoni, *Les banques françaises et la Grande Guerre: Journée d'études sous la direction de Fabien Cardoni* (Paris: Institut de la gestion publique et du développement économique, 2016), p. 6.

104. Herbert Feis, *Europe the World's Banker, 1870–1914: An Account of European Foreign Investment and the Connection of World Finance with Diplomacy before the War* (New Haven: Yale University Press, 1930), pp. 3–82.

105. Plumpe, Nützenadel, and Schenk, *Deutsche Bank*, p. 219.

106. George F. W. Young, "German Banking and German Imperialism in Latin America in the Wilhelmine Era," *Ibero-amerikanisches Archiv* 18, nos. 1–2 (1992): 31–66.

107. Yousef Cassis, *Capitals of Capital: A History of International Financial Centres, 1780–2005* (Cambridge: Cambridge University Press, 2005), pp. 50 and 92, table 3.3.

108. Jean-Marc Delaunay, "Le Crédit Lyonnais en Espagne, 1875–1939. La plus active des banques françaises au sud des Pyrénées," in *Le Crédit lyon-*

nais, 1863–1986: Études historiques, ed. Bernard Desjardins, Michel Lescure, Roger Nougaret, Alain Plessis, André Straus, p. 606 (Geneva: Librairie Droz, 2003).

109. Piet Geljon and Tom de Graaf, "Dutch Colonial and Imperial Banking: Different Ways of Entry and Exit," in *Colonial and Imperial Banking History,* ed. Hubert Bonin and Nuno Valério, p. 78 (London: Routledge, 2016).

110. SHD, 7 N 875, Etat-major de l'armée, 5ème bureau, Section de contrôle, "Note pour le Comité de restriction des approvisionnements et du commerce de l'enemi," 20 February 1916 [referring to the *Bulletin hebdomadaire* of the Comité R of 12 February 1916], pp. 1–2.

111. MAE, Blocus 1914–1920, Box 280, A378-4, Commission financière interministérielle, Procès-verbal de la 50ème séance, 4 September 1917, p. 1.

112. Ibid., p. 3.

113. This position was consistent with what the Sous-direction d'état du blocus had argued since 1916; a narrow financial formulation of the prohibition would allow it to be "presented as the logical consequence of the already existing commercial measures of blockade of which they would be nothing but the transposition into the realm of finance" (MAE, Blocus 1914–1920, A378-4, Blocus financier. Note de M. Sayous [Commission financière interministérielle], Zurich, 2 November 1916, p. 3).

114. SHD, 7 N 967, Blocus financier—Commission financière inter-ministérielle, Procès-verbal de la 45ème séance, 20 July 1917.

115. SHD, 7 N 967, Blocus financier—Tannery to Block, 28 October 1917, 11 November 1917.

116. SHD, 7 N 967, Procès-verbal de la 62ème séance, 8 December 1917, p. 3.

117. Hubert Bonin, *La France en guerre économique (1914–1919)* (Geneva: Droz, 2018), pp. 349–423.

118. Ibid., pp. 5–6.

Chapter Two. The Birth of Sanctions from the Spirit of Blockade, 1917–1919

1. Boris Kadomtsev, *The Russian Collapse: A Politico-Economic Essay* (New York: Russian Mercantile and Industrial Corporation, 1919), p. 59.

2. "Russia's Grain Artery," *The Weekly Northwestern Miller,* vol. 101, 10 March 1915, p. 639; "Dardanelles Is Key to Granary of Slavs," *Weekly Commercial News,* vol. 50, 3 April 1915, p. 3.

3. Boris E. Nolde, *Russia in the Economic War* (New Haven: Yale University Press, 1928).

4. Anthony J. Heywood, "The Logistical Significance of the Turkish Straits, Russo-Ottoman War and Gallipoli in Imperial Russia's Great War, 1914–1917," *Revolutionary Russia* 30, no. 1 (2017): 6–34.

5. Avner Offer, *The First World War: An Agrarian Interpretation* (Oxford:

Clarendon Press, 1989), pp. 354–367; Alexander Watson, *Ring of Steel* (London: Penguin, 2014), pp. 416–424.

6. Benjamin A. Coates, "The Secret Life of Statutes: A Century of the Trading with the Enemy Act," *Modern American History* 1, no. 2 (2018): 151–172; Nicholas Mulder, "The Trading with the Enemy Acts in the Age of Expropriation, 1914–49," *Journal of Global History* 15, no. 1 (March 2020): 81–99; Daniela L. Caglioti, "Aliens and Internal Enemies: Internment Practices, Economic Exclusion and Property Rights during the First World War," *Journal of Modern European History* 12 (2014): 448–459.

7. Léon Bailby, "La grande menace," *L'Intransigeant*, 2 August 1918, p. 1.

8. Richard V. Oulahan, "League to Rule by Economic Pressure; Use of Force by Nations Optional; Armaments Cut, Submarines Barred," *New York Times*, 2 February 1919, p. 1.

9. Cited in "Any Peace Proposal Must Come from Our Enemies Is Declaration of Germany," *Los Angeles Herald*, no. 33, 9 December 1915, p. 12.

10. The length of coastline to be blockaded—three thousand kilometers in the Mediterranean alone—was so enormous that this blockade was declared only in stages. The initial declaration covered the coast from Dedeağaç (Alexandropouli) on the Aegean coast of Thrace to Samos—effectively covering western Anatolia and the Dardanelles. Eugene Rogan, *The Fall of the Ottomans: The Great War in the Middle East* (New York: Basic Books, 2015), pp. 93–94; Lindsey Cummings, "Economic Warfare and the Evolution of the Allied Blockade of the Eastern Mediterranean: August 1914–April 1917" (MA thesis, Georgetown University, 2015), pp. 63–64; W. H. D. Doyle, "Naval Operations in the Red Sea, 1916–17," *Naval Review* 13 (1925): 648–667; "Naval Operations in the Red Sea, 1917–18," *Naval Review* 14 (1926): 48–56. Intermittent naval control to cut off food supplies functioned as a substitute for sending soldiers from the Indian Army into the Middle East. See TNA, CAB 37/122/159, Viceroy to Secretary of State for India, 7 November 1914.

11. Zachary J. Foster, "Why Are Modern Famines So Deadly? The First World War in Syria and Palestine," in *Environmental Histories of the First World War*, ed. Richard P. Tucker, Tait Keller, J. R. McNeill, and Martin Schmid, pp. 191–207 (Oxford: Oxford University Press, 2018).

12. The lower figure comes from George Antonius, *The Arab Awakening: The Story of the Arab National Movement* (New York: Capricorn Books, 1965), p. 241; the higher estimate is based on an examination of the German records by Linda Schatkowski-Schilcher, "The Famine of 1915–1918 in Greater Syria," in *Problems of the Modern Middle East in Historical Perspective: Essays in Honour of Albert Hourani*, ed. John Spagnolo (Reading, England: Ithaca Press, 1992), pp. 229–258.

13. Elizabeth Thompson, *Colonial Citizens: Republican Rights, Paternal Privilege, and Gender in French Syria and Lebanon* (New York: Columbia University Press, 2000), pp. 22–23.

14. Mustafa Aksakal, "The Ottoman Empire," in *Empires at War: 1911–1923*, ed. Robert Gerwarth and Erez Manela, pp. 30–31 (Oxford: Oxford University Press, 2014).

15. Eugene L. Rogan, *Frontiers of the State in the Late Ottoman Empire: Transjordan, 1850–1921* (Cambridge: Cambridge University Press, 1999), pp. 223–224.

16. Cummings, "Economic Warfare and the Evolution of the Allied Blockade," p. 96.

17. "1,200,000 Starving in Syria," *New York Times*, 22 October 1917.

18. Melanie S. Tanielian, *The Charity of War: Famine, Humanitarian Aid, and World War I in the Middle East* (Stanford, CA: Stanford University Press, 2017), pp. 51–77, 145–146.

19. The first studies of the German war economy were already being produced during the war itself. See, among others, August Skalweit and Hans Krüger, *Die Nahrungsmittelwirtschaft großer Städte im Kriege* (Berlin: Verlag der Beiträge, R. Hobbing, 1917); F. Lorentz and A. Thiele, "Die Wirkungen der Hungerblockade auf die Gesundheit der deutschen Schuljugend," in *Hunger! Wirkungen moderner Kriegsmethoden*, ed. M. Rubmann, pp. 17–36 (Berlin: Georg Reimer, 1919); August Skalweit, *Die deutsche Kriegsernährungswirtschaft* (Berlin and Leipzig: Deutsche Verlagsanstalt, 1927); Rudolf Meerwarth, Adolf Günther, and Waldemar Zimmermann, eds., *Die einwirkung des Krieges auf Bevölkerungsbewegung, Einkommen und Lebenshaltung in Deutschland* (Stuttgart and Berlin: Deutsche Verlagsanstalt, 1932); C. Paul Vincent, *The Politics of Hunger: The Allied Blockade of Germany, 1915–1919* (Athens: Ohio University Press, 1985); A. Roerkohl, *Hungerblockade und Heimatfront: Die kommunale Lebensmittelversorgung in Westfalen während des Ersten Weltkrieges* (Stuttgart: Steiner Verlag, 1991); N. P. Howard, "The Social and Political Consequences of the Allied Food Blockade of Germany, 1918–1919," *German History* 11, no. 2 (1993): 161–188; Watson, *Ring of Steel*, pp. 330–374; Mary Elisabeth Cox, "Hunger Games: Or How the Allied Blockade in the First World War Deprived German Children of Nutrition, and Allied Food Aid Subsequently Saved Them," *Economic History Review* 68, no. 2 (2015): 600–631.

20. Ernst Schuster and Hans Wehberg, *Der Wirtschaftskrieg: Die Maßnahmen und Bestrebungen des feindlichen Auslandes zur Bekämpfung des deutschen Handels und zur Förderung des eigenenen Wirtschaftsleben* (Jena: G. Fischer, 1917); Edwin J. Clapp, *Britisches Seekriegsrecht und die Neutralen im Kriege 1914/16* (Berlin: Siegfried Mittler und Sohn, 1916), p. 7.

21. Matthew Stibbe, *German Anglophobia and the Great War, 1914–1918* (Cambridge: Cambridge University Press, 2001); Alfred Hettner, *Englands Weltherrschaft und ihre Krisis* (Leipzig and Berlin: Verlag von B. G. Teubner, 1917); Otto Jöhlinger, *Die Britische Wirtschaftskrieg und seine Methoden* (Berlin: Springer Verlag, 1918).

22. Willi Prion, *Die Pariser Wirtschaftskonferenz* (speech to the Deutsche Wirt-

schaftliche Gesellschaft in Berlin, 23 November 1916) (Berlin: Carl Hey-
manns Verlag, 1917). See also Waldemar Koch, *Handelskrieg und Wirtschafts-
expansion. Überblick über die Maßnahmen und Bestrebungen des feindlichen
Auslandes zur Bekämpfung des deutschen Handels und zur Förderung des eigenen
Wirtschaftslebens* (Jena: G. Fischer, 1917).

23. Georges-Henri Soutou, *L'or et le sang: Les buts de guerre économiques de la
Première Guerre Mondiale* (Paris: Fayard, 1989), chapter XIII.

24. Erich Ludendorff, *My War Memories, 1914–1918* (London: Hutchinson,
1919), 2:517.

25. Erich Ludendorff, *The General Staff and Its Problems: The History of the Relations between the High Command and the German Imperial Government as
Revealed by Official Documents* (New York: E. P. Dutton, 1920), 2:494. See
also Vejas G. Liulevicius, *War Land on the Eastern Front: Culture, National
Identity, and Occupation on the Eastern Front* (Cambridge: Cambridge University Press, 2000).

26. Watson, *Ring of Steel*, pp. 257–276.

27. BL, RCP, MS 51093, O.1/99/287, William R. Robertson (C.I.G.S.), "Military Effect of Russia Seceding from the Entente," 9 May 1917, ff. 28–29.

28. Mary Davis, *Sylvia Pankhurst: A Life in Radical Politics* (London: Pluto
Press, 1999), p. 45.

29. TNA, CAB 23/3/68, War Cabinet meeting 220, 20 August 1917, p. 5.

30. SHD, 5 N 165, Fonds Clemenceau, Telegram by Balfour to British embas-
sies in Paris, Rome, and Washington, 26 January 1918, p. 2.

31. MAE, Blocus 1914–1920, Box 147, A374-6N, Roumanie, SIE No. 478, 13
April 1918.

32. Reinhart Koselleck, "'Erfahrungsraum' und 'Erwartungshorizont'—zwei
historische Kategorien," in Reinhart Koselleck, *Vergangene Zukunft. Zur
Semantik geschichtlicher Zeiten* (Frankfurt: Suhrkamp, 1989), pp. 349–375.

33. "The terms of the [Brest-Litovsk] Treaty made it plain that the blockade of
the Central Powers on which such immense naval efforts had been concentrated was to a large extent broken. The Germans obviously had Russia at
their disposal. The granaries of the Ukraine and Siberia, the oil of the Caspian, all the resources of a vast continent could, it seemed to us, henceforth
be drawn upon to nourish and maintain the German armies now increasing so formidably in the West, and the populations behind them" (Winston
Churchill, *The World Crisis*, vol. 4: *The Aftermath* [London: Folio Society,
2000 (1929)], p. 61).

34. BL, RCP, MS 51093, O.1/99/287, William R. Robertson (C.I.G.S.), "Military Effect of Russia Seceding from the Entente," 9 May 1917, f. 29.

35. TNA, CAB 25/91, "The Internal Situation in Germany during February
1918, Being the Forty-Third Month of the War," W. G. Max-Muller, 23
March 1918, p. 7.

36. SHD, 7 N 875, Conseil supérieur de guerre, "Les conséquences de la catastrophe russe en Asie," 10 March 1918, p. 1.

37. Ibid., p. 7. See "Aus der Denkschrift des Vereins deutscher Eisen- und Stahlindustrieller 'Die Wünsche der Eisenindustrie zum Friedensschluß mit Rußland' z. Hd. Von Generalfeldmarschall Paul v. Hindenburg," in Reinhard Opitz, ed., *Europastrategien des deutschen Kapitals, 1900–1945* (Cologne: Pahl-Rugenstein Verlag, 1977), pp. 409–411.

38. German interest in the region had been considerable. The Nikopol mines provided the main energy supply for the steel plants in Ekatineroslav that were largely French-, Belgian-, and German-owned. In 1912 and 1913 German firms had acquired large stakes in the Chiatura mines. John P. McKay, *Pioneers for Profit: Foreign Entrepreneurship and Russian Industrialization, 1885–1913* (Chicago: University of Chicago Press, 1970), pp. 44–46.

39. SHD, 4 N 14, Comité R, La question des matières premières dans les rapports des Alliés et des Empires Centraux: Le manganèse, No. 1407, 9 November 1918, p. 7.

40. Protokoll der Kriegszielbesprechung zwischen Reichsregierung und Oberster Heeresleitung unter Vorsitz von Kaiser Wilhelm in Spa, 2–3 July 1918, in Opitz, *Europastrategien des deutschen Kapitals*, p. 457.

41. BL, RCP MS Add 51093, Correspondence 1915–1918, Letter by Lansdowne to the editor of the *Daily Telegraph*, 29 November 1917, f. 50.

42. Cited in the *Carlisle Journal*, 29 December 1917.

43. Alexander Zevin, *Liberalism at Large: The World according to the Economist* (London: Verso, 2019), pp. 159–172.

44. "Economic Peace," *The Economist*, no. 3881 (12 January 1918): 39.

45. Cited in League to Enforce Peace, "Lord Robert Cecil's Plan," *League Bulletin*, no. 75, 22 February 1918, p. 150.

46. Léon Daudet, *La Guerre totale* (Paris: Nouvelle Librairie Nationale, 1918), p. 11.

47. Edmond Laskine, "L'arme économique," *La Liberté*, 5 March 1918, p. 1.

48. Archives Nationales, F 12 7985 and F 12 7967, Bureau d'études économiques, Procès-verbal, séance du 8 mars 1918; Procès-verbal, séance du 15 mars 1918.

49. Soutou, *L'or et le sang*, p. 561n243.

50. Charles P. Kindleberger, *A Financial History of Western Europe* (London: Allen and Unwin, 1984), p. 227.

51. Hassan Malik, *Bankers and Bolsheviks: International Finance and the Russian Revolution* (Princeton, NJ: Princeton University Press, 2018), pp. 129–161, 178–184.

52. SHD, 7 N 967, Blocus financier, Note pour la mission anglaise par Général Alby, 20 December 1917.

53. Malik, *Bankers and Bolsheviks*, pp. 226–227, table A.1.

54. Stephen White, *The Origins of Détente: The Genoa Conference and Soviet-Western Relations, 1921–1922* (Cambridge: Cambridge University Press, 1985), pp. 26–27.

55. SHD, 7 N 967, General Alby (Ministère de la guerre), "Note pour la mission anglaise," 31 March 1918.

56. The German government attempted to convince the Ottomans to nationalize all British and French investments and then sell these assets to German firms. Ulrich Trumpener, *Germany and the Ottoman Empire, 1914–1918* (Princeton, NJ: Princeton University Press, 1968), pp. 331–333.

57. SHD, 7 N 967, Homberg to Président [du Conseil des ministres], 8 April 1918, ff. 1–2.

58. SHD, 7 N 967, Liste des titres dont la sortie de France est interdite, 15 September 1918.

59. Martin Kitchen, "Hindenburg, Ludendorff and Rumania," *Slavonic and East European Review* 54, no. 2 (April 1976): 214–230.

60. MAE, Blocus 1914-1920, A374-6N, Roumanie, Service d'information économique, Circular No. 2381, 2 October 1918.

61. David Hamlin, *Germany's Empire in the East: Germany and Romania in an Era of Globalization and Total War* (Cambridge: Cambridge University Press, 2017), pp. 251–322.

62. Kaiser Wilhelm, Protokoll der Kriegszielbesprechung zwischen Reichsregierung und Oberster Heeresleitung unter Vorsitz von Kaiser Wilhelm in Spa, 2–3 July 1918; cited in Opitz, *Europastrategien des deutschen Kapitals*, p. 454.

63. Winfried Baumgart, "Das 'Kaspi-Unternehmen'—Größenwahn Ludendorffs oder Routineplanung des deutschen Generalstabs?" *Jahrbücher für Geschichte Osteuropas* 18, nos. 1–2 (March–June 1970): 47–126, 231–278.

64. David T. Zabecki, *The German 1918 Offensives: A Case Study in the Operational Level of War* (New York: Routledge, 2006).

65. A. E. Zimmern, *The Economic Weapon in the War against Germany* (New York: George H. Doran, 1918), p. 13.

66. Hugo von Freytag-Loringhoven, *Deductions from the World War* (New York: G. P. Putnam's Sons, 1918), p. 17.

67. Atticus, "The Economic Weapon and Imperial Unity," *The New Europe: "Pour la victoire intégrale"* 6, no. 73 (7 March 1918): 225–233, esp. p. 225.

68. "L'embouteillage économique," *Le Temps*, 6 July 1918, p. 1.

69. Data from SHD, 4 N 14, "Matières premières. Repartition dans le monde" [undated, summer 1918], and "L'embouteillage économique," *Le Temps*, 6 July 1918, p. 1. "Central Powers" includes European Russia and Romania but not Asiatic Russia. Totals of world supply do not add up to 100 percent because the resource shares of neutrals have been left out. Numbers for the cereals category are production averages of the years 1910–1914; for the textiles category they are averages of the years 1913-1914; data on mineral and combustibles production are from 1912; data on stimulants are from 1913; for rubber, 1915 production figures are used.

70. Extensive reports appeared throughout the year on rubber (28 December 1917), tin (10 May 1918), iron (18 May 1918), phosphates (25 May 1918), nickel (31 May 1918), copper (6 September 1918), oleaginous products (28 September 1918), chrome and cobalt (5 October 1918), aluminum (19 October 1918), and asbestos (31 December 1918) as economic weapons. Those

commodities of which the Central Powers now held a considerable portion of global supply, such as manganese, were also studied in a separate series of reports titled "La question des matières premières dans les rapports des Alliés et des Empires Centraux," most of which are collected in SHD, 4 N 14, Effets du blocus 1917–1918.

71. SHD, 5 N 277, Etat-major de l'armée, 2ème bureau, Section économique, "Note sur les besoins de l'Allemagne en denrées alimentaires et en matières premières d'industrie après la guerre," 24 May 1918, pp. 8–9, 9–10.

72. Commandant M., *L'arme économique des Alliés* (Paris: Bernard Grasset, 1918), p. 3.

73. "The Proposed German Boycott," *Drug and Chemical Markets* 4, no. 24 (20 February 1918): 30.

74. Cited in "Le banquet de la Chambre de commerce américaine," *La Croix*, 6 July 1918, p. 2.

75. "Against the Proposed Boycott," *American Economist*, vol. 61, 22 February 1918, pp. 89–90; "The International Boycott," *New York Times*, 18 February 1918, p. 10.

76. See especially Jan Lemnitzer's argument about Wilson's subtle mimicking of, rather than opposition against, British navalism: "Woodrow Wilson's Neutrality, the Freedom of the Seas, and the Myth of the 'Civil War Precedents,'" *Diplomacy and Statecraft* 27, no. 4 (2016): 615–638.

77. Arthur S. Link, ed., *The Papers of Woodrow Wilson*, vol. 56: *March 17–April 4, 1919* (Princeton, NJ: Princeton University Press, 1987), p. 158.

78. "Memorandum by President Wilson: Bases of Peace," 7 February 1917; in State Department, *Papers Relating to the Foreign Relations of the United States: The Lansing Papers, 1914–1920* (Washington, DC: GPO, 1914–1920), 1:19. Cited hereafter as FRUS: The Lansing Papers, 1914–1920.

79. "Memorandum by the Secretary of State. Notes on the Bases of Peace," 7 February 1917, and "Bases of Peace No. 2," in FRUS: The Lansing Papers, 1914–1920, pp. 20–22.

80. Giuliana Chamedes, *A Twentieth-Century Crusade: The Vatican's Battle to Remake Christian Europe* (Cambridge, MA: Harvard University Press, 2019), pp. 21–25.

81. John F. Pollard, *Benedict XV: The Unknown Pope and the Pursuit of Peace* (New York: Continuum Books, 1999), pp. 125–126.

82. This view was in keeping with the core idea behind the papal institution of the interdict. Reinhard Knittel, *La pena canonica dell'interditto—indagine storico-giuridica* (Rome: Pontificia Università Lateranense, 1998).

83. Benedict XV, "To the Heads of the Belligerent Peoples," 1 August 1917; in John Eppstein, *The Catholic Tradition of the Law of Nations* (London: Burnes, Oates and Washbourne, 1935), pp. 216–217. This was a historic turn for the Holy See: freedom of the seas had been formulated by Grotius in response to the closure of maritime space that Portugal and Spain had implemented in the sixteenth century with papal backing, the doctrine later defended by

English jurists such as John Selden as *mare clausum* against Dutch liberalism.

84. Edward House, *The Intimate Papers of Colonel House*, ed. Charles Seymour (New York: Houghton Mifflin, 1928), 3:156; cited in Agnes de Dreuzy, *The Holy See and the Emergence of the Modern Middle East: Benedict XV's Diplomacy in Greater Syria (1914–1922)* (Washington, DC: Catholic University of America Press, 2016), p. 27.

85. Wilson, "Reply to the Pope," 27 August 1917; in Arthur S. Link, ed., *The Papers of Woodrow Wilson*, vol. 44: *August 21–November 10, 1917* (Princeton, NJ: Princeton University Press, 1984), pp. 56–57.

86. On the history of this fundamental distinction between sovereignty and government, see Richard Tuck, *The Sleeping Sovereign: The Invention of Modern Democracy* (Cambridge: Cambridge University Press, 2015).

87. Klaus Schwabe, *Deutsche Revolution und Wilson-Frieden: Die amerikanische und deutsche Friedensstrategie zwischen Ideologie und Machtpolitik 1918/19* (Düsseldorf: Droste Verlag, 1971), pp. 75–87.

88. Soutou, *L'or et le sang*, pp. 527–530.

89. Wilson, "State of the Union Address," 4 December 1917; in Arthur S. Link, ed., *The Papers of Woodrow Wilson*, vol. 45: *November 11, 1917–January 15, 1918* (Princeton, NJ: Princeton University Press, 1984), pp. 194–202.

90. Ibid., p. 198.

91. Cited in "Calls War Boycott American Weapon," *New York Times*, 12 April 1918, p. 13.

92. Soutou, *L'or et le sang*, p. 548.

93. Erez Manela, *The Wilsonian Moment: Self-Determination and the International Origins of Anticolonial Nationalism* (New York: Oxford University Press, 2007); Larry Wolff, *Woodrow Wilson and the Reimagining of Central Europe* (Stanford, CA: Stanford University Press, 2020).

94. Cited in Special Representative (House) to Secretary of State, 29 October 1918; in FRUS, Supplement 1: *The World War*, vol. 1 (Washington, DC: GPO, 1933), pp. 405–406.

95. Herbert Houston, "Economic Pressure as a Means of Preserving Peace," *Annals of the American Academy of Political and Social Science*, vol. 66: "Preparedness and America's International Program" (July 1916): 29.

96. Cited in Norman Angell, *The World's Highway: Some Notes on America's Relation to Sea Power and Non-Military Sanctions for the Law of Nations* (New York: George H. Doran, 1915), pp. 355–356.

97. Benjamin A. Coates, *Legalist Empire: American Foreign Relations and International Law in the Early Twentieth Century* (New York: Oxford University Press, 2016), chs. 5–6.

98. Stephen Wertheim has shown that Wilson rejected the "legalist-sanctionist" model for the League proposed by arbitrationists such as Elihu Root, William Taft, and Theodore Roosevelt ("The League That Wasn't: American Designs for a Legalist-Sanctionist League of Nations and the Intellectual

Origins of International Organization, 1914–1920," *Diplomatic History* 35, no. 5 [November 2011]: 797–836, esp. 799–802).

99. Woodrow Wilson, Address on Unveiling the League Covenant Draft, 14 February 1919; in Lyman Powell and Fred Hodgins, eds., *America and the League of Nations: Addresses in Europe*, p. 164 (Chicago: Rand McNally, 1919).

100. F. N. Keen, *The World in Alliance: A Plan for Preventing Future Wars* (London: W. Southwood, 1915), p. 95.

101. See Sakiko Kaiga: "The Use of Force to Prevent War? The Bryce Group's 'Proposals for the Avoidance of War,' 1914–15," *Journal of British Studies* 57, no. 2 (April 2018): 308–332, and *Britain and the Intellectual Origins of the League of Nations, 1914–1919* (Cambridge: Cambridge University Press, 2021).

102. J. A. Hobson, *Imperialism: A Study* (New York: James Pott, 1902).

103. Norman Angell, *Europe's Optical Illusion* (London: Simpkin, Marshall, Hamilton, Kent, 1909).

104. Adam Tooze and Ted Fertik, "The World Economy and the Great War," *Geschichte und Gesellschaft* 40, no. 2 (April–June 2014): 214–238.

105. J. A. Hobson, *Towards International Government* (London: G. Allen and Unwin, 1915), p. 91.

106. Norman Angell, *America and the New World State: A Plea for American Leadership in International Organization* (New York: G. P. Putnam's Sons, 1915), pp. 56–58.

107. Angell, *The World's Highway*, pp. xvi, 341.

108. Hobson, *Towards International Government*, p. 94.

109. Angell, *The World's Highway*, p. 357; my emphasis.

110. Eugenio Rignano, *Les facteurs de la guerre et le problème de la paix* (Paris: Librairie Félix Alcan, 1915), pp. 45–46. Born to a Jewish family in Livorno in 1870, Rignano was trained as a natural scientist in Pisa and contributed research in the fields of engineering, mathematics, psychology, sociology, and political science.

111. MAE, PA-AP 29, Fonds Léon Bourgeois, P/16884, "L'arbitrage international," résumé de l'exposé de Edgard Milhaud, ff. 148–166; reproduced in part as "L'arbitrage international et les questions de puissance," in Edgard Milhaud, *Sur la ligne de partage des temps* (Neuchâtel: Editions de la Baconnière, 1948), pp. 34–39.

112. MAE, PA-AP 29, Fonds Léon Bourgeois, P/16884, "L'arbitrage international," p. 4, f. 152.

113. "'If all the peoples will commit to apply simultaneously and in solidarity the same sanctions—as soon, for example, as the court in the Hague will have pronounced a condemnation—it will suffice. The condemnation will not have to be pronounced. It will never be. The preventive action of equal penalties will be decisive" (ibid., p. 6, f. 154).

114. Jean-Noël Jeanneney, *François de Wendel en République: L'argent et le pouvoir (1914–1940)* (Paris: Éditions du Seuil, 2004 [1976]), p. 112.

115. Serge Audier, *Léon Bourgeois: Fonder la solidarité* (Paris: Editions Michalon, 2007).

116. MAE, PA-AP 29 P/16884, Comité national d'études, "Propositions de la sous-commission" [undated], p. 3, f. 116.

117. Ibid., 5 July 1916, ff. 116–118.

118. The other members included the Quai d'Orsay's legal experts André Weiss, Henri Fromageot, and Paul Matter; the career diplomats Pierre de Margerie (head of political affairs, Quai d'Orsay), Jean Goût, Jules Cambon (vice-chair), Gabriel Hanotaux (former foreign minister), and Fernand Pila; military officers Vice-Admiral Lucien Lacaze and Captain René Petit (who drew up the famous plan for a permanent international military staff to lead a League expeditionary force); and academics Ernest Lavisse and Paul Appell. See Peter Jackson, *Beyond the Balance of Power: France and the Politics of National Security in the Era of the First World War* (Cambridge: Cambridge University Press, 2013), pp. 178–182.

119. MAE, PA-AP 29 P/16054, Commission d'études pour une Société des Nations, Notes de 1ère séance, 28 July 1917, p. 4, f. 10: "Sommes-nous des idealists? Des rêveurs? Non—des *réalistes* hélas! Trop instruits par la sanglante épreuve qui désole l'humanité. Il y a un intérêt reel, primordial, vital, supérieur à tous les intérêts: la paix. Le droit seul la fondera, il faut assurer l'organisation du Droit" (emphasis in original).

120. "Le plan français de la Société des Nations," 28 September 1917; in Léon Bourgeois, *Le pacte de 1919 et la Société des Nations* (Paris: Bibliothèque Charpentier, 1919), p. 44.

121. Bourgeois, "Exposé des principes sur lesquels peut être constituée la Société des Nations," in Bourgeois, *Le pacte de 1919 et la Société des Nations*, pp. 204–205.

122. Jackson, *Beyond the Balance of Power*, pp. 185–186.

123. Bourgeois, "Exposé des principles," p. 205.

124. MAE, PA-AP 29 P/16054, Capitaine Petit, "Sanctions militaires," p. 2, f. 67.

125. French diplomats were not the only ones who supported an international army. Matthias Erzberger also pointed to the Great War as proof that multinational military forces could operate together. He invoked the eight-country expedition to suppress the Boxer Rebellion in China in 1900 as an example of what successful international policing to keep the peace could look like (*Der Volkerbünd: der Weg zum Weltfrieden* [Berlin: Hobbing, 1918], p. 137).

126. Angell, *The World's Highway*, p. 310.

127. MAE, PA-AP 29 P/16054, "Onze objections américaines à la creation d'une 'ligue pour imposer la paix,'" 1 November 1916, f. 166.

128. Grégoire Mallard: "'The Gift' Revisited: Marcel Mauss on War, Debt, and the Politics of Reparations," *Sociological Theory* 29, no. 4 (2011): 225–247, and *Gift Exchange: The Transnational History of a Political Idea* (Cambridge: Cambridge University Press, 2019), pp. 43–84.

129. "Can International Law Be Enforced? [Le droit international peut-il être

fortifié?]," [undated], 57 CdF 47-1, Marcel Mauss Papers, Collège de
France Archives, University of Paris. Since this document is in the Mauss
Papers but is unsigned, the identity of the author is not certain. My attri-
bution is based on conversations with Grégoire Mallard.

130. H. N. Brailsford, *The Covenant of Peace: An Essay on the League of Nations*
(New York: B. W. Huebsch, 1919), pp. 22–23.

131. Mark Mazower, *No Enchanted Palace: The End of Empire and the Ideological
Origins of the United Nations* (Princeton, NJ: Princeton University Press,
2009), pp. 28–65; John Darwin, *The Empire Project: The Rise and Fall of the
British World System, 1830–1970* (Cambridge: Cambridge University Press,
2009), pp. 250–254, 335.

132. Jan Smuts, *The League of Nations: A Practical Suggestion* (London: Hodder
and Stoughton, 1918), pp. 60–61.

133. Ibid., p. 61.

134. Joseph A. Maiolo notes that a positive verdict on blockade remained a
dominant but "unquestioned assumption" in the interwar period itself (*The
Royal Navy and Nazi Germany, 1933–1939: A Study in Appeasement and the
Origins of the Second World War* [Basingstoke: Macmillan, 1998], p. 112). Due
to the author's doubts about the overall effects on the German war economy, A. C. Bell's *A History of the Blockade of Germany and of the Countries
Associated with Her in the Great War, Austria-Hungary, Bulgaria, and Turkey,
1914–1919* (London: HMSO, 1937) was not published until 1961, twenty-
four years after its completion.

135. Positive judgments have come from strategic thinkers (Basil Liddell Hart
and Raoul Castex), politicians (Lloyd George and Winston Churchill), and
historians (Albrecht O. Ritschl, Brian Bond, B. J. C. McKercher, and Isabel
Hull). See, for example, Raoul Castex, *Théories stratégiques*, vol. 5: *La mer
contre la terre* (Paris: Economica, 2003 [1935]), p. 464; House, *The Intimate
Papers of Colonel House*, 1:163–164; Winston Churchill, *The World Crisis,
1911–1918* (New York: Free Press, 2005 [1931]), pp. 564, 577; Albrecht O.
Ritschl, "The Pity of Peace: Germany's Economy at War, 1914–1918 and
Beyond," in *The Economics of World War I*, ed. Stephen Broadberry and
Mark Harrison, pp. 41–76, esp. p. 52 (Cambridge: Cambridge University
Press, 2005); Brian Bond, "Attrition in the First World War: The Naval
Blockade," in Brian Bond, *Britain's Two World Wars against Germany: Myth,
Memory and Distortions of Hindsight* (Cambridge: Cambridge University
Press, 2014), pp. 88–99; B. J. C. McKercher, "Economic Warfare," in *The
Oxford Illustrated History of the First World War*, ed. Hew Strachan, pp. 119–
133 (Oxford: Oxford University Press, 2014); Isabel Hull, *A Scrap of Paper:
Breaking and Making International Law during the Great War* (Ithaca, NY:
Cornell University Press, 2014), pp. 169–170. Hew Strachan argues for the
"Corbettian" role of blockade in pushing the German high command into
risky land offensives leading to defeat ("Sea Power vs. Land Power: The
Geopolitics of Germany's Defeat in the First World War," lecture at the

Centre for British Studies, Humboldt-Universität zu Berlin, 10 May 2012).
A similar escalation-based argument centered around the 1917 decision for
unrestricted submarine warfare is made by Offer, *The First World War*, p. 76,
and Erik Sand, "Desperate Measures: The Effects of Economic Isolation
on Warring Powers," *Texas National Security Review* 3, no. 2 (Spring 2020):
24–26.

136. Holger Herwig, *The First World War: Germany and Austria-Hungary, 1914–
1918* (London: Bloomsbury, 2014), p. 410.

137. Michael Geyer, "Insurrectionary Warfare: The German Debate about a
Levée en Masse in October 1918," *Journal of Modern History* 73, no. 3 (September 2001): 459–527.

138. Charles Maier writes that "had the supreme command not wagered so desperately, attrition alone was unlikely to terminate the war for the allies
within a feasible time frame, that is, before allied as well as German public opinion started to falter" ("Wargames: 1914-1919," *Journal of Interdisci-
plinary History* 18, no. 4 [1988]: 837).

139. Conclusions based on U.S. Army intelligence studies of "variations in German morale" based on six metrics: the state of civilian morale, the Reich's
military position, the degree of political unity, the food situation in northern Germany, the condition of Austria-Hungary, and the rate of U-boat
sinkings. HIA, World War I Subject Collection, Box 18, Folder 19, "Graph
to Indicate Variations in German Morale, August 1914–October 1918."

140. Wilhelm Deist, "Verdeckter Militärstreik im Kriegsjahr 1918," in *Der Krieg
des kleinen Mannes: Eine Militärgeschichte von unten*, ed. Wolfram Wette
(Munich: Piper, 1992), pp. 146–167. On the Spring Offensive's "shock and
awe, 1918 style," see Alexander Watson, "Ludendorff in Total War: A Reassessment," lecture to First World War Research Group, Defence Studies
Department, Joint Services Command and Staff College, 19 May 2015.

141. Before the war Germany imported about a third of its food supply. Gerald
Feldman, *Army, Industry, and Labour in Germany, 1914–1918* (Princeton, NJ:
Princeton University Press, 1966), p. 98.

142. Gerd Hardach argued that "the tremendous decline of the Central Powers
between 1914 and 1918 was caused less by the blockade than by the ex-
cessive demands made on their economies by the war" (*The First World
War, 1914–1918* ([Berkeley and Los Angeles: University of California Press,
1981], p. 34); on the relatively larger welfare loss due to war requirements
than due to the blockade, see Mark Harrison, "Myths of the Great War,"
in *Economic History of Warfare and State Formation*, ed. Jari Eloranta, Eric
Golson, Andrei Markevich, and Nikolaus Wolf, pp. 151–152 (Singapore:
Springer, 2016).

143. Such fungibility involved not just sectors that were logical candidates for
reconversion to war production such as the steel, electrical, chemical, and
shipbuilding industries. The world-renowned artisanal pencil makers of
Franconia, for example, found new employment as gun-barrel makers in

the reorganized German war economy. Norman Stone, *The Eastern Front, 1914–1917* (London: Penguin, 2008 [1975]), p. 163.

144. Alexander Watson, *Enduring the Great War: Combat, Morale and Collapse in the German and British Armies, 1914–1918* (Cambridge: Cambridge University Press, 2008), pp. 184–231; David Stevenson, *With Our Backs to the Wall: Victory and Defeat in 1918* (London: Penguin, 2011), pp. 429–430.

145. The historical arguments to this effect were made by Gerd Hardach, *Der Erste Weltkrieg, 1914–1918* (Munich: Deutscher Taschenbuch Verlag, 1973), and Paul Kennedy, "Mahan versus Mackinder: Two Interpretations of British Sea Power," *Militärgeschichtliche Zeitschrift* 16, no. 2 (1974): 39–66, esp. 51.

146. Skalweit, *Die deutsche Kriegsernährungswirtschaft;* Gustav Gratz and Richard Schüller, *Die Wirtschaftliche Zusammenbruch Österreich-Ungarns* (Vienna: Hölder-Pichler-Tempsky, 1930), pp. 188–204; Richard Riedl argued that "in a far higher degree than is commonly assumed, it was the blockade, and the conditions of distress caused by it, that determined the outcome of the war and the fate of Austria" (*Die Industrie Österreich während des Krieges* [Vienna: Hölder-Pichler-Tempsky, 1932], p. 142). As Belinda Davis has argued, it was the state's involvement in managing food supplies that increased popular demands on it and contributed to the social unrest that led to the 1918 German Revolution (*Home Fires Burning: Food, Politics, and Everyday Life in World War I Berlin* [Chapel Hill: University of North Carolina Press, 2000]).

147. Hew Strachan, "The Limitations of Strategic Culture," in Hew Strachan, *The Direction of War: Contemporary Strategy in Historical Perspective* (Cambridge: Cambridge University Press, 2013), pp. 147–148.

148. Elisabeth Piller, *Selling Weimar: German Public Diplomacy and the United States, 1918–1933* (Stuttgart: Franz Steiner Verlag, 2021).

149. BA-BL, R 901/80905, "Errechnung der wirtschaftlichen Schäden des Reichs als Folge der britischen Handelsblockade (mit Stellungnahmen der Reichsbank, des Reichswirtschafts- und Reichsschatzamtes)," 3 December 1918. In this secret memorandum, Reichsbank president Rudolf von Havenstein opposed sharing Reich trade statistics with the Allies since these would show blockade-caused losses to have been smaller than the German government had publicly claimed. Havenstein also observed that "in the case of exports, one should point out, that even with free seas we would barely have been in a position to substantially raise them—save in the first year of the war perhaps—since the overwhelming majority of our industry was completely adjusted to army needs and the increasing shortage of workers, even when we could have imported sufficient raw materials, would have gradually brought our export industry to a standstill" (ibid., p. 27).

150. Mary Elisabeth Cox, *Hunger in War and Peace: Women and Children in Germany, 1914–1924* (Oxford: Oxford University Press, 2019), pp. 17–64, 205–338.

151. Christian Götter has noted the political utility of this historical view, as well as its connection to modern-day economic sanctions, despite the fact that "no unified research judgment on the British blockade exists" ("Von der militärischen Maßnahme zum politischen Machtmittel. Die Evolution der Wirtschaftsblockade im Ersten Weltkrieg," *Militärgeschichtliche Zeitschrift 75* [November 2016]: 364–365).

152. W. Arnold-Forster, "Sanctions," *Journal of the British Institute of International Affairs 5*, no. 1 (January 1926): 2–3. Arnold-Forster was citing the 762,796 deaths recorded by German public health expert Dr. Max Rubner in December 1918 (Reichsgesundheitsamt, "Schädigung der deutschen Volkskraft durch die völkerrechtswidrige feindliche Handelsblockade," in *Das Werk des Untersuchungsausschusses der Verfassunggebenden Deutschen Nationalversammlung und des Deutschen Reichstages 1918–1919* (Berlin, 1928), 6:398). See also Alice Weinreb, "Beans Are Bullets, Potatoes Are Powder: Food as a Weapon during the First World War," in Tucker, Keller, McNeill, and Schmid, *Environmental Histories of the First World War*, pp. 19–37.

153. Jay Winter's estimate of about three hundred thousand dead is a broadly accepted figure, but a large degree of uncertainty remains ("Some Paradoxes of the First World War," in *The Upheaval of War: Family, Work and Welfare in Europe, 1914–1918*, ed. Richard Wall and Jay M. Winter, p. 30 [Cambridge: Cambridge University Press, 1988]).

154. Viscount Cecil and W. Arnold-Forster, "The Freedom of the Seas," *Journal of the Royal Institute of International Affairs 8*, no. 2 (March 1929): 97.

155. Robert Cecil, *A Great Experiment: An Autobiography by Viscount Cecil* (London: Jonathan Cape, 1941), p. 68. As Phillip Dehne has shown, Cecil's presence and power played a large part in ensuring the economic weapon found its way into the structure of the League (*After the Great War: Economic Warfare and the Promise of Peace in Paris 1919* [London: Bloomsbury, 2019]).

156. Peter Yearwood, *Guarantee of Peace: The League of Nations in British Policy, 1914–1925* (Oxford: Oxford University Press, 2009), pp. 65–67, 76–87.

157. MAE, PA-AP 29, Capitaine Petit, "Sanctions militaires," ff. 65–76; BL, MS 51088, Robert Cecil, "Draft paper on Article 16," 8 December 1924, ff. 27–29.

158. BL, MS 51094, Robert Cecil, Record of interview with Colonel House at Paris, Thursday, 9 January 1919 [signed by Cecil, 10 January], f. 168.

159. BL, MS 51116, Covenant, President Wilson's draft, 1st ed. [undated, January 1919], pp. 4–6.

160. Contra accounts that claim Cecil always opposed military sanctions and only Bourgeois promoted a league army. The first conversations between House and Cecil in early January are recorded in the Cecil Papers but subsequently left out of his diary, perhaps because Cecil did not want to commit to supporting a policy to which Wilson would never agree (Dehne, *After the Great War*, pp. 70–71).

161. The negative obligation not to break the covenant was individual rather

than joint. Wilson, Miller, and Lansing opposed anything that could entail "joint coercion of an American Republic" by non-American nations (David Hunter Miller, *The Drafting of the Covenant* [New York and London: G. P. Putnam and Sons, 1928], 1:29–30).

162. "In order to secure world-peace I would pile up the dangers and risks in front of an intending breaker of the moratorium. Should the rigours of maritime warfare be mitigated at the peace and a measure of freedom be restored to the seas in the direction contended for by President Wilson, I would advocate the power of full revival of all these rigours as against such a law-breaker.... The question requires careful consideration whether such a State should be accorded the status of legalized war, and whether it should not be outlawed and treated as the common criminal that it is" (Smuts, *The League of Nations*, p. 62).

163. Although Lloyd George's cabinet considered Smuts's pamphlet "a most able and interesting document," and Cecil made sure that both Wilson and Clemenceau received copies of it in December 1918 and January 1919, it never became official British government policy. SHD, 5 N 165, Letter from Lord Derby to Clemenceau, 6 January 1919 [Smuts's *A Practical Suggestion* attached].

164. BL, RCP MS 51131, Diary, 5 February 1919.

165. BL, RCP MS 51116, British draft, "League of Nations. Draft Convention," 20 January 1919, f. 8.

166. Miller, *The Drafting of the Covenant*, p. 52.

167. BL, RCL MS 51116, Covenant, President Wilson's second draft [handwritten: "Lord Robert Cecil with the compliments of Woodrow Wilson"], 21 January 1919, f. 24.

168. In 1931, the British judge Anton Bertram concluded that with his modification, Miller "gave things a very sharp turn, which at the time was very imperfectly appreciated" ("The Economic Weapon as a Form of Peaceful Pressure," *Transactions of the Grotius Society* 17 [1931]: 139–174; esp. 145).

169. Daniela L. Caglioti, *War and Citizenship: Enemy Aliens and National Belonging from the French Revolution to the First World War* (Cambridge: Cambridge University Press, 2020), pp. 289–313; my emphasis.

170. BL, RCP MS 51117, Minutes, "The Commission of the League of Nations, February 7, 1919. Presided over by President Wilson," f. 20.

171. MAE, PA-AP 29 P/16054, "Commission de la Société des Nations, 8ème séance," 11 February 1919, p. 15, f. 97.

172. Cecil, *A Great Experiment*, pp. 64–65.

173. This paragraph read: "The Members of the League agree, further, that they will mutually support one another in the financial and economic measures which are taken under this Article, in order to minimise the loss and inconvenience resulting from the above measures, and that they will mutually support one another in resisting any special measures aimed at one of their number by the covenant-breaking State, and that they will take the

necessary steps to afford passage through their territory to the forces of any of the Members of the League which are co-operating to protect the covenants of the League."

174. BL, RCP MS 51117, Meeting of the subcommittee of the League of Nations Commission (Cecil, House, Bourgeois, Hymans, Vesnitch, and Venizelos) with neutrals, 20 March 1919, f. 36.

175. Cecil, "Conservatism and Peace," in Robert Cecil, *The Way of Peace: Essays and Addresses* (London: P. Allan, 1928), p. 77.

Chapter Three. The Peacewar, 1919–1921

1. Diary entry of Vance C. McCormick, 16 January 1919, in Suda Lorena Bane and Ralph Haswell Lutz, eds., *The Blockade of Germany after the Armistice, 1918–1919* (Stanford, CA: Stanford University Press, 1942), p. 40.

2. Henry Noel Brailsford, *Across the Blockade: A Record of Travels in Enemy Europe* (New York: Harcourt, Brace and Howe, 1919), pp. 46, 48–49.

3. C. Paul Vincent, *The Politics of Hunger: The Allied Blockade of Germany, 1915–1919* (Athens: Ohio University Press, 1985), pp. 60–156; Offer, *The First World War: An Agrarian Interpretation* (Oxford: Clarendon Press, 1989), pp. 386–401; Mary Elisabeth Cox, *Hunger in War and Peace: Women and Children in Germany, 1914–1924* (Oxford: Oxford University Press, 2019), pp. 205–240; Jörn Leonhard, *Pandora's Box: A History of World War I* (Cambridge, MA: Harvard University Press, 2018), pp. 818–826.

4. Suda Lorena Bane and Ralph Haswell Lutz, eds., *The Organization of American Relief in Europe, 1918–1919* (Stanford, CA: Stanford University Press, 1943); Bruno Cabanes, *The Great War and the Origins of Humanitarianism, 1918–1924* (Cambridge: Cambridge University Press, 2014), pp. 189–247; Elisabeth Piller, "German Child Distress, American Humanitarian Aid and Revisionist Politics, 1918–1924," *Journal of Contemporary History* 51, no. 3 (2016): 453–486.

5. The best study of the 1919 settlement as a conservative project of stabilization remains Arno Mayer, *Politics and Diplomacy of Peacemaking: Containment and Counter-Revolution at Versailles, 1918–1919* (New York: Knopf, 1967); the classic study of the domestic politics and political economy of restoration is Charles S. Maier, *Recasting Bourgeois Europe: Stabilization in France, Germany, and Italy in the Decade after World War I* (Princeton, NJ: Princeton University Press, 1975).

6. Georges-Henri Soutou, "1918: La fin de la première guerre mondiale?" *Revue historique des armées*, no. 251 (2008): 4–17.

7. Robert Gerwarth, *The Vanquished: How the First World War Failed to End* (London: Penguin, 2016), pp. 254–257.

8. The centrality of global monetary contraction to the repression of restive labor and socialist movements is emphasized by Adam Tooze, *The Deluge: The Great War and the Remaking of Global Order, 1916–1931* (London: Allen

Lane, 2014), pp. 353–373, and C. Maier, *Recasting Bourgeois Europe*, pp. 136, 138. The best study of the economic campaign against Bolshevik Russia is Norbert Horst Gaworek, "Allied Economic Warfare against Russia" (PhD diss., University of Wisconsin, 1970).

9. E. D. Morel, "The Peacewar," *Foreign Affairs* 2, no. 5 (November 1920): 69.

10. Zs. L. Nagy, "The Mission of General Smuts to Budapest: April, 1919," *Acta Historica Academiae Scientiarum Hungaricae* 11, no. 1/4 (1965): 163–185; Miklos Lojko, "Missions Impossible: General Smuts, Sir George Clerk and British Diplomacy in Central Europe in 1919," in *The Paris Peace Conference, 1919: Peace without Victory?* ed. Michael Dockrill and John Fisher, pp. 115–139 (London: Palgrave Macmillan, 2001); Holly Case, *Between States: The Transylvanian Question and the European Idea during World War II* (Stanford, CA: Stanford University Press, 2005), pp. 25, 66.

11. Harold Nicolson, *Peacemaking 1919* (London: Grosset and Dunlap, 1933), p. 298.

12. Leonard V. Smith, *Sovereignty at the Paris Peace Conference* (Oxford: Oxford University Press, 2018), p. 208.

13. Nicolson, *Peacemaking*, 307.

14. TNA, FO 608/220/1, Cecil to Balfour, 14 March 1919, f. 1.

15. On the effects of the disintegration of the Hungarian realm and the loss of Transylvania on private enterprise, see Máté Rigó, *Capitalism in Crisis: How Business Elites Survived the Collapse of Empires in Central Europe* (Ithaca, NY: Cornell University Press, forthcoming).

16. "Notes of a Meeting Held in M. Pichon's Room at the Foreign Office, Paris, on Friday, March 28th, 1919," in *Papers Relating to the Foreign Relations of the United States: The Paris Peace Conference* (Washington, DC: GPO, 1943–1947), 4:522–523. Cited hereafter as FRUS, Peace Conference.

17. TNA, FO 608/220/1, Smuts to Foreign Office, 22 April 1919, f. 83.

18. TNA, FO 608/220/1, Note from Nicolson to Cecil, 2 May 1919, f. 84.

19. TNA, FO 608/220/1, Dixon (secretary of Supreme Economic Council) to Maurice Hankey, 6 May 1919, f. 16.

20. Francis Déak, *Hungary at the Peace Conference: The Diplomatic History of the Treaty of Trianon* (New York: Columbia University Press, 1942), p. 78; Gerwarth, *The Vanquished*, p. 138.

21. TNA, FO 608/220/1, Nicolson to Cecil and Smuts, 15 May 1919, f. 80.

22. TNA, FO 608/221/1, Note by Crowe, 16 May 1919, f. 81.

23. Ibid., f. 37.

24. "Notes of a Meeting of the Heads of Delegations of the Five Great Powers held in M. Pichon's Room at the Quai d'Orsay, 4 August 1919," in FRUS, Peace Conference, 7:505.

25. Ibid., pp. 509–510.

26. Telegram from Allied Supreme Council to French minister in Belgrade, 4 August 1919; reproduced in FRUS, Peace Conference, 8:518.

27. Martin Motte, "La Séconde Iliade: Blocus et contre-blocus au Moyen-

Orient, 1914–1918," *Guerres mondiales et conflits contemporains*, no. 214 (April 2004): 39–53.

28. Historian and international relations thinker Edward Hallett Carr, then serving in the Foreign Office's Contraband Department, thought that the British Cabinet's unannounced decision on 10 December 1917 to cease delivering war material to Russia marked the start of the embargo—which he wholly supported. Seeing the Bolsheviks as a threat equal to the Germans, Carr advocated stopping food supplies: "The most likely thing to cause their collapse is I take it hunger in Petrograd and Moscow," he wrote, "and if we supply food there, we shall simply be defeating our own ends" (TNA, FO 382/1421, Minute from Carr for Sir Eyre Crowe, 29 December 1917; cited in Jonathan Haslam, *The Vices of Integrity: E. H. Carr, 1892–1982* [London: Verso, 1999], p. 21).

29. The Ministry of Blockade was disbanded on 10 July 1919, with much of its personnel returning to service in the Foreign Office and BoT. The ongoing blockade of Russia would be directed by these two bodies based on war cabinet instructions in consultation with the Committee of Imperial Defence and the Admiralty.

30. TNA, ADM 137/3033, Comité du blocus de l'Orient, 1ère séance, 26 February 1919, ff. 1–3.

31. SHD, 7 N 797, Commandant Chapouilly, "Rapport sur la situation en Russie," 5 February 1919, pp. 15, 16.

32. TNA, FO 608/230/19, "Blockade of Bolshevik Black Sea Coast," Note by Harmsworth to Cecil, 2 April 1919, f. 217.

33. TNA, FO 608/230/19, Minute by W. Selby, 17 May 1919, f. 445.

34. TNA, FO 608/230/35, "Relief for Russia," handwritten note by E. F. Wise, 17 May 1919, f. 442.

35. These were the terms in which his career was described by the Norwegian Christian Lange of the Nobel Committee upon awarding Cecil the Peace Prize in 1937. "Award ceremony speech," 10 December 1937, available at https://www.nobelprize.org/prizes/peace/1937/ceremony-speech/. Accessed 5 May 2020.

36. TNA, FO 800/250, Robert Cecil to Cecil Harmsworth, 23 April 1919, p. 2.

37. George H. Nash, *The Life of Herbert Hoover: The Humanitarian, 1914–1917* (New York: W. W. Norton, 1988), pp. 157–304; Glen Jeansonne, *Herbert Hoover: A Life* (New York: New American Library, 2016), pp. 91–121; Sophie de Schaepdrijver, *De Groote Oorlog: Het Koninkrijk België in de Eerste Wereldoorlog* (Amsterdam: Atlas, 1997); Clotilde Druelle, *Feeding Occupied France during World War I: Herbert Hoover and the Blockade* (Basingstoke: Palgrave Macmillan, 2019).

38. Hoover to President Wilson, "A Survey of Food Supplies Available in Case of an Early Peace," 4 November 1918; cited in Bane and Lutz, *The Blockade of Germany after the Armistice*, p. 7.

39. Offer, *The First World War*, p. 393.

40. Benjamin M. Weissman, *Herbert Hoover and Famine Relief to Soviet Russia, 1921–1923* (Stanford, CA: Hoover Institution Press, 1974).

41. SHD, 7 N 797, Capitaine Hage, Directeur de la Croix rouge danoise à Paris, to Commandant d'Harcourt, 2ème Bureau d'état major, Ministère de la guerre, 6 March 1919, f. 3.

42. House of Commons debate, 3 March 1919, in *Hansard*, vol. 33, pp. 84–85.

43. TNA, CAB 24/78/49, "Relaxation of the Blockade of Germany," Memorandum by the secretary of state for war, 25 April 1919, p. 1.

44. Norbert Horst Gaworek, "From Blockade to Trade: Allied Economic Warfare against Soviet Russia, June 1919 to January 1920," *Jahrbücher für Geschichte Osteuropas* 23, no. 1 (1975): 39–69.

45. House of Lords debate, 6 March 1919, in *Hansard*, vol. 33, p. 576.

46. Keith Jeffery, *The British Army and the Crisis of Empire, 1918–1922* (Manchester: Manchester University Press, 1984), p. 13.

47. French supreme commander Ferdinand Foch explicitly drew this link in February 1919. "When the Allied Armies are reduced to a point when it would be difficult to carry out any big military operations," he pointed out to Allied heads of government, "the blockade, which can be tightened or relaxed according to circumstances, will remain the best and most rapid means of enforcing the terms of the Armistice and of enforcing our will on Germany" (CAB 24/78/49, "Relaxation," p. 1).

48. TNA, FO 800/250, Robert Cecil to Cecil Harmsworth, 11 February 1919, ff. 11, 12.

49. House of Lords Debate, 6 March 1919, in *Hansard*, vol. 33, p. 579.

50. Israel Zangwill, *The War for the World* (New York: Macmillan, 1916), p. 333; David Edgerton, *The Rise and Fall of the British Nation* (London: Penguin, 2018), p. 55.

51. Margaret Jourdain, "Air Raid Reprisals and Starvation by Blockade," *International Journal of Ethics* 28, no. 4 (July 1918): 542–553.

52. *The Woman Patriot* 1, no. 30 (16 November 1918): 4.

53. Ute Daniel, *The War Within: German Working-Class Women in the First World War* (Oxford: Berg, 1997).

54. Belinda Davis, *Home Fires Burning: Food, Politics, and Everyday Life in World War I Berlin* (Chapel Hill: University of North Carolina Press, 2000), pp. 190–236.

55. Gertrude C. Bussey, *Women's International League for Peace and Freedom, 1915–1965: A Record of Fifty Years' Work* (London: Allen and Unwin, 1965).

56. A. Maude Royden, *The Great Adventure: The Way to Peace* (London: Headley Brothers, 1915); cited in Joy Milos, "Introduction: Peacemaking: The Christian Ideal," *Sewanee Theological Review* 54, no. 4 (Michaelmas 2011): 355.

57. "Actions towards Peace," WILPF Resolutions, 1st Congress, The Hague, Netherlands (1915), p. 2; available at: https://wilpf.org/wp-content/uploads/2012/08/WILPF_triennial_congress_1915.pdf. Accessed 15 December 2019.

58. Ethel Williams, "A Visit to Vienna," *Towards Peace and Freedom: Zurich Congress of the Women's International League for Peace and Freedom* (WILPF, 1919), p. 10.

59. "Demonstration at Trafalgar Square," *WIL Monthly News Sheet* (May 1919); cited in Sarah Hellawell, "Antimilitarism, Citizenship and Motherhood: The Formation and Early Years of the Women's International League (WIL), 1915–1919," *Women's History Review* 27, no. 4 (2018): 558.

60. "Resolutions Presented to the Peace Conference of the Powers in Paris," 2nd Congress, Zurich, Switzerland, 1919, p. 1; available at: https://wilpf .org/wp-content/uploads/2012/08/WILPF_triennial_congress_1919.pdf. Accessed 15 December 2019.

61. Lucian Ashworth, "Feminism, War and the Prospects for Peace," *International Feminist Journal of Politics* 13, no. 1 (2011): 25–43; Jan Stöckmann, "Women, Wars, and World Affairs: Recovering Feminist International Relations, 1915–39," *Review of International Studies* 44, no. 2 (April 2018): 215–235.

62. Mary Elisabeth Cox, "Hunger Games: Or How the Allied Blockade in the First World War Deprived German Children of Nutrition, and Allied Food Aid Subsequently Saved Them," *Economic History Review* 68, no. 2 (2015): 600–631.

63. German-language newspapers were full of dramatic headlines; "Der Krieg gegen Kinder und Greise," *Vorwärts*, issue 58 (1 February 1919); "Die Hungerblockade der Kinder," *Frankfurter Zeitung*, issue 444 (19 June 1919).

64. Jane Addams, *Peace and Bread in Time of War* (Urbana: University of Illinois Press, 2002 [1922]), p. 95.

65. Ibid., p. 136.

66. "Presidential Address Delivered by Jane Addams," 10 July 1921, in *Report of the Third International Congress of Women* (Geneva: Women's International League for Peace and Freedom, 1921), p. 2.

67. House of Commons debate, 4 August 1919, in *Hansard*, vol. 119, p. 23; Christine A. White, *British and American Commercial Relations with Soviet Russia, 1918–1924* (Chapel Hill: University of North Carolina Press, 1992), ch. 4. Up to that point, the Treaty of Brest-Litovsk had served as a justification for the Allies to blockade Russia. When the Armistice ended hostilities, this belligerence by extension rather than proclamation became increasingly untenable.

68. Harmsworth admitted that an Allied request for German cooperation concerned not an "actual legal blockade" but merely "the exercise of economic pressure" on Russia (House of Commons debate, 3 November 1919, in *Hansard*, vol. 120, p. 1123).

69. C. V. Wedgwood, *The Last of the Radicals: Josiah Wedgwood, M.P.* (London: Jonathan Cape, 1951), pp. 126–136.

70. Military professionals also preferred to keep war and peace neatly separated; Joseph Kenworthy, an Asquithian Liberal MP and ex-Royal Navy

officer, confronted the prime minister's denial that a blockade against the Bolsheviks existed. If there was no such blockade, then why, Kenworthy demanded, did British firms trading with Russia require export licenses? "Are we to understand that there is a blockade, but it is not to be called a blockade?" he asked. Lloyd George stuck to his earlier disavowal, saying that the Bolshevik government had simply not given "a clear understanding on two or three essential matters," but he refused to say to the legislature what these were (House of Commons debate, 28 June 1920, in *Hansard*, vol. 131, pp. 27–28).

71. "To Save Russia: An Appeal to Humanity by Mr Paul Birukoff," Special Supplement to *Foreign Affairs*, November 1919, pp. 17–18.

72. Cited in "Mr. Morel in Glasgow," *Foreign Affairs*, 1, no. 7 (January 1920): 16.

73. "Un grand crime se commet: Nous protestons," *L'Humanité*, 26 October 1919.

74. Edwin L. James, "Demand a Halt in Riga Advance. Peace Council's Powers Put to the Test by the War in the Baltic Provinces," *New York Times*, 12 October 1919, p. 8.

75. "Entente, Baltikum, Sowjetblockade," *Vorwärts*, no. 523, 13 October 1919.

76. Cited in 106th session of the National Assembly, 23 October 1919; in *Verhandlungen des Reichstages*, vol. 330 (1919/20) (Berlin, 1920), p. 3359.

77. Jürgen Zarusky, *Die deutschen Sozialdemokraten und das sowjetische Modell. Ideologische Auseinandersetzung und außenpolitische Konzeptionen, 1917–1933* (Munich: R. Oldenbourg Verlag, 1992), pp. 97–98.

78. SHD, 7 N 797, Ministère des affaires étrangères, Jacques Seydoux to prime minister and minister of war, 15 November 1919, Lettre du département au sujet du blocus de la Russie bolcheviste (communiquée à Londres, Rome, Washington, Berne, Madrid, La Haye, Copenhague, Christiania, Helsingfors, Varsovie, Prague, Vienne, Stockholm, Sofia, Belgrade, Bucarest).

79. *Pravda*, 21 January 1920.

80. SHD, 7 N 797, Quai d'Orsay circular, 29 January 1920.

81. "Explains Cooperatives; Russian Organization Is Strictly Economic, Says Dr. Sherman," *New York Times*, 29 February 1920, p. 21. The American political scientist and journalist Leo Pasvolsky, himself the son of Russian émigrés, suspected that the lifting of the blockade on the cooperatives was "a camouflaged decision to enter into direct communication with the Soviet Government" ("Lifting the Blockade," *New York Times*, 25 January 1920; reproduced in Committee for the Regeneration of Russia, *The Blockade of Soviet Russia* [New York: Committee for the Regeneration of Russia, 1920], pp. 37–39). Columbia University president Nicholas Murray Butler thought that reestablishing commercial links with Bolshevik Russia was tantamount to "selling the principles of America for money." Cited in SHD, 7 N 797, Report by General Collardet, "Rapport sur le mouvement 'social' aux États-Unis," 13 July 1920, p. 6.

82. Anthony J. Heywood, *Modernising Lenin's Russia: Economic Reconstruction, Foreign Trade and the Railways* (Cambridge: Cambridge University Press, 2004), p. 78.

83. House of Commons debate, 10 February 1920, in *Hansard*, vol. 125, pp. 43, 46.

84. Ibid., p. 46.

85. Geoffrey Hosking, *The First Socialist Society: A History of the Soviet Union from Within*, 2nd enlarged ed. (Cambridge, MA: Harvard University Press, 1993), pp. 119–131; Stephen Kotkin, *Stalin*, vol. 1: *The Paradoxes of Power, 1878–1928* (New York: Penguin, 2014), pp. 661–723.

86. Litvinov declared to the SEC representatives that "the reestablishment of economic relations is as important for the Entente as it is for Russia, for reasons of raw materials and the grain that she can provide. . . . All depends on transport. A condition indispensable for exports is the lifting of the blockade" (MAE B.82.4, 1920–1921, Conseil supreme économique, June 1919–March 1920, "Notes prises aux réunions des délegués du CSE avec la mission commerciale russe à Copenhague, séance du 7 avril 1920," p. 4).

87. Andrew J. Williams, *Trading with the Bolsheviks: The Politics of East-West Trade, 1920–39* (Manchester: Manchester University Press, 1992), pp. 55–150.

88. Phil H. Goodstein, *The Theory of the General Strike from the French Revolution to Poland* (Boulder, CO: East European Monographs, 1984).

89. Brigitte Studer, *Reisende der Weltrevolution: Eine Globalgeschichte der Kommunistischen Internationale* (Frankfurt: Suhrkamp, 2020).

90. Mayer, *Politics and Diplomacy of Peacemaking*, pp. 853–873. One of the only directly successful parts of the strike occurred in Yugoslavia, where the Communist Party organized walkouts by workers and mass refusals to serve by soldiers that prevented the Yugoslav Army from joining the Czechoslovaks and Romanians in their campaign to overthrow the Kun government in Budapest. Vilko Vinterhalter, *In the Path of Tito* (Tunbridge Wells: Abacus Press, 1972) p. 513n3; Josip Broz Tito, *Yugoslav Communists and the International Workers' Movement* (Belgrade: Socialist Thought and Practice, 1983), p. 290.

91. Arnold-Forster, "Democratic Control and the Economic War," *Foreign Affairs* 9, no. 1 (March 1920): 11.

92. Ibid.

93. Gerwarth, *The Vanquished*, pp. 165–166; Johannes Erger, *Der Kapp-Lüttwitz-Putsch: Ein Beitrag zur deutschen Innenpolitik, 1919–1920* (Düsseldorf: Droste, 1967); Erwin Könnemann and Gerhard Schulze, eds., *Der Kapp-Lüttwitz-Putsch: Dokumente* (Munich: Olzog, 2002).

94. Albert S. Lindemann, *The Red Years: European Socialism versus Bolshevism, 1919–1921* (Berkeley: University of California Press, 1974), p. 105.

95. Sean McMeekin, *History's Greatest Heist: The Looting of Russia by the Bolsheviks* (New Haven: Yale University Press, 2009), p. 142.

96. Alan Bullock, *The Life and Times of Ernest Bevin: Trade Union Leader, 1881–1940* (London: William Heinemann, 1969), p. 134.

97. Cited in John Callaghan, *The British Labour Party and International Relations: A History* (New York: Routledge, 2007), p. 74.

98. A historian of this episode concludes it was "Labour-inspired opinion which led the British government to put pressure on the Poles into accepting the severe peace terms offered by the Russians" (L. J. Macfarlane, "Hands Off Russia: British Labour and the Russo-Polish War, 1920," *Past and Present*, no. 38 [December 1967]: 144); Martin Ceadel, *Semi-Detached Idealists: The British Peace Movement and International Relations, 1854–1945* (Oxford: Oxford University Press, 2000), p. 245.

99. Trade Agreement between His Britannic Majesty's Government and the Russian Socialist Federal Soviet Republic, 16 March 1921; in Richard H. Ullman, *The Anglo-Soviet Accord* (Princeton, NJ: Princeton University Press, 1972), pp. 474–478.

100. David S. Foglesong, *America's Secret War Against Bolshevism: U.S. Intervention in the Russian Civil War, 1917–1920* (Chapel Hill: University of North Carolina Press, 1995), pp. 231–271.

101. As Tehila Sasson has argued, "Interwar humanitarianism was not opposed to imperialist thought, but rather built upon it" ("From Empire to Humanity: The Russian Famine and the Imperial Origins of International Humanitarianism," *Journal of British Studies* 55 [July 2016]: 521).

102. Gaworek, "From Blockade to Trade," pp. 58–68.

103. Peter van Ham, *Western Doctrines on East-West Trade: Theory, History and Policy* (Basingstoke: Macmillan, 1992), pp. 51–53.

104. Cited in "Lloyd George Defends Trading with Russia Because of Mutual Dependence of Nations," *New York Times*, 23 March 1921, p. 1.

105. C. Maier, *Recasting Bourgeois Europe*, p. 150.

106. MAE, B.82.4, Note by M. du Halgouet, 19 April 1920, p. 3.

107. George Young, *The New Germany* (London: Constable, 1920), p. 127.

Chapter Four. Calibrating the Economic Weapon, 1921–1924

1. Cited in "League Council Opens Sessions," *New York Times*, 31 July 1920, p. 3.

2. MAE, PA-AP 29, P/16054, Commission d'études pour une Société des Nations, 1ère séance, 28 July 1917, f. 10/I.

3. Sami Sarè, *The League of Nations and the Debate on Disarmament (1918–1919)* (Rome: Edizioni Nuova Cultura, 2013), pp. 168–178.

4. League of Nations (LoN) Archive A.20/48/20, C.20/41/49, "Economic Weapon of the League."

5. LON, C.20/4/152.V, Memorandum about the "Economic Weapon of the League of Nations," December 1920.

6. Cecil, House of Commons Parliamentary Papers (HCPP), series 5, vol. 139, Friday, 18 March 1921, pp. 2044–2047. See also A. J. Marder, *From the Dreadnought to Scapa Flow: The Royal Navy in the Fisher Era, 1904–1919*, vol. 5: *Victory and Aftermath (January 1918–June 1919)* (New York: Oxford University Press, 1970).

7. David Edgerton, "Liberal Militarism and the British State," *New Left Review* 1, no. 185 (January–February 1991): 138–169. See also David Edgerton, *Warfare State: Britain, 1920–1970* (Cambridge: Cambridge University Press, 2006), pp. 48–57.

8. W. Arnold-Forster, "The Future of Blockades—Part II," *Foreign Affairs* 2, no. 3 (September 1920): 37.

9. The blockade origins of the main institution for French foreign economic policy remain understudied. MAE, B.83.4, Société des Nations (SdN)/Blocus, "Note au sujet de blocus" [undated; probably 1921], p. 8.

10. Georges-Henri Soutou, "Die deutschen Reparationen und das Seydoux-Projekt 1920–21," *Vierteljahrsheft für Zeitgeschichte* 23 (1975): 237–270.

11. MAE, B.83.4, Société des Nations (SdN)/Blocus, "Note au sujet de blocus," p. 1.

12. MAE, B.83.4, "Questionnaire relative à la mobilisation économique prévu par la commission d'études," 2 May 1921, p. 8.

13. MAE, B.83.4, "Application de l'arme économique comme mésure préventive (résumé de la sous-commission inter-ministérielle du blocus)," p. 13.

14. See, for example, Nicholas A. Lambert's application of the paradigm of a quick "strategy of economic warfare" to the realm of cyber-warfare—where the idea of a sudden surprise attack with catastrophic effects, a "digital Pearl Harbor," is popular ("Brits-Krieg: The Strategy of Economic Warfare," in *Understanding Cyber Conflict: 14 Analogies*, ed. George Perkovich and Ariel E. Levite, pp. 123–145 [Washington, DC: Georgetown University Press, 2017]). For a useful historical corrective to techno-futurist optimism about rapid-acting war-winning weapons, see Lawrence Freedman, *The Future of War: A History* (London: Allen Lane, 2017), ch. 1.

15. MAE, B.83.4, Minutes of meeting by the Commission inter-ministerielle du blocus, 28 May 1921, pp. 1–18; Peter Jackson, *Beyond the Balance of Power: France and the Politics of National Security in the Era of the First World War* (Cambridge: Cambridge University Press, 2013), p. 376.

16. Pedro Pablo Figueroa, *Diccionario biográfico de estranjeros en Chile* (Santiago: Imprenta moderna, 1900), pp. 11–12.

17. José Luis García Ruiz, "Pablo Garnica Echevarría," Asociación española de historia económica, 28 February 2015; available at http://www.aehe.es/2015/02/28/pablo-garnica-echevarria/.

18. Dietrich Schindler, "Max Huber—His Life," *European Journal of International Law* 18, no. 1 (2007): 81–95.

19. Jackson, *Beyond the Balance of Power*, p. 373.

20. G. R. Rubin, "Finlay, William, second Viscount Finlay (1875–1945)," *Ox-*

ford Dictionary of National Biography (Oxford: Oxford University Press, 2004).

21. *Carnegie Endowment for International Peace Yearbook 1922*, no. 11 (Washington, DC, 1922), p. ix; MAE 378-1, Box 266, Note sur les comités de restriction organisés dans les pays allies, 27 October 1916.

22. In the introduction to its report the IBC stated that "it could not omit to deal with the political considerations which are involved in the application of Article 16" (LON A.28.1921.V, "International Blockade Committee: Report submitted by the Committee to the Council," 29 August 1921, p. 3).

23. The act versus state of war distinction had been made the previous year in the assembly's sixth committee meeting by Cecil. Amos Taylor, "Economic Sanctions and International Security," *University of Pennsylvania Law Review* 74, no. 2 (December 1925): 155–168, 160.

24. LON, A.28.1921.V, "International Blockade Committee: Report," p. 4.

25. "Perhaps for the first time, statesmen had to grapple with the principles and paradoxes of international deterrence" (Peter J. Yearwood, *Guarantee of Peace: The League of Nations in British Policy, 1914–1925* [Oxford: Oxford University Press, 2009], p. 166).

26. LON, A.28.1921.V, "International Blockade Committee: Report," p. 6.

27. Norman Angell, *The Fruits of Victory* (New York: Century, 1921), p. 55.

28. Anne-Monika Lauter, *Die französische Öffentlichkeit, der Rhein, und die Ruhr (1921–1923)* (Essen: Klartext, 2006).

29. SHD, 4 N 92, État-major Maréchal Foch, No. 234/1, "Note sur l'application des sanctions," 19 February 1921, p. 6.

30. MAE, B.82.9.1, High Commissioner Paul Tirard to Briand, 18 February 1921, p. 2; "World Coal Production in 1921," *Science* 55, no. 1422 (31 March 1922): 341.

31. Fehrenbach in the seventy-eighth session of the Reichstag on 8 March 1921; in *Verhandlungen des Reichstages*, vol. 347: *1920* (Berlin, 1921), p. 2722.

32. See especially the seventy-sixth session of the Reichstag on 5 March 1921; in ibid., pp. 2658–2678.

33. Moses's diagnosis was that "The Phariseeism of our ruling classes is thus becoming clear everywhere and at every moment. . . . Just like in the Middle Ages at the time of the Black Death people staggered from one lustful activity to another, so do the propertied circles in Germany today, while the broad mass of the people starves, freezes, and sinks into the grave. . . . When the sanctions will have their effect, then the misery among the proletariat, even though this will hardly seem possible, will double, triple, and increase tenfold. Certainly, the average philistine [*Durchschnittsphilister*] will not see this frightful misery at all" (cited in eightieth session of the Reichstag, 10 March 1921, in ibid., p. 2809).

34. MAE, B.82.9.1, Sanctions. Considérations générales, 18 February—25 March 1921, "Protestation allemande auprès du Secretariat général de la S.D.N. contre les sanctions prises par les Alliés," Peretti de la Rocca aux représentants français à Berne et Stockholm," 18 March 1921, p. 2, f. 222.

35. MAE, B.82.9.1, Jacques Seydoux, "Note au sujet Memorandum allemand à la Société des Nations," 19 March 1921, p. 3, f. 242.

36. MAE, B.82.11, Exécution du Traité de Versailles. Nouvelles Sanctions (février–juin 1921), "Attaché militaire de France au Danemark à M. le Ministre de la Guerre," 9 April 1921, ff. 72–73.

37. MAE, B.82.11, Tel. 320 from St. Aulaire (London) to Quai d'Orsay (Paris), 26 April 1921, f. 119.

38. MAE, B.82.11, Stephen Osusky to Briand, 4 May 1921, ff. 184–185.

39. One difference between the French occupations of 1921–1925 and imperialist controls such as the Chinese Maritime Customs Service and the Ottoman Public Debt Administration was that whereas the latter were international bureaucracies grafted onto national governments, the system envisioned by the French to extract reparations from the Ruhr intended to bypass the German state altogether. Hans van de Ven, *Breaking with the Past: The Maritime Customs Service and the Global Origins of Modernity in China* (New York: Columbia University Press, 2014); Murat Birdal, *The Political Economy of Ottoman Public Debt: Insolvency and European Financial Control in the Late Nineteenth Century* (London: I. B. Tauris, 2010).

40. Hanns Christian Löhr, *Die Gründung Albaniens. Wilhelm zu Wied und die Balkan-Diplomatie der Großmächte 1912–1914* (Frankfurt: Peter Lang, 2010), pp. 71–88, 173–206.

41. James N. Tallon, "Albania's Long War, 1912–1925," *Studia Historyczne* 4 (2014): 437–455.

42. Löhr, *Die Gründung Albaniens*, pp. 162–163.

43. MAE, PA-AP 29 P/14613, Paul d'Estournelles de Constant to Bourgeois, 10 September 1920, f. 104.

44. Peter Bartl, "Die Mirditen—Bemerkungen zur nordalbanischen Stammesgeschichte," *Münchner Zeitschrift für Balkankunde* 1 (1978): 27–69; Bobi Bobev, "Le conflit entre l'Albanie et le Royaume des Serbes, des Croates et des Slovènes en 1921 et la position de l'Italie," *Études balkaniques* 1 (1980): 87–100; Michael Schmidt-Neke, *Entstehung und Ausbau der Königsdiktatur in Albanien (1912–1939). Regierungsbildungen, Herrschaftsweise und Machteliten in einem jungen Balkanstaat* (Munich: Oldenbourg, 1987), pp. 83–87.

45. MAE, PA-AP 29 P/14613, Eric Drummond to Bourgeois, 2 November 1921, f. 109.

46. "Balkan War Looms; Serbs Fight Albania," *Chicago Tribune*, 21 September 1921, p. 1.

47. MAE, PA-AP 29 P/14613, "Note pour le représentant de la France au Conseil," 12 November 1921, p. 4, f. 118.

48. Maurice Fanshawe, *Reconstruction: Five Years of Work by the League of Nations* (London: George Allen and Unwin, 1925), p. 265.

49. George F. Kohn, "Organization and Work of the League of Nations," *Annals of the American Academy*, 1924, pp. 21–22.

50. "Great Britain Acts to Protect Albania: Calls on League Council to Check Jugoslav Invasion without Delay," *New York Times*, 9 November 1921.

51. "Albania. First Public Meeting Held on Thursday November 17th, 1921, at 10.30 A.M."; reprinted in Benjamin B. Ferencz, *Enforcing International Law: A Way to World Peace* (London: Oceana, 1983), 1:316.

52. *Records of the Third Assembly of the League of Nations* (Geneva, 1922), pp. 33–37; Yearwood, *Guarantee of Peace*, pp. 207–208.

53. MAE, PA-AP P/14613, L. Bourgeois, "Note sur la convocation du Conseil de la SdN en vue des mesures à prendre aux termes de l'article 16 du Pacte au regard du gouvernement serbe-croate-slovène pour refus ou retard d'exécution de la décision de la Conférence des Ambassadeurs," p. 4, f. 135.

54. Björn Opfer-Klinger, "Albanien als Krisen- und Kriegsgebiet, 1908–1921," *Militärgeschichtliche Zeitschrift* 73 (2014): 23–50.

55. Frank Paul Walters, *A History of the League of Nations* (London: Oxford University Press, 1952), 1:161.

56. "Seeking Peace," *The Economist* 94, no. 4090 (14 January 1922): 39; Layton, a New Liberal economist who had worked as Lloyd George's right-hand man at the Ministry of Munitions during the war, was briefly appointed by his boss to lead the League Economic and Financial Section in 1920 before being succeeded by Arthur Salter. Alexander Zevin, *Liberalism at Large: The World according to the Economist* (London: Verso, 2019), pp. 177–185.

57. "The Mosul Question and the League," *The Economist* 95, no. 4144 (27 January 1923): 134.

58. "L'Albanie et la Société des Nations," *Le Figaro*, 19 November 1921, p. 2.

59. Stanislas Jeannesson, *Poincaré, la France et la Ruhr, 1922–1924: Histoire d'une occupation* (Strasbourg: Presses Universitaires de Strasbourg, 1998).

60. Minutes of conference with Germany at Spa, 13 July 1920, in *Documents on British Foreign Policy* (DBFP), series 1: 1919–1925, vol. 8: *Conversations and Conferences (1920)* (London: HM Printing Office, 1958), pp. 582–583.

61. MAE, B.41.5, Relations commerciales, "Note par J. Seydoux," 26 March 1921, f. 14.

62. MAE, B.82.4, Délibérations internationales, réunion du Conseil suprême à Paris (August 1921), p. 12.

63. TNA, T 160/115/13, British consulate in Cologne to FO, 13 April 1922, f. 4.

64. MAE, SdN/Blocus 815, Sous-commission inter-ministerielle pour l'étude des questions de blocus. Procès-verbal de la 5ème séance," 18 April 1921, p. 31.

65. Nicholas Mulder, "'A Retrograde Tendency': The Expropriation of German Property in the Versailles Treaty," *Journal of the History of International Law / Revue d'histoire du droit international* 22, no. 1 (May 2020): 15–20.

66. Walter A. McDougall, *France's Rhineland Diplomacy, 1914–1924: The Last Bid for a Balance of Power in Europe* (Princeton, NJ: Princeton University Press, 1978), pp. 139–144.

67. MAE, Ruhr 2, "Note au sujet de l'attitude probable de l'Allemagne en cas probable d'occupation prochaine du bassin de la Ruhr," 26 April 1921, f.

81; Hermann J. Rupieper, *The Cuno Government and Reparations, 1922–1923: Politics and Economics* (The Hague: Martinus Nijhoff, 1979), p. 82.

68. Jeannesson, *Poincaré, la France et la Ruhr*, p. 242.

69. Sally Marks, "The Myths of Reparations," *Central European History* 11, no. 3 (September 1978): 243–244.

70. One of the most pernicious legacies of the Ruhr occupation in German nationalist discourse was the demonization of African soldiers in French service as racial intruders attacking the German national body. Peter Collar, *The Propaganda War in the Rhineland: Weimar Germany, Race and Occupation after World War I* (London: I. B. Tauris, 2013).

71. Poincaré to Senate, *Journal officiel*, 29 June 1922; cited in Tel. 348 by Cheetham (Paris) to London, 1 July 1922, T 160/115/13, German Reparation. Payments + Conditional Moratorium, f. 10.

72. TNA, T 160/115/13, Application of sanctions in event of Germany not complying with requirements of Reparations Commission, C 16722/99/18, Memorandum by Joseph Addison, 4 December 1922, p. 2.

73. SHD, 2 N 237, "Au sujet des sanctions économiques immédiatement applicables à l'Allemagne," 14 January 1923.

74. "The Shifting Balance," *The Economist*, no. 4149 (3 March 1923): 480.

75. Peter J. Yearwood, "'Consistently with Honour': Great Britain, the League of Nations and the Corfu Crisis of 1923," *Journal of Contemporary History* 11, no. 4 (October 1986): 559–579; Walters, *A History of the League of Nations*, pp. 249–254.

76. "Signor Mussolini's Mistake," *The Times*, 1 September 1923.

77. As cited in Yearwood, *Guarantee of Peace*, p. 254.

78. TNA, FO 371/8615, Treasury to Foreign Office, 4 September 1923, pp. 1–2.

79. TNA, FO 371/8616, Admiralty to Foreign Office, 6 September 1923.

80. Treasury to Foreign Office, 5 September 1923, in DBFP series 1, vol. 24, no. 655, pp. 986–987.

81. Gian Giacomo Migone, *The United States and Fascist Italy: The Rise of American Finance in Europe* (Cambridge: Cambridge University Press, 2015), pp. 71–74.

82. Salandra to Mussolini, 3 and 5 September 1923, in *I Documenti Diplomatici Italiani* (DDI), series 7: *1922–1935*, vol. 2 (27 aprile 1923–22 febbraio 1924) (Rome: Istituto Poligrafico dello Stato, 1955), pp. 265, 283.

83. Romeo Bernotti, *Cinquant'anni nella Marina militare* (Milan: Edizione Mursia, 1971), pp. 132–133. See also the memorandum by Minister of the Navy Paolo Thaon di Revel to Mussolini, 13 September 1923, in DDI, series 7, vol. 2, pp. 347–348.

84. Helena Swanwick, *Builders of Peace, Being Ten Years' History of the Union of Democratic Control* (London: Swarthmore Press, 1924), p. 177.

85. Yearwood, "Consistently with Honour," p. 574.

86. Orest Babij, "The Advisory Committee on Trade Questions in Time of War," *Northern Mariner* 8, no. 3 (July 1997): 3. This was much the same

conclusion reached by the French Foreign Ministry's blockade committee in 1922. MAE, B.83.4, "Note sur l'organisation du blocus en temps de guerre," 28 August 1922, p. 9.

87. Elisabetta Tollardo, *Fascist Italy and the League of Nations, 1922–1935* (London: Palgrave Macmillan, 2016); Roberta Pergher, *Mussolini's Nation-Empire: Sovereignty and Settlement in Italy's Borderlands, 1922–1943* (Cambridge: Cambridge University Press, 2018).

88. Aristotle A. Kallis, *Fascist Ideology: Territory and Expansionism in Italy and Germany, 1922–1945* (London: Routledge, 2000), pp. 109–110.

89. Though the Covenant banned recourse to war, it did not, strictly speaking, prohibit the use of force, which allowed governments to claim a right to reprisals under traditional international law. See James Barros, *The Corfu Incident of 1923: Mussolini and the League of Nations* (Princeton, NJ: Princeton University Press, 1965), p. 311.

90. Mussolini to Salandra (Geneva), repeated to all diplomatic missions abroad, 1 September 1923, in DDI, series 7, vol. 2, p. 244. Il Duce also mentioned the British bombardment of Alexandria in 1882, the French seizure of the Greek island of Mytilene in 1901 to obtain payment for debts from the Ottoman Empire, and the U.S. reprisal action against Veracruz in 1914.

91. Frederick Pollock, "Reprisals and War," letter to the editor of *The Times*, 10 October 1923, p. 11. British measures to contain the Greco-Turkish War of 1897 had been far more violent than what France, Belgium, and Italy were doing to Germany. During the Cretan rebellion against Ottoman rule, an international Admirals Council had made itself master of the island, fought and shelled Cretan insurgents, hanged locals who had killed British citizens, and forced the withdrawal of Ottoman forces from Crete under threat of naval bombardment.

92. Charles R. Smith, "Reparations and Sanctions: A Discussion of the Legality of the Occupation of the Ruhr," *North American Review* 219, no. 819 (February 1924): 173.

93. "The German Default," *Daily Telegraph*, 19 April 1921.

94. The League Special Committee of Jurists convened to study the crisis concluded that "measures of coercion . . . not meant to constitute acts of war may or may not be consistent" with the covenant—an ambiguous response pointing to the legal loophole that Mussolini exploited in the covenant. See Special Committee of Jurists, "Report: Interpretation of Certain Articles of the Covenant and Other Questions of International Law," *League of Nations Official Journal* 5 (1924): 523.

Chapter Five. Genevan World Police, 1924–1927

1. Zara Steiner, *The Lights That Failed: European International History, 1919–1933* (Oxford: Oxford University Press, 2005), pp. 379–383; Patrick O. Cohrs, *The Unfinished Peace after World War I: America, Britain and the Stabilisation*

of Europe, 1919–1932 (Cambridge: Cambridge University Press, 2006), pp. 201–205; Peter J. Yearwood, *Guarantee of Peace: The League of Nations in British Policy, 1914–1925* (Oxford: Oxford University Press, 2009), pp. 211–250, 282–325; Robert Boyce, *The Great Interwar Crisis and the Collapse of Globalization* (Basingstoke: Palgrave Macmillan, 2009), pp. 130–134; Peter Jackson, *Beyond the Balance of Power: France and the Politics of National Security in the Era of the First World War* (Cambridge: Cambridge University Press, 2013), pp. 420–423; Oona Hathaway and Scott J. Shapiro, *The Internationalists: How a Radical Plan to Outlaw War Remade the World* (New York: Simon and Schuster, 2017).

2. David Mitrany, *The Problem of International Sanctions* (London and New York: Humphrey Milford, Oxford University Press, 1925). On Mitrany's thought, see Or Rosenboim, *The Emergence of Globalism: Visions of World Order in Britain and the United States, 1939–1950* (Princeton, NJ: Princeton University Press, 2017).

3. Jackson, *Beyond the Balance of Power*, pp. 427–513.

4. This draft treaty was drawn up by an eleven-person American Committee on Disarmament and Security that Shotwell had brought together in early 1924 at the Columbia University Club. Carl Bouchard, "Le 'Plan américain' Shotwell-Bliss de 1924: Une initiative méconnue pour le renforcement de la paix," *Guerres mondiales et conflits contemporains*, nos. 202–203 (April–September 2001): 203–225; Hathaway and Shapiro, *The Internationalists*, pp. 116–119.

5. LON, R8/39107/39081, "Protocol for the Pacific Settlement of International Disputes," adopted by the Fifth Assembly of the League of Nations on 2 October 1924, p. 6.

6. LoN, ASP, Box 120, Arthur Salter, "The Economic Weapon of the League," 29 September 1919, pp. 5–6.

7. LoN, ASP, Box 120, Alexander Loveday, "Economic Information Required by Weapon," 8 October 1924, p. 5.

8. Charles DeBenedetti, "The Origins of Neutrality Revision: The American Plan of 1924," *The Historian* 35, no. 1 (November 1972): 84.

9. V. C. Scott O'Connor, *The Empire Cruise* (London: Riddle, Smith and Duffus, 1925).

10. TNA, ADM 18671/215, Admiralty to Rear Admiral Aubrey C. H. Smith, 17 September 1924, f. 4.

11. Cristopher Bell, *The Royal Navy, Seapower and Strategy between the Wars* (Basingstoke: Palgrave Macmillan, 2000), pp. 1–48.

12. BL, RCP MS 51088, Cecil, draft paper on Article 16, 8 December 1924, p. 1, f. 27. The quote is from Eyre Crowe, the Foreign Office's German expert.

13. BL, RCP MS 51088, Cecil, note attached to draft paper on Article 16, p. 2, f. 26.

14. "The British and Americans in their anxiety to keep the Covenant as mild as possible cut down the provisions with regard to security to the lowest

point. . . . If therefore it is now desired to strengthen the provisions with regard to disarmament it is natural that the provisions with regard to security should also be strengthened" (ibid., Cecil to Hankey, 14 January 1925, f. 34, p. 2).

15. SHD, 2 N 6, Conseil supérieur de défense nationale, "Séance du 15 novembre 1924: Organisation des travaux préparatoires à l'application du Protocole de Genève pour le règlement pacifique des différends internationaux, les sanctions, l'assistance mutuelle et la réduction des armements. Notes ayant servi à l'établissement de la minute du procès-verbal," pp. 20, 32–33.

16. Ibid.

17. LoN, ASP, Box S120, A. E. Felkin to John Fischer Williams, 6 November 1924, p. 2.

18. TNA, CAB 4/12 CID Paper 559-B, "Report of the Sub-Committee on the Geneva Protocol," January 1925, p. 11.

19. As Foreign Secretary Austen Chamberlain put it, "It is a fundamental condition of British policy, I might almost say a condition of the continued existence of the British Empire, that we should not be involved in a quarrel with the United States" (note by Chamberlain, 12 October 1925, in DBFP, series 1: 1919–1939, vol. 27 [London: HM Printing Office, 1958], p. 866).

20. TNA, CAB 4/12 CID Paper 559-B, "Report of the Sub-Committee," p. 14.

21. SHD, 2 N 9, Rapport fait au CSDN au nom de la Commission d'études, 10 November 1924, p. 3.

22. DeBenedetti, "The Origins of Neutrality Revision."

23. James T. Shotwell, introduction to "Protocol for the Pacific Settlement of International Disputes," *International Conciliation* 10, no. 204 (December 1924): 528–529.

24. Miller argued that "the very uncertainty and the vagueness of the sanction, the ignorance of the potential aggressor as to what will happen if the aggression takes place, would be much more effective than any precise knowledge could be" ("Sanctions," *Proceedings of the Academy of Political Science in the City of New York* 12, no. 1, International Problems and Relations [July 1926]: 47).

25. Miller, then working as a Wall Street lawyer, predicted that "the effect of [these measures] upon business interests would be instant. . . . In a world built up on a basis of credit, the result would be for the aggressor unavoidable panic . . . the fall in the exchange value of the currency. . . . There could hardly be a more impressive lesson of the danger of violating . . . the economic sanction here provided [which] brings to bear upon the aggressor state the whole post-war experience of Europe" (cited in "A Practical Plan for Disarmament. Draft Treaty of Disarmament and Security Prepared by an American Group, with Introduction and Commentary by James Thomson Shotwell," *International Conciliation* 10, no. 201 [August 1924]: 355).

26. LoN, ASP, Box S120, Letter from Emily G. Balch (Women's International

League for Peace and Freedom, Vienna) to Mr. Huntington Gilchrist (League Secretariat), 3 November 1924.

27. LoN, ASP, Box S120, Letter from A. E. Felkin to Gilchrist, 2 December 1924, p. 2.

28. The important global influence of these laws has recently received attention from James Q. Whitman, *Hitler's American Model: The United States and the Making of Nazi Race Law* (Princeton, NJ: Princeton University Press, 2018), pp. 34–43.

29. LOC, Arthur Sweetser Papers, Box 72, "The Protocol and the United States," ca. November 1924, p. 5. Fearing a Japanese challenge to their own anti-Asian immigration regimes, the British Dominions of South Africa, Australia, and New Zealand also thought the amendment was "not one which it would be safe to accept" (LoN, Box S120, Memorandum by Henry Strakosch [SA] on the Geneva Protocol, 9 October 1924, p. 4).

30. David D. Burks, "The United States and the Geneva Protocol of 1924: 'A New Holy Alliance?,'" *American Historical Review* 64, no. 4 (July 1959): 891–905.

31. Frederick F. A. Pearson to Charles Evans Hughes, 1 November 1924, National Archives, Maryland, State Decimal Files (NADF) 511.3B1/242; cited in Burks, "The United States and the Geneva Protocol," p. 893.

32. The signatories were Albania, Belgium, Brazil, Bulgaria, Chile, Czechoslovakia, Ethiopia, Finland, France, Greece, Haiti, Latvia, Liberia, Paraguay, Poland, Portugal, Spain, Uruguay, and Yugoslavia.

33. Stephen A. Schuker, *The End of French Predominance in Europe: The Financial Crisis of 1924 and the Adoption of the Dawes Plan* (Chapel Hill: University of North Carolina Press, 1976); Tooze, *The Deluge: The Great War and the Remaking of World Order, 1916–1931* (London: Allen Lane, 2014), pp. 440–461.

34. "Kurzer Überblick über die Ergebnisse der London-Konferenz," 19 August 1924, in *Akten der Reichskanzlei: Die Kabinette Marx I/II* Bd. 2 (Boppard am Rhein: Boldt, 1973), pp. 983–984.

35. Christoph Kimmich, *Germany and the League of Nations* (Chicago: University of Chicago Press, 1976); Joachim Wintzer, *Deutschland und der Völkerbund* (Paderborn: Ferdinand Schöningh, 2006).

36. Peter Krüger, *Außenpolitik der Republik von Weimar* (Darmstadt: Wissenschaftliche Buchgesellschaft, 1985), p. 264; Ralph Blessing, *Der mögliche Frieden: Die Modernisierung der Außenpolitik und die deutsch-französischen Beziehungen, 1923–1929* (Munich: R. Oldenbourg Verlag, 2008), p. 279.

37. Jürgen Spenz, *Die diplomatische Vorgeschichte des Beitritts Deutschlands zum Völkerbund, 1924–1926* (Göttingen: Müsterschmidt, 1966).

38. On Stresemann's League diplomacy, see Christian Baechler, *Gustave Stresemann (1878–1929): De l'impérialisme à la sécurité collective* (Strasbourg: Presses Universitaires de Strasbourg, 1996); on his political development, see Jonathan Wright, *Gustav Stresemann: Weimar's Greatest Statesman* (Oxford: Oxford University Press, 2002).

39. The early analysis of the Covenant produced by the famous jurists Walter Schücking and Hans Wehberg, *Die Satzung des Völkerbundes* (Berlin: Franz Vahlen, 1921), was a key reference work for much of the German ruling class, which was heavily staffed with legally trained bureaucrats.

40. Peter Wilson, *The Heart of Europe: A History of the Holy Roman Empire* (Cambridge, MA: Harvard University Press, 2016).

41. Sébastien Schick, "Reichsexekution," in *Les mots du Saint-Empire—un glossaire*, ed. Falk Bretschneider and Cristophe Duhamelle; available at https://saintempire.hypotheses.org/publications/glossaire/reichsexekution; accessed 15 April 2018. See also Raimund J. Weber, *Reichspolitik und reichsgerichtliche Exekution: Vom Markgrafenkrieg (1552–1554) bis zum Lütticher Fall (1789/90)* (Wetzlar: Gesellschaft für Reichskammergerichtforschung, 2000).

42. The Holy Roman Empire's powers of federal execution were vested in the German Confederation, which initiated four federal interventions in the nineteenth century. The power was retained and incorporated into the infamous Article 48 of the Weimar Constitution, which gave the president emergency powers to rule by decree. The Weimar Republic undertook three federal executions in as many years: against the far-left "free state" of Gotha in 1920 and against Communist-SPD state governments in Saxony and Thuringia in October and November 1923. Deutsche Liga für Völkerbund, *Deutschland und der Völkerbund* (Berlin: Verlag von Rainer Hobbing, 1926), pp. 11, 161, 175; Ludwig Waldecker, *Die Stellung der menschlichen Gesellschaft zum Völkerbund: Ein Versuch zum Kampf um die Weltorganisation* (Berlin: Verlag von Carl Heymann, 1930), pp. 41, 75; Ernst Jäckh and Wolfgang Schwarz, *Die Politik Deutschlands im Völkerbund* (Geneva: Librairie Kundig, 1932), p. 38; Karl Anton Rohan, "Bundesexekution and internationalen Polizeimacht," *Europäische Revue* 11 (1935): 795; Spenz, *Die diplomatische Vorgeschichte der Beitritt Deutschlands*, pp. 38, 99, 193; Peter Weber, "Ernst Jäckh and the National Internationalism of Interwar Germany," *Central European History* 52, no. 3 (September 2019): 402–423.

43. Heinrich Weiler, *Die Reichsexekution gegen den Freistaat Sachsen unter Reichskanzler Dr. Stresemann im Oktober 1923. Historisch-politischer Hintergrund, Verlauf und staatsrechtliche Beurteilung* (Frankfurt: Rita G. Fischer Verlag, 1987).

44. PAAA, R 96751, Stresemann to German Embassy in Moscow, 14 March 1925, p. 2.

45. Cited in F. Gaus and H. von Dirksen, "Entwurf von Richtlinien für die Fuhrung der weiteren politischen Besprechungen mit Russland," 29 May 1925; in Akten zur deutschen auswärtigen Politik ADAP, series A, 1918–1925, vol. 13 (Göttingen: Vandenhoeck and Ruprecht, 1967), p. 182.

46. PAAA, R 96751, B. v. Bülow and F. Gaus, "Bedeutung des Artikel 16 der Völkerbundsatzung für Deutschland" [undated, ca. 1925], p. 9.

47. "Final Protocol of the Locarno Conference, 1925 (and Annexes), together

with Treaties between France and Poland and France and Czechoslovakia," *American Journal of International Law* 20, no. 1 (Supplement: Official Documents) (January 1926): 32.

48. Baechler, *Gustave Stresemann*, p. 663; Jean-Michel Guieu, "Les allemands et la Société des Nations (1914–1926)," *Les cahiers Irice* 8, no. 2 (2011): 82.

49. Luther declared that "the possibility, that we will in one way or another have to participate in a disciplinary procedure [*Exekutionsverfahren*] against a state which we ourselves do not at all regard as a peace-breaker [*Friedensbrecher*], that is to say, as an attacker, is excluded from the start." When right-wing parliamentarians countered that "that is not how Briand and Chamberlain put it!," Luther cried back, "But gentlemen, just read Article 16!" (123rd session of the Reichstag, 23 November 1925; in *Verhandlungen des Deutschen Reichstags*, III. Wahlperiode 1924, vol. 388 [Berlin: Druck und Verlag der Reichsdruckerei, 1926], pp. 4477–4478).

50. J. Paul-Boncour, "L'article seize," *L'Oeuvre*, 24 October 1925.

51. PAAA, R 96751, German minister v. Mutius in Copenhagen to AA, Berlin, 31 October 1925.

52. Ludwig Geßner, "Die Gefahren des Völkerbund-Artikels 16," *Münchener Neueste Nachrichten*, 25 December 1925.

53. Article 3 of the Treaty of Berlin read, "If on the occasion of a conflict of the kind mentioned in Article 2, or at any other time where neither of the signatories are in any hostilities, a coalition is formed among third powers with the goal of imposing an economic or financial boycott against either of the signatories, then the other signatory will not join such a coalition" (PAAA, R 96752, German-Soviet Treaty of 24 April 1926, pp. 2–3).

54. Arnold-Forster, "Der Sanktionskrieg des Völkerbundes," *Der Friedenswart* 27, no. 7 (July 1927): 202–203.

55. TNA, CAB 24/95/54, Establishment of a Blockade Advisory Committee, 19 December 1919.

56. David Edgerton, *Warfare State: Britain, 1920–1970* (Cambridge: Cambridge University Press, 2006), pp. 15–58.

57. Avner Offer, *The First World War: An Agrarian Interpretation* (Oxford: Oxford University Press, 1989), chs. 5–9; Nicholas Lambert, *Planning Armageddon: British Economic Warfare and the First World War* (Cambridge, MA: Harvard University Press, 2012), pp. 121–126. The CID's interest in the 1920s in the new realm of "grand strategy" considered both the political objectives of war and the military factors that had to be kept in mind in peace. The term "grand strategy" was first used by the British officer and military theorist J. F. C. Fuller, whose *The Reformation of War* (London: Hutchinson, 1923) contained a chapter titled "The Meaning of Grand Strategy," a realm he saw as "a military brain, an organ which can control the entire defence forces of the nation" (xiii–xiv).

58. Though the existence of the ATB has been acknowledged by historians, there is only one short essay that discusses its work: Orest Babij, "The

Advisory Committee on Trade Questions in Time of War," *Northern Mariner* 8, no. 3 (July 1997): 1–10; the committee's existence is mentioned or discussed in Huw Dylan, *Defence Intelligence and the Cold War: Britain's Joint Intelligence Bureau, 1945–1964* (Oxford: Oxford University Press, 2014), pp. 12–13; Joseph A. Maiolo, *The Royal Navy and Nazi Germany, 1933–1939: A Study in Appeasement and the Origins of the Second World War* (Basingstoke: Macmillan, 1998), pp. 112–115; Christopher Price, *Britain, America and Rearmament in the 1930s: The Cost of Failure* (Basingstoke: Macmillan, 2001), pp. 10–11; Nicholas Tracy, *Attack on Maritime Trade* (Basingstoke: Macmillan, 1991), pp. 175–184; and Donald Cameron Watt, "British Intelligence and the Coming of the Second World War in Europe," in *Knowing One's Enemies: Intelligence Assessments before the Two World Wars*, ed. Ernest R. May, pp. 244–245 (Princeton, NJ: Princeton University Press, 1984).

59. Hew Strachan, "Strategy and Contingency," in Hew Strachan, *The Direction of War: Strategy in Historical Perspective*, p. 237 (Cambridge: Cambridge University Press, 2013).

60. BL, RCP Add MS 51088, M. P. A. Hankey to Cecil, "An Introduction to the Study of Disarmament," 4 August 1925, pp. 16–17, ff. 53–54.

61. On the "fourth arm" of defense constituted by economic stability see George Peden: *Rearmament and the British Treasury, 1932–1939* (Edinburgh: Scottish Academic Press, 1979), pp. 83–84, 100–103, and "Financing Churchill's Army," in *The British Way in Warfare: Power and the International System, 1856–1956: Essays in Honor of David French*, ed. Keith Nelson and Greg Kennedy, pp. 277–300 (Farnham: Ashgate, 2010); Price, *Britain, America and Rearmament*, ch. 1; John Darwin, *The Empire Project: The Rise and Fall of the British World System, 1830–1970* (Cambridge: Cambridge University Press, 2009), p. 519.

62. Robert W. D. Boyce, *British Capitalism at the Crossroads, 1919–1932: A Study in Politics, Economics, and International Relations* (Cambridge: Cambridge University Press, 1987).

63. BL, RCP, Hankey to Cecil, 10 February 1926, f. 65. Baldwin explicitly wanted someone of Cecil's stature to run the ATB because he thought that economic pressure was so important it required someone of cabinet minister rank. Recent works on British internationalism, such as Helen McCarthy, *The British People and the League of Nations: Democracy, Citizenship and Internationalism, c. 1918–48* (Manchester: Manchester University Press, 2011), and Gaynor Johnson, *Lord Robert Cecil: Politician and Internationalist* (Farnham: Ashgate, 2013), focus on Cecil's public-facing activities but not on his involvement in the ATB. His continued contribution to strategic planning in 1926–1927 also qualifies Peter Yearwood's claim that Cecil's influence in Whitehall never recovered from the blow suffered during the Corfu crisis (*Guarantee of Peace*, pp. 274, 277–278).

64. TNA, CAB 47/1, Advisory Committee on Trade Questions in Time of War, seventh meeting, 6 May 1926, p. 4, f. 148.

65. Alan Gaukroger, "The Director of Financial Enquiries: A Study of the Treasury Career of R. G. Hawtrey, 1919-1939" (PhD diss., University of Huddersfield, 2008); Clara Elisabetta Mattei, "Treasury View and Post-WWI British Austerity: Basil Blackett, Otto Niemeyer and Ralph Hawtrey," *Cambridge Journal of Economics* 10 (2017): 1-21.

66. The Department of Overseas Trade was an institutional outgrowth of the economic warfare of 1914-1918, which had confronted the Cabinet with the lack of economic knowledge of many Foreign Office diplomats and the need for the BoT to extend its activities to foreign affairs. Ephraim Maisel, "The Formation of the Department of Overseas Trade, 1919-1926," *Journal of Contemporary History* 24, no. 1 (January 1989): 169-190.

67. TNA, CAB 47/1, Advisory Committee on Trade Questions in Time of War (ATB), conclusions of the second meeting, 28 November 1924, p. 6, f. 120.

68. TNA, CAB 47/1, ATB, Fourteenth meeting, 19 April 1929, p. 9, f. 212.

69. On this first mention of "the economic weapon, i.e., interference with German commerce," see "Attitude to Be Adopted towards Belgium in Event of Germany Violating Her Neutrality during Anglo-German War," memorandum by Cecil Hurst, 16 February 1912, Document 150, in Kenneth Bourne and D. Cameron Watt, eds., *British Documents on Foreign Affairs*, part I, series F: *Europe, 1848-1914*, vol. 5: *The Low Countries II: Belgium, 1893-1914*, ed. David Stevenson, pp. 335-336 (Frederick, MD: University Publications of America, 1987).

70. TNA, CAB 47/1, ATB, Thirteenth meeting of the Standing Committee on Bunker Control, 21 November 1927. Between 1913 and 1930 the consumption of British bunker coal in global shipping fell by a third, from thirty to twenty million long tons. The percentage of coal-powered vessels fell from 89 percent in 1914 to 52 percent in 1934, whereas the number of oil-fueled ships rose from 3 to 30 percent in the same twenty-year period. John Bradley, *Fuel and Power in the British Empire* (Washington, DC: GPO, 1935), pp. 23, 26.

71. TNA, CAB 47/1, ATB, Seventh annual meeting, 6 May 1926, p. 3, f. 147.

72. TNA, CAB 47/1, ATB Paper 31, Robert Cecil, "Blockade Machinery. Memorandum by Chairman," 29 April 1926.

73. TNA, CAB 47/1, ATB Eighth meeting, 21 July 1926, p. 3, f. 155.

74. For this reason, Hankey had already communicated to the League back in 1921 that "His Majesty's Government have the power to impose any prohibition on trade, financial relations and intercourse which may be necessary to give effect to Article 16 of the Covenant and that no legislation 'ad hoc' is required to enable their obligations under this Article to be fulfilled" (LON, Box R322, International Blockade Committee—Replies by certain governments to the questionnaire circulated by the Secretary-General, File 10/11230/1230, Response by H.M. Government, 5 May 1921).

75. TNA, CAB 47/1, Paper ATB-65, Arnold-Forster, "Sanctions and Trading

with the Enemy" [written 26 December 1926; presented to ATB, 24 September 1928], p. 2, f. 198.

76. Arnold-Forster: "Maritime Law and Economic Pressure," *Journal of the Royal United Service Institution*, no. 70 (February 1925): 442–466, and "Sanctions," *Journal of the British Institute of International Affairs* 5, no. 1 (January 1926): 1–15. The latter was subsequently presented to the ATB by Charles Hipwood of the BoT in the ATB's eighth meeting on 21 July 1926.

77. Darwin, *The Empire Project*, pp. 375–393; the concept of the "Eurasian imperial seam" comes from Michael Geyer and Charles Bright, "Global Violence and Nationalizing Wars in Eurasia and America: Geopolitics of War in the Nineteenth Century," *Comparative Studies in Society and History* 38, no. 4 (1996): 622–634.

78. "Puzzle d'Asie," *L'Intransigeant*, 9 February 1922, p. 3.

79. See, for example, Henderson (Constantinople) to Foreign Secretary Curzon, 28 January 1923, in FO 424/256, "Turkey. Further Correspondence Part III, 1923 Jan.–Mar.," p. 263; Rumbold (Lausanne) to Curzon, 16 June 1923, in FO 424/257, "Turkey, Further Correspondence Part IV, Apr.–Jun. 1923," p. 327.

80. Edward Mead Earle, *Turkey, the Great Powers, and the Baghdad Railway: A Study in Imperialism* (New York: Russell and Russell, 1966 [1923]), pp. 322, 329–336; Sevtap Demiric, "Turco-British Diplomatic Manoeuvres on the Mosul Question in the Lausanne Conference, 1922–1923," *British Journal of Middle Eastern Studies* 37, no. 1 (April 2010): 57–71.

81. Quincy Wright, "The Mosul Dispute," *American Journal of International Law* 20, no. 3 (July 1926): 453–464; Aryo Makko, "Arbitrator in a World of Wars: The League of Nations and the Mosul Dispute, 1924–1925," *Diplomacy and Statecraft* 21, no. 4 (2010): 631–649; Peter J. Beck, "'A Tedious and Perilous Controversy': Britain and the Settlement of the Mosul Dispute, 1918–1926," *Middle Eastern Studies* 17, no. 2 (April 1981): 256–276.

82. "The Mosul Question and the League," *The Economist*, no. 4144, 27 January 1923, p. 134.

83. TNA, CAB 47/1, ATB fifth meeting, 16 December 1925, p. 2, f. 141.

84. TNA, CAB 4/14, CID Paper 660-B, "Possible Action by the League of Nations to Bring Economic Pressure to Bear upon Turkey, Report by ATB," 14 December 1925, p. 2.

85. Beck, "A Tedious and Perilous Controversy," p. 270.

86. The considerations of various actors in the British imperial ruling class and government apparatus are well covered by historians in the "retreat from China" debate. See Roberta A. Dayer, *Bankers and Diplomats in China, 1917–1925: The Anglo-American Relationship* (Totowa, NJ: Frank Cass, 1981); Edmund S. K. Fung, *The Diplomacy of Imperial Retreat: Britain's South China Policy, 1924–1931* (New York: Oxford University Press, 1991); Phoebe Chow, *Britain's Imperial Retreat from China, 1900–1931* (London: Routledge, 2017); Robert Bickers, *Out of China: How the Chinese Ended the Era of Western Domi-*

nation (Cambridge, MA: Harvard University Press, 2017). My thanks to Jamie Martin for emphasizing the importance of this historiography.

87. C. Martin Wilbur and Julie Lien-ying How, *Missionaries of Revolution: Soviet Advisers and Nationalist China, 1920–1927* (Cambridge, MA: Harvard University Press, 1989), pp. 297–310; Chan Lau Kit-ching, *China, Britain and Hong Kong, 1895–1945* (Hong Kong: Chinese University Press, 1990).

88. Michael Share, "Clash of Worlds: The Comintern, British Hong Kong and Chinese Nationalism, 1921–1927," *Europe-Asia Studies* 54, no. 4 (June 2005): 601–624.

89. Ming K. Chan, "Hong Kong in Sino-British Conflict: Mass Mobilization and the Crisis of Legitimacy, 1919–1926," in *Precarious Balance: Hong Kong between China and Britain, 1842–1992*, ed. Ming K. Chan, with the collaboration of John D. Young, p. 49 (Abingdon: Routledge, 2015).

90. André Malraux, *Les Conquérants* (Paris: Bernard Grasset, 1928), pp. 35–36.

91. TNA, FO 371/11620, "China Political (cont.). Anti-British Boycott in South China," January–February 1926.

92. BL, RCP MS 51088, Hankey to Cecil, 18 August 1925, f. 58.

93. MAE, SdN/Blocus D.23.79, "Note: Blocus du port de Canton par des navires britanniques," 21 August 1925, f. 1.

94. Enforcing non-discrimination was the essence of the Open Door policy. Under the unequal treaties, China had lost its right to autonomously set tariffs.

95. TNA, CAB 47/1, CID Paper 681-B, "Blockade of the Approaches to Canton, Report by ATB," 26 March 1926. Present were fourteen representatives of the Treasury, Foreign Office, Dominions Office, India Office, Colonial Office, War Office, Admiralty, Department of Overseas Trade, and BoT, as well as former Hong Kong governor Stubbs.

96. Ibid., pp. 2–3.

97. Robert J. Horrocks, "The Guangzhou-Hongkong Strike, 1925–1926: Hongkong Workers in an Anti-Imperialist Movement" (PhD diss., University of Leeds, 1994), pp. 199–216.

98. "The Week in China," *The Economist*, no. 4374, 25 June 1927, p. 1329.

99. Share, "Clash of Worlds," p. 609. See also TNA, FO 371/12501/9132, "Report on the Hong Kong–Canton Strike," March 1926, p. 3.

100. See Ming K. Chan, "Labor and Empire: The Chinese Labor Movement in the Canton Delta, 1895–1927" (PhD diss., Stanford University, 1975), pp. 308–356.

101. An Interdepartmental Committee on Eastern Unrest had identified the hand of Communist agents in upheavals in China, Afghanistan, Persia, and Turkey; Baldwin's Conservatives were convinced the British 1926 general strike had been a Soviet plot. Keith Neilson, *Britain, Soviet Russia and the Collapse of the Versailles Order, 1919–1939* (Cambridge: Cambridge University Press, 2006), pp. 52–53; John Fisher, "The Interdepartmental Committee on Eastern Unrest and British Responses to Bolshevik and Other

Intrigues against the Empire during the 1920s," *Journal of Asian History* 34, no. 1 (2000): 1–34.

102. Harriette Flory, "The Arcos Raid and the Rupture of Anglo-Soviet Relations, 1927," *Journal of Contemporary History* 12 (1977): 707–723.

103. TNA, FO 800/261, Foreign Secretary Chamberlain to Lloyd George, 30 May 1927, p. 3, f. 19.

104. Stephen Kotkin, *Stalin*, vol. 1: *The Paradoxes of Power, 1878–1928* (New York: Penguin, 2014), pp. 616–619, 631–635, 721; Francis Delaisi, "Oil and the Arcos Raid" (2 parts), *Foreign Affairs* 9, nos. 4–5 (October–November 1927): 106–108, 137–138.

105. TNA, CAB 47/3, Papers Nos. 51–80 (March 1927–April 1931); Paper ATB-55/CID-845-B, "Economic Pressure on Soviet Russia," 28 November 1927; Neilson, *Britain, Soviet Russia and the Collapse of the Versailles Order*, p. 56.

106. TNA, CID-845-B, "Economic Pressure on Soviet Russia," p. 10.

107. LoN, R2646/10A/1098, Economic Sanctions—Situation in Russia (1927–1928), Letter by Melchior, "Moskauer Eindrücke," pp. 11–12.

108. Steiner, *The Lights That Failed*, p. 355.

109. James Barros, *The League of Nations and the Great Powers: The Greek-Bulgarian Incident, 1925* (Oxford: Clarendon Press, 1970).

110. Steiner, *The Lights That Failed*, p. 358.

111. Mark Mazower, *Greece and the Inter-War Economic Crisis* (Oxford: Oxford University Press, 1991), p. 22.

112. Barros, *The League of Nations and the Great Powers*, pp. 16–18; Bernhard Stettler, *Die Stellung der Schweiz zum Sanktionssystem des Völkerbundes: Von 1919 bis zum Anwendung gegen Italien 1935/36* (Bern: Peter Lang, 1977), p. 191. Pangalos was described by League deputy secretary-general Frank Paul Walters as "if not the wickedest, without doubt the stupidest of the dictators who darkened the face of Europe between the world wars" (Walters, *A History of the League of Nations* [London: Oxford University Press, 1952], 1:313).

113. "Telegram from the Acting President of the Council to the Greek and Bulgarian Governments," *League of Nations Official Journal*, Sixth Year, 36th (Extraordinary) Session (23 October 1925), p. 1696.

114. LoN, Arthur Salter Papers (ASP), Box S119, Salter to Mr. Cummings (League of Nations Union), "Ultimatum from Greece to Bulgaria," 13 December 1926.

115. LoN, ASP, Box S119, Note from Salter to Drummond about possible economic sanctions on Greece, October 1925, with handwritten comment by Drummond, 28 October 1925.

116. LoN, ASP, Box S119, Salter, "Greco-Bulgar Incident. Sanctions," 21 January 1926, p. 2.

117. "League Prepared to Use Blockade," *New York Times*, 23 October 1925, p. 1.

118. LoN, ASP S119, "Greece," October 1925, pp. 3–6. Indeed, Barros argues that "undoubtedly the most important consideration was [Greece's] mili-

tary weakness and susceptibility to naval blockade and harassment, a condition that the decision-makers in Athens did not lose sight of" (*The League of Nations and the Great Powers*, p. 119).

119. Edwin L. James, "League Jubilant over Balkan Peace: Tribute to Wilson," *New York Times*, 31 October 1925, p. 1.

120. Adam Tooze and Martin Ivanov, "Disciplining the Black Sheep of the Balkans: Financial Supervision and Sovereignty in Bulgaria, 1902–38," *Economic History Review* 64, no. 1 (2010): 30–51.

121. LoN, ASP S119 Folder No. 54/4, "Bulgaria," 24 October 1925, pp. 2–3.

122. Barros, *The League of Nations and the Great Powers*, pp. 78–81.

123. Van Hamel had been a journalist for the Dutch newspaper *NRC* and owed his job to a fortuitous meeting with Drummond at the Paris Peace Conference in 1919; doubtless Drummond was strongly attracted by the prospect of having the League's legal work performed by a fervently pro-British and anti-German liberal from a country usually known for its even-handed neutrality between London and Berlin. Van Hamel also produced an important work of diplomatic history validating Dutch alignment with British sea power throughout history: *Nederland tusschen de mogendheden: de hoofdtrekken van het buitenlandsch beleid en de diplomatieke geschiedenis van ons vaderland sinds deszelfs onafhankelijk volksbestaan onderzocht* (Amsterdam: Van Holkema and Warendorf, 1918).

124. LoN, ASP S119, J. A. Van Hamel, "Sanctions," 17 November 1925, p. 6.

125. Ibid., p. 7.

126. King's College Archive Center (KCAC), Arthur Elliott Felkin Papers, Box 2/1/12, "Note on Arbitration, Security and Disarmament. Resolution of the 3rd Commission," 22 September 1927, p. 4.

Chapter Six. Sanctionism versus Neutrality, 1927–1931

1. PAAA, R 96751, Artikel 16 (1921–1925), Letter from Ludwig Meyr to Konni Zilliacus, March 1925.

2. "Declaration Concerning Wars of Aggression," League of Nations Resolution (24 September 1927), *League of Nations Special Supplement* 53 [1927]: 22.

3. The history of the Kellogg-Briand Treaty is the subject of Oona Hathaway and Scott Shapiro, *The Internationalists: How a Radical Plan to Outlaw War Changed the World* (New York: Simon and Schuster, 2017).

4. Viscount Cecil and W. Arnold-Forster, "The Freedom of the Seas," *Journal of the Royal Institute for International Affairs* 8, no. 2 (March 1929): 89.

5. Norman Angell, "Is the Conference Bunk?" *Foreign Affairs* 12, no. 6 (March 1930): 279; John D. Coogan, *The End of Neutrality: The United States, Britain, and Maritime Rights, 1899–1915* (Ithaca, NY: Cornell University Press, 1981).

6. James T. Shotwell, "La liberté des mers" (Deuxième partie), *Journal de Genève*, no. 176, 29 June 1928.

7. George L. Ridgeway, *Merchants of Peace: Twenty Years of Business Diplo-*

macy through the International Chamber of Commerce, 1919–1938 (New York: Columbia University Press, 1938), pp. 21–194; Clotilde Druelle-Korn, "The Great War: Matrix of the International Chamber of Commerce, a Fortunate Business League of Nations," in *The Impact of the First World War on International Business*, ed. Andrew Smith, Kevin D. Tennet, and Simon Mollan, pp. 103–120 (New York: Routledge, 2017).

8. F. W. Bitter and A. Zelle, *No More War on Foreign Investments: A Kellogg Pact for Private Property* (Philadelphia: A. Dorrance, 1933).

9. On this break within British New Liberalism, especially the dissociation of free trade from laissez-faire, see Anthony Howe, *Free Trade and Liberal England, 1846–1946* (Oxford: Clarendon Press, 1997), pp. 274–308; on French social liberalism, see Serge Audier, *La pensée solidariste: Aux sources du modèle sociale républicain* (Paris: Presses Universitaires de Paris, 2010); on the emergence in the 1920s United States of a "new liberalism that emphasized the 'economic' and neglected the 'cultural,'" see Gary Gerstle, "The Protean Character of American Liberalism," *American Historical Review* 99, no. 4 (October 1994): 1043–1073.

10. On neoliberals' separation between property (*dominium*) and sovereignty (*imperium*), see Quinn Slobodian, *Globalists: The End of Empire and the Birth of Neoliberalism* (Cambridge, MA: Harvard University Press, 2018), pp. 121–181.

11. Cecil and Arnold-Forster, "The Freedom of the Seas," p. 95.

12. SHD, 7 N 875, 5ème Bureau [Logistics], "Note au sujet de la guerre économique" [undated; ca. early 1916].

13. J. M. Keynes, *Two Memoirs: Dr Melchior, a Defeated Enemy, and My Early Beliefs* (London: Rupert Hart-Davis, 1949), p. 24; Douglas J. Newton, *British Policy and the Weimar Republic* (Oxford: Clarendon Press, 1997), pp. 342–343.

14. KCAC, JMK CO/2/61, Felkin to Keynes, 16 October 1924, p. 3.

15. LoN, ASP, Box S120, Letter from J. M. Keynes to A. Elliot Felkin, 29 October 1924, p. 2.

16. SHD, 2 N 6, CSDN Séance du 22 avril 1926, "Rapport fait au CSDN au nom de la Commission d'études au sujet des questions à examiner par la commission préparatoire de la reduction des armaments," 3 March 1926, p. 11.

17. MAE, B.28.1s/d (1924–1927), Comité supérieur économique de la défense nationale/Conseil supérieur de la défense nationale, 1 janvier 1924–31 décembre 1927, Letter from Briand to Serrigny, "Action économique à l'étranger en temps de guerre," 8 December 1927.

18. MAE, B.28.1w, "Rapport relative au fonctionnement des commissions de défense nationale concernant les produits et industries déficitaires pendant l'Exercice, 1926–1927," 1 December 1927.

19. MAE, Série SDN No. 815 (Arbitrage Sécurité Désarmament, 1920–1927), "Mesures d'entr'aide économique," 20 September 1926, p. 6.

20. Kalervo Hovi, *Interessensphären im Baltikum. Finnland im Rahmen der Ost-politik Polens, 1919–1922* (Helsinki: Studia Historica / Societas Historica Finlandiae, 1984).

21. Rudolf Kiszling, *Die militärischen Vereinbarungen der Kleinen Entente, 1929–1937* (Munich: R. Oldenbourg, 1959); Jozef Korbel, *Poland between East and West: Soviet and German Diplomacy toward Poland, 1919–1933* (Princeton, NJ: Princeton University Press, 1963); Ozer Carmi, *La Grande-Bretagne et la Petite Entente* (Geneva: Imprimerie Droz, 1972); Vladimir Streinu, *La Petite Entente et l'Europe* (Geneva: Institut Universitaire de Hautes Études Internationales, 1977); Eliza Campus, *The Little Entente and the Balkan Alliance* (Bucharest: Editura Academiei Republicii Socialiste Românâ, 1978); Kalervo Hovi, *Alliance de Revers: The Stabilization of France's Alliance Policies in East Central Europe* (Turku: Turun Yliopisto, 1984); Magda Ádám, *The Little Entente and Europe (1920–1929)* (Budapest: Akadémiai Kiadó, 1993); Zara Steiner, *The Lights That Failed: European International History, 1919–1933* (Oxford: Oxford University Press, 2005), pp. 270–309.

22. "This conflict between the vital interests of small exposed states and the efforts of the League of Nations with a view to reducing the military budgets of its members must be solved by the League itself" (LON, C.513.1926. IX, Propositions des délégations française, polonaise et finlandaise à la commission préparatoire de la conference du désarmement, 3 September 1926, p. 3).

23. LoN, R478/10/59171/57661, Memorandum by G. Roos to Eric Drummond, 3 May 1927, p. 2.

24. Rapport de M. de Brouckère sur la question I (b) de la proposition de la délégation française à la Commission préparatoire de la Conférence du désarmement (LON, C.301.1926, p. 4), Genève, 1 December 1926; in A.14.1927.V, Rapports et résolutions concernant Article 16 du Pacte (Geneva, 1927), pp. 60–72.

25. "If the Council only met after war has been declared, it thus neglected or lost the opportunity of doing anything more than intervening in war instead of preserving peace" (Brouckère in ibid., p. 70).

26. Ibid., p. 72.

27. MAE, Affaires Juridiques, Fonds Fromageot, Article 16/Allemagne (1927), Letter from Berthelot to Briand, 25 January 1927, pp. 4–6.

28. PAAA, R 96752, Telegram by von Bülow to AA, 31 May 1926.

29. PAAA, R 96752, Telegram by von Bülow to Stresemann, 4 June 1925, f. 5.

30. LoN, R478 10/57661/57661, Annexe au procès-verbal du Comité financier, 7 mars 1927. Résumé de la première discussion sur l'aide financière à un état victim d'aggression, préparé par le Dr. Pospisil, président du Comité financier, p. 2.

31. Nathan Marcus, *Austrian Reconstruction and the Collapse of Global Finance 1921–1931* (Cambridge, MA: Harvard University Press, 2018); Jamie Martin, *Governing Capitalism in the Age of Total War* (Cambridge, MA: Harvard Uni-

versity Press, forthcoming). For biographies, see Nicole Piétri, "L'oeuvre d'un organisme technique de la Société des Nations: Le Comité financier et la reconstruction de l'Autriche (1921–1926)," in *The League of Nations in Retrospect: Proceedings of the Symposium, Geneva, 6–9 November 1980 / La Société des Nations: Rétrospective* (Berlin: Walter de Gruyter, 1980), pp. 324–328.

32. LoN, R 478/10/57661/60186 C.336.M.110.1927.II, Financial Committee, Report to the Council on the work of the twenty-seventh session of the committee, 8–14 June 1927. This was quite a substantial amount—the League's largest loans in the 1920s were the Austrian reconstruction loan of 1923 (£33.78 million), and the Greek settlement loan (£12.3 million) and Hungarian stabilization loan (£14.38 million), both issued in 1924. See Yann Decorzant and Juan H. Flores, "Public Borrowing in Harsh Times: The League of Nations Loans Revisited," Working Papers in Economic History, Universidad Carlos-III de Madrid, September 2012, p. 13, table 1.

33. LoN, R 478/10/57661/57661 F/26ème session/P.V. 9, Annexe au procès-verbal du Comité financier, 7 March 1927.

34. LoN, R 478/10/57661/57661 F. 391, Statement by Director Ryrto [*sic*] Ryti regarding the proposal of financial assistance to states victims of aggression, [undated; March 1927], pp. 3–4. Ryti had brought the Finnish markka onto the gold standard the year before.

35. PAAA, R 96753, January–July 1927, Melchior to Stresemann, 4 January 1927. Both in its design and in the political problems of shared liability for debt that it tried to overcome, Melchior's proposal bears a striking resemblance to the European Union's crisis-fighting finance bodies, the European Financial Stability Facility and the European Stability Mechanism, created in 2010–2012.

36. LoN, R 478, 10/61946/57661, Financial assistance to states victims of aggression; discussion at eighth session of the Assembly, extracts from discussions in Third Committee of Assembly on 22 September 1927, p. 7.

37. MAE, Série SDN No. 815, M. de Chalendar, "Note au sujet de l'étude des mesures d'assistance financière à prévoir en faveur d'un état victime d'une aggression," 22 January 1927.

38. Financial Committee to Drummond, 13 October 1927; in LON, C.40.1928. IX, "Study of Economic and Financial Relations of the Various States with a View to the Possible Application of Article 16 of the Covenant," 15 February 1928, p. 4.

39. LoN, E.371, Serruys to Drummond, 29 December 1927, "Relations économiques entre différents pays. Réponse du Comité économique à la demande du S.G. concernant la réunion des informations à ce sujet," p. 2; for Serruys's professional self-conception, see his "L'Oeuvre économique de la S.D.N.," *La Revue des Vivants* 3 (1929); Laurence Badel, *Un milieu libéral et européen: Le grand commerce français, 1925–1948* (Paris: Comité pour l'histoire économique et financière de la France, 1999).

40. Patricia Clavin, *Securing the World Economy: The Reinvention of the League of Nations, 1920–1946* (Oxford: Oxford University Press, 2013), pp. 47–123; Madeleine Lynch Dungy, "Writing Multilateral Trade Rules in the League of Nations," *Contemporary European History* 29 (April 2020): 1–16.

41. LoN, E.371, Serruys to Drummond, 29 December 1927, p. 3.

42. Bradley Bordiss and Vishnu Padayachee, "'A Superior Practical Man': Sir Henry Strakosch, the Gold Standard and Monetary Policy Debates in South Africa, 1920–23," *Economic History of Developing Regions* 26, no. 1 (2011): 114–122.

43. Sir Henry Strakosch, "The Convention on Financial Assistance," *International Affairs* (Royal Institute for International Affairs) 10, no. 2 (March 1931): 210.

44. KCAC, JMK CO/2/132, Letter from J. M. Keynes to A. E. Felkin, 12 August 1928.

45. Strakosch, "The Convention on Financial Assistance," p. 216.

46. See Strakosch's short pamphlet, *A Financial Plan for the Prevention of War* (London: London General Press, 1929). *The Economist* saw the convention as a "formidable deterrent to war makers" ("Finance and Peace," in vol. 109, no. 4488 [31 August 1929]: p. 389); Alexander Zevin, *Liberalism at Large: The World According to the Economist* (London: Verso, 2019), pp. 191, 202.

47. The convention's initial signatories were Albania, Austria, Belgium, Bolivia, Britain, Australia, Bulgaria, Ireland, Czechoslovakia, Cuba, Denmark, Spain, Estonia, Ethiopia, Finland, France, Greece, Latvia, Lithuania, Norway, the Netherlands, Peru, Persia, Poland, Portugal, Romania, Sweden, and Yugoslavia; Germany and Italy signed in 1931. *League of Nations—Official Journal* 11 (November 1930): 1648–1679.

48. Hathaway and Shapiro, *The Internationalists*, pp. 158–182, 396–415.

49. Gerry Simpson, "Writing the Tokyo Trial," in *Beyond Victor's Justice: The Tokyo War Crimes Trial Revisited*, ed. Yuki Tanaka, Timothy L. H. McCormack, and Gerry Simpson, p. 25n9 (Leiden: Martinus Nijhoff, 2011).

50. "The Ambassador in Great Britain (Houghton) to the Secretary of State," 19 May 1928; in FRUS, 1928 (Washington DC: GPO, 1942), 1:68.

51. Edwin M. Borchard argued that "it would be difficult to conceive of any wars that nations have fought within the last century, or are likely to fight in the future, that cannot be accommodated under these exceptions. Far from constituting an outlawry of war, they constitute the most definite sanction of specific wars that has ever been promulgated" ("The Multilateral Pact 'Renunciation of War,'" address delivered at the Williamstown Institute of Politics, August 22, 1928).

52. Henry Cabot Lodge, "The Meaning of the Kellogg Treaty," *Harper's* (December 1928), pp. 28–41.

53. B. J. C. McKercher, *The Second Baldwin Government and the United States, 1924–1929* (Cambridge: Cambridge University Press, 1984), pp. 34–44.

54. Cited in "American Warning to the League: Effect of Sanctions on Trade,"

The Observer, 30 October 1927. Lord Robert Vansittart, Chamberlain's more pragmatic and pro-European colleague, thought in 1927 that "a war with America would indeed be the most futile and damnable of all, but it is not 'unthinkable,' and we shall the more surely avoid it by cutting that word from our vocabulary" (cited in Kori Schake, *Safe Passage: The Transition from British to American Hegemony* [Cambridge, MA: Harvard University Press, 2017], p. 252).

55. "The Next Step," *The Economist,* no. 4409 (25 February 1928): 359.

56. Cited in Edward House, *The Intimate Papers of Colonel House,* ed. Charles Seymour (Boston: Houghton Mifflin, 1928), 4:168. Professor Seymour describes the Anglo-American naval discussions about armament as "the most serious and delicate of the entire Peace Conference" (LoN, ASP, Box S119, "The Freedom of the Seas" [abstract from *The Intimate Papers of Colonel House*], 1928, p. 7).

57. LoN, ASP, Box S118, Freedom of the Seas, Salter to Raymond Buell, 26 May 1928, pp. 1–2.

58. Ibid., p. 2.

59. Lisa McGirr, *The War on Alcohol: Prohibition and the Rise of the American State* (New York: W. W. Norton, 2016).

60. W. Arnold-Forster, "Maritime Law and Economic Pressure," *Journal of the Royal United Services Institution,* no. 70 (February 1925): 456.

61. *Freedom of the Seas: Old and New* (London: Labour Party, 1929).

62. Arnold-Forster, "Freedom of the Seas: Old and New. Draft Pamphlet," Labour Party International Department, February 1929, p. 13.

63. Raymond Buell, "Sea Law under the Kellogg Pact," *New Republic,* 15 May 1929, pp. 349–351.

64. David Miller, *The Pact of Paris—A Study of the Kellogg-Briand Treaty* (New York: G. P. Putnam's Sons, 1928), p. 132. See the critical review by Edwin Borchard in *American Journal of International Law* 23, no. 2 (April 1929): 487–489.

65. Harold Josephson, "James Thomson Shotwell: The Historian as Activist," (PhD diss., University of Wisconsin–Madison, 1968), p. 222.

66. L. H. Woolsey, "The Porter and Capper Resolutions against Traffic in Arms," *American Journal of International Law* 23, no. 2 (April 1929): 379–383.

67. "Porter Resolution Tabled. House Committee Says Time Is Too Short to Consider Arms Embargo," *New York Times,* 20 February 1929, p. 4.

68. MAE, Série SDN No. 816, "Le Sénateur Borah et la liberté des mers," note from Claudel to Briand, 1 February 1929, p. 4; Claudel to Briand, 27 March 1928, p. 2.

69. Between 1921 and 1928, the United States was the world's third-largest international arms exporter after Britain (the undisputed first) and France, producing about one-fifth of the world's arms exports. This ranking includes heavy equipment and small arms but excludes aircraft (in which the United States was the premier producer) and warships (in which it came in

seventh). Keith Krause, *Arms and the State: Patterns of Military Production and Trade* (New York: Cambridge University Press, 1992), p. 74, table 3.

70. MAE, Série SDN, Box No. 816, *Izvestia* article on Capper Resolution, 14 February 1929, f. 98.

71. MAE, Série SDN, Box No. 817, "Étude sur la liberté des mers," January 1932, pp. 11–12.

72. Sir Julian Corbett, *The League of Nations and Freedom of the Seas* (London: Oxford University Press, 1918), pp. 10–11.

73. "'Freedom of the Seas': Sir Richard Webb on War Difficulties," *The Times*, 3 January 1930, p. 3.

74. Ger van Roon, *Kleine landen in Crisistijd. Van Oslostaten tot Benelux, 1930–1940* (Amsterdam: Elsevier, 1985). On the interwar erosion of neutrality, see Nils Ørvik, *The Decline of Neutrality, 1914–1941: With Special Reference to the United States and the Northern Neutrals* (London: Frank Cass, 1971); on neutrals and the sanctionist system, see John F. L. Ross, *Neutrality and International Sanctions: Sweden, Switzerland, and Collective Security* (Westport, CT: Praeger, 1989).

75. M. W. W. P. Consett, *The Triumph of Unarmed Forces (1914–1918): An Account of the Transactions by Which Germany during the Great War Was Able to Obtain Supplies Prior to Her Collapse under the Pressure of Economic Forces* (London: Williams and Norgate, 1923); B. J. C. McKercher and Keith E. Neilson, "'The Triumph of Unarmed Forces': Sweden and the Allied Blockade of Germany, 1914–1917," *Journal of Strategic Studies* 7, no. 2 (1984): 178–199.

76. J. F. C. Fuller, *The Reformation of War* (London: Hutchinson, 1923), pp. 96, 98.

77. Victor Mogens, "Freedom of the Seas and Submarine Warfare: Comments of a Neutral," *Foreign Affairs* 3, no. 9 (March 1922): 142.

78. Arnold-Forster, "Freedom of the Seas: A Belligerent's Reply," *Foreign Affairs* 3, no. 10 (April 1922): 158.

79. Arnold-Forster, "Maritime Law and Economic Pressure," p. 456.

80. Miroslas Gonsiorowski, *Société des Nations et problème de la paix* (Paris: Rousseau, 1927), 2:422.

81. This point emerges clearly from studies of pro-peace and pro-League civic movements, such as the following: Christian Birebent, *Militants de la paix et de la SDN: Les mouvements de soutien à la Société des Nations en France et au Royaume-Uni, 1918–1925* (Paris: L'Harmattan, 2007); Helen McCarthy, *The British People and the League of Nations: Democracy, Citizenship and Internationalism, c. 1918–1948* (Manchester: Manchester University Press, 2011); Michael Pugh, *Liberal Internationalism: The Interwar Movement for Peace in Britain* (Basingstoke: Palgrave Macmillan, 2012).

82. H. F. Crohn-Wolfgang, "Randstaatenpolitik," *Weltwirtschaftliches Archiv* 17 (1921/1922): 94–108.

83. PAAA, R 96754, Von Bülow, Aufzeichnung über die Note Finnlands und den Völkerbund vom 15.6.1927, 14 July 1927. See also the reflections on the

destabilizing effects of collective security provisions in an incomplete non-universal League by State Secretary Carl von Schubert, "Aufzeichnung," 1 December 1927.

84. "Aufzeichnung über die Unterredung swischen dem Herrn Reichsminister Curtius und den Herren Tardieu und Briand im Restaurant 'Anjema' im Haag, am 4. Januar 1930 von 9–11 Uhr 45 abends"; in ADAP, series B: *1925–1933*, vol. 14:1. Januar bis 30. April 1930 (Göttingen: Vandenhoeck & Ruprecht, 1980), pp. 18–19.

85. "Aufzeichnung des Reichsministers des Auswärtigen Curtius," 4 April 1930; in ADAP, series B: *1925–1933*, vol. 14, pp. 437–438.

86. "Vortragender Legationsrat von Bülow an Botschaftsrat Dieckhoff (London)," 24 January 1930; in ADAP, series B: *1925–1933*, vol. 14, pp. 121–123.

87. Rhiannon Vickers, *The Labour Party and the World*, vol. 1: *The Evolution of Labour's Foreign Policy, 1900–51* (Manchester: Manchester University Press, 2003), p. 94; B. J. C. McKercher, *Transition of Power: Britain's Global Loss of Pre-Eminence to the United States* (Cambridge: Cambridge University Press, 1999), pp. 38–42.

88. Adam Tooze, *The Deluge: The Great War and the Remaking of Global Order, 1916–1931* (London: Allen Lane, 2014), pp. 491–492; Donald J. Lisio, *British Naval Supremacy and Anglo-American Antagonisms, 1914–1930* (Cambridge: Cambridge University Press, 2014), pp. 313–315.

89. "Armistice Day Address. November 11, 1929," in *Public Papers of the Presidents of the United States: Herbert Hoover, March 4 to December 31, 1929* (Washington, DC: GPO, 1974), p. 377. The observation made by Hoover was acute; the same tradeoff between navies and tariffs provides the framework for the account of nineteenth-century globalization and war developed by Avner Offer, *The First World War: An Agrarian Interpretation* (Oxford: Clarendon Press, 1989).

90. PAAA, R 96755, Telegram Nr. 104 from Adolf Müller (Bern) to AA (Berlin), 14 November 1929, pp. 1–2.

91. "Europe Sees Hoover Clash with League in Food Ship Plan; Holds the Economic Blockade, Geneva's Strongest Weapon, Would Be Nullified," *New York Times*, 13 November 1929, p. 1.

92. Steven W. Roskill, *Naval Policy between the Wars*, vol. 2: *The Period of Reluctant Rearmament, 1930–1939* (London: Collins, 1968), p. 47.

93. MAE, Série SDN, Box No. 817, Note summarizing the dossier of freedom of the seas by Aubert et Basdavant, "État actuel de la question de liberté des mers," 14 October 1931, p. 8, f. 103.

94. MAE, Série SDN, Box No. 817, French ambassador to United States Claudel to Briand (foreign affairs minister), 29 November 1930, p. 2.

95. This lecture is reproduced as "Das Zeitalter der Neutralisierungen und Entpolitisierungen," in *Positionen und Begriffe im Kampf mit Weimar–Genf–Versailles, 1923–1939* (Berlin: Duncker and Humblot, 1988), pp. 120–133.

96. "Der Völkerbund und Europa" [1928], in *Positionen und Begriffe*, pp. 88–97.

97. Among his contemporary appreciators was Bülow in the German Foreign Ministry, to whom Schmitt was a useful radical who "writes with a very skillful pen [*Gewandte Feder*]" (PAAA, R 96753, Telegram by von Bülow to Martius, 21 June 1927, p. 2).

98. Carl Schmitt, *The Nomos of the Earth in the International Law of the* Jus Publicum Europaeum (New York: Telos Press, 2003), p. 235.

99. A point that emerges from Peter Jackson, *Beyond the Balance of Power: France and the Politics of National Security in the Era of the First World War* (Cambridge: Cambridge University Press, 2014).

100. George Egerton, "Collective Security as Political Myth: Liberal Internationalism and the League of Nations in Politics and History," *International History Review* 5, no. 4 (November 1983): 496–524. The term "liberal internationalism" was rarely used in the early twentieth century; when it was, it was to describe a specific policy choice for individual states, not a structural or institutional order. In the 1920s and 1930s the few mentions of liberal internationalism were usually contrasts with protectionism or imperialism, especially in the Allied treatment of Germany, where "liberal" meant generous instead of harsh treatment. See Donald R. Taft, review of George Young, *The New Germany, Journal of International Relations* 11, no. 4 (April 1921): 628–631. For the term's use to denote an organized system of free trade, see Lionel C. Robbins, "The Economics of Territorial Sovereignty," in *Peaceful Change: An International Problem*, ed. C. A. W. Manning, p. 57 (New York: Macmillan, 1937); Ridgeway, *Merchants of Peace*, pp. 342–360. For the concept's modern use to connote a structural order characterized by formal inter-state equality, the protection of a measure of individual rights and freedoms, and a normative commitment to popular self-government, see Fred Halliday, "Three Concepts of Internationalism," *International Affairs* 64, no. 2 (Spring 1988); Tony Smith, *America's Mission: The United States and the Worldwide Struggle for Democracy* (Princeton, NJ: Princeton University Press, 1994); G. John Ikenberry: *After Victory: Institutions, Strategic Restraint, and the Rebuilding of Order after Major Wars* (Princeton, NJ: Princeton University Press, 2001), and *A World Safe for Democracy: Liberal Internationalism and the Crises of Global Order* (New Haven: Yale University Press, 2020), p. 13n20. For historical application to countries engaged in internationalism with a strong domestic liberal tradition (most prominently late Victorian, Edwardian, and interwar Britain), see Casper Sylvest, *British Liberal Internationalism, 1880–1930* (Manchester: Manchester University Press, 2013). The League's successful preservation of empire and comfortable incorporation of authoritarian and anti-liberal states into its various organs makes it questionable if the epithet "liberal" can be applied to the interwar order as a whole; for a critical consideration of these issues, see David Petruccelli, "The Crisis of Liberal Internationalism: The Legacies of the League of Nations Reconsidered," *Journal of World History* 31, no. 1 (March 2020): 111–136.

Chapter Seven. Collective Security
against Aggression, 1931–1935

1. Pitman B. Potter, review of David Davies, *The Problem of the Twentieth Century*, *American Political Science Review* 26, no. 2 (April 1932): 382–383.

2. George Egcrton, "Collective Security as Political Myth: Liberal Internationalism and the League of Nations in Politics and History," *International History Review* 5, no. 4 (November 1983): 496–524.

3. Margaret Doxey, *Economic Sanctions and International Enforcement* (London: Oxford University Press, 1971), p. 93. The same argument for the signaling role of sanctions is made in the influential study by G. Clyde Hufbauer, J. J. Schott, and Kimberley Ann Elliott, *Economic Sanctions Reconsidered: Supplemental Case Materials* (Washington, DC: Institute for International Economics, 1990), pp. 33–40.

4. For Carr, the issue was the refusal of the British state to back up sanctions with military force since "the military and economic weapons are merely different instruments of power" (Edward Hallett Carr, *The Twenty Years' Crisis, 1919–1939: An Introduction to the Study of International Relations*, revised 2nd ed. [New York: Harper and Row, 1964; first published 1939], p. 109).

5. Charles Kindleberger, *The World in Depression, 1929–1939* (Berkeley: University of California Press, 1973), p. 240.

6. Zara Steiner, *The Lights That Failed: European International History, 1919–1933* (Oxford: Oxford University Press, 2005), p. 358.

7. The teleology of such historical judgments is clear in Oona Hathaway and Scott J. Shapiro, *The Internationalists: How a Radical Plan to Outlaw War Remade the World* (New York: Simon and Schuster, 2017), p. 173; Lori Fisler Damrosch, "Collective Economic Sanctions: Nonforcible Responses to Threats to Peace," in *The Dumbarton Oaks Conversations and the United Nations, 1944–1994*, ed. Ernest May and Angeliki E. Laiou, p. 62 (Washington, DC: Dumbarton Oaks Research Library and Collection, 1998).

8. For example, Elizabeth Borgwardt argues that before the creation of the United Nations "there were no ultimate sanctions through which an international security organization could impose its judgments"—a claim that elides the importance of Article 16 in interwar history (Borgwardt, *A New Deal for the World: America's Vision for Human Rights* [Cambridge, MA: Harvard University Press, 2005], p. 154).

9. Dorothy Borg, *The United States and the Far Eastern Crisis of 1931–1933* (Cambridge, MA: Harvard University Press, 1964).

10. Donald S. Birn, *The League of Nations Union, 1918–1945* (Oxford: Clarendon Press, 1981).

11. Cited in J. A. Thompson, "Lord Cecil and the Pacifists in the League of Nations Union," *Historical Journal* 20, no. 4 (1977): 949; on party alignment, see Helen McCarthy, *The British People and the League of Nations:*

Democracy, Citizenship and Internationalism, c. 1918–48 (Manchester: Manchester University Press, 2011), pp. 46–78.

12. Anton Bertram, "The Economic Weapon as a Form of Peaceful Pressure," *Transactions of the Grotius Society* 17 (1931): 164, 166.

13. Frederick G. Tryon, "The Economic Aspects of Sanctions," in *Program for an Investigation and Report on Economic Sanctions and American Policy* (New York: Twentieth Century Fund, June 1930), pp. 21–60; quote on p. 21. This resource distribution improved slightly as Mexico would join the League in 1931 and the Soviet Union in 1934.

14. The ten-man committee included Wilsonian legal advisers (Joseph Chamberlain and John Foster Dulles), businessmen and financiers (William Crocker, Lucius Eastman, Edward Hurley, James Mooney, and Bolton Smith), and foreign affairs hands (Harold Moulton and the former ambassador to London, Alanson Houghton).

15. Cited in *League of Nations Official Journal, Special Supplement*, no. 93 (Geneva, 1931): 59–60.

16. The standard account is Christopher Thorne, *The Limits of Foreign Policy: The West, the League, and the Far Eastern Crisis of 1931–1933* (London: Macmillan, 1972). See also Steiner, *The Lights That Failed*, pp. 707–754; Akira Iriye, "The Manchurian Incident: Japan's Revisionist Militarism, 1931–1932," in *The Cambridge History of China*, vol. 13, part 2: *Republican China, 1912–1949*, ed. John K. Fairbank and Albert Feuerwerker (Cambridge: Cambridge University Press, 1986); Ian Nish: "Some Thoughts on Japanese Expansion," in *Imperialism and After: Continuities and Discontinuities*, ed. Wolfgang J. Mommsen and Jürgen Osterhammel (London: German Historical Institute, 1986), and "Intelligence and the Lytton Commission, 1931–1933," in *Decisions and Diplomacy: Essays in Twentieth-Century International History in Memory of George Grun and Esmonde Robertson*, ed. Dick Richardson and Glyn Stone (London: Routledge, 1995).

17. On the repeated use of boycotts in the preceding decade, see Banno Junji, "Japanese Industrialists and Merchants and the Anti-Japanese Boycotts in China, 1919–1928," in *The Japanese Informal Empire in China, 1895–1937*, ed. Peter Duus, Ramon H. Myers, and Mark R. Peattie, pp. 314–329 (Princeton, NJ: Princeton University Press, 1989).

18. Hoover Institution Archives (HIA), Stanley Hornbeck Papers (SHP), Box 369, Folder "Economic Sanctions," Consul General Arthur Garrels, "Present Position of Japan's Commercial Interests and Trade in China," 2 November 1931, p. 1.

19. George E. Sokolsky, "China Fights Again with the Boycott; a Weapon She Has Used Many Times Is Now Pointed toward Japan Once More," *New York Times*, 8 November 1931, p. 3.

20. For an argument that traces the roots of the Mukden Incident to the effects of *Chinese* economic pressure on Japan in the summer of 1931, see Donald A. Jordan, *Chinese Boycotts versus Japanese Bombs: The Failure of China's "Revo-*

lutionary Diplomacy," *1931–1932* (Ann Arbor: University of Michigan Press, 1991).

21. As the Japanese liberal Yusuke Tsurumi put it to American readers of *Foreign Affairs* earlier that year, "Japan has been caught unawares within three unsurmountable walls: the tariff wall, the migration wall and the peace wall. The first wall excludes Japan's manufactured goods from other countries. The second cuts off the migration of her people. And the third prohibits the readjustment of the unequal distribution of territories among nations with different density of population" ("Japan in the Modern World," *Foreign Affairs* 9, no. 2 [January 1931]: 262).

22. TNA, FO 371 F 590/1/10, Arthur Salter to John Simon, 2 February 1932.

23. Quincy Wright, "When Does War Exist?" *American Journal of International Law* 26 (1932): 362–368.

24. LOC, Arthur Sweetser Papers, Box 29, Letter from Sweetser to Drew Pearson, 6 October 1960, f. 5.

25. Herbert Hoover, *The Memoirs of Herbert Hoover, 1920–1933: The Cabinet and the Presidency* (London: Macmillan, 1952), pp. 366, 370; Thorne, *The Limits of Foreign Policy,* pp. 196–197.

26. Castle argued that "there can be no doubt that a boycott, universally applied, would bring a nation to its knees, but at a cost that would be almost worse than war. Except in a country able to feed itself from its own resources it would mean starvation. Starvation means revolution and the collapse of all government. Before this happens, to be sure, there would probably be war. A boycott implies a blockade and I know of no measure more certain to lead to war than blockade" (HIA, SHP, Box 369, Folder Sanctions #1, Transcript of speech by Under Secretary of State William R. Castle at General Conference of the Methodist Episcopal Church, Atlantic City, 6 May 1932).

27. HIA, SHP, Memorandum 793.94/4314, "Manchuria Situation. B. Economic Boycott," 6 December 1931.

28. R. A. Lamont, "United States Maintains Position as the Leading Exporter Nation," *Commerce Reports,* Washington, DC, 25 April 1932.

29. George Soule, "The Fallacy of a Boycott," *Harper's Magazine* 164, no. 984 (May 1932): 706.

30. TNA, CAB 47/4 Report ATB 86 (CID Paper No. 1083-B), "Economic Sanctions against Japan," March 1932, p. 8.

31. HIA, SHP, Box 369, Folder "Economic Sanctions," Allen T. Klots, "Memorandum of Conversation with Miss Emily Greene Balch, Mr. Tucker P. Smith, Mr. Ray Newton," 2 March 1932, p. 2.

32. Carrie A. Foster, *The Women and the Warriors: The U.S. Section of the Women's International League for Peace and Freedom* (Syracuse, NY: Syracuse University Press, 1995), p. 195.

33. Cited in Thorne, *The Limits of Foreign Policy,* p. 222.

34. For Dean's views on sanctions, see "The United States and Sanctions," *For-*

eign Policy Bulletin, 9 July 1930, pp. 181–182; Dorothy Detzer, *Appointment on the Hill* (New York: Henry Holt, 1948).

35. Garrard Glenn, "War without Guns," *Virginia Quarterly Review* 8, no. 1 (July 1932): 389.

36. "Butler for Boycott as Weapon of Peace," *New York Times*, 4 April 1932, p. 18.

37. Committee on Economic Sanctions, *Reports of Research Findings* (New York: Twentieth Century Fund, 1931), p. 222.

38. "Urge Treaty to Give Kellogg Pact Teeth. Members of Butler Committee Suggest Nations Agree to Joint Economic Action," *New York Times*, 2 March 1932, p. 7.

39. "Urges a Boycott Plan as Curb on Conflicts. Head of Twentieth Century Fund Tells Castle Concerted Embargo Would Uphold Kellogg Pact," *New York Times*, 9 May 1932.

40. "Are Sanctions Necessary to International Organization?" *Foreign Policy Association* pamphlet, nos. 82–83 (June 1932).

41. Raymond Buell, in "Are Sanctions Necessary to International Organization?" pp. 13, 17.

42. John Dewey, in ibid., pp. 28, 33, 38.

43. Donald A. Jordan, *China's Trial by Fire: The Shanghai War of 1932* (Ann Arbor: University of Michigan Press, 2001).

44. Japan was not the first member state to abandon Geneva, however; Costa Rica had left the League in 1925 and Brazil had done so in 1926.

45. Sobei Mogi and H. Vere Redman, *The Problem of the Far East* (Philadelphia: J. B. Lippincott, 1935), p. 116.

46. Thomas W. Burkman, *Japan and the League of Nations: Empire and World Order, 1914–1938* (Honolulu: University of Hawaii Press, 2008), pp. 77–80.

47. Ian Nish, *Japan's Struggle with Internationalism: Japan, China and the League of Nations, 1931–1933* (Abingdon: Routledge, 1993).

48. There were other internationalisms that remained possible for Tokyo, such as a Locarno Pact for the Far East among Japan, China, Manchukuo, and the Soviet Union, or a revival of the Anglo-Japanese Entente. Burkman, *Japan and the League of Nations*, pp. 174–175, 198–206.

49. Michael Geyer, "Etudes in Political History: Reichswehr, NSDAP, and the Seizure of Power," in *The Nazi Machtergreifung*, ed. Peter D. Stachura, pp. 101–119 (London: George Allen and Unwin, 1983).

50. Avraham Barkai, *From Boycott to Annihilation: The Economic Struggle of German Jews, 1933–1943* (Hanover, NH: University Press of New England, 1990), pp. 17–23; Christoph Kreutzmüller, "Picketing Jewish-Owned Businesses in Nazi Germany: A Boycott?" in Christoph Kreutzmüller, *Boycotts Past and Present: From the American Revolution to the Campaign to Boycott Israel* (Cham: Palgrave Macmillan, 2019), pp. 97–114.

51. Samuel Untermeyer, *Civilization's Only Weapon against Hitlerism* (New York: Non-Sectarian Anti-Nazi League, 1934); Moshe R. Gottlieb: "The

First of April Boycott and the Reaction of the American Jewish Community," *American Jewish Historical Quarterly* 57, no. 4 (June 1968): 516–556, and "The Anti-Nazi Boycott Movement in the United States: An Ideological and Sociological Appreciation," *Jewish Social Studies* 35, nos. 3–4 (July–October 1973): 198–227; Rona Sheramy, "There Are Times When Silence Is a Sin: The Women's Division of the American Jewish Congress and the Anti-Nazi Boycott Movement," *American Jewish History* 89, no. 1 (2001): 105–121.

52. The Board of Deputies of British Jews, for example, chose to pursue a more cautious approach for fear of retaliation against the German Jewish community. Sharon Gewirtz, "Anglo-Jewish Responses to Nazi Germany, 1933–39: The Anti-Nazi Boycott and the Board of Deputies of British Jews," *Journal of Contemporary History* 26, no. 2 (1991): 255–276.

53. Christian Lange, "An American Discussion of International Sanctions," *New Commonwealth*, April 1933, p. 4.

54. The Chatham House findings were also shared with the State Department, where they reached the eyes of Stanley Hornbeck, whose interest in economic pressure went beyond his responsibility for Far Eastern affairs and extended to their general use. HIA, SHP 67008, Box 369, Folder "Sanctions #1," Letter from Royal Institute of International Affairs (29 March 1933) sent to State Department, 24 April 1933.

55. MAE, Série SDN, No. 817, Ambassador Claudel (Washington, DC), "Note pour Monsieur Herriot," 26 April 1933, pp. 2, 4; "Paris Encouraged by Davis's Speech; Press Holds Geneva Pledge Goes Far toward Assuring Security French Seek. Range Urged to Disarm. Blum Proposes Action in Gratitude for Our Abandoning Policy of Freedom of the Seas," *New York Times*, 26 May 1933; Warren F. Kuehl and Lynne Dunn, *Keeping the Covenant: American Internationalists and the League of Nations, 1920–1939* (Kent, OH: Kent State University Press, 1997), p. 195.

56. TNA, CAB 47/4 ATB-101 (CID Paper 1118-B), "Economic Pressure on Germany," 30 October 1933, p. 14. The downbeat assessment of the ATB in October chimed with Admiralty studies of the effects of a British blockade of Germany in May 1933. These assessments fitted into a broader desire to stave off war before Britain could restore its global maritime dominance along a two-power standard, which Admiralty experts did not expect to attain until at least 1942. Joseph A. Maiolo, *The Royal Navy and Nazi Germany, 1933–1939: A Study in Appeasement and the Origins of the Second World War* (Basingstoke: Macmillan, 1998), pp. 112–116.

57. Adam Tooze, *The Wages of Destruction: The Breaking and Making of the Nazi Economy* (London: Viking, 2006), pp. 73–74.

58. Harold James, *The Deutsche Bank and the Nazi Economic War against the Jews: The Expropriation of Jewish-Owned Property* (Cambridge: Cambridge University Press, 2001), pp. 23–27.

59. Hans-Erich Volkmann, *Ökonomie und Expansion: Grundzüge der NS-Wirtschaftspolitik* (Munich: R. Oldenbourg, 2003), pp. 107–109.

60. This measure attracted much criticism from American and British shipping firms; one American shipping executive warned that "any German policy which would restrict American trade would automatically react to the detriment of Germany" (cited in "Best Spirit," *Time* 22, no. 8 [21 August 1933]: pp. 13–14).

61. Peter Krüger and Erich J. C. Hahn, "Der Loyalitätskonflikt des Staatssekretärs Bernhard Wilhelm von Bülow im Frühjahr 1933," *Vierteljahrshefte für Zeitgeschichte* 20, no. 4 (1972): 376–410.

62. Bernhard von Bülow, "Die Außenpolitische Lage Deutschlands (März 1933)," in Günter Wollstein, "Eine Denkschrift des Staatssekretärs Bernhard von Bülow vom März 1933. Wilhelminische Konzeption der Außenpolitik zu Beginn der nationalsozialistischen Herrschaft," *Militärgeschichtliche Zeitschrift* 13, no. 1 (1973): 77–94; 87, 89.

63. PAAA, RZ 101 Büro RAM, Handakten Neurath, "Deutsche Außenhandelspolitik," memorandum by Bülow, 24 March 1933, f. 32; Eckart Teichert, *Autarkie und Großraumwirtschaft in Deutschland, 1930–1939: Außenwirtschaftspolitische Konzeptionen zwischen Wirtschaftskrise und Zweitem Weltkrieg* (Munich: R. Oldenbourg, 1984), p. 133; Sören Dengg, *Deutschlands Austritt aus dem Völkerbund und Schachts "Neuer Plan": Zum Verhältnis von Aussen-und Aussenwirtschaftspolitik in der Übergangsphase von der Weimarer Republik zum Dritten Reich (1929–1934)* (Frankfurt: P. Lang, 1986), pp. 355–356; Stephen G. Gross, *Export Empire: German Soft Power in Southeastern Europe, 1890–1945* (Cambridge: Cambridge University Press, 2015), pp. 264, 269.

64. Cited in Wollstein, "Eine Denkschrift," pp. 84, 85.

65. Jürgen Förster, *Die Wehrmacht im NS-Staat: Eine strukturgeschichtliche Analyse* (Munich: R. Oldenbourg, 2009), p. 27.

66. BA-MA, RH 2/25 Oberkommando des Heeres, "Landesverteidigung—Allgemeines: 1933–1935"; Vorbereitungen für ein bewaffneten Widerstand gegen feindliche Sanktionen nach dem Austritt Deutschlands aus dem Völkerbund." Document 140-C in Trial of the Major War Criminals before the International Military Tribunal (IMT), vol. 34, pp. 487–491.

67. Gerhard L. Weinberg, *Hitler's Foreign Policy, 1933–1939: The Road to World War II* (New York: Enigma Books, 2005), pp. 132–136.

68. Michael Geyer, *Aufrüstung oder Sicherheit: Die Reichswehr in der Krise der Machtpolitik, 1924–1936* (Wiesbaden: Franz Steiner Verlag, 1980), p. 380.

69. German Ambassador Hassell in Rome to Foreign Ministry in Berlin, 5 and 12 January 1934; in Documents on German Foreign Policy (DGFP), series C, vol. 2: *1933–1934* (Washington, DC: GPO, 1959), pp. 306, 345.

70. James Barros, *Betrayal from Within: Joseph Avenol, Secretary-General of the League of Nations, 1933–1940* (New Haven: Yale University Press, 1969). For an analysis of how "in the 1930s actors within and outside the League of Nations looked to the authoritarian states for examples how to organize the international order in ways framed as offering alternatives to the seemingly defunct liberal order," see David Petruccelli, "The Crisis of Liberal

Internationalism: The Legacies of the League of Nations Reconsidered," *Journal of World History* 31, no. 1 (March 2020): 111–136.

71. Kuehl and Dunn, *Keeping the Covenant*, pp. 178–202.

72. In 1912, President Taft had prohibited the export of weapons to Mexico. President Coolidge used the same powers in 1922 to prevent American arms from fanning the escalating Chinese civil war, and in 1927 he applied them against insurgent forces during the U.S. intervention in Nicaragua. Edwin Borchard, "Comment: The Arms Embargo Resolution and International Law," *Yale Law Journal* 42, no. 7 (May 1933): 1109–1112, 1112n18.

73. See Joseph P. Chamberlain, "Enforcing Economic Sanctions," *International Conciliation* 11 (1926): 287–291.

74. Joseph P. Chamberlain, "Embargo as a Sanction of International Law," *American Journal of International Law* 27 (April 1933): 68.

75. Robert A. Divine, *The Illusion of Neutrality: Franklin D. Roosevelt and the Struggle over the Arms Embargo* (Chicago: University of Chicago Press, 1962), p. 41.

76. MAE, Série SdN No. 817, Arbitrage Sécurité Désarmement: Article 16, janvier 1930–septembre 1935, "Note au sujet des idées américaines d'embargo sur les exportations d'armes," 4 February 1933, p. 2.

77. Divine, *The Illusion of Neutrality*, pp. 47, 53–54.

78. Cited in "Mr. Baldwin in Glasgow," *The Times*, 24 November 1934, p. 7.

79. Bruce W. Farcau, *The Chaco War: Bolivia and Paraguay, 1932–1935* (Westport, CT: Praeger, 1996). Paraguay mobilized a national army equipped with rifles and hand grenades from Belgium, Danish machine guns, French mortars, American trucks, and a mix of German and British artillery; it also operated a small navy of Italian-made gunboats. Bolivia brought together a larger army of one hundred thousand, commanded by the German World War I veteran Hans Kundt, and supplied this force with a similar mix of foreign equipment, including Czech rifles, German submachine guns, British tanks and artillery, and Swiss anti-aircraft and machine guns, while maintaining an air force of American aircraft. See Alejandro de Quesada, *The Chaco War, 1932–35: South America's Greatest Modern Conflict* (Oxford: Osprey Publishing, 2011), pp. 6–35.

80. MAE, Série SDN, No. 316, "Bolivie et Paraguay (Conflit du Chaco): Embargo," French League section in Geneva to Quai d'Orsay, "Note pour la sous-direction d'Amerique," 20 January 1933, pp. 1–3.

81. Leslie B. Rout, Jr., *Politics of the Chaco Peace Conference, 1935–1939* (Austin: University of Texas Press, 1970), chs. 3–4.

82. The French manufacturer Brandt, for example, rushed off a shipment of 90 mortars and 100,000 grenades just before the arms controls took effect. MAE, Série SDN, Box 316, "Note pour la sous-direction d'Amerique," 1 June 1934. The Curtiss-Wright Export Corporation, the foreign sales branch of a large American aircraft manufacturer, was indicted for planning to sell machine guns to Bolivia; after the company sued the Roosevelt

administration for impeding its right to freely trade abroad, the case went all the way up to the Supreme Court before being adjudicated in the government's favor. Charles A. Lofgren, "United States vs. Curtiss-Wright Export Corporation: An Historical Reassessment," *Yale Law Journal* 83, no. 1 (November 1973): 1–32.

83. LON, C.54.M.24.1935.VII, "Rapport du comité consultative sur la situation crée par les réponses de la Bolivie et du Paraguay," 24 January 1935.

84. MAE, Série SDN, Box 317, Bolivie et Paraguay (Conflit du Chaco): Embargo, août 1934–novembre 1935, Telegrams Nos. 9–10 from Dussol (Asunción) to Quai d'Orsay (Paris), 6 February 1935, pp. 1–2. French foreign minister Laval promptly reassured his ambassador in Asunción that no such procedure was in the works: the European countries were merely following League recommendations. MAE, SDN 317, Tel. No. 9, Foreign Minister Laval to Dussol (Asunción), "Analyse. Le Paraguay et l'embargo," 8 February 1935.

85. "League and Chaco. Difficulties of Peace Plan," *The Times*, no. 46918, 22 November 1934, p. 13.

86. Manley O. Hudson, *The Chaco Arms Embargo: Report Presented by the American Committee in Geneva to the Special Committee of the United States Senate Investigating the Munitions Industry on September 1, 1935* (Washington, DC: GPO, 1935), pp. 15–19.

87. The politically useful but historically misleading stigmatization of the multifarious opponents of U.S. global supremacy as supporters of "isolationism" has been documented and countered by Stephen Wertheim, *Tomorrow, the World: The Birth of U.S. Global Supremacy* (Cambridge, MA: Harvard University Press, 2020). See also the important corrective by Brooke L. Blower, "From Isolationism to Neutrality: A New Framework for Understanding American Political Culture, 1919–1941," *Diplomatic History* 38, no. 2 (2014): 345–376.

88. See, for example, Alan Dobson's claim to this effect in his brief history of the failure of U.S. sanctions efforts in the 1930s in *US Economic Statecraft for Survival, 1933–1991: Of Sanctions, Embargoes and Economic Warfare* (New York: Routledge, 2002), p. 35.

89. On the Soviet turn to collective security, see the skeptical account by Jiří Hochman, *The Soviet Union and the Failure of Collective Security, 1934–1938* (New York: St. Martin's Press, 1984), in which Hochman highlights opportunism and anti-capitalist suspicion, and Jonathan Haslam, *The Soviet Union and the Struggle for Collective Security in Europe, 1933–1939* (Ithaca, NY: Cornell University Press, 1984), in which Haslam argues that while desirous of the security advantages of the League, Stalin also pursued self-strengthening because he lacked confidence in the Western democracies' commitment to alliance with him. See also Geoffrey Roberts, "A Soviet Bid for Coexistence with Nazi Germany, 1935–1937: The Kandelaki Affair," *International History Review* 6, no. 3 (August 1994): 466–490, and the im-

portant study by Sabine Dullin, *Des hommes d'influence: Les ambassadeurs de Staline en Europe, 1930–1939* (Paris: Presses Universitaires de Paris, 2001).

90.   TNA, CAB 47/5 ATB 106, "Economic Pressure on Germany: Possible Action by the League," 29 January 1934, p. 13.

91.   This view is confirmed by Tooze, *The Wages of Destruction*, pp. 71–78.

92.   Bülow to Konstantin von Neurath, August 1934; cited in *Nazism, 1919–1945: A Documentary Reader*, ed. J. Noakes and G. Pridham, 3:662 (Exeter: University of Exeter, 1988).

93.   Tooze, *Wages of Destruction*, pp. 90–94. By the end of the decade just a fifth of German trade was conducted using "free" foreign exchange, with the rest settled through clearing arrangements. See also "German Exchange Control, 1931–1939: From an Emergency Measure to a Totalitarian Institution," *Quarterly Journal of Economics* 54, no. 4 (August 1940): 54–76.

94.   R. J. B. Bosworth, *Mussolini* (London: Verso, 2002), pp. 297–298.

95.   Giorgio Rochat, *Militari e politici nella preparazione della campagna d'Etiopia: Studio e documenti* (Milan: F. Angeli, 1971), pp. 104–107; George Baer, *The Coming of the Italian-Ethiopian War* (Cambridge, MA: Harvard University Press, 1967), pp. 29–35; G. Bruce Strang, "Places in the African Sun: Social Darwinism, Demographics and the Italian Invasion of Ethiopia," in *Collision of Empires: Italy's Invasion of Ethiopia and Its International Impact*, ed. G. Bruce Strang, pp. 11–32 (Farnham: Ashgate, 2013); Robert Mallett, *Mussolini in Ethiopia, 1919–1935: The Origins of Fascist Italy's African War* (Cambridge: Cambridge University Press, 2015), pp. 70–71.

96.   My narrative of the road to the Italo-Ethiopian War follows the superb study of Esmonde M. Robertson, *Mussolini as Empire-Builder: Europe and Africa, 1932–1936* (London: Macmillan, 1977), pp. 70–83, 100–102.

97.   TNA, CAB 47/5, Paper ATB 117, Annex I: "Economic Measures with the Object of Restraining German Rearmament" (Communicated by M. Leger at Stresa), 6 April 1935, pp. 6–8.

98.   Edward E. Ericson, *Feeding the German Eagle: Soviet Economic Aid to Nazi Germany, 1933–1941* (Westport, CT: Greenwood, 1999), p. 17. The French proposal left open the option of measures combining mutual support with pressure on Germany—including a financial blockade of the Reich. The French government considered international action better than a unilateral response to unilateral German rearmament, "hence we have passed from Stresa to Geneva" (Eighty-Fifth [Extraordinary] Session of the Council. Minutes, 16 April 1935, p. 3). After Stresa the Council appointed a special "Committee of Thirteen," which in its deliberations underlined "the value, as a means of preventing war, of the pressure to be brought to bear through the use of the financial weapon" (LoN, ASP S121 LON C.O.S.C./2, "Committee of Thirteen Set Up for the Purpose of Proposing Measures to Render the League Covenant More Effective in the Organisation of Collective Security," 23 May 1935, p. 4).

99.   Walter L. Duranty, "Economic Weapon Aimed at Germany: Threat of

Pressure, Evidenced at Stresa, Is Seen as Cause of Compromise Spirit," *New York Times*, 13 April 1935, p. 8.

100. Zara Steiner, *The Triumph of the Dark: European International History, 1933–1939* (New York: Oxford University Press, 2011), p. 103.

101. John Fischer Williams, "The League of Nations and Unanimity," *American Journal of International Law* 19, no. 3 (July 1925): 475–488. However, when a dispute or war led to the invocation of Article 16, "for the purpose of such unanimity the vote of the covenant-breaking state, if a member of the Council, would not be counted" (ibid., p. 484n29). When Ethiopia appealed to Article 16 in October 1935, the Council could thus approve economic sanctions against Italy, one of its permanent members, without procedural delays.

102. Frédéric Dessberg, *Le triangle impossible: Les rélations franco-soviétiques et le facteur polonais dans les questions de sécurité en Europe, 1924–1935* (Brussels: P.I.E. Peter Lang, 2009).

103. J. Calvitt Clarke III, "Soviet Appeasement, Collective Security and the Italo-Ethiopian War," in Strang, *Collision of Empires*, pp. 261–286.

104. Haslam, *The Soviet Union and the Struggle for Collective Security*, p. 49.

105. Michael Jabara Carley, "'Only the USSR Has . . . Clean Hands': The Soviet Perspective on the Failure of Collective Security and the Collapse of Czechoslovakia, 1934–1938 (Part I)," *Diplomacy and Statecraft* 21 (2010): 202–225.

106. Cited in Stephen Kotkin, *Stalin*, vol. 2: *Waiting for Hitler, 1929–1941* (London: Allen Lane, 2017), p. 244.

107. Diary entry for 2 July 1935, in Gabriel Gorodetsky, ed., *The Complete Maisky Diaries* (New Haven: Yale University Press, 2013), 1:130–131. The Soviets were not prima facie hostile toward Fascist Italy since they saw Nazi Germany as the bigger threat, against which they hoped to build a ring of anti-German allies including France, Czechoslovakia, Yugoslavia, and hopefully Britain. Thus Stalin and Litvinov's collective security policy was anti-Nazi rather than anti-Fascist in character. See J. Calvitt Clarke III, *Russia and Italy against Hitler: The Bolshevik-Fascist Rapprochement of the 1930s* (Westport, CT: Greenwood, 1991).

108. Cited in E. M. Robertson, *Mussolini as Empire-Builder*, p. 133.

109. Martin Laberge, "La France et la Méditerrannée: Objectifs politiques et stratégiques, 1930–1940" (PhD diss., University of Montreal, 2005), pp. 118–151.

110. For the Anglo-French disagreement on sanctions on Germany in the spring of 1935, see Steiner, *The Triumph of the Dark*, p. 89.

111. Buell expected that "League machinery might also come into play should the German army suddenly occupy Austria, Danzig or Memel, with or without a declaration of war. . . . Should the League Council find that Germany had acted illegally and was the aggressor, it could authorize the great powers—Britain, France, Italy and the Soviet Union—to apply sanctions

against Germany. . . . From the legal point of view the Allied powers and other members of the League might be joining in a 'just war' against the German aggressor. Thus League machinery may be used to aid the Allied powers, morally at least, in their struggle with Germany" (in Herbert Briggs and Raymond Buell, "American Neutrality in a Future War," *Foreign Policy Reports* 11, no. 3 [April 10, 1935]: 29).

112. TNA, AIR 8/200, Chiefs of Staff, "Imperial Defence: Revision of Defence Requirements," 28 May 1935, p. 1.

113. TNA, CAB 47/5, Paper ATB 117, "Report on the French Memorandum for the Exercise of Economic Pressure on Germany without There Being a State of War," 6 June 1935, p. 5.

114. Mallett, *Mussolini in Ethiopia, 1919–1935*, p. 165.

115. Paul Corthorn, "The Labour Party and the League of Nations: The Socialist League's Role in the Sanctions Crisis of 1935," *Twentieth-Century British History* 13, no. 1 (2002): 62–85.

116. James's argument against sanctions rested on the risk of provoking war. As he put it, "If you are for sanctions, you are closing the Suez Canal. That can be done only by warships. You therefore must tell the sailors of the Fleet that you as a revolutionary are in support of this action. But Mussolini may attack. From start to finish he has never been bluffing, and it is madness to think that he will climb down now. The moment he attacks, war begins. How is the sanctionist now to make propaganda to the Fleet and tell the sailors to turn Imperialist war into Civil war? No true Marxist can play these games with the proletariat" (cited in "I.L.P. Abyssinian Policy," *Controversy: Internal Discussion Organ of the I.L.P.* [October 1935]).

117. Adom Getachew, *Worldmaking after Empire: The Rise and Fall of Self-Determination* (Princeton, NJ: Princeton University Press, 2019), p. 69.

118. The effect of this embargo was vastly different from that imposed during the Chaco War. Unlike the relative balance of force which marked that conflict, in the summer of 1935 Italy had progressed very far with its military preparation for the invasion of Ethiopia, which remained under-equipped and could only have imported adequate military supplies from abroad. S. K. B. Asante, "The Italo-Ethiopian Conflict: A Case Study in West African Response to Crisis Diplomacy in the 1930s," *Journal of African History* 15, no. 2 (1974): 291–302. In retrospect, it is clear that the impartial embargo was a major reason for the Ethiopians' eventual military defeat. Baer, *The Coming of the Italian-Ethiopian War*, p. 224.

119. "The Situation in Europe. Mr. Baldwin and Germany," *The Times*, 28 May 1935, p. 18.

120. Polanyi, "Markstein 1935," in Michele Cangiani and Claus Thomasberger, eds., *Chronik der großen Transformation. Artikel und Aufsätze (1920–1945), Band 2: Die internationale Politik zwischen den beiden Weltkriegen* (Marburg: Metropolis Verlag, 2003), p. 266.

Chapter Eight. The Greatest Experiment in Modern History, 1935–1936

1. "British Stand for World Peace," *The Times*, 12 September 1935; p. 12; Raymond Buell, "Geneva Threatens Sanctions," *Foreign Policy Bulletin* 14, no. 47 (20 September 1935).

2. LoN, Sean Lester Archives, Diary (1935–1947), vol. 1, entry for 17 November 1935, pp. 24–25.

3. George W. Baer, *Test Case: Italy, Ethiopia and the League of Nations* (Stanford, CA: Hoover Institution Press, 1976).

4. A. J. P. Taylor, *The Origins of the Second World War* (New York: Simon and Schuster, 1961), p. 96.

5. G. Bruce Strang, "'The Worst of All Worlds': Oil Sanctions and Italy's Invasion of Abyssinia, 1935–1936," *Diplomacy and Statecraft* 19, no. 2 (2008): 210–235.

6. Cristiano A. Ristuccia, "The 1935 Sanctions against Italy: Would Coal and Oil Have Made a Difference?" *European Review of Economic History* 4, no. 1 (2000): 85–110.

7. It was a fact evident at the time in studies such as Paul Einzig, *Behind the Scenes of International Finance* (London: Macmillan, 1931), and Ragnar Nurkse, *International Currency Experience: Lessons of the Interwar Period* (Geneva: League of Nations, 1944), the implications of which have since been documented further by Adam Tooze, *The Wages of Destruction: The Breaking and Making of the Nazi Economy* (London: Viking, 2006), pp. 71–96, 214, 232–234; Barry Eichengreen and Marc Flandreau, "Rise and Fall of the Dollar, or When Did the Dollar Overtake Sterling as the Leading Reserve Currency?" *European Review of Economic History* 13, no. 3 (2009): 377–411; Nicholas Crafts and Peter Fearon, "Lessons from the 1930s Great Depression," *Oxford Review of Economic Policy* 26, no. 3 (Autumn 2010): 285–317; and Stefan J. Link, *Forging Global Fordism: Nazi Germany, Soviet Russia, and the Contest over the Industrial Order* (Princeton, NJ: Princeton University Press, 2020), pp. 16, 102, 115–117, 134.

8. The argument in the following chapters is congruent with the account of collective security as intercontinental alliance warfare in Thomas Bottelier, "Associated Powers: Britain, France, the United States and the Defence of World Order, 1931–1943" (PhD diss., King's College London, 2019).

9. Sino-Japanese conflict in the 1930s has always lent itself to a "long" periodization of World War II. See Saburo Ienaga, *The Pacific War, 1931–1945* (New York: Pantheon, 1978), and S. C. M. Paine, *The Wars for Asia, 1911–1949* (Cambridge: Cambridge University Press, 2006); a useful application of the long war frame to Italy is John Gooch, *Mussolini's War: Fascist Italy from Triumph to Collapse, 1935–1943* (New York: Pegasus Books, 2020).

10. League of Nations, *World Economic Survey* (Geneva: Imprimerie de Genève, 1935), p. 11. This figure was measured in "old" (pre-April 1933) U.S. gold dollars.

11. Barry Eichengreen and Douglas A. Irwin, "Trade Blocs, Currency Blocs and the Reorientation of World Trade in the 1930s," *Journal of International Economics* 38 (1995): 1–24. Eichengreen and Irwin use the statistics gathered by EFO in its *Survey of World Trade, 1938* (Geneva: League of Nations, 1939).

12. Paul Bairoch, *Economics and World History: Myths and Paradoxes* (Chicago: University of Chicago Press, 1993), pp. 5, 9.

13. In fact there were only two years during the 1930s—1932 and 1933—when global trade volumes were below 1913 levels (at 95.9 and 94.4 percent, respectively). Giovanni Federico and Antonio Tena-Junguito, "World Trade 1800-1938: A New Synthesis," *Revista de Historia Economica—Journal of Iberian and Latin American Economic History* 37, no. 1 (March 2019): 9–41 and appendix D.18.

14. League of Nations, *World Economic Survey: Fifth Year, 1935/36* (Geneva: League of Nations, 1936), p. 64; Christian Saint-Etienne, *The Great Depression, 1929–1938: Lessons for the 1980s* (Stanford, CA: Hoover Institution Press, 1984), p. 30, table 1.13.

15. Even in 1931–1940, aggregate global migration was equal to that of the highly mobile 1896–1905 period, levels far in excess of anything seen in the mid-nineteenth century. The perception that the depression inaugurated a hostile world pulling up the drawbridges to immigrants is strongly Eurocentric; except for the 1920s, pan-Asian migration was higher in the 1930s than in any other decade in the previous eighty years. See Adam McKeown, "Global Migration, 1846–1940," *Journal of World History* 15, no. 2 (June 2004): 165, fig. 1.

16. Harold James, "Deglobalization: The Rise of Disembedded Unilateralism," *Annual Review of Financial Economics* 10 (2018): 219–237.

17. Derek H. Aldcroft, *Studies in the Interwar European Economy* (Abingdon: Routledge, 1997), table 4.3.

18. Christof Dejung, "The Boundaries of Western Power: The Colonial Cotton Economy in India and the Problem of Quality," in *The Foundations of Worldwide Economic Integration: Power, Institutions and Global Markets, 1850–1930*, ed. Christof Dejung and Niels P. Petersson, p. 137 (Cambridge: Cambridge University Press, 2013).

19. Gelina Harlaftis, *A History of Greek-Owned Shipping: The Making of an International Tramp Fleet, 1830 to the Present Day* (London: Routledge, 1996), pp. 189–191, table 6.3.

20. Ibid., p. 195, fig. 6.9.

21. SHD, 2 N 237, Capitaine de vaisseau Leclerc (Collège des hautes études de défense nationale), "La Marine allemande, Conférence du 28 décembre 1938."

22. John R. Bradley, *Fuel and Power in the British Empire* (Washington, DC: GPO, 1935), p. 26.

23. TNA, CAB 4/17, "Advisory Committee on Trading and Blockade in Time of War, Fourth Annual Report," 21 December 1927 (CID-852B).

24. Anand Toprani, *Oil and the Great Powers: Britain and Germany, 1914–1945* (Oxford: Oxford University Press, 2019), pp. 8–13.

25. Edward H. Shaffer, *The United States and the Control of World Oil* (Abingdon: Routledge, 1983), table 4.4. The dissipation of the fin-de-siècle British control over coal due to the rise of oil mirrored a larger pattern of reduced British hegemony in terms of control of raw materials, in the fifteen years between 1913 and 1928, the empire's share of global production fell in oil, iron ore, silver, copper, tin, graphite, phosphates, potash, and salt. See Bradley, *Fuel and Power*, p. 28.

26. Edward Sampson, *Mineral Resources and International Strife* (Princeton, NJ: University Extension Fund, Herbert L. Baker Foundation, 1938), pp. 8–9.

27. The "major minerals of commerce" category was used in British and American industry surveys and Department of the Interior Studies. *Minerals Yearbook 1935* (Washington, DC: Department of the Interior, 1935), pp. 19–20.

28. Bradley, *Fuel and Power*, p. 2.

29. "Empires and Raw Materials," *The Economist* 121, no. 4809 (26 October 1935): 793.

30. TNA, CAB 47/4, Report ATB 92, "Italy. The Possibilities of the Exercise of Maritime Economic Pressure upon Italy. Part I," March 1931, p. 3.

31. SHD, 7 N 3571, Désarmement naval, "Importations par voie de mer," Tableau des importations par voie de mer en temps de guerre par l'Italie (mai 1933).

32. Mario Alexander May, "Fuelling Fascism: British and Italian Economic Relations in the 1930s, League Sanctions and the Abyssinian Crisis" (PhD diss., London School of Economics, 2000), pp. 32–37; Gian Giacomo Migone, *The United States and Fascist Italy: The Rise of American Finance in Europe* (Cambridge: Cambridge University Press, 2015), pp. 319–324.

33. TNA, CAB 47/5 ATB 120, "Economic Pressure on Italy," 18 September 1935, p. 7.

34. Ibid., p. 8. The remaining 27 percent of Italian export earnings came from exports to just three non-League states: the United States, Germany, and Argentina. All reserve figures henceforth are quoted at contemporary exchange rates.

35. TNA, CAB 47/5 ATB 127, Revisions and updates to ATB 120, "Economic Pressure on Italy," 27 September 1935, Annex I: Economic Pressure on the East African Expeditionary Forces, p. 22.

36. George W. Baer calls this the "instrumentalist" approach in "Sanctions and Security: The League of Nations and the Italo-Ethiopian War," *International Organization* 27, no. 2 (March 1973): 165–179.

37. Hoare's commitment to a combined arms and import embargo is clear from a report dated 16 September from the chargé d'affaires at the U.S. Embassy in London, Ray Atherton, reporting on a conversation with the British foreign secretary immediately upon his return from Geneva: "Sir

Samuel reiterated that the imposition of sanctions would be a gradual one along the lines of the 1921 Resolutions. The first question to be posed was whether League members and non-League members would refrain from selling arms and munitions and implements of war to Italy and, secondly, since foreign exchange was vital to Italy, whether they would also agree to cease purchasing from Italy" (cited in a memorandum by Wallace Murray [chief of Near Eastern Affairs at the State Department], "Possible Situations in Which This Government May Find Itself in Connection with the Italo-Ethiopian Crisis," 18 September 1935, HIA, SHP, Box 369, Folder Sanctions #1).

38. SHD, 2 N 151, "Étude sur le programme des sanctions économiques que l'on pourrait éventuellement appliquer à l'Allemagne," [undated, mid-1935], p. 7.

39. See, for example, the extensive analysis "How Will Sanctions Work?" in the *Washington Post*, 30 September 1935 — four days *before* the war broke out.

40. TNA, CAB 47/1 ATB, Minutes of meetings 1924–1938, Minutes of twenty-first meeting, 25 September 1935, Report on the best form of economic pressure to exert on Italy (Paper ATB 122).

41. Emilio De Bono, *Anno XIII: The Conquest of an Empire* (London: Cresset Press, 1937), p. 220.

42. Angelo del Boca, *The Ethiopian War, 1935–1941* (Chicago: University of Chicago Press, 1969), p. 18; Nicola Labanca, *La guerra d'Etiopia, 1935–1941* (Bologna: Il Mulino, 2015), p. 74.

43. Giorgio Rochat, *Guerre italiane in Libia e in Etiopia: Studi militari, 1921–1939* (Treviso: Pagus Edizioni, 1991), pp. 99-176.

44. John Elliott, "League Action as a Warning," *New York Herald Tribune*, 24 October 1935.

45. Alfred Zimmern, "The League's Handling of the Italo-Abyssinian Dispute," *Royal Institute for International Affairs* 14, no. 6 (November–December 1935): 751–768.

46. Ibid., 766. See also Albert E. Highley, *The Actions of the States Members of the League of Nations in Application of Sanctions against Italy, 1935/1936* (Geneva: Imprimerie du "Journal de Genève," 1938).

47. "The economic factor will be largely determinative for Italy in her East African campaign, military experts here believe. . . . These views are predicated on professional military judgments that, while Italy can conquer Ethiopia, it will be a long and costly effort. This opinion is supported by the progress of the Italian armies to date" ("Sanctions Vital, U.S. Experts Say. They Declare Cost Will Be the Deciding Factor in Italy's Ethiopian Campaign," *New York Times*, 11 October 1935).

48. "Sanctions, and the Italian Loan," *New York Herald Tribune*, 22 October 1935.

49. "Great Powers Maneuver on Sanctions," *Foreign Policy Bulletin* 14, no. 52 (25 October 1935).

50. As the *Washington Post* wrote, "At the present rate of depletion, the gold

reserves would not hold out many months even if Italy were free to sell in all parts of the world. . . . In short, a League import embargo, if firmly enforced, is calculated within a short time to limit Italy's foreign purchases to amounts that can be paid for by the restricted volume of goods sold to the handful of countries unwilling to join in collective action in behalf of peace" ("Effective Sanctions," 22 October 1935).

51. See Hugh Temperley's articles on Italy's prospects for military action in Abyssinia in *Daily Telegraph*, 21 and 22 August 1935; SHD, 7 N 2809, Dossier 1, 3ème trimestre 1935, "Campagne en Abyssinie," Telegram No. 692, French military attaché Voruz to Minister of War, 22 August 1935, p. 2.

52. TNA, CAB 47/5 ATB 130, R. D. Hawtrey and S. D. Waley, "Sanctions and Italy's External Costs. Memorandum Prepared by Treasury Representatives," 3 October 1935. Without sanctions, Hawtrey and Waley estimated that Italy would exhaust itself in as little as eighteen months and as much as four years, depending on its economic response.

53. MAE, Série K (Afrique), Direction politique et commerciale, Carton 82, Dossier 81/2, Ethiopie, Box 110, Conflit italo-ethiopien. Sanctions prises contre l'Italie (Application de l'Article 16 du Covenant), "Conflit italo-abyssin. Sanctions économiques. Note pour le ministre," 4 October 1935, p. 5.

54. ATB 130, "Sanctions and Italy's External Costs"; "Effective Sanctions," *Washington Post*, 22 October 1935.

55. Michele Fratianni and Franco Spinelli, *A Monetary History of Italy* (Cambridge: Cambridge University Press, 1997), p. 153.

56. Richard Pankhurst, *The Ethiopians* (Oxford: Blackwell, 1998), p. 228.

57. Felice Guarneri, *Battaglie economiche tra le due guerre*, vol. 1: *1918–1935* (Milan: Garzanti, 1953), p. 407.

58. HIA, U.S. Department of State Records, 44006, Box 1, Folder 1-1, "The Imposition of Sanctions: Documents Concerning the Experience of States Participating in the Application of Article 16 of the Covenant of the League of Nations to Italy, 1935–1936," p. 1.

59. *World Petroleum* (New York: R. Palmer, 1936), 7:56.

60. Michael L. Roi, "'A Completely Immoral and Cowardly Attitude': The British Foreign Office, American Neutrality, and the Hoare-Laval Plan," *Canadian Journal of History* 29, no. 2 (1994): 333–352.

61. Migone, *The United States and Fascist Italy*, pp. 326–342.

62. W. Phillips (Rome) to Hull (Washington, DC), 14 November 1935; Franklin D. Roosevelt Presidential Library, Folder Italy-Phillips; cited in Migone, *The United States and Fascist Italy*, p. 364.

63. HIA, SHP, Box 369, Hornbeck to Cordell Hull, 25 October 1935, p. 2.

64. Raymond Buell, "Geneva Threatens Sanctions," 20 September 1935; see also "Experts See Help of U.S. to League. Analysis of Neutrality Act Lists Possible Cooperation in Non-Military Sanctions. Report by R. L. Buell Asserts President Can Keep Raw Materials from Italy," *New York Times*, 28 September 1935.

65. Vera Micheles Dean, "The League Applies Economic Sanctions," *Foreign Policy Bulletin* 14, no. 51 (18 October 1935): 2.

66. MAE, Série SDN, Art. 16, Box No. 818, Note "Remis à l'Ambassadeur d'Angleterre," 18 October 1935, p. 6.

67. The secret Anglo-French negotiations picked up where earlier peace negotiations before the start of the war had ended; thus Hoare, Eden, and other British officials were, "well before Hoare met Laval in Paris and the British General Election and even before the commencement of the Italo-Ethiopian hostilities, psychologically committed to the principle of sweeping Italian gains at Ethiopian expense" (James C. Robertson, "The Hoare-Laval Plan," *Journal of Contemporary History* 10, no. 3 [July 1975]: 433–464, 440). See also W. N. Medlicott, "The Hoare-Laval Pact Reconsidered," in *Retreat from Power: Studies in Britain's Foreign Policy of the Twentieth Century*, vol. 1, ed. David Dilks, pp. 118–138 (London: Macmillan, 1981).

68. "France Stands By," *Evening Star*, 30 November 1935; Maisky diary entry for 14 December 1935, in Gabriel Gorodestsky, ed., *The Complete Maisky Diaries* (New Haven: Yale University Press), 1:146.

69. Del Boca, *The Ethiopian War, 1935–1941*, pp. 70–84.

70. Livingston Hartley, "Oil Sanction Impasse," *Washington Post*, 1 January 1936; Strang, "The Worst of All Worlds," pp. 217–218.

71. MAE, Série SDN, Art. 16, Box No. 818, De Laboulaye (Washington, DC) to Joseph Paul-Boncour, 27 December 1935, Telegram 1466, f. 55.

72. Robert A. Divine, *The Illusion of Neutrality: Franklin D. Roosevelt and the Struggle over the Arms Embargo* (Chicago: University of Chicago Press, 1962), pp. 136–138.

73. MAE, Série SDN, Art. 16, Box No. 818, Laval to De Laboulaye (Washington, DC), 6 January 1936.

74. Hiram Johnson, "Neutrality," Senate Hearings, 74th Congress, 2nd Session (January 1936), pp. 142–143.

75. MAE, Série SDN, Art. 16, Box No. 818, De Laboulaye (Washington, DC) to Paris, 11 January 1936, Tels. 61–62, f. 142.

76. John H. Spencer, "The Italian-Ethiopian Dispute and the League of Nations," *American Journal of International Law* 31, no. 4 (October 1937): 614–641.

77. Herbert Matthews, *Eyewitness in Abyssinia* (London: Martin Secker and Warburg, 1937), pp. 177–188.

78. J. Calvitt Clarke III, "Soviet Appeasement, Collective Security and the Italo-Ethiopian War," in *Collision of Empires*, ed. G. Bruce Strang, p. 281 (Farnham: Ashgate, 2013).

79. Lowell R. Tillett, "The Soviet Role in League Sanctions against Italy, 1935–36," *American Slavic and East European Review* 15, no. 1 (1956): 11–16.

80. Daniel Yergin, *The Prize: The Epic Quest for Oil, Money and Power* (New York: Simon and Schuster, 1991), p. 332.

81. LON, C.L. 216.1936.II.A.Annex XVI, "Memorandum from the Government of the Union of Soviet Socialist Republics, January 21, 1937," p. 115. While Litvinov and Maisky supported international coercive sanctions under the umbrella of the League, Stalin was focused on the German threat. To the Soviet leader, this was not antithetical to maintaining and even deepening economic relations with the Reich. In many ways the pattern of German-Soviet trade relations gave Moscow a stronger hand as the Nazi economy began to mobilize resources ever more intensively for war. See Edward E. Ericson: "Karl Schnurre and the Evolution of Nazi-Soviet Economic Relations, 1936–1941," *German Studies Review* 21, no. 2 (May 1998): 263–283, and *Feeding the German Eagle: Soviet Economic Aid to Nazi Germany, 1933–1941* (Westport, CT: Greenwood, 1999), p. 24.

82. D. A. Farnie, *East and West of Suez: The Suez Canal in History, 1854–1956* (Oxford: Oxford University Press, 1969), p. 601.

83. Coleman Phillipson and Noel Buxton, *The Question of the Bosphorus and Dardanelles* (London: Stevens and Haynes, 1917), pp. 15–16; Joseph A. Obieta, *The International Status of the Suez Canal* (The Hague: Martinus Nijhoff, 1970), p. 46.

84. Heinrich Rheinstrom, *Die völkerrechtliche Stellung der internationalen Kanäle* (Budapest: Réai, 1937).

85. LoN, PCIJ, The SS Wimbledon, United Kingdom and others v. Germany, Judgment, PCIJ Series A, No. 1, 17 August 1923. The case concerned Germany's obligation under Article 380 of the Versailles Treaty to keep the Kiel Canal open to warships and ships carrying war materials at the time of the Polish-Soviet War of 1920. J. H. W. Verzijl, *International Law in Historical Perspective*, vol. 3: *State Territory* (Leiden: A. W. Sijthoff's Uitgeversmaatschappij, 1970), p. 238.

86. See, for example, Heinrich Triepel, *Internationale Wasserläufe: Kritische Betrachtungen* (Berlin: F. Dümmler, 1931).

87. MAE, Série K, Ethiopie, Box 110, Conflit italo-ethiopien: Sanctions prises contre l'Italie, Note de M. Dasderat, Dans le cas où il y aurait à prendre contre l'Italie les sanctions prévues par l'article 16 du Pacte de Société des Nations, celles-ci pourraient-elles comprendre une interdiction de passage, pour les navires italiens, dans le canal de Suez?, 30 August 1935.

88. Raymond Buell, *The Suez Canal and League Sanctions* (Geneva: Geneva Research Center, 1935). A similar proposal for internationalization had already been made by Arnold-Forster in the context of debates about the future of the Turkish Straits in the fall of 1922. See W. Arnold-Forster, "Britain and Blockade," *Foreign Affairs* 4, no. 5 (November 1922): 108.

89. TNA, CAB 47/5 ATB 132, "Payment of Suez Canal Duty on Italian Ships," 28 October 1935.

90. TNA, CAB 47/1, Committee of Imperial Defence. Advisory Committee on Trading and Blockade in Time of War. Conclusions of the twenty-second meeting, 3 October 1935, p. 3.

91. Ibid., p. 8.

92. TNA, CAB 47/1, ATB Notes of meetings, eleventh meeting, 17 January 1927, p. 3, f. 190.

93. James Thomas Emmerson, *The Rhineland Crisis, 7 March 1936: A Study in Multilateral Diplomacy* (Ames: Iowa State University Press, 1977); Richard Davis, "Mésentente cordiale: The Failure of the Anglo-French Alliance. Anglo-French Relations during the Ethiopian and Rhineland Crises, 1934–1936," *European History Quarterly* 23, no. 4 (1993): 513–528; Michael L. Roi, *Alternative to Appeasement: Sir Robert Vansittart and Alliance Diplomacy, 1934–1937* (Westport, CT: Greenwood, 1997); Stephen A. Schuker, "France and the Remilitarization of the Rhineland, 1936," in *The Origins of the Second World War*, ed. Patrick Finney, pp. 206–221 (London: Arnold Press, 1997); Jean-Baptiste Duroselle, *France and the Nazi Threat: The Collapse of French Diplomacy, 1932–1939* (New York: Enigma Books, 2004); Alexander Wolz, *Die Rheinlandkrise 1936: Das Auswärtige Amt und der Lokarnopakt 1933–1936* (Munich: Oldenbourg, 2014).

94. TNA, CAB 47/5 Paper ATB 140, "Imposition of Sanctions against Italy, Review of the Forecasts in the Light of Subsequent Events," 6 October 1936, p. 13.

95. Cited in Renzo de Felice, *Mussolini: Il Duce*, vol. 2: *Lo stato totalitario, 1936–1940* (Milan: Einaudi, 1965), p. 701n3.

96. Haile Selassie, "Appeal to the League of Nations," 30 June 1936; available at https://www.mtholyoke.edu/acad/intrel/selassie.htm. Accessed 20 April 2021.

97. Insofar as Britain and France took the third paragraph's "mutual support" provisions seriously, they discussed only how they would come to each other's military aid if either country ended up in a war with Italy over the sanctions—a very different meaning of "support" than the financial support envisioned by the small states. Franklin D. Laurens, *France and the Italo-Ethiopian Crisis, 1935–1936* (The Hague: Mouton, 1967), pp. 190–209.

98. "Arms Embargoes Sanction Proposed. Keynes Urges Prohibition of Commercial and Financial Transactions with Italy. Export Boycott Sought," *New York Times*, 28 September 1935, p. 6.

99. C.447.M.234.1935.VII, Wolde Mariam, "Request by the Ethiopian Government for Financial Assistance from the Members of the League of Nations," *League of Nations Official Journal* 17, no. 1 (January–June 1936): pp. 24–26.

100. "Dispute between Ethiopia and Italy: Draft Resolutions Submitted by the Ethiopian Delegation," *League of Nations Official Journal* 151, Special Supplement (1936): 60, 68–69; Baer, *Test Case*, p. 298.

101. On the intricacies faced by Greece during the sanctions on Italy, see James Barros, *Britain, Greece and the Politics of Sanctions: Ethiopia, 1935–1936* (Atlantic Highlands, NJ: Humanities Press, 1982).

102. Constantine Brown, "This Changing World," *Washington Evening Star*, December 1935.

103. Vera Micheles Dean, "A Farewell to Sanctions," *Foreign Policy Bulletin* 15, no. 37 (July 10, 1936).

104. Moritz Bonn, "How Sanctions Failed," *Foreign Affairs*, January 1937.

105. Letter to M. C. Gillett, 19 April 1936, in W. K. Hancock and Jean van der Poel, eds., *Selections from the Smuts Papers*, vol. 6: *1934–1945* (Cambridge: Cambridge University Press, 1966), pp. 389–390.

106. BL, RCP Add MS 51140, N. Angell, "Draft Manifesto of the Next Five Years Group," 13 July 1936, p. 17.

107. Ibid., p. 9. On the Next Five Years Group, see Martin Ceadel, *Living the Great Illusion: Sir Norman Angell, 1872–1967* (Oxford: Oxford University Press, 2009), pp. 319–326. Members included Arnold-Forster, Cecil, Lionel Curtis, H. A. L. Fisher, Harold Macmillan, Gilbert Murray, and Arthur Salter, among others. See Thomas C. Kennedy, "The Next Five Years Group and the Failure of the Politics of Agreement in Britain," *Canadian Journal of History* 9 (1974): pp. 45–68.

Chapter Nine. Blockade-phobia, 1936–1939

1. Karel Čapek, *War with the Newts* (London: Penguin Classics, 2010 [1936]), pp. 321–322.

2. LoN, ASP S120, Memorandum by Loveday, "Economic Information Required by Weapon," 8 October 1924, p. 6.

3. Hans Langelütke, "Das Rohstoffproblem in der neueren Literatur," *Weltwirtschaftliches Archiv* 47 (1938): 5. For a representative sample of this literature just from the years 1936–1937, see *Raw Materials and Colonies* (London: Royal Institute for International Affairs, 1936); Ferdinand Friedensburg, *Die mineralischen Bodenschätze als weltpolitische und militärische Machtfaktoren* (Stuttgart: Enke, 1936); Wilhelm Ziegelmayer, *Rohstoff-Fragen der deutschen Volksernährung. Eine Darstellung der ernährungswirtschaftlichen und ernährungswissenschaftlichen Aufgaben unserer Zeit* (Dresden: Theodor Steinkopf, 1936); *Le commerce international de certaines matières premières et denrées alimentaires par pays d'origine et de consommation* (Geneva: League of Nations, 1937); Brooks Emeny, *The Strategy of Raw Materials: A Study of America in Peace and War* (New York: Macmillan, 1937); Corrado Gini, "Problems of the International Distribution of Population and Raw Materials," *Annals of the American Academy of Political and Social Science* 189 (January 1937): 201–214.

4. How a structural perception of inferiority vis-à-vis the Anglo-American powers motivated Hitler in particular is the overarching argument of Adam Tooze, *The Wages of Destruction: The Breaking and Making of the Nazi Economy* (London: Viking, 2006). Dale C. Copeland argues that "declining expectations of future trade were critical to the support needed to initiate war" (*Economic Interdependence and War* [Princeton, NJ: Princeton University Press, 2014], pp. 140–142). See also Dale C. Copeland, "Economic Interdependence and the Grand Strategies of Germany and Japan, 1925–1941," in *The Challenge of Grand Strategy: The Great Powers and the Broken*

Balance between the World Wars, ed. Jeffrey W. Taliaferro, Norrin M. Ripsman, and Steven E. Lobell, pp. 120–146 (Cambridge: Cambridge University Press, 2012). On the destabilizing role of rapid competitive armament, see Joseph A. Maiolo, *Cry Havoc: How the Arms Race Drove the World to War, 1931–1941* (New York: Basic Books, 2010).

5. Eckart Teichert, *Autarkie und Großraumwirtschaft in Deutschland, 1930–1939: Außenwirtschaftspolitische Konzeptionen zwischen Wirtschaftskrise und Zweitem Weltkrieg* (Munich: R. Oldenbourg, 1984); Michael Barnhart, *Japan Prepares for Total War: The Search for Economic Security, 1919–1941* (Ithaca, NY: Cornell University Press, 1988); and Alessio Gagliardi, *L'impossibile autarchia: La politica economica del fascismo e il Ministero scambi e valute* (Soveria Mannelli: Rubbettino, 2006).

6. For a good overview of the ideological drive toward autarky in science and technology, see Tiago Saraiva and Norton Wise, "Autarky/Autarchy: Genetics, Food Production and the Building of Fascism," *Historical Studies in the Natural Sciences* 40, no. 4 (Fall 2010): 419–428.

7. On the long tradition of the "closed commercial state" in Germany since the late eighteenth-century contributions of Johann Gottlieb Fichte, see Isaac Nakhimovsky, *The Closed Commercial State: Perpetual Peace and Commercial Society from Rousseau to Fichte* (Princeton, NJ: Princeton University Press, 2011); Keith Tribe, *Strategies of Economic Order: German Economic Discourse, 1750–1950* (Cambridge: Cambridge University Press, 1995). Karl Hardach argued that the blockade of 1914–1918, a "bitter experience of an imposed, involuntary autarky, was to influence future German economy policy, especially after 1933" (*The Political Economy of Germany in the Twentieth Century* [Berkeley: University of California Press, 1976], p. 12).

8. An important case study concerning metals is Jonas Scherner, "Lernen und Lernversagen. Die 'Metallmobilisierung' im Deutschen Reich 1939 bis 1945," *Vierteljahrshefte für Zeitgeschichte* 66, no. 2 (2018): 233–266.

9. This chapter uses the nexus between ideology, political economy, and strategy to go beyond narrow diplomatic readings of how the Ethiopian sanctions of 1935–1936 were interpreted by the Nazi leadership—for example, David Baldwin's suggestion that League sanctions were "counterproductive" in that they did not impress Hitler (*Economic Statecraft* [Princeton, NJ: Princeton University Press, 1985], pp. 157–158).

10. Barnhart, *Japan Prepares for Total War*, p. 76.

11. The most up-to-date general account of this process is Robert Boyce, *The Great Interwar Crisis and the Collapse of Globalization* (Basingstoke: Palgrave Macmillan, 2009).

12. LoN, ASP, Box S119, Remarks by M. Da Mata in minutes of the eighty-fifth (extraordinary) session of the Council, 17 April 1935, p. 3. "In the present economic and financial state of the world," Da Mata said, "I think these sanctions may often be not only inoperative against the violator but dangerous, if not punitive, to those applying them."

13. On theories and recurring motifs of autarky, see Eric Helleiner, "The Re-

turn of National Self-Sufficiency? Excavating Autarkic Thought in a De-Globalizing Era," *International Studies Review*, 2021, pp. 1–25.

14. Luigi Einaudi, "Autarchia o autarcia?" *Rivista di storia economica* 2, no. 4 (1937): 369–370.

15. Stefan J. Link, "How Might 21st-Century De-Globalization Unfold? Some Historical Reflections," *New Global Studies* 12, no. 3 (2018): 358.

16. Link rightly argues that "thirties-style autarky . . . owed its radical nature to the severity and complexity of the Great Depression" (ibid., p. 362).

17. For an analysis that illustrates how autarchy was aimed at "alter[ing] the relationship between globalization and sovereignty," see the outstanding study by Ted Fertik, "Steel and Sovereignty: The United States, Nationalism, and the Transformation of World Order, 1898–1941" (PhD diss., Yale University, 2018), pp. 20–21; Jan Kofman, *Economic Nationalism and Development: Central and Eastern Europe between the Two World Wars* (Boulder, CO: Westview Press, 1997); Eric Helleiner and Andreas Pickel, eds., *Economic Nationalism in a Globalizing World* (Ithaca, NY: Cornell University Press, 2005); Thomas David, *Nationalisme économique et industrialisation: L'experience des pays d'Europe de l'Est (1789–1939)* (Geneva: Droz, 2009); Henryk Szlajfer, *Economic Nationalism and Globalization: Lessons from Latin America and Central Europe* (Leiden: Brill, 2013).

18. League of Nations, *World Economic Survey: Fifth Year 1935/36* (Geneva: League of Nations, 1936), pp. 185–186. The EFO mentioned that the bloc constituted by the United States, the British Empire, Scandinavia, Portugal, Japan, and China (which contained 54 percent of global trade by gold value) kept commerce under little administrative interference.

19. Helmut Maier, *Chemiker im "Dritten Reich": Die Deutsche Chemische Gesellschaft und der Verein Deutscher Chemiker im NS-Herrschaftsapparat* (Weinhein: Wiley-VCH Verlag, 2015), p. 176.

20. Cited in L. Zani, *Fascismo, autarchia, comercio estero: Felice Guarneri, tecnocrata al servizio dello "Stato Nuovo"* (Bari: Laterza, 1988), p. 72.

21. C. K. Leith, *World Minerals and World Politics* (New York: McGraw-Hill, 1931), p. 149.

22. As one American commentator wrote, "If our planning can be so improved as to provide national economic independence, then economic sanctions will be ineffective" (John Gullet, "Economic Planning *versus* Economic Sanction," *Harvard Business Review* 10, no. 3 [April 1932]: 360).

23. Carl Freytag, *Deutschlands "Drang nach Südosten": Der Mitteleuropäische Wirtschaftstag und der "Ergänzungsraum Südosteuropa" 1931–1945* (Vienna: Vienna University Press, 2012), pp. 54–60.

24. Guenther Stein, "The Yen and the Sword," *Pacific Affairs* 12, no. 1 (March 1939): 5–12; Michael Schiltz, *The Money Doctors from Japan: Finance, Imperialism, and the Building of the Yen Bloc, 1895–1937* (Cambridge, MA: Harvard University Asia Center, 2012).

25. Amedeo Gambino, "Le relazioni economiche tra l'Italia e l'Albania," *Rivista Internazionale di Scienze Sociali* 11, no. 3 (May 1940): 408–423.

26. Anthony N. Stranges, "Friedrich Bergius and the Rise of the German Synthetic Fuel Industry," *ISIS* 75, no. 279 (1984): 643–667.

27. Anand Toprani, *Oil and the Great Powers: Britain and Germany, 1914–1945* (Oxford: Oxford University Press, 2019), pp. 169–198.

28. G. Bruce Strang, "'The Worst of All Worlds': Oil Sanctions and Italy's Invasion of Abyssinia, 1935–1936," *Diplomacy and Statecraft* 19, no. 2 (2008): 219–225.

29. David Edgerton, *Britain's War Machine: Weapons, Resources and Experts in the Second World War* (Oxford: Oxford University Press, 2011), p. 189. The strategic importance that the anti-Comintern powers attached to freedom from severable imports—something not pursued by planners within the intercontinentally dispersed French and British maritime empires—adds a key distinction to the general autarkic trend described in Maiolo, *Cry Havoc*.

30. "Labor Conditions in Japan," *Monthly Labor Review* 61, no. 4 (October 1945): 651–668; TNA, CAB 47/1, ATB 120, Appendix II, "Detailed Analysis of Italy's Economic Vulnerability," p. 6.

31. The centrality of cotton, wool, and silk imports to German and Italian employment convinced French and British planners that sanctions on these items were not useful as a way to cripple fascist war potential since their effects would be "social" and not "military." This shows that to European sanctionists, the economic weapon was most of all a means of containing strategic threats to peace, not a political tool to foment regime change—indeed toppling Hitler and Mussolini with sanctions on fiber imports was explicitly ruled out as dangerous and destabilizing. SHD, 2 N 151, "Sanctions applicables à l'Allemagne, 1935."

32. Jonas Scherner, "The Beginnings of Nazi Autarky Policy: The 'National Pulp Programme' and the Origin of Regional Staple Fibre Plants," *Economic History Review* 61, no. 4 (2008): 867–895.

33. U.S. Department of Agriculture, "World Wool Prospects," October 1936, pp. 12–14; Gerda Blau, "Wool in the World Economy," *Journal of the Royal Statistical Society* 109, no. 3 (1946): pp. 179–242; Economic Intelligence Service, *The Network of World Trade: A Companion Volume to "Europe's Trade"* (Geneva: League of Nations, 1942), p. 30, table 12, "World Exports of Twenty-Six Products in 1938."

34. Tiago Saraiva, *Fascist Pigs: Technoscientific Organisms and the History of Fascism* (Cambridge, MA: MIT Press, 2016), pp. 21–42. Italian agronomists also studied German techniques with interest. V. Gayda, *I "quatro anni" del Terzo Reich (L'autarchia in Germania)* (Rome: Edizioni Roma, 1938).

35. Alexander Nützenadel, *Landwirtschaft, Staat und Autarkie: Agrarpolitik im faschistischen Italien, 1922–1943* (Tübingen: Max Niemeyer, 1997); Carol Helstolsky, "Fascist Food Politics: Mussolini's Alimentary Sovereignty," *Journal of Modern Italian Studies* 9, no. 1 (2004): 1–26.

36. TNA, CAB 47/5, ATB 120, "Economic Pressure on Italy, Appendix II. Detailed Analysis of Italy's Economic Vulnerability," 18 September 1935, p. 5.

37. U.S. Department of Commerce, *Economic Review of Foreign Countries, 1937* (Washington, DC: GPO, 1938), p. 51.

38. Vera Zamagni, "Italy: How to Lose the War and Win the Peace," in *The Economics of World War II: Six Great Powers in International Comparison*, ed. Mark Harrison, p. 191, table 5.8, "Italian Agricultural Production and Consumption" (Cambridge: Cambridge University Press, 2000).

39. Gianni Toniolo, *L'economia italiana dell'Italia fascista* (Rome: Laterza, 1980), pp. 139–146; Marcello de Cecco, "The Economy from Liberalism to Fascism," in *Liberal and Fascist Italy*, ed. Adrian Lyttelton, pp. 62–82 (New York: Oxford University Press, 2002).

40. As the prospect of an invasion of Austria loomed in June 1934, Mussolini also confided to his finance minister, Guido Jung, that the lira had to be kept on gold since he needed its strength in case of war—with Germany! Roberto Gualtieri, "Da Londra a Berlino: Le relazioni economiche internazionali dell'Italia, l'autarchia e il Patto d'acciaio (1933–1940)," *Studi Storici* 46, no. 3 (July–September 2005): 625–659.

41. William G. Welk, "League Sanctions and Foreign Trade Restrictions in Italy," *American Economic Review* 27, no. 1 (March 1937): 96–107, esp. 98–100; Maiolo, *Cry Havoc*, pp. 67–72.

42. Zani, *Fascismo, autarchia, commercio estero*. On Guarneri's deliberately misleading self-representation as a "rational" technocrat resisting "ideological" regime opponents—a narrative similar to that crafted after World War II by Albert Speer in relation to the Nazi regime—see Gualtieri, "Da Londra a Berlino," pp. 636–637. The best account of Guarneri's role is found in the work of Alessio Gagliardi: "Il Ministero per gli scambi e valute e la politica autarchica del fascismo," *Studi Storici* 46, no. 4 (October–December 2005): 1033–1071, and *L'impossibile autarchia*.

43. Mariangela Paradisi, "Il commercio estero e la struttura industriale," in *L'Economia italiana nel period fascista*, ed. Pierluigi Ciocca and Gianni Toniolo, pp. 271–328 (Bologna: Il Mulino, 1976).

44. Rolf Petri, *Von der Autarkie zum Wirtschaftswunder: Wirtschaftspolitik und industrieller Wandel in Italien 1935–1963* (Tübingen: Max Niemeyer, 2001), pp. 34–38, 60–125, 234–293; Welk, "League Sanctions and Foreign Trade Restrictions," p. 104; Maiolo, *Cry Havoc*, pp. 147–150.

45. Petra Terhoeven, *Ora alla patria: Donne, guerra e propaganda nella giornata delle Fede fascista* (Bologna: Il Mulino, 2006).

46. Victoria de Grazia, *How Fascism Ruled Women: Italy, 1922–1945* (Berkeley: University of California Press, 1992), pp. 77–78; Kate Ferris, "Fare di ogni familia italiana un fortilizio: The League of Nations' Economic Sanctions and Everyday Life in Venice," *Journal of Modern Italian History* 11 (2006): 117–142.

47. The writer Carlo Emilio Gadda later described Mussolini as a "thief of saucepans and pots of all peoples: with the excuse of making war on England" (*That Awful Mess on the Via Merulana*, trans. William Weaver [New York: NYRB Classics, 2000 (1957)], p. 206).

48. Luigi Filippo de Magistris, *Per Non Dimenticare: Testo atlante antisanzionista* (Milan: G. de Agostini e Figli, 1936).

49. Giuseppe Parenti, "L'efficacia delle 'controsanzioni' italiane," *Rivista Internationale di Scienze Sociali* 44, no. 7 (July 1936): 355–365.

50. Gagliardi, *L'impossibile autarchia*, pp. 146, 182.

51. Alberto Caracciolo, "Introduzione," in *La Banca d'Italia tra l'autarchia e la guerra, 1936–1945* (Rome: Laterza, 1992), pp. 21–30; Gianni Toniolo, "The Bank of Italy, A Short History, 1893–1998," in *Sveriges Riksbank and the History of Central Banking*, ed. Rodney Edvinsson, Tor Jacobson, and Daniel Waldenström, p. 312 (Cambridge: Cambridge University Press, 2018).

52. MAE, Rélations commerciales, 1918–1940, Italie, Box 39, Leroy-Beaulieu to Paris, 20 December 1935; cited in Gualtieri, "Da Londra a Berlino," p. 634n31.

53. Gagliardi, "Il Ministero per gli scambi e valute," pp. 1033–1071. See also Henry Siefke Miller, *Price Control in Fascist Italy* (New York: Columbia University Press, 1938).

54. Constantine E. McGuire, *Italy's International Economic Position* (New York: Macmillan, 1926), p. 26.

55. Francesco Cesarini, "Alle origini del credito industriale: La gestione dell'IMI dalla costituzione ai provvedimenti per l'autarchia (1931–1938)," in Banco di Roma, *Banca e industria fra le due guerre*, vol. 2: *Le riforme istituzionali e il pensiero giuridico* (Bologna: Il Mulino, 1981), pp. 81–180; Marianna Cavazza Rossi and Pasquale Saraceno, "Sergio Paronetto e la politica autarchica dell'IRI," in *Pensare l'Italia nuova: La cultura economica milanese tra corporativismo e ricostruzione*, ed. Giuseppe De Luca, pp. 231–243 (Milan: FrancoAngeli, 2007); Giovanni Farese, *Dare credito all'autarchia: L'IMI di Azzolini e il governo dell'economia negli anni Trenta* (Naples: Editoriale Scientifica, 2009); on the important role of IRI head Alberto Beneduce, see F. Bonelli, "Alberto Beneduce, il credito industriale e l'origine dell'IRI," in *Alberto Beneduce e i problem dell'economia italiana del suo tempo*, ed. P. Armani, pp. 71–85 (Rome: Edindustria, 1985).

56. The austere budgets of 1937 and 1938 in fact retarded colonial development, providing only for basic functions such as road construction and dashing the hopes of the Italian "Africanist" lobby for more ambitious settlement schemes. Roberta Pergher, *Mussolini's Nation-Empire: Sovereignty and Settlement in Italy's Borderlands, 1922–1943* (Cambridge: Cambridge University Press, 2018), pp. 117–160.

57. Zamagni, "Italy: How to Lose the War and Win the Peace," pp. 198–199, table 5.13, "Italian Public Expenditure, Revenues and Deficit, 1933–1947."

58. TNA, FO 371 20403, Drummond to London, 20 November 1936; cited in Gualtieri, "Da Londra a Berlino," p. 640n55.

59. "Industrie tessili e dell'abbigliamento: Meraviglie del prodotto tessile italiano al convegno di Forlì," *L'industria nazionale* 22, no. 1 (January 1937): 9–11; G. Sessa, "L'industria della canapa e del lino," in *L'indipendenza eco-*

nomica italiana, ed. L. Lojacono, pp. 269-271 (Milan: Hoepli, 1937); Mauro Santoro, *L'autarchia tessile del regime fascista: Il ginestrificio di Cariati (1935-1943)* (Cosenza: Editoriale Progetto, 2000).

60. Emanuela Scarpellini, *Italian Fashion since 1945: A Cultural History* (Cham: Springer, 2019), pp. 75-76.

61. Marcella Spadoni, *Il gruppo SNIA dal 1917 al 1951* (Turin: Giappichelli, 2003), pp. 9-17.

62. "Artificial Wool Production in Italy," *Nature* 140, no. 3556 (25 December 1937), p. 1090.

63. Angelo Tarchi, *Autarchia dei carburanti* (Florence: Carlo Cya, 1938); Alessio Zanardi, *Dall'autarchia all'austerity: Ceto politico e cultura d'impresa nell'industria nazionale del metano (1940-1973)* (Rome: Aracne Editrice, 2012).

64. Gustav Egloff, "Motor Fuel Economy of Europe," *Industrial Chemistry and Engineering* 30 (October 1938): 1091-1104; Charles Will Wright, "Progress in the Petroleum Producing Countries in Europe during 1938," *International Petroleum Trade* 8, no. 1 (25 January 1939): 14.

65. Marino Ruzzenenti, *L'autarchia verde: Un involontario laboratorio di green economy* (Milan: Jaca Book, 2011).

66. *L'autarchia del minerale italiano: Guida della mostra, 18 novembre-9 maggio XVII E.F.* (Rome: Circo Massimo, 1938). On Italian Fascist advertising, see Karen Pinkus, *Bodily Regimes: Italian Advertising under Fascism* (Minneapolis: University of Minnesota Press, 1995).

67. F. Caprotti, *Mussolini's Cities: Internal Colonialism in Italy, 1930-1939* (Youngstown, NY: Cambria Press, 2007). In these land reclamations, agricultural development was crowned by the construction of new towns. Tommaso Stabile: *Le Bonifiche in Italia e nei Territori d'Oltremare* (Vela: Velletri, 2000), and *La Bonifica di Mussolini: Storia della Bonifica Fascista dell'Agro Pontino* (Rome: Settimo Segillo, 2002).

68. Patrizia Dogliani, *L'Italia fascista: 1922-1940* (Florence: Sansoni, 1999), p. 224.

69. Alberto Vacca, *Carbonia e i problemi dell'industria carbonifera sarda (1936-1976)* (Cagliari: Della Torre, 1985).

70. Massimo Carta, *Perché Carbonia* (Cagliari: Ettore Gasperini Editore, 1981), p. 124.

71. Massimo Borgogni, *Tra continuità e incertezza: Italia e Albania (1914-1939): La strategia politico-militare dell'Italia in Albania fino all'Operazione "Oltre Mare Tirana"* (Milan: FrancoAngeli, 2007), pp. 141-142.

72. Bernd Jürgen Fischer has written of "Count Ciano's invasion of Albania" in *Albania at War, 1939-1945* (West Lafayette, IN: Purdue University Press, 1999), pp. 5-32; Davide Rodogno, *Fascism's European Empire: Italian Occupation during the Second World War* (Cambridge: Cambridge University Press, 2006), pp. 50-59.

73. Andrea Vento, *In silenzio gioite e soffrite: Storia dei servizi segreti italiani dal Risorgimento alla Guerra fredda* (Milan: Il Saggiatore, 2010), p. 441n24;

Libero Lenti, "Gli scambi internazionali dell'Albania," *Giornale degli economisti e annali di economia* 2, nos. 7–10 (July–October 1940): 548, table 6.

74. G. Fauser, "La benzina sintetica in Italia," *L'industria nazionale. Rivista mensile dell'autarchia* 24, nos. 11–12 (November–December 1939): 13–17.

75. Mario Perugini, *Il farsi di una grande impresa: La Montecatini tra le due guerre mondiali* (Milan: FrancoAngeli, 2014), pp. 323–328, 336.

76. Ibid., p. 338. The Mexican government of Lázaro Cárdenas had nationalized Western oil firms in 1938 and temporarily pursued a neutralist policy, from which Mussolini briefly profited. Noel Maurer, "The Empire Struck Back: Sanctions and Compensation in the Mexican Oil Expropriation of 1938," *Journal of Economic History* 71, no. 3 (September 2011): 590–615.

77. Alan S. Milward, *War, Economy and Society, 1939–1945* (Berkeley: University of California Press, 1977), p. 37.

78. On the value of Spanish iron ore to Italy, see Ulrich von Hassell (Rome) to Berlin, 27 October 1937, in DGFP, series D, vol. 1 (Washington, DC: GPO, 1949), pp. 19–20; John R. Hubbard, "How Franco Financed His War," *Journal of Modern History* 25, no. 4 (1953): pp. 390–406; Charles E. Harvey, "Politics and Pyrites during the Spanish Civil War," *Economic History Review* 31, no. 1 (February 1978): pp. 89–104; Stanley Payne, *The Franco Regime, 1936–1975* (Madison: University of Wisconsin Press, 1975), p. 155; Robert H. Whealey, *Hitler and Spain: The Nazi Role in the Spanish Civil War* (Lexington: University Press of Kentucky, 1989), p. 86, table 2, "Annual Export of Iron Ore from Spanish Morocco, 1936–1938."

79. Robert H. Whealey, "How Franco Financed His War: Reconsidered," *Journal of Contemporary History* 12, no. 1 (January 1977): 133–152.

80. Giuseppe Tattara, "Power and Trade: Italy and Germany in the Thirties," *Vierteljahrschrift für Sozial-und Wirtschaftsgeschichte*, no. 3, 1992, pp. 457–500.

81. Under the bilateral German-Italian clearing agreement of 14 April 1935, reciprocal deliveries of goods had to be equally proportioned. Manfred Funke, *Sanktionen und Kanonen: Hitler, Mussolini und der internationale Abessinienkonflikt 1934–36* (Düsseldorf: Droste, 1970), pp. 71–73.

82. "La manifestazione di un atteggiamento fondamentalmente non amichevole" (Felice Guarneri, *Battaglie economiche tra le due guerre*, vol. 1: *1918–1935* [Milan: Garzanti, 1953], pp. 391–392).

83. Funke, *Sanktionen und Kanonen*, pp. 68–69.

84. Gualtieri, "Da Londra a Berlino," p. 650; Toprani, *Oil and the Great Powers*, p. 197; Maximiliane Rieder, *Deutsch-italienische Wirtschaftsbeziehungen. Kontinuitäten und Brüche 1936–1957* (Frankfurt: Campus Verlag, 2003), p. 118.

85. Angela Raspin, *The Italian War Economy, 1940–1943: With Particular Reference to Italian Relations with Germany* (New York: Garland Publications, 1986).

86. "Marie Antoinette and Sanctions," *Time* 26, no. 16 (14 October 1935): 24.

87. Cited in Anne O'Hare McCormick, "Europe: Italy Boasts That Sanctions Only Made Her Stronger," *New York Times*, 19 November 1937, p. 16.

88. Wolfgang Birkenfeld, *Der synthetische Treibstoff 1933–1945. Ein Beitrag zur nationalsozialistischen Wirtschafts- und Rüstungspolitik* (Göttingen: Messerschmidt Verlag, 1964); Peter Hayes, *Industry and Ideology: IG Farben in the Nazi Era* (Cambridge: Cambridge University Press, 1987), pp. 32–80.

89. Suzanne Heim, *Autarkie und Ostexpansion: Pflanzenzucht und Agrarforschung im Nationalsozialismus* (Göttingen: Wallstein Verlag, 2002); Jonas Scherner, *Die Logik der Industriepolitik im Dritten Reich* (Stuttgart: Franz Steiner Verlag, 2008). On the importance of food security in Nazi ideology, see Gesine Gerhard, *Nazi Hunger Politics: A History of Food in the Third Reich* (Lanham, MD: Rowman and Littlefield, 2015), pp. 19–46.

90. Tooze, *The Wages of Destruction*, pp. 203–240.

91. PAAA, RZ 209, Referat Völkerbund, R 96758, "Die Lage Deutschland sim Falle der Verhängung von Völkerbundssanktionen gegen Italien," 7 October 1935, p. 13

92. Hans Steinberger, "Der deutsche Außenhandel in Kriegszeit," *Deutsche Wehr* 15 (1 August 1935); cited in French intelligence report found in SHD, 2 N 151, "Le commerce exterieure en temps de guerre," p. 3.

93. PAAA, R 96758, Artikel 16, October–November 1935, Note "Die Genfer Sanktionsbeschlüsse," Bd. 8, Vbd. 1313/55 (undated), p. 11.

94. Cited in memorandum by Konstantin von Neurath, 22 November 1935, in DGFP, series C, vol. 4 (April 1935–March 1936) (Washington, DC: GPO, 1962), p. 849.

95. Projecting old memories of the 1914–1918 hunger blockade, the tone in which newspapers described the crisis quickly moved from the formal to the fearful. Heinz A. Ludwig, "Italien unter Blockade. Die Auswirkungen der Sanktionen von Rom aus gesehen," *Wiener Wirtschaftswoche*, 13 November 1935.

96. Bülow to German Embassy in Rome, 7 November 1935; in DGFP, series C, vol. 4, pp. 798–799.

97. Ibid., p. 799.

98. Trial of the Major War Criminals before the International Military Tribunal (IMT), vol. 36, Document 406-EC, "Sitzungsbericht zur 11. Sitzung der Reichsverteidigungsausschusses, 6.12.1935," p. 463.

99. Ibid., p. 477.

100. Hjalmar Schacht, *Deutschland und die Weltwirtschaft. Vortrag vor dem "Bund der Freunde der Technischen Hochschule," München, am 7. Dezember 1935* (Berlin: Druckerei der Reichsbank, 1935), p. 11. On this speech as evidence of Schacht's conflicted approach to stabilization, see Teichert, *Autarkie und Großraumwirtschaft*, p. 125.

101. "Ölsanktion als Kampfmittel," *Preußischer Zeitung*, no. 334, 3 December 1935; Heinz Gernhuber, *Der italienisch-abessinische Konflikt und das Völkerrecht* (Königsberg: Otto Kümmel, 1937), pp. 98–99.

102. Helmut Mejcher, *Die Politik und das Öl im Nahen Osten* (Stuttgart: Klett-Cotta, 1980), 1:169. Soviet exports resumed later but fell by half from their 1935 level. Toprani, *Oil and the Great Powers*, p. 175n35.

103. Maj. a. D. Dr. W. Hedler, "Deutsche Rohstofflage und die Rohstoffwirtschaft im Kriege," *Militär-Wochenblatt* 120, no. 32 (25 February 1936).

104. Von Hassell to Berlin, 14 February 1936; in DGFP, series C, vol. 4, p. 1143.

105. George W. Baer, *Test Case: Italy, Ethiopia and the League of Nations* (Stanford, CA: Hoover Institution Press, 1976), pp. 221–231.

106. TNA, CAB 47/5 ATB 137, "Exercise of Economic Pressure on Germany without There Being a State of War," 12 March 1936, p. 18.

107. Tooze, *The Wages of Destruction*, pp. 207–222; Peter Longerich, *Hitler: A Biography* (New York: Oxford University Press, 2019), pp. 448–450; Toprani, *Oil and the Great Powers*, pp. 174–176.

108. Nazi Conspiracy and Aggression, 1945–1946 (NCA), vol. 7, Document EC-407, "Minutes of the 12th Meeting of the Reich Defence Council, 14 May 1936," pp. 463–464.

109. The first historian to point this out was Wilhelm Treue, "Hitlers Denkschrift zum Vierjahresplan, 1936," *Vierteljahrshefte für Zeitgeschichte* 3, no. 2 (1955): 188–202. Maiolo notes that "Mussolini's 23 March speech on autarky prefigured (and certainly helped to inspire) Hitler's Four-Year Plan memorandum" (*Cry Havoc*, p. 148).

110. Göring told his interrogators at Nuremberg that the Four-Year Plan's two aims had been, first, to make Germany secure against any crisis in agriculture and, second, "[make Germany] able to withstand a blockade, to the greatest extent possible" (IMT, vol. 9, "Vernehmung Görings zum Vierjahrenplan, 14. März 1946," p. 283).

111. *Der Vierjahresplan: Zeitschrift für nationalsozialistische Wirtschaftspolitik* 1, no. 2 (February 1937): 93.

112. Arthur Schweitzer, "Der ursprüngliche Vierjahresplan," *Jahrbücher für Ökonomie und Statistik* 168 (1956): 348–396; Dieter Petzina, *Autarkiepolitik in dritten Reich. Der nationalsozialistische Vierjahresplan* (Stuttgart: Deutsche Verlagsanstalt, 1968), pp. 30–48; Tooze, *The Wages of Destruction*, pp. 222–230; on the plan's efforts to boost German iron ore extraction through the Reichswerke Hermann Göring, see Fertik, "Steel and Sovereignty," pp. 301–360.

113. IMT, vol. 7, Document NI-051, "Minister President General Goering on the Execution of the Four-Year Plan. The Speech in the Big Assembly Hall of the 'Preussenhaus' on 17 December 1936," pp. 815, 816.

114. Accordingly, racial ideologues in the Nazi Party claimed that "when the Roman nation was fighting for the establishment of its empire and for the expansion of its living space [*Lebensraum*], it was the Jew who stoked the sanctions war to force Italy to its knees" ("Italiens Rassenpolitik," *Neues Volk* 7, no. 1 [1939]: 9).

115. Albrecht Haushofer, "Berichterstattung aus der atlantischen Welt," *Zeitschrift für Geopolitik* 12, no. 9 (September 1935): 556.

116. Paul Einzig, *Bloodless Invasion: German Economic Penetration into Danubian States and the Balkans* (London: Duckworth, 1938); Alice Teichova, "Über das Eindringen des deutschen Finanzkapitals in das Wirtschaftsleben der Tsechoslowakei vor dem Münchener Diktat. Ein Beitrag zur ökonomischen Geschichte des Imperialismus," *Zeitschrift für Geschichtswissenschaft* 5 (1957): 1160–1180; Alan S. Milward, "The Reichsmark Bloc and the International Economy," in *The "Führer State": Myth and Reality: Studies on the Structure and Politics of the Third Reich*, ed. Gerhard Hirschfeld and Lothar Kettenacker (Stuttgart: Klett-Cotta, 1981); Bernd-Jürgen Wendt, "Südosteuropa in der nationalsozialistischen Grossraumwirtschaft," in Hirschfeld and Kettenacker, *The "Führer State,"* pp. 414–428; Alfred Kube, "Außenpolitik und 'Grossraumwirtschaft': Die deutsche Politik zur wirtschaftlichen Integration Südosteuropas 1933 bis 1939," in *Wirtschaftliche und politische Integration in Europa im 19. und 20. Jahrhundert*, ed. Helmut Berding, pp. 185–211 (Göttingen: Vandenhoeck and Ruprecht, 1984); Stephen G. Gross, *Export Empire: German Soft Power in Southeastern Europe, 1890–1945* (Cambridge: Cambridge University Press, 2015), pp. 253–391.

117. Roland Schönfeld, "Deutsche Rohstoffsicherungspolitik in Jugoslawien, 1934–1944," *Vierteljahrshefte für Zeitgeschichte* 24 (1976): 215–258; Pierre L. Siklos, *War Finance, Reconstruction, Hyperinflation and Stabilization in Hungary, 1938–48* (New York: St. Martin's Press, 1991), pp. 45–48.

118. Cited in *Deutschlands wirtschaftliche Lage an der Jahreswende 1935/36* (Berlin: Reichs-Kredit Gesellschaft, 1936), p. 79.

119. Cited in Freytag, *Deutschlands "Drang nach Südosten,"* p. 229. Freytag points out that whereas in the early 1930s, German industry had desired a breakout into new markets to sell its goods, recover market share, and deal with overcapacity—and was willing to import from countries that bought in return—by 1937–1938 the relationship had inverted; with armaments production now gobbling up gargantuan amounts of raw materials, export became simply a means to earn the foreign exchange needed for importing the vital inputs.

120. Michael Ebi, *Export um jeden Preis: Die deutsche Exportförderung von 1932–1938* (Stuttgart: Steiner, 2004).

121. Teichert, *Autarkie und Großraumwirtschaft*, pp. 180–205.

122. The continued possibility of exchanging luxury goods in a world economy of great spaces—not unlike premodern intercontinental trade—was rhapsodized by the Nazi journalist Ferdinand Fried (1898–1967). See his "Die Überwindung des Kapitalismus," *Odal: Monatsschrift für Blut und Boden* 5, no. 12 (June 1937): 961–962. See also Joshua Derman, "Prophet of a Partitioned World: Ferdinand Fried, 'Great Spaces,' and the Dialectics of Deglobalization, 1929–1950," *Modern Intellectual History*, 2020, pp. 1–25.

123. Albrecht O. Ritschl, "Nazi Economic Imperialism and the Exploitation of the Small: Evidence from Germany's Secret Exchange Balances, 1938–1940," *Economic History Review* 54, no. 2 (2001): 324–345. Ritschl finds that contrary to the hopes of the *Mitteleuropa* enthusiasts in the German busi-

ness community, the countries in the Danubian basin were a net drain on German foreign exchange reserves into 1938–1939. This lends support to the idea that what Germany sought was less an escape from the depression than politically *secure* trade ties.

124. Hossbach memorandum, 10 November 1937; in DGFP, series D, vol. 1 (September 1937–September 1938) (Washington, DC: GPO, 1949), p. 31.

125. Address in Berlin, 28 September 1937; cited in *Hitler. Reden und Proklamationen, 1932–1945*, ed. Max Domarus, 2:738 (Wiesbaden, R. Löwit, 1973).

126. Christian Leitz, *Economic Relations between Nazi Germany and Franco's Spain, 1936–1945* (Oxford: Oxford University Press, 1996); Pierpaolo Barbieri, *Hitler's Shadow Empire: Nazi Economics and the Spanish Civil War* (Cambridge, MA: Harvard University Press, 2015).

127. Felix Butschek, *Die österreichische Wirtschaft 1938 bis 1945* (Vienna: Österreichisches Institut für Wirtschaftsforschung, 1978), p. 45; Tooze, *The Wages of Destruction*, pp. 245–247.

128. The initial order to prepare this plan had been given to the CID by the chiefs of staff in April 1937, but it had been suspended in December 1937, when, following the escalation of the Sino-Japanese conflict, the minister for coordination of defense directed the economic war planners to plan against Japan. After the Anschluß in March 1938, the ATB refocused economic war contingency planning on its original target, Germany, and the first plan was ready four months later. See TNA, CAB 47/5, Walter Elliott, "Plan for Economic Warfare against Germany. Memorandum by the Chairman," 22 July 1938, p. 1.

129. SHD, 5 N 579, "Étude pour le président Daladier, des décisions à prendre au CSDN," 13 September 1938.

130. Katriel Ben-Arie, "Czechoslovakia at the Time of 'Munich': The Military Situation," *Journal of Contemporary History* 25, no. 4 (October 1990): 431–446.

131. MAE, Relations commerciales to secrétariat-général de la Défense nationale, "L'expansion allemande en Europe Centrale et sud-orientale" [based on Memorandum No. 1086 from the French Embassy in Berlin of 13 October 1938], 25 October 1938, p. 14.

132. Alexander Görner, *Die deutsche Kriegswirtschaft 1914 und 1939* (Munich: Deutsche Verlagsanstalt, 1939), p. 17; S. Gross, *Export Empire*, pp. 253–329.

133. Toprani, *Oil and the Great Powers*, pp. 190, 196–197.

134. Cited in Domarus, *Hitler*, 3:1053.

135. Herbert Sirois, *Zwischen Illusion und Krieg: Deutschland und die USA 1933–1941* (Paderborn: Ferdinand Schöningh, 2000), pp. 162–167; David Reynolds, *From Munich to Pearl Harbor: Roosevelt's America and the Origins of the Second World War* (Chicago: Ivan R. Dee, 2001), pp. 41–50.

136. "Memorandum by the director of the Economic Policy Department, 30 March 1939: Economic Tension with the United States of America Caused by the Incorporation of the Protectorate of Bohemia and Moravia" in DGFP, series D, vol. 6 (London: HMSO, 1956), pp. 159–160.

137. Nuremberg Military Tribunals (NMT), vol. 7, Document EC-282, "Work Report of Dr. C. Krauch, Plenipotentiary General for Special Questions of Chemical Production of Minister President, Field Marshal Goering, Submitted to the General Council of the Four-Year Plan," 20–21 April 1939, p. 953; Tooze, *The Wages of Destruction*, pp. 307–308.

138. Christopher Clark has, in the context of the outbreak of World War I, defined "temporal claustrophobia" as "a sense that time was running out, that in an environment where assets were waning and threats were growing, any delay was sure to bring severe penalties" (*The Sleepwalkers: How Europe Went to War in 1914* [London: Penguin, 2012], p. 247).

139. The collective security view of the LNU was clear; defending the boycott of the Soviet Olympics of 1980, Philip Noel-Baker still maintained that "a general trade embargo would have rendered Hitler helpless in 1937–8" ("Sheer Hypocrisy That Our Athletes Should Ignore," letter to the editor of *Manchester Guardian Weekly*, 16 June 1980, p. 14).

140. "German Need of Raw Materials," *Financial Times*, 22 May 1939, p. 7.

141. On the fourth anniversary of the League sanctions against Italy in 1939, Mussolini said that "the division between the economy of peace and the economy of war is simply absurd. . . . Even in types of peace other types of war are being waged, which in their turn prepare our armed warfare. Therefore, it is the fact, or rather the imminent fatality, of armed warfare that ought to dominate and that does dominate economy" (cited in "Economy of War Affirmed to Italy," *New York Times*, 19 November 1939, p. 32).

142. Josef Kölble, *Arbeitskraft schafft Wirtschaftsfreiheit: Rohstofffragen und Sozialprobleme der Gegenwart* (Leipzig: v. Hase and Koehler Verlag, 1938), pp. 80–84; Rudolf von Xylander, "Der Sanktionskrieg des Völkerbundes gegen Italien," *Deutsche Wirtschaft-Zeitung* 17 (1938): 545–550; Gerhard Herrmann, "Italiens Imperium im Aufbau II," *Zeitschrift für Geopolitik* 15, no. 1 (1938): 283.

143. Carl Burckhardt, *Meine Danziger Mission 1937–1939* (Munich: Callwey, 1960), p. 348. Its full context is Hitler's statement (reported by Burckhardt) that "everything I undertake is aimed at Russia; when the West is too dumb and too blind to understand this, I will be forced to reach an agreement with the Russians, to defeat the West, and then after its defeat I will turn with all my combined forces against the Soviet Union. I need the Ukraine, so that they cannot again starve us out like in the last war." The veracity of the quote has been disputed by Paul Stauffer, *Zwischen Hofmannsthal und Hitler: Carl J. Burckhardt. Facetten einer aussengewöhnlicher Existenz* (Zurich: Verlag Neue Zürcher Zeitung, 1991), pp. 187–201. See Golo Mann, "Kritik: Carl J. Burckhardts Danziger Mission," *Merkur* 14, no. 148 (June 1960): 573–576; Percy Ernst Schramm, "Brach Danzigs wegen der Zweite Weltkrieg aus?" *Die Zeit*, 1 July 1960. See also Andreas Hillgruber, "Quellen und Quellenkritik zur Vorgeschichte des Zweiten Weltkrieges," in *Kriegsbeginn 1939. Entfesselung oder Ausbruch des Zweiten Weltkriegs?*, ed. Gottfried Niedhart, p. 373 (Darmstadt: Wissenschaftliche Buchgesellschaft, 1976). How-

ever, Hitler's mention of the possession of Ukraine as a biopolitical insurance policy against a repetition of the 1914–1918 blockade seems entirely plausible in light of both his *Zweites Buch* (written in 1928 but published only in 1961), as well as the late-night ravings in which he engaged during the late summer and fall of 1941, when German armies were conquering Ukraine; recorded in Werner Jöchmann, ed., *Monologe im Führerhauptquartier 1941–1944: Aufgezeichnet von Heinrich Heim* (Munich: Albrecht Knaus, 1980); Burckhardt could not have known about either before writing *Meine Danziger Mission* in 1960.

144. IMT, vol. 26, Document 798-PS, "Ansprache des Führers vor den Oberbefehlshabern am 22. Aug. 1939," p. 343.

145. Andreas Hillgruber, *Die Zerstörung Europas: Beiträge zur Weltkriegsepoche, 1914 bis 1945* (Frankfurt: Propyläen, 1988), pp. 208–212; Gerhard L. Weinberg, *Hitler's Foreign Policy, 1933–1939: The Road to World War II* (New York: Enigma Books, 2005), pp. 639–645; Tooze, *The Wages of Destruction*, pp. 321–325.

146. Barnhart, *Japan Prepares for Total War*, pp. 23, 27–34; Maiolo, *Cry Havoc*, p. 27; Janis Mimura, *Planning for Empire: Reform Bureaucrats and the Japanese Wartime State* (Ithaca, NY: Cornell University Press, 2011), p. 18.

147. Mark R. Peattie, *Ishiwara Kanji and Japan's Confrontation with the West* (Princeton, NJ: Princeton University Press, 1975), pp. 27–83.

148. Louise Young, *Japan's Total Empire: Manchuria and the Culture of Wartime Imperialism* (Berkeley: University of California Press, 1998); Ortrud Kerde, "The Ideological Background of the Japanese War Economy: Visions of the 'Reformist Bureaucrats,'" in *Japan's War Economy*, ed. Erich Pauer, pp. 23–38 (London: Routledge, 1999).

149. Yoshihisa Tak Matsusaka, *The Making of Japanese Manchuria, 1904–1932* (Cambridge, MA: Harvard University Asia Center, 2001), pp. 214–223, 250–258.

150. Mark Metzler, *Lever of Empire: The International Gold Standard and the Crisis of Liberalism in Prewar Japan* (Berkeley: University of California Press, 2005), pp. 32–35, 240–256.

151. British sanctions planners were aware of this sympathy. See TNA, CAB 47/5 ATB 120, "Economic Sanctions against Italy, July 1935, Appendix I. International Cooperation in the Exercise of Pressure on Italy," p. 3.

152. Reto Hoffmann, *The Fascist Effect: Japan and Italy, 1915–1952* (Ithaca, NY: Cornell University Press, 2015), pp. 89–108.

153. Chalmers Johnson, *MITI and the Japanese Miracle: The Growth of Industrial Policy, 1925–1975* (Stanford, CA: Stanford University Press, 1982); Nakamura Takafusa, "The Japanese War Economy as a 'Planned Economy,'" in Pauer, ed., *Japan's War Economy*, pp. 9–22; Yoshiro Miwa, *Japan's Economic Planning and Mobilization in Wartime, 1930s–1940s: The Competence of the State* (Cambridge: Cambridge University Press, 2015).

154. Yasukichi Yasuba, "Did Japan Ever Suffer from a Shortage of Natural Re-

sources before World War II?" *Journal of Economic History* 56, no. 3 (September 1996): 543–560.

155. TNA, CAB 47/5 ATB 155, "Economic Sanctions against Japan," 5 November 1937, p. 12, Annex I. Principal Japanese imports by weight, 1936, showing proportion supplied by British Empire and United States and possible alternative sources of supply.

156. In September 1936, the Japanese launched the first Five-Year Plan for Manchuria, whose aim was to use Stalinist-inspired economic planning to create a Japanese version of the Nazi *Großraumwirtschaft*, a "unified economic region" (*koiki kokumin keizai*). Mimura, *Planning for Empire*, pp. 95–97; Kerde, "The Ideological Background of the Japanese War Economy," p. 29.

157. Guarneri, *Battaglie economiche*, p. 394.

158. Metzler, *Lever of Empire*, pp. 255–256.

159. G. C. Allen, *A Short Economic History of Japan, 1867–1937* (London: Routledge, 2003), 1:135–136; C. Johnson, *MITI and the Japanese Miracle*, pp. 133–134; Leon Hollerman, *Japanese Dependence on World Trade: An Approach toward Economic Liberalization* (Princeton, NJ: Princeton University Press, 1967), p. 225.

160. Akira Kudo, *German-Japanese Business Relations: Co-operation and Rivalry in the Inter-War Period* (London: Routledge, 1998), pp. 110–147. The first Japanese synthetic fuel production had begun in 1931 at Yongan in northern Korea; a second plant was built in 1937 at Aoji-ri. Another complex was erected by the Manchukuo government, the Imperial Fuel Development Company, and the Nitchitsu chemical corporation at Jilin in eastern Manchuria in 1938. Jilin was the third dedicated synthetic fuel plant in the world to start operation after IG Farben's Leuna plant and the Imperial Chemical Industries plant at Billingham in 1935. Dennis L. McNamara, *The Colonial Origins of Korean Enterprise, 1910–1945* (Cambridge: Cambridge University Press, 1990), p. 109; Barbara Molony, *Technology and Investment: The Prewar Japanese Chemical Industry* (Cambridge, MA: Harvard University Press, 1990), pp. 226, 229, 231; Aaron Stephen Moore, *Constructing East Asia: Technology, Ideology, and Empire in Japan's Wartime Era, 1931–1945* (Stanford, CA: Stanford University Press, 2013), p. 170.

161. Cited in 893.0146/549, Memorandum by the Assistant Chief of the Division of Far Eastern Affairs (Hamilton), 10 July 1937, in FRUS, 1937, vol. 3 (Washington, DC: GPO, 1943), p. 134.

162. Cited in Barnhart, *Japan Prepares for Total War*, p. 89.

163. S. C. M. Paine, *The Wars for Asia, 1911–1949* (Cambridge: Cambridge University Press, 2006), pp. 131–133.

164. Cited in Rana Mitter, *Forgotten Ally: China's World War, II 1937–1945* (New York: First Mariner Books, 2014), p. 94.

165. Margharita Zanasi, *Saving the Nation: Economic Modernity in China* (Chicago: University of Chicago Press, 2006), pp. 197–203.

166. In Geneva, Columbia-educated Chinese diplomat Wellington Koo, a long-standing advocate of U.S.-Chinese friendship, implored the League to initiate economic sanctions to defend China, a member state, against Japan, a non-member state. LON C.300.M.176.1938.VII, "Communication de la delegation chinoise," 11 September 1938.

167. Ken-ichi Arakawa, "Japanese Naval Blockade of China in the Second Sino-Japanese War, 1937–41," in *Naval Blockades and Seapower: Strategies and Counter-Strategies, 1805–2005*, ed. Bruce A. Elleman and S. C. M. Paine, pp. 105–116 (London: Routledge, 2006); Imperial Japanese Navy lawyers cited the great power pacific blockade of Montenegro in 1913 and the Entente's 1916 blockade of Greece as precedents. MAE Série SDN No. 356, Bureau du Japon, "Observations sur l'affaire sino-japonaise," 20 September 1937.

168. There were good reasons to avoid openly declaring war. A de jure war would have opened the way to an extended Japanese blockade of the Western Treaty ports through which the Chinese Nationalists were receiving arms. LON, Com.Cons./Requête chinoise/2, "Extrait du compte rendu stenographique de la séance de l'assemblée, tenue le 15 septembre 1937, à 10h.30," 17 September 1937, p. 8.

169. The Third Neutrality Act included cash-and-carry provisions, which required exporters to limit their ordinary exports to belligerents to only those goods that they could pay for directly. This benefited countries with larger foreign exchange reserves such as Britain and France; in the Sino-Japanese conflict, however, Paris saw it as "an unmerited and dangerous advantage for Japan" (MAE, Série SDN, No. 818, Tels. 114-118, De Laboulaye [Washington, DC] to Quai d'Orsay [Paris], 28 January 1937). As the French regretfully noted, "The thesis of a total embargo on raw materials is definitely rejected" (Tel. 444, Georges Bonnet [DC] to Paris, 28 April 1937, f. 289).

170. MAE, Série SDN, No. 356, Directeur politique adjoint, "Conflit sino-japonais," 6 September 1937, p. 2.

171. Cited in FRUS, Japan 1931–1941, vol. 1 (Washington, DC: GPO, 1943), pp. 379–383.

172. John McVickar Haight, "Roosevelt and the Aftermath of the Quarantine Speech," *Review of Politics* 24, no. 2 (April 1962): 233–259.

173. John Franklin Carter, "We, the People: Warning Issued That Sanctions against Japan Would Hurt U.S. Commerce," *Evening Star*, 12 October 1937. Carter, who worked as a speechwriter for Henry Wallace before starting his column *We the People* in the *Evening Star*, argued that sanctions failed to address the manifest inequality of the Versailles order. He continued: "The lesson of the post-war decades is that even the most successful act of military and economic repression (we starved and killed the Germans into abject surrender in 1918) is powerless to solve the problems arising from economic and social inequalities in international relations. . . . If Mr. Roosevelt

is a great statesman, however, he will accompany his threats of democratic reprisals with an offer of economic appeasement and political satisfaction for the social security of the 'have-nots,' internationally as well as in domestic matters. This means he must persuade the British, French, Dutch and Portuguese empires to modify exclusive colonial policies and to give Germany, Italy and Japan a chance to earn a living for their people under the present political status quo."

174. "If We Boycott Japan," *New York Times*, 12 October 1937.

175. TNA, CAB 47/1, ATB minutes of twenty-fifth meeting, 4 November 1937, p. 1.

176. There was one paradox, however, caused by the substitution effect of raw material inputs: any action to interfere with Japanese exports would mean that fewer raw materials would be used up by civilian industry and thus could be allocated to military production; in the short run, then, an anti-export embargo would not stop the war economy. CAB 47/5 ATB 155, Economic Sanctions against Japan, 5 November 1937, p. 3.

177. TNA, CAB 47/1, ATB minutes of twenty-fifth meeting, pp. 5–7.

178. Metzler, *Lever of Empire*, p. 253; G. Bruce Strang, "Imperial Hubs and Their Limitations: British Assessments of Imposing Sanctions on Japan, 1937," in *British World Policy and the Projection of Global Power, 1830–1960*, ed. T. G. Otte, pp. 276–304 (Cambridge: Cambridge University Press, 2019).

179. TNA, CAB 47/5 ATB 155, Economic Sanctions against Japan, p. 6.

180. Richard A. Harrison, "A Neutralization Plan for the Pacific: Roosevelt and Anglo-American Cooperation, 1934–1937," *Pacific Historical Review* 57, no. 1 (February 1988): 47–72.

181. Cited in John Morton Blum, *From the Morgenthau Diaries*, vol. 1: *Years of Crisis, 1928–1938* (Boston: Houghton Mifflin, 1959), p. 489; Reynolds, *From Munich to Pearl Harbor*, p. 38.

182. Cited in Blum, *From the Morgenthau Diaries*, 1:262; available at https://www.fdrlibrary.marist.edu/_resources/images/morg/md0134.pdf. Accessed 14 December 2018. See also Harold L. Ickes, *The Secret Diary of Harold L. Ickes*, vol. 2: *The Inside Struggle, 1936–1939* (New York: Simon and Schuster, 1955), pp. 274–276.

183. TNA, T 160/693/11, Treasury Secretary John Simon to Neville Chamberlain, 18 December 1937, ff. 26–27.

184. As Simon put it to Chamberlain, the ATB had provided "strong reasons against this sort of economic nagging, and we have our Italian experience!" (ibid., p. 27). The Simon-Morgenthau exchange also gave occasion to the rather awkward discovery by the British of the American version of their own Trading with the Enemy Act, which Roosevelt had already used for domestic purposes in 1933. The British could not understand how an economic warfare law targeting property could be reapplied for purposes of foreign exchange control, and they were quite appalled by the suggestion (ibid., Note from Hopkins to S. D. Waley, Phillips, and Warren Fisher, 20

December 1937, ff. 41–42). Treasury Permanent Secretary R. V. N. Hopkins cautioned that "economic sanctions designed to hamper the nature of war are intensely provocative and I should think the Japs are the last people on which to try them unless [a] battle fleet is over there" (handwritten comment on memorandum by Sir Frederick Leith-Ross, 20 December 1937, f. 38).

185. MAE, Série SDN, No. 367, January–August 1938, Service française de la SDN, No. 7, "Note. Appel du gouvernement chinois," 22 April 1938, pp. 1–2.

186. LOC, Norman Davis Papers, Box 8, Letter from Lord Cecil to Norman Davis, 30 June 1938; letter from Davis to Cecil, 13 July 1938.

187. Warren S. Hunsberger, "The Yen Bloc in Japan's Expansion Program," *Far Eastern Survey* 7, no. 22 (9 November 1938): 251–258.

188. Barnhart, *Japan Prepares for Total War*, pp. 91–96.

189. Mitter, *Forgotten Ally*, p. 146.

190. Paine, *The Wars for Asia*, pp. 144–145; Stephen Kotkin, *Stalin*, vol. 2: *Waiting for Hitler, 1929–1941* (London: Allen Lane, 2017), p. 1003n152.

191. Benjamin H. Williams, "The Coming of Economic Sanctions into American Practice," *American Journal of International Law* 37, no. 3 (July 1943): 393, 394n15; Arthur N. Young, *China and the Helping Hand, 1937–1945* (Cambridge, MA: Harvard University Press, 1963).

192. Blum, *From the Morgenthau Diaries*, pp. 483–484, 506–508, 519, 526–527.

193. C. Johnson, *MITI and the Japanese Miracle*, pp. 139–141; Barnhart, *Japan Prepares for Total War*, pp. 137–146.

194. Donald Cameron Watt, *How War Came: The Immediate Origins of the Second World War, 1938–1939* (New York: Pantheon, 1989), p. 356.

195. TNA, CAB 47/5, ATB 201, "Economic Measures to Restrain Japan from Further Action Inimical to British Interests in the Far East," 20 July 1939, p. 5.

196. John D. Meehan, *The Dominion and the Rising Sun: Canada Encounters Japan, 1929–1941* (Vancouver: University of British Columbia Press, 2004), pp. 181–184.

197. Edward S. Miller, *Bankrupting the Enemy: The U.S. Financial Siege of Japan before Pearl Harbor* (Annapolis, MD: Naval Institute Press, 2007), pp. 73–75.

198. Mimura, *Planning for Empire*, p. 187.

199. Paine notes that "Japan had invaded China in pursuit of national security through autarky. Yet its military strategy made its economic goals unattainable by causing the collapse of the Chinese economy" (*The Wars for Asia*, p. 167).

200. E. B. Schumpeter, ed., *The Industrialization of Japan and Manchukuo, 1930–1940: Population, Raw Materials and Industry* (New York: Macmillan, 1940).

201. E. B. Schumpeter, "The Yen Bloc: Program and Results," *Annals of the American Academy of Political and Social Science* 215, America and Japan (May 1941): 30.

202. HIA, SHP, Box 369, Folder Sanctions #2, Letter [with written comment by Hornbeck] from Elizabeth Boody Schumpeter to the editors of *Pacific Affairs*, "The Problem of Sanctions in the Far East," 14 January 1940, p. 15.

203. Ibid., p. 17. Schumpeter also foresaw the denouement of U.S. economic pressure almost two years before the attack of Pearl Harbor: "If Japan is confronted with a choice between complete submission (which would reduce her to a third rate power) or a final desperate attack in the South Seas, I believe it probable that the militarist party would choose to attack" (ibid., p. 16).

Chapter Ten. The Positive Economic Weapon, 1939–1945

1. Antonín Basch, *The New Economic Warfare* (New York: Columbia University Press, 1941), p. xii.

2. For a view of Rooseveltian internationalism as emergent global democracy promotion, see G. John Ikenberry, *A World Safe for Democracy: Liberal Internationalism and the Crises of Global Order* (New Haven: Yale University Press, 2020), pp. 141–176.

3. Mark Mazower, *Dark Continent: Europe's Twentieth Century* (London: Allen Lane, 1998); Andrea Orzoff, "Interwar Democracy and the League of Nations," in *The Oxford Handbook of European History, 1914–1945*, ed. Nicholas Doumanis, pp. 261–281 (Oxford: Oxford University Press, 2016).

4. Thomas Bottelier, "'Not on a Purely Nationalistic Basis': The Internationalism of Allied Coalition Warfare in the Second World War," *European Review of History* 27, nos. 1–2 (2020): 152–175.

5. W. N. Medlicott, *The Economic Blockade*, 2 vols. (London: HMSO, 1952); Alan S. Milward: *The German Economy at War* (London: Athlone Press, 1965), pp. 13, 48, 115, and *War, Economy and Society, 1939–1945* (Berkeley: University of California Press, 1977), pp. 294–328; Lance E. Davis and Stanley L. Engerman, *Naval Blockades in Peace and War: An Economic History Since 1750* (New York: Cambridge University Press, 2006), pp. 239–320; Geoffrey Till, "Naval Blockade and Economic Warfare in the European War, 1939–45," in *Naval Blockades and Seapower: Strategies and Counter-Strategies, 1805–2005*, ed. Bruce A. Elleman and S.C. M. Paine (London: Routledge, 2006), pp. 117–130; Michael Geyer and Adam Tooze, eds., *The Cambridge History of the Second World War*, vol. 3: *Total War: Economy, Society and Culture* (Cambridge: Cambridge University Press, 2015), pp. 27–195.

6. Ludwig Dehio, *Gleichgewicht oder Hegemonie: Betrachtung über ein Grundproblem der neueren Staatengeschichte* (Krefeld: Scherpe Verlag, 1948); Georges-Henri Soutou, "Was There a European Order in the Twentieth Century? From the Concert of Europe to the End of the Cold War," *Contemporary European History* 9, no. 3 (November 2000): 329–353.

7. F. P. King, *The New Internationalism: Allied Policy and the European Peace,*

1939–1945 (Newton Abbot: David and Charles, 1973); Robert C. Hilderbrand, *Dumbarton Oaks: The Origins of the United Nations and the Search for Postwar Security* (Chapel Hill: University of North Carolina Press, 1990).

8. Warren Kimball, *The Most Unsordid Act: Lend-Lease, 1939–1941* (Baltimore: Johns Hopkins University Press, 1969); Robert Huhn Jones, *The Roads to Russia: United States Lend-Lease to the Soviet Union* (Norman: University of Oklahoma Press, 1969); George C. Herring, *Aid to Russia, 1941–1946: Strategy, Diplomacy, the Origins of the Cold War* (New York: Columbia University Press, 1973); Leon Martel, *Lend-Lease, Loans, and the Coming of the Cold War: A Study of the Implementation of Foreign Policy* (Boulder, CO: Westview Press, 1979); Roger Munting, "Lend-Lease and the Soviet War Effort," *Journal of Contemporary History* 19 (1984): 495–510; Henri Dunajewski, "Le lend-lease américain pour l'Union soviétique," *Revue d'études comparatives Est-Ouest* 15, no. 3 (1984): 21–89; Alan P. Dobson, *US Wartime Aid to Britain* (London: Croom Helm, 1986); Hubert P. Van Tuyll, *Feeding the Bear: American Aid to the Soviet Union, 1941–1945* (New York: Greenport Books, 1989); Albert L. Weeks, *Russia's Life-Saver: Lend-Lease Aid to the U.S.S.R. in World War II* (Plymouth: Lexington Books, 2004); for its macro-economic effects on the Soviet economy, see Mark Harrison, *Soviet Planning for Peace and War, 1938–1945* (Cambridge: Cambridge University Press, 1985), pp. 153–154.

9. Paul A. C. Koistinen, *Arsenal of World War II: The Political Economy of American Warfare, 1940–1945* (Lawrence: University Press of Kansas, 2004); James T. Sparrow, *Warfare State: World War II Americans and the Age of Big Government* (New York: Oxford University Press, 2011); Mark R. Wilson, *Destructive Creation: American Business and the Winning of World War II* (Philadelphia: University of Pennsylvania Press, 2016).

10. The global reflation of the 1940s is examined in the underappreciated study by A. J. Brown, *The Great Inflation, 1939–1951* (New York: Oxford University Press, 1955).

11. Charles Maier, "The Politics of Productivity: Foundations of American International Economic Policy after World War II," in Charles Maier, *In Search of Stability: Explorations in Historical Political Economy* (Cambridge: Cambridge University Press, 1987), pp. 121–152; Eric Helleiner, *Forgotten Foundations of Bretton Woods: International Development and the Making of the Postwar Order* (Ithaca, NY: Cornell University Press, 2014); David Engerman, *The Price of Aid: The Economic Cold War in India* (Cambridge, MA: Harvard University Press, 2018).

12. Igor Lukes, *Czechoslovakia between Stalin and Hitler: The Diplomacy of Edvard Beneš in the 1930s* (New York: Oxford University Press, 1996), pp. 190–224; Igor Lukes and Erik Goldstein, eds., *The Munich Crisis, 1938: Prelude to World War II* (London: Frank Cass, 1999); Louise Grace Shaw, *The British Political Elite and the Soviet Union, 1937–1939* (London: Frank Cass, 2003), pp. 5–30; Hugh Ragsdale, *The Soviets, the Munich Crisis, and the Coming of World War II* (Cambridge: Cambridge University Press, 2004), pp. 28–52.

13. LON, "La 19ème Assemblée et l'application facultative des sanctions économiques," 11 October 1938.

14. Gabriel Gorodetsky, *The Grand Delusion: Stalin and the German Invasion of Russia* (New Haven: Yale University Press, 2001), p. 4.

15. David E. Kaiser, *Economic Diplomacy and the Origins of the Second World War: Germany, Britain, France, and Eastern Europe, 1930–1939* (Princeton, NJ: Princeton University Press, 1980), pp. 284-315; G. Bruce Strang, "Once More unto the Breach: Britain's Guarantee to Poland, March 1939," *Journal of Contemporary History* 31, no. 4 (October 1996): 721-752; see also G. Bruce Strang, "John Bull in Search of a Suitable Russia: British Foreign Policy and the Failure of Anglo-French-Soviet Alliance Negotiations, 1939," *Canadian Journal of History* 41 (Spring-Summer 2006): 47-84.

16. Robert Boyce and Joseph A. Maiolo, "Introduction," in *The Origins of World War Two*, ed. Robert Boyce and Joseph A. Maiolo, p. 6 (Basingstoke: Palgrave Macmillan, 2003). Peter Jackson notes that "ideological clashes over the identity of France had a devastating effect on efforts to construct a new external policy" ("France," in Boyce and Maiolo, *The Origins of World War Two*, p. 99). Anita J. Prazmowska argues that "Poland's unwillingness to consider the benefits of supporting the Soviet policy of collective security left it unprepared for the consequences of the failure of Moscow's efforts, which led directly to a *rapprochement* with Germany and joint action against Poland" ("Poland," in Boyce and Maiolo, *The Origins of World War Two*, p. 157). See also Michael Jabara Carley: "End of the 'Low, Dishonest Decade': Failure of the Anglo-French-Soviet Alliance in 1939," *Europe-Asia Studies* 45, no. 2 (1993): 303-341, and *1939: The Alliance That Never Was and the Coming of World War II* (Chicago: Ivan R. Dee, 1999); on Chamberlain's role, see Shaw, *The British Political Elite*, pp. 114-127.

17. Geoffrey Roberts: *The Soviet Union and the Origins of the Second World War: Russo-German Relations and the Road to War, 1933–1941* (New York: Macmillan, 1995), pp. 62-91, and *Stalin's Wars: From World War to Cold War, 1939–1953* (New Haven: Yale University Press, 2006), pp. 30-43; Gorodetsky, *The Grand Delusion*, pp. 7-9.

18. Adam Tooze, *The Wages of Destruction: The Breaking and Making of the Nazi Economy* (London: Viking, 2006), pp. 319-321.

19. Angelo Tasca, *Deux ans d'alliance germano-soviétique, août 1939-juin 1941* (Paris: Fayard, 1949), p. 123.

20. Although officially neutral, Finland had since 1930 developed a covert military alliance with Estonia that included plans and exercises for a joint blockade of the Gulf of Finland. See Jari Leskinen, *Vaiettu Suomen Silta: Suomen ja Viron salainen sotilaallinen yhteistoiminta Neuvosoliiton varalta vuosina 1930–1939* [The silenced bridge of Finland: Secret military cooperation between Finland and Estonia against the Soviet Union, 1930-1939] (Helsinki: Suomen Historiallinen Seura, 1997), with an English summary of his argument on pp. 450-459.

21. The general view of an aggressive Soviet attack is nuanced by Stephen

Kotkin, *Stalin*, vol. 2: *Waiting for Hitler, 1929–1941* (London: Allen Lane, 2017), pp. 706–729; see also Zara Steiner, *The Triumph of the Dark: Interwar International History, 1933–1939* (New York: Oxford University Press, 2011), p. 938.

22. HIA, Herbert Hoover Papers (HH), Box 90, Folder 1, "The Crusade against Famine in World War II," pp. 38–39. U.S. food aid to Finland would have to cross the Anglo-French blockade of the European continent, however. American conservatives' support for a small people fighting communism shows that the supposed "neutralists" of the 1930s could turn very quickly into active interventionists. It also prefigured later campaigns to help anti-Communists fighting the USSR—an arc from Mannerheim's Finns in 1939 to the Afghan *mujahideen* in 1979.

23. *Report to American Donors, December 1939–July 1940* (New York: Finnish Relief Fund, 1940).

24. The Roosevelt administration used the Export-Import Bank to grant loans to the Finns because a Congress-approved credit was deemed unacceptable to the neutralist opposition. Richard H. Sherman, "Development of Export-Import Bank Loan Policy to 1944" (PhD diss., University of Wisconsin–Madison, 1957), p. 113.

25. "Finland and Russia," *Manchester Guardian*, 13 December 1939, p. 6.

26. This was a controversial decision since of the sixteen Council members, two were absent (Iran and Peru); three abstained (China, Greece, and Yugoslavia); and two were parties to the dispute and thus could not vote (Finland and the Soviet Union). Moreover, three members (South Africa, Egypt, and Bolivia) had entered the body only the previous day, on the instigation of London and Paris.

27. It is important to note that as founding members of the Genevan organization, neither Japan in 1931 nor Italy in 1935 was expelled from the League directly for aggressive war. Leo Gross, "Was the Soviet Union Expelled from the League of Nations?" *American Journal of International Law* 39, no. 1 (January 1945): 35–44.

28. HIA, SHP, Box 369, Folder "Sanctions," Tel. 2985, Ambassador William Bullitt (Paris) to Secretary of State Cordell Hull, 16 December 1939.

29. SHD, 2 N 237, Delanda (Minister of War) to CSDN, "Au sujet des renseignements sur la situation en Allemagne," 21 December 1939; Medlicott, *The Economic Blockade*, 1:45.

30. François Bédarida, *La Stratégie secrète de la drôle de guerre: Le Conseil suprême interallié, septembre 1939–avril 1940* (Paris: Éditions du CNRS, 1979); John C. Cairns, "Reflections on France, Britain and the Winter War Prodrome, 1939–1940," *Historical Reflections / Réflexions Historiques* 22, no. 1 (Winter 1996): 211–234; David Edgerton, "Controlling Resources: Coal, Iron Ore and Oil in the Second World War," in Geyer and Tooze, *The Cambridge History of the Second World War,* 3:133, 139.

31. Charles O. Richardson, "French Plans for Allied Attacks on the Caucasus Oil Fields, January–April 1940," *French Historical Studies* 8, no. 1 (1973):

130–156; Patrick Osborn, *Operation Pike: Britain versus the Soviet Union, 1939–1941* (Santa Barbara, CA: Praeger, 2000). Charles de Gaulle later criticized these actions as needless distractions from confronting the Nazi threat. "Certain circles took Stalin for the enemy, not Hitler. They were more concerned about striking at Russia either by coming to the aid of Finland, or by bombing Baku, or by landing in Istanbul rather than with the question of how Germany could be defeated" (*Mémoires de guerre*, vol 1: *L'Appel, 1940–1942* [Paris: Librairie Plon, 1954], p. 26).

32. Annie Lacroix-Riz, *Le choix de la défaite: Les élites françaises dans les années 1930* (Paris: Armand Collin, 2010).

33. Despite the centrality of Swedish ore to the Nazi war economy, it is not evident that stronger pressure on Stockholm or World War I–style export rationing would have had a decisive effect on industrial production in the Third Reich. See Alan S. Milward: "Could Sweden Have Stopped the Second World War?" *Scandinavian Economic History Review* 15, no. 1 (January 1967): 127–138, and *War, Economy and Society, 1939–1945*, pp. 309–310.

34. John Morton Blum, *From the Morgenthau Diaries*, vol. 2: *Years of Urgency, 1938–1941* (Boston: Houghton Mifflin, 1965), p. 134.

35. TNA, CAB 47/1, Minutes of twenty-fourth meeting, 11 June 1937, p. 7.

36. TNA, CAB 47/5 ATB 197, "Handbook of Economic Warfare," 24 July 1939.

37. Medlicott, *The Economic Blockade*, 1:1.

38. Fredric Sondern, "Contraband Control: Britain's Ministry of Economic Warfare Seeks a Death Grip on Germany's Trade," *Time* 15 January 1940, p. 44.

39. Paul Einzig, *Economic Warfare, 1939–1940* (London: Macmillan, 1941), p. 20.

40. BL, RCP Add MS 51140, W. Arnold-Forster, "Rationing Neutrals in the Blockade," 3 December 1939, f. 122.

41. BL, RCP Add MS 51088, Lord Cecil to Minister of Economic Warfare Ronald H. Cross, 11 January 1940, f. 114.

42. Germany's stocks of monetary reserves and raw materials were in fact far lower than many British and French analysts imagined, and the Reich underwent an enormous import squeeze in the first months of the war. Tooze, *The Wages of Destruction*, pp. 332–335.

43. Medlicott, *The Economic Blockade*, 1:133–138.

44. National Academy of Sciences, *Managing Materials for a Twenty-First-Century Military* (Washington, DC: National Academies Press, 2008), p. 134.

45. Stephen Wertheim, *Tomorrow, the World: The Birth of U.S. Global Supremacy* (Cambridge, MA: Harvard University Press, 2020), pp. 47–62.

46. Alan Milward was right to argue that in the short run "the conquest of territory was a highly effective riposte to economic blockade" (*War, Economy and Society, 1939–1945*, pp. 312, 317); the best overview of initial German responses to the blockade is Rolf-Dieter Müller, "The Mobilization

of the German Economy for Hitler's War Aims," in Bernhard R. Kroener, Rolf-Dieter Müller, and Hans Umbreit, *Germany and the Second World War,* vol. 5: *Organization and Mobilization of the German Sphere of Power,* part 1: *Wartime Administration, Economy, and Manpower Resources, 1939–1941* (Oxford: Clarendon Press, 2000), pp. 457–473.

47. On Iberian-German economic relations, see Herbert Feis, *The Spanish Story: Franco and the Nations at War* (New York: Alfred A. Knopf, 1948), and Christian Leitz, *Economic Relations between Nazi Germany and Franco's Spain, 1936–1945* (Oxford: Oxford University Press, 1996). On economic warfare in the Iberian Peninsula, see Donald G. Stevens, "World War II Economic Warfare: The United States, Britain, and Portuguese Wolfram," *The Historian* 61, no. 3 (Spring 1999): 539–555; Antonío Louca, *Nazigold für Portugal: Hitler und Salazar* (Vienna: Holzhausen, 2002); Hugh Rockoff and Leonard Caruana, "A Wolfram in Sheep's Clothing: Economic Warfare in Spain and Portugal, 1940–1944," *Journal of Economic History* 63, no. 1 (2003): pp. 100–126; on resource diplomacy with Turkey, see Murat Önsoy, "The World War Two Allied Economic Warfare: The Case of Turkish Chrome Sales" (PhD diss., Friedrich-Alexander-Universität, Nuremberg, 2009).

48. Leonard Caruana and Hugh Rockoff, "An Elephant in the Garden: The Allies, Spain, and Oil in World War II," *European Review of Economic History* 11, no. 2 (August 2007): 159–187.

49. Archivo de Ministerio de Asuntos Exteriores, 2246 E. 75; cited in Caruana and Rockoff, "An Elephant in the Garden," pp. 168–169.

50. Alan P. Dobson, *US Economic Statecraft for Survival, 1933–1991: Of Sanctions, Embargoes and Economic Warfare* (New York: Routledge, 2002), pp. 37–39; Medlicott, *The Economic Blockade,* 1:476–477.

51. John H. Crider, "Ban Affects Japan. U.S. Supply of Materials in Her War on China Can Be Cut Off. Oil to Spain Stopped," *New York Times,* 26 July 1940, pp. 1, 7.

52. Not everything about this policy was immediately clear; newspapers and businessmen were surprised that U.S. tankers continued to supply the Soviets with oil on the California-Vladivostok route, even as fuel supplies to Spain and Japan were being stopped. "Use of U.S. Tanker Granted Russians: Maritime Board Approves Chartering, after Denials to Spain and Japan. Export Ban Proclaimed," *New York Times,* 27 July 1940, p. 2.

53. For example, the "moral" (i.e., voluntarily privately imposed) embargoes on deliveries of aircraft in July 1938 and on aluminum, magnesium, molybdenum, and aviation fuel refining knowledge in December 1939.

54. Stanley G. Payne, *Franco and Hitler: Spain, Germany and World War II* (New Haven: Yale University Press, 2008), pp. 61–145, 243–248.

55. Blum, *From the Morgenthau Diaries,* 2:358–359.

56. Akira Iriye, *The Origins of the Second World War in Asia and the Pacific* (Abingdon: Routledge, 1987), ch. 5; Saburo Ienaga, *The Pacific War, 1931–1945: World War II and the Japanese* (New York: Pantheon, 1978), pp. 131–150.

57. League of Nations, *Statistical Year-Book of the League of Nations, 1940–1941* (Geneva: League of Nations, 1941), p. 128; Anand Toprani, *Oil and the Great Powers: Britain and Germany, 1914–1945* (Oxford: Oxford University Press, 2019), p. 13.

58. Alexander Igolkin, "The Sakhalin Anomaly," *Oil of Russia*, no. 1, 2004.

59. S. C. M. Paine, *The Wars for Asia, 1911–1949* (Cambridge: Cambridge University Press, 2006), p. 146.

60. L. de Jong, *Het Koninkrijk der Nederlanden in de Tweede Wereldoorlog 1939–1945, Deel 11a Nederlands-Indië I: Tweede Helft* (Leiden: Martinus Nijhoff, 1984), pp. 695–696.

61. Harry Bernstein, "Mexico's War with Japan," *Far Eastern Survey* 11, no. 24 (November 1942): 246.

62. Medlicott, *The Economic Blockade*, 1:416–419, 474.

63. "Bombing and Blockade," *The Economist* 139, no. 5070 (26 October 1940): 512.

64. Richard William Barnes Clarke, *Britain's Blockade* (Oxford: Clarendon Press, 1940).

65. Richard Overy, *The Bombing War: Europe, 1939–1945* (London: Penguin, 2013), pp. 225–226.

66. The best general work on this conjuncture remains the global history by Andreas Hillgruber, *Hitlers Strategie: Politik und Kriegführung 1940–1941* (Bonn: Bernard und Graefe Verlag, 1965), on which this chapter relies.

67. "Weisung Nr 21. Fall Barbarossa vom 18. 12. 1940," in Gerd R. Überschar and Wolfram Wette, eds., *"Unternehmen Barbarossa": Der deutsche Überfall auf die Sowjetunion 1941: Berichte, Analysen, Dokumente* (Paderborn: Schöningh, 1984), pp. 298–300.

68. Blum, *From the Morgenthau Diaries*, 2:364–365.

69. LOC, ASP, F. P. Walters to Arthur Sweetser, 20 December 1940, pp. 1–2.

70. Adam Tooze and James R. Martin, "The Economics of the War with Nazi Germany," in Geyer and Tooze, *The Cambridge History of the Second World War*, 3:42.

71. Peter Jackson, *Beyond the Balance of Power: France and the Politics of National Security in the Era of the First World War* (Cambridge: Cambridge University Press, 2013), p. 102, notes that Lend-Lease would have been inconceivable in 1916–1917; the argument here is that the intervening decades of discussion about organized international aid to the victims of aggression *did* make Lend-Lease conceivable by late 1940. For Monnet's use of the phrase "arsenal of democracy," see Jean Monnet, *Memoirs* (London: Collins, 1978), p. 160.

72. Rana Mitter, *Forgotten Ally: China's World War II, 1937–1945* (New York: First Mariner Books, 2014), p. 235.

73. Craig Stockings and Eleanor Hancock, *Swastika over the Acropolis: Reinterpreting the Nazi Invasion of Greece in World War II* (Leiden: Brill, 2013), p. 60.

74. Hoover, *Addresses upon the American Road*, vol. 3: *1940–1941* (New York: C. Scribner's Sons, 1941), p. 57.

75. Susan Dunn, *Blueprint for War: FDR and the Hundred Days That Mobilized America* (New Haven: Yale University Press, 2018), p. 165.

76. Indeed, Britain was as of January 1941 already in far-reaching military collaboration with the Greek Army. Stockings and Hancock, *Swastika over the Acropolis*, pp. 49–56.

77. Arthur D. Gayer, *The Problem of Lend-Lease: Its Nature, Implications, and Settlement* (New York: Council on Foreign Relations, 1944), p. 2.

78. The political scientist Benjamin Williams was pellucid about the dual structure of the economic weapon: "The purposes of the negative sanctions were to shut off American materials and dollars from the aggressor nations. . . . The purpose of the positive sanctions was to give the victims and opponents of aggression easier access to American materials" ("The Coming of Economic Sanctions into American Practice," *American Journal of International Law* 37, no. 3 [July 1943]: 394, 387–388).

79. U.S. Senate, *To Promote the Defense of the United States: Hearings before the Committee on Foreign Relations*, Seventy-Seventh Congress: First Session on S.275 (Washington DC: GPO, 1941), p. 831; "U.S. Weighs Economic Weapons in Aid-Britain Plan; Still Held in Reserve, They May Yet Bring Strong Pressure on the Axis. Impounding of German, Italian and Japanese Funds Suggested," *New York Times*, 12 January 1941, p. 3.

80. William Hardy, *America, Britain, and Russia: Their Co-operation and Conflict, 1941–1946* (New York: Oxford University Press, 1953), p. 778. The links between Lend-Lease and Article 16 were evident to critics such as international jurist Edwin Borchard, who called Lend-Lease "a direct brainchild of the jaundiced philosophy of Article 16 of the League of Nations Covenant, which implied that the good countries would in common deliberation choose the 'aggressor,' i.e. any nation in revolt against the status quo, and then combine to starve, suppress and if necessary exterminate such 'aggressor.' . . . There has been a tendency in this country for some years to assume the sole management of the policy of selecting and then suppressing aggressors. This was strongly manifest in the desire to chastise Japan in 1931 and to impose sanctions on Italy in 1935. It reaches its apotheosis in this bill" (Borchard in U.S. Senate, *To Promote the Defense of the United States*, pp. 653–654).

81. Dunn, *Blueprint for War*, p. 168.

82. Between 1931 and 1935 Yugoslavia sold four times as much to Italy as it had to Britain and France; under the sanctions its trade with Italy fell by two-thirds, a wrenching adjustment for the Balkan state. Giuseppe Parenti, "L'efficacia delle 'controsanzioni' italiane," *Rivista Internationale di Scienze Sociali* 44, no. 7 (July 1936): 360; Perica Hadži-Jovančić, *The Third Reich and Yugoslavia: An Economy of Fear, 1933–1941* (London: Bloomsbury, 2020), pp. 97–100.

83. J. B. Hoptner, *Yugoslavia in Crisis, 1934–1941* (New York: Columbia University Press, 1962), p. 235.

84. David A. T. Stafford, "SOE and British Involvement in the Belgrade Coup d'État of March 1941," *Slavic Review* 36, no. 3 (September 1977): 399–419. Edward Stettinius noted that Lend-Lease deliveries had arrived too late to help "the Yugoslav people [who] overthrew the[ir] Government" (*Lend-Lease: Weapon for Victory* [New York: Macmillan, 1944], 91).

85. LON, ASP, Box 120, Letter from J. M. Keynes to A. E. Felkin, 29 October 1924, p. 2.

86. J. M. Keynes, *How to Pay for the War: A Radical Plan for the Chancellor of the Exchequer* (New York: Harcourt, Brace, 1940), pp. 82–86.

87. Blum, *From the Morgenthau Diaries*, 2:248.

88. Lend-Lease was passed in no small part due to the proselytizing efforts of Wendell Wilkie, Roosevelt's erstwhile Republican opponent for the presidency in 1940, on whose campaign team Raymond Buell had worked as a foreign affairs adviser. Wertheim, *Tomorrow, the World*, p. 120.

89. Donald Cameron Watt, "Every War Must End: Wartime Planning for Postwar Security in Britain and America in the Wars of 1914–1918 and 1939–1945: The Role of Historical Example and of Professional Historians," *Transactions of the Royal Historical Society* 28 (1978): 159–173; Mark Mazower, *No Enchanted Palace: The End of Empire and the Ideological Origins of the United Nations* (Princeton, NJ: Princeton University Press, 2009), pp. 14–18.

90. LOC, ASP, Box 30, Letter from Arthur Sweetser to R. L. Buell, 9 April 1941. This referred to Clarence Streit's book *Union Now with Britain* (New York: Harper and Brothers, 1941); Wertheim, *Tomorrow, the World*, p. 94.

91. LOC, ASP Box 30, Letter from Arthur Sweetser to Cecil, 1 July 1941, p. 3.

92. LOC, ASP Box 30, Letter from Arthur Sweetser to Cecil, 9 May 1941, pp. 1, 2.

93. Jürgen Förster, "Hitler's Decision in Favour of War against the Soviet Union," in *Germany and the Second World War*, vol. 4: *The Attack on the Soviet Union*, ed. Horst Boog, Jürgen Förster, Joachim Hoffmann, Ernst Klink, Rolf-Dieter Müller, and Gerd R. Ueberschär, pp. 13–51 (Oxford: Clarendon Press, 1998).

94. "Freezing of German and Italian Assets in the United States," 14 June 1941, in *Department of State Bulletin* (Washington, DC: GPO, 1941), 4:718.

95. V. Muthesius, *Autarchia Europea* (Rome: Quaderni di politica e di economia contemporanea no. 18, 1940), p. 11.

96. BA-BL, R 3601/2360 RWM memorandum, "Die ernährungswirtschaftliche Blockadefestigkeit Deutschlands und Kontinentaleuropas," November–December 1940; on the crucial conjuncture, see Hillgruber, *Hitlers Strategie*, pp. 352–377; Tooze, *The Wages of Destruction*, pp. 411–420; Toprani, *Oil and the Great Powers*, pp. 199–230; Edgerton, "Controlling Resources," p. 131.

97. Trial of the Major War Criminals before the International Military Tribunal (IMT), vol. 36, Document EC-126, "Wirtschaftspolitische Richt-

linien für Wirtschaftsorganisation Ost, Gruppe Landwirtschaft," 23 May 1941, p. 145.

98. Alex J. Kay, *Exploitation, Resettlement, Mass Murder: Political and Economic Planning for German Occupation Policy in the Soviet Union, 1940–1941* (New York: Berghahn Books, 2006), pp. 39–40; Kim Priemel, "Scorched Earth, Plunder, and Massive Mobilization: The German Occupation of Ukraine and the Soviet War Economy," in *The Consequences of Nazi Hegemony for Europe*, ed. Jonas Schermer and Eugene White, pp. 389–426 (Cambridge: Cambridge University Press, 2016).

99. BA-MA, OKW/WiAmt/Z1/II Nr. 6250/42 geh., "Auszug aus den Arbeitsrichtlinien des Reichsministers für die besetzten Ostgebiete für die Zivilverwaltung," 1 September 1942; see also pamphlets such as *Deutschland blockadefest, Europa blockadefest* (Gauschulungsamt der NSDAP, 1942), and the memoranda by Theodor Oberländer, collected in *Der Osten und die deutsche Wehrmacht: 6 Denkschriften aus dem Zweiten Weltkrieg über die Behandlung der Sowjetvölker* (Ingolstadt: Mut Verlag, 1984), pp. 43, 48; Götz Aly and Susanne Heim, *Vordenker der Vernichtung: Auschwitz und die deutsche Pläne für eine neue europäische Ordnung* (Hamburg: Fischer, 1991), pp. 234–282; Ulrich Herbert, *Geschichte Deutschlands im 20. Jahrhundert* (Munich: C. H. Beck, 2015), p. 434.

100. Blum, *From the Morgenthau Diaries*, 2:256–259, 262.

101. Stettinius, *Lend-Lease*, pp. 121–124.

102. William L. Langer and S. Everett Gleason, *The Undeclared War, 1940–1941* (New York: Harper and Brothers, 1953), p. 558.

103. "War of the factories" was a phrase used by the ordoliberal German economist Volkmar Muthesius, *Der Krieg der Fabriken* (Berlin: Im Deutschen Verlag, 1941). See also Jeffrey Fear, "War of the Factories," in Geyer and Tooze, *The Cambridge History of the Second World War*, pp. 94–121; for a contemporary application in the study of Nazi and Soviet wartime production, see Stefan J. Link, *Forging Global Fordism: Nazi Germany, Soviet Russia, and the Contest over the Industrial Order* (Princeton, NJ: Princeton University Press, 2020), pp. 172–206.

104. Michael Barnhart, *Japan Prepares for Total War: The Search for Economic Security, 1919–1941* (Ithaca, NY: Cornell University Press, 1988), p. 215.

105. M. Wilson, *Destructive Creation*, p. 61.

106. David Reynolds believes that avoiding war remained the core objective of the Roosevelt administration, summarizing its overall posture as a "deterrent policy of oil sanctions and reinforcement of the Philippines, backed by a readiness to keep talking to gain time" (*From Munich to Pearl Harbor: Roosevelt's America and the Origins of the Second World War* [Chicago: Ivan R. Dee, 2001], pp. 139–144, 143). By contrast, Marc Trachtenberg has contended that the United States pursued an aggressive rollback policy, willingly risking war through intensifying sanctions while rejecting a Pacific settlement with Tokyo in the Hull-Nomura talks (*The Craft of International*

History: A Guide to Method [Princeton, NJ: Princeton University Press, 2006], pp. 79-139). What both sides in this debate agree on, however, is that the ratcheting up of economic sanctions in the second half of 1941, whether it was de facto or de jure, and intentionally pursued on Roosevelt's part or secretly arranged by his advisers behind his back, had the effect of pushing Japan to a decision for war.

107. Hornbeck's first memorandum advocating economic sanctions went back to December 1931, but in the context of the Sino-Japanese War he had supported American pressure since at least the end of 1938. See HIA, SHP, Box 369, Folder "Sanctions #1," Telegram from Hornbeck to Mr. Sayre, 22 December 1938, p. 1.

108. Joseph C. Grew, *Turbulent Era: A Diplomatic Record of Forty Years, 1904-1945* (Boston: Houghton Mifflin, 1952), 2:1279-1280.

109. William Diebold Jr., "Japan's Vulnerability to American Sanctions," *Studies of American Interests in the War and the Peace* (New York: Council on Foreign Relations), 23 November 1940, p. 3.

110. "The Congress Is Asked for an Oil Pipeline to Supply Middle Atlantic Refineries with Crude Oil, May 20, 1941," in *Public Papers of the Presidents of the United States: Franklin D. Roosevelt: 1941* (New York: Harper, 1950), 10:173-174; David Edgerton, *Britain's War Machine: Weapons, Resources and Experts in the Second World War* (Oxford: Oxford University Press, 2011), pp. 184, 188.

111. Stephen J. Randall, "Harold Ickes and United States Foreign Petroleum Planning, 1939-1945," *Business History Review* 57, no. 3 (Autumn 1983): 367-387.

112. Joan Maria Thomàs, *Roosevelt and Franco during the Second World War: From the Spanish Civil War to Pearl Harbor* (New York: Palgrave Macmillan, 2008), pp. 169-170.

113. *Pearl Harbor Attack: Hearings before the Joint Committee on the Investigation of the Pearl Harbor Attack, Seventy-Ninth Congress*, part 5 (Washington, DC: GPO, 1946), p. 2114.

114. Jonathan G. Utley, *Going to War with Japan, 1937-1941* (New York: Fordham University Press, 1985), pp. 153-156; Edward S. Miller, *Bankrupting the Enemy: The U.S. Financial Siege of Japan before Pearl Harbor* (Annapolis, MD: Naval Institute Press, 2007); Roland H. Worth, *No Choice but War: The United States Embargo against Japan and the Eruption of War in the Pacific* (Jefferson, NC: McFarland, 1995).

115. Harold Ickes, *The Secret Diary of Harold L. Ickes*, vol. 3: *The Lowering Clouds, 1939-1941* (New York: Simon and Schuster, 1965), p. 588.

116. Barnhart, *Japan Prepares for Total War*, p. 231; Blum, *From the Morgenthau Diaries*, 2:378-380; Reynolds, *From Munich to Pearl Harbor*, pp. 150-151. My thanks to Noriko Kawamura for driving this point home.

117. Akira Hara, "Japan: Guns before Rice," in *The Economics of World War II: Six Great Powers in International Comparison*, ed. Mark Harrison, p. 240 (Cambridge: Cambridge University Press, 1998).

118. Cited in Noriko Kawamura, "Emperor Hirohito and Japan's Decision to Go to War with the United States: Reexamined," *Diplomatic History* 31, no. 1 (2007): 60.

119. Robert J. C. Butow, *Tojo and the Coming of the War* (Stanford, CA: Stanford University Press, 1969), p. 314.

120. Weeks, *Russia's Life-Saver*, p. 141, table 1.1.

121. "Führerhauptquartier, 9.17 Abends und in der Nacht zum 9.1941," in Werner Jöchmann, ed., *Monologe im Führerhauptquartier 1941–1944: Aufgezeichnet von Heinrich Heims* (Munich: Albrecht Knaus, 1980), p. 46.

122. "Führerhauptquartier, 25.9.1941, Abends," in Jöchmann, *Monologe im Führerhauptquartier*, p. 53.

123. Jöchmann, *Monologe im Führerhauptquartier*, p. 24. Hitler added: "The Four-Year Plan hit the English like nothing before because they felt the [German] state is no longer vulnerable to blockade [*Blockadeschwach*]; they would have offered me a loan if that would have made me discard the Plan."

124. This is compellingly argued based on Russian-language sources in Boris V. Sokolov, "The Role of Lend-Lease in Soviet Military Efforts, 1941–1945," *Journal of Slavic Military Studies* 7, no. 3 (September 1994): 567–586, and Alexander Hill, "British Lend-Lease Aid and the Soviet War Effort, June 1941–June 1942," *Journal of Military History* 71, no. 3 (July 2007): 773–808; M. Harrison, *Soviet Planning for Peace and War*, pp. 257–262.

125. Chargé in Finland (McClintock) to Secretary of State, 20 February 1943, Document 163, in FRUS, 1943, vol. 3: *The British Commonwealth, Eastern Europe, the Far East* (Washington, DC: GPO, 1963), p. 240.

126. Weeks, *Russia's Life-Saver*, p. 141, table 1.1.

127. A point made well by Mark Edele, "Who Won the Second World War and Why Should You Care? Reassessing Stalin's War 75 Years after Victory," *Journal of Strategic Studies* 43, nos. 6–7 (2020): 1039–1062.

128. HIA, SHP, Box 369, Folder "Sanctions #2," Memorandum by Hornbeck, "Withdrawal of Americans from Far East," 2 October 1941, pp. 1–2. The term *juramentado* referred to attacks by Moro swordsmen against Spanish and U.S. colonial forces in the Philippines.

129. Winston S. Churchill to Franklin D. Roosevelt, 5 November 1941; in Martin Gilbert, ed., *The Churchill War Papers*, vol. 3: *The Ever-Widening War, 1941* (New York: W. W. Norton, 2000), p. 1412.

130. Jeffrey Record, *A War Which It Was Always Going to Lose* (Washington, DC: Potomac Books, 2011), ch. 1.

131. Willem Remmelink, ed., *The Invasion of the Dutch East Indies (Compiled by the War History Office of the National Defence College of Japan)* (Leiden: Leiden University Press, 2015), pp. xxxi, 1–2, 4.

132. IMT, vol. 35, Document 423-D, "Aufzeichnung über das Gespräch des Führers mit Botschafter Oshima am 3. Januar 1942 im Beisein des Reichsaußenministers in der Wolfsschanze," pp. 101, 102.

133. David L. Roll, *The Hopkins Touch: Harry Hopkins and the Forging of the Alliance to Defeat Hitler* (London: Oxford University Press, 2013), pp. 172–175.

134. Gayer, *The Problem of Lend-Lease*, p. 5; Koistinen, *Arsenal of World War II*, p. 266.

135. *A Brief Historical Statement of the Office of Economic Warfare, Office of Lend-Lease Administration, Government Corporations, Office of Foreign Economic Co-ordination, Office of Foreign Relief and Rehabilitation Administrations, with Exhibits* (Washington, DC: United States Foreign Economic Administration, 1944), p. 7.

136. *The Office of Exports: Purpose and Organization*, 7 December 1942 (Washington, DC: Board of Economic Warfare, 1942), p. 5.

137. "Board of Economic Warfare," in *United States Government Manual, Summer 1943* (Washington, DC: Office of War Information, 1943), p. 133.

138. Henry Wallace, *The Price of Free World Victory*, address before the Free World Association, New York City, 8 May 1942 (Washington, DC: GPO, 1942), p. 2.

139. Cited in Donald G. Stevens, "Organizing for Economic Defense: Henry Wallace and the Board of Economic Warfare's Foreign Policy Initiatives, 1942," *Presidential Studies Quarterly* 26, no. 4, Intricacies of U.S. Foreign Policy (Fall 1996): 1126–1139.

140. Wallace, *The Price of Free World Victory*, p. 3.

141. LOC, ASP, Box 30, Letter from Cecil to Sweetser, 23 November 1942.

142. HIA, NCFSD, Box 27, Folder 32, "What Must Be Done to Start Relief," 3 May 1943, p. 2.

143. Jessica Reinisch, "Internationalism in Relief: The Birth of UNRRA," *Past and Present* 210, no. 1 (2011): 258–289.

144. Norman Angell expressed this absolutist view with characteristic force: "There never has been and there never will be a body of law, a status quo, which all those living under it regard as completely just. It was the truth which we ignored after the last peace, and which helped to wreck it. We could not, we said, help China to defend herself in 1931 because there might be something to be said for Japan, confronting a continent racked with disorder; nor the Ethiopians in 1935 because they had failed to abolish slavery and ate raw meat; nor, later, the Spanish Government against Nazi-Fascist invasion because some loyalists burned down churches; nor co-operate with Russia for mutual defense because she was Communist or 'godless'" (cited in "Divergent Views in United Nations Handicap to Peace," *New York Times*, 17 January 1943).

145. Cited in "Adoption of Policy on Sanctions Urged. Dr. Leith of WPB Calls for Step to Deal with Aggressors in Testing Society Talk," *New York Times*, 29 June 1944.

146. "The decline in the weight of foreign trade is due, for the most part, to the conspicuous cleavage of the world commercially. Blockade and counter-blockade measures led to the segregation of three main areas having no communication with one another except through those tiny rivulets of trade which a few neutrals were still allowed to carry on outside their respective geographical blocs. The central points of attraction and radiation

in these blocs have been Germany for Continental Europe, Japan for the Far East, and the United States for Latin America and (through the mechanism of lend-lease) for the United Nations as a whole" (Bank for International Settlements, *Fourteenth Annual Report: 1st April 1943–31st March 1944* [Basel: BIS, 1944], p. 46).

147. Mark Harrison, "The Soviet Union: The Defeated Victor," in Harrison, *The Economics of World War II*, p. 292.

148. The commitment to collective security evinced by both the Soviets and the Chinese should stand as a refutation of Western-centric accounts of the formation of the United Nations that misleadingly portray the Moscow Conference of foreign ministers in October 1943 as one in which Hull and Eden "convinced their Soviet and Chinese counterparts to support a future collective security organization," as one recent book puts it (W. Nester, *Globalization, War, and Peace in the Twenty-First Century* [New York: Palgrave Macmillan, 2010], p. 132).

149. *The Future International Authority: Draft Pact with Commentary* (London: Executive Committee of the League of Nations Union, 1944).

150. "This country would be willing to do far more on a straight security basis than on the other and broader phases of international cooperation" (LOC ASP, Box 30, Letter from Sweetser to Cecil, 8 February 1944).

151. BL, RCP MS Add 51086, Letter from Cecil to James Gascoyne-Cecil, 4th Marquess of Salisbury, 3 September 1942.

152. House of Lords Debate of 9 May 1944, in *Hansard*, vol. 131, pp. 640–641, 644.

153. LOC, ASP, Box 30, Letter from Cecil to Sweetser, 23 February 1944, p. 2.

154. Memorandum C. Security. The Military Aspect of Any Post-War Security Organisation, in "Tentative Proposals by the United Kingdom for a General International Organization," 22 July 1944, in FRUS, 1944, General (Washington, DC: GPO, 1948), 1:686.

155. "United States Tentative Proposals for a General International Organization, July 18, 1944," in FRUS, 1944, 1:654.

156. See Cordell Hull, *The Memoirs of Cordell Hull* (New York: Macmillan, 1948), 2:1602–1609; Memorandum by the Executive Committee on Foreign Economic Policy, 14 August 1944, in FRUS, 1944, 1:285–286.

157. Lori Fisler Damrosch, "Collective Economic Sanctions: Nonforcible Responses to Threats to Peace," in *The Dumbarton Oaks Conversations and the United Nations, 1944–1994,* ed. Ernest May and Angeliki E. Laiou, pp. 61–70, esp. pp. 63–67 (Washington, DC: Dumbarton Oaks Research Library and Collection, 1998).

158. "Memorandum on an International Security Organization, by the Soviet Union," 12 August 1944, Document 415 in FRUS, 1944, 1:710–711.

159. "Article 41 of the [UN] Charter again gave the 'easy' route of economic and financial sanctions a respectable place in the United Nations' arsenal, but only as a part of a sweeping plan of response to the problem of preserv-

ing peace" (Rita and Howard J. Taubenfeld, "'The Economic Weapon': The League and the United Nations," *Proceedings of the American Society of International Law* 58 [1964]: 186).

160. The thirteen others had been those countries that had agreed to declare war on Germany by the end of February 1945, as Churchill, Stalin, and Roosevelt had requested at Yalta; this allowed countries such as Argentina, Egypt, and Turkey to attend but excluded neutrals like Ireland, Portugal, Spain, and Switzerland. G. Roberts, *Stalin's Wars*, p. 240.

161. Memorandum by French Ministry of Foreign Affairs, 21 March 1945, in *The United Nations Conference on International Organization* (Washington, DC: GPO, 1946), p. 380.

162. MAE, Série SDN, Box No. 817, Art. 16, Memorandum "Éléménts pour M. Massigli," 8 July 1935, pp. 1–3.

163. Roosevelt's desire to obtain a sixth permanent seat for Brazil failed. Hilderbrand, *Dumbarton Oaks*, pp. 122–125; Andrew Williams, "France and the Origins of the United Nations, 1944–1945: 'Si la France ne compte plus, qu'on nous le dise,' *Diplomacy and Statecraft* 28, no. 2 (2017): 215–234.

164. Lord Strabolgi in House of Lords Debate of 9 May 1944, in *Hansard*, vol. 131, p. 655.

165. Brooke L. Blower notes how compared to the League Covenant, the UN Charter was "far more hostile to neutral powers" ("From Isolationism to Neutrality: A New Framework for Understanding American Political Culture, 1919–1941," *Diplomatic History* 38, no. 2 [2014]: 367n43). See also Jürg Martin Gabriel, *The American Conception of Neutrality after 1941* (New York: St. Martin's Press, 1988).

166. Medlicott, *The Economic Blockade*, 1:3.

167. Edwin Borchard, "The Impracticability of 'Enforcing' Peace through 'Sanctions,'" editorial comment, *Yale Law Journal* 55, no. 5 (1946): 971–972.

168. As Alan Milward wrote, "The power which had most sustained the international law of neutrality in the past now became its most virulent enemy" (*War, Economy and Society, 1939–1945*, p. 306).

169. Mazower, *No Enchanted Palace*, p. 198.

170. David L. Gordon and Royden Dangerfield, *The Hidden Weapon: The Story of Economic Warfare* (New York: Harper and Brothers, 1947), pp. 228–229.

Conclusion: From Antidote to Alternative

1. Atticus, "The Economic Weapon and Imperial Unity," *The New Europe: "Pour la victoire intégrale"* 6, no. 73 (7 March 1918): 226.

2. A good overview is Lance E. Davis and Stanley L. Engerman, *Naval Blockades in Peace and War: An Economic History since 1750* (New York: Cambridge University Press, 2006), pp. 383–415.

3. Christian Lange, "An American Discussion of International Sanctions," *New Commonwealth*, April 1933, p. 4.

4. Helena Swanwick, *Collective Insecurity* (London: Jonathan Cape, 1937), p. 216.

5. Lisa L. Martin, *Coercive Cooperation: Explaining Multilateral Economic Sanctions* (Princeton, NJ: Princeton University Press, 1992).

6. Joy Gordon, *Invisible War: The United States and the Iraq Sanctions* (Cambridge, MA: Harvard University Press, 2010).

7. Idriss Jazairy, "Un tiers de la population mondiale habite dans des pays touchés par des sanctions, affirme un expert de l'ONU," September 2015; available at http://www.unmultimedia.org/radio/french/2015/09/un-tiers-de-la -population-mondiale-habite-dans-des-pays-touches-par-des-sanctions -affirme-un-expert-de-lonu/. Accessed 20 February 2018.

8. For an overview of trends in 729 multilateral and bilateral sanctions cases between 1950 and 2016, see Gabriel Felbermayr et al., "The Global Sanctions Database," *European Economic Review* 129 (October 2020): 1–23, article 103561.

9. Albert O. Hirschman, *National Power and the Structure of Foreign Trade* (Berkeley: University of California Press, 1945), p. 81.

10. Alan S. Milward, "Economic Warfare in Historical Perspective," in *East-West Trade and the Cold War*, ed. Jari Eloranta and Jari Ojala, p. 201 (Jyväskylä: University of Jyväskylä, 2005).

11. Michael Mastanduno, *Economic Containment: CoCom and the Politics of East-West Trade* (Ithaca, NY: Cornell University Press, 1992).

12. A search for active OFAC sanctions using the Sanctions Explorer by C4ADS yields 16,726 individuals and organizations; available at https://sanctions explorer.org/search. Accessed 12 January 2021.

13. Peter Schwab, *Cuba: Confronting the U.S. Embargo* (New York: Macmillan, 1999); Xin-zhu J. Chen, "China and the US Trade Embargo, 1950–1972," *American Journal of Chinese Studies* 13, no. 2 (October 2006): 169–186; Suk Hi Kim and Semoon Chang, eds., *Economic Sanctions against a Nuclear North Korea: An Analysis of United States and United Nations Actions since 1950* (Jefferson, NC: McFarland, 2007).

14. Giovanni Arrighi, "The Political Economy of Rhodesia," *New Left Review* 1, no. 39 (September–October 1966): 35–65; George W. Sheperd, ed., *Effective Sanctions on South Africa: The Cutting Edge of Economic Intervention* (New York: Praeger, 1995); David M. Rowe, *Manipulating the Market: Understanding Economic Sanctions, Institutional Change, and the Political Unity of White Rhodesia* (Ann Arbor: University of Michigan Press, 2001). For an excellent examination of sanctions against South Africa's apartheid regime, which concludes that "their contribution to ending apartheid was actually rather modest and ultimately determined by contextual factors," see Lee Jones, *Societies under Siege: Exploring How International Economic Sanctions (Do Not) Work* (Oxford: Oxford University Press, 2015), pp. 52–92. The role of the stagflation, oil, and debt crises of the 1973–1989 period in the downfall of both regimes is significant. On earlier efforts to pressure Pretoria, see

Simon Stevens, "Boycotts and Sanctions against South Africa: An International History, 1946–1970" (PhD diss., Columbia University, 2016); on the role of Cuban intervention and South African defeat in the Angolan Civil War, see Piero Gleijeses, *Visions of Freedom: Havana, Washington, Pretoria, and the Struggle for Southern Africa, 1976–1991* (Chapel Hill: University of North Carolina Press, 2013).

15. Trita Parsi, *Losing an Enemy: Obama, Iran, and the Triumph of Diplomacy* (New Haven: Yale University Press, 2017); Richard Nephew, *The Art of Sanctions: A View from the Field* (New York: Columbia University Press, 2017); Kevan Harris, "Of Eggs and Stones: Foreign Sanctions and Domestic Political Economy in the Islamic Republic of Iran," in *Economic Shocks and Authoritarian Stability: Duration, Financial Control, and Institutions*, ed. Victor Shih, pp. 72–96 (Ann Arbor: University of Michigan Press, 2020).

16. Anthony Lake, "Confronting Backlash States," *Foreign Affairs* 73, no. 2 (March–April 1994): 45–46; on the proliferation of sanctions in this period, see David Cortright and George A. Lopez, *The Sanctions Decade: Assessing UN Strategies in the 1990s* (Boulder, CO: Lynne Rienner, 2000).

17. Giuliano Garavini, *The Rise and Fall of OPEC in the Twentieth Century* (Oxford: Oxford University Press, 2019).

18. L. Martin, *Coercive Cooperation*, pp. 234–237.

19. The concept was first developed by David A. Baldwin, *Economic Statecraft* (Princeton, NJ: Princeton University Press, 1985), and has since been taken up with gusto by academics and foreign policy analysts as well as policymakers. See Daniel Drezner, *The Sanctions Paradox: Economic Statecraft and International Relations* (Cambridge: Cambridge University Press, 1999); Robert D. Blackwill and Jennifer M. Harris, *War by Other Means: Geoeconomics and Statecraft* (Cambridge, MA: Harvard University Press, 2016); William J. Norris, *Chinese Economic Statecraft* (Ithaca, NY: Cornell University Press, 2018).

20. On the inadvertent reinvention of U.S. hegemony through financialization and capital imports, see Greta Krippner, *Capitalizing on Crisis: Political Origins of the Rise of Finance* (Cambridge, MA: Harvard University Press, 2011), pp. 86–105.

21. Henry Farrell and Abraham Newman, "Weaponized Interdependence," *International Security* 44, no. 1 (Summer 2019): 42–79; Adam Tooze, *Crashed: How a Decade of Financial Crises Changed the World* (New York: Penguin, 2018), pp. 202–219.

22. David A. Baldwin, "The Sanctions Debate and the Logic of Choice," *International Security* 24, no. 3 (1999–2000): 80–107; Jonathan Kirshner, "Economic Sanctions: The State of the Art," *Security Studies* 11, no. 4 (2002): 160–179.

23. In its widely cited 2000 study of economic sanctions in the twentieth century, the Peterson Institute of International Economics (PIIE) judged sanctions to be "at least partially successful" in 34 percent of cases. This

study found that their success rate varies notably across different goals: to get minor policy changes, sanctions work about half of the time, but to disrupt military action or achieve regime change, their odds of success are between one in five to one in four. Gary Clyde Hufbauer, Jeffrey J. Schott, Kimberly Ann Elliott, and Barbara Oegg, *Economic Sanctions Reconsidered*, 3rd ed. (Washington, DC: Peterson Institute for International Economics, 2007), pp. 158–159. Political scientist Robert Pape has convincingly challenged the PIIE study and argued that of its 40 supposed successes out of 115 cases examined, only 5 stand up to real scrutiny in the sense that the policy success in question can be feasibly attributed to economic coercion ("Why Economic Sanctions Do Not Work," *International Security* 22, no. 2 [1997]: 90–136, and "Why Economic Sanctions Still Do Not Work," *International Security* 23, no. 1 [1998]: 66–77).

24. Felbermayr et al., "The Global Sanctions Database," p. 12, fig. 7.
25. Kevan Harris, "Shock without Success: Effects and Effectiveness of Economic Sanctions on Iran," *Democracy and Autocracy* 18, no. 2 (June 2020): 19–24.
26. Herodotus, *The Histories*, book 9, trans. Tom Holland (New York: Viking, 2013), p. 639.

Index

Notes and tables are indicated by n and t following the page number. Photographs are indicated by italic page numbers.